TUDOR ENGLAND

Lucy Wooding is the Langford Fellow and Tutor in History at Lincoln College, Oxford. She is an expert on Reformation England and its politics, religion and culture, and the author of *Henry VIII*.

Further praise for *Tudor England*:

'A brilliant sketch of political, religious and social change under the Tudor monarchs.'

George Bernard, author of *Who Ruled Tudor England?*

'Essential reading . . . Deftly fusing social, religious and political history, *Tudor England* is an outstanding achievement.'

Elizabeth Norton, author of *The Lives of Tudor Women*

'Beautifully written . . . A deeply humane text, in which so many contemporary voices are given a sympathetic hearing.'

Ian Archer, University of Oxford

'A treasure trove, exploring Tudor history from every angle . . . Combines narrative panache with rigorous new research.'

Joanne Paul, author of *The House of Dudley*

'An extraordinary book . . . With great clarity and engaging prose, we are offered stimulating reappraisals of each regime, all of them bristling with fresh ideas.'

David Robinson, *Country Life*

T0002886

TUDOR ENGLAND

A HISTORY

LUCY WOODING

YALE UNIVERSITY PRESS
NEW HAVEN AND LONDON

For Misha, Vanya and Roma

Copyright © 2022 Lucy Wooding

First published in paperback in 2023

All rights reserved. This book may not be reproduced in whole or in part, in any form (beyond that copying permitted by Sections 107 and 108 of the U.S. Copyright Law and except by reviewers for the public press) without written permission from the publishers.

All reasonable efforts have been made to provide accurate sources for all images that appear in this book. Any discrepancies or omissions will be rectified in future editions.

For information about this and other Yale University Press publications, please contact:
U.S. Office: sales.press@yale.edu   yalebooks.com
Europe Office: sales@yaleup.co.uk   yalebooks.co.uk

Set in Minion Pro by IDSUK (DataConnection) Ltd
Printed in Great Britain by Clays Ltd, Elcograf S.p.A

Library of Congress Control Number: 2023938309

ISBN 978-0-300-16272-1 (hbk)
ISBN 978-0-300-27332-8 (pbk)

A catalogue record for this book is available from the British Library.

10 9 8 7 6 5 4 3 2 1

CONTENTS

ILLUSTRATIONS

Plates

1. *The Whitehall Mural*, by Remigius van Leemput, 1667. Royal Collection Trust / © Her Majesty Queen Elizabeth II 2022 (RCIN 405750).

2. *The Gospels of the fower Evangelistes . . .*, 1571. Courtesy of Lincoln College, University of Oxford.

3. Ruins of Fountains Abbey, Yorkshire. © Gaertner / Alamy Stock Photo.

4. *Seven Corporal Works of Mercy*, medieval wall paintings in St Peter and St Paul's church in Pickering, North Yorkshire. © Paul Heaton / Alamy Stock Photo

5. *King Henry VII*, by an unknown Netherlandish artist, c.1505. © National Portrait Gallery, London.

6. *Henry VIII's Joust*, Westminster Tournament Roll. © College of Arms MS Westminster Tournament Roll, 1511, membranes 25–6. Reproduced by permission of the Kings, Heralds and Pursuivants of Arms.

7. *Solomon and the Queen of Sheba*, by Hans Holbein the Younger, c.1534. Royal Collection Trust / © Her Majesty Queen Elizabeth II 2022 (RCIN 912188).

8. *Henry VIII and the Barber Surgeons*, attributed to Hans Holbein the Younger, c.1541. © Worshipful Company of Barbers / © Courtesy of the Worshipful Company of Barbers, Barber-Surgeons' Hall, London, UK / Bridgeman Images.

9. *Edward Prince of Wales*, by Hans Holbein the Younger, c.1538. Andrew W. Mellon Collection, National Gallery of Art, public domain.

10. *Mary I*, by Hans Eworth, 1554. © The Picture Art Collection / Alamy Stock Photo.

11. *Sieve Portrait of Queen Elizabeth I*, by Quentin Metsys the Younger, c.1583. © incamerastock / Alamy Stock Photo.

12. Elizabeth I's locket ring, c.1575. By kind permission of the Chequers Trust © Mark Fiennes Archive. All rights reserved 2022 / Bridgeman Images.

13. The four heraldic Dacre Beasts, c.1520. © Victoria and Albert Museum, London.

14. Decorative overmantel, Plas Mawr, Conwy. © David Angel / Alamy Stock Photo.

15. *Mary Neville, Lady Dacre*, by Hans Eworth, c.1555. © The Picture Art Collection / Alamy Stock Photo.

16. A Black trumpeter, John Blanke. © College of Arms MS Westminster Tournament Roll, 1511, membrane 28. Reproduced by permission of the Kings, Heralds and Pursuivants of Arms.

17. *The Ambassadors*, by Hans Holbein the Younger, 1533. © The Picture Art Collection / Alamy Stock Photo.

18. *The Armada Portrait*, attributed to George Gower, c.1588. © The Picture Art Collection / Alamy Stock Photo.

19. A rood screen in All Saints, Morston, Norfolk. © Griffin Art / Alamy Stock Photo.

20. Triangular Lodge, Rushton, Northamptonshire. © Steve Taylor ARPS / Alamy Stock Photo.

21. Banner of the Five Wounds of Christ, c. sixteenth century. His Grace The Duke of Norfolk, Arundel Castle. © Bridgeman Images.

22. *The Family of Henry VIII*, British School, c.1545. Royal Collection Trust / © Her Majesty Queen Elizabeth II 2022 (RCIN 405796).

23. *A Fête at Bermondsey*, by Marcus Gheeraerts the Elder, c.1571. Public domain.

24. Interior of the Shakespeare Globe Theatre, London. © Martin Bache / Alamy Stock Photo.

ACKNOWLEDGEMENTS

It is a joyful task to be able to thank the many people who have helped bring *Tudor England* into existence. To Heather McCallum at Yale, who first asked me to write this book and who has been an extraordinarily astute, patient and supportive editor through the long years it has taken me to finish it, I owe all gratitude. I am also indebted to Katie Urquhart and the team at Yale for all their hard work and professionalism, and to the anonymous readers for their very helpful suggestions.

Since October 2016, I have been lucky enough to work at Lincoln College Oxford, and there could not have been a more congenial atmosphere in which to finish a book. Lincoln is a college like no other: the warmth of its community and the standards of academic excellence upheld by fellows and students alike have supplied both encouragement and motivation. In particular, I have been fortunate enough to work alongside Perry Gauci, whose enduring patience and abiding good humour are legendary – many generations of Lincoln alumni will know what I am talking about. To him, and to our colleagues Sam Brewitt-Taylor and Joshua Bennett, I owe a great debt of gratitude for their support, forbearance and unfailing cheerfulness.

The wider population of early modern scholars at Oxford comprises a formidable array of talent, and it is an exceptional privilege to work among them. In particular, I am profoundly grateful to Ian Archer, Alexandra Gajda and Steven Gunn, all of whom, out of the kindness of their hearts, found time to read the book – in Steve's case, with exceptional nobility, whilst immured with Covid. They have done much to improve it. Aude de Mézerac-Zanetti supplied both scholarly advice and affectionate encouragement. I also owe a great deal to other cherished colleagues, especially Vincent Gillespie: teaching alongside Vincent has truly been one of the most inspiring experiences of my life. For both wisdom and good fellowship, I would like to thank George Bernard, Matthew Kempshall, Melanie Marshall, Peter Marshall, David Parrott, Susan Royal, Alec Ryrie, Adam Sutcliffe and Alexandra Walsham.

I have been privileged to teach on the subject of Tudor England for nearly three decades now. I would like to record my gratitude to the successive generations of students with whom I have discussed all the themes in this book over those years – at Queen's University Belfast, King's College London and, most recently, the University of Oxford. Students teach their tutors far more than they ever realize, and impart the kind of energy and enthusiasm that keep every university alive. In particular, the early modern postgraduate community here at Oxford is comprised of especially gifted and lovely people, to whom we all owe a special debt for keeping us going through the long and difficult months of lockdown. Above all, I thank my beloved Lincolnites for being such a delight and inspiration. I hope some of the generations to come will find this book useful.

That this book was finished at all is a testament to friendship. Tony Claydon has been saving me from various forms of crisis at regular intervals ever since my second year as an undergraduate, and again stepped in to rescue me from despair in the dark days of 2021. To him and his husband, Jeremy Gregory, I owe all love and gratitude. Ross Moncrieff agreed, in the long and painful summer of 2020, to help out with a little editorial work, but rapidly assumed instead a role somewhere between literary advisor and life coach, and I owe him more than I can say. Joseph Hopper was both helpful and calming. Ebrahim Hanifehpour, with great generosity, read some of the manuscript to give me the student perspective, and I thank him, too, for his insightful comments. To the many friends who cheered me on, again thanks – especially to Kate and Matt, who read pieces of the book and said heartening things, and to a host of other friends without whom I could not have coped. I also have to thank – from the bottom of my heart – Aleksandra Edwards, who has helped to look after my family for ten years now, and on whose resourcefulness, cheerfulness and affection we all depend. Even closer to home, my mother's creative energy and intellectual curiosity have been lighting up the world for over nine decades, and never cease to inspire and entertain. My dear husband would have found it all a lot easier if this had been a book about Russian history; but he has been my faithful companion through this, as through many other trials. Finally, I have to thank our lovely children, who have put up so philosophically with their often stressed, frequently inattentive mother; who have tried hard not to roll their eyes when I talk about the Tudors; and who (along with the dog Byelka, who deserves a mention) have made life worth living throughout all the time this has taken. Misha, Vanya, Roma, I promise you don't have to read it, but this book is for you, with all my love.

INTRODUCTION

> Rightly therefore is it sayd of Cicero, speaking of antiquitie, that historie
> is the witnesse of truth, the glasse of times: and not to understand what
> was done before we were borne, is to live alwayes as children.[1]

There was no such thing as 'Tudor England' until long after the last Tudor
was dead.[2] This epoch was created in retrospect, pieced together out of
countless memories and a great deal of selective forgetting. Many modern
depictions of the Tudor past continue to distort the historical record, and
are often a travesty of the real thing. In popular culture, Tudor England
exists as a succession of clear, jewel-like images, as glowing as the Tudor
portraits we know so well, and as deceptive. Its story can be framed as a
melodrama about a glamorous but dysfunctional royal family, depicted as
the era of artistic subtlety and splendour that produced Elizabethan drama,
hailed as an age of religious awakening, or acclaimed as laying foundations
for the modern bureaucratic state. These are mostly just fables, however,
stitched together to create a beguiling picture, at times compounded of
benign sentiment alongside the misinformation; at other times, more trou-
blingly, founded on religious bias or political prejudice. Fabricated notions
of the Tudor era have been used over the centuries to support everything
from the averred prerogatives of parliament to the claims of different sects
within the Church of England; they have been blithely appropriated for
accounts of the beginning of empire or the dawn of secularism.[3] Nowadays
they are used as the backdrop for novels, rattling with modern assumptions, prettified to be peddled as a commodity in scores of giftshops,
sensationalized by journalists and television personalities, frequently

commercialized beyond all recognition. For all that this popular enthusiasm can be inspiring at times, it can also be deeply misleading. The Tudors deserve more profound and careful scrutiny.

Tudor England in its own time was nothing like it looks on a screen.[4] The truth is at once more complicated, more intractable and much more interesting. There were many different political, social and religious changes taking place in the years between 1485 and 1603. At the same time, international alliances were shifting; wars were fought on land and at sea; famines and epidemics ravaged communities; schools and colleges were founded; books were written and printed as never before; villages, towns and cities battled with social problems and attempted to promote social harmony; men, women and children worked, suffered, celebrated and died. This book tells some stories which may seem familiar – of kings and queens, battles and rebellions, palace intrigue and political crisis. It interweaves such stories with less familiar accounts of what it was like to walk through the Tudor landscape; to live the life of a peasant woman or an urban artisan; to exercise authority as a noblewoman or as a lawyer; to follow the rhythm of the ritual year in one of the thousands of rural parishes; and to struggle to maintain communal solidarity in the face of unprecedented social challenges. Escaping from the stranglehold of the usual Tudor narratives, this book aims to give a broader picture, looking at the whole of Tudor England, not just the pieces we already recognize.

Much of what follows is intended, therefore, to disregard expectations. We might even question the accuracy of speaking of 'the Tudors' in the usual sense.[5] Henry VII, his son and his three grandchildren did not regard themselves as a new and distinctive dynasty, but constantly sought refuge in the memory of their medieval predecessors. As Henry VII struggled to establish himself before his accession, the title he used was not 'Tudor' but 'Richmond', the title carried by his father which linked him to his Lancastrian forebears.[6] Far from the grandiose figures of legend, the members of this family were all in their different ways dogged by terrible insecurity, their questionable claim to the throne underlying all their apparent assurance. Never more than three steps away from disaster, they wove tapestries out of the different threads of the past – Plantagenet, Lancastrian, Yorkist – to clothe the bare walls of their makeshift kingship with the illusion of longevity. They appealed to Arthurian legend, to the memory of Edward III and Henry V, the chivalric rituals of the Order of the Garter, and the great victories of the Hundred Years War.[7] Despite the pageantry and display of the Tudor Court, when Elizabeth died in 1603, her funeral cortège proudly, and a little pathetically, displayed the arms of her Yorkist ancestors – a tacit admission that the Tudor claim had never quite taken root. Her successor James I made a point of tracing his direct lineage from Henry VII, casting the previous four monarchs as a sterile off-shoot unworthy of too much attention.

If 'Tudor' remains a questionable concept, what should we understand by 'England' between 1485 and 1603? There was some stately rhetoric lavished upon the idea and ideal of England in these years, but in reality, the nature and the scope of England were still under negotiation in the years covered by this book. For most of the Tudor era, Scotland was a hostile country, Ireland was a thorny political problem, and Wales was still recognizably a separate country, for all that it had been assimilated into the English administrative system, whilst the Cornish still spoke a separate language.[8] This book deals solely with England and Wales, as the territories ruled by the Tudor monarchs, since the histories of Scotland and Ireland deserve a level of attention which was not within the scope of this work.[9] It is also wary of assuming that even England and Wales together formed either a coherent or an enduring polity. The slow absorption of the Welsh into English administration from the 1530s onwards created an unprecedented sense of Welsh territorial integrity, even as it sought to integrate the two countries.[10] Meanwhile, female rule between 1553 and 1603 always held out the possibility that the realm might be subsumed within a larger dominion if either Mary I or Elizabeth I married. In 1600, Thomas Wilson's book, *The State of England*, identified twelve possible claimants to the throne after Elizabeth's death, including the Infanta Isabella of Spain and the duke of Parma, who might have absorbed England within a European Catholic empire.[11] The very frontiers of the kingdom remained fragile, permeable, debatable.

Tudor England was also heavily dependent upon the rest of Europe for intellectual and cultural inspiration, new technologies and trade. William Caxton was only able to bring printing to London because he had observed the commercial value of books when governor of the English merchants in Bruges, and learned how to make them in Cologne.[12] From the crafting of armour and warships to the acquisition of Greek and Hebrew learning, England constantly had to appeal abroad for help. Tudor monarchs expended time, money and diplomatic effort in raising England's profile abroad, but they strained to compete with other realms. Hampton Court Palace was an attempt to emulate the great Italian *palazzi*, and Henry VIII treasured the one gifted Italian craftsman who had worked on Fontainebleau when he managed to persuade him into his service.[13] Thomas Tallis wrote 'Spem in alium', his great forty-part motet, allegedly because a nobleman listening to an Italian song in thirty parts had asked testily 'whether none of our Englishmen could sett as good a songe'.[14] English scholars worked hard to keep up with developments abroad, while the Tudor nobility aped the grander fashions of Italy, France and the Netherlands in their houses, gardens, education and statecraft. As religious divisions emerged, both Catholicism and Protestantism were conceptualized as international movements, and the English took refuge within networks of scholars, reformers and exiles across the continent. It is impossible to understand Tudor England without appreciating its European context.

Tudor England was deeply preoccupied with its own historical past.[15] It was in the first century BC, in a Rome sharply self-conscious about its own history, that Cicero uttered the words which head this introduction; words that were avidly taken up by John Foxe, the martyrologist, in 1571 to affirm history as the 'witnesse of truth'. 'What incomparable delectation, utility and commodity shall happen to emperors, kings, princes and all other gentlemen by reading of histories', wrote Thomas Elyot in his 1531 *Boke Named the Governour*, written to educate the next generation of those destined to rule. Richard Carew, writing his *Survey of Cornwall*, had some doubts about the fable that the county had been named after a cousin of Brutus who wrestled a giant; but he was held back by the fact that 'I reverence antiquitie, and reckon it a kind of wrong, to exact an over-strict reason for all that which upon credite shee delivereth.'[16] A guide to how history should be written and read, published in 1574 and dedicated to the earl of Leicester, praised him for reading history 'not as many doe, to passe away the tyme, but to gather thereof such judgement and knowledge as you may therby be the more able, as well to direct your private actions, as to give Counsell lyke a most prudent Counseller in publyke causes, be it matters of warre, or peace'.[17] In Devon in 1593, the yeoman Robert Furse, knowing death was near, wrote a book of advice for his small son, including the admonition 'to rede the old crownekeles and shuch like awnshyente hystoryes', since it was 'a shame for a man to be ignorante' of his own past.[18]

The polemical force of history-writing was realized more and more by the Tudors precisely because it was in the sixteenth century that history became more contested than ever before, caught up in the conflicts of the Reformation. With Catholics and Protestants both laying claim to the true and ancient Christian faith, the study of the Christian past took on a new edge. The appearance of the four gospels in Anglo-Saxon in 1571 was not a peaceful piece of antiquarianism, but a volley fired in a culture war (see plate 2). Foxe, in his introduction, argued that 'for want of true history, truth hath lacked witnesse . . . new thynges were reputed for olde, and olde for new'.[19] He was trying to show that Elizabethan Protestantism was far more deeply rooted in English history than its detractors alleged. Foxe's work shows the potential of history, deployed here in pursuit of a deeply partisan purpose, which made the Anglo-Saxons, with their vernacular versions of the Scriptures, out to be proto-Protestants. It was this kind of appropriation of the historical agenda which led William Camden, perhaps the greatest of Elizabethan historians, to denounce the hot-headed zeal-otry of some of his contemporaries.[20] He grieved at 'the declamations and exclamations of the ecclesiastical sort of people on both sides, who for the most part are very fiery and vehement' and tried, by contrast, to fashion a newly detached and dispassionate kind of history.[21] The work attempted in this book, of dispelling some of our prejudices and assumptions about Tudor England, is in part founded on a historical awareness, which the sixteenth century itself brought to birth.

This book is written with the simple objective of unfolding the story of English history between 1485 and 1603 and, in the process, bringing together some of the remarkable findings uncovered by recent historical research. In the last fifty years or so, we have seen significant advances in historical writing. Anthropology, sociology and the history of race have provided important fresh perspectives.[22] Women's history, gender history and 'history from below' have transformed our view of society, popular culture and the political process, while the study of mentalities has added a kind of 'history from within'.[23] Art history and the study of material culture have added new depth and detail to the picture.[24] Revisionist views of the Reformation, in particular with an emphasis on Catholic history, have turned upside-down many of the easy assumptions of our Protestant past.[25] Kings, bishops, bureaucrats and playwrights have stepped aside to make room for women writers, peasant leaders, thoughtful Londoners, prophetic artisans, woodcarvers and painters, prostitutes and spies. The historical landscape of the late fifteenth and sixteenth centuries is no longer dominated by fortresses and palaces; we can now also make out the cottages and the river courses, the growing towns and the monastic houses, the fenlands and the holy wells, the city streets and taverns. The history of the Tudor dynasty needs to be set alongside the history of every other family at that time, and the politics of the parish are now scrutinized just as closely as the politics of the Court. The desire to give a fuller picture has dictated the structure of the book, in which the five core chapters that narrate the political history of each successive reign are interwoven with thematic chapters that deal with social, cultural and religious develop-ments. The reader will need to move between accounts of fast-paced polit-ical change on the one hand, and explorations of more gradual evolutions on the other; but the hope is that the end result will prove all the richer for this variegated approach, and give a truer sense of the varied experiences of Tudor men and women.

This book rests upon a great many other books. Not only does it pay grateful tribute to the many outstanding scholars who work in this area, but it also acknowledges a profound debt to the books written in the fifteenth and sixteenth centuries. Early modern men and women seem to have been in love with words: they displayed an astonishing mastery of their language, from the sublime fantasies of playwrights to the stately pronouncements of parliamentary statutes, from the sharp poignancy of prayers crafted in adversity to the rich insults of street quarrels found in legal court records. Their age was a great age of literature, in which their words found their way onto the printed or handwritten page as treatises, plays, sermons, poems, ballads, almanacs, petitions, proclamations and polemics. The power of the written word was celebrated by poets, and condemned by those who burned the works they feared.[26] These Tudor words also have a history, touched with the excitement of the first age of printing, crafted at a time when the English language was itself evolving.[27] Translating the Bible into English produced a wealth of new words such as 'scapegoat' and 'atonement'; rendering the church service from Latin into English produced a new language of prayer; the inventiveness of the Elizabethan dramatists added words such as 'lustrous' and 'swagger', 'radiance' and 'moonbeam'. Tudor writers themselves were intensely aware of how their language was being enriched.[28] Their choice of words to translate sixteenth-century bibles shows how they thought about everything from their servants to their landscape; the words in which Shakespeare described the hopes and fears of kings convey how his contemporaries viewed those in power; phrases plucked from Roman history illustrate how an Elizabethan might construct his own political integrity.[29] To study the Tudor period is to encounter a great many literary voices, some raised in exhortation, advice and instruction, some in protest, warning or denunciation; and from these early modern texts can be fashioned a human story.[30] This book seeks to make those many voices audible, in all their ardour, vehemence, contradiction and complexity.

One final theme links the experience of early modern England to our own time. The late fifteenth and early sixteenth centuries saw the world changing around them at a pace never before experienced. New inventions such as printing, and advances in navigation or in military technology pushed back the boundaries of the mind, the known world and the threats posed by war. New diseases ravaged the continent of Europe, and were exported to the New World: syphilis, with its degradation and agony, or sweating sickness, which could kill within a day. Old certainties were challenged, as women ruled nations, and rulers not only contemplated bigamy but tried to justify it from the Old Testament. Most of all, any sense of a world united under one God was irretrievably broken apart. It was challenged from the outside by the advance of the Islamic world to the gates of Vienna in the 1520s and by the discovery of non-Christians in newly encountered lands in north or south America, Africa or India. It was challenged from within by ongoing disputes about Jewish identity and scholarship; by fears about the workings of the Devil; and above all, by the profound and deadly divisions between different kinds of Christians.

In the face of these challenges, many early modern men and women responded with extraordinary levels of courage, inventiveness and compassion. At a time when it was considered acceptable by many to aspire to military conquest, to enslave newly encountered populations, to burn heretics and to execute witches, there were voices which spoke up against all of these things. When governments in a panic enacted draconian punishments for vagabondage, riot or heresy, pardons were used to soften their impact; and parish constables and parish priests, exercising both kindness and common sense, might quietly avoid implementing the laws in question. When rebellions broke out, the Tudor authorities, even in times of instability, mostly contented themselves with prosecuting the ringleaders, while pardoning the ordinary folk involved.[31] Alongside such pragmatic moderation there was a flowering of idealism the like of which this country has seldom seen. From the skilful ironies of More's *Utopia*, through the careful pleas of a succession of reforming church councils and the patient instruction of the official church homilies, to the troubled ambivalence of Shakespeare's Shylock, Lear or Hamlet, there was a striving to understand the pitfalls of human existence and to build a better world. Works of instruction were written on every conceivable subject – from how to educate a prince in wisdom and justice to how to manage a household; from the arts of archery or angling to the art of dying. Each one held out a new set of aspirations. At a time when the very structures of power depended on a shared ideology of justice, obedience and charity, the ideological strength which Tudor society was capable of showing puts our own to shame. Faced with the threat of apocalypse, people found a new level of resourcefulness, took guidance from the ancients and strove to build afresh. For all their many failures, their levels of political, social and religious engagement remain astounding, and worthy of contemplation.

CHAPTER I

LANDSCAPE AND SEASCAPE

In one of the most isolated corners of the British Isles, in the far south-west of Pembrokeshire, lies the small, secluded cove called Mill Bay, where Henry of Richmond, the prospective Henry VII, came ashore on 7 August 1485. Landing his forces here, far out of sight of all human settlement, underlines just how covert and anxious an enterprise this was. Henry kissed the ground, we are told, as an exile returning home; a reminder of his Welsh identity, which would prove so crucial in the weeks ahead. He made the sign of the cross and spoke the opening words of Psalm 42, '*Judica me, Deus, et discerne causam meam*' – Judge me, O God, and distinguish my cause. As a verse spoken at the start of mass, these words were perhaps recognizable even to those who spoke no Latin. Henry was staking his claim to divine protection, as he set out to claim the throne.[1] He then embarked on the long journey across Wales and England that would culminate at the battle of Bosworth Field. The sea voyage, the sheltered cove, the rugged Welsh landscape, the long trek across to Leicestershire: this was where the Tudor story began.

History does not unfold in a vacuum. The struggles and triumphs of the Tudor regime were rooted in the soil. Power was enacted in the mud of the battlefield, built up in bricks and mortar into palaces, and imprinted on the countryside in the form of castles and fortifications. Military campaigns were subject to the weather and the challenges of the terrain. Trade involved hazardous sea voyages, and the difficulties of transporting goods across land. Above all, for the majority of the Tudor population, their daily task was to extract sustenance from the earth, rivers, forests and seas around them, to scrape iron from the ground, mine tin or quarry stone. Surroundings shaped identity: in 1519, tenants in Gloucestershire petitioning to save their land from enclosure emphasized that this was land 'that they were borne unto', and more than anything else, what stood out in the recollections of the old was the land that they had worked all their lives.[2] Landscape and seascape also held religious, mythical and providential meaning. The land was a repository of memory, scarred by past battles and rebellions, or more gently shaped by the usage of generations. Parish boundaries were marked out by the yearly procession of those who lived within their limits.[3] The cultivation of land was all-important: Robert Cecil in 1601 could tell the parliament, 'whosoever doth not maintain the Plough, destroys this Kingdom'.[4] To make sense of the characters and events of Tudor England, it is necessary to understand the landscape through which those characters moved, and in which those events unfolded. History books might more often tend to begin with dynastic marriages or great battles; but to come close to the real history of the time, we need first to know about the woods and fields, mountains and rivers, towns and cities, and England's relationship with the seas that surrounded it.[5]

For Tudor men and women, the landscape around them was full of meaning. It was not by accident that rivers contained fish, forests were full of deer and crops grew in the field: it was through the benevolence of God. Providence shaped the contours of the hills and the shifting patterns of the weather. The greatest poets of the age would be intensely concerned with the land, not just as a thing of beauty, but as a spur to human virtue and a setting for human endeavour. Shakespeare's Forest of Arden was a place of innocence, where people might learn honesty; and Prospero's island was a place of coiling enchantments, in which human integrity was tested.[6] Thomas Wyatt, imagining himself exiled to his home in the country, striding through the frost and snow, saw the landscape as the embodiment of liberty, in contrast to the choking and corrupting intrigues of the Court.[7] If everyday life was close in all practical aspects to the natural world, the life of the imagination was just as deeply rooted in the soil.

It was widely believed that landscape shaped temperament. A report on Sussex submitted to the Privy Council in 1587 noted that 'it borders south on the sea and north on the wild: in which two places commonly the people be given much to rudeness and wilfullness', and made the practical suggestion that, in consequence, it might need more magistrates than other areas.[8] The medieval romance *Sir Gawain and the Green Knight* reminded its readers of the 'wayward people' found in the 'wilds of the Wirral'.[9] William Harrison, the Elizabethan cleric who contributed his description of England to Holinshed's *Chronicles*, thought that the country's position and climate made its inhabitants hungry, rendering 'the heate of our stomaches to be of somewhat greater force … than [among] the inhabitants of the hotter regions'.[10] Tudor commentators generally portrayed their country in terms of human interaction with it. Harrison, who was, he claimed, 'the first … so particularly to describe this Isle of Britain', began with religion and the way the landscape was carved up into bishoprics, before turning to castles and palaces, and the military capabilities of the country.[11] Robert Wyer, who published a chronicle in 1532, began his description of England with its measurements; then listed the number of parishes and bishoprics; and then the number of shires and towns.[12] Caxton in 1480 published a work by the fourteenth-century monk Ranulf Higden, a description of England which also began with dimensions, and then moved on to its 'worthyness and prerogatives' and 'mervailles and wondres', before describing highways, rivers, towns and shires.[13]

Land was a source of blessing, as well as sustenance. Wells, rocks and trees could be imbued with divine grace. The holy wells of St Anne at Buxton or St Winefride at Holywell, both marked by chapels, probably reflect attempts to claim for Christianity sites that had possessed supernatural properties in pre-Christian days.[14] St Winefride's spring had been visited by Henry V and Edward IV, so when Lady Margaret Beaufort paid for the construction there of a chapel whose badges intertwined royal and sacred symbolism, she was usefully reinforcing her son Henry VII's claim to the throne.[15] Other features of the landscape bore the imprint of miraculous encounters: the deep crevice in the cliffs at Lundy Top in Cornwall was where St Minver had fought the Devil, whilst strange snake-shaped rocks near Whitby were serpents petrified by the prayers of St Hilda.[16] Even when Protestantism had challenged the idea of sacrality invested in material objects, many Protestants still saw something sacred in trees and stones, wheat fields and hanging vines.[17] The Bible taught that the landscape of the Holy Land had been imbued with miraculous power, and when it was translated into English, the flora and fauna of the Near East were transmuted into the oak trees, owls and sparrows of the English landscape.[18]

Between 1485 and 1603, the landscape of England underwent some profound transformations. Its monastic houses were torn down and many castles were left to crumble. The first of these changes was the most brutal, crammed into just a few short years between 1536 and 1540.[19] Perhaps a third of the land in England was transferred from church ownership to the Crown, amid the widespread destruction of some monastic buildings and the conversion of others into anything from secular cathedrals to farm buildings.[20] In due course, monastic land passed into the hands of nobility and gentry: in Norfolk, for example, the gentry increased their holding from 67 per cent of manors in 1535 to 78 per cent in 1565; and in Yorkshire, over 25 per cent of gentry families came to own some monastic land.[21] The ruins of monasteries such as Fountains Abbey in Yorkshire, Glastonbury Abbey in Somerset, Wenlock Priory in Shropshire or Battle Abbey in East Sussex became permanent features of the countryside, an embodiment of desecration and a focus for unease and nostalgia for centuries to come (see plate 3).[22] John Speed, describing Dorset in his atlas of Britain in 1611, noted how the abbeys of Sherborne and seven others in the county had been destroyed by the hand of Henry VIII, 'which lay with such waight upon their faire buildings, that he crushed the juice thereof into his owne Coffers'.[23]

Castles withdrew more gradually from the Tudor landscape. The right to fortify a dwelling required royal licence; although 380 such licences were granted in the fourteenth century, the number fell to 80 in the fifteenth.[24] Thornbury Castle in Gloucestershire, built by the duke of Buckingham between 1511 and his execution for treason in 1521, is one place where the fortified house of the fifteenth century meets the Renaissance mansion of the sixteenth (see illustration 1). Buckingham had a licence to crenellate; but the south range, with its great windows, the gardens and deer park, were more modern features. Henry VIII's fortifications from the 1540s, along the south coast, were called castles, but Deal Castle, Wardour Castle and others were, in truth, fortified gun batteries. The Tudor antiquarian John Leland, having toured England, recorded with sadness many castles in ruins: Appleby in Westmorland was a 'ruinous castle wherein the prisoners be kept'; Hereford had once been 'one of the fairest, largest and strongest castles of England' but 'now the whole castle

1. Thornbury Castle, Gloucestershire

tendith towards ruin'.[25] George Owen, describing Pembrokeshire in the 1590s, commented with more satisfaction on how the castles which had once held the 'destroyers and disinheritors' of Wales stood in ruin, while the houses 'of the gentlemen and people . . . flourish and increase'.[26] Those castles still standing tended to be on the edges of the kingdom, such as Carmarthen ('very fair and double walled') or Scarborough ('exceedingly goodly, large and strong'). The prospect of a threat from the sea was still something to be taken seriously: in 1557, Thomas Stafford briefly captured Scarborough Castle in his abortive rebellion against Mary I.[27]

Political eminence was usually proclaimed by building work. The comment of Suetonius on the Emperor Augustus – that he found Rome brick and left it marble – was often cited; and when Harrison assessed the reign of Henry VIII, his chief praise was for his building works: 'a perpetual precedent unto those that do come after'.[28] Those who achieved positions of influence drove home the point in material form. Thomas Cromwell's political success was consolidated by acquiring his Mortlake estate, emphasizing the triumph of the brewer's son from Putney turned baron of

Wimbledon.[29] Sir Thomas Lovell, faithful servant to Henry VII, built three grand houses; his palace of Elsyng in Enfield, Middlesex, had moat, towers, gatehouse, chapel and two royal suites of rooms for when the king and queen visited.[30] Houses such as Hardwick Hall, Burghley House, Wollaton Hall or Longleat pronounced the wealth and aspirations of the Elizabethan nobility. Elsewhere, the vicissitudes of fortune left their mark: Baconsthorpe Castle in Norfolk was built and ruined in the space of just a few generations – hostage to the vagaries of the wool trade; meanwhile, the ruins of Surrey Place on the heights above Norwich bear witness to the rise and fall of one of the most brilliant and difficult Tudor nobles: the poet Henry Howard, earl of Surrey, executed in 1547.

Most people lived in the countryside, and most of those – perhaps three quarters of the population as a whole – lived south and east of the line between the Severn and the Humber. It has been estimated that in 1520, 95 per cent of the population was living in either villages or very small towns (although even a small town could have substantial economic or political importance).[31] Changes here were slow, piecemeal and diverse. Many farmers continued to use medieval strip-farming methods, although profits from the wool trade encouraged many to enclose land for sheep farming. Some villages, such as that of Wharram Percy in Yorkshire, abandoned around 1500, vanished altogether as arable land was given over to sheep; others remained relatively unchanged throughout the era.[32] Although the details are debated, somewhere between 1350 and 1850 there was a shift from a society of small farmers to one of larger farms reliant on wage-labourers; in some parts of the country this was a sixteenth-century development, but there was a great deal of regional variation.[33] In the manor of Havering in Essex, the population doubled between 1500 and 1620, landholding became concentrated in the hands of a small number of large-scale landowners, and the position of the middling sort and the poor worsened; but Havering, within London's orbit, was far from typical.[34]

Change often prompted lamentation. In the *Discourse of the Commonweal*, written in 1549 (and printed in 1581), the husbandman protested that 'these enclosures do undo us all'.[35] A work pointedly entitled *The Decaye of England only by the Great Multitude of Shepe*, addressed to the Privy Council and the House of Lords, argued that where once arable farming had provided livelihood for thousands, now 'they have nothynge, but goeth about in England from dore to dore' begging, whilst some, 'because they will not begge . . . doeth steale, and then they be hanged, and thus the Realme doeth decay'.[36] Harrison took issue with landowners who ejected tenants and fashioned their lands into hunting parks, replacing corn, cattle and people with 'wild and savage beasts, cherished for pleasure and delight'.[37] Concerns over depopulation went back to before 1485. Henry VII's parliament passed a statute to combat the 'pulling down and wilfull waste of houses and Townes within this his realme, and leyeng to pasture londes which custumeably have ben used in tilthe'. This act imagined that where two hundred people had once lived, there were now just 'two or three herdemen', whilst 'the residue fall in ydelnes'; in consequence, husbandry was decayed, 'churches destroied, the service of God withdrawen, the bodies there buried not praied for, the patrone and Curates wronged, the defence of this land ageyn oure ennemyes outwarde febled and impaired'.[38] This kind of lament was to remain central to all kinds of political commentary.[39] Thomas More's *Utopia* in 1516 imagined his idealistic protagonist Hythlodaeus inveighing against England's sheep, 'that commonly are so meek and eat so little; now, as I hear, they have become so greedy and fierce that they devour human beings themselves'.[40] In 1597, Francis Bacon, addressing the Commons, pictured a once-peopled landscape given over to 'nought but Greenefeildes a Sheapheard and his Dogg'.[41] The *Book of Common Prayer* of 1552 included a prayer that landlords might 'not rack and stretch out the rents of their houses and lands', but ensure 'that the inhabitants thereof may both be able to pay the rents, and also honestly to live, to nourish their families, and to relieve the poor'.[42] In truth, the pressures upon the English landscape were more complicated and regionally varied than much of this language suggests; and economic distress was frequently the consequence of many different pressures that were harder to see or to control, such as fluctuations in the cloth trade or government devaluation of the coinage. Despite this, the transformation of the land, and the plight of the poor, remained a core element in Tudor rhetoric.

With population figures rising only slowly in the fifty years after 1485, land shortages were not at first a problem, and in the late fifteenth and early sixteenth centuries standards of living were comparatively high, whilst greater diversity in trade, mercantile expansion, the growth of towns and changes in farming all brought greater wealth to certain sectors of society – something which left its traces upon both town and countryside. Harrison in the 1570s observed distrustfully that houses were now customarily built with oak, which previously had been reserved for churches and great houses: 'when our houses were builded of willow, then had we oaken men; but now that our houses are come to be made of oak, our men are not only become willow but a great many ... altogether of straw, which is a sore alteration'.[43] In the second half of the sixteenth century, however, concerns about poverty became acute, and with good reason. The population grew quickly after around 1550, and this placed a strain on many communities as prices rose. The land was, in many areas, not very rich, so animals were needed to fertilize it, but livestock prices were rising sharply.[44] Arable farming needed to provide food not just for people, but also for the horses and oxen that were the source of all power for transport and agriculture, as well as for other livestock. Wood was needed for fuel and for building, but timber prices had risen perhaps fivefold.[45] In the seventeenth century, coal would replace wood as fuel (something that was already happening in London in the 1570s) and bricks would supply building materials, whilst changing patterns of cultivation would improve soil fertility and grazing; but these changes were still in the future.[46] The Elizabethan countryside seemed to many disfigured by conflict, with common land violated, roads contaminated by vagrants and beggars, and impoverished yeomen and gentry no longer providing the hospitality of yesteryear.

Landscape, then as now, was itself a historical document, an archive of occupation and aspiration, and a record of conflict.[47] Much of this remains visible: lines carved in the soil by centuries of strip-farming, clay pits, chalk pits or the abandoned bell pits of fifteenth-century miners.[48] Windmills and cathedrals, almshouses and palaces, drovers' roads and stone bridges dating from the late fifteenth and sixteenth centuries are still landmarks today. England's canal system achieved its first tentative advances in the sixteenth century. Great houses carved out hunting demesnes around them: Nonsuch Park remains, though Nonsuch Palace is gone, and the great London parks attest to Henry VIII's desire for both royal magnificence and fresh food. Other records exist, too, which are not carved in earth or stone: the Tudors wrote avidly about the world around them, leaving us everything from guidebooks on surveying or farming to poetry about the marriage of rivers, interweaving the pragmatic and the idealistic. 'Now pause with your selfe, and view the end of all your labours in an Orchard: unspeakeable pleasure, and infinite commoditie', wrote the Elizabethan cleric and gardener William Lawson.[49] William Camden, perhaps the greatest historian of the age, wrote of how his country delighted the beholder 'with so gallant and glittering varieties . . . which way so ever they glance'. He helped found the Society of Antiquaries in 1586 both to map the topography and to understand the antiquity and mythology of the land.[50] Tudor England was a landscape shaped as much by the ideas of its inhabitants, as by the tools they wielded.

'This blessed plot'

Much about the landscape of Tudor England remained hidden to its inhabitants; but during the sixteenth century, they became increasingly curious about it.[51] These inquiries were not without their difficulties: Harrison recorded that he had 'intended at the first to have written at large, of the number, situation, names, quantities, townes, villages, castles, mounteines, fresh waters, plashes or lakes, salt waters, and other commodities' of Britain, but that his hopes of 'information from all parts of England' were disappointed, so that he had to rely on 'that which I knew my selfe either by reading, or such other helpe as I had alreadie purchased and gotten of the same'.[52] Harrison confessed that he himself, apart from journeys to Kent, or between London, Oxford and Cambridge, 'never travailed 40 miles in all my lyfe'.[53] John Leland was commissioned by Henry VIII to survey the monastic libraries up and down the country.[54] His experience gave him a taste for topography, and led to the six years of travelling recorded in his *Laboryouse Journey* of 1549, where he claimed that

> there is almost neyther cape nor baye, haven, creke or pere, ryver or confluence of ryvers, breches, washes, lakes, meres, fenny waters, mountaynes, valleys, mores, hethes, forestes, woodes, cyties, burges, castels, pryncypall manor places, monasteryes and colleges, but I have seane them and noted in so doynge a whole worlde of thynges verye memorable.[55]

Camden's *Britannia* of 1586 sought to provide a sense of the ancestry and beauty of his land: 'the glory of my country encouraged me to undertake it', he wrote. And he reproached any who might condemn his work, for being 'strangers in their owne soile, and forrainers in their owne City'.[56] Yet the landscape of Tudor England was, of course, very varied, and the extent to which Yorkshire differed from Devon, Lancashire from Essex, made it difficult to generalize. Contemporaries often regarded different parts of the kingdom as if they were different countries, and noted language barriers: 'Oure language is also so dyverse in yt selfe / that the commen maner of spekyng in Englysshe of some contre / can skante be under-stondid in some other contre of the same londe.'[57] It was also changing, in some places quite quickly. When Richard Carew wrote his *Survey of Cornwall* in 1602, he noted how 'the state of our Countrie hath undergone so manie alterations, since I first began these scriblings', and concluded that 'a wonder it were, that in the ceaselesse revolution of the Universe, any parcell should retaine a stedfast constitution'.[58]

It was generally agreed that the island of Britain was triangular, but with varying degrees of precision: a visiting Venetian unhelpfully compared it to Sicily, while Harrison thought it like a triangle, wedge or 'bastard sword', with the bottom corners in Cornwall and Kent, and the topmost point in Caithness. Its precise location with regard to the rest of Europe was a little unclear – the same Venetian described its setting with wild inaccuracy: 'Germany being opposite to her to the north, France to the east and south, and Spain to the south, a little to the west.'[59] In another account of England, written in 1545 in classical Greek by Nicander Nucius, a Corfiot traveller, Britain was described as the largest island in the world, after Ceylon and the semi-mythical Thule.[60] Another early sixteenth-century account thought Ireland bigger than England, its northernmost point on a level with Dumfries in Scotland, and its southernmost tip aligned with St Michael's Mount in Cornwall.[61] Others came closer to accuracy: Robert Wyer opined that the length of England 'from Cateney in the marche of Scotlande / to Totnes in Devenshyre / is foure hondred myles', and that the breadth from St David's to Dover was 300 miles; he also thought the circumference of the isle was 4,360 miles, which was not a bad approximation.[62]

Some have interpreted the growing interest in mapping this landscape as a shift towards viewing the land as a commodity, preparing the way for the commercial and imperial attitudes of the future, or have taken 'carto-graphic silence' about certain features of the landscape as a sign of patriar-chal domination.[63] It is true that many early maps were commissioned by landowners wanting both to know and to proclaim the extent of their estates.[64] The Sheldon tapestry maps, woven in the 1590s for Sir Ralph Sheldon to display at his house in Weston in Warwickshire, grandly depict that house on the same scale as a small town. Yet they also include reflec-tion on the beauty of the land: 'Thine eye wolde make thin hart rejoyce to see so pleasant grounde', says the text woven into the map of Worcestershire. Map makers might also have a religious agenda. John Speed, author of the first atlas to include detailed maps of all the counties of England, was also known for his compilation of biblical genealogies, and had developed his cartographical skills by producing a map of biblical Canaan. He repre-sented his atlas as a manifestation of God's power, and England as a blessed realm 'whose Climate, Temperature, Plentie and Pleasures, make it to be as the very Eden of Europe', adding 'pardon me I pray if affection passe limits'.[65] Speed was also motivated by history. In 1601, he published, appar-ently at the request of his patrons, *A Description of the civill warres of England*, a map of England which recorded all the battles fought there since 1066. He expressed his resolve to follow it up with another map of English victories overseas, 'a matter of more honour to our Country and pleasure to our Countrey men'.[66] Speed depicted England etched with past conflicts, at a time when it was feared that Elizabeth I's death might provoke another civil war. His work had a pioneering flavour, attempting as it did a new level of detail – although not always successfully: on a map of Wiltshire, Speed made a note to himself to query the name of the village of North Burcombe, and then forgot about it; the village remained on the map as 'Quaere' for over a hundred years, until the oversight was corrected.[67] Overall, his maps showed the workings of history and providence more than they claimed domination.

It was in the sixteenth century that the English first learned the art of surveying land in scientific detail, partly as disputes over rights and boundaries rendered more precise information necessary. For centuries, surveyors had used the guide written by Walter of Henley in the thirteenth century, published by Wynkyn de Worde in 1510; but in 1523, Anthony Fitzherbert published his *Husbondrye*, and many other works followed.[68]

In 1537, Richard Bernese, a Benedictine monk from Merton Priory in Surrey who was one of Henry VIII's surveyors, was still measuring land using a wooden rod or a cord treated with white wax and rosin to stop it stretching or shrinking. Twenty years later, Leonard Digges was discussing the use of such instruments as the geometrical square, cross-staff or carpenters' square, and in a work of 1571, finished after his death by his son, he surveyed a host of mathematical instruments, including the theodolite.[69] In 1582, Edward Worsop attacked the many errors made in surveying, some because of the incomprehensibility of books which 'can not bee understoode of the common sorte'; he sought to provide 'a plaine and popular discourse' that was accessible to 'the understanding of every reasonable man'.[70] He advised where instruments might be purchased, and explained such mysteries as what was meant 'by this word, Parallel' and 'Howe much money is lxxx and iiii penies?' (the answer to the latter question being 7s).[71] His book defended his profession, acknowledging that people were often fearful when their land was surveyed, but reassuring his readers that good surveyors were a defence against bad landlords.[72] If Worsop bore witness to a growing expertise, he also testified to the anxiety surrounding land tenancy in the Elizabethan age.

To the Venetian visitor, the English landscape seemed one of abundance, with 'pleasant undulating hills, and beautiful valleys . . . agreeable woods, or extensive meadows or lands in cultivation; and the greatest plenty of water springing everywhere'. These observations were based on just two journeys – from Dover to London and from London to Oxford – but they still give a vivid idea of what England looked like around 1500. He thought it 'truly a beautiful thing to behold one or two thousand tame swans upon the river Thames', noting more pragmatically that swans were 'eaten by the English like ducks and geese'. He was surprised that the English had no objection to crows, rooks or jackdaws, which he considered birds of ill omen, and that there were penalties for destroying them, since 'they say that they keep the streets of the towns free from all filth'. He recorded that kites were 'so tame, that they often take out of the hands of little children, the bread smeared with butter, in the Flemish fashion, given to them by their mothers'.[73] Like most foreign visitors, the Venetian also commented on the weather, observing that rain 'falls almost every day during the months of June, July and August'.[74]

Beauty and utility were closely linked. Rivers were deemed beautiful, in part because they also provided food and transport: when William Herbert, earl of Pembroke, refashioned his garden with five ornamental ponds, he ensured that they were 'replete with fisshe'.[75] Harrison recorded the 'infinit number of swans' on the Thames, alongside 'the two thousand wherries and small boats, whereby three thousand poore watermen are maintained'. He also rejoiced in 'the fat and sweet salmons', which the Venetian visitor described as 'a most delicate fish, which they seem to hold in great estimation', whilst Richard Carew's *Survey of Cornwall* contained an ode to the salmon, 'king of fish'.[76] One treatise on fishing agreed that 'the Samon is moste statelye fysshe' but disliked the pike, because 'he devoureth so manye as wel of his owne kinde as of other, I love him the lesse'.[77] Fishing also provided food for the soul, and was to be undertaken 'pryncypally for your solace and to cause the helthe of your body and specyally of your soule'. Fishing in solitude, 'ye maye serve god devowtly in sayenge affectuously youre custumable prayer. And thus doynge ye shall eschewe and voyde many vices'.[78] Even if the fisherman caught nothing, there were consolations: 'atte the leest he hath his holsom walke and mery at his ease. a swete ayre of the swete savoure of the meede floures' listening to 'the melodyous armony of fowles'. And 'yf the angler take fysshe: surely thenne is there noo man merier than he is in his spyryte'.[79] Even when other forms of hunting were deplored, fishing managed to preserve its reputation, helped by the recollection that some of the apostles had been fishermen. William Perkins, the puritan divine who condemned other animal sports, himself remained a keen angler; and Alexander Nowell, Elizabethan dean of St Paul's, had his portrait painted of himself with not just a bible, but also his fishing tackle.[80]

Living creatures which inhabited the Tudor landscape had both symbolic and pragmatic importance. 'Go to the ant, thou sluggard: consider her ways, and be wise', said the Book of Proverbs. Animals, like many other aspects of God's creation, were believed to instruct humankind. Bishop Richard Fox, founding his new college of Corpus Christi in Oxford in 1517, envisaged it as a garden in which his scholars would labour industriously like bees. One of the earliest works printed by Caxton was a poem by John Lydgate, in which the horse, the goose and the sheep debated their comparative value, reckoned in terms of which of them 'avayleeth most a man'.[81]

The powerful religious symbolism of the 'paschall lambe without spot all whyte' was cited alongside the profits of the wool trade and the health benefits of mutton broth without any sense of incongruity.[82] Horses, meanwhile, were of enormous importance. A 1561 book on the art of riding declared itself 'very necessary for all gentlemen, souldyours, servingmen, and for any man that delighteth in a horse'.[83] This was a translation from the Italian of the best-selling work by Federico Grisone; the translator, Thomas Blundeville, published widely on the care of horses. He noted that 'Grison attributeth so much honor and praise to a horse, as he sayeth, that the worthye state of knighthoode, toke his first beginning of this beaste.'[84] The knight on horseback remained the basic unit of military strength, and therefore an integral feature of political authority. Robert Dudley very nearly made the transition from being Elizabeth I's master of horse to being her consort. Blundeville, dedicating his book to Dudley, noted that anyone who kept a horse for his own use should also keep 'a horse mete for service in the fielde', reproaching those who did not do so. He urged Dudley to press Elizabeth to enforce statutes about horse-breeding, hoping to excel 'al other nations in this exercise, as they now excel us': with proper provision of horses, 'our enemies would always be afrayde to attempt any enterprise against us'.[85] Lydgate's poem asserted that there was no other beast 'so notable to man in pees and werre' than the horse, and remarked on the reliance of heroes of the past upon their steeds, recalling Alexander the Great and Perseus, and their horses Bucephalus and Pegasus.[86]

Some creatures were believed to be dangerous. Camden commented censoriously on the kind of crow with a red bill and feet that was found in Cornwall, which 'the inhabitants have found to be an Incendiarie, and theevish beside. For, oftentimes it secretly conveieth fire-sticks setting their houses a fire and as closely filcheth and hideth little peeces of money.'[87] The appearance of more striking animals usually contained a providential warning. A 'rare or rather most monstrous fishe' caught off the coast of Holland in 1566 was the subject of a broadside ballad that drew some dire conclusions from its appearance (see illustration 2). It was seen as a reproach for human degeneracy, while the creature's red tail – 'fower cornered like to a priestes Cap' – was taken as divine condemnation of popery.[88] Three years later, near Ipswich, a catch of seventeen monstrous fishes prompted more positive reflections on the 'straung and marveylous

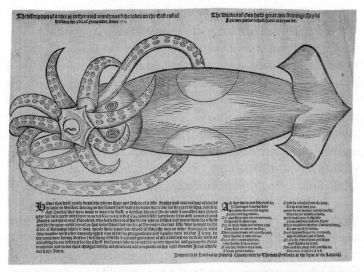

2. An Elizabethan ballad, 'The discription of a rare or rather most monstrous fishe taken on the East cost of Holland the xvii of November, anno 1566'

handye workes of the Lord', since they were found to be 'verye good meate, eyther rosted or bakt'; when baked, they apparently tasted 'lyke red Deere'. The author's only regret was that the men of Ipswich had not anticipated how good they might taste, and had therefore not profited from them as they might have done.[89]

Camden's account of England brought together the 'nature of the soile' with 'some of the most signall, and ancient families therein'.[90] His land-scape was indistinguishable from its inhabitants. Yet the landscape of Tudor England was less peopled than it had been two centuries before, when the Black Death struck. Population figures are elusive and unreliable for this period, but the population of England in 1600 was probably still less than it had been in 1300, with some areas emptier than they had been under Roman rule.[91] Even between Dover, London and Oxford, the Venetian visitor thought the land 'very thinly inhabited'.[92] The sixteenth century was to see rapid population growth, however. The last great medi-eval famine had struck between 1437 and 1440, and by the Tudor period the peasantry had a reasonably healthy diet, whilst diseases associated with poor nutrition, such as leprosy, were in decline.[93]

To contemporaries, it appeared that their world was becoming more crowded; poverty and vagabondage was an increasing problem, and anxieties about the use and ownership of land were rife. Land was chiefly organized into manors, which remained the basis of landownership throughout this period. The lord of the manor controlled the manorial court; the rights to woodland and pasture, fishing and mining; the provision of markets and fairs; and the holdings of his tenants. Even freeholders, who owned their land, were usually bound to attend meetings of the manorial court, although the more prosperous might pay to be excused this obligation.[94] Serfdom was largely gone from the English countryside, defeated by the plague and its aftermath: the reduction in the availability of labour had increased its value and facilitated its mobility. Tudor peasants mostly held their land by copyhold tenure, whereby their tenancy was either guaranteed for life or could be inherited by subsequent generations. This was confirmed by a scrap of parchment bearing a copy of the entry on the manorial roll. Copyhold tenants needed to pay their rent, as well as a fine when land was passed on; but otherwise they could buy, sell and rent out the land without interference.[95] Familial ties remained strong, however, and more often than not, generations of the same family worked the same land.

County boundaries may have had administrative significance, but it was the nature of the land which marked out settlement patterns in England at this time. Sussex, for example, comprised three distinct areas: the forested Weald and the chalk Downs were sparsely populated, while most people lived in the arable coastal lands.[96] In general, richer agricultural land saw a mingling of sheep and arable farming, commonly with nucleated village settlements; more wooded and upland areas produced pastoral farming, with people living on isolated farms or in small hamlets.[97] The Venetian visitor thought the English negligent in not growing more grain, but felt they compensated for this with an 'immense profusion of every comestible animal, such as stags, goats, fallow-deer, hares, rabbits, pigs, and an infinity of oxen, which have much larger horns than ours . . . But above all they have an enormous number of sheep, which yield them quantities of wool of the best quality'.[98] Agricultural life was augmented by many other opportunities, such as fishing, mining or clothworking. These occupations were often seasonal: miners in the tin mines of Devon, Cornwall and Somerset, or the lead mines of Worcestershire, Derbyshire,

County Durham, Northumberland and Westmorland, would work the mines once the spring ploughing and lambing was over, but return home for harvest time. In the 1540s, one John Philips, a prosperous peasant farmer with 35 acres of arable land and 24 acres of pasture to his name, augmented his income by mining in the 'meers' near Wells; this seems to have brought him an annual haul of over a hundredweight of ore.[99] Mining, less labour intensive than arable farming, could be successfully combined with pastoral farming: the mining of lead, iron or tin was not a particularly skilled occupation, since it mostly required scratching out ore from a lead rake, iron-stone bed or a trench of alluvial tin. Silver mining required more expensive equipment and skilled technology to drive deep into the argentiferous deposits in hard rock.[100] The real challenge of any mining endeavour, however, was transport. Cornish tin miners had the sea for the import of charcoal for smelting and the export of tin to London; copper miners in the Lake District sent the ore by sea to the smelters based in South Wales. The mining of coal only began to grow in significance towards the end of the sixteenth century, especially in Northumberland and County Durham, with the coal shipped out of Newcastle.[101] Coal had little of its later importance, being chiefly viewed as a cheap fuel for the poor; but Londoners in the 1590s complained about the monopoly on it held by the Hostmen of Newcastle, who were deemed to be driving up the price.[102]

Clothmaking was the industry most deeply rooted in the English countryside. This often flourished in pastoral areas, where gavelkind or partible inheritance – the division of land equally between one's descendants (*cyfran* in Welsh) – was still practised, and where common land was widely available.[103] This created both the need for a supplementary income and the opportunity to raise it. The Wiltshire wool trade, one of the oldest rural trades in the country to feed a national market, flourished in those parts of the countryside given over to dairy farming, far more than on the Salisbury Plain, where sheep and corn husbandry was dominant.[104] The clothmaking industry in the environs of Kendal in what was then Westmorland, or in Suffolk near Sudbury, might reflect the combination of these different elements; the strange decline of clothmaking in Hertfordshire in the early sixteenth century might reflect the shift towards corn-producing arable farming around that time.[105]

These rural industries were an attempt to eke out an existence in an unstable world. Harvests were unpredictable and might fail every four to five years, so rural households tended to diversify their occupations. Spinning wool, or flax, or hemp, was a common endeavour; late medieval depictions of women often showed them spinning, frequently whilst doing something else as well, such as watching over sheep or saying their prayers. Knitting woollen stockings was a common employment in the Pennines and Yorkshire: an octogenarian from the village of Dent, then in West Yorkshire (now in Cumbria), when questioned in the 1630s about the customs of his village, opined that tenants with just a few acres to farm 'could not maintain their families were it not by their industry in knitting coarse stockings'.[106] In 1580, when Richard Hakluyt made a list of commodities to take to China, he included mariners' caps, envisaging that if a market could be found for these, it might greatly help the poor, who could then live by knitting them.[107]

Most rural endeavour therefore involved high levels of collaboration within communities. Strip-farming was dependent on communal effort, and not just at harvest time. It was the exception, rather than the rule, that the owner of a piece of land was also the person who farmed it: although there were substantial numbers of freehold tenant farmers and farming landowners, the concept of absolute ownership of land was still unfamiliar to the common law system.[108] This necessitated collaboration between owners, tenants and labourers. Mines were often part owned, as were fishing boats and mercantile ships. Cooperation within the family unit was also essential. The 1570 survey of Norwich, which identified over 2,300 paupers, found that almost every household had some form of income, and most women and children were employed in some way.[109] This was an economy fuelled by familial, neighbourly or communal obligation.

This communal ideal was to be sorely tested, particularly in the latter part of the period. The pressure of a growing population, compounded by war, plague and harvest failure, led to growing anxiety about the poor and their potential for disruption, signalled by attempts to control their place in the landscape. In 1589, an act forbidding the construction of cottages with less than four acres of ground reflected the fear that poor families in ramshackle housing could become a burden on the community. This act insisted that only one family could inhabit any dwelling.[110] In Swallowfield,

Wiltshire, in 1596, the town meeting enacted that anyone keeping 'any inmates' (implying impoverished lodgers or poor relations) should be reported to the justices of the peace (JPs) and denied poor relief.[111] These were attempts to turn back an inexorable tide, as cottages were shared and tenancies subdivided to house the swelling ranks of the poor.[112] The requirement that vagrants should be returned to their birthplace, or to the parish they had lived in for the previous three years, was laid down in 1504; by 1598 this had been reduced to one year, reflecting the difficulties that parish officers faced.[113] In some places, the arrival of potential labourers from elsewhere might be welcome, but in others it was a weighty burden. In Elizabethan Hertfordshire, some communities almost doubled in size, and there were complaints about outhouses being converted into dwellings and cottages being constructed.[114] The poor traditionally drew subsistence from the land, gleaning spare grain from cornfields, gathering sticks in the forest, grazing their meagre flocks on common land – and when all this failed, asking for poor relief from the parish. The fear was that the village would not have the resources, natural or man-made, to support them.

Women were particularly vulnerable to being driven out of the parish, with widespread anxiety about unmarried mothers and illegitimate children. The standard response to any woman arriving with a bastard child, or giving birth to one in the town, was to 'banyshe her the parryshe', and pregnant women could be hounded over parish boundaries as their time drew near.[115] Identity was deeply rooted in the parish. When an Elizabethan man from Northamptonshire was accidentally killed on a piece of land whose ownership was contested by two villages, he was buried in the village of Stanion, only for his body to be exhumed and reburied at Geddington, lest Geddington's claim on the land where he had died be undermined: even in death, you were expected to be in the right place.[116] England was covered by a web of invisible parish boundaries, which delineated the boundaries of belonging and in which the lives of the poor could be helplessly enmeshed. These boundaries were marked out by processions at Rogationtide: the 'beating of the bounds', which was such an essential part of parish life that it survived the Reformation.[117] Beer consumed at points along the route was not meant solely to cheer, but also to fix in the memory where the boundary lines lay; where boundaries were disputed, processions were all the more likely to survive in popular tradition.[118] Children were taken along to impress on them the extent of their parish, and many in old age recorded this childhood experience: one Norfolk fisherman recalled how, when he was 'but a child his father . . . tooke him by the eare and bad him remember the Crosse waie . . . because it was the uttermost bownd of there Towne'.[119]

Features of the Tudor landscape which are still visible today are resonant of stability and continuity; but at the time, the inhabitants of the country saw it altering all around them. The many complaints about the conversion of arable land to sheep pasture were in part a lament for a lost world. The peasant farmer of old was contrasted with the hordes of rootless wage-labourers, and with the beggars and vagabonds of Elizabethan England. Abbey ruins were stark features of a past destroyed, and London suburbs crawled out beyond the city walls, whilst English sailors voyaged to unknown lands. The landscape which could seem both beautiful and blessed was, to some, fixed and invariable in its features, but to others it was dangerously unstable and changing fast.

Gardens and forests

Human endeavour was mostly concerned with wresting a livelihood from the soil, but there were places where the natural world could be a place of cultivation and perfect order, where humankind exercised control. 'My garden sweet, enclosed with walles strong' was how George Cavendish imagined Cardinal Wolsey describing his gardens at Hampton Court.[120] The work of the Flemish philosopher Justus Lipsius, translated into English in 1595, described gardens as a 'withdrawing place from the cares and troubles of this world', and the garden became a place of sanctuary, respite and renewal in Tudor literature.[121] There was a correspondence between human experience and that of nature; the same divine benevolence caused people and plants alike to flourish, and the movement of the planets was held to influence both.[122] By contrast, forests could be places of mystery and subversion. As the property of the Crown, forests were largely empty, a refuge for outlaws and wild beasts. Shakespeare's Forest of Arden was a 'desert inaccessible', or a 'desert city', because it was 'unpeopled', a lawless enclave where women could become men, and kings could be humbled.[123] The legends of Robin Hood, located by the Tudors in Barnsdale Forest rather than Sherwood, and the fantasy of the rich conquered by the poor were well known: three separate groups of rebels in the 1490s, in Derbyshire and Staffordshire, cast themselves as the famous outlaw and his band.[124] Woods and forests were also a vital resource, and when they were encroached upon there was great anxiety.[125] A statute 'for the preservacion of Woodes', passed in 1543, warned that unless woods were protected, there would be no timber left for the building of houses and ships, or for fuel and firewood.[126] There could be conflict over rights and privileges within a forest, where the royal prerogative to hunt met the ancient rights of plough-bote, firebote and housebote, the entitlement to take timber to mend tools, provide fuel or repair a house.[127] If gardens were a place of calm, the forest could be a place of turmoil and conflict.

Gardens offered spiritual refreshment, evoking the lost Garden of Eden, as well as more practically providing food, medicine, cosmetics and colours for paints and textiles.[128] The herbalist John Gerard opined that, among all things created by God, 'none have provoked mens studies more, or satisfied their desires so much as Plants have done'. He envisaged the earth covered with plants 'as with a robe of embroidered worke, set with Orient pearles, and garnished with great diversitie of rare and costly jewels'.[129] Important conversations were frequently held in gardens: in a mid-Tudor dialogue debating the country's troubles, a significant moment in the conversation was marked by a move 'to the garden under the vine where is a good, fresh, and cold sitting for us in the shadow'.[130] In More's *Utopia*, the characters conversed in a garden, and it was a mark of the Utopians' civilization that Hythlodaeus had 'never seen any gardens more productive or elegant than theirs'.[131] Writing for the nuns of Syon Abbey, their librarian saw their garden in terms of divine resonance: he told them to behold the herbs and trees, 'smellynge the floures and fruytes with theyr swetnesse' and then to marvel at 'the grete power of god in his creatures'.[132] Roses, lilies, cowslips, marigolds and violets were scattered through Tudor poetry and plays, just as herbs and flowers were scattered indoors to keep the air sweet. In 1512, the almoner to the Browne family at Cowdray Park was told to keep the hall clean 'and sweete with bowes, and flowers, in their seasons'.[133] When Elizabeth I travelled, she took her own strewing woman with her to keep her rooms strewn with herbs, of which meadowsweet was her favourite.[134]

Some of the aesthetics usually associated with later centuries can be found in Tudor ideas about gardens, including architectural framing, and an enthusiasm for hermitages and grottoes.[135] William Knight, Henry VIII's ambassador to Rome, came back to Horton Court in Gloucestershire, and built a loggia there – a Renaissance reworking of the medieval cloister (see illustration 3).[136] Sir Edward Stradling, sheriff of Glamorganshire, antiquarian and champion of the Welsh language, having travelled in Italy, constructed an Italianate terraced garden descending to the sea at his castle of St Donat's.[137] Francis Carew employed French gardeners at Beddington in Surrey to build his water-garden with grottoes and fountains. Carew and Thomas Cecil met as envoys in Paris in the 1560s, where they seem to have collaborated in importing orange, lemon, pomegranate and myrtle trees.[138] Rosemary, Madonna lilies, lupins and bay trees had all been imported before 1485, but the Tudor era saw the arrival of cyclamen, snowdrops and star of Bethlehem. In 1534, Henry VIII's royal fruiterer planted 105 acres of orchards in Kent, bringing grafts of apple trees from France, and cherry and pear trees from the Low Countries.[139] William Cecil, planting his garden at Stamford in the 1580s, employed advisors from France and Flanders.

Royal gardens proclaimed their superiority with heraldic beasts on poles: the painting of Henry VIII and his family at Whitehall (see plate 22) depicts the gardens with snarling creatures perched on top of columns bearing pennants. When Robert Dudley entertained Elizabeth I at his castle of Kenilworth, his gardens were given a royal touch with a statue of his own heraldic beast, the bear with ragged staff – perhaps a gentle indication of his marital suitability.[140] Whitehall gardens also contained a banqueting house, and Elizabeth had another of these built at the end of the terrace at Windsor Castle: the word 'banquet' at this stage meant a feast of sweet things at the end of a meal, for which the guests might move to another location. Artifice was prized and garden designers might also be responsible for constructing stage scenery.[141] Accounts frequently recorded gifts of fruit and vegetables being brought to Court. When Elizabeth was to visit Francis Carew at his house in Surrey, he covered one of his cherry trees with a tent of canvas to stop the fruit from ripening until the visit was imminent, allowing the queen to eat cherries 'at least one month after all cherries had their farewell of England'.[142]

3. The Renaissance loggia at Horton Court in Gloucestershire

Yet gardens were not just for the wealthy. All country households and many town dwellers had gardens: peasant holdings would be described as a 'messuage and a curtilage' or a 'cottage and a close'.[143] Presents of fruit were important in the ritual of gift-giving, so vital to maintaining social bonds: 'it is better to give an apple than to eat it' was a late medieval proverb.[144] It was noted during Elizabeth I's coronation procession how a 'branche of Rosemary geven to her grace with a supplication by a poore woman about flete bridge, was seen in her chariot til her grace came to westminster'.[145]

Many important popular festivals celebrated the natural world. When Philip Stubbes attacked the rites of the Lords of Misrule in his work of 1583, *The Anatomie of Abuses*, he recalled how the revellers would dance into the churchyard, 'where they have commonly their Sommerhaules, their bowers, arbors, and banqueting houses set up, wherin they feast, banquet and daunce al that day, & (peradventure) all the night too'.[146] He also dwelt with loathing on the practice of 'maying', when in the month of May people went out 'to the woods, groves, hils and mountains, where they spend all the night in plesant pastimes, and in the morning they return bringing with them birch and branches of trees, to deck their assemblies withall'.[147] Stubbes thought these celebrations were presided over by Satan, but for the less puritanical, they were a cherished element of the ritual year.

One of the most popular gardening books of the time, Thomas Hill's treatise of 1563, was seemingly aimed at city gardeners, appealing to Varro, who had advised that gardens be placed near cities, 'for the commodytye (as he sayd) of violets, Roses: and many other thynges … which the cyti hath nede of', including spinach, marigolds, thyme and rosemary.[148] The outskirts of the city had market gardens to provide food for Londoners, and houses within the city also had gardens, as did the monastic houses: that of St Mary Spital in Bishopsgate provided for the largest infirmary in late medieval London, and when the property was sold after the Dissolution, its gardens were listed as a key part of the assets.[149] In Holy Trinity Priory at Aldgate, acquired by the duke of Norfolk after the Dissolution, the priory church itself became an open space in which a banqueting house was lodged, and the former nave became a garden.[150] Other cities were also known for their greenery: there were nurseries in York and Norwich, and the striped rose 'Rosa Mundi' was first found in Norwich in the sixteenth century. A lease of land in York in 1541 was made, on condition that fruit trees should be planted there.[151] Many of the sixty or so livery companies also kept gardens attached to their halls. The Clothworkers' Hall had a vine, regularly tended, and a garden with eglantine, hyssop, rosemary, speedwell and thyme; accounts list payments for weeding and buying watering pots. In the 1560s, the gardens of the Carpenters' Hall bought seeds from abroad, including beet, camomile, chicory, endive, lavender, lettuce, marigold, rosemary, sage and parsley.[152] From the 1550s, the Banbury family ran a business supplying seeds and plants from Tothill Street in Westminster.[153] Gardens showed the human capacity for harnessing nature; they could, as Gerard promised, produce 'a flourishing shew of Summer beauties in the midst of Winters force'.[154]

Forests also had their uses. Wood was essential for fuel and building; glassworks and ironworks were based in woodlands, and tanners used bark to condition leather.[155] As the basis of England's navy, trees were equated with national strength. It took nearly 4,000 trees to build a warship, and the story circulated that the Spanish Armada had orders, if conquest failed, that they should at least destroy the Forest of Dean.[156] Most buildings were timber-framed: Grundle House in Stanton, Suffolk, a farmhouse built in the late fifteenth century, contains around 350 trees, although half of them were less than 9 inches in diameter at the base, whilst the fifteenth-century roof of Norwich Cathedral used around 680 oaks, around 15 inches in diameter. To build the towers of Nonsuch Palace, Henry VIII obtained fifteen huge oaks, each 80 feet long.[157] John Manwood's 1598 treatise on the laws of the forest reproached those who 'contemptuously commit . . . heynous spoiles and trespasses therin', and acts of parliament from 1483 to 1585 sought to protect young trees and to prevent the conversion of woodland to pasture or tillage.[158]

The fascination of the forest also lay in its more mysterious and intractable nature. Forests were 'very auncient things', which 'Kings and Princes of this Realme have always mayntained . . . for places of pleasure and delight for their recreation'.[159] Manwood noted that the creatures therein had been the king's since before the time of Canute.[160] Forests were kept empty of settlement to preserve game for hunting, so that in otherwise fairly densely populated areas they were empty enclaves.[161] They were defined by their 'places of Secresie' for the 'abode of the wild beasts', namely 'the Hart, the Hynde, the Hare, the Boare and the Wolfe'.[162] They were a foil to the city, or the orderliness of cultivated ground. Timon of Athens, furiously spurning his city, turned instead to the woods, to find the 'unkindest beast more kinder than mankind'; the forest in *Titus Andronicus* was the setting for rape and murder.[163] In *A Midsummer Night's Dream*, the characters escape the tyranny of Athenian law and courtly society to enter the woods, where the boundaries between dream and reality are blurred and magic reigns; and in Sir Thomas Wyatt's sonnet, Love flees 'unto the heart's forest' to hide in darkness and secrecy.[164]

Manwood was fantasizing, however, when he imagined forests teeming with boars and wolves: the last wild boars in England had been killed in the Forest of Dean in the thirteenth century.[165] The forest was cast as a place of lawlessness and danger, as a necessary backdrop to Tudor notions of civilization. Thomas Churchyard, in 1587, saw the Welsh as progressing towards a more enlightened condition by grubbing up their trees to plough the ground, 'where sturdie Okes did stand'.[166] At the same time, forests became a focus for nostalgia. The Elizabethan poet Michael Drayton recalled the time when 'this whole country's face was forestry'; and lamenting the loss of the monasteries in 1589, Francis Trigge recalled not only the monks' charity, but also 'their planting of woods'.[167] At the start of the Tudor period, Sir Thomas Malory's knights had ridden into the forest to prove their courage and their chivalry amidst supernatural enchantments; and towards the end of Elizabeth's reign, Edmund Spenser's *Faerie Queene* contained forests even more allegorical, even more dangerous.[168] In an age of rapid and troubling change, forests and woodland suggested continuity with the past, whether as a source of sustenance, or as a space of mythical enchantment and unlicensed liberty.

Towns and cities

Towns accounted for only 5–10 per cent of the population, but they were growing. Under Tudor rule, they established new links with the countryside through trade and the growth of the cloth industry, stretching out by means of roads and waterways to connect with the rest of the country. London and its suburbs, whose population increased rapidly in this period, was unique: even compared to its European rivals it was huge.[169] Norwich and Bristol were the next biggest cities, but this period also saw the growth of Hull, Newcastle, King's Lynn and Liverpool, chiefly as a result of expanding foreign trade.[170] Of the fifteen to twenty towns with a population of over 5,000 by the end of the century, nine were ports. Tudor towns have often been described in terms of crisis and decay, and provincial towns certainly contrasted with the prosperous, variegated anomaly that was the city of London.[171] The towns have also been viewed as diametrically opposed to the rural areas that accounted for most of English society. Some social commentary of the time disparaged town dwellers as parasites upon the face of the land: Francis Trigge insisted that 'the plowe maintaines all trades'.[172] Yet towns did not exist in isolation: their economies, their cultural patterns and their population all had deep roots within the surrounding landscape. The picture of crisis and decay has been both overstated and oversimplified. Some towns were blighted by fluctuations in population or trade, and some by epidemics; yet this varied a great deal according to the region or the trade concerned. Overall, the picture was one of growth and increased prosperity, whilst London, despite all the challenges, continued to grow at an astonishing pace.

While only 3 per cent of people in England in 1500 lived in cities of 10,000 or more, that was still a greater proportion than in Scotland or Scandinavia, and was similar to the figure for France (though lower than in the more urbanized societies of Italy and the Low Countries). By 1600, the proportion had risen to around 6 per cent.[173] Figures for urban dwellers remain debatable, however, because it is uncertain what constituted a town: the modern tendency to categorize according to size of population ignores the importance of small towns as centres of distribution. If by 1600 there were fewer than 20 towns with a population of 5,000 or more, there were nevertheless over 600 towns that held markets.[174] These left lasting traces on the urban landscape: the market hall in Shrewsbury or the market cross at Malmesbury give some sense of the importance of those towns as trading hubs. The butter cross in Witney indicates how larger towns would have had separate centres for the marketing of different commodities: Tudor Scarborough had at least five crosses, including for butter and corn. Exeter's Guildhall dated from the mid-fifteenth century, but in 1591 the Renaissance portico was added to provide a focus for the market. A hook in the ceiling for weighing scales still remains as a reminder of the moral importance of correct weights and measures.[175]

Much seaborne trade centred upon the greater ports. The coal trade out of Tyneside is estimated to have doubled between the 1570s and the 1590s.[176] Material remnants of this are now scarce, although Bessie Surtees House in Newcastle demonstrates the wealth of the Tudor merchant class.[177] A great deal of trade, especially in lumber and coal, used quite small seaside towns as points for distribution, treating the sea as 'a great river around the country'.[178] Trade in the south-west was often between Cornwall and Wales, and the Tudor merchant's house still standing in Tenby gives an idea of the prosperity this might engender. Blakeney in Norfolk is another example of small-scale local trading by sea: in 1587, Blakeney imported coal from Newcastle, timber from Arundel, fish from Blyth, oats from Lynn and groceries from London; only vegetables and building materials came from abroad, shipped from the Netherlands. At the same time, Blakeney's little port saw the export of malt, rye, peas, butter and saffron.[179] Its parish church of St Nicholas, patron saint of sailors, had two towers to guide ships home from sea; extensive medieval and early modern graffiti of ships there were votive offerings to the saint for his protection.

Larger towns and cities were the focus for their provinces, drawing in migration and trade, sending out news and merchandise.[180] Their importance was not purely economic, for they were also political rallying points: Exeter Guildhall displayed the sword and cap of maintenance given by Henry VII in thanks for the city's loyalty against Perkin Warbeck. They were also places in which the church hierarchy was most firmly rooted: Chester gained new status and prosperity from being made a bishopric in 1540; it also prospered from serving as a base from which to reach Ireland.[181] York was the religious capital of northern England, the seat of government administration for the north, a bulwark against the Scottish menace and the focal point of England's largest county. It possessed one of the few mints other than the one in the Tower of London, and its archdiocese stretched from Cumberland to Nottinghamshire (even after the creation of the diocese of Chester, it accounted for perhaps a tenth of England's population). The Ouse was navigable to York and beyond, connecting the city by water to the rest of England's coasts and waterways, and to the rest of the continent.[182] York served as a focus and engendered a sense of identity among northerners. In his attempt to put to rest the animosities that had fuelled the Pilgrimage of Grace, Henry VIII promised to call a parliament at York, and later made an unprecedented royal progress there in 1541, securing the submission and affirming the loyalty of his northern subjects.

Towns provided a nexus for trade between communities, and with other countries. Port books introduced in 1565 to regulate customs dues were applied to 122 maritime centres. The sixteenth century also saw the development of a network of postal routes.[183] In 1565, London was connected by just two postal roads to Dover and Berwick; but by 1605, the routes reached to Portsmouth, Penryn, Padstow and Barnstaple; through Birmingham to Holyhead, Carlisle and Penrith; and through Bristol and Swansea to Dale, Ludlow, Margate and Sandwich.[184] Towns were developing new links with the countryside, as the lure of cheap labour encouraged cloth merchants to practise 'putting out', getting their cloth woven in village households before being brought to town for sale and distribution. This kind of outsourcing could keep costs down and help avoid the restrictions of urban regulation. There was also a steady flow of people back and forth, with seasonal migration to the towns for work, and back to the countryside at the busiest times in the agricultural year, prompting the development of toll roads, bridges and canals. Exeter Ship Canal was constructed in 1566 with a new form of lock, the pound lock. The first act of parliament to promote inland navigation was secured for the River Stour in 1515 by the city of Canterbury, which argued that the city was 'now of late in grete ruyne and decaye' and needed the river to be deepened, scoured and cleared of mills and dams, from the village of Great Chart down to the port at Sandwich.[185]

England's capital was a city like no other, so far as its Tudor inhabitants were concerned. And there was some basis for their claims: London was enormous, with a population of perhaps 50,000 people in 1500 that had grown to around 200,000 by the end of the century. The original city of London, sheltered within walls that echoed those of Roman Londinium, was spilling over and reaching out down the Strand towards the separate settlement of Westminster, where the Palace of Westminster and the Abbey with the shrine of Edward the Confessor, king and saint, embodied both royal and sacred authority. Within its walls, the city was overlooked by the spire of St Paul's Cathedral to the west and the Tower of London to the east, and there were over a hundred distinct parishes, each with its parish church.[186] There were also thirty-nine religious houses. It was said that there was a cross on every street corner: the greatest of these, like the Eleanor Cross at Cheapside, formed a part of civic pageantry during coronation processions and the receptions held for Emperor Charles V in 1522 and King Philip II in 1554. After the Reformation, this Eleanor Cross proved a continual source of aggravation to Puritans, although it was not finally destroyed by religious zealots until 1643.[187]

The River Thames, which ran along London's southern flank, had only one crossing-point, which gave London Bridge exceptional importance as both a thoroughfare and a symbolic portal. The severed heads and limbs of traitors impaled there warned against wrong-doing. By the Elizabethan period, the city was expanding in all directions, reaching out towards Clerkenwell, Islington and Hackney in the north, and to the east along the river. The parish of Stepney in the marshes built a gallery for its parish church in the 1580s to cope with an increasing population. Southwark, south of the Thames and beyond the reach of city regulations, hosted a number of growing concerns, from theatres to brothels. The city walls had last been overhauled in 1477, so by 1600 they were no longer convincing defences; and the drawbridge on London Bridge had not worked since before 1500. But then London had not faced an army of any note since 1471.[188] The two great wharves of the city were at Billingsgate and Queenhithe; but increasingly the river to the east was becoming a centre for shipping, and by 1600 international voyages were leaving from Deptford, Wapping and Ratcliffe.

The Greek visitor of 1545, Nicander, marvelled at the Thames and at how 'the Ocean, swollen by the tide, thrusts the water upstream' for six hours, before returning the other way. To him, the Tower of London appeared like an acropolis armed with many guns.[189] To the Venetian visitor, London abounded 'with every article of luxury, as well as with the necessaries of life'. He was impressed by the Strand, where 'there are fifty-two goldsmith's shops, so rich and full of silver vessels, great and small, that in all the shops in Milan, Rome, Venice and Florence put together, I do not think there would be found so many of the magnificence that are to be seen in London'.[190] London's chief provision was of luxuries, including the books sold around St Paul's, although it was also the centre of the coaching and goods transport system. More importantly, however, it was the political hub of the nation. News of what was happening in London could soon spread to the rest of the country. Perhaps a sixth of the population of England dwelt at one point or another in the capital, and this circulation of its citizens could help make London an engine of change in the country at large.[191]

To hold London was to hold England, or so it was believed. The city was the objective of almost every coup or rebellion, from Henry VII's conquest in 1485 to the earl of Essex's abortive uprising in 1601. This was not just symbolism: London contained the armoury, the mint and frequently the royal family, too. It commanded the Thames, which was England's link to the rest of the world, and increasingly the focus of its overseas trade. As a result, the London chronicles provide an invaluable source for Tudor history, from Fabyan's chronicle which reflects the preoccupations of the great city companies, to the diary of Henry Machyn, a London chronicler with Catholic sympathies, who left an account of the extraordinary happenings of the 1550s.[192] If London was the backdrop to many of the plays written in the sixteenth century, this only reflected the extent to which it was already a stage on which political and social dramas were daily enacted, from the theatre of punishment to the grandeur of a coronation to the

Midsummer revels. The most successful political players of the time were usually those who also knew how to play a London crowd.

For Thomas Starkey, London was the new Rome, offering an opportunity for a new order of government based on classical virtue and civic duty. John Stow began his *Survey of London* by comparing the foundation of Rome by gods to that of London, founded by Brutus, a descendant of Venus.[193] William Caxton, publishing a translation of Cato's *Distichs*, dedicated it to 'the noble auncyent . . . Cyte of london', to which he felt a profound debt, 'as to my moder / of whom I have receyved my noureture and lyvynge'; Caxton worried that the city was being damaged by the pursuit of profit and the neglect of civic duty. Like Starkey, he wanted the citizens of London to take the citizens of Rome as their model: 'the noble Romayns', who, for the sake of their city, would 'put theyr bodyes and lyves in Ieopardy and to the deth'.[194] This idealization of London was embodied in Thomas Wyatt's poem 'Tagus, Farewell', when, as ambassador, he bade farewell to Spain and described the pull to return to his own city, 'the town which Brutus sought by dreams', and to the service of king and country.[195] By contrast, Henry Howard, earl of Surrey, in political disgrace, described London as a concentration of vice, comparing her to Babylon (albeit largely to divert attention from his own unruly behaviour).[196] It was easy to characterize the city in this way. In 1593, perhaps prompted by the cruel visitation of the plague, Thomas Nashe turned from his usual bawdy or satirical prose to write *Christs Teares Over Jerusalem*, 'a quintessence of holy complaint'.[197] In it, he pleaded with God to feel the same compassion for London as he had for his own city of Jerusalem.[198]

Between 1485 and 1603, London witnessed substantial changes. Perhaps the two most significant were the loss of the monastic houses and the acquisition of the Royal Exchange, constructed between 1566 and 1568. London was full of religious houses: Blackfriars, Austin Friars, Charterhouse, Greyfriars. It had good connections with the Observant Franciscans attached to the royal palaces at Greenwich and Richmond, and with the royal foundations of Sheen and Syon on the river near Hampton Court. Monasteries were deeply integrated within city society. They maintained hospitals: some such as Cheapside, St Augustine Papey and Elsing Spital were lost during the Reformation; however, St Mary of Bethlehem was preserved and granted to the city. St Bartholomew's was refounded by

Henry VIII in 1544, and St Thomas' Hospital (previously dedicated to St Thomas Becket) was refounded by Edward VI. The Savoy Hospital, founded by Henry VII and dissolved by Edward VI, was refounded by Mary I. Some former monastic houses were adapted to become houses of the nobility: part of Austin Friars was taken by Thomas Cromwell; as his status increased, he acquired more of the property and began planning stables, a tennis court and a bowling alley. Confiscated after his execution, it passed to the Drapers' Company, whilst its church was given to the Dutch Protestants during Edward VI's reign. St Bartholomew's Priory went to Richard Rich and Holy Trinity Priory Aldgate passed to Thomas Audley; meanwhile, the Charterhouse was rebuilt by Sir Edward North and then by the duke of Norfolk.[199]

Built by the banker Thomas Gresham, the Royal Exchange was designed by a Flemish architect in imitation of the Bourse at Antwerp – another example of England emulating its European neighbours. One of Gresham's friends had written to him in 1561, marvelling that business prospered, 'considering what a city London is and that in so many years they have not found the means to make a bourse but must walk in the rain when it raineth, more like pedlars than merchants'.[200] The Royal Exchange was Gresham's response, and was a significant addition to the urban landscape. Thomas Smith, in 1549, commented on how the city was filling up with shops full of glittering luxuries: 'gaye daggers, knives, swordes, and girdles, that is able to make anie temperate man to gase on them and to bie sumwhat'.[201] Not everyone thought this level of cosmopolitanism an asset: William Harrison commented on how people moved between 'Spanish guise . . . French toys . . . the High Almain fashion' and even 'the Morisco gowns', adding disparagingly that 'except it were a dog in a doublet, you shall not see any so disguised as are my countrymen of England'.[202]

If London was both a political crucible and an intangible ideal, it was also a fluid and volatile society. The high mortality rates – a consequence of overcrowding and poor sanitation – meant the diseased city was only kept alive by a constant influx of immigrants: it has been estimated that by the later sixteenth century, around 4,000 new arrivals each year were needed to sustain London's population. Some were foreigners; a high proportion were apprentices; and many came from the country, so there was always uncertainty as to a Londoner's true origins. A common slander was to accuse a woman of having had a bastard child elsewhere, or of having left because of some other social crime.[203] The mobility of Londoners was striking, both within its walls and in the movement of people from rural areas to the city and back again.[204] Within the hundred or more parishes packed together, tensions ran high and boundaries mattered. Dwellings were close together, families were crowded, temporary lodgers were common and privacy was rare. Many defamation suits rested on evidence of words that had been overheard – sometimes from a house across the street, but usually in shared yards or on doorsteps.[205]

The freedom of London's women to walk the streets was noted by foreign visitors. In part, this was because women were heavily involved in the various economic activities, from brewing to shopkeeping; there were also many servants, from house-servants going to market to washerwomen plying their trade, and all sorts of women ate and drank in alehouses. Other less salubrious trades also flourished: prostitution continued unabated, despite Henry VIII's ban on brothels in 1546. London's women were a force in their own right: in the summer of 1535 there was a demonstration by some of them at Greenwich in favour of Princess Mary, whose exclusion from the succession had aroused much indignation.[206]

London could be cast as a crucible of sin, ambition and strife. Elizabethan ballads could reproach the city as if it were a person: 'Pray England pray, and London leave thy wicked trade.'[207] For Stow, by contrast, 'the propagation of Religion, the execution of good policie, the exercise of Charity, and the defence of the countrey, is best performed by townes and Cities: and this civill life approcheth nearest to the shape of that misticall body whereof Christ is the head, and men be the members'.[208] His beloved city was the embodiment of love both human and divine, its citizens working 'together in good amity'.[209] His survey of 1598, however, was deeply imbued with nostalgia and a sense of loss.[210] The city of his youth had changed beyond recognition; he grieved that the rich no longer maintained traditions of hospitality and charity, and that the newly affluent had little sense of responsibility towards the poor; great houses were converted into tenements, the indigent were clustered in alleys, and the fields outside the city were 'encroached upon by building of filthy cottages'.[211] Stow's observations were coloured in part by his Catholic sympathies; but his more Protestant contemporary Thomas Bentley also deplored the spoliation of churches, and was nostalgic for the communal gatherings of earlier times.[212] By the end of the century, in a London four times the size of Henry VII's city, boundaries of all sorts had been overwhelmed; Bridewell and Bethlem had become bywords for crime and madness; and appeals to a sense of community and civic duty constantly harked back to the past.[213] The fervency of London's defenders was in itself a reflection of the bewildering speed at which the city was changing.

Seascape

It is a fact of enormous importance, and yet one infrequently discussed, that Tudor England was largely surrounded by water. The sea was the country's chief defence, the conduit for its trade and a major source of sustenance. The sea was also both mysterious and dangerous, a landscape of its own, 'rich and strange', which brought forth 'sea-sorrow' from 'contentious waves'.[214] The salt water of the ocean corresponded to the saltiness of blood, sweat and tears, and sea voyages could be times of trial.[215] The translator of a 1536 navigational guide advised mariners to 'let god stere', and to take as their shipmates St George, St Mary and St John for safety's sake. The sea was also a place for strange portents. In 1590, when France was riven with religious wars, a pamphlet reported how one of Elizabeth's ships, the *Vanguard*, had encountered vessels from the Netherlands, whose sailors told how 'in a place called Bell Ile, the Sea round about them was of the coulour of blood, for the full space of halfe an houre, and nothing was to be seene but bloud, so farre as they could discerne, and taking up the water in their buckets, they could not perceive it from bloud'.[216]

St Nicholas, protector of seafarers, was a prominent saint in coastal communities: at Great Yarmouth, where the church was dedicated to St Nicholas, the oblations offered in 1504–05 on the saint's feast day totalled 43s 11d, almost equalling the Christmas offering, and only outstripped by the 68s 4d offered at Easter.[217] The chapel of St Anne at Brislington, near Bristol, received the offerings made by pilgrims in a host of model ships; it protected the ferry crossing that was established over the Avon in the early sixteenth century.[218] The Chapel of Our Lady in the Rock on the shore at Dover, which Henry VIII visited in 1532, also watched over the shipping there; after surviving shipwreck in 1530, the French ambassador made a bequest to it.[219] Even the English Channel might seem fearsome in a small Tudor vessel: the Greek visitor Nicander wrote of his awe and wonder at the ocean, 'boundless and inscrutable', even though he had only sailed from Calais to Dover.[220]

The practical dangers of travelling by sea were well known. Thomas Bentley's 1582 compendium of prayers for women included one for those whose men were at sea, as merchants or travellers. It listed the 'divers calamities' which threatened: 'to be tossed at the pleasure of the wind and waves . . . dashed violentlie upon the maine rocks, or to sticke in the quicksands, or to be despoiled . . . by the tyrannie of pirats'. References to sea travel tended to recall the prophet Jonah as a reassuring example of God's ability to save, and Bentley's prayer reminded God that the use of ships was not the product of 'anie humane invention', but a divine mystery revealed unto Noah. Nonetheless, shipwrecks figured prominently in Tudor literature. The martyrologist John Foxe described how the biblical translator William Tyndale narrowly escaped when shipwrecked off the coast of Holland, casting him as a modern equivalent of St Paul.[221] Shakespeare's plays contain so many references to seafaring that some have insisted, rather implausibly, that the playwright had been a sailor at some point.[222] The sea was a force which could disrupt, terrify and estrange.

Yet the Tudor era was an age of discovery, when the encounter with new stretches of ocean and newfound countries beyond them broke apart the already unravelling medieval notion of Christendom as a bounded world.[223] England's trading links were growing apace in the sixteenth century. John Sanderson, a misanthropic London merchant, travelled to Constantinople, Egypt and the Holy Land, visiting Antioch, Aleppo, Tripoli and Damascus.[224] On his first voyage to Constantinople, he recalled, 'the shipp came aground and put us all in extraordinary feare'; trying to board a small boat in Rhodes harbour, he was nearly drowned when it capsized; on a later voyage between Alexandria and Cairo, his ship was wrecked near Rosetta. He listed the losses of this last adventure: 'all provision of wood, wine, and houshold stufe; also five person drowned; others saved by swimming . . . myselfe and three more most miracolously in the boate, for which I ever geve thankes to God Almightie'.[225]

Despite the dangers, perseverance could bring riches. Cornwall may have been 'shouldered out . . . into the farthest part of the Realme', wrote

Richard Carew, but it was 'in the trade way betwene Wales, Ireland, Spaine, France and Netherland', which meant 'lesse peril' and fewer costs.[226] Many parts of England had a close relationship with the sea. The fishing trade was vital to a country that fasted from meat twice a week, and all through Lent and Advent. Thomas Bodley's wealth was in large part because his wife was the daughter of a pilchard merchant; he used it to endow Oxford's university library.[227] Luxury goods and exotic foodstuffs also depended on seagoing trade: Nicander noted that London merchants imported olive oil from the Peloponnese and wine from Crete.[228] The Crown also had a close relationship with the sea, since fishing fleets contributed to the navy in times of war. Investments in trading ventures might also, therefore, bolster naval defence capabilities.[229] In 1558, at war with France, Mary I issued a proclamation against those 'Shipmasters, maryners, gonners, Sea farynge men, and watermen' who had disappeared on commercial ventures, leaving only 'the refuse, and basyst sort of men of servyce' to furnish the royal navy. She instructed that nobody was to leave, 'out of any havon, ryver, creke, or place', without special licence, and ordered all those at sea to return immediately.[230]

The liminality of the sea was underlined by the questionable legality of much that took place there. State-sponsored piracy was an integral part of warfare. In July 1557, for example, Philip and Mary issued a proclamation aimed at the 'most loving, faithful, and obedient' inhabitants of coastal areas, who might be willing to equip a ship 'at their own costs . . . for the annoyance of their majesties' enemies, the Frenchmen and Scots'. This proclamation went on to safeguard anything they might acquire in this way.[231] Piracy also happened in peacetime. Since the Admiralty Court had first been established in 1340, it had issued 'letters of marque', granting permission for reprisals by those who claimed that their ships had been menaced by foreign craft. This permission could be exploited in various ways. From the 1530s onward, after England had broken with the papacy, another element was added to tensions at sea. Robert Reneger, merchant of Southampton, had a prosperous business taking grain to Spain and returning with wine, woad, iron, oil, soap, raisins and figs, which were distributed to Newbury, Winchester and Basingstoke. One voyage, however, was intercepted by a French warship and a Portuguese caravel, its crew assaulted and its cargo stolen. The attackers, it was reported, spoke of the English as 'most erronyouse lutheryans'.[232] That the English were seen not just as enemies, but also as heretics, brought a new level of animosity into play.

In July 1563, Elizabeth I licensed the seizure of French shipping, responding to an initiative by France that encouraged its citizens 'to invade, take, offend, and endamage all Englishmen and other her majesty's subjects, either by sea or land . . . by taking them prisoners and putting them to ransom'.[233] A month later, she had to issue another exasperated proclamation, explaining that her subjects should not feel free to harass any French people 'living quietly' or falsely claim that people were French as an excuse to seize them and their goods.[234] Yet another month later, in September 1563, she was ordering naval forces to protect Spanish vessels from French attacks.[235] The difficulties of regulating behaviour at sea were given voice in a proclamation of February 1564 against those who had nonetheless been harassing Spanish shipping; it noted that because the number of ships at sea preparing to fight the French 'are so great . . . and of so divers port towns and countries . . . it appeareth very hard how a good account may be made of every of them, being so many'.[236] Elizabeth's response was to implement the dubious policy of encouraging people in coastal areas to inform on offenders. The behaviour of those at sea often remained, however, beyond the reach of authority.

In 1536, a translated work on navigation was published in English: the translator related that he had been asked by a 'sad / ingenyous and cyrcum-specte maryner of the cyte of London' to turn it from French to English, but he was nervous about the finished product, 'for I came never on the see nor by no coste therof'.[237] This sense of unfamiliarity with the sea was echoed by other works on navigation. As in so many things, Tudor England learned from its neighbours. The Venetian pilot Battista Testa Rossa, visiting London during Mary I's reign, brought his own navigating manual with him and left it behind when he departed. His techniques were considerably more sophisticated than English practice at this time.[238] The first navigation manual printed in English, in 1561, was a translation of a Spanish original.[239] Its usefulness and popularity is attested by the nine further reprints and updated editions which followed over the next seventy years. Sixteen other texts were translated, mostly from Spanish and Dutch, between 1575 and 1590.[240] One of the first English works, *A Regiment for the Sea*, published in 1577 by William Bourne, gave the impression that navigation was still a science alien to English culture. Bourne felt moved to remind his reader why navigational lore was useful, 'for that wee be invironed rounde aboute with the Sea', and then had to define what navigation actually was.[241]

More's *Utopia* purported to be the tale of the traveller Hythlodaeus, who 'with a black sun-burned face, a long beard, and a cloak cast homely about his shoulders' was obviously a mariner, full of stories about 'strange and unknown peoples and countries'. Travel literature sold well, and it brought with it an acquaintance with seafaring. One of the characters in *Utopia* noted how the voyages of Amerigo Vespucci were 'in print, and abroad in every man's hands'. When Hakluyt published his *Principall Navigations* in 1589, the title page had a hasty addition: 'Whereunto is added the last most renowned English Navigation, round about the whole Globe of the Earth.'[242] A book called *The Libell of Englyshe Polycye* in the 1430s had urged the English government to establish sovereignty over the seas around its coast and to build a navy to dominate trade; when Hakluyt included it in his work, the plea to keep the sea like a fortified city wall protecting England had a more pointed resonance.[243]

* * *

The landscape in which we live is constructed as much by our imagination as by earth, stones, wood and water. It is an archive in itself of the histories played out there, a repository of treasures and affections, a place where memory is both forged and preserved.[244] Landscape also exists in the mind, a world which we shape with our longings and understanding, and which shapes us in return.[245] For most of the Tudor period, sanctity and history were etched upon the landscape, to be celebrated or contested. As Tudor commentators surveyed this beloved land, they could observe both change and decay. At the very end of the period, as James VI of Scotland ascended the throne, Francis Trigge wrote a work dedicated to the new king, pleading for 'the restoring of . . . ancient Commons and liberties, which late Inclosure with depopulation, uncharitably hath taken away'. Trigge saw landowners greedily gathering together lands previously held in common, thereby depriving the poor of their ancient rights; he observed despondently that where once 'God hath beene praised with many mouthes, there now shreeking Owles, and other uncleane birds make their nestes'. The results of this were concrete and worrying: 'whereas your

Maiestie might have had great choice of Souldiers, and able men for service in warre . . . now there is almost none to be had, but a Sheepheard and his dogge'. In a work that was both economic analysis and religious exhortation, Trigge argued that enclosure led to the decay of tillage and the depopulation of towns, and was against Christian charity and the ancient liberties and customs of England, concluding that 'Inclosure with depopulation is a sinne whereof God shall make especiall inquiry at the day of Iudgement.'[246]

If the sixteenth-century English landscape was more malleable and changeable than we might expect, by far the greatest change came about in attitudes towards the land and all its features. Tudor society saw a new inquisitiveness about the nature and significance of the natural world, in which there were many places of solace, but where, too, signs of trouble could be clearly written, from economic strains to the disputed sacrality of sites previously revered. It was against this backdrop that the dramas of the era were played out. Landownership remained the basis of power, and the key to all local politics. Some landowners, inevitably, exploited their tenants.[247] Many tenants fought back, however, on the grounds of ancient custom, and it is evident that the gentry respected this, and usually sought a conciliatory, rather than combative, stance on the question of rents and entry-fines.[248] As legal records attest, questions of land ownership, tenancy and farming rights were often the medium through which power was brokered in the localities. Human connections to the land were a key part of the identity of Tudor men and women, and lay at the heart of popular memory, since the daily battle to extract a living from field, forest, river and sea remained the determining factor in the lives of the majority of the population.

The landscape was also the backdrop to questions of national politics. The sovereignty which was won in the 1480s in the muddy fields of Leicestershire and Nottinghamshire, at the battles of Bosworth Field and Stoke, was reinforced in military action in 1497 on Blackheath, outside London, and again in the north of England in 1537, in both East Anglia and Devon in 1549, near London in 1554, and in the north in 1569. That sovereignty was then consolidated by the Tudor palaces built or enlarged at Richmond, Greenwich, Nonsuch and many other places besides, including Whitehall and St James' in Westminster and London. On a more daily basis, it was enacted in royal processions through city and countryside, where hunting forays helped bind together the mutual loyalties of the monarchs and their subjects. Henry VIII's response to rebellion in the north was to progress to York, just as Elizabeth consolidated her sometimes questionable role as Protestant queen in her many progresses.[249] The assize judges sent out on circuits and the proclamations broadcast in market squares across the country were practical reinforcement of public order and the royal will, respectively; and the coastal fortifications of the 1540s and 1580s embodied the protective capability of government, as well as its vulnerability. To understand truly the Tudor era, we must situate our imagination within the natural world in which the Tudors lived, worked, fought and died.

CHAPTER 2

'HIS WIT ALWAYS QUICK AND READY'
THE REIGN OF HENRY VII

It takes uncommon skill to launch a successful invasion of England. Julius Caesar may have managed it, but Napoleon failed. William the Conqueror in 1066 had established a claim before he set sail and William III in 1688 was invited in. Success has usually required substantial military backing. Yet in August 1485, a young man with a handful of ships and about 2,000 men landed near Milford Haven, across the bay from Pembroke Castle, the place where he had been born twenty-eight years before. Within two months, he had crossed Wales and England, defeated the anointed king in battle, taken London and been crowned in Westminster Abbey. Over the next twelve months, he pacified England, established his court, married a Yorkist princess and fathered a male heir. Henry VII, contrary to the historical myths that surround him, was an exceptionally talented king – forceful, intelligent and resourceful. It is seldom acknowledged, but he was probably the most effective and impressive of the Tudor monarchs.

Henry's reputation today is as an avaricious, reclusive and – compared to his successors – very dull man. In his own time, however, he was known for his magnificence, his strength of character and his astounding achievements.[1] With a combination of military flair, energetic management and showmanship, he rescued a deeply unnerved and divided country from recurring civil war, and brought comparative order and stability to government. He was capable and perceptive; and to judge from his tight-knit family and the loyal service of his closest advisors, he was probably also likeable. Whatever subsequent centuries have claimed, many contemporaries saw his abilities. An English elegy from 1509 referred to 'the puyssaunt and myghty henry' and called him 'Hector in batayll, Ulyxes in polecy'.[2] Sir Thomas Elyot, writing twenty years after Henry's death, noted the terrible state of the country in 1485, but opined that 'by his most excellent wit, he in a few years, not only brought this realm in good order and under due obedience, revived the laws, advanced Justice, refurnished his dominions and repaired his manors', but was such a good diplomat that 'all other princes either feared him or had him in a fatherly reverence'.[3] The Italian scholar Polydore Vergil, papal tax collector and historian, gave this description of the king (see plate 5):

> His body was slender but well built and strong; his height above the average. His appearance was remarkably attractive and his face was cheerful, especially when speaking ... His spirit was distinguished, wise and prudent; his mind was brave and resolute and never, even at moments of the greatest danger, deserted him ... In government he was shrewd and prudent, so that no one dared to get the better of him through deceit or guile. He was gracious and kind and was as attentive to his visitors as he was easy of access. His hospitality was splendidly generous.[4]

Vergil concluded, however, by saying that such virtues were 'obscured latterly only by avarice'. He had to say this, because it was the required opinion once Henry VIII's reign had begun. It was a judgement that would come to dominate the historical memory of Henry VII, but it was not universally agreed at the time. During the king's lifetime, a Venetian envoy thought him 'a man of vast ability'; a Spanish envoy, observing him instructing his son, commented that 'there could be no better school in the world than the society of such a father ... He is so wise and attentive to everything; nothing escapes his attention'.[5] Thomas Wriothesley called him 'the famous prince namyd in his tyme for his wisdome le doyen de roys'.[6] John Fisher, bishop of Rochester and future saint, who preached Henry's funeral sermon, recognized 'his wytte always quycke and redy, his reason pyththy and substancyall, his memory fresshe and holdynge, his experyence notable, his counseylles fortunate and taken by wyse delyberacyon, his speche gracyous in dyverse languages, his persone goodly and amyable'.[7]

To Francis Bacon, one of the earliest historians of Henry's reign, and undoubtedly one of the most able, Henry was wise and skilled, 'this

Solomon of England', a man who loved peace and yet was valiant; a just king, a maker of good laws, a man who 'had nothing in him of vainglory, but yet kept state and majesty to the height, being sensible that majesty makes the people bow, but vainglory bows to them'.[8]

Such positive assessments of Henry have usually been dismissed as flattery, while the accusations of avarice have been taken as objective commentary.[9] In reality, it was the comments about avarice that were flattery; crucially, however, they were meant to flatter a different king. Henry VII was cast as a distrustful miser in the tense first few months of his son's reign. His reputation was a casualty of Henry VIII's attempts to strengthen his own credibility as ruler. It is undeniable that Henry VII sought to exercise close control over his court and his nobility – with good reason, since he encountered betrayal many times. Given the vulnerability of his position, these attempts to keep a tight rein on the political classes should be seen as intelligent management, which largely succeeded, rather than as something vindictive and repressive. There are plenty of examples of Henry VII being merciful. He issued pardons after 1485 and the uprising of 1487, and he gave the pretender Lambert Simnel, who had tried to supplant him, a job in his kitchens, in marked contrast to his predecessor Richard III, who had crushed the rebels of 1483.[10] The bonds Henry used to keep his more wayward subjects on the straight and narrow were mostly suspended fines; he did not extract money, so much as threaten to do so in the event of any misdemeanour.[11] But those of his subjects who had a great deal of wealth did not like having this threat hanging over them, and when he died, the chattering classes of Tudor London came together by unspoken agreement to pressurize the new king into a style of government which would give them more freedom of action, even as his humbler household servants mourned their dead king. As Edward Hall observed in his chronicle, 'Wonder it were to write of the lamentacion that was made, for this Prince emongest his servauntes, and other of the wisest sort, and the joy that was made for his death, by suche as were troubled, by rigor of his law.'[12]

By praising the new king's generosity, and uttering pious condemnation of the previous king's avarice, those who shaped popular opinion were skilfully influencing Henry VIII. Among them were some powerful propagandists. Thomas More, who had already defended the city of

London in parliament against novel forms of raising revenue, wrote a Latin poem to celebrate Henry VIII's coronation. 'This day is the end of our slavery, the fount of our liberty, the end of sadness, the beginning of joy', he wrote – a curiously rude thing to say about the new king's father.[13] He characterized the previous reign as a time when people feared 'laws put to unjust ends'.[14] 'Tight-fistedness is well and truly banished', wrote William Blount, Lord Mountjoy, praising his new monarch, whom he knew very well. 'Our king's heart is not upon gold or jewels or mines of ore, but upon virtue, reputation and eternal renown.'[15] These men were not stating a fact, so much as outlining an agenda for the new king. To do so, they had to cast the old king as fatally tainted by his miserliness. A poem by Erasmus which has recently come to light, scribbled in the margin of an early copy of More's *Utopia*, asks 'Why is it that no Englishman mourned your death, Henry?' He noted that 'neither a licentious crowd nor a hater of the whip and discipline laments the departure of the diligent doctor'.[16] This clear-sighted commentator from the Netherlands was well practised at recognizing self-interest at work.

The verdict on Henry VII's avarice enshrined in Vergil's history was to be the basis for nearly every other sixteenth-century account.[17] Henry VIII's very first piece of legislation was a general pardon, which suggested that from now on, justice would be done and men would be able to live and work in peace, without any of the 'rigour' with which they had previously been 'vexed'.[18] Copies of this pardon were printed and distributed within twenty-four hours of it being signed, a slick deployment of print technology. Other utterances reinforced the message. At Henry VII's funeral in St Paul's, John Fisher praised him for keeping his land 'many a daye in pease and tranquyllyte', but recalled what Henry had said during his last Lenten confession, when he promised 'a true reformacyon of all them that were offycers and ministres of his lawes', so that justice henceforth 'truly and indyfferently myght be executed in all causes'. This was language which, perhaps intentionally, echoed the terms of the general pardon.[19] In this skilful piece of oratory, Fisher carefully shredded the dead king's reputation under the guise of reverent commemoration. He held Henry accountable for injustice, corruption and persecution, although Fisher praised the old king's resolve at the last to become 'a newe chaunged man'.[20] Henry had wept for three quarters of an hour, Fisher recalled, when receiving the sacrament of penance. In his eagerness to emphasize the king's contrition, Fisher arguably brought into question one of the most sacred principles of his priestly vocation by discussing the circumstances of the king's confession and subsequent promises made to his confessor. We might conclude that he was under strong pressure to create this portrayal of a contrite king.

The devastating effects of this negative portrayal have lingered ever since, compounded by the awkwardness of Henry VII's 'liminality', poised as he was between the medieval period and the age of Renaissance and Reformation.[21] Since Henry neither knew he was on the brink of a new era, nor claimed to be the founder of a new dynasty, this is entirely an invented problem, in which he is made a victim of the modern habit of slicing history into identifiable chunks. Another difficulty has been the historical tendency to study the workings of government as if conducting an audit, focusing attention on administration and finance to the exclusion of other elements. Henry's rule demands an appraisal that looks beyond the bureaucratic mechanisms of government. In particular, his reign looks very different if we appreciate for how much of his time as king England was on a war footing, combating threats at home and abroad. The king faced military challenges from Ireland, Scotland and the Low Countries, sent expeditions to Brittany, an army to northern France, and won battles at Bosworth, Stoke and Blackheath. The taxes which prompted rebellions in Yorkshire and Cornwall in 1489 and 1497 were levied to defend the realm against attack. Ireland was a particular focus of anxiety, since Richard, duke of York had been posted there during the 1450s, creating loyalties to the Yorkist cause that would linger for decades to come.[22] The Calais garrison was another Yorkist stronghold: about 200 soldiers abandoned the city after Bosworth, only to reappear on the Yorkist side at Stoke in 1487.[23] Henry established the royal dockyard at Portsmouth, improved his artillery, built two great warships and reinforced his control of Berwick and the borders, Wales and Ireland.[24] He wanted his subjects to 'lyve in rest and peas for many yeres to come', but this was not easily achieved.[25] This was a king who never lost a battle, but could never lower his guard. Following the example of other European courts, he established the yeomen of the guard from among those who had fought for him at Bosworth, and whom he trusted.[26] He was always on the defensive, for very good reason. As Vergil wrote, 'throughout his life Henry was destined never to draw a peaceful or idle breath, since right from the start he began to be vexed by the seditions of his subjects, so much so that, because of these, he was never permitted to be relaxed or carefree'.[27]

Henry VII pulled his country together after the kind of political disintegration England had seldom witnessed. He fought off every challenger to keep the country comparatively stable and strong, his monarchy authoritative and affluent, his dynasty respected, the rule of law re-established. In so doing, he demonstrated just how much strength a clever and capable monarch might accrue, so it should come as no surprise that the political elite at times viewed his activities with unease or alarm, and tried to steer his impulsive young successor down a different path. Walter Raleigh, looking back across the century at Henry VII's achievements, thought him a 'politicke Prince . . . who by the ingine of his wisdome, beat downe and overturned as many strong oppositions both before and after hee ware the crowne as ever King of England did'.[28] The ruler who could turn failure, exile and disgrace into power, peace and prosperity was someone to be feared, as well as admired.

England in 1485

When Henry of Richmond set out from France to conquer England in August 1485, this was not the only event of importance that year. In this society of over two million inhabitants, there was a keen interest in political affairs; but most people had more immediate concerns than what was happening to the country's leadership. In the depths of the countryside, it was coming up to harvest time. Churches up and down the land had just celebrated the feast of the Transfiguration, and were preparing for the feasts of St Lawrence and the Assumption: this last was a feast so important that it would linger in popular memory long after its abolition.[29] Robert Fabyan, the great London chronicler, who was also a draper, sometime sheriff and alderman, noted Henry's welcome in London, from the 'mayer and aldernmen in scarlet, and the cytezyns in violet'; but Fabyan also noted the arrival of the sweating sickness shortly afterwards, which claimed the lives of two lord mayors in quick succession.[30] There was plague, too, in London that year, and so the Flemish printer William de

Machlinia published three editions of *A litill boke . . . agenst the pestilence*, translated from the Latin by the Swedish bishop Benedict Canutus. This warned that changeable summer weather, clouds of flies, falling stars, comets, thunderstorms and great winds all presaged an attack of the plague; more practically, it confirmed that plague sores could be contagious and advised treatment, which comprised everything from godly living to 'fumigacion of herbes', blood-letting and mustard plasters.[31] That year, the same printer also produced the first ever printed collection of parliamentary statutes, *Nova Statuta*, combining statutes from the fourteenth and fifteenth centuries, with an index that divided them up under a variety of headings, ranging from apparel and apprentices to victuallers and wines.[32]

It was also in 1485 that William Caxton published a life of Charlemagne; the book's colophon quietly registered the upheavals of that year, noting that the work had been finished in June, in 'the second yere of kyng Rychard the thyrd', but was printed in December, in 'the fyrst yere of kyng Harry the seventh'. It recorded the conversion of King Clovis to Christianity, stressing that the king 'was vyctoryous of hys enemyes by cause he byleved in Ihesus Cryste'; the connection between virtue and victory was perhaps especially on people's minds at the time.[33] Caxton also printed a stirring account of St Winifred, beheaded by a king's son and would-be rapist for resisting him; her attacker the prince, reproached by St Beuno, dropped dead, his body melted, 'and his soule drowned in helle', before Winifred was miraculously restored to life.[34] The penalties in the case of princes guilty of homicide may also have given people pause for thought at this time. As Hall's chronicle observed, had Richard III 'suffered his nephewes to have lyved and reigned, no doubt but the realme had prospered' and he would have been as 'muche praysed and beloved as he is nowe abhorred'.[35]

In London, in the parish of St Mary at Hill, the churchwardens Harry Vavasour and John Baker were reckoning up the expenses of the last two years. They had considerable rental income, in houses and shops, and their tenants included priests, a butcher, an ironmonger, a goldsmith, a gardener, two grocers and several widows. Outgoings included payments to priests for keeping various obits (commemorative masses said on the anniversary of someone's death). There were payments to labourers and carpenters, and for the purchase of nails, board, sand and sacks of lime.

The wardens also paid out sixpence for birch boughs at midsummer, threepence for a new key to the rood loft door, 10s for mending the organs, and 12d to William Paris for his work in watching the Sepulchre overnight at Easter (and for the bread and ale that presumably sustained him in this task). Five shillings also went on wine at the tavern for the singers who sang on St Barnabas eve 'and at many other festes of the yer'. These calculations went on with little regard for the change of regime being consolidated just 2 miles away in Westminster.

In Canterbury, William Selling, the prior of the Benedictine abbey of Christ Church, was working on his translation from Greek into Latin of a sermon by St John Chrysostom. Selling had been born near Canterbury and educated at the school run by the Benedictines; becoming a monk, he had been sent to study at the priory's house in Oxford for ten years, and he had also gone to study in Italy at Bologna, visiting Padua and Rome, and learning Greek there. As prior, he had created a library to house Latin and Greek manuscripts and encouraged his monks to study. He would be part of the delegation sent by Henry VII to Rome to thank the pope for his marriage dispensation, which was crucial to securing the king's hold on his throne.[36] Meanwhile, in Compton Pauncefoot, 30 miles or so southeast of Glastonbury, Sir William Pauncefoot's will of 1485 left a bequest to build a south aisle in the church of St Mary the Virgin, where he could be buried, and endowed a chantry there, specifying the use of three yards of crimson silk, three yards of tawny silk and two yards of black silk 'beyng in my cofer at Cometon Paunssefote' for vestments for the chantry priest. At the same time, he left money for the poor and bequests to churches from the surrounding villages of North and South Cadbury, Maperton, Blackford, Yarlington, Weston Bampfylde and Charleton, sketching out the extent of his sphere of influence in one corner of Somerset.[37] The will of Sir John Blount, Lord Mountjoy, made the same year, suggested a different focus, requesting burial in the church of Greyfriars in London, where his father was buried; he left the church a vestment of white with red orphreys, and his best chalice. In keeping with the simplicity of the Franciscan order, he stipulated that there should be 'no grete pompyous herse about my body', but that money should instead be given to the poor.[38] Even against the background of political upheaval, the vastness of eternity could compel more serious attention.

In Lincolnshire, the Crowland Abbey chronicler was adding to the monastery's record.[39] He included some commentary on national affairs, recording the death of Richard III at Bosworth and Henry VII's marriage to Elizabeth of York, 'which had from the first been hoped for'. Far more important to him, however, were the monastery's bitter struggles with their hostile neighbours, who were disputing its landholding. 'In these matters, which were long in dispute, you might have seen the lamb contending with the wolf, the mouse with the mouse-catcher.' The chronicler was outraged at the behaviour of these foes, who in 'proof of their extreme cruelty . . . wantonly pierced a dog that had been set watch by the cellarer . . . with their arrows'.[40] From the vantage point of rural Lincolnshire, a dead dog might assume parallel significance with a dead king.

Henry would always retain a clear sense of the people he governed and their quotidian concerns. It is possible to trace this through his account books, which demonstrate the king's preoccupations as he must have seen them – all heaped together, great matters alongside small ones, rather than separated out into distinct categories by historians. Payments for jewels and building works appear beside rewards for espionage, gifts to musicians and grants to his mother. On a single page, we find the huge sum paid to the undertaker who organized his son's funeral, £566 16s 'for the buriall of my lorde prince', alongside £6 given to a bookseller for 'the gardyn of helth' (a herbal by Anthony Verard) and 6s 8d 'to a mariner that brought an Egle'.[41] We see regular offerings at mass – the usual amount was 6s 8d – and weekly gifts of alms to the poor, which tended to be 37s 11d. Sermons on important occasions were splendidly rewarded: 'Item to the Precher that preched afore the kinge upon Ascencon day 40s.'[42] Ten shillings went to the Lord Privy Seal's fool, 20s to 'my Lady York mynstrels' and 40s 'to the Walshmen on Saint David day'. A smaller payment of 3s 4d went to a woman 'for a neste of leveretes' – these young hares would have been considered a delicacy. There was also a payment of 13s 4d 'to the Kings norysshe sonne' – in other words, to the child of the king's wet nurse who had suckled him thirty-five years earlier.[43] In these painstaking records of pounds, shillings and pence we see the full scope of Henry's kingship and all the intricate obligations of kingship laid bare. They act as a reminder that political transactions were also personal connections, and that they operated at every level of society.

The shadows of the past

The events of 1485 were unexpected. Richard III had usurped the throne and was thought to have had his nephews murdered; but nonetheless, he had a brilliant reputation as a military leader, and he was the crowned and anointed king. Months earlier, he had issued a proclamation against 'Henry Tydder and others ... rebelles and traitours', casting Henry as a troublesome outlaw.[44] To use the name 'Tudor' here was a calculated insult, making reference to the undistinguished ancestry of Henry's grandfather Owen Tudor.[45] Henry's grandmother on his father's side had been Henry V's widow, Queen Katherine – admittedly royal, but unhelpfully French – whose marriage to Owen had been mildly scandalous. Henry's great-grandfather on his mother's side had been John Beaufort, marquess of Somerset, who was the son of Edward III's son, John of Gaunt. This Beaufort line was Henry's most direct royal link, but there was a problem with it. The Beauforts were John of Gaunt's illegitimate children by his mistress, Katherine Swynford, legitimized when their parents married in later life, but by an act which ruled out any possible right to the crown. Henry of Richmond, in short, had no good claim to the throne at all. The Crowland Abbey chronicle recorded that, on hearing of Henry's arrival, Richard 'rejoiced, or at least seemed to rejoice, writing to his adherents ... that now the long wished-for day had arrived, for him to triumph with ease over so contemptible a faction'.[46]

Richard III could not afford to be too complacent, however. Fifteenth-century England had long been in a state of political unease, which periodically flared up into violence on a frightening scale. Since 1399, four kings had been deposed, one of them twice, and three of them had been murdered.[47] This unprecedented set of problems, rather unhelpfully christened 'the Wars of the Roses' by the eighteenth-century philosopher David Hume, provides a tortured background to both the achievements and the anxieties of Henry VII and his descendants. To call it 'the Wars of the Roses' is to imply that there was some clarity of purpose involved, a straightforward contest between the Lancastrians and the Yorkists. The reality was more complicated, and although dynastic elements were a part of the picture, more fundamental were the recurrent political crises. What is indisputable, however, is the carnage that the turmoil caused. From

Henry VII's perspective, there were two conclusions to be drawn. One was the hopeful thought that royal authority might be dependent less on the right of succession than on a more indefinable compound of personal dynamism, military success and political skill. This was what made it possible in 1485 for the laws of inheritance to be overridden by considerations of political credibility. The second conclusion was more sobering. It was clear from England's recent history that the price of political failure had now been clearly set as deposition and death.

The consequences of this for Henry VII and his successors were profound. The nightmare of civil war was to lurk as a shadowy, vengeful possibility in the minds of all the Tudor rulers, never to be entirely vanquished. It subjected the exercise of Tudor royal authority to constant evaluation of its political plausibility. The memory of civil strife was an ever-present feature of Tudor culture. Shakespeare made the Wars of the Roses the basis of seven of his plays, delineating the 'purple testament of bleeding war', and summing up the significance of 1399, when it all began, as destined to shower the landscape 'with faithful English blood'.[48] This emphasis on the human cost of civil war should help underline one essential feature of Tudor England. Kings might be appointed by God (in both their own and their subjects' minds) and they might possess authority and wealth; yet their power was contingent on the good opinion of their subjects no less than in a modern democracy. If they lost that good opinion, they ran the risk of losing their crown – not swiftly, by decorous electoral process, but slowly and painfully, through resistance, rebellion, civil strife, and often culminating in violent death.

By 1485, Richard III's credibility was dwindling, as he was held responsible for the murder of his brother's sons. There was no clear alternative claimant to the English crown; this was one of the reasons why Richard had taken the calculated gamble of eliminating the young Edward V and his brother. Henry of Richmond was by no means an obvious candidate. His chief strength seemed to lie in the promise of marriage to Edward IV's eldest daughter Elizabeth, and the backing of her mother, the dowager queen. This offered some hope of a final resolution to the dynastic problems of the past century. To those acquainted with Henry's determination, his intelligence and his ability to inspire loyalty in his small band of followers, there was hope of a final resolution to the political problems, too; but few people in England knew much about him. When he set sail from France in August 1485, his attractions as a king were highly theoretical. Yet despite its close acquaintance with bloodshed and upheaval, the fifteenth century was a highly theoretical age. It knew the principles of good government only too well; now it had to hope that this untried exile could put them into practice.

Henry had almost no experience of the country he was to govern, and very little experience of anything except exile and danger. The French chronicler Philippe de Commynes recalled Henry saying that ever since the age of five he had been guarded and hidden like a fugitive.[49] When he was born in Pembroke Castle on 28 January 1457, his father was already dead and his mother was only thirteen years old. Both mother and child had nearly died during childbirth, and their position was precarious, reliant as it was on the protection of Henry's uncle Jasper, earl of Pembroke.[50] When Henry VI was deposed in 1461, it left the young Henry Tudor as little more than an awkward appendage to a dynasty in crisis. In the reign of Edward IV, the young Henry with his Lancastrian ties was a minor irritant, soon stripped of the earldom of Richmond. Aged four, he was separated from his mother and made ward of the Yorkist Sir William Herbert. The wardship cost Herbert £1,000, so Henry was not an insignificant prize, but was by no means a major figure.[51] Brought up alongside the Herbert children in Raglan Castle, he was envisaged as a husband for Maud Herbert in due course; 'neutralizing' someone through marriage was a common approach during the Wars of the Roses. During the 'readeption' of Henry VI, who returned to power for just six months in 1470, Henry may have travelled to London to meet his royal cousin; but when Edward IV returned, Henry of Richmond and his uncle Jasper fled back to Pembroke, and in October took ship from Tenby to Brittany, to begin their years in exile.

Henry's formative years were therefore spent as a chancer, a putative rebel, a stranger in a land that might turn hostile at any time, and a potential pawn in international relations.[52] He was not a powerful figure, although he was important enough to be tradeable.[53] In 1483, Duke Francis of Brittany agreed to support Henry's involvement in the rebellion of the duke of Buckingham against Richard III. With fifteen ships and five thousand men, Henry sailed from Brittany, only to have his ships scattered by adverse winds. He returned as the uprising failed, and Buckingham was executed, but the episode alerted Richard III to the threat from across the Channel, now augmented by the fact that some of the rebels who escaped had joined Henry in exile. Richard offered Brittany an alliance, provided it handed Henry over. Warned in time, Henry crossed the French border disguised as a servant, evading arrest in Brittany by just days. Buckingham's uprising had nearly cost Henry his life, but it had raised his standing. It was now that he began to emerge as a potentially credible claimant to the throne. On Christmas Day 1483, in the solemn setting of Rennes Cathedral, Henry promised to marry Edward IV's daughter Elizabeth as soon as he was king. All those present swore homage to him. Their names can be guessed from the 104 persons attainted by Richard III's next parliament, in January 1484. Details of these shadowy months in which Henry plotted in France are scarce, but two things stand out. One was Henry's ability to secure commitment from his closest advisors. The other was his sheer nerve. In November 1484, he took an unprecedented step and assumed the title of king.[54]

It must have taken extraordinary courage to launch an invasion in 1485, on the back of a failed uprising, with the support of just a few close friends, with troops that were a motley collection of French, Scots, Breton and English, and with his credibility largely resting on a promise to marry a princess who might, at any point, be forcibly married to his opponent. In all the uncertainty, it seems oddly touching – as well as politically astute – that Henry should have chosen to land within sight of his birthplace and childhood home, which perhaps represented all the security he had ever known. As he marched through Wales, he garnered new supporters, partly on the basis of his Welsh ancestry; these included Sir Rhys ap Thomas, who added another 2,000 men to his forces.[55] Henry himself did not speak Welsh, and yet he knew the value of his birthright. Of the three banners he marched under, one bore the arms of St George and another proclaimed his Lancastrian heritage. But the third showed a red dragon on white and green – the arms of Cadwallader, who had prophesied that his descendants would recover the land of the Britons.[56] Henry made intelligent use of this: there were at least 35 bards hard at work around 1485, spreading the idea that he was the fulfilment of the prophecy.[57] Cadwallader's arms were prominent during Henry's coronation, and the king brought Welsh bards to court and rewarded his Welsh followers, from the archers in his bodyguard to his old nurse; in addition, in 1507 he granted the Welsh the charter of liberties they had sought for decades.[58] Foreign envoys noted this: a pageant prepared for his entry into Worcester in 1486 spoke of 'Cadwaladers Blodde' and hailed Henry as 'the Fulfiller of the Profecye'.[59] Vergil, too, dwelt on the significance of the prophecy, and an Italian visitor in 1498 described Henry simply as 'a Welshman'.[60] So the red dragon of Wales became part of the Tudor badge, alongside the Beaufort portcullis and Edmund Tudor's greyhound, and Henry VII was proclaimed Cadwallader's heir, last king of the Britons.

Henry's dubious claim to the throne meant he needed all the help he could get, and he made intelligent use of anything that could possibly be framed as an asset. At Bosworth Field, his fate hung in the balance as he faced Richard's larger forces. Henry's mother's third husband, Thomas Stanley, together with his brother William Stanley, were there along with around 2,000 men; but they waited to see which way the battle went before committing themselves to Henry's cause, clearly feeling that he had only an outside chance of success. In all, Henry may have had up to four or five thousand men; Richard probably had more like six or seven thousand. Yet the earl of Northumberland held back on Richard's side and did not engage, and at a crucial moment the Stanleys decided to weigh in. Just as significantly, Richard III was killed while attacking Henry in person. In retrospect, it would seem to Richard's former subjects that God had spoken on that day.[61] It is reported by Francis Bacon that, as soon as the victory was his, Henry 'caused *Te Deum Laudamus* to be solemnly sung in the presence of the whole army upon the place'. Bacon called it 'a kind of military election'. As Henry entered London, 'trumpeters went in front with the spoils of the enemy, thundering forth martial sounds'.[62] He went first to St Paul's Cathedral, and there offered up his standards. It was not clear to everyone that divine providence had intervened, however. The city of York recorded that King Richard had been 'pitiously slane and murderd, to the grete hevyness of this Citie'.[63] In so far as Henry had been made king, it was in large part with Yorkist support – not because he was a likely candidate, but as a reflection of the hostility felt towards Richard III by former supporters of Edward IV. If Henry's appeal was that he was more plausible than the man they saw as both usurper and murderer, it was hardly a ringing endorsement.[64]

Henry's success owed a great deal to his supporters. In particular, his authority as king would owe much to the involvement of two exceptionally powerful women. His mother, Lady Margaret Beaufort, had protected her exiled son by every means available to her, including through her marriage to Thomas Stanley, which expanded her already considerable territorial holdings and brought her into collaboration with the Woodvilles – the family of Edward IV's queen – in the administration of Cheshire and North Wales.[65] These Yorkist links enabled her to work towards Henry's marriage to Elizabeth of York, and prompted the decisive intervention of the Stanleys at Bosworth. Once Henry had gained the throne, Lady Margaret and Queen Elizabeth between them did a great deal to ensure that he kept it. Lady Margaret was an exceedingly forceful woman. John Fisher, at her funeral, recollected her saying that she had wanted to go on crusade: 'yf the crysten prynces wolde have warred upon the enmyes of his faith, she wold be glad yet to go folowe the hoost and helpe to wasshe theyr clothes for the love of Jhesu'.[66] If this last observation was an expression of Christian devotion, it was also Lady Margaret declaring her eagerness to go to war. She remained closely involved with her son's rule throughout her lifetime, lodging close to his chambers in most of the royal palaces.[67] From 1499, she signed herself 'Margaret R', which might have been meant as 'Margaret Richmond', but looked uncannily like 'Margaret Regina', the signature of a queen.[68]

Lady Margaret Beaufort is an outstanding example of the kind of eminence which a high-born woman could achieve. The first parliament of Henry's reign declared her *femme sole*, a woman free to act independently of her husband.[69] Her vast landholdings stretched from Lancashire to Devonshire, London to Northamptonshire, and as a landowner she was diligent and ambitious, building, improving and leaving her portcullis badge on everything from Westminster Abbey to the churches of Langport in Somerset and Sampford Peverell in Devon.[70] Her foundations of Christ's College and St John's College Cambridge still bear her heraldic devices. Many men who began their careers as her household servants or estate officers later served her son. Reginald Bray managed her estates and legal affairs from the 1460s onwards. His first service to Henry was in 1469, when he took him to buy a bow and arrows; after Henry became king, he served as chancellor of the duchy of Lancaster, treasurer of England, MP for Hampshire, governor of Carisbrooke Castle and the Isle of Wight, steward of Oxford University and knight of the garter.[71] He would oversee the building of Henry's warships just as he sustained his demesne lands.[72] Hugh Oldham, a priest from Salford and an Oxford graduate, entered Lady Margaret's service in 1492, becoming chancellor of her household and later bishop of Exeter. In 1503, he was one of the select group laying the foundation stone of Henry VII's Lady Chapel in Westminster Abbey.[73] Family loyalty and length of service were to prove key features of Henry VII's regime.

Elizabeth, meanwhile, was one of the major reasons why that regime stood a chance. She was Henry's key to the Yorkist backing, without which he could not survive. Margaret and Elizabeth seem to have worked harmoniously together from the first. They often wore similar dress at court festivities to emphasize their closeness, and Margaret walked immediately after Elizabeth in formal processions.[74] Henry often referred to them in the same breath, 'the Queen and my mother'. It is characteristic that when, in May 1487, Henry heard about the rebellion in Ireland, his first thought was to send 'for our dearest wife and for our dearest mother to come unto us'.[75] These women were as valuable to him as any loyal magnate, and their account books indicate that their favour and patronage were sought through gifts given by the political elite. In 1495, when anxieties were running high, Elizabeth brokered the marriages of her sisters Anne and Katherine to Thomas Howard and William Courtenay, sons of the earls of Surrey and Devon, respectively, thus drawing two powerful noble families closer to the Crown. When John Skelton presented verses to the king on St George's Day, 1488, he included the queen and the king's mother in his description of the knights of the garter all sumptuously arrayed for the feast day, noting 'the queen's grace and thy mother clothed in the same'.[76] They made a formidable team.

So much emphasis has been placed on Henry's later reputation for the fear he inspired that the faithful support at the heart of his regime has been overlooked. The men and women who supported him made his safety and success their life-long work. Those who had served him in exile, such as Owen ap Griffith or Robert Baggar, and those who had survived the battle of Bosworth Field, became the yeomen of the guard, the king's own personal bodyguard. This was one of his first initiatives as king and, as Vergil observed, was undertaken 'that he might thereafter be better protected from treachery'.[77] Other loyal servants were men such as Christopher Urswick, born in Furness in Lancashire and sent to be educated at Cambridge by the Stanleys. Urswick was Lady Margaret Beaufort's chaplain and confessor. He had known Henry as a child, and was a key player in the conspiracy before 1485, travelling to Brittany in 1484, fleeing with him to France, and then accompanying him to Milford Haven and on to Bosworth. Henry sent him with his military standard after the battle of Stoke to the shrine of the Virgin at Walsingham, 'to place the standard there as a memorial to the favour he had received from God'.[78] For the rest of his life, Urswick would serve Henry as chaplain, confessor and diplomat.

Henry's success as king was a collaborative effort. His accession in 1485 was brought about as much by his mother's skill as his own. His foreign policy successes were secured by the marriage of one daughter to the Scottish king and the betrothal of another to the future Charles V, both alliances brokered by his mother.[79] The consolidation of his authority rested on the diligent work of his 'new men', the lawyers and administrators whom Perkin Warbeck in 1497 would dismiss as Henry's 'caitiffs and villains of simple birth'.[80] Men such as Reginald Bray, Thomas Lovell, Henry Wyatt, Richard Guildford, Robert Southwell, John Hussey, John Mordaunt, Edward Poynings and Thomas Brandon sustained the judiciary, the administration and Henry's security generally. Their heraldic badges proclaimed their loyalty to the new Tudor dynasty, but also admitted their recent arrival among the ranks of the nobility and gentry. Bray bought up manors that had in the past belonged to families called Bray, as if to impart the illusion of ancient lineage to his newly minted status.[81] The wives of these men often served Elizabeth and Henry's daughters: Lady Bray was beside the queen through all the years from the christening of her first-born son Arthur to the queen's death and funeral.[82] It made the work of sustaining Henry's rule a family affair in more senses than one.

Henry's loyal followers served in his Council, in parliaments, in the law courts, and held office both at Court and in the localities as JPs, sheriffs, tax commissioners, and keepers of castles and forests.[83] The particular importance of the Council, which took on unprecedented responsibility in Henry's reign, underlines both how much help Henry needed in holding everything together, and also how skilled he was at drawing on the expertise, as well as the reliability, of those around him. Those who rendered him this political service also fought to defend their king and advance his cause. Hussey claimed that in wartime, 'I never left friend of mine at home that was able to serve you.'[84] Guildford was knighted at Milford Haven; Lovell on the battlefield of Stoke; Brandon and Hussey at Blackheath in 1497. Henry deserves to be seen not as the avaricious bureaucrat of legend, but as a resolute and audacious man who could draw on the support and ingenuity of loyal friends and servants in desperately difficult times.

'The times were rough': consolidating power

Francis Bacon, writing just over a century after Henry VII's death, noted that 'the times were rough, and full of mutations and rare accidents'.[85] When Henry seized the throne in 1485, he unavoidably reinforced some unhelpful precedents from the recent past. If one young adventurer with family ties to royalty, some foreign backing and a lot of courage could turn himself into a king, others could perhaps pull off the same feat. Successful kingship was in part a question of good theatre: two of the pretenders to the throne who threatened Henry VII's rule were chosen for their looks. Lambert Simnel was the son of an Oxford organ builder, groomed to look like the earl of Warwick; Perkin Warbeck was the blond, handsome son of a Flemish boatman, who, when he walked through the streets of Cork dressed in the silks which his master hoped to sell, caught the attention of a group of Yorkist conspirators. They decided to cast him in the role of Richard, duke of York, the younger of the two 'princes in the Tower'; the confident hand in which he signed himself 'Rychard off England' in a letter from Edinburgh in 1496 suggests he was a good learner.[86] Kingship required an assured performance.

The precedent which Henry had set never ceased to haunt him, and the weakness of his claim to the throne was never entirely overcome. The Crowland chronicler noted how his first parliament confirmed the king's claim 'not so much by right of blood as of conquest and victory in warfare', but also noted that 'some persons . . . were of opinion that words to that effect might have been more wisely passed over in silence'.[87] This parliament came together just eleven weeks after the victory at Bosworth, and was the obvious source of reinforcement for Henry's fragile new authority; but it also underscored the difficulties he faced.[88] From the immediate threats in the 1480s from Viscount Lovell, the de la Poles and Lambert Simnel, through the protracted threat from Perkin Warbeck and the treachery of William Stanley in the 1490s, to the menace of the earl of Suffolk after 1502, when Henry was also fatally weakened by the death of his eldest son and his queen, the spectre of deposition never ceased to haunt the king.

The first challenge came only months after Henry's coronation in October 1485, as he went on a royal progress to the Yorkist heartlands in the north of England. In the north, he would confront those of his subjects most likely to challenge his rule, possibly encouraged by the likelihood of invasion from Scotland (although conversely, this threat also meant that many of them had, since September, been serving on commissions of array, rallied to defend England against the Scots).[89] Henry had just celebrated Easter in Lincoln when he heard that Richard III's close associate Viscount Lovell and his fellow Yorkist, Humphrey Stafford, had together broken sanctuary and were trying to raise the Ricardian loyalists. Lovell aimed to take York, Stafford to take Worcester. Few answered their call, and Lovell, in a pattern which others would repeat, took refuge with Richard's sister Margaret of York, dowager duchess of Burgundy, in her court at Mechelen. Henry brought those of the northern nobles and gentry who had seemed lukewarm in their support for him to London and placed them under bonds for their future good behaviour, just to make sure of them. Stafford, who had fled back to sanctuary, prompted a legal enquiry as to whether this was permissible for traitors; it was judged that it was not, and Stafford was executed for treason.[90] Indictments were brought against others, including the bailiff and commonalty of Worcester for not keeping a better guard upon their city gates.[91] If Henry VII could lead an army with flair and resolve, he was also skilled at following up on the legal details.

Lovell and Stafford had already been attainted in the first parliament of the reign; they had nothing to lose by rebelling. More worryingly, Lovell was joined in the Netherlands at the start of 1487 by John de la Pole, earl of Lincoln. Nephew to Edward IV, raised at his Court and knighted alongside Edward's own sons, Lincoln posed a serious threat. He had carried the orb at Richard III's coronation, and many had regarded him as

Richard's heir apparent. The matter was all the more concerning in that Lincoln had initially supported Henry VII, heading the enquiry into Stafford's treason and attending Prince Arthur's christening. The conspirators did not attempt to advance Lincoln himself as a claimant to the throne; instead, they fixed on Lambert Simnel, whom they claimed was the earl of Warwick, son of Edward IV's brother, the duke of Clarence. With Margaret of Burgundy's help, the conspiracy came together in Ireland, and in May 1487 Simnel was crowned 'Edward VI' in Dublin, an act witnessed by many Irish lords, including the earl of Kildare, and several Irish bishops. The gold circlet used to crown him had been taken from a nearby statue of the Virgin Mary, but if this was a conspiracy which lacked polish, it still had menace. Margaret of Burgundy had supplied German and Swiss mercenaries, perhaps 1,500 men in all; Lincoln had some Yorkshire men; and Kildare supplied around 4,000 Irish kerns (warriors). It was a serious force which, in June 1487, landed on Piel Island, off the coast of Furness, and marched through Lancashire North of the Sands towards Richard III's old heartland of Wensleydale. It was a landing reminiscent of Henry's own arrival at Milford Haven.

The Simnel affair was a test of how convincingly Henry had made himself king. When the two armies met near Nottingham, by the village of East Stoke, the king's army was probably twice the size of the rebel force of around 8,000. If most of the nobility had rallied to Henry's cause, still some Yorkist commanders in Simnel's forces fought to the death, a worrying testimony to their commitment.[92] John de la Pole was killed in the battle, removing a significant Yorkist contender from play. Simnel was captured and Henry, in a gesture both humane and intelligent, gave him a job in the kitchen, rather than having him executed; this move underlined both the flakiness of the attempted usurpation and the king's mercy. The dowager Queen Elizabeth Woodville and her eldest son, the marquess of Dorset, were arrested for their complicity, which may well have been another way of demonstrating Henry's pre-eminence over people whose support he had previously needed. It is certain that with victory at Stoke, Henry's authority was reaffirmed. Bernard André, in his life of the king, described it as his 'second triumph', equal to Bosworth.[93] The parliament that met in November 1487 had a more confident tone and the 'Te Deum' was sung in celebration in all the city churches.[94]

Yet the threats continued to recur. Two years later, trouble again arose in Yorkshire. In April 1489, Henry Percy, earl of Northumberland, was murdered – partly owing to his own unpopularity, but also in protest at the king's taxes.[95] One worrying element of this was that one of the ringleaders, Sir John Egremont, managed to evade capture and flee to Margaret of Burgundy's court. The presence of a Yorkist enclave in Mechelen was a constant trial to Henry, since Margaret proved keen to shelter any possible challenger to his rule. Bernard André described her as 'the ringleader' of the Yorkists, casting her as a jealous Juno to Henry's Aeneas.[96] In the 1490s, she helped support an even more protracted and serious challenge from Perkin Warbeck, the teenager with the arresting countenance who was seized upon by the Irish, the French and the Burgundians in turn, all hopeful of dislodging (or at least destabilizing) Henry. From Cork, he went to Harfleur and thence to Mechelen, where he was welcomed by Margaret of Burgundy as her nephew. Emperor Maximilian was encouraged by his links to plotters at the English court and helped plan a landing in Kent to coincide with renewed rebellion in Ireland; when both failed, Warbeck sailed to Scotland, where, with the king's encouragement, he married James IV's cousin, Katherine Gordon. As the Milanese envoy observed in 1497, 'the Scots, who have nothing to lose, are always willing for a war with England'.[97] James and Warbeck together crossed the border in September 1496; and although they soon withdrew in disarray, Henry VII mobilized an army against Scotland at the start of 1497. That army had to be turned around, however, to confront rebellion in the south-west of England, whilst Warbeck travelled via Ireland to land in Cornwall, where he mustered around 8,000 men and laid siege to Exeter. He had managed to menace Henry from almost every point of the compass.

Henry was also threatened from the heart of his own household. Sir William Stanley, his mother's brother-in-law, and his supporter at Bosworth, had been made chamberlain of the royal household, and John Radcliffe, Lord Fitzwalter, was his household steward. Stanley had helped defeat Lambert Simnel's rebellion, and had put down a rising in Yorkshire in 1489 in the king's name, and his rewards were such that he was reputed to be the richest commoner in England.[98] Yet both Stanley and Radcliffe were found to be plotting in support of Warbeck, whom they seem to have genuinely believed to be Edward IV's younger son.[99] William Stanley had also been a loyal servant of Edward IV, and when Edward's sister Margaret of Burgundy declared that Perkin Warbeck was indeed Richard of York, Stanley offered his support. He was convicted of treason in 1495, his brother having presided at his trial.[100] To find this canker at the centre of his own court was especially shattering. Henry's response was to create a Privy Chamber as the core of his household community, a safe space among those he thought he could trust.[101] After ten years in power, he could not feel at peace even in his own home.

Warbeck's forces were defeated, and he was finally captured at Beaulieu Abbey in Hampshire, imprisoned and eventually executed, as were the two men who had first seen his potential in Cork eight years earlier. The only person who perhaps emerged well from the affair was Warbeck's wife: Bernard André made a touching scene out of Henry's chivalrous forgiveness and protection of her, and she went on to marry three more times and enjoy a long life as lady of the manor at Fyfield in Oxfordshire.[102] If Warbeck had been a chancer and opportunist, he had still been supported by the rulers of France, Burgundy, Scotland and the Empire, and had given Henry almost a decade of uncertainty. It is against this background that Henry's careful husbanding of both authority and wealth needs to be set. As the Milanese envoy remarked in 1497, 'this treasure of his, which every one supposes to be very great, he has accumulated because he has no one whom he can trust, except the paid men at arms'.[103] After Warbeck's execution in 1499, the most serious challenge was over; but the presence abroad after 1501 of the earl of Suffolk (brother to John, earl of Lincoln, who had supported Lambert Simnel and been killed at Stoke) and his brother Richard de la Pole meant that the king could never relax his guard.

Trouble could come when it was least expected. In 1502, Henry's position was severely weakened by the death of Prince Arthur. At one stroke, he lost a child, an heir and – since the prince's death put an end to his marriage to Katherine of Aragon – the most valuable alliance of his reign. This was both a personal and a political catastrophe. Less than a year later, after giving birth prematurely, Queen Elizabeth died on her thirty-seventh birthday. The death of 'one of the most gracious and best beloved Princesses in the world' left Henry stricken.[104] It had been a happy marriage and a powerful political partnership. Elizabeth had been his safeguard against Yorkist antagonism, his talisman against a resurgence of the Wars of the

Roses. The loss underlined once more the fragility of his rule. The threat of a Yorkist challenge to Henry's weak claim to the throne, and the possibility of betrayal at home and invasion from abroad were constant features of Henry's time as king.

'A wise man, and an excellent king'

The scale of the difficulties which Henry VII encountered makes his achievements as king all the more impressive. His reign was not a move towards despotism, constitutionalism or modernity, whatever some of the theories that have been spun around all three might suggest. Yet Henry had inherited a fractured polity and a bruised and divided nobility, and he was attempting to rule them on the basis of a very shaky claim to the throne, so he had to prioritize those elements of government that he could depend upon over those that were likely to prove unreliable. He started from the tried and tested loyalties of a few close friends and family, and then extended his rule through an administration controlled from the centre and a network of those he could trust in the provinces, reinforced by the rule of law. It was as if a formerly flourishing tree now had only some of its branches healthy and intact, whilst others were broken and barren. Henry made sure he rested the weight of government on those boughs that could still stand the strain, and he grafted onto the tree of state some fresh shoots to help restore its vitality.

Historians have tended to focus on the technicalities of Henry's rule, but contemporaries were more impressed by his magnificence.[105] 'He well knew how to maintain his royal majesty and all which appertains to kingship at every time and in every place', wrote Vergil.[106] In York in 1486, on the eve of St George's Day, with news of a threatened insurrection spreading, Henry appeared crowned in the morning and in his garter robes at evensong.[107] Royal grandeur conveyed a many-layered message: that the king possessed not just wealth, but also the capacity for military skill, sincere piety, wise generosity and intelligent judgement. And this had to be communicated to the widest possible array of spectators, most of whom were beyond the reach of the written word. When Bernard André wrote his life of the king, he constructed it as a drama, giving Henry thrilling speeches at key moments. Successful kingship was a sophisticated performance, put on for a highly diverse and (by now) quite anxious audience. For this, Henry VII was careful to provide the right stage. At St George's Chapel in Windsor and King's College Chapel in Cambridge, he extended and decorated buildings founded by kings before him, emphasizing dynastic continuity. He used the best workmen available in England, such as the Janyns family of masons from Oxford, who had helped build All Souls College and the tower of Merton College Chapel; Henry set them to work afresh at Eton and Windsor. He also brought in talented foreigners, such as Pietro Torrigiano, who built his tomb. The Savoy hospital on the Strand recalled Italy's most famous hospital, that of Santa Maria Nuova in Florence; Henry wrote to Francesco Portinari, whose ancestors had founded the hospital in 1288, to ask his advice.[108] Above all, the architectural glories of the Lady Chapel in Westminster Abbey, where he lies buried, demonstrate the scope of his ambition (see illustration 4). Henry left precise instructions in his will for armorial decorations to fill the chapel, 'in as goodly and riche maner as suche a work requireth, and as to a Kings werk apperteigneth'.[109] When, in 1545, the antiquarian John Leland saw the completed chapel, he described it as 'the wonder of the entire world'.[110]

Another statement of Henry's intent was to be found at Richmond. The ancient royal palace of Sheen, favoured by the Plantagenets, was now partially ruined. Henry V had planned to rebuild it, enhancing its splendour with a threefold monastic foundation; but he only fulfilled part of this plan, founding, in 1415, the Brigittine monastery at Syon and the Charterhouse at Sheen. Henry VII constructed a formidable new complex of palace and monasteries, re-christened Richmond, echoing his former title. The house of Observant Franciscans that he founded there was connected to the palace, so the king could walk from his privy chambers to his private chapel within the priory church.[111] Ostentation on this scale required money. John Fortescue, the lawyer and political theorist who wrote during the Wars of the Roses, listed the costs of government, and wrote 'it is necessary that the king has such treasure that he may make new buildings when he wants to, for his pleasure and magnificence'.[112] Fortescue also regarded 'rich clothes and rich furs ... and other jewels and ornaments' as necessary, as well as 'rich hangings and other apparel for his houses; vessels, vestments, and other ornaments for his chapel'; it was

4. Fan vaulting in the Lady Chapel at Westminster Abbey

expected that a king should incur 'such other noble and great costs, as befits his royal majesty'.[113] These were not the playthings of the rich, but necessary props in the theatre of kingship. The administration of finance and the splendour of the royal court were inextricably linked in a single political objective. Appropriately enough, Henry also made intelligent use of the coinage: he was responsible for the first gold sovereign, the heaviest gold coin ever struck in England, which copied the grandeur of the *real d'or* of Burgundy and depicted the king wearing a closed imperial crown, one of the first Tudor uses of imperial symbolism.[114]

The question of finance has long preoccupied historians, particularly those anxious to know whether Henry was indeed initiating a more 'modern' form of government. But this kind of question increasingly seems both anachronistic and irrelevant.[115] The changes which Henry made to his financial administration were not part of any ideological re-conception of the workings of government; like everything else he did, they were an intelligent response to circumstances, driven by the pressing need to secure his regime, and building on the expertise and initiative of his closest advisors. At the start of his reign, financial affairs were in the hands of the Exchequer; but like his Yorkist predecessors, Henry increasingly moved financial affairs under the more personal management of the Chamber – not so much out of a desire to innovate, but rather to maximize the flexibility of the system and capitalize on the proximity of some very capable individuals. The most concerted attempt to reconfigure government finance seems to have been prompted in 1494 by the threat posed by Perkin Warbeck.[116] In later reigns, however, Chamber finance would become less responsive, and in 1554 a reorganized Exchequer would again assert its control over government finance. There was no desire for progress for its own sake at the centre of Tudor government, but a pragmatic and urgent need for efficient and immediate solutions.

Henry was lucky that his reign coincided with a boom in cloth exports, which rose by 61 per cent during his reign, even though wool exports declined by 30 per cent over the same period. He worked hard to encourage English trade, pursuing diplomatic links, defending the privileges of English merchants, and even lending money to both English and Italian merchants to stimulate trade. He also brought in a book of rates in 1502–03, which codified the valuation of goods liable for customs dues and became a standard element of Tudor customs policy.[117] He was resolute enough to innovate when it came to finance. The attempted income tax of 1489 caused a tax revolt in Yorkshire, so Henry did not try that experiment again. He also attempted a benevolence (a financial exaction cast in the guise of a voluntary gift) in 1491, which had been tried by Edward IV in 1475 but had been resented; this took over five years to collect and was also not very successful.[118] The use of a parliamentary subsidy, however, was an important innovation that would become a standard form of taxation. In 1504, Henry asked for a feudal aid for the knighting of his eldest son and the marriage of his eldest daughter. This was an ancient feudal right, but his eldest son had been knighted in 1489 and was already two years dead, whilst his daughter had been married the year before, so his justification seemed thin. Parliament instead offered a subsidy of £40,000. It is a mark of Henry's intelligence that, rather than attempt a confrontation, he instead graciously accepted a lower subsidy of £30,000.[119] He did not want financial gain to compromise political stability. When Henry's authority was threatened by pretenders, he did not hesitate to sacrifice customs income for the sake of security, cutting trading links with the Netherlands in 1496 in response to their backing for Warbeck, and threatening trade embargoes again in 1499 and 1505 as a consequence of Burgundian backing for Yorkist rebels.[120] Money was important, but only as a source of political strength.

Henry's relations with his nobles have been variously interpreted. Bacon, writing his history in exile from the faction-ridden Court of James VI and I, was full of approval for a Court where the ambitions of the nobility were kept under control.[121] Others have cast the suppression of the nobility as less of an achievement, and more like repression.[122] Some have criticized Henry for autocratic leanings, or for Machiavellian tendencies.[123] As a Spanish envoy once said, 'he would like to govern England in the French fashion' – although he went on to add more prosaically, 'but he cannot'.[124] Historians have frequently suggested that Henry caused the downfall of high-ranking courtiers, the illegal confiscation of property and the break-down of trust in government. It is certainly true that he placed great confidence in a few trusted counsellors, chosen less for their noble blood than for their intelligence and political acuity. It is also true that he used a greater number of royal representatives to govern the shires, where previously the local nobility and gentry might have taken care of matters. This could be seen as a new form of monarchy, or a badly misjudged version of an older system.[125] It might, however, be more accurate and less anachronistic to see his policies as a series of intelligent, but quite hasty, responses to some weighty political problems. Henry's reign has too often been viewed as an exercise in administration, rather than appreciated as being crisis management for much of the time.

In particular, Henry is known, and often condemned, for his use of bonds and recognizances. Those whom he suspected of disloyalty, or knew to be corrupt, were required to vow reformation, on the understanding that if they broke their word, they would be liable for a huge fine.[126] Others were kept under scrutiny in other ways: when granting office to Richard Empson, Henry VII signally altered the grant from one for life to one held at the king's pleasure.[127] Throughout his reign, he dealt strictly with those in breach of their duties. Corrupt customs officers were chased up just as much as those who evaded customs were prosecuted and fined.[128] Lands confiscated after acts of attainder against traitors were restored to their heirs piecemeal, and Henry made it clear that his favour had to be earned, and that the efforts to earn it had to be sustained.[129] This was not, however, the campaign of fear that has often been depicted. Henry's policies could only work if he could rely on his nobility and gentry to implement his authority. Gentry whose loyalty was questionable were kept on a tight leash, but more often than not they were also kept in royal service. When Sir John Hussey, who had fought for Henry at Stoke, was found to be corrupt as master of the king's wards, Henry kept him on, but under threat of punishment; the consequence was that he worked twice as hard.[130] In 1506, Giles, Lord Daubeney, came under suspicion of corruption as lieutenant of the Calais garrison; he was removed from Calais and fined £2,000, but continued as the king's chamberlain. Richard Grey, earl of Kent, entered into a recognizance for £10,000 that he would behave, and was required to stay at court 'soo that he bee seen daily ones in the day within the kinges house'.[131] Henry was adept at fashioning potential enemies into obedient royal servants. Sometimes he even managed to turn them into friends. Thomas Howard, who had fought for Richard III at Bosworth and spent three years in the Tower after Henry's accession, was gradually rehabilitated as earl of Surrey after long years of loyal service to the new regime, becoming lord treasurer in 1501 (and in the next reign duke of Norfolk).

Given the awkward circumstances of Henry's accession, it is hardly surprising that his relationship with the nobility was initially more wary than that of his predecessors. There were only a few he could rely on with certainty. His uncle Jasper, for example, was made duke of Bedford two months after Bosworth; Jasper's marriage to the duke of Buckingham's widow Katherine, sister to Edward IV's queen, was another union of Lancastrian and Yorkist. Once the first couple of years had passed, however, Henry's reign saw greater stability within the ruling elites, and the majority of his nobility were neither disaffected nor treasonous.[132] Henry Bourchier, earl of Essex, was a former Yorkist, cousin to Queen Elizabeth and a prominent courtier; he enjoyed wealth and influence in Essex, Hertfordshire and Suffolk and built a grand house at Halstead; he served Henry loyally and continued to prosper into Henry VIII's reign.[133] Many close to the king were people he had learned to trust before 1485. Charles Somerset, Lord Herbert, was a Beaufort cousin who had been with Henry in exile; he was entrusted with many important missions, particularly abroad. John de Vere, earl of Oxford, was a flamboyant magnate whose military expertise was crucial to

Henry's success in 1485; he was recognized as hereditary lord great chamberlain, carried the king's train at his coronation and set the crown on Henry's head at the coronation banquet, later becoming lord admiral, constable of the Tower, knight of the garter and godfather to Prince Arthur. He commanded troops at Stoke in 1487, in Yorkshire in 1489, in France in 1492 and in Cornwall in 1497. He lived in state, built extensively at his seat of Castle Hedingham, had a noted choir and was a patron of Caxton.[134] Henry was not incapable of good relations with his nobility.

Alongside such magnates, Henry also relied on lawyers and churchmen who had risen to prominence through talent, rather than birth. The growing number of lawyers in royal service in part reflected just the expansion of judicial business, but it also underlined Henry's intelligent reliance on men of ability. The irony is, of course, that most of Henry's 'new men' who served him loyally were promoted into the higher gentry or nobility in consequence. The churchmen on whom he relied frequently rose from lowly backgrounds to achieve greatness through their careers. John Morton, from a middling gentry family, became cardinal archbishop of Canterbury and a great patron, responsible for the spire of Canterbury Cathedral and the great brick gatehouse that still adorns Lambeth Palace. Richard Fox, from a similar background, became bishop of Winchester and founder of Corpus Christi College Oxford. Twenty years earlier, Fortescue had warned against the potential partiality of 'the greatest lords in the land', who were inclined to work for their own benefit or for that of 'their cousins, their servants, tenants, or such other as they owed favour to'. He had recommended instead the use of twenty-four paid counsellors, chosen 'from the wisest and best disposed men that can be found in all the parts of this land', who would take no rewards from anyone, except their salary from the king. He said they would be like the justices of the King's Bench and the Common Pleas, which was high praise from Fortescue. In short, he was earnestly recommending some degree of detachment from the nobility, with all its passions and partialities, and greater reliance on a more professional group of advisors, chosen for their skill, bound by oath, modestly rewarded by the king alone, and more interested in matters of state than in their own prosperity and that of their followers.[135] Henry was more prepared to work with the nobility than this, but his handling of his administration did have a flavour of Fortescue's advice.[136]

Parliaments were another obvious source of stability, if handled intelligently. Parliament was the place in which the king's authority was displayed in all its regal dignity, where his legal responsibilities were articulated and where his financial needs might be met. It was also the place where the political classes came together to communicate and collaborate. The 224 representatives of the boroughs, towns and ports and the 74 knights from the shires sat in the Commons, which met in either the chapter house or the refectory of Westminster Abbey. The nobility and senior clergy sat in the Lords, which met in Westminster Palace.[137] Parliament was simultaneously the most important communal manifestation of the king's royal standing, the highest court in the land, a nexus of communication, a source of royal income and a valuable source of justification in time of need. The levels of legal awareness and the competence of the administrative process under Henry VII sat particularly well with parliamentary attitudes and expectations.[138] The historical tendency to look for conflict between a king and his parliaments finds few footholds in Henry's reign. Although his parliaments were capable of voicing their doubts about some of Henry's initiatives, they were both supportive and energetic – never more so than in 1495, when the parliament rallied to combat the threat from Perkin Warbeck.[139]

Law was a great source of strength for Henry VII. It might seem like a dull, dry kind of subject, but law possessed extraordinary potential to revolutionize government. In the face of repeated failures by previous monarchs to safeguard stability, the legal system acquired new status and significance. Fortescue had perceived as much before Henry of Richmond had ever set sail. His work, *In Praise of the Laws of England*, was written as a book of instruction for Henry VI's son, Prince Edward, who was destined never to be king, since he died at Tewkesbury in 1471. In a dialogue, a grave statesman teaches a young energetic prince the true value of the law, explaining that not only the laws of the Bible, 'but also all human laws, are sacred, inasmuch as law is defined by these words, "Law is a sacred sanction commanding what is honest and forbidding the contrary." ' This work gave lawyers a status analogous to that of priests.[140] In a time when all the usual rules about order, deference and kingship seemed to have broken down, it made sense to cling to a set of principles that were less vulnerable to alteration.

One other vital buttress of Henry VII's regime was the perception that he was subject to the will of God. His political life had been a series of gambles which had, astoundingly, succeeded, and in this he and his contemporaries read the providence of the Almighty at work. His claim to the throne had been sanctioned at Bosworth by divinely ordained victory in battle (for in the fifteenth century there was no other kind of victory). For the rest of his life, Henry was to remain attentive to the demands of his faith and deferential to the supernatural powers. He was the first king to employ a court astrologer, imported from Piacenza in Italy; one of the finest manuscripts in the king's collection was a collection of astronomical, astrological and prophetic works, which included the prophecy of Merlin allegedly foretelling the arrival of the Tudor dragon.[141] A belief in astrology was at this point entirely compatible with Christian faith; one of the most enthusiastic patrons of astrology at Henry's court was Richard Fitzjames, bishop of London and warden of Merton College Oxford, where he caused an astrological gateway to be built. If the stars were aligned in Henry's favour, he had only God to thank. To this end, his religious patronage was lavish, carefully targeted and highly visible. He sought to capitalize on the reputation for sanctity which surrounded the memory of Henry VI, and his greatest building work, the Lady Chapel at Westminster Abbey, was intended to be the burial place of both of them. Celebrating his first Eastertide as king, he worshipped publicly in Lincoln Cathedral, on Maundy Thursday washing the feet of twenty-nine paupers (one for each year of his life) and on Good Friday blessing cramp rings.[142] Only kings had the capacity for channelling divine grace to heal their subjects, and so his participation in this ceremony was good for his authority as well as his soul, and Henry was careful never to neglect it.[143]

Religion was not just a matter of public display. Royal authority could hinge on private morality, particularly in times of uncertainty. Henry VII's strongest case against Richard III rested on his supposed murder of his nephews. In Edward Hall's chronicle, the speech which Henry supposedly gave on the eve of Bosworth had asked: 'what can be a more honest, goodly, or godly quarrel, than to fight against a captain being an homicide and murderer of his own blood and progeny?'[144] Whether or not Henry actually said this, the fact that the chronicler envisaged such a plea is testimony enough to the strength of the king's claim. Even the proposed marriage to

Elizabeth of York, perhaps the most important bulwark of Henry's claim to the throne, was tied in to this: Richard III was described as 'a tyrant more than Nero', who had 'not only murthered his nephew . . . bastarded his noble brethren, and defamed his virtuous and womanly mother', but also plotted to force himself upon his niece.[145] Moral integrity, manifest through decorous and wholesome family relations, was an assurance of political probity. Richard III, playing the same game, had issued a proclamation against Henry before the battle, emphasizing how he was 'discended of bastard blood bothe of ffather side and of mother side'.[146]

Tudor writers excelled in providing advice literature for princes, where the importance of education for any future ruler was continually emphasized, and Henry VII would take great care over the instruction of his two sons.[147] Yet between the ages of fourteen and twenty-eight, Henry's own youth had been chiefly shaped by the experiences of flight, exile, conspiracy and military campaigning. It is no surprise that his approach to government seems to have had an experimental flavour at times. He took inspiration from the grandeur of the Burgundians; borrowed the idea of a privy chamber and a royal bodyguard from the kings of France; and lifted notions of household finance from his Yorkist predecessors. Meanwhile, in some of his ideas about law, justice and finance, he might well have been drawing on the work of Sir John Fortescue.[148] Henry was not a Machiavellian prince who aimed to rule by commanding fear, rather than love and loyalty; he did not have the luxury of time in which to construct a new theory of politics. He was an intelligent and resourceful ruler, besieged on all sides, doggedly pursuing stability and the resumption of order and deference in political life.

War and diplomacy

In November 1501, it seemed that Henry's energetic efforts had finally gained him international recognition. In St Paul's Cathedral, his heir Prince Arthur married Katherine of Aragon, Infanta of Castile and daughter to the two most powerful rulers in Europe. Henry ensured that this diplomatic triumph achieved the greatest possible visibility. Within the cathedral, which was London's biggest interior space, a raised walkway covered in red cloth had been constructed, stretching from the great west door to the stage before the altar where the marriage was to be solemnized. The altar was laden with gold vessels and jewelled reliquaries, and on the platform stood the archbishop of Canterbury and eighteen bishops. The three central actors were the bride and groom, and the groom's brother Prince Henry, who conducted the bride along the walkway towards the altar; all three were dressed in white, their clothes stiff with jewels. This wedding was a tribute to Henry's transformation from penniless exile to strong and wealthy ruler. As the couple left the cathedral after the marriage, they beheld a mountain crafted out of precious metal, crowned by three kings under three trees, planted firmly outside the west door. On the top of this mountain, between the kings of Spain and England sat the mythical King Arthur, with a red dragon in the branches above him. This conceit was called 'Rich Mount', a reference to both the king's original title of Richmond and the elaborate royal palace of that name that he had built beside the Thames.[149] Londoners pressing close to drink the wine that flowed magically from the heart of the mountain may not have thought too hard about the symbolism, but Henry had scrutinized the plans for this wedding very carefully, and was determined to make his point. Yet there were other, less positive signs to be read. This marriage had taken longer than anticipated to arrange: there had been a pretender to the throne to clear out of the way first and a bout of plague to endure. Above all, international relations were always volatile and changeable. Despite all Henry's hopes of this grand alliance, less than five months after this wedding, Arthur would be dead.

Henry's diplomatic endeavours cannot be separated from his domestic concerns, and both revolved around issues of hard-won security.[150] Henry's own survival before becoming king had been entirely dependent upon relations between Brittany and France. The man who had crossed the border between the two in disguise one night did not need to be told how swiftly the balance of power, or the configuration of alliances, could change. After 1485, the recurring challenges to his kingship had been most dangerous when the parties involved had drawn on backing from the Netherlands, Ireland or Scotland, and Henry's foreign policy was, first and foremost, an attempt to negate such threats from abroad. The willingness of Margaret of York, now duchess of Burgundy, to countenance any Yorkist pretender continued to prove a particular menace. In 1489 and 1492,

Henry tried to lessen Habsburg aggression by sending small forces to help secure that dynasty's rule in the Netherlands, and in 1492 his invasion of France appealed to the old Anglo-Burgundian-Breton alliance.[151] The concern with emergent nationalism that once used to preoccupy historians has long since been proved anachronistic.[152] Henry's concerns were with his personal and dynastic security: that was what gave the kingdom as a whole the best chance of deriving peace and prosperity.[153]

If Henry was a realist, he was not unambitious. By providing support to the duchess of Brittany in 1489, his primary interest was to secure a useful bulwark against France; but the Treaty of Redon also ensured that Brittany was bound to assist England 'if it should happen in the future that the said king of England be moved to arms . . . for his right or those of his progenitors or ancestors, either for Normandy, Gascony or for any other part of France, or for the Crown of France itself'.[154] This suggests that he was as ready as his Plantagenet forebears to revive the English claim to France, given the chance.[155] He also prepared to send a force of 10,000 men to fight in Brittany; it was the Bretons, wary of too much English military might, who scaled it down to 6,000. He ensured that they would provide transport across the Channel, reimburse his expenses and give two strategic towns, fortified and victualled, into English control.[156] In 1497, he was prepared to launch a forthright invasion of Scotland.[157] The notion that he was reluctant to wage war is another common misapprehension.

The war in France in 1492 was part of the complicated and fluctuating tensions between France, Brittany, England and the Netherlands.[158] It was, in part, a response to French backing for Perkin Warbeck: Charles VIII was seeking to undermine Henry, in order to improve his chances of annexing Brittany. Henry was also keen to counter French domination of north-western Europe more generally. The speech with which parliament opened in 1491 had been particularly bellicose and critical of French ambition.[159] War was declared in August, although the invasion fleet of over 700 ships did not in fact reach Calais until October.[160] The offensive required the Anglo-Habsburg alliance as its foundation, however, and Emperor Maximilian proved unreliable. Before the campaign could slide into disaster, Henry brokered the Treaty of Étaples with the French, securing an annual pension of £5,000 from them, and more importantly an agreement to stop backing Yorkist pretenders and rebels.

From the workings of Chamber finance to the management of JPs in the localities, nothing Henry did was unconnected to the risk of invasion and usurpation. His domestic policies are perhaps best understood in the context of the wider threats he faced, and in both military and administrative affairs Henry could innovate where necessary. He brought in artillery experts from abroad and built a firing range to test new weapons at Mile End outside London; by 1497, he had over 200 gunners.[161] He commissioned the first English warship to have cannon on a lower gun-deck behind portholes. He made sure that town authorities arrested soldiers who left their units without permission.[162]

Nor was he concerned solely with military technicalities. His early years had taught him the importance of sustaining morale and a sense of identity. From an order placed in London by the Crown in 1490 for several thousand brigandines in white, with the red cross of St George, it appears that Henry may have been the first king to put an English army into a standard uniform.[163] He also ensured that his 1502 letter to Pope Alexander VI – in which he promised to support a future crusade, as long as other Christian princes did likewise – was printed for distribution, in order to underline both his godly commitment and the shrewdness of his bargaining techniques.[164] In 1492, he created a new coin, presumably for distribution in conquered French territory, with the French coat of arms held within a Tudor rose.[165]

All of Henry's diplomatic endeavours also paid close attention to trade. Between 1487 and 1489, he signed trade treaties with Brittany, Spain and the Habsburgs. In the Treaty of Medina del Campo of 1489, professions of friendship came alongside guarantees of safe conduct for citizens and shipping, and an agreement to reduce customs dues.[166] Beyond this, there was also an agreement of mutual aid in any war against France.[167] Henry's reputation is for 'military underachievement', yet he both won and defended his crown in open combat, and never lost a battle.[168] He also sent the biggest army to France of any fifteenth-century English king, and secured terms at Redon, Étaples and Medina del Campo which strengthened England's wealth and prestige. Most of all, the repeated attempts by the Irish, the Scots, the French and the Burgundians to back a series of Yorkist pretenders were defeated. It is impossible to separate out Henry's efforts to build good alliances, strengthen his financial situation, guard against potential conspiracies, and project an image of vigorous, martial and godly kingship. It should be clear that he had considerable success on all these fronts.

Closing years

About 1497, an anonymous poet composed a tribute in French to Henry VII, likening him to Hercules in his twelve labours. The comparison was a bit contrived at times, but the slaying of the wild boar of Arcadia equated neatly with the defeat of Richard III, whose emblem had been a white boar. The poem made the point, however, that Henry's labours were far from over, the victory not yet won. '*Faulce Envye est tousjours en dement / Le destruyre par son sort venymeux*' (Treacherous Envy is always raging / To destroy him by her venomous fate).[169] This was a not unreasonable commentary on the events of his lifetime. By 1499, of course, the deaths of Perkin Warbeck and the earl of Warwick had removed two notable threats. Yet there were still many hostile forces to contend with: significantly, in the eyes of the poet, Margaret of Burgundy was an Amazon and Emperor Maximilian was a dragon. At the start of the new century, grief and danger circled. In June 1500, Henry's third son Edmund died, aged sixteen months. In 1501, Edmund de la Pole, earl of Suffolk, and his brother Richard, took refuge in the court of Maximilian. September of that year saw the death of Cardinal John Morton, who had proved so valuable a counsellor to Henry. By 1501, the king was also feeling his age, complaining of his failing eyesight in a letter to his mother. As the grand dynastic marriage between Arthur and Katherine of Aragon was being brokered, the traitorous group surrounding the de la Poles was being rounded up and investigated. Then, in April 1502, Prince Arthur died, just months after his wedding. Henry sent for the queen when the news came, 'saying that he and his Queene would take the painful sorrows together'. Elizabeth had to plead with him in his grief to remember his own well-being, 'the comfort of his realme and of her'. She tried to console him by reminding him of his own near-miraculous survival, and 'howe that God had left him yet a fayre Prince, two fayre Princesses and that God is where he was, and we are both young ynoughe'. Their anxiety for the succession was inextricably bound up with the pain of losing a child. Having delivered this comfort, Elizabeth then returned to her own apartments, where 'motherly remembraunce of that great losse smote her so sorrowful to the hart that those about her were faine to send for the King to comfort her'.[170] Private pain was inseparable from public grief.

Ten months later, Queen Elizabeth herself was dead. Her premature child, Princess Katherine, also died after a few days. Henry had lost his beloved wife and the chief source of his security. He shut himself away to mourn, and was soon severely ill himself. A few months later, Princess Margaret departed for Scotland; in the book of hours that Henry gave her was a request that she should pray for him. That summer, Henry also lost his oldest friend and counsellor, Sir Reginald Bray, whom Vergil thought deserved the title 'pater patriae', father of the country.[171] The dynasty, and with it the stability of the realm, depended on the life of Henry's sole remaining son, Prince Henry, only twelve years old when his mother died. If the last seven years of Henry VII's reign have an austere feel about them, the explanation lies in these two calamitous years in which the king lost his wife, two of his sons, a newborn daughter, and several of his most trusted friends and advisors. These were also years in which he continued to be plagued by the threat of rebellion and usurpation, spearheaded by the remaining disaffected Yorkists surrounding the de la Poles.

The king's own health suffered: after 1506 he all but gave up hunting, which was a worrying indication of the severity of his illness. There was obviously something wrong with his throat: he was described as suffering from quinsy, and at times he could neither eat nor drink; he may also have suffered from pulmonary tuberculosis.[172] In February 1508, he was too ill to go from Richmond to Westminster for the mass commemorating the queen's death, which previously he had never failed to attend. In such circumstances, his fears for the security of the realm, always present, were heightened still further.

The consequence was a series of measures intended to secure obedience and preserve stability. Perhaps the most obvious point about these policies – though one often overlooked – is that they succeeded. In 1509, the throne would pass peacefully to Henry VIII, who, right from the first, was equipped with experienced counsellors, a healthy income and a functioning administration. For all of that, he had his father to thank. It should be noted that the use of bonds and recognizances continued under

Henry VIII, despite the outcry against them, which was encouraged by the new king.[173] The protests made by certain interested parties whose independence or wealth was threatened by Henry VII's attention to detail have been allowed to obscure the enormously important fact that, for the first time in nearly a century, a regime change had taken place without civil strife, bloodshed or the threat posed by minority rule. This was an achievement that each and every one of Henry's successors would struggle to match.

Two years before the king died, in 1507, England suffered another outbreak of the sweating sickness. To Vergil, with the benefit of hindsight, this seemed a metaphor for Henry's reign: 'I myself consider it was a portent of the death of Henry himself who "in the sweat of his brow" (that is to say, only with difficulty) acquired the kingdom in the first place, and who ended his reign in many exertions.' Henry's life had indeed been characterized by constant exertion. He had ascended to the throne against overwhelming odds: after a childhood fraught with danger, he had grown to adulthood in exile; and as a bargaining chip in international affairs, he had several times only narrowly escaped capture. As king, he had constantly faced challenges that ranged from hostile foreign powers to treachery at home, even in the heart of his own household and family. He had seen five of his eight children die, and had lost his beloved wife whilst she was still young. None of this had lessened his determination to secure his throne, the succession, and the safety and stability of his kingdom. He had proved himself a military leader both daring and shrewd, an astute and effective politician, an accomplished diplomat, and a wise and efficient administrator. He had protected his family, inspired his friends to years of loyal service, pardoned most of his enemies and ruthlessly struck down the few who refused to yield. He had restored a bankrupt, fractured and diseased polity to health and security. It was from his legacy that sixteenth-century England was able to derive its political strength. It is a bitter irony that the man whose success laid the foundations for all the achievements of the Tudor era that followed nevertheless remained the most shadowy and underappreciated Tudor of them all. The workings of historical reputation are savage and frequently unjust. Henry VII deserved a different fate.

CHAPTER 3

'WITH MY OWN EYES TO SEE'
EARLY TUDOR RELIGION

Henry VII's path to the throne had started in the town of Vannes in Brittany, and throughout his life he sustained his devotion to its patron saint, St Vincent, regularly sending gifts to Vannes Cathedral.[1] Henry was always conscious, too, of the special protection of the Virgin Mary, whom he described in his will as the saint 'to whom in al my necessities I have made my continuel refuge, and by whom I have hiderto in all myne adversities ever had my special comforte and relief'.[2] The presence of the saints was keenly felt by the inhabitants of early Tudor England, who perceived the providence of God constantly at work in the world. Decisions were strongly influenced by the obligations of Christian charity, just as daily occupations were framed by regular patterns of worship. Work and pleasure, art and music, family life and political office – all were moulded by religious belief and practice. The shape of each year was dictated by the rhythms of Christian worship. No understanding of life in Tudor England is complete without an understanding of the intricacies, the wonders, the imperatives and the energies of religious life.

The Christian ritual year saw the redemption offered at Easter coincide with the springtime, and Christmas provided the symbolism of new life at the darkest time of the year. Everyday life fitted into this framework. Business transactions and legal documents were dated according to feast days; even today, rents are often due at Michaelmas. The great festivals of Christmas, Palm Sunday, Easter and Pentecost were marked in royal court and village alike; the great fasts of Advent and Lent, and the weekly fasts on Wednesdays and Fridays, and on the eve of saints' days, were an accepted part of life, while local loyalties were expressed through devotion to a host of different local saints. During the half century after Henry VII's accession in 1485, the Church saw both material and spiritual investment at every level, from the founding of new institutions and the expansion of existing churches, to the development of new feast days and the arrival of a vigorous print culture. All of these were underpinned by the continuing strengths of monastic observance, liturgical tradition and popular religious custom. All forms of Christianity idealize notions of regeneration, and early Tudor religion saw many different debates unfold about how to build better religious institutions and stronger patterns of devotion. Within these debates, however, lay a consensus that the religious life was the best chance of peace and comfort in this world, as well as salvation in the next. The Church's role as the source of reconciliation and charity within the community, the glue which held society together, was so essential to religious understanding that it would survive the Reformation more or less intact.[3]

Tudor England may have witnessed the invention of Protestantism, but only for the last two or three decades of its existence was it a convincingly Protestant country. And this came after a series of painful transformations that left some still defiantly Catholic and many more still quietly wedded to aspects of past belief and practice. The idea that the Church of England sprang into existence when Henry VIII broke with Rome in 1533 is yet another historical myth, compounded of wishful thinking and confessional propaganda. Anglicanism was, and remains, a complicated hybrid, pieced together over several centuries; and the sixteenth-century contribution to it was highly problematic. The Tudor era deserves to be remembered as an age in which England experienced a flowering of late medieval Catholic piety, unprecedented in its cultural scope and sophistication and marked by unusual levels of popular involvement.

The early Tudor Church has almost always been studied in the light of the Reformation, which transformed it from the 1530s onwards. Any critical voice, or religious initiative, has been seized upon as a precursor of religious change. This pattern was set by the Protestant propagandists of the mid-sixteenth century, above all John Foxe, whose vast book, *Actes and Monuments of these latter and perilous dayes, touching matters of the church*, first published in 1563, immortalized a vision of Christian history that has dominated the history of the English Reformation to the present day.[4] Seeking historical validation for his fledgling Protestant Church,

Foxe rewrote the entirety of the Christian past to make it appear that the Protestant faith was the true faith of Christ and his apostles, submerged by superstition during the Middle Ages but never entirely extinguished, kept alive in every age by a few valiant souls, before its triumphant re-emergence in the sixteenth century. Surveying the late medieval Church, Foxe picked out any individuals he found there who seemed to have critical or evangelical tendencies, and claimed them as proto-Protestants. These included not just actual dissenters, such as the Lollards, but anyone who ever expressed a reforming impulse.[5] His huge work (which after revision ended up several times longer than the Bible) may be one of the most influential history books ever written. It certainly ensured that the history of the late medieval Church was written almost entirely as an assessment of its strengths and weaknesses.[6]

The debate rumbles on as to whether the late medieval Church should be seen as corrupt and decaying, or flourishing and vigorous.[7] Assessed as an institution, it is not hard to find failures, anomalies and contradictions. 'Religion' in the early Tudor period, however, was not about institutional structures or intellectual propositions; it was the very fabric of life. Above all else, it was a body of believers.[8] Authority structures, clerical hierarchies, canon law and doctrinal disputes were on the periphery of religious life, not at its centre. It is no accident that the most positive assessments of pre-Reformation religion have come from historians who focus on the life of the parish, the loyalties of ordinary people and the rhythms of the ritual year.[9] Even then, some have mistakenly assumed that the strength of this popular Church lay in its unswerving adherence to tradition, its fixed allegiance to time-honoured beliefs and practices.[10] Some fundamental tenets were, of course, largely unchanged by time; but the true strength of the late medieval Church lay in its adaptability and its responsiveness to popular need. And here, perhaps, its greatest asset would, in the end, prove an accessory to its downfall; for, as we shall see in later chapters, when religious change first began to reach the parishes, many assumed that the promise of reformation was no different from earlier reforms.[11] Accustomed to periodic bursts of enthusiasm for preaching, education, religious printing or clerical reform, early Tudor society did not appreciate where Henry VIII's policies might lead them. It would be not the weaknesses of the late medieval Church, but its strengths that would help bring about its downfall.

This period also saw the continuation of more agitated debates prompted by England's own native heresy, Lollardy, and new discussions prompted by humanist and Lutheran ideas from abroad. In particular, there was much concern for clerical morals and education, and personal piety, alongside more technical doctrinal questions, such as the wisdom of translating Scripture or the correct use of religious images. These deliberations were primarily the preoccupation of the small literate elite. The late medieval Church was not a monolithic construction, ready to crack and crumble at the first assault. It was a variegated, malleable, vigorous institution, which spoke a multiplicity of languages – scriptural, liturgical, ritual and symbolic – and which was engaged in a series of conversations about most aspects of its belief and practice. Religion was not a state-sponsored ideology, although when applied as a form of political sanction it could be tremendously powerful; it was a state of being and a pattern of life. The Church comprised a fluid and changeable pattern of ideas, traditions, ceremonies and loyalties, all bound together by sufficient shared expectations and convictions to impart a measure of stability. It was a tapestry full of colour and variety, backed by a web of stout threads of doctrine and devotional practice.

The 1530s saw the process begin of a gradual, piecemeal unravelling of this extraordinary tapestry, and the channelling of religious energies into new and more radical forms of expression. But for far too long, that part of the story has dominated the historical narrative. The richness of religious life between the 1480s and the 1530s deserves far more historical attention than it often gets. Even when political and religious forces combined to begin breaking apart older constructs of both doctrine and devotion, traditional religion demonstrated not only considerable tenacity, but also remarkable flexibility; and for most of the span of this book, society remained predominantly more Catholic than Protestant. Even after the Elizabethan settlement – itself a hasty and imperfect creation – had been absorbed into the rituals, language and communities of parish, city and state, the symbols and sympathies of the country's Catholic past would continue to resonate.

Sensing the sacred

The remnants of Catholic England are still clearly visible today, to be read in the grandeur of England's cathedrals and ruined abbeys, or on the painted walls, stained glass windows and great wooden ceilings of the surviving medieval parish churches. This longevity can make for confusion. Parish churches today are predominantly built on pre-Reformation foundations, and thousands of them are substantially the same buildings in which Henry VII's subjects heard mass. This offers the chance of interrogating walls, windows, carvings and paintings for answers about early Tudor religion, but it also seduces the observer into imagining that the Anglican rituals of the modern day might approximate to the church rituals of five centuries ago, an impression encouraged by the pseudo-medievalism of much Victorian church restoration and reorganization. Modern religion is deeply concerned with words, doctrines and uniform participation: a religion of the mind, even if it is also a religion of the heart. Tudor religion was necessarily the faith of the illiterate, experienced through ritual, gesture, drama and music. It was less an intellectual endeavour than a passionate sensory encounter. Sermons and treatises sought to provoke and sustain love, grief, ardour and compassion. One of the most popular religious tracts of these years was Nicholas Love's *Mirror of the Blessed Life of Christ*, of which over sixty manuscript copies and nine printed editions survive.[12] This work defended the fictional 'ymagynacyons' it used in recounting Christ's life as being catalysts for the emotions, leaving the believer 'stered and ravysshed to love and desyre ghoostly [spiritual] invysyble thynges'.[13]

Many of the feelings engendered could be stark and terrible. At the heart of this belief system, and at the centre of every ritual, God hung in agony on a cross, his blood the bitter price of human salvation.[14] The emblem of the crucifixion was the symbol most often depicted, and late medieval devotion was profoundly preoccupied with Christ's sufferings.[15] The popular treatise *Dives and Pauper* described how the devout should behold the picture of Christ on the cross. 'See how his armes and hondes be spradde a brode on the tree / in token that he is redy to . . . kysse the / and to take the to his mercy'.[16] Christ's 'mervelous and bounteuous love' for humankind was held to exceed 'alle other loves as apperith well by the paynfull passion and tormentis that he suffryd for the redempcyon therof'.[17] The idea of Christ's wounded side as a place wherein the soul might take refuge was a commonplace; so too the image of Christ as a mother suckling the thirsty believer with his blood.[18] The common vice of swearing by 'God's blood' or 'God's heart' was held literally to dismember the bleeding body of Christ.[19] In the image of the 'Sunday Christ', those who worked on the sabbath were warned that they were lacerating the body of Christ with the tools they used.[20] Religious images engendered powerful reactions. The anchorite Julian of Norwich wrote of how she envisaged her own passionate response to the Crucifixion:

> I wanted to be actually there with Mary Magdalene and the others who loved him, and with my own eyes to see and know more of the physical suffering of our Saviour, and the compassion of our Lady and of those who there and then were loving him truly and watching his pains. I would be one of them and suffer with him.[21]

The Church was aware of the challenges faced by the illiterate populace. Sermons made a vigorous effort to reach out to ordinary people. Nicholas Love's work was meant for 'them that ben of symple understandynge', who, like children, needed to be fed with 'mylke of lyght doctryne and not with sadde meet of grete clergye and of hyghe contemplacyon'.[22] Religious devotion was described in terms of the 'imitation of Christ', which was also the title of the late medieval bestseller by Thomas à Kempis, circulated in manuscript in both Latin and English, and published in English in 1504 and 1531.[23] Outward performance provided the structure for inward contemplation. Churchwardens' accounts record payments for palms on Palm Sunday, candles at Candlemas, canopies on Corpus Christi, all to be carried in procession. At St Mary at Hill, in the church year from 1487 to 1488, twopence was expended on 'childern, goyng on processyon on holye thursdaye', eightpence 'for ij dossen and o halffe Roose garlondes on seynte Barnabees daye' and 3s 4d for 'belles for the canapye on corpus christi daye', while another ninepence was for 'a latyn bell to go with the sacrament'.[24] Processions which brought a community together in the streets mirrored the religious ideal of all creation coming together within the mystical body of Christ.[25]

At the start of life in the sacrament of baptism, and at the end of life in the sacrament of extreme unction, the priest anointed forehead, eyes, nostrils, lips, ears, breast, hands and feet with holy oil.[26] These were the gateways into mind and heart, and to balance the worldly temptations which might use such portals, the Church provided holy images for the faithful to see, incense for them to smell, candles to hold and pax boards to kiss, music to hear and holy bread to taste. In a fifteenth-century poem, 'How the Good Wife Taught Her Daughter', the mother impressed upon her daughter the importance of going to church, 'For you fare best that whole day / When God you have seen.'[27] At a time when the consecration of the eucharistic bread and wine was believed to transform it into Christ's real flesh and blood, it was possible to set eyes on God each day, and beholding the consecrated host was believed to be of almost equal importance to eating it.[28] The interior of the church was intended to act as a *biblia pauperum*, a bible for the poor, and every wall-painting, stained-glass window or carving in wood or stone told a story.[29] These were often arranged in something akin to a cartoon strip: the example from Pickering in North Yorkshire (see plate 4) depicts the seven corporal works of mercy. These crude, heartfelt pictures seem a world away from the elegant depictions in missals and books of hours, and yet the precepts common to both display the emotive force which they shared.[30] It was not just that images were 'books for the laity'.[31] Images were believed to change the beholder, and the act of seeing was a sensory experience which could result in a spiritual transformation.[32] As one fifteenth-century defence of images argued, 'they be ordained to stir man's affection and his heart to devotion, for often man is more stirred by sight than by hearing or reading'.[33] Those who prayed before the image of the crucifix were, in their imagination, in Jerusalem, standing at the foot of the cross. Extracts from the book of Margery Kempe, published in 1501, described how she could not see any kind of suffering – be it the crucifix, or a man beating a child or striking an animal – without thinking that 'she sawe our lorde beten or wounded', and being consumed by grief.[34]

Visual communication was supported by auditory effects. The music of the late medieval Church ranged from the sophisticated works of John Dunstaple or John Sheppard to the simple chants used in the parish churches. Great cathedrals, abbeys and collegiate foundations such as Eton, or the Oxford and Cambridge colleges, routinely used polyphonic music by 1500, known as 'pricksong', because the notes had to be pricked out upon the page.[35] Parochial records are patchy, but Latin polyphony was clearly not as alien to parish church life as we used to think.[36] It was certainly common in towns, where local guilds might share the costs of providing music: in Louth, the Lady Guild paid the salaries of chaplains and clerks, which included the master of the choristers, whilst the church-wardens paid for the copying of new music.[37] The proliferation of chantry foundations in the late medieval period, where masses were said for the soul of the founder, also provided resources for church music.[38] Acoustic jars set into church walls or within trenches in the church floor, and choirstalls built against walls or soundboards, or on raised hollow plat-forms, were all devices used to heighten the sound; such jars can still be seen in St Andrew's Church in Lyddington, Rutland.[39] Parish clerks, who from the mid-fifteenth century seem usually to have been laymen, were commonly expected to play the organ and to sing polyphony, and some also composed church music.[40]

In an age of pungent smells, religion also made powerful use of scents. The saintly were believed to give off the odour of sanctity when they died. The sweetness of incense in church would have made a marked difference from the everyday human and farmyard smells. The censer, or thurible, at St Paul's Cathedral weighed over 13 pounds, and could swing the length of the nave.[41] In 1530, Richard Whitford published a book called *The Pomander of prayer*, which expressed the hope that 'lyke as a Pomaunder ... made warme with contynuaunce in a mannes hande gyveth a fragrant and swete smell / so I trust this pomaunder of prayer ... wyll gyve a fragraunt smell of spyrytuall conversacyon and lyvynge to the devout reders of it'.[42] Divine utterances were described as sweet tasting: 'O my god thy wordes ben to me more swetter than hony, or other savours and swete lycour', a holy man was recorded to have said, in a work of 1495.[43] And sanctity could be transferred through touch: the laying on of hands in blessing, the kiss of peace during mass, the sprinkling with holy water. On Good Friday, at the 'creeping to the cross', the crucifix was brought down into the body of the church for the faithful to approach, barefoot and on their knees, and kiss it, a ritual performed by everyone from the king to the poorest peasant.[44]

Reformation conflicts would bring about a preoccupation with codifi-cation and categorization of written texts, where heresy was defined in numbered points and the text of the Bible was scrutinized, and deployed as a weapon, as never before. But for the first half century of Tudor rule, older, more varied and mutable channels of religious truth still predomi-nated. The many different mediations of the life of Christ offered as a focus for contemplation were not an imprecise or fabricated account of biblical truth, as later reformers would claim, so much as an imaginative pathway to religious experience. In this the later medieval understanding of imagination was very different from that of today. Where modern attitudes celebrate imagination for its creative potential, the medieval view of imagination was as a central component in the process of cognition. Late medieval religious writers would subsequently be criticized for rendering devotion fanciful; but to contemporaries, imaginative and emotive devotion was a direct route to religious truth.[45]

Religion was desperately needed. The prevalence of poverty, disease, war and famine in the decades after 1485 made the promise of comfort, healing and retribution for injustice all the more telling. Religious teachings showed a sharp awareness of the plight of the poor. John Mirk's sermons reminded his congregations how Christ had also suffered, 'in the same flesshe and blode as one of us / and layde in a cradell more poorely than ony of us'.[46] There was a triumphalism in his portrayal of the Last Judgement as the day when 'poore people shall sytte with cryst' and condemn the rich 'for the grete wronges that they dyde to them'.[47] Late medieval religion could contain some very unsettling messages for the wealthy. The *Danse Macabre*, or the 'Dance of Death', which reminded the rich and powerful that death would come for them as surely as for the peasant, was painted around the cloister of St Paul's Cathedral, with a poem by John Lydgate underlining its meaning. In the church of St Mary Magdalene in Newark, a dancing skeleton presents a carnation to a young man ostentatiously dressed and fingering his purse, and tells him 'As I am today, so you will be tomorrow.' The radicalism of this message is an important reminder of the capacity of religion for social levelling.[48]

Practical provision for the poor was interwoven with the patterns of religious life.[49] Religious institutions regularly gave alms to the poor at their gates; monastic houses often had an almonry, a building specifically dedicated to the purpose. At Westminster Abbey, the almonry was a complex of buildings on the west side. Thomas More wrote of how the poor pressed around it in such numbers that he had to turn his horse to ride a different route. He also remarked that 'as farre as ever I harde, the munkes use not to sende awaye many unserved'.[50] Food was set apart every day for the poor, and monks were encouraged to donate additional food from their own portions; there was also a tradition of commemorating a monk who had passed away by serving his food each day for thirty days or more, and at the end of the meal giving the untouched food to the poor.[51] Commemorations of the dead nearly always had some element of charitable giving involved, and at funerals and obits (annual commemorations of the departed) money was handed out, one or two pennies to every supplicant, at a time when a penny could buy a day's supply of food. Lady Margaret Beaufort instructed her executors to hand out 32,000 pennies on the day of her death, and the same amount again on the day of her funeral.[52] Towards the other end of the social scale, Katherine Robbyns of the village of Morebath in Devon, a farmer's wife of middling wealth, had bread and ale doled out at her funeral and month's mind, and provided beef and mutton served with raisins and mustard for the mourners.[53] Simon Appleby, the last anchorite of London Wall who died in 1537, left provision for twopence to be given to each of fourteen children carrying tapers at his funeral, and to fourteen poor people besides; he also specified that 'there be expended at the time of my burial in buns, cheese and ale ... eight shillings and fourpence'.[54] At the end of the Tudor period, the Elizabethan Poor Laws would put in place a system of poor relief (which endured until the nineteenth century) that centred on the parish; this had its roots in the expectations of the medieval Church that charity was an integral part of religious observance, and that where people prayed, they should also give to the poor. Many parishes would go on providing charity on the basis of this tradition late into the seventeenth century.[55]

Later in the sixteenth century, Protestants would cast themselves as educators and philanthropists; but the late medieval Church was already energetically founding schools, colleges and hospitals, often through the agency of religious guilds. The Guild of the Holy Cross in Stratford-upon-Avon, founded in the thirteenth century, nurtured the school where Shakespeare would one day study; the Guild chapel was rebuilt in the 1490s, the almshouses were constructed around 1500 and the school was refounded in 1553. In the Collegiate Church of Manchester, the Guild of St Saviour and the Name of Jesus was founded in 1506, with a splendid Jesus Chapel that today stands within Manchester Cathedral, and the Guild of Our Lady and St George founded a chantry in 1523; meanwhile, Manchester Grammar School grew out of another of the chantry foundations.[56] Those with wealth and influence used them both to build for the future, with a particular emphasis on furthering education alongside piety. Bishop John Alcock founded Jesus College Cambridge in 1496 and endowed a chantry and school at Holy Trinity, Hull, which would, in due course, become Hull Grammar School. There were many such foundations in the century before the break with Rome.[57]

The fact of these foundations was an admission that many things within the early Tudor Church needed improvement. There was particular concern about the morals and education of the clergy, the ignorance of the laity and the worldliness of the higher clergy, who often had significant political roles. On the whole, such criticisms were not meant to condemn the Church: they were expressed by individuals within the institution who were attempting to improve it. Those who complained about their clergy usually wanted them to do a better job, not a different one. The parishioners of Sturry in Kent complained in 1511 that their vicar sang mass only once or twice a week, and reported plaintively 'we have asked the vicar for masses to be sung more frequently, and he answers, "Would you have me sing masses when I don't feel like it?"'[58] Most examples of 'anticlericalism' were of a similar type, seeking to improve the clergy, not undermine them.[59] Those who criticized the Church's response to the poor and uneducated were often the self-same people as were founding almshouses, hospitals, colleges and schools. Those who commented on the clergy's lack of education or virtue usually took steps to improve them. Perhaps the most strenuous criticism during the first fifty years of the Tudor Church was that voiced by John Colet, who, as dean of St Paul's, launched a tirade against his fellow clergymen in 1511. By the time his sermon was reprinted in English in 1530, it was being cast as an early blow struck for the Protestant cause; but at the time of its delivery in Latin, before the Convocation of Canterbury, it was meant as a powerful call for renewal from within.[60]

The history of early Tudor religion is probably also the best form of social history we have available to us. Few other sources take us so immediately to the heart of people's most deeply felt emotions, their hopes and their fears, or tell us so much about their communities. It is precisely because the Church was such an integral part of society that it was inevitably flawed. Individual church communities were dogged by the same problems as any other social group: there were tensions, disagreements and even aggression. When, in 1523, one Londoner fell out with his priest, he threatened violence, 'that all other knave priests shall beware by thee'.[61] These were isolated incidents, however, not intimations of a steady decline. The potency of late medieval religion lay not in conformity, but in consensus. If not everyone was equally engaged in religious life, few doubted that the Church was the source of sanctity and succour alike. In around nine thousand parish churches and over eight hundred religious houses, at wayside crosses and holy wells, by open-air pulpits, walking in processions, watching mystery plays and saying their prayers at home, the Tudor population constantly encountered what they considered to be the divine. Art, architecture, music, drama and literature were all conduits of religious devotion. In the marketplace, the tavern, the guildhouse and the workshop, taking in the harvest or plying a trade, the sense of the sacred could be equally vivid. Since God was for them both the source and the objective of all communal ties, there was no part of life that was not touched by faith.

'My soul doth magnify the Lord'

In 1483, William Caxton published *The Golden Legend*, England's version of one of the most popular books of the Middle Ages, and a monumental achievement for the new technology of print.[62] The woodcut image on the frontispiece depicted a crowd of saints divided evenly into male and female groupings, with the Trinity hovering overhead (see illustration 5). On the left stood St Peter with his keys, St Lawrence with his gridiron and St Edmund with his crown and arrow; the right-hand group contained St Catherine with her wheel, St Mary Magdalen with her pot of ointment and St Barbara with her tower, among many others. The women were as numerous and as recognizable as the men. On the following page, Caxton included two images, of the Annunciation and the Crucifixion. In the first, the Virgin Mary has just looked up from a book laid open on her lap. In the second, the mocking soldiers on one side of the cross are quietly reproached by the group on the other side, comprising the Virgin Mary, two other female disciples and St John.

These images silently make an important point: namely, that women had just as central a role in late medieval Christianity as men.

5. The frontispiece from William Caxton's edition of the *Legenda Aurea* by Jacopo da Voragine

Religious culture was packed with powerful women who were mothers, warriors, martyrs and queens. When it came to the religion of the dispossessed, the hungry, the outcasts and the sinners, the women in Christian tradition were arguably even more important than the men, because not only was the Virgin Mary seen as the particular protectress of those in need, but the other women of the gospel stories were held to represent the most wretched and degraded members of society, who were nonetheless brought to salvation and recast as figures of strength. Depictions of Christ, meanwhile, contained elements of both male and female, with the idea of Christ as nurturer, healer and protector often cast in the language of motherhood.[63] Julian of Norwich wrote of how 'in our Mother, Christ, we profit and grow', and compared Christ to a woman in labour, who out of suffering brings life.[64] The Virgin Mary as the Mother of God often acquired a form of parity with God the Father in religious imagination. The nuns of Syon meditated on a different aspect of the Virgin Mary's life on each day of the week, and on Saturday they dwelt on 'how she was taken up in to heven ... and sette moste nyghe the blessed Trinyte above all creatures'.[65] Iconography of the coronation of the Virgin often cast her as a kind of additional member of the Trinity; the statues known as 'Vierge ouvrage' were statues of the Virgin which could be opened up to reveal the Father and the Son.[66] In images of the weighing of souls at the Last Judgement, Mary appeared as a merciful queen, dropping her rosary into the weighing scales to save a sinner's soul from the devils who were clamouring for it on the other side.

Christian thought can pose a radical challenge to some common views of gender hierarchies. Mary was the focus of heartfelt popular devotion, depicted as the forgiving mother of the helpless, merciful even to criminals. And if this outpouring of devotion to Mary emphasized her warmth, it also underlined her immense power. Mary's virginity was a source of strength. 'Maydyn and moder, both jentill and fre', rejoiced one verse, preserved in the commonplace book of a London grocer in the 1530s.[67] It takes some readjustment of modern attitudes to see virginity as a liberation, but that was how Tudor men and women understood it. Mary's grief and suffering was also a form of empowerment, at a time when such emotions were seen as a path to closeness to God. Pain was a currency of both love and power. Margery Kempe, like many other religious adepts, welcomed suffering: 'That day that she suffred noo trybulacyon for oure lordes sake she was not mery ne gladde / as that daye whan she suffred trybulacyon.'[68] In particular, the Virgin Mary's anguish at the Crucifixion was a central devotional theme. Nicholas Love described Mary witnessing Christ's sufferings as if she hung on the cross with him: 'she henge in soule with her sone on the crosse / and desyred Inwardly rather to have dyed that tyme with hym / than to have lyved lenger'.[69] In the late fifteenth and sixteenth centuries, around one child in every five died before attaining adulthood. The anguish of suffering mother and dying child would have been immediately recognizable, emotive in the same way as the many images of the *Pietà*, Mary mourning over the dead body of Jesus, which were found in English homes and churches. Love's description of how Mary, a grieving mother, stood beside the cross and 'torned never her eyene' from her dying child would have had a powerful resonance.

The emotions which emerge from women in the meditations, songs, poems, sermons and plays of late medieval religion are sometimes shocking in their extremity. Their emphasis on intermingled grief and ecstasy, and their welters of blood and tears, have led many historians to be dismissive of what they perceive as feminized and irrational. Margery Kempe's 'excessive emotional piety' has been labelled as showing 'pathologically neurotic traits'.[70] One of the most respected historians of English monasticism described fifteenth-century religion as 'contaminated' by 'emotional and idiosyncratic devotion, manifesting itself in visions, revelations and unusual behaviour'.[71] The distinctiveness of fifteenth-century devotional patterns should be recognized, however, as testimony to growing popular engagement with religious life, and in particular its ability to reach out to the most uneducated element within society. If this rendered it at times more vivid in its expressions, it also gave it great energy and diversity. Fifteenth-century paintings on the walls of parish churches could be crude, but they were striking. Corpus Christi processions might be noisy affairs, but they brought an entire community together. Mystery plays might be full of slapstick humour and bawdy jokes, but they also conveyed the chief stories of the Bible with unforgettable vigour.

In practical terms, religious life was heavily dependent on the industry and enthusiasm of women in each parish and household. St Margaret's, Westminster has surviving pre-Reformation parish accounts spanning fifty-eight years, which show that 972 women purchased seats in church during that period, compared with 316 men.[72] In the Devon parish of Morebath, where statues of Jesus, St George, St Anthony, St Sunday and St Loy kept company with those of St Anne, two statues of the Virgin Mary and one of the revered local saint St Sidwell, it was up to both the men and women of the parish to keep the lights before them burning. The funds for this were kept in different 'stores', and it was the Maidens' store, for which the wardens were two young women, who kept the lights burning before the statue of the Virgin, the High Cross and St Sidwell.[73] There was a strong sense that certain saints were the particular preserve of women: the medieval diocesan statutes for Worcester and Canterbury had made church attendance compulsory for women on the feast days of St Agnes, St Agatha, St Margaret and St Lucy.[74] The frequent use of housekeeping metaphors in sermons suggests an appeal to a female audience, and the late medieval cult of St Sitha saw her depicted as a housewife with a bunch of keys at her waist. Women left bequests of precious garments and jewellery to their church, whereas men were more likely to leave money; in 1518, one woman left her church her wedding gown to be made into a vestment, and another accompanied a gift of her best clothes with instructions on how to protect them from moths.[75] Women might even serve as churchwardens, although this was unusual.[76]

Caxton's image of the Virgin quietly reading a book suggests another important point: that the advances in printing and literacy might benefit women, as well as men. The gentle transition from manuscript to print culture saw the 'books of hours' – those medieval prayer books that were so frequently the focus of female piety, and of which over 800 manuscripts still survive – giving way to their more humble successor, the Tudor primer.[77] The written word also helped underline the importance of women within the Church. Manuscript and printed lives of the saints suggest that many of the most influential saints of the fifteenth century were female, and they all broke the mould in some way. St Catherine of Siena was a townswoman; St Bridget of Sweden was married with eight children. Three female saints from Liège had their lives translated into English in the fifteenth century, alongside an account of Catherine of Siena; a manuscript of these stories survives in the Bodleian library.[78] All these women were unusual. St Marie D'Oignies had been a Beguine, and was married; Elizabeth of Spalbeek was the first person known to bear the *stigmata* after St Francis; Christina the Astonishing lived up to her name by being impervious to flame and coming back to life at her own funeral. All three had been given to extreme mortification of the flesh.[79] These popular late medieval saints showed how stereotypes of sanctity were themselves being challenged by new patterns of religious life.

It is a common assumption that religion helped express and perhaps augment the misogyny endemic in late medieval and early modern society. It is true that there was much discussion of how Eve brought evil into the world by succumbing to temptation in the Garden of Eden; and many clerical commentators – who were, of course, all men – commented on how women's weak wills and strong emotions made them susceptible to sin. Many historians have taken the accusations levelled at Eve out of context, however, overlooking the far greater emphasis on how

Mary brought salvation into the world.[80] The record has been skewed by the fact that so many surviving voices from the past are male, but the female voices of religious adepts such as Julian of Norwich or Margery Kempe, or literate gentry women from the Paston, Stonor, Plumpton, Armburgh and Cely families whose letters survive, or the high-born women who not only wrote letters, but also patronized writers and publishers, suggest a slightly different story.[81] The tendency of historians to look first to Latin learning for a long time led to the vigorous vernacular culture (in both English and French) of urban, monastic, gentry and noble women being overlooked; but recent work has uncovered the networks of female readers, writers and patrons.[82] Girls did not attend the larger grammar schools, but some were clearly able to access schooling.[83] Statues of St Anne teaching the Virgin Mary to read were widely circulated.[84] Some religious women were great patrons, such as the king's mother, Lady Margaret Beaufort, who had 'dyvers bokes in Frensshe', some of which she translated; but many were of humbler status, such as the Suffolk gentle-woman Thomasin Hopton, who on her death in 1498 left her two grand-daughters a book of saints' lives and a life of the Virgin Mary, respectively, while she bequeathed her son two service books and a book by the poet Thomas Hoccleve.[85]

Women did more than aspire to participate on the fringes of a literary religious culture dominated by men: they shaped religious life to their own aspirations and modes of existence. This is hinted at in some of the more homely imagery used by female authors: Julian of Norwich described the droplets of blood on Christ's forehead as being arranged like the scales of herring, and the drops of blood that fell from him as being like water dripping from the eaves after a rain shower.[86] Lady Margaret Beaufort made sure that the edition of the *Imitation of Christ* which she sponsored, and partly translated was designed to speak directly to the laity. Her other published translation, *A Mirroure of golde for the synfull soule,* was also very practical in its intentions – and seemingly popular, since it ran to three editions.[87] The prominence of female saints, and the women of the Bible, in religious drama, literature, art and song, and the vigorous engage-ment of women in parish life, suggest far greater parity in religious life than we might expect.

Looking in holy books

There was plenty that was new in early Tudor religion, including in the religious life of the more educated. Many of the greatest late medieval works of spiritual direction and inspiration dated from the period before print: alongside the works of Julian of Norwich and Margery Kempe were the writings of Walter Hilton, Richard Rolle, Thomas Hoccleve, John Lydgate and others, all dating from the fourteenth or fifteenth centuries. When Caxton set up his printing press in a corner of Westminster Abbey, such works found a new life in printed form. He clearly hoped for a broad audience: *The doctrinal of sapyence*, published in 1489, was 'for symple peple', both for 'the prestes to lerne and teche to theyr parysshens' and also 'for symple prestes that understonde not the scriptures'. Caxton related Bede's story of the learned bishop who was turned away from preaching because his sermons were too abstruse and replaced by one with less knowledge, but whose sermons were 'more playn' and who used parables 'by whyche he prouffyted moche more unto the erudicion of the symple peple'.[88] The extent to which such works really did shape popular perception remains debatable, but early Tudor authors and printers were trying hard to reach their public. John Foxe would later insist that the 'science of Printyng' brought light into the world, 'by which light, darkenes began to be espyed, and ignoraunce to be detected, truth from errour, religion from superstition to bee discerned'.[89] This confident appropriation of print for the Protestant cause has obscured the fact that for the first half century after Caxton, the printed word was expounding the traditional faith: not challenging the existing reliance on symbol and ritual, but augmenting it.[90]

There were also important advances at the more academic level. Humanists were scholars seeking to rediscover the lost glories of the classical past, but their interests went beyond just Cicero and Livy. Jesus Christ had also been a subject of the Roman Empire; the New Testament might also be viewed as a classical text; and, at least in northern Europe, the Renaissance was as much about understanding St Paul and the early Church Fathers as it was about comprehending Plato. There was immense intellectual excitement about the study of classical Latin, Greek and Hebrew, and about the rediscovery of texts by Greek saints or Hebrew scholars which might elucidate Christian understanding. Greek texts began to appear in monastic libraries from the mid-fifteenth century onwards, whilst the brief moment of reunion between the Eastern Orthodox and the Western Latin churches in the 1440s prompted a new level of enthusiasm for the writings of St John Chrysostom and other Eastern Fathers.[91] It was once held that the English failed to appreciate or embrace the Renaissance, but this was when humanism was mistakenly defined as something highly Italianate and largely secular.[92] Many English scholars did study in Italy, but it was often religious inspiration that they found there; and for the English, Machiavelli was far less influential than the Dutch humanist Erasmus.[93] In particular, Erasmus's views on education had a huge impact on society, including the royal children and the pupils at St Paul's school in London, founded in 1511.[94] Erasmus was a scholar of extraordinary range and ability, who also cultivated fame and influence. He argued for the regeneration of education, a new and vivid appreciation of the Bible, the reproach of superstition and corruption, and a fervent, evangelical and transformative interior faith. He inspired several generations of scholars to be eloquent, angry, mischievous, innovative and subversive.

In 1516, Erasmus created a sensation with his translation of the New Testament from Greek into Latin. Learning Greek and Hebrew enabled scholars to read the Bible in its original languages, and humanists were fired with enthusiasm for the idea of a more immediate encounter with Scripture. Their comments were seized upon by later historians and hailed as an indication of emergent Protestant thinking, but in fact the religious conclusions drawn from these encounters with the Bible were usually far from dissenting. John Colet gave lectures on St Paul's epistles in Oxford in the late 1490s, generating much excitement; but his conclusions were so much in tune with late medieval piety that his Victorian biographers edited them out of the historical record.[95] Protestant polemic would give the impression that the Bible in English had been denied to the laity until Tyndale published his illicit translation of the New Testament in 1526; but in reality, English bibles were allowed with permission from the church authorities, and recent research has suggested that the vast majority of the many English bibles which still survive in manuscript were used by ordinary believers.[96] At the start of the sixteenth century, there were calls for a printed English Bible. Thomas More in 1528 wrote, 'we ley people shall in this matter ere longe ... be well and fully satysfyed and contente'.[97] His opposition to Tyndale's New Testament of 1526 was founded on the use which Protestants made of it: harmful 'not by the occasyon yet of the englysh translacion / but by the occasyon of theyr owne lewdnes and foly'. And he argued that it would be best, whilst guarding against error, to 'let a good thynge go forth'.[98]

A devotional work of 1491 talked of three ways of approaching holy writ. One was the 'flesshely' approach used by the very clever, of which the author wrote disapprovingly, 'the more kunnynge that they have the more they ben blowen and fillid wyth pryde'. A second approach was 'bestely', as readers sought 'in a symple maner' what they needed for the health of their soul, but remained 'necligent and slow to profyte in fervour of charite and love to god'. The proper method was 'sprituel and goostly', in which increase of understanding meant that their 'soules and . . . affection ben fillid wyth the wisdom of god'.[99] The population at large received an amount of biblical instruction through various means. Parish sermons, mostly given in English, were based on Bible passages, and by the fifteenth century the importance of hearing sermons was heavily emphasized. *Dives and Pauper* opined that it was more beneficial to the soul to hear a sermon than to attend mass, and this notion was echoed by the Brigittine monk Richard Whitford in his best-selling *Werke for Housholders*, a guide to domestic spirituality.[100] Bible stories formed the basis of miracle plays, and were depicted in wall-paintings, whilst Christmas carols told the stories of the nativity, the coming of the Magi and the massacre of the innocents by King Herod. These were not just narrative sources: they also explored the meaning of the text. Even the juxtapositions of biblical scenes on the walls of the parish church were meant to suggest an analytical pattern, as the depiction of the Last Judgement, for example, was linked to depictions of the seven corporal works of mercy, evoking Christ's description in the Gospel of Matthew (chapter 25), of how at the Last Judgement people would be commended for feeding the hungry, housing the homeless and other works of charity.[101]

The arrival of print was not a sharp disjunction with the past; indeed, early books were crafted to look like manuscripts, with elaborate initials at the start of bodies of text, sometimes even coloured in by hand after printing.[102] These early publications could be sharply satirical in their castigation of contemporary abuses, such as Alexander Barclay's translation of the *Stultifera Navis* of Sebastian Brandt, published in English as *The Ship of Fools*. For the most part, the proliferation of devotional treatises, lives of saints, sermons, Bible paraphrases and harmonies, and prayer books only reinforced the preoccupations and enthusiasm of early Tudor religion, reflecting the innovatory thinking of scholars, at the same time as reaching out to the populace at large.

In particular, the blending together of intellectual endeavour, traditional piety and pastoral responsibility was a feature of many of England's monastic houses. Monasteries had always been centres of book production, with manuscripts produced in their *scriptoria* by skilled scribes. Once the printing press arrived in England, the monastic orders swiftly adapted to its use: there were presses in the Benedictine abbeys of Abingdon and Tavistock in the 1520s, and in the 1530s St Augustine's, Canterbury and St Alban's also established printing presses.[103] Monasteries likewise embraced humanism. Robert Joseph, monk of Evesham, whose letter book survives, copied out examples of the lectures and texts he used when teaching; his work was saturated with enthusiasm for the classical authors of the past and the humanist pioneers of his own day.[104] Richard Whitford was a humanist, a friend of More and Erasmus, who acquired an international reputation before taking monastic vows at Syon in 1511, bringing with him his books for the college library. His facility as a popular writer would lead to a succession of best-selling books in the 1520s and 1530s.[105] Yet his enthusiasm for reform and renewal did not in any way incline him towards Lutheranism; his *Pype or Tonne* of 1532 was a spirited defence against the new heresy.

Monasticism tends not to figure very much in accounts of the early Tudor Church because it was so completely annihilated by Henry VIII: not just destroyed as an institution, but discredited as a concept.[106] The reports of the royal commissioners in the 1530s were devastating on two crucial levels: first, the *Valor Ecclesiasticus* gave a detailed account of precisely how much each house was worth, providing a powerful incentive for the regime to confiscate them; second, the reports sneered at the monasteries so comprehensively for being corrupt, decadent and superstitious that their reputation has never recovered. Richard Layton wrote to Thomas Cromwell in words which dripped with sarcasm, for example, about the prior of Maiden Bradley, who 'hath but 6 children . . . His sons be tall men waiting upon him, and he thanks God he never meddled with married women, but all with maidens the fairest could be got . . . The Pope, considering his fragility, gave him licence to keep an whore.'[107] Set alongside this striking indictment of one corrupt house, the reports of other commissioners noting virtue, learning, chastity and good order seem unexciting.

Here is yet another example of the early Tudor Church obscured by Protestant rhetoric. Monasticism was a distinctive feature of the Tudor landscape, and something which bound together every corner of the land, from the wilds of Northumbria to the busy streets of London. The cathedrals of Canterbury, Carlisle, Winchester, Worcester, Durham, Ely, Norwich and Rochester, and the vast bulk of Westminster Abbey are all testimony to its prominence, ubiquity and capacity for grandeur. The post-Reformation Church would rely for much of its strength and substance on what had gone before: in Chester, Bristol, Peterborough, Gloucester and Oxford, abbeys were converted in the 1540s into new cathedrals, and since Tudor times former monastic churches in Ripon, St Albans and Southwark have also become cathedrals. The ruins of abbeys from Furness to Glastonbury, Whitby to Godstow, Tintern to Lindisfarne, stand witness to the ubiquity of monasticism, as do the many monastic churches that remain in use as parish churches today – from Cartmel Priory to Beverley Minster and those that still bear the name of abbey at Bath, Dore, Sherborne and Hexham. Monasteries converted into great houses still stand at Battle, Buckfast, Beaulieu, Bisham, Forde and Ecclesfield. And from Blackfriars Bridge in London, to the Greyfriars Roads that may be found in Coventry, Bedford, Cardiff and Milton Keynes, to the Whitefriars Roads in London, Harrow and Rugby, street names recall the presence of the friars in early Tudor towns and cities. Nearly every inhabitant of England around 1500 would have been within walking distance of a monastic house.

Monasticism was expunged from England by Henry VIII, in an extraordinary campaign of state-sponsored violence that took only four years to accomplish its ends, with just a few communities managing to sustain an existence in hiding or in exile. Just because they were done to death in the 1530s, however, does not mean that monasteries and priories were manifestations of a dying tradition. The dissolution of several small and moribund houses before the Reformation, to provide funds for the foundation of colleges, can give the misleading impression that an older form of religious institution was being replaced by something more vibrant. Cardinal Wolsey dissolved twenty-one small houses to found his Oxford college in 1525; Lady Margaret Beaufort fashioned St John's College on the site of an Augustinian hospital with funds from two small and decaying nunneries.[108] University colleges, however, were just another manifestation of the monastic ideal, which was experiencing an era of unusual vitality just before the Reformation, building on patterns of educational expansion and institutional reform established in the late fourteenth and early fifteenth centuries.[109] Monasticism was a force to be reckoned with in early Tudor England. It helped institution-alize the printing press and produced a thriving culture of vernacular religious literature; it was a major force within the universities; it supplied some of the greatest churchmen of the age; and in a final irony, the religious houses would also be responsible for providing some of the greatest of the English Protestant reformers: John Bale, Robert Barnes, Miles Coverdale, William Roy and Jerome Barlow, among others.[110]

Monasticism around 1500 was demonstrating its adaptability. In the towns, the vitality of the orders of friars – Franciscan, Dominican, Carmelite and Augustinian – was increasingly supplemented by the foundation of collegiate churches, such as the college of Manchester (which in the nine-teenth century would become Manchester Cathedral).[111] Rural collegiate churches in Pleshey, Fotheringhay, Rotherham and Ottery St Mary combined parish worship with liturgical and commemorative provision. Monasticism was built around the principle of a community maintaining a daily act of worship, and in the late medieval period not just colleges, but also hospitals and almshouses perpetuated this principle: the monastic ideal was a pliable and adaptable one.[112] The collegiate foundation was particularly flexible. It could provide enhanced parochial care, as in Manchester; serve as the focus of royal patronage and military dedication, as in St George's, Windsor; answer the city's demand for good preachers, as in Whittington College in London; or focus on educational provision, as in the foundation between 1496 and 1525 of the colleges of Jesus, Christ's and St John's in Cambridge, and Brasenose, Corpus Christi and Cardinal College (later refounded as Christ Church) in Oxford.[113] Contemporaries seem to have regarded the different kinds of institution as equivalent: Whitford moved seamlessly from being a humanist scholar at Queen's College Cambridge to being a monk at Syon; Bishop Richard Fox considered founding a monastery, before deciding instead to found Corpus Christi College Oxford; monks staffed colleges; and colleges metamorphosed into monasteries.[114]

One historical difficulty is that monasticism is often discussed as though it were a single phenomenon, whereas in reality monastic orders and houses varied greatly. Criticism found easy targets: contemporary literature poked fun at monks and friars, and visitation reports sternly recorded the number of houses with a superfluity of dogs.[115] Yet although there were houses where discipline was lax and walls needed repair, there were also the great houses renowned for their piety and learning, and the foundation of colleges, almshouses and hospitals did not mean that the larger abbeys were on the way out. The great houses included the Brigittines at Syon; the Carthusians in London, Sheen and Mount Grace; the Cistercians in the countryside at Furness, Fountains, Whalley and Sawley; and the grand Benedictine houses, which included York, Durham, St Albans, Bury St Edmunds, Canterbury, Worcester and Westminster. Will bequests usually reflected local loyalties, but some monasteries had a national, or even international, reputation. East Anglian wills, for example, mostly record bequests to local houses, but the exceptions were the three Charterhouses, or Carthusian monasteries, of London, Sheen and Mount Grace, and the Brigittines of Syon, which received bequests from all over the country.[116]

The Brigittine house at Syon, founded by Henry V in 1415, was the sole example of this order in England. It was a joint house of sixty nuns and twenty-five monks, under the rule of an abbess, and was famous for its library and its book-learning.[117] The library catalogue, compiled between 1504 and 1523, included over 1,300 titles, and its standards were strictly maintained; meanwhile, younger nuns were instructed to help the older nuns 'in beryng of hevy bokes'.[118] The monks had an obligation to produce works of instruction for the nuns, who seem to have been able to read in English, though not always in Latin. The author of one work explained that he had translated it from the Latin, 'for asmoche as many of you / thoughe ye can synge and rede / yet ye can not se what the meanynge therof ys'.[119] This gave rise to an extraordinary publishing campaign from 1500 onwards, in which a succession of books sought to make a simplified version of monastic devotion accessible to the laity.[120] For if the Brigittines were renowned for their learning, they were also a force within popular religion.

Visitors came in such numbers that special confession houses were built within the monastery compound to cater for the crowds who came on pilgrimage and to hear the sermons, for which Syon was famous. Preaching was a central obligation for the monks, and any brother writing a sermon was given three days off choir duty to prepare. Syon's devotional life managed to knit together the rarefied perceptions of the educated, monastic and lay alike, with the more unsophisticated needs of the uneducated laity. In 1500, a papal dispensation allowed brothers to bless rosaries for pilgrims, and Syon had a distinctive set of 'pardon beads', which it distributed to the faithful, with an indulgence attached to those who used them devoutly; there was also a Brigittine rosary of sixty-three beads that was still being used by recusants after the Reformation. For the more articulate, the prayers known as the 'Fifteen Oes of St Bridget' were emotional pleas of great beauty and intensity. These prayers were so deeply embedded in popular memory and practice that they survived the Reformation, being reprinted in an Elizabethan Prayer Book of 1578.[121]

Late medieval monasticism was able to make a clear and practical connection between educated ideas of piety and reform and the preoccupations and patterns of popular devotion. What one distinguished historian of monasticism dismissed as the 'indefinable spirit of rusticity' in English monasteries may in fact have been one of its chief strengths.[122] Certainly the publications emerging from monastic presses in the early years of the sixteenth century all put heavy emphasis on the need to convey religious teaching in 'a playne style / without ynkehorne [overly scholarly] termes'.[123] Whitford's *Werke for Housholders*, written while he was still a monk at Syon, offered advice to those who did not know what to say in confession, or who were embarrassed about saying their prayers in a shared bedroom: he suggested that prayers should be said by the household all together, partly so that those who were too old to admit without shame that they did not know their prayers could quietly learn them 'by use and custome' without humiliation.[124] There was a practicality here alongside religious zeal, all briskly and eloquently expressed in print. The monastic ideal was being packaged for dissemination among the laity, with the aspiration that each individual household might prove a monastery in miniature. This was not a new idea, as the many late medieval writings on the 'mixed life' testify, but it was gaining a new audience in the early Tudor period.

Monastic communities were not without their tensions and scandals. Whitford knew 'by experyence' that many monks did not live up to their vows, and described these as 'heretykes / sysmatykes and very traytours unto the ordinances of theyr rule'.[125] He was also firmly critical of those who were secretive about the details of their monastic rule, and his earliest publication was a translation of the rule of St Augustine, in which he stated bluntly that 'every lawe shold be openly knowen', that only heretics and wrongdoers 'kepe theyr maters secrete'.[126] Yet some of the earliest martyrs of the Reformation were monks and friars. William Peto, the head of the Observant Franciscans, was brave enough to stand up to Henry VIII and preach against his plans for a divorce in 1532, reminding him of the fate of the biblical King Ahab, who was thrown to his death and had dogs lick his blood. Many of the Carthusians of the London Charterhouse resisted Henry, and were executed or died in chains, later becoming a rallying point for dissident English Catholics.[127] John Feckenham, a Benedictine monk of Evesham, was imprisoned under Edward VI, but under Mary became the abbot of the restored and reformed abbey of Westminster. Under Elizabeth, he suffered further imprisonment and died in 1584, still renowned for his piety and charity, having (among other bequests) set up a public aqueduct at Holborn and a market cross in Wisbech.[128] William Peryn, a Dominican friar, spent time in exile abroad, but returned under Mary to be prior of the refounded priory of St Bartholomew at Smithfield; he also published one of the most important devotional works of the Marian restoration.[129] All these people, fierce partisans for the old faith, had grown up in England and found their vocation in the years before the Dissolution.

Tudor monasticism was emphatically not on the way out; indeed, in the years before it fell foul of Henry VIII's ambitions and insecurities, it was arguably on the way up. The most famous English houses had an international reputation, and at home they were the focus of popular devotion, drawing financial support from every layer of society. The poor depended upon them for alms; travellers relied on their hospitality; in rural areas they were great farming concerns. The great houses near London were particularly known for their asceticism and scholarship, and provided refuge for men such as Thomas More, who frequently withdrew to the London Charterhouse to pray, think and write. Their books spread their distinctive brand of piety and created a vernacular tradition of religious literature, and their most talented luminaries fostered biblicism and reform. It is little wonder that their disappearance was to be lamented by Protestants, as well as Catholics. Many thought they should have been kept as centres of learning; many more lamented the loss of their libraries and schools; and the dwindling of charity was widely noted. Some even felt the misuse of land through enclosure and the appropriation of common land were a result of the Dissolution.[130] As Robert Aske would say, defending those who joined the Pilgrimage of Grace in 1536, 'when the said abbeys stood, the said people not only had worldly refreshing in their bodies, but also spiritual refuge'.[131]

'Men mad with marveylous folysshnes'[132]

For some, their faith demanded a radical show of commitment which meant turning away from mainstream practice. Among these were England's home-grown heretics, the Lollards, followers – at least in part – of the fourteenth-century Oxford don John Wyclif. Wyclif's own ideas went from being startling but interesting to excessive and concerning during his lifetime, less because of their own internal logic than as a result of the changing political and ecclesiastical circumstances in which they were received.[133] Wyclif was never formally deemed heretical during his lifetime, but his views were condemned by the Council of Constance in 1415, and his bones were exhumed and burned in 1428. Those who upheld his ideas, or versions of them, were called Lollards by their critics, for reasons that no one has satisfactorily explained.[134] Lollards were by turn outspoken and secretive; they tended to be critical of the clergy and passionate about reading the Bible in English; they could be sceptical about the sacraments and scathing about ritual practices which they deemed superstitious. They were not as rational as their later admirers liked to make out, and could be eccentric, and sometimes violent. They have been seen as early Protestants by many, most signally by the first Protestants themselves, who energetically claimed a family relationship and created the impression of a causal link by publishing old Lollard works afresh from the 1530s onwards.[135] This has given a misleading impression of clarity to what was in reality a many-sided and often inchoate phenomenon. Historians have argued vigorously about

Lollard identity right from the inception of the movement, when contemporaries were not sure whether to class Lollardy as theological heresy or as social and political subversion.[136] Some assert the idea of a coherent Lollard theology.[137] Others see Lollardy more as a 'series of attitudes from which beliefs evolved', or cast it as more of a social than an ideological movement.[138] Some have dismissed both its consistency and its importance as a movement, claiming that it was largely given form by the formulaic questions used by interrogators during heresy trials.[139]

It is never easy to address the history of a movement whose sole identifying label is a term of abuse. Contemporaries freely applied the term 'Lollard' to anyone they disagreed with or saw as morally suspect, nonconformist or just plain peculiar; and those who identified and prosecuted heretics often did so out of alarm at their failure to fit in with societal norms, or from fear of popular insurrection. For its persecutors, heresy perhaps existed largely in the eye of the beholder, being a useful tool to reinforce either their own religious commitment or the probity of the political regime of the moment.[140] Not all heretics were necessarily Lollards: it is possible to identify individuals who displayed ideas or behaviour apparently consonant with Lollardy even before it had been invented, which shows that Wyclif cannot be held responsible for all religious deviance in the late medieval period.[141] Much historical attention has focused on the inherent coherence (or not) of Lollard thought, with no clear conclusions.[142] Many who were attracted by Lollard ideas never entirely left the orthodox Church, and most of the preoccupations associated with Lollardy echoed views expressed, perhaps more moderately, by orthodox believers. If Lollards were angry with the pretensions and the corruption of some of the clergy, this was just a fiercer version of what many were suggesting. Lollard arguments for having the Bible translated into English echoed those of many others. Lollard insistence that richly jewelled images and donations to pilgrimage sites diverted money from the needy were quietly echoed by those who gave alms to the poor and requested simple funerals without pomp. The views of Erasmus on pilgrimages, the worship of images, priestly morality and church wealth were just a more subtle, elegant and Latinized expression of what a Lollard said when he asserted that 'no pilgrimages ought to be made to any saints or locations, but only to poor people'.[143] For some individuals, it was their commitment to the worship of God that led them to disparage the lesser worship of images or saints: one Robert Hilles deposed, for example, 'that it was not nede to pray to any seynt but oonly to God'.[144] The ways in which their faith was sustained by their communal ties, held within their parish boundaries, also mirrored the more temperate faith of their contemporaries. These dissenters were perhaps not so much diametrically opposed to mainstream religion, as expressing a concentrated distillation of it.

One aspect of Lollard thought seemed a more decisive departure, involving a rejection of the miraculous, and a denial of the power of sacred spaces, rituals and ceremonies. Some refused to accept the miracle of the eucharist, insisting that 'it is but brede and not Crists body' and that 'all other sacraments and teching of the holy churche . . . be not profitable for mannys soule nor anything worth'.[145] This was not a disavowal of faith: these were deeply religious people, and some of them were prepared to die, rather than recant these opinions. Rather, it was a rejection of the tangibility of late medieval religion and of its intermingling with the material world, in favour of a faith that was interior and that could be expressed only in words. Such a world-view questioned the idea of the sacred as something specific to any particular location: as one Coventry Lollard said in 1486, 'to go to church to pray is pointless because people can pray equally well in their own house as in a church'.[146] Yet even this was a starker, more emphatic expression of questions that were being raised more generally at the time. Many contemporaries emphasized the need to put inward conviction above outward demonstration; to witness the holy with the eyes of the soul, rather than the body. Lengthy debates about the use of images interrogated how far material objects could act as conduits of the divine.[147] Those who reproved the unthinking worship of statues did not necessarily question whether the eucharistic bread and wine were truly the body and blood of Christ, but the same principle was at stake. Lollard zeal turned this unease about the limits of the miraculous into something more jarring and counter-cultural, but there was a strong family resemblance between these different questioning minds.

At the start of the Tudor period, Lollardy was still in existence, and some Lollards were energetically (if sporadically) persecuted in the early decades of the sixteenth century. In the early years of Henry VIII's reign, Lollards were found in such disparate places as Kingston-upon-Thames, Devizes,

Colchester, Coventry and London.[148] Undoubtedly some individuals, families and networks identified themselves with a dissenting tradition, and upheld what they saw as a coherent religious viewpoint.[149] It would, however, be hard to say for sure how far they anticipated later Protestantism or how far they had truly departed from the religious preoccupations of their contemporaries. Later Protestant commentators reinforced the impression that English society in the fifteenth century was divided into the orthodox (whom they saw as deluded) and the heretics (who carried the true faith). Lollards were depicted as a loyal band of Christians enduring persecution for the sake of gospel truth, and Foxe was more approving of their radicalism than later attempts to cast him as a kind of Anglican apologist cared to recognize.[150] In fact, it seems clear that there was no simple and distinct division of loyalties, and the line between orthodox and heterodox views was often far from evident. Some of the early Lollard ideas had been taken from disputes within the Franciscan order.[151] In common-profit books – a kind of late medieval scrapbook – we find Lollard and anti-Lollard texts copied out side by side, implying more an interest in the debate than any partisan identification with one side or the other.[152] One manuscript collection of tracts on the subject of vernacular Scripture put works by Lollard sympathizers together with works by those who clearly opposed them.[153] When, in 1530, an early Protestant compilation of tracts in favour of an English Bible was published, one of the works it contained was by the orthodox writer Richard Ullerston, who had written both in favour of vernacular Scripture and in condemnation of Lollardy. Orthodox reformers mingled ideas and modes of delivery with the unorthodox.

Lollard trials in the years 1510–14 were framed by the anxieties of Henry VIII's early years and the upheaval of war with France and Scotland simultaneously. The level of concern was not particularly high, however: in these early sixteenth-century trials, fewer than three hundred people seem to have been under suspicion in parts of Kent, the Chilterns, Coventry and London, and less than a dozen seem to have suffered execution for heresy.[154] In the Chilterns in 1521, the bishop of Lincoln, John Longland, examined around three hundred and fifty suspects: around fifty were compelled to recant and four were burned.[155] These proportions are significant: the Tudor prosecution of heresy produced very few actual executions, and may have been most important at the time as a chance for

Tudor bishops to display their diligence. Most of the evidence of persecutions came from John Foxe's careful excavation of the details nearly fifty years later, as he pursued his mission to give English Protestantism the dignity of a history. The proceedings in Kent, for example, assiduously recounted by Foxe, occupy just a few pages in Archbishop William Warham's register, and there is little evidence of any further persecution of Lollards during Warham's tenure from 1503 to 1532.[156]

The Lollards of Kent in 1511–12 were asked about their views on the eucharist: one William Baker of Cranbrook repented that he had argued 'that the blissed sacrament of the aulter ys not Crists very body, flesshe and bloode, but oonly materiall bred, affermyng that God made man but man cowde not make Gode'.[157] Views concerning pilgrimages, images, the other sacraments and the powers of the priesthood were all examined, and there was some consistency here. But equally, one man believed that Christ had been made man since the beginning of the world; another denied that Christ had ever been human at all. The individual who asserted 'that Crist was not incarnatt nor borne of our lady the virgin Mary, nor deed suffer passion for the redempcion of mannys soule, nor dide aryse from deth' was at odds with every kind of Christian.[158] Yet a few key things did emerge from these early Tudor trials, apart from any noted theological consistency. One was that Lollardy, like the more orthodox expressions of Christianity, was a communal affair. The fifty-three people accused in Kent came from just a handful of towns and villages, and over half of them lived in the villages of Tenterden, Benenden, Rolvenden, Cranbrook, Halden and Wittersham, with several groupings from the same family.[159] They had talked over their ideas in one another's houses – 'yn the wynter tyme', said one, conjuring up an image of cold evenings spent talking by the fireside. These communal ties also seemed to stretch back several generations, and in some of the affected areas it is possible that a tradition of Lollardy stretched back over a century, and had become an aspect of local identity for its adherents.[160]

Lollardy was not the fundamental challenge to the late medieval Church that its later admirers wanted it to be. The number of its adherents in the early Tudor period remained small, prosecutions were sporadic and executions relatively rare. Ironically, evidence of Lollard opinion might be a better source for understanding the orthodox belief of the time, rather than the origins of Protestantism. Lollard objections were more often than not a strident version of popular opinion, rather than a challenge to it. The Lollard from Coventry who deplored pilgrimages to shrines of the Virgin, 'because people can equally well venerate the Blessed Virgin next to the fire in a kitchen', was stating more irritably what Richard Whitford also thought when he encouraged household prayers.[161] His friend who thought 'it would be better to give money to the poor than to offer money to images of Christ and of other saints, which are dead wood and stones', was making a bolder statement of the unease about the use of images that appeared in works like *Dives and Pauper*.[162] Lollard ideas were not so much diametrically opposed to the deeply held convictions of late medieval religion, as a concentrated form of both its intense devotion and its levels of involvement in religious debate.

* * *

Religious institutions like to insist on their unchangeability, priding themselves on transmitting the faith and practice of ages in uncorrupted form. Historians, by contrast, discover that there was a large gap between what churches claimed to be and what they actually were. The capacity for adaptation and innovation in the early Tudor Church has often been overlooked, as has the astonishing intricacy of popular religious culture. To move away from dogmatic definitions into the everyday manifestations of religion within society is to step from the hard ground of intellectual certainties into a rich and confusing world full of oddities, contradictions and powerful emotions. It was through a consideration of the lives of ordinary men or women that the history of Tudor religion took on a new dimension, which turned older assumptions upside down. Patient work in the archives reveals that however much Henry VIII might insist that the pope's authority was invalid, and however much Edward VI might seek to destroy all religious imagery and replace the mass with an English liturgy, their subjects had more enduring loyalties to their religious beliefs and traditions.

Etheldreda Swan, living near Cambridge, had no great wealth, but when she died, she left 1s each to the high altar, the bells and the torches of her parish church; 20d for church repairs; and 6s 8d to another church nearby. She spent only 7d on her own funeral, including 2d for the bellringers, but left 13s 4d for the light that burned in front of the Virgin Mary's image. She also left her best coverlet and a sheet to one of the chapels in her church, a platter to one confraternity in her parish, and a brass pot, silver spoon and some pewter dishes to another.[163] To consider her viewpoint, and that of others like her, is not just to uncover new evidence: it is to take a different approach to the question. Early Tudor religion was more than just 'a ritual method of living'.[164] It was the fabric of society, the framework for space and time, a conduit for human emotion, and a promise of divine love and protection; and the faith of these years put down deep roots within English communities. The expectations of Christian morality and the rhythms of the church year were something that bound together the whole of Tudor society, and even those with but a lukewarm interest in piety and devotion had to acknowledge the patterns and imperatives of religious life.

Above all, those who attempted to rule Tudor England had, of necessity, to acknowledge and respect the belief systems which they shared with their subjects. Many – if not most of them – seem to have held a sincere faith, and to have participated in the rites of the Church with more than just an eye to social convention. When Henry VII wrote his will and left his soul in the 'moost mercifull handes of hym that redemed and made it', he must have known how miraculous had been his preservation, and he gratefully ascribed his successes as king to divine intervention and protection.[165] Nobles built chapels within their grand houses, and left money to build chantries in their parish churches once they were gone.[166] As we shall see, even Henry VIII, who had such a strong sense of his own majesty and such confidence in his own opinions, made daily obeisance before his God. In his will, he acknowledged the 'giftes and benefites of Almighty god given unto us in this transitory life', and admitted his 'feare that we have not worthely received the same'. He also observed that the more someone held honour and authority in the world, 'the more he is bounde to love serve and thank god and the more diligently to endevor himself to do good and charitable woorkes to the lawde honour and praise of almighty god and the profit of his sowle'.[167] Everything that happened in Tudor England was framed by beliefs about spiritual obligation and providential meaning. The needs of the dead were as pressing as those of the living; the wonder-working saints who dwelt in the courts of heaven were no less real, and their patronage no less sought after, than the glittering courtiers in Tudor palaces. And if the powers of the king were deemed subject to the powers of God, both might occupy a similar place in Tudor imagination.

CHAPTER 4

SUFFERING IN LIFE AND CONSOLATION IN DEATH

Every aspect of society in Tudor England was interconnected. We cannot understand Tudor monarchs and their courtiers without understanding the lives of those who farmed their lands, served in their households and died in their wars. Authority was indivisible from social responsibility, because nearly every person of status was a landowner and therefore had a duty to care for his workers: these connections were no less strong for being hierarchically arranged. There were also any number of horizontal ties binding people together. John Banister, writing a guidebook for his fellow surgeons in 1578, observed that nobody could exist in isolation: 'Nothing joyeth without societie of other.'[1] These ties were needed. It is easy to assume that pre-modern societies were more static than our own; but in reality, much of Tudor society was changing fast, and by 1603 would bear the marks of some swift (and sometimes painful) transformations that occasioned many expressions of nostalgia for a world that was vanishing.[2] At the same time, reactions to those changes drew on deep-seated moral convictions about communal obligation, prompting responses – both ideological and practical – that were sophisticated, inventive and often surprisingly effective.

Poverty, disease, war and civil strife all coloured the early modern era, and the distress that they caused left traces that are still visible today. Relics of past trauma comprise everything from iconoclasm in churches and graffiti in prisons, to dead cats stowed in roof spaces as protection against witchcraft.[3] The struggles of this time left ideological traces in the legal system, and found voice in the literature of the age. The Protestant liturgy created in 1549, a variant of which is still used in many churches today, embodied heartfelt pleas for benign weather, good harvests and freedom from plague and invasion. The pathos of the closing prayer of evening worship is particularly eloquent: 'Lyghten our darkenes we beseche thee, O lord, and by thy great mercy defende us from all perilles and daungers of thys nyght.'[4] The perils and dangers of a dark night in early modern England were manifold.

Despite difficult times, bonds of affection and obligation endured.[5] If life in Tudor England was tough, wells of compassion could be deep and the ties between neighbours strong. Preachers admonished their listeners 'to be ever redy to geve our selfes to our neighbors, and asmuch as lyeth in us to study with all oure indevour, to doo good to every man'.[6] Neighbourly duty could also be more pragmatically defined, as by the man in Norfolk who, in 1582, described it as 'good will for good will and one good toorne for another'.[7] Even when negotiating a business deal, there was an expectation that, if dealing with someone less affluent than yourself, 'you must endeavor that it be more to his commodity than yours'.[8] Faced with famine, disease and death, Tudor society might have been forgiven for adopting a defeatist attitude; but in many places, the opposite seems to have been true. In the modern world, the word 'society' is used to describe a passive unit, but in the sixteenth century 'society' was something voluntary and purposeful.[9] Men and women entered into society deliberately, and with the intention of creating something positive. The first Tudor book to use 'society' in the title – an Elizabethan work by the lawyer John Barston – identified five forms of such association: country, town, craft or guild fellowship, family and 'societie of friends'. The purpose of association was the 'common wealth' or 'commonweal', which was not just a static entity, but also a shared ideal. 'For who knoweth not, that every societie of people, is established for common weale?' asked Barston.[10] He took it as read that 'all good men will endeavour to live in unitie and concorde'.[11] It was a view central to Tudor religious observance: the communion service from the 1549 *Book of Common Prayer* included the exhortation, 'to reconcile your-selfes to your neighbors . . . putting out of your heartes al hatred and malice against them, and to be in love and charitie with all the worlde'.[12]

In Swallowfield in 1596, when the chief inhabitants were drawing up rules for their community, they explained: 'This we have don to the end we may the better and more quyetly lyve together in good love and Amyte.'

This was not just pious idealism: their articles also included such practical suggestions as that everyone who spoke at their meetings should be heard 'quyetly one after an other', that 'no man shall skorne an others speeche', and that participants should promise not to fall out with one another 'nor offer to goe to lawe' until everyone had listened to an account of the problem, so that 'all stryfes may be ended before any mallece take roote, for pacyfyinge of wiche grieffes every of us promysethe to do the best he can'.[13] In the constitutions of guilds, the founding statutes of schools and colleges, family correspondence, treatises on married life, royal proclamations and parliamentary statutes, countless practical provisions were made to engender and preserve harmony. Tudor men and women made strenuous efforts to enable everyone to 'live quietly' one with another, in an era that was anything but quiet.

Unity and division

When Tudor theorists described their own society, they provided a vision of a neatly regulated hierarchy. Most of those surveying the commonwealth arranged it into ranks, or orders, but it is notable that no two commentators came up with quite the same pattern. Edmund Dudley, in 1509, divided society into the traditional three groupings of clergy, nobility and commonalty. William Harrison, writing in Elizabeth's reign, divided it into gentlemen, citizens and burgesses, yeomen, and a fourth category comprising day labourers, servants and poor husbandmen and craftsmen, people with 'neither voice nor authoritie' who were 'to be ruled and not to rule other'. Sir Thomas Wilson, writing around 1600, used five divisions, each with many different layers, and including in the ranks of the lesser gentry a substantial number of professional men, such as lawyers, clergy and other graduates.[14] The social hierarchy was understood to be flexible, subject not just to birth and wealth, but also to occupation and education. And all commentators seemed to accept the principle of social mobility: wealthy yeomen might quite readily become gentry. Thomas Smith, scholar, diplomat and parliamentarian, gave a detailed description of freemen who did not claim to be gentry, 'and yet they have a certaine preheminence and more estimation than laborers and artificers, and commonly live welthilie, keepe good houses, do their businesse and travaile to get riches'. He noted how they bought up the land of 'unthriftie gentlemen', and by educating their sons and leaving them land 'doe make their saide sonnes by those meanes gentlemen'.[15] Shakespeare, whose father had sought the right to a heraldic device before losing all his money, renewed this campaign as soon as he was sufficiently wealthy, and in 1596 was granted a crest and a motto by the London College of Heralds. He would sign his will 'William Shakespeare ... gentleman'. Ben Jonson mocked these social pretensions in a play of 1599, in which Shakespeare's motto of *Non sanz droict* 'Not without right' was gleefully parodied as 'Not without mustard'; yet this kind of status was clearly worth having.[16] Social mobility could work the other way, too: the younger sons of gentry might turn from the land to craft or a trade, and indeed a substantial minority of apprentices were drawn from the gentry.[17] Anxieties about social status were prevalent not because the gradations were rigid, but precisely because they were so fluid. Sumptuary laws warned against dressing in a manner inappropriate to one's station in life, but the frequent reiteration of those laws shows just how ineffective they were.[18] Tudor society was protean, fast-changing and hard to control.

It was also predominantly youthful. The young were often cast as troublemakers, and youth as a liminal stage of life full of dangers.[19] Yet it appears that nearly half the population in 1600 was under the age of twenty-one, which made for recurring social tensions.[20] To study the experience of the young in Tudor society is to come face to face with the inbuilt contradiction of communities which preached the values of temperate, moral, orderly behaviour, while the young drank and fought in taverns, had sexual relations outside marriage, undermined good order in the household and rioted in the streets.[21] Puberty arrived much later than in the modern world; early marriage was rare, and yet young people often left home in their early teens, so the years of youth were long and precarious, and interminable years in service or apprenticeship could lead to frustration.[22] They also frequently involved hardship and vulnerability, not least since perhaps a quarter of fourteen-year-olds, at the age when they were apprenticed, were already fatherless.[23] Servants, too, were for the most part young, mobile and potentially disruptive, and they made up a large part of most communities: almost a quarter of the population of Coventry in 1523.[24] Times when social inversion was expected, such as the Shrovetide festivities before the hardships of Lent, often spilled over into violence, and it was apprentices and serving-men who were often at the forefront.[25] Those who combined being young with being lawless vagabonds were punished with unusual severity.[26]

These dramas of life and death were played out in the shadow of past apocalypse. In 1348, just over a hundred years before Henry VII was born, the plague had for the first time arrived in England and at least a third – and perhaps half – of the population had died.[27] Plague was never far away during this period: it returned at regular intervals, moving between cities, often with those who could afford to move fleeing before it. Sometimes there would be a more manageable bout, but a serious outbreak could still devastate a city. In the plague years of 1593 and 1603, it was the young who were particularly hard hit: George Marrow, a London carpenter, buried three of his children, as well as two of his servants in 1603.[28] Even without epidemics, mortality rates were high. 'Broken' families are often considered a modern phenomenon, but most Tudor families were scarred by loss, and many people would marry two or three times, rendering families a complicated mixture of step-parents and step-siblings, as spouses died and were replaced.[29]

Meanwhile, the economic challenges of the sixteenth century were transforming society. Population increase and inflation are not exclusively modern problems: between 1485 and 1603, the population of England roughly doubled and the price of grain increased sixfold. In 1524–25 the population was around 2.4 million; it reached around 3 million by 1560, and rose to around 4 million by 1603.[30] Enough of this population lived close enough to the poverty line to turn a harvest failure into a famine. One author, in the dearth of the 1590s, lamented the condition of 'thousands of our poore Christian brethren, whereof some cannot labor, and many are without labor, and those which labor can hardly maintain themselves by their labor'.[31] There was a great deal of regional variation, but on the whole, the wealthy landlord or prosperous yeomen might do very well out of the changing circumstances, whilst the poor frequently became poorer.[32] Tudor commentators perceived that the number of poor was increasing from the 1540s onwards, and they were almost certainly correct. Elizabethan surveys suggest that at least 20 per cent of the community lived on the margins of subsistence.[33] The Elizabethan writer who sagely observed that the poor 'are always the greater part in any societie' reflected the general view.[34] Censuses from towns suggest that between 5 per cent and 22 per cent of the population lived in poverty.[35] When, in 1556, a year blighted by famine and disease, Archbishop Thomas Cranmer made his last speech before being burned alive, it was not for himself that he wept, but for the poor, reminding the rich that 'if ever they had any occasion to shew their charity, they have now at this present, the poor people being so many, and victuals so dear'.[36]

In the face of these challenges, Tudor society proved remarkably resilient and resourceful. At every level, people took responsibility for preserving the peace, ministering to the poor, reducing crime and encouraging reform. They founded hospitals, endowed universities, built colleges and schools, made charitable bequests, and served in parliament, in the judiciary, as churchwardens, parish constables and overseers of the poor. Poverty, vaga-bondage and lawless or immoral behaviour were widely accepted as being the responsibility of the community as a whole. Responses were often sporadic or inconsistent, and sometimes harsh or impractical, but they were persistent and could be surprisingly successful. Political and legal centrali-zation allowed for a nationwide response in the form of the poor rate, a compulsory tax levied in parishes from 1572 onwards which provided cash payments for the poor.[37] The Statute of Artificers, passed in 1563, attempted to codify a large body of legislation concerning labour and employment after the famines, epidemics and labour shortages of the 1550s. In part, it tried to get everyone into work, compelling men between the ages of 12 and 60, and women between the ages of 12 and 40, to work in agriculture, and forbidding servants to leave their parish without permission. It also laid down regulations for both wage-labourers paid by the day, or servants on annual contracts, including the setting of wage rates each year by the JPs of each county. The penalties for giving (or asking for) wages higher than the rate included fines and imprisonment.[38] Such initiatives were far from perfect, but they had a value that was ideological, as well as practical.

In the pre-Reformation period, the well-attested view that poor people were far closer to heaven than the rich could not help but shape wider social attitudes; after the Reformation, Protestant attitudes rendered charity an indispensable part of godly living, and some radical religious thought included powerful advocacy for the dispossessed. The Protestant polemicist Robert Crowley, in an epigram of 1550, wrote of a leasemonger who dreamt on his deathbed of a great crowd of poor folk, waiting patiently for justice to be done; the oppressed were 'promised rewarde', whilst the avaricious were 'certayne to have hell'.[39] A prayer from a popular Elizabethan Prayer Book interceded for those 'snarled and intangled in the extreem penury of things needfull for the body' and implored mercy for the poor: 'when they be disapoynted of the thinges which they doe so mightely desire, their harts are cast down, and quaile for excesse of grief'.[40] A Paul's Cross preacher in 1594 reproached his audience for their complacent individualism: 'why then doe we purchase lands as if wee would dwell alone, and lay up money as if we would live alone upon the earth?' He condemned those who built lofty buildings whose foundations were 'strife and discord, the morter whereof is tempered with the tears of widowes, the windowes beautified with the spoile of Orphanes, the beams and supporters, of the fal of good yeomen?'[41]

If the helpless poor merited compassion, vagrants (or 'sturdy beggars') were a different matter. There was widespread condemnation of those who had the capacity to work, but did not do so. Edmund Dudley regarded unemployment as 'the very mother of all vice', and vagrants were condemned as perpetrating every kind of immorality.[42] Not least, they were condemned for taking the charity needed by the more deserving poor: the puritan writer Philip Stubbes called them 'drone bees, that live upon the spoil of the poor bees' and thought they should be imprisoned and, if persistent, hanged.[43] Vagrants were understood to have separated themselves voluntarily from the social body. So ingrained were these social attitudes that it was believed that the undeserving poor had a rival form of community: a tract of 1561 by John Awdelay, *The Fraternity of Vagabonds*, listed nineteen orders of vagrant and twenty-five of knaves bound together in a society with a language of its own, which the Elizabethans called 'rogues' cant'.[44] Thomas Harman, in a work of 1567 described two hundred types of vagabond, based on his own independent research trips into the underworld. He provided a rich seam of material for later writers and dramatists concerning the 'abhominable, wicked and detestable behaviour of all these rowsey, ragged rabblement of rakehelles' in a work which, whilst purportedly condemning it, at the same time took gleeful, unspoken delight in the richness of vagabond culture.[45]

Every member of Tudor society might be supposed to have a support network. One problem with vagabonds was that they were 'masterless men': governments legislated busily to make sure that each one was assigned a master, weaving them back into the fabric of society.[46] It was once thought that the early modern period saw a shift from the pre-modern notion of 'community' as an integrated grouping based on personal links and obligations to a more modern, mechanistic and impersonal 'society' – a theory now regarded as mistaken.[47] There was, however, change afoot that led to an often anxious interrogation of concepts of social obligation. Two long-standing corporate ideals came under attack in the 1530s, when Henry VIII's break with Rome called into question the notion of a united Christendom, and when the dissolution of the monasteries destroyed what, for many, had been the epitome of the ideal community. Closer to home, the three most recognizable communities were those of the Church, the manor house and the alehouse; and all three experienced conflict from the mid-sixteenth century onwards. The rituals and furnishings of the Church were hotly contested; the charity and hospitality associated with the mano-rial lord were frequently eroded by economic strain; and alehouses became the target of religious commentators bent upon a reformation of manners. Social commentary increasingly featured laments for a vanished past.

Society had many lines of defence, not least in law, which could offer protection for the poor, as well as for the rich.[48] Customary law, in partic-ular, had a broad impact on society.[49] Villages, towns, craft guilds and occupational groups such as miners all had their own traditions, which could take legal form – as in the case of the lead miners of Derbyshire, whose defiance of attempts by landowners and the Crown to limit their rights to free mining would stretch far into the seventeenth century.[50] The values of rents and fines were often recorded in writing; but knowledge concerning grazing rights, or the use of commons, was frequently held in oral tradition, even though the written record was slowly becoming more dominant.[51] The testimonies of the oldest inhabitants of any community might be taken as authoritative: in 1565, a seventy-year-old husbandman in Gloucestershire pronounced upon the customs of his manor of Southam, adding as further testimony that 'he hathe heard bothe his grandfather and his own father, sometyme beying tenants of Southam, so say and declare'.[52]

Society also possessed methods of reconciliation. Before the Reformation, different members of the parish would kiss the pax board during mass in order of rank; after the Reformation, the same differentiation was achieved by the churchwardens seating everybody in the parish church in order of importance. Processions, whether sacred or secular, bound a community together in a single ritual act, but also demonstrated the wealth and authority of those who walked at the front, or under cloths of estate, or who held banners or staffs of office.[53] Historians have sometimes been guilty of assuming that early modern communities were essentially harmonious, and that the flood of Tudor rhetoric exhorting charitable and cooperative behaviour illustrates a time before the growth of individualism had destroyed communal identity.[54] In reality, idealism and dysfunction existed side by side, and the rhetoric of neighbourliness might be taken as an indication of how frequently effort was needed to heal social divisions. The very rituals intended to celebrate and strengthen the ties of community could themselves be turned into a vehicle for antagonism. Corpus Christi processions celebrated unity, but they could equally be used to underline the divisions within the town.[55] Kissing the pax board was intended as a ritual which bound the congregation together, but the order in which the pax board was venerated could equally give rise to disagreements. One London woman threw the pax to the ground in fury in 1496, because another woman had kissed it before her; and another Londoner used the pax board to assault his priest.[56] It took an intricate hierarchy of courts, ecclesiastical and civil, and a range of informal interventions to defuse tension and dispense justice.[57]

Communities could be bound together by opposition to threats from both within and without. Parishes might work together to expel alien or disruptive elements.[58] More frequently, however, it was the quietly recurring rhythms of the ritual year that helped to reinforce communal ties at Christmas and Easter, at ploughing and harvest, with church ales, maying, processions and holy days. Community was not a static entity, but a series of relationships in constant need of reaffirmation.[59] It was the patterns of life, the constant reiteration of connections between family, neighbours, parishioners, guild members and townsfolk, which kept knitting back together the fabric of society, even as economic distress, religious division and political crisis tore rents within it.

Women and children

If Tudor society was self-conscious about the ties of community, it usually tended to leave another key set of relationships more idealized or parodied than diligently examined. Sex and gender were considerations which shaped every encounter. Often gender was passed over without comment; but it could also be caricatured in ways which, though they amused or admonished contemporaries, provide highly unreliable guides for the historian. Then, as now, sexual stereotypes were a good way of selling cheap print. Broadsheets, pamphlets and ballads were full of men cast either as steadfast citizens or unruly subversives, and of women caricatured as fragile innocents, relentless scolds or vicious wantons. Jokes about the opposite sex made good entertainment, but are unreliable as a commentary on gender relations.[60] Ballads could carry mixed messages: one Elizabethan ballad that conveyed 'a warning to al London dames' reminded them how beauty fades and advised them to pay attention to virtue and charity; but at the same time it heaped lavish praise on those self-same London women, whose fame spread throughout the world, renowned as they were 'For beauties kyndely grace.'[61]

It remains difficult to uncover the experiences of women, who are often less visible through political, judicial or financial records than men, and who wrote a much smaller proportion of the books of the time. Many sources suggest separate spheres, with women occupying the domestic space, without legal rights or independent wealth. Legal records demonstrate that if crimes such as murder, sodomy and bestiality were largely the preserve of men, infanticide, witchcraft and fornication (meaning premarital sex) were usually ascribed to women. Sermons and books of religious instruction prescribed virtuous male leadership and quiescent female obedience. The picture is one of patriarchy, the word most commonly applied to the gender relations of this period, and often held to be the dominant cultural framework, in which women were both victims and colluding agents.[62] Yet recent work on both women's history and the history of masculinity has challenged the simplicity of this picture of a divided society.[63] We now have a better idea of how masculine ideals concerning authority, wealth, honour and sexual prowess could oppress men just as much as feminine ideals could daunt the lives of women.

Patriarchal values could leave large swathes of society, male and female alike, marginalized and disempowered.

Patriarchy remains a tricky concept, not least since it remains an enduring phenomenon, and a continuing problem, in the modern world. It is important to realize that there have been many different varieties of patriarchy across history, and the Tudors had their own distinct version.[64] Tudor men had more legal rights than Tudor women; they also had legal rights over those women if they married or fathered them. Women's property became the property of their husband after marriage. This legal situation was reinforced by ideas commonly held about women: both religious ideology and scientific theory emphasized the inferiority of the female sex. Yet to Thomas Platter, travelling through England in 1599, the women had 'far more liberty than in other lands and know just how to make good use of it' – a view echoed by other commentators.[65] The theoretically inferior position of women jars with the strong-minded, boisterous and intelligent women of Tudor literary culture, and with the many women who appear to advantage in legal, urban and parish records. One foreign commentator said as much about the women in England, although he was clearly talking about women with a certain level of prosperity:

> Although the women there are entirely in the power of their husbands except for their lives, yet they are not kept so strictly as they are in Spain or elsewhere. Nor are they shut up but they have the free management of the house or housekeeping . . . They go to market to buy what they like to eat. They are well dressed, fond of taking it easy, and commonly leave the care of household matters and drudgery to their servants . . . All the rest of their time they employ in walking or riding, in playing at cards and otherwise, in visiting their friends and keeping company . . . and all this with the permission and knowledge of their husbands.[66]

Perhaps above all, we should beware of making easy assumptions that all of Tudor society shared common views of gender roles. Thomas Smith, who as Cambridge professor of civil law, secretary to Edward VI and Elizabethan ambassador might be held to belong firmly to the establishment, nevertheless saw husband and wife as equal partners: 'ech obeyeth and commaundeth other, and they two togeather rule the house'.[67] Some legal constraints may have put women at a severe disadvantage, but did not necessarily impinge on daily life; and some legal constraints may have been less binding than they at first appear. Women made considerable use of the legal system themselves to defend their property and reputation.[68] Rape cases were pursued with vigour, and it seems probable that the low conviction rates were more indicative of stringent expectations concerning reliable legal evidence than prejudice against women.[69] Nor, when it came to violence, were women limited to verbal weapons: assault cases show that women, too, used both knives and fists to defend their cause; although when women killed, it was usually believed to be through witchcraft, or a case of infanticide.[70]

Commentary on marriage suggests a more egalitarian model than we might expect. If the theory was often one of male authority and female subordination, the evidence suggests that in practice marriage was widely understood to have a measure of equality, an expectation of affectionate companionship and a dread of marital strife.[71] 'Mariage being the chiefe ground and preservation of all societies, is nothing else but a communion of life betweene the husband and the wife, extending it selfe to all the parts that belong to their house', was one aphorism. 'Marriage with peace, is this worlds paradice; with strife, this lifes purgatory.' In descriptions of marriage, mutuality was a recurrent theme:

> A good husband must be wise in wordes, milde in conversation, fayth-full in promise, circumspect in gyving counsaile, carefull in provision for his house, diligent in ordering his goods, patient in importunity, jealous in bringing up his youth. A good wife must be grave abroade, wise at home, patient to suffer, constant to love, friendly to her neigh-bours, provident for her houshold.[72]

There were also conduct books, which prescribed a more unequal power relationship.[73] The Calvinist William Perkins defined a husband as 'he that hath authority over the wife', but even here a lot was open to individual interpretation.[74] Where the head of the household was believed to rule as God's representative on earth, much depended on whether people conceived of God as loving and benevolent, or stern and judgemental.[75]

The Puritan Richard Rogers, who kept a diary, recorded in the 1580s his fears about losing his wife in childbirth. He felt it was his religious duty to consider what might happen if God 'should part us', but confessed 'alas this . . . is hard'. He was worried about marrying again, about who would care for household and children; but he also listed as a chief worry the loss of 'so fitt a companion for religion, huswifery, and other comf[orts]'.[76] Here was a many-layered understanding of marriage. In general, it is clear that relationships between the sexes were much debated, considered and contested; and that if there were inequalities, there could also be sympathy, cooperation and trust.[77]

Marriage was not always easy. Thomas Bentley, an Elizabethan church-warden, published *The Monument of matrones*, a seven-book compilation of prayers and meditations by, and about, a succession of virtuous biblical and political figures, including Queen Elizabeth.[78] It included a prayer 'to be used of the wife that hath a froward and bitter husband', hoping to provide 'a present remedie against the mischiefe of divorcement and sepa-ration'. The prayer pleaded for divine grace to open the man's 'wits and senses' to perceive the true nature of marriage, 'and thereby become unto me not so bitter a despiser and hater, but a true lover, sweet freend, and godlie governour'. In heartfelt language, it asked for help, 'for if we thus bite and devour one another, it cannot possible be, but we shall be consumed one of another'.[79] Divorce for the unhappily married was not common, yet it was not impossible; and from the strenuous condemnation of those who disapproved, it is clear that it did sometimes happen.[80] Thomas Becon's homily of 1547 against whoredom and adultery, reissued as part of the Elizabethan homilies, spoke of how whoredom was to blame for 'the divorces: which (nowe a dayes) be so comonly accustomed and used'.[81] Church courts could grant an annulment of a marriage on grounds of pre-contract (having previously promised to marry someone else), bigamy, consanguinity, affinity or impotence, all of which rendered a marriage contract invalid. In the case of a marriage deemed valid, divorce could only be granted on grounds of cruelty and adultery, but it left both parties unable to marry whilst the other lived.[82] Common law courts could not dissolve the marriage bond, but they could bind either party to keep the peace or pay maintenance: in 1540, Margery Acton sued her husband, who told the court that he would accept any reasonable decision about maintenance payments.[83] If the couple were of higher status, the case might come before the Privy Council. Moral sanction could also be applied: the Clothworkers' Guild in 1602 reprimanded one of their beadles for beating his wife, and threatened him with losing his job unless he reformed.[84]

There were also those who did not marry. It is hard to be sure, but in this period probably between a tenth and a fifth of women remained single throughout their lives.[85] Given that most people would not marry until their late twenties, and that spouses frequently died, the number of men and women in a community who were single at any given point must have been quite high. A homily of 1547 told those graced with chastity to 'prayse God for his gift, and seke all meanes possible to maynteyne the same', envisaging a single life given over to Bible-reading, meditation and prayer.[86] It was not usual, but it was not uncommon either for unmarried women to go on living in the family home, supported by a legacy from their parents.[87] Urban communities, with a high concentration of servants and high mortality rates, might contain a particularly large proportion of unmarried and widowed women.[88] This could foster anxiety among those in authority. In 1584, Manchester's court leet complained about unmarried women 'abusing themselves with young men and others having not any man to control them to the great dishonour of God and evil example of others'.[89] Yet an attempt to counter prostitution in Coventry in 1492, by banning single women under the age of fifty from keeping house in their own right, provoked stern opposition from the honest women of the city.[90]

It should not be assumed that patriarchy was the same thing as misogyny. Tudor society was not without its expressions of misogyny, but they tended to be the preserve of specific groups or individuals – from young unmarried men vying for credibility to anti-Catholic commentators attacking a Catholic queen.[91] A more educated kind of misogyny was also a recurrent feature of much Tudor entertainment, yet this was not straight-forward either. A popular Elizabethan collection of aphorisms contained such gems as 'Womens sorrowes are eyther too extreame, not to bee redressed, or else tricked up with dissimulation, not to be beleeved', under-lying the common belief that women were both excessive in their emotions and untrustworthy. Yet observations such as 'A woman of good lyfe, feareth no man with an evill tongue' suggested a more positive view, as did the concluding aphorism: 'That man which is married to a peaceable and vertuous woman, beeing on earth, hath attained heaven, being in want, hath attained wealth, beeing in woe, hath attained weale, being in care, hath attained comfort'.[92] Male limitations could also be clear-sightedly assessed. Thomas Elyot, discussing the care of very young children, advised that they should be kept from witnessing any dishonesty or hearing any 'wanton or unclene' words. He concluded briskly that 'for that cause all menne, excepte phisytyons onely, shulde be excluded and kepte out of the nursery'.[93]

There was a set of biological constraints which no woman could ignore. Whilst the modern world has increasingly questioned the relationship between gender constructs and biological identity, in the Tudor era the materiality of the body was considered foundational to gender. Each stage of a woman's life was marked in blood – from menstruation through child-birth to menopause – underlining the distinctiveness of female experience.[94] It was believed, too, that the baby in the womb was nourished by the mother's blood.[95] The lives of most women were marked by procreation: the standard guide to midwifery in the period was called *The Birth of mankynde, otherwyse named the womans booke*.[96] This sought to give instructions to midwives who could read, and envisaged the text being read aloud to those who could not. Its references to 'easy or uneasy, diffi-cult, or dolorous delyveraunce' are a reminder of the difficulties of child-birth.[97] Women were perhaps not so much more likely to die giving birth than more modern women: the likelihood was somewhere between sixteen and twenty-five women in every thousand.[98] Nevertheless, the risk was real. Women were also deemed vulnerable during pregnancy, when it was believed that looking upon someone or something ugly could result in a deformed child.[99] If a mother's health was too robust during pregnancy, it could lead to fears that the unborn baby was not thriving: the expectation was that the mother should feel frail and sick. She might also be frightened and melancholic.[100] There was no help but the reassurance and experience of other women in the community, and the providence of God.[101]

Yet motherhood was also seen as a divinely appointed miracle.[102] The humanist Juan Luis Vives discussed in 1523 the question of a mother's influence over her children, in particular asserting the importance of breast-feeding, arguing that a mother might 'more truly reken her daughter her owne' if she had not only carried her in the womb and given birth to her, but had also breast-fed her. It gave a touching picture of the mother's love for the daughter 'whom she hath nourished with her owne blod / whose slepes she hath cherished in her lappe / and hath cherfully accepted and kyssed the fyrst laughes / and fyrst hath ioyfully herde the stameryng of hit / covetyng to speke / and hath holden harde to her brest / prayenge hit good lucke and fortune'.[103] This might suggest to modern readers a constricted domestic role for Tudor women; yet this work was dedicated to Katherine of Aragon, the daughter of one of the most powerful early modern rulers, Queen Isabella of Castile, and it envisaged the rule of her daughter Mary as a future queen. The capacity to produce new life was a source of power, and the importance of child-bearing was at the heart of dynastic politics, just as much as it was at the centre of so many women's life experience. Thomas Bentley's inclusion of two prayers for pregnant queens in his *Monument of matrones* underlined the political significance of childbirth. Comparing the queen to the Virgin Mary, Bentley's prayers asked for a royal child 'in bodie beautifull and comelie, in pregnant wit, notable and excellent, in mind noble and valiant'.[104] Childbirth was both a private happening and a political act. The inability of Katherine of Aragon to bear a healthy son, Anne Boleyn's miscarriage of 1536, Mary I's phantom pregnancy of 1555 and Elizabeth I's barren state were all as instrumental in shaping England's political fortunes as any of the broader shifts in economic conditions or political relations.

Even at the village level, the business of childbirth was something in which women wielded unassailable authority and from which men were excluded. Elite pregnant women were 'confined' some time before the birth in a birthing chamber, sealed from the elements but also from incursion by men.[105] After the birth, women remained in a female-only space until their churching, a ritual of readmission to the church community, which was also a ceremony of purification. It would be easy to read the phenomenon of churching as symbolic of a woman's marginalized position in society, except that evidence suggests that it was a ritual in which women took great pride and pleasure, and which they retained after the Reformation long into modern times. A woman of Barking was brought before the archdeacon's court in Essex in 1597 for having had too much fun at her churching and spending several hours in the tavern.[106]

Religious change turned childbirth into a potential source of conflict in the sixteenth century.[107] In medieval England, the intercessory and miraculous elements of religion were most keenly felt in times of trouble, and for women in labour, the intervention of the Virgin Mary was eagerly sought. Relics, and girdles which had been kept wrapped around statues of the Virgin, were a common aid.[108] Prayers to an array of powerful female saints were used by the woman in labour and her helpers. This confederacy of strong women was broken apart by Protestantism. Relics were banished, prayers were to be directed only to God, and midwives were watched with suspicion lest they preserve any habits from the past. In 1538, the Protestant bishop of Salisbury, Nicholas Shaxton, issued orders to his priests that they should instruct midwives to prevent the use of girdles, and not allow women in labour 'to make any foolish vow to go in pilgrimage to this image or that image after her deliverance'.[109] Nonetheless, childbirth remained a moment heavily imbued with sacred significance; Bentley's prayers included the admission that without divine help, 'all womens helpe, and all physicke is in vaine'.[110] His book also contained several prayers to be said by midwives, making clear the continuing importance of their role, 'working togither' with God 'to helpe and ease woman . . . in this case and time of their sore labour'.[111] Unease at the potential influence wielded by these women in the birthing chamber remained.

The raising of children was a heavy responsibility at a time of high infant mortality. Perhaps a quarter of all children died before the age of one, and a similar proportion died before the age of ten.[112] Bentley had himself buried his newborn son and a wife who died in childbirth, and he included some anguished prayers for those in difficulties or on the brink of death. The place of children within early modern society has been debated at length. It was once assumed that Tudor men and women could not have been as attached to their children as their equivalents in later centuries, because the child mortality rate was so devastatingly high that it must have militated against a strong bond of affection. It was argued that family relationships were distant and cold and little affection was shown to children.[113] Historical sources are not always forthcoming about emotions, but it is clear that a great many parents loved their children, were fearful when they fell ill and felt devastated when they died.[114] It is a poignant fact that children, often invisible in the historical record, become most evident when they are sick or dying, when their experiences are most likely to be recorded.[115] John Dee, the astrologer and physician, kept a diary of events, illnesses and accidents in the lives of his children, just as he kept a careful account (in Greek characters) of his wife's menstruation.[116] Richard Rainolde, writing his book on rhetoric in 1563, used the example of the question 'is it good to marry?' to illustrate how to address a rhetorical question. One of the objections against the married state was that it could produce 'greate care, and pensivenesse of minde, by losse of children, or wife, whom thou loveste'. Yet among the responses to this and other arguments for the burdens of married life was the suggestion that to 'laboure for thy wife, whom thou loveste, and deare children, thy pleasure, the ioye easeth thy labour'.[117] Thomas Wilson, discussing the rhetorical arts needed to make a good sermon, advised the preacher to dwell on the plight of the unfortunate. 'For if fleshe and bloude move us to love our children, our wyfes, and our kynsfolke: muche more should the spirite of God and Christes goodnes towardes man stirre us to love our neighbours moste entirely'.[118] He had no difficulty believing that men loved their wives and children.

Childhood did not last long in Tudor England. Babies from high-status families were breast-fed by wet nurses, or weaned within their first year, though babies from humbler backgrounds were not weaned until a later stage. Boys were thought to need breast-feeding for longer than girls.[119] At around the age of seven, children began to dress in versions of adult clothing, and those prosperous enough began education, whilst their poorer contemporaries might begin work in the fields. Surveys showed that in struggling households the children worked as hard as any to stave off ruin.[120] Nevertheless, there was a concept of childhood, and a sense of comradeship between children.[121] The Tudor schoolmaster William Horman, in a book of Latin and English translations for schoolchildren, included the sentence, 'I wyll bye a rattell to styll my baby for cryenge', and dolls, puppets, tops and hobbyhorses can all be found in the records; meanwhile, the trade in imported puppets and dolls was lucrative enough for the government in 1582 to impose a tax on them.[122] Some puritan commentators opined that children were treated too indulgently by the parents.[123] The Elizabethan minister John Northbrooke, complaining about 'the naughty, and wanton, and foolish bringing up of children', warned 'what joly yonkers and lustie brutes these wilbe, when they shall come to be Citizens and intermedlers in matters of Common wealth'.[124] More congenial were the views of Erasmus, who set a standard of thoughtfulness which tempered some of the sterner injunctions about the disciplining of the young, describing children as 'the most precious of your possessions' and urging teachers to show 'gentleness and kindness'.[125] Thomas Elyot, writing in the 1530s, also advised that a child should be 'pleasauntly trayned' by tutors 'of moche affabilitie and patience'. He warned that 'by a cruel and irous mayster, the wyttes of chyldren be dulled', and pointed out that beating children would only hinder learning. He recommended instead using conscience to instil discipline and praise to inspire: 'desyre of prayse addeth to a sharpe spurre to theyr dysposition towarde lernynge and vertue'.[126] Taking account of all these variations, it is still clear that the love, playfulness, anxiety and grief of Tudor parenting was far closer to our own experience than we ever used to think.[127]

Men and war

To be a man in Tudor England could be an anxious business. The patriarchal ideal was as problematic for many men as it was for women, and many men struggled to respond adequately to it.[128] It is clear that masculine ideals varied: the head of a household might be expected to conform to patriarchal notions of authority, competence, prosperity, hospitality and control of wife and children; conversely, an apprentice might seek to prove his manhood through displays of bravura, comradeship, a measure of violence and some heavy drinking.[129] Even those who managed to achieve wealth and influence as the head of a family might be plagued by anxieties about their wayward wives, as the prominence of plays, ballads and jests about cuckoldry serves to illustrate. Nor was the patriarchal ideal reliant on the control of women alone: asserting authority over subordinate men in the household was equally important. The proliferation of jokes revolving around the undermining of patriarchal authority by a man's wife and apprentice makes the point neatly. Manhood could be dominated as much by jealousy, guilt and fear, as by feelings of superiority.[130]

Masculine honour and authority relied on a complicated mixture of elements, including age, wealth, occupation, vigour, education and physical prowess. Fertility was important and impotence was a serious problem.[131] Men could feel menaced by women's powerful sexuality, which was perceived as potentially rendering them lascivious and insatiable, placing great expectations on male performance.[132] Popular literature, ballads and songs were full of stories of luckless men outwitted by libidinous wives, who caroused with their lovers and left their husbands looking foolish. The case of Alice Arden, who in 1551 was convicted for inciting her lover to murder her husband, was widely discussed, and became the basis of a ballad and of the 1590 play *Arden of Faversham*, perhaps precisely because what we might call gender politics were no less fascinating or contentious then than they are now.[133] Even more complexity surrounds *The Taming of the Shrew*, which can be read as a discourse on misogyny and patriarchal power, or as a complex debate about the redundancy of patriarchal precepts and a celebration of headstrong, witty women.[134]

Puritan divines might insist on the need for a man to exercise godly authority over his wife, but other commentators were more practical. Fitzherbert, in his *Boke of Husbandry*, spoke gravely of the 'dylygence and labour, that [be]longeth to an housbande, to thy lyvyng, thy wyves, they chyldrens, and they servauntes', but also made it clear 'that seldome doth the housbaunde thryve, without the leve of his wyfe'. He expected a wife to work hard, but he emphasized that her principal obligation was 'to love hir housbande, above father and mother, and above all other men', painting a picture of a companionate marriage both affectionate and practical.[135] This seems at odds with the legal reinforcement of the principle of male superiority: Alice Arden was burnt alive as punishment for her crime, because a wife's murder of her husband was deemed to be treason, equivalent to the crime of a servant murdering his or her master.[136] Some historians have taken the law at face value and assumed that it 'turned a woman into a non-person'.[137] Men were legally entitled to beat their wives, even if not 'outrageously' or 'violently', and were generally only brought to law if the level of violence was deemed to be life-threatening.[138] There was also a London by-law that forbade wife-beating after nine o'clock at night because of the noise. On the other hand, others have pointed to the gulf between theory and practice. The way that neighbours rallied in cases of domestic abuse to protect the woman and reproach the man suggests that violence against women was largely deplored.[139]

Few aspects of masculinity remained uncontested.[140] Tudor men were prone to bursting into tears in times of trial, and yet this was often classified as indecent, or even bestial behaviour, particularly by those with aspirations to Renaissance civility. Yet King Arthur and his knights had wept, and there remained those who thought that intense emotion might make tears justifiable. When Shakespeare's Coriolanus was moved to weep by his mother's pleading, the general beside him was disgusted; but within the wider ethical framework of the play, Coriolanus's tears saved both himself and the city of Rome.[141] For many men, the struggle to achieve a solid reputation and avoid shame was a life-long challenge, which required both public probity and domestic harmony, neither achieved with ease. Men were deeply concerned with their 'fame', or standing in society, and particularly sensitive about slurs regarding sexual misconduct or weakness.[142] To call a man a cuckold was a bitter insult. Even harmonious relationships where the man was deemed to hold authority placed a burden of expectation on the husband: as Kate acknowledges at the end of *The Taming of the Shrew*, whether seriously or satirically it is hard to say:

Thy husband is thy lord, thy life, thy keeper,
Thy head, thy sovereign, one that cares for thee,
And for thy maintenance commits his body
To painful labour both by sea and land,
To watch the night in storms, the day in cold,
Whilst thou liest warm at home, secure and safe,
And craves no other tribute at thy hands
But love, fair looks, and true obedience.[143]

Historians have speculated whether the early modern period saw a crisis in gender relations.[144] This idea, once stated, was almost immediately called into question; but undoubtedly there were some profound tensions concerning gender roles in the Tudor era.[145] Since male honour was largely dependent on relationships with women, and because the most profound challenges to male honour came from unruly, libidinous or domineering women, issues of conjugal relations and domestic harmony were energetically contested in the church courts. An increase in such disputes often reflected other social and economic tensions at work, but there was more continuity than crisis at work in gender relations.[146]

Tudor men may have had more opportunities to exercise authority and achieve independence than their female equivalents, but this was offset by the stark fact that all adult males might be called upon to fight the wars that were a recurrent feature of this period. Included in Bentley's *Monument of matrones* was a prayer 'to be used of the wife for hir husband being a Captaine or Souldiour, and gone a war-fare'. It lamented the malice that had brought into the world 'discord, tumults, seditions, wars, bloud-sheading, man-slaughter, destruction of realmes and countries, cities and villages', and it pleaded with God 'to assist my husband', asking for an angel to be sent 'that he may pitch his tents among them'.[147] The prevalence of war and its human cost in this period is something often overlooked, and yet it was a recurring feature. War turned many men into vagrants, although it is also true that many soldiers had been vagrants to begin with: the fact that some beggars chose to pose untruthfully as military veterans suggests that theirs was a predicament that Tudor society viewed with concern.[148] Almanacs and prophecies which foretold war were widely bought, copied and shared: one reader in 1544 copied out the warning of imminent war, which would see many men 'spowled and slayne howses castelles and ceytes shalbe taken brent and destrowed'.[149]

Military prowess was a crucial ingredient of masculinity. Musters made careful distinctions between the relative fighting capabilities of the men they reviewed, and many men seem to have taken it as a compliment to be rated one of the 'choyce menne'.[150] The phenomenon of the duel, which historians used to assume was a survival from medieval chivalry, was in fact an import from Renaissance culture in mainland Europe.[151] As one Elizabethan commentator observed, it had been unknown in England 'till our youth beganne to travell straunge Countreys, and so brought home strange manners'; nonetheless, the duel soon became a fixture.[152] This was also a society liberally supplied with weaponry. Armour could be more problematic, but musters for twenty-seven counties in 1522 suggest enough bows and bills for nearly all of the men raised, and household inventories show swords, bows and handguns kept in bedchambers, halls and parlours.[153] The place of war in Tudor society has important resonance for the contested question of gender roles. In the playful debate from Erasmus's colloquy 'Puerpera', the new mother mounts a spirited attack on male claims to strength. 'Now, – though you make a special point of boasting of your martial valor – there's not a single one of you who, if he once experienced childbirth, would not prefer standing in a battle line ten times over to going through what we must endure so often.'[154] If this underlines how familiar some of the early modern rhetoric about the battle of the sexes might sound, it also alludes to a truth frequently overlooked. However dismal the experiences of some early modern women, standing in battle lines was not something they were called upon to do.

The inevitable corollary of war was disease, mutilation and death, and the last of these was often the kindest. To live on as a disabled veteran in Tudor society was a difficult fate. Yet there was provision for returning veterans. When Henry VIII established six new cathedrals in 1540, he specified that they should provide employment for some of the veterans 'decayde' or 'maimed' in his wars. One man 'sore hurt and maimed' at Blackheath was made constable of Tenby Castle, and Mary I planned a new hospital in London for 'pore, impotent and aged souldiers'.[155] Before the Reformation, such men could be granted the right to collect alms for indulgences, or could seek alms from the monastic houses; after the Reformation, almshouses, hospitals and livery companies tried to fill the gap. Still, people went on giving charity to wounded soldiers: the porter in the dialogue of 1535, *The hye way to the spyttell hous*, listed 'maymed souldyours' as one of the categories of people received in his hospital.

Despite principles of superiority enshrined in law, therefore, Tudor men were never straightforwardly the beneficiaries of the patriarchal order. Human relationships remained complex and often contested, but the ideal was more often one of mutual love and respect than of domination and submission. The expectation that men would possess and deploy both physical and moral strength in a range of circumstances was both exacting for all and troubling for many, and the experiences of war were terrifying, its consequences frequently devastating.

Feasting and fasting

Food was a central preoccupation of Tudor life: not just a source of nutrition, but a badge of status, a means of occupation, a major item of expenditure and a symbol of the sacred.[156] In the first printed collection of statutes, published in 1485, the index contained categories for laws about cheese and butter, victuallers and wines.[157] Food and drink were common currency: rents paid in kind were often rendered as foodstuffs; payments to officials could be in the form of game; and offerings to patrons were frequently edible. Food could be a tool of diplomacy: visiting dignitaries were often presented with wine, sugar or marzipan on visits to towns, and Pope Leo X once gave Henry VIII a gift of 100 parmesan cheeses.[158] Fraternities were bound together by their feasts, and indeed the word 'companion' was understood to mean 'bread sharer' (from the Latin *cum pane*) in late medieval England.[159] Gifts of food reinforced social ties at every level, between neighbours in the village (where the 'help ale' was a way of assisting the poor) or between different urban groupings who paid tribute in traded goods, such as sugar loaves, wine or spices.[160]

Bread was the most important commodity for the poor, capable of carrying religious sanction through its association with the eucharist and biblical symbolism generally; the cost of grain was of vital political importance, since grain shortages might result in riots.[161] During the good harvests of the later fifteenth century, barley bread had been replaced as a staple by wheaten bread, although commentators thought it worrying that labourers now expected this.[162] For the very poor who were short of flour, acorns could be ground up to use as a substitute, but this was a pitiful sign of indigence.[163] The poorer sort used thick slices of bread as trenchers, or plates, for the rest of their food, and bread was also customarily crumbled into pottage to thicken it. Pottage was the main daily dish for ordinary people: somewhere between porridge and thick soup, it contained cereals, pulses, herbs, vegetables and sometimes meat. In a collection of exercises for Latin translation, Vives provided a description of a cauldron suspended on a pot-hook over the fire; in it simmered a broth containing meat, cereal, rice and vegetables.[164]

The symbolism surrounding bread underlined the extent to which Tudor society could be dependent upon it. Harrison commented on town dwellers who could not grow their own grain: 'for wheaten bread, they eat it when they can reach unto the price of it, contenting themselves in the meantime with bread made of oats or barley: a poor estate, God wot!'[165] The use of false weights and measures was one of the worst social crimes: a sermon from the 1550s warned gravely that 'deceitfull weyghtes, and double measures' were to be avoided as assiduously as the 'sword of Satan'.[166] Urban authorities paid close attention to weights and measures: in Leicester in 1520, there were attempts to 'set standards as of the quality of bread sold to the poor', for the sake of 'the comonwelth off the towne'.[167] Corrupt dealings were opposed on the grounds that they would cause suffering among the lowest orders of society: the lord mayor of York in 1555 went on a personal tour of the market, ordering one butcher with inflated prices to sell at a cost 'reasonable to the poor'.[168] Hugh Plat, responding to the famines of the 1590s, called down the wrath of heaven upon those who raised their prices in times of dearth, and asked indignantly, 'why should the rich men feast, when the poore are ready to famish?'[169]

Social status, and social climbing, could be demonstrated by the food which people ate. The royal court made a point of consuming foodstuffs that were exotic, or rare, or only briefly in season: Henry VIII seems to have pioneered the breeding of pheasants, and rejoiced in sweet cherries, cucumbers, radishes and early peas.[170] Conspicuous consumption was a mark of the great household, although it was also used in alehouses and taverns.[171] Above all, the ability to provide hospitality was essential to any kind of social standing.[172] Andrew Borde warned those seeking to set up in a mansion house that they should be sure that they could muster the necessary lavish provision for household, friends and neighbours: it was madness, he argued, 'to set up a great howse' if you were 'not able to kepe man nor mowse'.[173] The duty of hospitality had been a central obligation of the pre-Reformation clergy and a central part of monastic provision for the poor, so much so that it was enshrined in church law.[174] After the Reformation, it was still expected of anyone who kept a manor house, although it could sometimes indicate enduring Catholic loyalties, as with the Petre family of Ingatestone in Essex, whose account books indicate that during the winter of 1551–52 they fed the local poor every day.[175] Nor was it only the great who were expected to dispense hospitality. John Heritage, born in Warwickshire in 1470, spent most of his working life in Moreton-in-Marsh in Gloucestershire, and was a yeoman farmer, wool merchant, trader and moneylender. He grew up in a household of about sixteen, including his parents, seven siblings and servants. An inventory of 1495 shows that the kitchen could comfortably feed a large group of people, with three spits, an array of pots and pans, and ale brewed in the bakehouse; it also pictures the household gathered for meals at the long table in the hall, with John's father at the head of the table in the only chair, and everyone else on benches. There was a linen tablecloth, pewter plates, and silver spoons for important occasions.[176]

Subtle distinctions were made between fare that was good and generous, and that which was luxurious, which was of questionable morality. Here again, degrees of social status were important: those who lived in a manner inappropriate to their station in life could be censured. The Privy Council was concerned in 1596 by the 'increase of luxury in London' and urged better regulation of 'both public assemblies and private diett', although this should be set against the background of famine that year.[177] There were also health considerations. Fresh fruit and vegetables could be viewed with suspicion. 'It is wryten in the lyf of saynt Benet that a religious woman with a gredenes, receyved a wycked spiryte in etynge [eating] of letuse in the gardeyn', recorded Thomas Betson of Syon.[178] William Harrison liked the fact that exotic plants could be brought from the New World to decorate the gardens of the rich, but he thought it the height of folly to actually eat such strange things as mushrooms and aubergines. The oddity of foreigners was also characterized by what they ate. Dutch immigrants or merchants were called 'butter-tubs' or 'butter-mouths', whilst people looked askance at Turks on account of their extreme fasting.[179] Nonetheless, by the end of the century, foreign cookery books were being translated into English. *Epulario or the Italian Banquet*, published in 1598, may have been the first to introduce the English to the idea of cooked cheese.[180]

The giving and consumption of food underlines an important political point about Tudor England: namely, that the most important relationships were always understood as having a personal element. William Cecil, Lord Burghley, advising his son Robert on the rules of political life, told him how to maintain a friendship with anyone eminent: 'Compliment him often with many, yet small, gifts, and of little charge. And if thou hast cause to bestow any great gratuity, let it be something which may be daily in sight.'[181] The Lisle family in Calais maintained their links with Henry VIII by sending everything from boar's head to sturgeon, as well as the quails that Jane Seymour craved while pregnant.[182] Their envoy in London could begin a letter by announcing that 'I presented the King with the cherries in my lady's name, which he was very glad of, and thanks you and her both for them.'[183] The Lisles adopted a particularly familiar tone in their exchanges to underline the point that they really were family: Arthur, Lord Lisle, was Elizabeth of York's illegitimate brother. Thomas Cromwell's accounts record the rewards dispensed to those who brought gifts such as artichokes, quinces and porpoise; and Robert Dudley responded to tributes, including a brace of puffins from the earl of Derby.[184] The rarity of certain foodstuffs, or the fact that – like cherries – they were only briefly in season, heightened the value of the gift.

Fresh water was not widely available, particularly in an urban setting, and the Tudors consumed enormous quantities of beer. Manual workers, sailors and soldiers were assumed to need 4 quarts (over 4 litres) of beer for their daily allowance.[185] There was little concern over alcohol consumption, although Thomas Elyot did observe the longevity of the Cornish, who drank mostly water, and commented that men and women brought up on milk and butter were a lot healthier than those who drank ale and wine.[186] Pregnant women necessarily drank a fair amount of alcohol, which may have contributed to late miscarriages; but they were advised to avoid strong drink.[187] Ale, beer and cider, like milk, were mostly produced at home, or close to home.[188] Wine was believed to have health-giving properties, and Elyot recalled the opinion of Plato that it 'norysheth and comforteth, as well all the body, as the spirites of man'. He thought that God 'dyd ordeyne it for mankynde, as a remedy agaynstd the incommodities of aege, that thereby they shulde seme to retourne unto youth and forgette hevynes', but advised that 'yonge men shoulde drynke lyttell wyne, for it shall make them prone to fury, and to lecherye'.[189]

Fasting was a regular part of Tudor life, both before and after the Reformation. In the pre-Reformation period, everyone abstained from meat and dairy on Wednesdays and Fridays, on the eve of important saints' days, and throughout Advent and Lent. One of Protestantism's attractions was that it dispensed with these requirements. However, the threat to the fishing trade was such that Friday fasting was hastily restored during Edward VI's reign – although it remained unpopular, as the attempts to regulate butchers' sales on fast days indicate.[190] In later Protestant culture, it became common to mark times of mourning, or special intercession, with fast days. Public fasts might be held in parish, town or by the nation at large in response to a particular crisis, whilst the godly might keep private fasts, accompanied by prayer and almsgiving, in pursuit of greater personal sanctity.[191] The response to the terrible famines of the 1590s, after three consecutive harvests had failed, was to declare public fasts on Wednesdays and Fridays – with the pious objective of showing penitence to a providential God for the sins that had merited such punishment, and with the practical objective of giving the food saved to the starving poor. The Council interpreted God's displeasure as a response to the 'excesse in dyett' and 'nedeles waste and ryotous consumpcion' prevalent throughout the kingdom.[192] In more private fashion, many dedicated Protestants resumed the medieval practice of fasting the night before receiving communion.[193]

In 1599, in a decade that had seen the death rate rise to over 50 per cent above average, Richard Gardiner of Shrewsbury published *Profitable Instructions for the Manuring, Sowing and Planting of Kitchen Gardens very Profitable for the Commonweal and Greatly for the Help and Comfort of Poor People*.[194] He recorded with pride how, with less than 4 acres of land, he had grown hundreds of cabbages and carrots to sustain the poor people of his town in the last dearth: 'there were many hundreds of people well refreshed thereby, for the space of twentie daies when bread was wanting amongst the poore in the pinch or fewe daies before Harvest'.[195] He left his book, with detailed instructions on the growing of vegetables, as a last word, hoping to benefit the town he had cherished and defended: 'now in my olde age, or last dayes, I would willinglie take my last farewell with some good instructions to pleasure the generall number'. His love of gardening was indissolubly linked to his love for his town and its community, and his duty to God, and he wrote his book in order 'that God may be glorified in his good gifts, the generall number the better comforted, and the poore the better releeved with Garden stuffe'.[196] Even the growing of cabbages could be a way to strengthen society, in soul as well as body.

Sleep and sex

Sleep was a subject discussed by those seeking to regulate health in body and soul. Thomas Elyot wrote approvingly that moderate sleep aided digestion, rendering 'the body fatter, the mynde more quiete and clere, the humours temperate'.[197] Andrew Borde also praised moderate sleep,

> for it doth make parfyte degestyon, it doth nourysshe the blode, and doth qualyfye the heate of the lyver, it doth acuate, quycken, and refressheth the memory, it doth restore nature, and doth quyet all the humours and pulses in man, and doth anymate, and doth comforte all the naturall and anymall and spyrytuall powers of man.

His final accolade was that 'such moderate slepe is acceptable in the syght of God'.[198]

Immoderate sleep, by contrast, could bring on all sorts of diseases of the brain, including epilepsy and apoplexy. At a time when human health was believed to be governed by the four humours, which rendered people either sanguine, choleric, melancholic or phlegmatic, those governed by the first two needed only seven hours' sleep, but phlegmatic individuals might sleep for nine hours or more.

Tudor sleeping patterns were quite unlike our own. Sleeping was usually a communal activity; only babies slept alone, out of a fear that they could be smothered. Tudor beds like the 'Great Bed of Ware', which is over 10 feet wide, reflect this. Beds were valuable items: with all their furnishings, they could be worth £10 or more.[199] They were the site of marital encounters, friendly confidences, childbirth and death, and a great many dramas unfolded around them.[200] It was important to be considerate of others when sleeping. Erasmus's instructions for children admonished them: 'If thou lye with a bedfelowe / lye stylle / and make nat bare they selfe with tumblyng / nor vexe nat thy bedfelowe with pullynge of the clothes.' He also observed that in the bedchamber, 'sylence is laudable'.[201] Borde's advice – 'To slepe grovelynge upon the stomacke and belly is not good' – reflected the fact that beds were usually shared. He advised that, in the event of digestive problems, 'better it is to lay your hande or your bedfelowes hande over your stomacke'.[202] There were two 'sleeps' each night. The first sleep lasted until around midnight, when in a period of wakefulness, it was possible to catch up on one's correspondence, say one's prayers or have sex. Then came a second, longer sleep.[203]

The sharing of beds often caused troubling behaviour – from the homesick apprentices who wet the bed, to those prompted to unlawful sexual activity by proximity. One Essex man was brought before the arch-deaconry court in 1587 for sharing a bed with his wife and his maid, and for coming very late to church: it is not clear that the two crimes were deemed to be related, but they were both taken as indications of moral slackness. His defence was that he did not own enough beds for them to sleep apart.[204] The use of truckle beds often allowed servants to observe the infidelities of their masters or mistresses. Beds could be found all over the house, in parlours and kitchens, although towards the end of the sixteenth century they were increasingly being relocated to bedchambers.[205] Pillows, in the view of William Harrison, who was suspicious of anything luxurious, should only be used by women in childbed.

Tudor humour frequently revolved around sex, and jokes, ballads and proverbs on the subject were plentiful. Keys in locks, swords in scabbards, pestles in mortars, and a range of fruit and vegetables could all provide sexual innuendo.[206] Formal discussion of sex, on the other hand, was unusual, and what there was might well be put into Latin for the sake of discretion. Discussing the highly sensitive question of the king's possible impotence after his disappointing marriage to Anne of Cleves, Henry VIII's physicians referred in Latin to his nocturnal emissions, which they took as proof of his virility.[207] The notebook of Thomas Betson, Syon's physician librarian, contained a chapter written in Latin on the uses of urine for diagnosing illness; he probably used Latin because this chapter dealt mostly with women's illnesses. At least Betson tackled the subject: the Elizabethan physician John Banister, discussing anatomy, dealt with the male genitalia without inhibition, even commenting on how the foreskin moved 'in the acte of venerie, now upward, now downeward, to the exceedyng delectation of the Female'; but he would not even mention the female organs: 'I am from the begynnyg perswaded, that, by liftyng up the vayle of Natures secretes, in womens shapes, I shall commit more indecencie agaynst the office of *Decorum* then yeld needefull instruction to the profite of the common sort.'[208]

Some advice was forthcoming. Borde thought that 'veneryous actes before the fyrste slepe' were to be avoided, implying that sex was best attempted in the middle of the night; he also thought it inadvisable on a full stomach.[209] Tudor literature usually upheld the view that women were far more libidinous than men, with hearty sexual appetites which their husbands could find difficulty in satisfying.[210] Jest-books suggest that women had strong views about their sexual preferences and often enjoyed sex, which medical authorities deemed to be very good for their health, and capable of curing various physical and mental disorders.[211] It was inequalities in social status that could turn sex into a form of oppression – in particular, the widely held acknowledgement that women servants might be easy prey for their masters and other men of the household. This gave rise to many jokes, proverbs and anecdotes, as well as to the misery that is more soberly related in legal records.[212]

Sexual encounters were closely linked to the question of procreation. This was so much the case that same-sex relationships between women were considered less significant than those between men, since no waste of seed was involved.[213] The primary purpose of marriage was to produce children. The 1559 *Book of Common Prayer* gave instructions for a certain prayer to be omitted from the marriage service if the wife was beyond the age of child-bearing: namely, that the new couple 'be fruytfull in procreation of Chyldren' and live long enough to see 'theyr chyldrens chyldren, unto the thyrde and fourth generation'.[214] The conception of children required compatibility, however. As the seventeenth-century herbalist Nicholas Culpeper asked, 'If their hearts be not united in love, how should their seed unite to cause conception?'[215] More practically, it was believed that conception could only occur if both man and woman achieved orgasm. This had tragic consequences in rape cases where the woman conceived, which was held to demonstrate her willingness.[216] However, it did mean that advice literature encouraged men to promote a woman's sexual pleasure, increasing the chances of conception.[217]

Much of the religious commentary concerning sex was of a highly condemnatory nature, as churchmen such as Thomas Becon inveighed against 'adultery . . . whoredom, fornication, and uncleannesse', which they feared had 'not onely braste [burst] in, but also overflowed almost the whole world'. Becon lamented that 'thys vice is growen unto such an heighth, that in a maner emonge many, it is coumpted no synne at all, but rather a pastime, a dalliaunce, and but a touch of youth: not rebuked, but wynked at: not punished, but laughed at'.[218] The church courts had the unenviable job of dealing with sexual misconduct, which constituted so much of their business that they were known as the 'bawdy courts' or 'bum courts'; in Leicester, in 1521–22, for example, of about 140 cases, over 100 concerned sexual transgressions, involving 174 people.[219] The Reformation created some confusion over who was responsible for the punishment of sexual sins. On a theoretical level, reformers argued over whether adultery should be punished in Old Testament style, with the death penalty.[220] Shakespeare's *Measure for Measure* interrogated the morality of civic authorities imposing 'strict statutes and most biting laws' to provide 'needful bits and curbs to headstrong jades', when those implementing such laws might themselves be of dubious reputation.[221] Shakespeare was only the most eloquent of the commentators who saw little wisdom in the rigorous punishment of sexual offences. Here he kept unlikely company with the martyrologist John Foxe, who thought sinners should be treated with charity and toleration.[222]

Prostitution was a part of life, and indeed early pornography consisted largely of writings about prostitutes.[223] The brothels, or 'bawdy houses', of Southwark were an established part of London's topography. Puritan commentators such as Philip Stubbes warned that consorting with prostitutes would bring physical degeneration, disease and death: 'it hurteth the memorie, it weakeneth ye whole body, it bringeth it into a consumption, it bringeth ulcerations, scab, scurf, blain, botch, pocks and biles'.[224] Southampton had a licensed brothel, in part to accommodate the demands of sailors from the Italian galley fleets which regularly used the port; but elsewhere, alehouses and taverns might be suspected of a sideline in 'promoting bawdry', which could involve a range of sexual offences, including prostitution.[225] Matthew Baker, one of Henry VII's esquires of the body, was charged with running a brothel actually within the Palace of Westminster, and prostitution was rife in Westminster generally, no doubt a reflection on the workings of the Court and government there.[226]

Same-sex relationships could be the target of condemnation, but they were also the subject of some ambiguity. Thomas Beard's condemnation in 1597 of 'Effeminate Persons, Sodomites, and Other Suchlike Monsters' decried how the king of Assyria 'shamed not to paint his face . . . and to attire his body with the habites and ornaments of women'; he offered a general denunciation of 'filthinesse and villany', but without giving any clear sense of quite what he understood by the 'infamous lusts' and 'unnaturall sinnes' he was condemning.[227] There was little sense of homosexual identity, so moral and legal proscription tended to focus on particular sexual acts, particularly sodomy, which was deemed an unnatural crime.[228] Henry VIII's revision of canon law put 'buggery committed with mankind or beast' in the same category.[229] Given the intimacy of both male and female friendship, where individuals of the same sex frequently slept together, homosexual relations had many opportunities to flourish; but for the historian looking back through time, it is often hard to assess the finer nuances of love, friendship, sexual attraction and emotional commitment. Authorities were usually mostly concerned with illicit heterosexual encounters.[230] There were some individuals accused of buggery, such as

Nicholas Udall, the headmaster of Eton, or Edward de Vere, earl of Oxford; but on the whole, there were remarkably few examples of such accusations, particularly compared to some of the evidence from mainland Europe, where cities such as Florence or Bruges saw frequent cases. It is not clear whether this demonstrates cultural inhibitions against discussing same-sex encounters or a relative unconcern.[231] Same-sex relationships between women are even harder to uncover from the sources, although they were discussed by medical writers. The writings of Leo Africanus, published in English in 1600, described Moroccan women with 'a damnable custom to commit unlawful venery among themselves', who would 'burn in lust' for fair women 'no otherwise than lusty younkers do towards young maids'. In the context of something exotic and foreign, it was possible to discuss such a subject openly; but on the whole, the sources remain frustratingly silent.[232]

Disease and death

A ballad addressed to the women of London in Elizabeth I's reign warned them to remember how Death hovered close at hand: 'How quickely some are taken hence / Not youthfull yeares may make defence.' It reminded them of how 'strange diseases' were on the increase, and recommended prayer, a life of virtue and charity towards the poor as the best response.[233] If the Tudors at times seem to have been obsessed with the threat of illness, they had good cause.[234] Particularly in cities, plague recurred on a regular basis; almost every inhabitant of Tudor England would have experienced at least one serious local outbreak in their lifetime.[235] In Norwich, the plague came in 1579–80 and killed around 6,000 people, a third of the citizens; and between then and 1603 there was a serious outbreak in the city every five years. The city became one of the first to keep formal tallies of the dead, and soon the authorities in other cities started to do likewise (see illustration 6): by the end of the century these bills of mortality would start to appear in print.

The horrors of plague in the 1590s jolted the usually scurrilous writer Thomas Nashe into an unexpectedly religious vein, acknowledging the scourge as the hand of God, striking in punishment for sin: 'Hys hande I may well terme it, for on many that are arrested with the Plague, is the

6. A bill of mortality from around 1512

print of a hand seene, and in the very moment it first takes them, they feele a sencible blow gyven them, as it were with the hande of some stander by.'[236] Thomas Dekker put it succinctly: 'Cease vexing heaven, and cease to die.'[237] One manuscript work on medical remedies advised 'take a quart of the repentance of Nineveh and put thereto both your handfuls of fervent [faith] in Christ's blood, with as much hope and charity of the purest you can get in God's shop and put it into the vessel'.[238] There remained some confusion as to the best way to respond: one devotional manual instructed anyone sick with the plague not to call a physician, since medicine could not 'infringe the ordinance of God, nor once save us from his anger'.[239] On the other hand, in 1603 the preacher John Balmford took issue with the sceptical 'which denieth the Pestilence to be contagious', and advised his flock to stay away from church and avoid visiting the poor, lest they spread infection.[240]

In 1564, just three months after Shakespeare had been baptized in Holy Trinity Church in Stratford-upon-Avon, the burial register recorded '*hic incepit pestis*', 'here begins the plague'. Over two hundred people died in that outbreak, including four children on young William Shakespeare's street. The plot of *Romeo and Juliet*, written in 1595, turned on the failure of the messenger to reach Romeo, locked up in a house for fear that it was a place where 'the infectious pestilence did reign'.[241] Responses to this threat were varied, but often energetic. Some suggested remedies which may have helped a little: one treatise recommended that windows were kept open, and there was particular concern about the plague being trans- mitted via clothing, which was probably one way in which the infected fleas were transferred. Less convincingly, a treatise of 1584 argued that 'no one medicine is better . . . than Triacle' – not treacle in the modern sense, but a kind of salve made of many ingredients, which the author thought good not only for plague, but also for 'the Cough, the Collick, the Stone, the Palsie, the Jaundise, the Agew, the Dropsie, the Leprosie, the headach, for dull hearing, for dimnesse of sight, to provoke appetite, to appease greedie desire, for melancholy, sadnesse, heavinesse of the minde'.[242] Dekker, driven to writing verse, rather than plays, when the theatres closed in the plague outbreak of 1603, compiled a jest-book full of funny stories relating to the plague. He told his readers: 'If you read, you may happilie laugh; tis my desire you should, because mirth is both Phisicall [i.e. medic- inal], and wholesome agains the Plague.'[243] It seems probable that laughter was at least as helpful as treacle; but actual remedies were few and far between, and fear of the plague was widespread.[244]

To the spectre of plague, which had terrified society since its arrival in England in 1348, and the known horror that was influenza were added the new diseases of sweating sickness and syphilis.[245] Nobody quite under- stood how 'the sweat' was passed from one individual to another, but this was an illness that could strike and kill within just twelve hours. It appeared in 1485, and there were four subsequent waves until 1551, when it vanished, never to return. Syphilis was understood to be a venereal disease, and its associations with both sex and death made it a rich seam for the black humour of the age. 'A pox o' your throat, you bawling, blasphemous, incharitable dog', was a representative early modern imprecation.[246] Syphilis was the great pox. Its lesser cousin was called smallpox to distin- guish the two, but the lesser version was also greatly feared, and nearly killed Elizabeth I in 1562. Disease levelled boundaries and emphasized the shared human condition.[247] The itinerant German medical practitioner Valentine Russwarin may have been a foreigner running his medical practice from a temporary stall on the London streets, but he treated William Cecil for the gout, and was naturalized as an English citizen in 1574. The threat of disease, then as now, could overcome social barriers.

As well as the infectious diseases that led to frequent epidemics, there were any number of chronic illnesses that had a profound effect upon Tudor society. Many of them were visible, as the number of references to sores, boils, scurvy and similar blights attests. There was extensive use of cosmetics to conceal skin blemishes, many of which only compounded the problem. Scurvy might be most immediately associated with mariners, but it could also affect urban populations deprived of fruit and vegetables. The widespread prevalence of kidney stones reflected the consumption of disproportionate amounts of meat and fish by those who were sufficiently wealthy. When Russwarin set up his stall near the Royal Exchange, he displayed a collection of bladder stones that had been successfully removed from his former patients, alongside testimony of his ability to operate on cataracts and an ointment which professed to cure skin diseases.[248] Health was always closely linked to diet, and one of the biggest killers at this time was malnutrition and its consequences. There were high mortality rates in the opening years of the sixteenth century, and again in the 1540s, the 1550s and the 1590s. Harvest failures played a significant part in this.[249] Thomas Elyot's book, *The Castell of Helth*, was as much a dietary guide as a medical treatise, including as it did such observations as 'appulles eaten soone after that they be gathered, are colde, hard to digest, and do make yll and corrupted bloudde'; apples kept until the winter were, by contrast, 'ryght holsom . . . specially yf they be rosted or baken'.[250]

The Tudors were not only concerned with diseases of the body: diseases of the mind and spirit also loomed large. Melancholy, insomnia, grief and madness were prevalent, and much discussed, particularly from 1580 onwards, perhaps reflecting growing social, political and religious tensions.[251] The early modern era understood very well the connection between emotion and well-being. The physician and writer Andrew Borde prescribed humour as vital to his patients' health, 'for myrth is one of the chefest thynges of Physycke the which doth advertyse every man to be mery, and to beware of pencyfulnes'.[252] Alongside his works on medicine, he accordingly produced jest-books such as *Merry Tales of the Mad Men of Gotham* and *Scoggin's Jests*, both published around 1540. It was believed that family and fellowship were the best support for those troubled by insanity. Bethlehem hospital was the only institution established for the mentally ill, and it was expected that most people suffering from a mental malady would live with their families; the Elizabethan poor laws classified impoverished lunatics with the deserving poor as people worthy of assistance.[253]

The practice of medicine had to be undertaken with care, lest it appear an affront to divine providence.[254] Prayer was the first defence against illness, as well as a necessary preparation for death.[255] The work of physicians, apothecaries, herbalists and healers was often coterminous with the work of the clergy, and both prayers and remedies were used freely by both. Monasteries were also hospitals and repositories of medical knowledge. Thomas Betson, monk and librarian, had a small notebook listing 700 herbal plant names and remedies, alongside pieces of canon law, history, star maps and information about secret writing, inks and codes, which seem to have fascinated him. Schoolmasters as well as clergy might practise medicine, just as barber-surgeons were frequently also trained in netmaking, music or the textile trades.[256] Most mothers had a store of medical lore, sometimes written in the family Bible, alongside recipes and children's drawings.[257] Medicine was a fledgling profession. Dissection was still rare, and its findings unpredictable: the Elizabethan John Banister claimed to have once found a bone in a man's heart.[258] The Royal College of Physicians was founded in 1518, to license practitioners and to prosecute the unqualified and unlicensed. The Guild of Surgeons had originated in the fourteenth century, and waged a brisk turf war with the Worshipful Company of Barbers (incorporated in 1462), until the two were brought together in the Company of Barber-Surgeons in 1540. This event was immortalized two years later by Hans Holbein, in a painting in which Henry VIII appears to be harnessing the power of the Gospel in the pursuit of health (see plate 8). Its Latin inscription notes how plague had 'profaned the land of the English, harassing men's minds and besetting their bodies' until God instructed their king to 'undertake the office of a good Physician'.

Suggestions for remedies were plentiful and – from a modern perspective – unconvincing. Thomas Betson's cure for gout involved taking an owl, baking it to powder and turning it into an ointment; John Feckenham, the last abbot of Westminster Abbey, had a similar recipe, but involving a jay.[259] Betson also had an alternative version, with the ointment made from a very old, thin dog, killed and stuffed with frogs between the two Marian feasts of the Assumption in August and the Nativity of the Virgin in September. More plausible were the suggestions for painkillers derived from poppies or henbane. The majority of Betson's remedies were for eye complaints, which must have been a particular affliction for monks reading by poor light, in an atmosphere suffused with candle and wood smoke.

Tudor authorities on health could also show understanding of the holistic approach to well-being, which has only recently resurfaced in modern medical discourse. Borde's *Dyetary of helthe* began by considering where and how a man should build his house, 'in a pure and fresshe ayre for to lengthen his lyfe'.[260] A treatise on fishing from the 1490s thought that the three remedies of 'a mery thought', with 'labour not outrageous' and 'dyete mesurable' would keep all illness at bay.[261] It was also acknowledged that the poor might have something to teach the rich when it came to the preservation of health. William Bullein's medical treatises equated much in the life of the poor with common sense and good health. *The Government of Health* appeals to the example of how 'the miserable ragged beggar called Irus, was more happier in his povertie with quietnes and mirth, than was the gluttonous beast, and monstrous man king Sardanapalus, with all his golden glorie, court of ruffians, and curtizans which came to a shamefull ende'.[262]

This levelling effect was also evident at the deathbed, when all attempts at medical treatment had failed. Death imparted a sombre kind of equality to Tudor society: in the work *Disce Mori: Learne to Die*, published in 1601, the man on his deathbed is depicted pointing at the young knight in armour and telling him, 'As thou art, I once was. As I am, thou shalt be.'[263] This was elaborated upon in any number of places. Depictions of hell usually featured crowned and mitred heads amid the throng. Popular verse and popular print reminded their audience that death came for rich as well as poor. The Tudors discussed death at length, and with a close familiarity born of common acquaintance with loss. It was said that John Fisher, bishop of Rochester and confessor to Lady Margaret Beaufort, placed a skull on his dining table to remind himself of his own mortality as he ate; perhaps unsurprisingly, he is also reported as eating very little. The same skull was placed on the altar when he said mass. Fisher's friend

John Colet, dean of St Paul's Cathedral and founder of St Paul's School, was born to comparatively wealthy parents: his father Henry Colet was a mercer who was twice mayor of London. Yet Colet was their sole surviving child out of twenty-two in total. It was a commonplace of Tudor preaching that people should be ready for death at any moment.[264]

The importance of making a good death was widely accepted and commonly reiterated in popular culture. In medieval culture, the deathbed could be seen as a battleground between God and the Devil over the soul of the person who lay dying. Medieval woodcuts depicted the angels and saints among the friends of the sufferer defying the attempts of demons to snatch the soul away to hell (see illustration 7). Protestant culture dismissed the notion of Purgatory, but still had a healthy respect for the Devil, which rendered Protestant deathbeds just as much a potential location for a spiritual battle. The moneylender Richard Allington on his deathbed was troubled by apparitions, which brought home to him the evils of usury by which he had made his fortune, and he gave away his ill-gotten gains to the tune of £1,800.[265] It is easy to see this preoccupation with death as gloomy or morbid, but in fact it was intended to be practical and comforting. Richard Whitford told his readers briskly to put away 'that chyldyssh vayne and folyssh feare, and drede of deth, that many persones have'.[266] Puritan preaching could overstretch the point: Thomas Playfere the preacher reminded his listeners in 1595 that 'the day of our death is better then the day of our birth. For when we are borne we are mortall: but when we are dead we are immortal.' He insisted that the godly 'are merrie at their dying day'.[267] This was perhaps excessive, but the idea that a deathbed should be a holy place, and one where the community came together to comfort the dying person, was so essential to early modern society that it survived the Reformation with more continuity than most other aspects of religious culture. In the pre-Reformation Church, the *Ars Moriendi*, literally 'the art of dying', prepared people for death; after the Reformation, there were Protestant equivalents of these tracts that urged the dying, who had once been told to fix their eyes on the crucifix, to look instead with the 'eyes of your faith' upon Christ.[268] Every rite of passage for the Tudors was a collective experience, a reflection of the connectivity which defined their communities.

* * *

7. A woodcut illustration of the deathbed from *Ars Moriendi* ('The Art of Dying')

In the 1590s, the marriage of Marion and Griffin Jones was in trouble. Among other things, he accused her of trying to kill him by leaving sharp knives in the bed; she claimed (somewhat implausibly) that she had accidentally mislaid them whilst cooking. What is remarkable is how many people tried to help this pair, including their minister, his curate, the churchwardens, other parishioners, the lord mayor, the court of the Clothworkers' Guild and the local wardmote (local court). In the end, they settled on a separation, and Marion agreed to pay her husband a living allowance.[269] There was clearly no question but that their private difficulties were also a matter of common concern. Tudor men and women had a powerful sense of their obligation to maintain the ties between them. Hugh Plat, proffering advice against famine, reminded his readers of Seneca's advice 'that we ought rather to prevent then relieve the necessity of a friend'.[270] There could be no good in selfishness: 'there ought to be one purpose, and inclination in all men, that a like utilitie, and of all thinges, may be to every one. Which if any man do snatch unto him selfe, all humane felowship is dissolved.'[271] The value of the commonwealth was universally held, for it was society's natural body: 'And he that endevoreth nothing to further it, is unnaturall, like as he that hindreth the same, is, as a rotten member, worthy to be cut away.' Good will was 'the bulwarke of the common wealth.'[272] It was on this shared understanding that the Tudor state rested, with the fragile authority of the Tudor monarchs given substance and strength by the structures and imperatives of society at large.

CHAPTER 5

'GLORIOUS KNIGHT AND CHRISTIAN KING'
THE REIGN OF HENRY VIII

It is telling that the most famous image of Henry VIII is also the most unreal. The Holbein portrayal of the king (see illustration 8) depicts him as quite literally larger than life, his breadth and bulk a physical impossibility. Yet in the splendour of the picture the distortions are lost to sight. It might serve as a metaphor for Henry's reign as a whole: apparently magnificent, but on closer inspection an exercise in political dissimulation, unforgettable but deceptive. Henry ruled with energy and ambition: he built palaces and constructed policies on a scale never previously imagined; he raised the largest armies ever seen in England; he launched a religious revolution that changed both government and society as never before; and his family dramas would not have been out of place in a Greek tragedy. The most immediate aspects of his reign are fascinating enough: the underlying tensions are just as compelling, whilst the damage that he wrought in the lives of his subjects deserves equal attention, being both complicated and pitiful. Of all the Tudors, his legacy was the most long-lasting; it has also proved abidingly divisive.[1]

The original version of Holbein's image was painted on the wall of the King's Privy Chamber in Whitehall Palace around 1537 (see plate 1). For all its message of dynastic continuity and family solidity, the fact remains that the other three people depicted – Henry VII, Elizabeth of York and Jane Seymour – all died before their time, with each of their deaths leaving the country in jeopardy. It is characteristic that this grandiloquent statement about Henry's sovereignty was constructed at a time when he was facing a series of disasters. Henry himself had almost died after a jousting accident at the start of 1536; his queen had miscarried a male child, and

8. Hans Holbein's drawing of Henry VIII

months later had been found guilty of multiple adulteries and beheaded; his beloved illegitimate son Henry Fitzroy had died; and half his kingdom had risen in rebellion, mustering an army bigger than Henry's own. The king's joy at the birth of a legitimate son and heir in October 1537 was then tainted by the death of the child's mother, Jane Seymour, just ten days later. Somewhere in the midst of these disasters, Henry oversaw the painting of the image that was to immortalize him: in the face of grave instability, his instinct was to display his power and strength. This was a bold and defiant impulse, and it worked far better than Henry had any right to expect; but it was still papering over the cracks. Much of Henry's reign remained peopled by ghosts, overshadowed by fear; his magnificence was constructed from smoke and mirrors, as he sought to distract from his political instability.

Henry VIII is, to this day, the most immediately recognizable of all England's monarchs, and his sense of majesty, his dynamism, his ruthlessness – all set against a backdrop of profound uncertainty – render the dramas of his reign peculiarly fascinating. He aroused both fierce loyalty and dread during his lifetime, prompting panegyrics from some and accusations of tyranny from others.[2] Modern judgement also remains divided. For his first twentieth-century biographer, Henry was a statesman, ruthless but effective. For later historians, he was a ruler who yielded power to others, swayed by his wives or his courtiers, 'a bit of a booby and a bit of a baby', the capricious and impulsive figure depicted in the film *A Man for All Seasons*.[3] More recent commentators have argued over the importance of faction, and whether the king was perhaps more forceful and engaged than previously admitted.[4] There has also been a new interest in Henry's cultural setting. Fashioning himself as a Renaissance prince, Henry recruited poets, writers, painters, musicians and architects to glorify the royal image.[5] From this wealth of images and opinions, it is hard to extract an authentic picture of the man.

Many who knew Henry well seem to have responded to him not just with awe, but with affection. Charles Brandon was, in 1509, just an esquire in the old king's funeral procession, but he rose to become duke of Suffolk on the basis of his friendship with Henry, and ended as his brother-in-law.[6] Thomas Cranmer, for whom the king caused many difficulties, held his hand as he lay dying, and seems to have mourned him sincerely.[7] More remarkably, his discarded wives could still speak of him with devotion. Katherine of Aragon wrote in her last letter to him, 'Lastly, I make this vow, that mine eyes desire you above all things.'[8] Anne Boleyn, on the scaffold, said to the crowd, 'I pray God save the king and send him long to reign over you, for a gentler nor a more merciful prince was there never, and to me he was ever a good, a gentle, and sovereign lord.'[9] Anne of Cleves, often held to be the lucky one who escaped his clutches without harm, remained his friend for the rest of his life. These levels of attachment should warn us not to make easy assumptions. Henry has been depicted, unconvincingly, as the Tudor Stalin; but in the eyes of his contemporaries, he was a charismatic leader, a sturdy protector, a man flawed and sometimes loathed, guilty of some terrible acts, and yet almost universally acknowledged as a figure of strength. He gave the fledgling dynasty an unprecedented degree of splendour, and his military activities raised England's profile abroad even as they emptied the treasury. He could be unpredictable and vindictive, but he could also be clever, energetic, innovative and impressive. He remained a political icon long after he was dead, and all three of his children traded on his memory. It would be easy to caricature him as vengeful, volatile and frightening, but the truth was a lot more intricate and varied.

In 1534, Henry had the law on treason redrafted. A traitor was defined as someone culpable not just by his actions, but by his words. This concept had been mooted in medieval times, but it was Henry VIII who put it firmly into statute law.[10] In particular, the act specified that it was treasonous to 'slanderously and maliciously publish and pronounce, by express writing or words, that the King our sovereign lord should be heretic, schismatic, tyrant, infidel or usurper of the crown'.[11] Obviously some people were saying precisely that about their king. Elsewhere on the continent, Henry was being cast as an infidel: a picture in the Charterhouse in Naples depicts him in a turban as the Great Turk, torturing and murdering the London Carthusians; and in 1538, Pope Paul III called for a crusade against the schismatic ruler of England.[12] Yet Henry was clearly capable of exercising great charm, and he commanded loyalty and dedicated service from many.[13] At a time when Europe as a whole was testing out the possibilities of sovereignty, exploring the potential and the pitfalls of centralized royal authority, Henry VIII was an object lesson in just how far kingship could be extended, and at what cost. 'Glorious knight and Christian king' was how Edmund Dudley, in his treatise on kingship, envisaged God greeting the king at the end of his labours.[14] But Dudley wrote this shortly before he was beheaded for treason by the young Henry VIII, in the first judicial murder of his reign. Everything that Henry strove to achieve came at a price.

The golden age

Henry's reign began with a lie. For two days, his father's death was kept a secret, and Henry pretended he was still prince of Wales as he celebrated St George's Day, whilst he and his closest advisors readied themselves for possible challenges.[15] We read of one groom of the Privy Chamber emerging 'with a smyling countenance' from the room where Henry VII's corpse lay, to tell Archbishop Warham that the king wished to speak with him.[16] Almost as soon as the announcement had been made of Henry VII's death, his administrators, Richard Empson and Edmund Dudley, were sent to the

Tower. Strategically chosen scapegoats, both were sufficiently notorious to make the gesture worthwhile, but neither was of high-enough status to make it dangerous. Henry's public pronouncements promised 'reformation' of the 'great extremity' which had been oppressing his subjects.[17] This ability to twist popular sentiment into a political tool, to assume the high moral ground and to insist that those who displeased him must be traitors would be distinguishing features of the reign. Underlying it all was the apprehension of potential danger. In 1509, Henry VIII was not the only potential successor to the throne. Just a few years before, the Yorkists Edmund de la Pole and Edward Stafford, duke of Buckingham, had been considered by some 'grett personages' as possible claimants.[18] Henry's throne was never as secure as he made it seem.

Yet by some, the start of Henry's reign was hailed as a great moment. Lord Mountjoy, Erasmus's patron, wrote 'Heaven smiles, earth rejoices; all is milk and honey and nectar.'[19] His was just one voice in a chorus of adulation. Thomas More wrote a set of Latin poems: the presentation copy showed a Tudor rose and a Spanish pomegranate lavishly intertwined under a golden crown. It was as if there was a conspiracy to launch Henry on a wave of enthusiasm. In reality, the political classes were encouraging their seventeen-year-old king to take the direction they wanted. Henry was already keen to distance himself from his father's reputation, and his nobles and courtiers applauded as he moved towards a more lavish style, and a more open demeanour. The young king swiftly acquired a reputation for magnificence, creating a court where access to the king was far easier than in the previous reign.[20] There were other changes, too. Henry VII had ruled with the help of a few trusted individuals. Henry VIII would be open to the flattery and comradeship of many more, but would not command the same kind of loyalty from a small and trusted cohort, and where he felt betrayed, he would be vengeful. Those closest to Henry VII, such as Bray, Morton or his queen, had been secure in their intimacy with the king, and had died peacefully in their beds. Those closest to Henry VIII nearly all died miserable or violent deaths.

The systematic destruction of Henry VII's reputation after 1509 was meant to provide a foil for a new and more beguiling image of kingship, and Henry took to this with the enthusiasm to be expected of any young, intelligent and athletic man who has just had power and wealth placed in his hands. Despite his ostentatious rejection of Henry VII's legacy, Henry VIII still quietly maintained his father's policies, and retained most of his Council. One of his first acts as king was to marry Katherine of Aragon, the symbol of Henry VII's greatest diplomatic triumph, allegedly in fulfilment of his father's dying wish. He was also playing safe. Katherine was well known to him, and Henry would always prefer to marry women he knew: the one time he married a foreign royal bride, the usual course of action for sixteenth-century monarchs, it ended in disaster. Katherine was an immediate source of security; it is probable the king did not want to begin lengthy marriage negotiations elsewhere, with powers that might well spurn his offer. Moreover, a Spanish alliance was the necessary prerequisite for making war on France.

From the start of the reign, it was clear that Henry intended war. Historical preoccupation with his administration, or his religion, or his court, has obscured the fact that this was his guiding passion. This was not just a profligate desire for excitement: there was a more profound objective, namely a potential solution to the problem of dynastic instability. If one clear lesson could be gleaned from the fifteenth century, it was that political control was best consolidated by victory in battle; nothing made a king look more convincing. From the start of his reign, Henry VIII seems to have decided that his majesty would be better conveyed by martial success than by his father's bonds and recognizances. He revived the chivalric militarism of his Plantagenet forebears, laying fresh emphasis on jousting, and – most unusually – participating in it himself; surviving score cards show that he was genuinely skilled.[21] The chronicler Edward Hall rejoiced at a king so 'lusty, young, and courageous' who so 'greatly delighted in feats of chivalry', though he also noted that some feared 'lest some ill chaunce might happen to the king'.[22] In celebration of his first-born son in 1511, Henry jousted as 'Sir Loyal Heart', his caparison decorated with gold 'K's and hearts, as the proclaimed lover of his queen (see plate 6). He followed his father in revering the cult of St George and maintaining the Order of the Garter: the 'Black Book' recording garter ceremonies in sumptuous detail dates from the 1530s. He changed the oath taken by new knights, so that they no longer swore to defend just the order, but also the 'honors, quarrels, rights, dominions and cause' of their king.[23] Not all of this worked: the new company of the 'King's Spears', intended to train the younger nobles as an elite corps to defend the king's person, had to be disbanded in 1515 as they were too expensive. Yet the themes of martial skill, chivalric display, noble piety and dedication to the king were all skilfully developed and interwoven as the reign wore on. Recycling the past in order to reconfigure the future was always something Henry did well.

By October 1511, a Holy League had been formed, comprising England, Spain, the papacy, the Holy Roman Empire and the Swiss. Henry might have dreamt of the Hundred Years War, but his allies were more concerned with French incursions into Italy that had ravaged the country since the 1490s, with consequences as various as Machiavelli's arresting political commentaries and the spread of syphilis. Henry's objective was to claim back English territories in France, but he also trumpeted his exalted intention of protecting the papacy from French aggression. In 1513, war was finally achieved. Henry was promised, if he won, the papal title 'Most Christian King', previously used by the kings of France. He named his new cannons 'the Twelve Apostles', apparently without irony; took the Chapel Royal with him to France, just as Henry V had done; and commissioned the publication of John Lydgate's *The Historye, Sege and Dystruccyon of Troye*, which could be read as a celebration of chivalric honour by Henry V's favourite poet.[24] It was characteristic of Henry to seek ideological sanction for his bellicose ambitions: he also badgered the pacifist-inclined dean of St Paul's, John Colet, into preaching 'on the right of Christians to wage war', to inspire 'even the spiritless and timid'.[25]

Henry arrived in Calais to a deafening welcome; the firing of the gun salutes could be heard back in Dover. It was two days after his twenty-second birthday. He rode through the city, gloriously decked out in armour and cloth-of-gold tunic, to ask divine blessing on his enterprise at the church of St Nicholas. His armour was emblazoned with the cross of St George, and he wore a brooch of St George in his hat, again emphasizing his links to the medieval past (St George had been adopted as England's patron saint in the course of the Hundred Years War). Yet military success was to prove frustratingly elusive. Henry's allies had different priorities: his fickle father-in-law, Ferdinand of Aragon, concluded a truce between Spain and France before the campaign was even under way. A slight skirmish was solemnly celebrated as the 'Battle of the Spurs', but its immortalization says more about the sophistication of propaganda at this time than about

Henry's military skill. The small town of Thérouanne was captured and promptly razed to the ground; the city of Tournai was a more splendid capture, but still the campaign failed to live up to expectations. It is ironic that the real victory of 1513 was that of Katherine of Aragon, left as regent in England, whose army crushed the Scots at Flodden on 9 September. This not only removed the threat of Scottish invasion in the king's absence, but it also altered the balance of Anglo-Scots relations substantially in England's favour. The king returned home for the winter, and although he fully intended to campaign again the next year, his allies thought differently. Most unhelpfully, the new Pope Leo X was seeking peace with the French, and successfully brought them to the Fifth Lateran Council of 1513 – a hopeful advance towards religious reform, but a blow to Henry's self-fashioning as the champion of Rome. It was an early and painful lesson in the difficulties of early modern warfare, and the first of a series of grandiose visions which never quite came to fruition.

Henry proved adaptable. War had disappointed him, so he made what capital he could from peace. In 1514, he concluded an honourable treaty with France, blessed by the papacy, including an alliance between King Louis XII and Henry's sister Princess Mary. Mary was eighteen, Louis was already in his fifties, and it was clear that Mary was not happy at the match; but her husband died after only three months – worn out by his exertions in the bedchamber, it was said – and Mary swiftly married the man she loved, Charles Brandon, duke of Suffolk and comrade-in-arms to the young king. Meanwhile, the regime continued to explore the political potential of peace-making, and in 1518 signed the Treaty of London, a mutual defence treaty intended to safeguard Europe from the destabilizing effects of war. The papacy sent the legate Cardinal Campeggio to ratify the treaty, but Henry kept him waiting until Cardinal Wolsey had also been granted the status of *legate a latere*; at the solemn mass in St Paul's to inaugurate the treaty, Wolsey officiated under a cloth of estate, on a dais raised five steps high.[26] If Henry was going to accept papal sanction, it was going to be on equal terms, not as a suppliant. Richard Pace, the king's secretary, preached a sermon at this mass which glorified the 'most invincible King Henry, whom Almighty God has endowed with so rare a genius, so deep a wisdom, so notable a piety and care for religion'. His comment that 'all could see you would have won had you chosen to continue in the war' was an awkward acknowledgement that Henry had, in fact, not won. Pace praised him for initiating 'universal peace among all Christian princes', but it was still making the most of disappointed hopes.[27]

Henry's instincts as king were at first thoroughly traditional. In a letter of 1519 to Pope Leo X, he avowed his willingness to go on crusade, still a beguiling thought to many European rulers. Offered the opportunity to invest in discovery of the New World, he was far less enthusiastic than his father. (Later, in 1537, Sebastian Cabot would have his request for royal patronage turned down.) Henry's ideas of empire were entirely contemporary. In 1519, St George's Day was kept with great solemnity, with a requiem mass for Maximilian, the Holy Roman Emperor, who had been a knight of the garter. Shortly thereafter, Henry began to manoeuvre himself into the running for election as the next Holy Roman Emperor – a proposition that nobody but Henry considered plausible, since the Empire was traditionally a Habsburg preserve, and the expected candidate was Charles, duke of Burgundy (and since 1516, King Charles I of Spain). Francis I of France also declared his intention of standing for election. It is hard to imagine that Henry expected his bid to be taken seriously; while his rivals handed out bribes, Henry's agent, Pace, only promised the electors rewards. It is telling, though, that Henry had the self-belief to imagine himself in this role. It would not be the last time that his grandiose imagination was at odds with political reality.

It was in these years that Henry met both of his rivals face to face. Charles V landed at Dover in May 1520, motivated by Henry's developing friendship with Francis I to stake his own claim to a special relationship. It helped that Charles was nephew to Katherine of Aragon. Henry certainly treated him as family, rushing to Dover to see him and embracing him as they met on the stairs. The three-day visit was an important acknowledgement of Henry's status, but he was still effectively a pawn in the power-play between Charles and Francis. Henry was prepared to go to extraordinary lengths to achieve European recognition, however, most notably when he met Francis I at the Field of Cloth of Gold. This diplomatic summit was the wonder of contemporaries – and for good reason. England emptied itself of its king, its nobility, much of its portable wealth and about five thousand people. A whole temporary palace was built in a field just outside Calais, with tapestries, wine fountains, cloth-of-gold draperies, musicians and every aspect of court ceremonial. The encounter between two ancestral enemies was a tense and momentous occasion, and the impact of the moment when the two kings rode forward and then embraced was considerable. This was political theatre at its best. The very ground beneath their horses' hooves had been reshaped, the landscape sculpted, so that neither side might appear to occupy the higher ground. Careful damage limitation was called for when Francis threw Henry during a wrestling bout, with all sides diplomatically agreeing that the kings were evenly matched. On the last day, the tiltyard was converted into a chapel, and Wolsey celebrated mass. This was the ultimate expression of harmony and concord, uniting the living and the dead with the angels and the saints – as well as (on this occasion at least) the English with the French. Richard Pace again preached on the subject of peace, perhaps with slightly greater conviction than two years before.[28] As a consolidation of the Treaty of London, the effort failed, since war with France resumed in 1522; yet as a display of strength and majesty, and a tribute to the ideal of a lasting European peace, it had significant value.[29]

Henry may have sought validation by aspiring to win glory in the same way as Henry V had a century earlier; but he lived in a rapidly changing world and, despite his limitations, he was too intelligent to ignore the implications of this. Developments in military technology, political thought, religion, literature, music and art all shaped his role as king. Henry had a talent for seizing upon gifted individuals and useful ideas and exploiting them to the full. He was determined from the first to restore England's military reputation, copying or borrowing new technologies from mainland Europe. He imported German armourers, as well as armour, and by 1515 had established armouries at Southwark and Greenwich. One of his first initiatives, in January 1510, was to order the construction of two new ships, the *Mary Rose* and the *Peter Pomegranate*, rose and pomegranate together symbolizing Henry's union with Katherine. The *Mary Rose* was the most advanced vessel the country had ever seen, frequently used as the admiral's flagship, a troop-carrier before the victory at Flodden and a key part of Henry's navy until she was lost at the battle of the Solent in 1545.[30] Another warship, the *Henry Grace à Dieu*, or *Great Harry*, prompted the chronicler's remark that 'suche another . . . was never seen before in England'.[31] Henry developed fortifications at Berwick and Calais, crucial strategic bases for war against Scotland and France, and began new dockyards at Portsmouth. Having captured Tournai, he worked to improve its defences, clearly envisaging it as a crucial pivot for further conquests in northern France. His ambition and expenditure raced ahead until, towards the end of his reign, in 1544, he put into France one of the largest armies in history, meanwhile drawing on Italian expertise to lace the south coast of England, from Kent to Cornwall, with defensive fortifications that would still be in use during the Napoleonic wars, over two centuries later.[32]

Military innovation went alongside new conceptions of politics. The civil wars of the fifteenth century, still a painful memory, and the initiatives of Henry VII's reign had prompted some intense evaluation of the political process. The importance of counsel, informed and sage advice from men of experience, was painstakingly described and idealized by statesmen and commentators.[33] Thomas More's discussion in *Utopia* of whether men of wisdom and integrity should serve at Court, or should distance themselves as far as possible from the power-brokerage there, underlines how deeply the political process was under scrutiny at this time.[34] The politeness with which Henry wrote to his chief subjects perhaps indicates his own awareness of how much he needed them.[35] Many people at Henry VIII's court were keen to advise him, proffering advice on local government, foreign conquest, religious and educational reform, and dynastic alliance. It used to be held that Henry VIII was susceptible to factional pressure, and that most of the important decisions of his reign were taken by his ministers.[36] Many around him clearly feared as much, particularly when the king was young. Erasmus translated Plutarch's advice on 'How to distinguish between flatterers and friends' for Henry.[37] Thomas Elyot warned that noble natures might be particularly susceptible: 'as the wormes do brede mooste gladly in softe wode and swete, so the mooste gentyll and noble wyttes, inclined to honour, replenished with most honest and curtaise [courteous] maners, do sonest admytte flaterars, and be by them abused'.[38] These concerns about the workings of faction should not, however, be wrestled by modern historians into some vague simulacrum of party politics.[39] Nor should we forget the dominant role of leadership within Tudor culture. Henry's reputation for strength, both at the time and since, is in large part precisely because he was not easily influenced. If ministers such as Wolsey or Cromwell had enormous power, it was because Henry had chosen them to wield that power; their fall from grace was equally striking, once their usefulness to the king had been compromised. It was Henry who was the directing force in the politics of the time, and concerns about counsel underline not the role of his counsellors, so much as the importance of his decisions.[40]

Nonetheless, Henry could not rule alone. In particular, his ambitions repeatedly outstripped his financial resources, requiring negotiation with his subjects. Henry VIII managed to institutionalize the parliamentary subsidy – arguably an improved form of taxation, as well as a more lucrative one – in part through Wolsey's management.[41] The subsidy, based on a direct assessment of individual wealth and income, has been described as a system 'several centuries ahead of its time'. It was certainly the single most effective attempt to deal with the problem of financing an ever-expanding government until the upheavals of the seventeenth century.[42] The failure of the 'Amicable Grant' (an anodyne label for what was, in effect, a forced levy) in 1525, however, shows that there were limitations to Henry's power to command resources.[43] Henry and Wolsey eventually resigned themselves to the fact that this particular tax was unworkable and played out a little drama, in which Wolsey took the blame and asked forgiveness, and Henry magnanimously chided and forgave him, and withdrew the attempted exaction. This episode demonstrates the limits of Henry's authority, the need for taxation to be based on popular cooperation and the necessity of his at least appearing to consult his subjects' opinions. It underlines just how far Henry's sovereignty was negotiated between ruler and ruled.

Henry also paid attention to the world of learning, which increasingly became a key element in his self-fashioning. He extended patronage to such men as Erasmus and More, backing Erasmus's 1516 publication of the New Testament in Greek and Latin, and instructing More to defend the new school of thought concerning Greek pronunciation in the universities.[44] The humanist learning, piety and patronage exercised, in particular, by Katherine of Aragon, Anne Boleyn and Katherine Parr, was a crucial adjunct to the king's authority.[45] Henry was siding here with the most advanced thinking in intellectual circles, embracing the Renaissance impetus to rediscover the classical past and, in the process, revitalize Church and society. It made him look both erudite and fashionable, and it could also have a direct political application. In 1521, Henry authored the book *Assertio Septem Sacramentorum*, which defended the sacraments against Martin Luther's recent attack. His reward was the papal title he had long wanted: *Fidei Defensor* or 'Defender of the Faith'. The assistance he had from scholars in writing this book set a pattern, which he would repeat many times in the years ahead. He had discovered that a pious and persuasive academic argument could make a powerful political tool.

Music and art could also be co-opted to project a convincing picture of majesty. At the Field of Cloth of Gold, Henry's international ambition had been framed with splendid fabrics, painted interiors, tapestries, armour and jewels; his temporary palace was so full of windows of Flanders glass that the French called it a 'crystal palace'; and the temporary chapel had a pearl-studded crucifix standing over 4 feet high on the high altar.[46] Henry was also accompanied to France by the choir of the Chapel Royal and other musicians. He himself was a good musician, and composed as well as performed: the manuscript called *Henry VIII's Songbook* contains thirty-four pieces attributed to the king. At his death, his inventory recorded that he possessed seventy-two flutes, seventy-six recorders and twenty-five viols. He brought organists from the Netherlands and Venice, and a viol ensemble of Sephardic Jews from Italy.[47] At Court, it was in 1512 at Epiphany that a new form of entertainment was introduced from Italy, called a masque, 'a thyng not seen afore in Englande', as Edward Hall commented.[48] Every form of cultural display was used: by the time of his death, Henry had the largest collection of tapestries ever owned by a European monarch.[49]

Gift-giving was a crucial part of this. Each gift received by the king elicited some return from him, underlining the reciprocity of kingship.[50] Small gifts of food were continually arriving at the gates of the palace, to be rewarded in turn, usually with a gift of money: 5s was given 'to a poor woman in Reward for bringing a present of Apples to the King's grace'; 20s to a servant of the abbot of Gloucester who brought baked lampreys. Servants of the nobility and gentry also came bearing game, fish and cheese; and in November 1529, the earl of Westmorland sent a servant with a spaniel.[51] A variant on gift-giving was the commissioning and dedication of books. When a copy of the *Res gestae Alexandri Magni*, or 'Deeds of Alexander the Great', was dedicated to Henry and Katherine of Aragon together, it was a subtle tribute to the majesty and erudition of both.[52] John

Skelton, Henry's tutor, had also compared him to Alexander, with the corollary that this cast Skelton in the role of Aristotle.[53] When the Spanish humanist Juan Luis Vives, who had designed a plan of studies for Princess Mary, published a book on the education of women, he dedicated it to Katherine of Aragon, praising 'the holiness of your life and your ardent zeal for sacred studies'.[54] Rituals of exchange, friendship, patronage and admission to intimacy with the royal family were all forms of power-brokerage, and political exchange and communication. Henry was careful to construct every aspect of his public persona, portraying himself as intelligent, pious, athletic, magnanimous, just, skilled, sophisticated and, above all, strong.

In 1525, the Habsburg defeat of the French at the battle of Pavia confirmed Charles V's ascendancy so resoundingly that England's long-standing tradition of making war with France required reconfiguration. The Treaty of Westminster in 1527 revived the idea of an Anglo-French alliance within a wider rearrangement of international relations. In a symbolic act of great importance, in January 1528, in St George's Chapel Windsor, Francis I of France was made a knight of the garter, the first French king ever to be given this chivalric honour, which had itself originated from the age-old conflict between the two countries.[55] Celebrations of this new treaty were held at Greenwich Palace in the spring of 1527, and the welcome laid on at Greenwich for the French delegation included a new banqueting house, and a 'disguising house', or amphitheatre, for the performance of masques, which had a ceiling painted by Holbein with the planets and signs of the zodiac. These celebrations at Greenwich in 1527 were, in a sense, Henry's apotheosis as a Renaissance prince.[56] A week after the Treaty of Westminster was signed, Charles V's troops sacked Rome and set in motion the train of events that would culminate in the destruction of much of Henry's stability. In retrospect, 1527 was also to prove a watershed year for the not unrelated reason that Henry was beginning to contemplate ending his marriage to Katherine, which had produced only one living child, his daughter Mary. He had begun to fix on Anne Boleyn as the consort he needed, and as the companion of his mature kingship. Henry was thirty-six years old, and increasingly confident in his wielding of authority. In Cardinal Wolsey he had a minister of consummate ability, with the European prestige sufficient for him to be considered a potential pope. The king had worked hard to establish a military reputation, and had created a Court known for its splendour, piety and learning. He had acquired a level of faith in his own abilities which promised great things ahead.

The first half of Henry's reign has often been overlooked by historians, who have focused on the great upheavals which took place after 1529; but it is impossible to understand fully the events of the later decades without appreciating the role that Henry had fashioned for himself between 1509 and 1529. In his grandeur, his military and imperial ambitions, his capacity for innovation and his preoccupation with humanist learning and theology, he laid the foundations for what was to happen next. Tudor kings required a range of abilities far wider than any modern leader: they needed to fight their own wars, dispense their own justice, and at the same time project all the style and charisma of the modern celebrity, as well as balancing their books and overseeing an administration. And for the first twenty years, Henry performed all this with considerable skill. There were times, however, when he brushed aside the reciprocal nature of his bond with his subjects, and relied too heavily on his divinely sanctioned authority. From 1529 onwards, he would become sufficiently beguiled by a new conception of his authority to neglect the need for balance. The successes of his first two decades gave Henry the level of self-belief necessary for him to embark on the wholesale transformation of Church and state that would reconfigure both the theory and the practice of kingship, with startling results. Yet Henry was also to discover that his subjects were minded to cling on to older notions of reciprocal responsibility, and that in consequence, his capacity for destruction would prove greater than his ability to build anew. He would find that he did not have the popular loyalty, the sophisticated administrative machinery, the financial resources, the ideological coherence or the powers of coercion to turn all his aspirations into reality. The years ahead were to be difficult for all concerned.

The 'King's Great Matter'

Henry VIII is notorious for his six wives, but the motivation behind this apparent excess is seldom properly appreciated. The idea of Henry as a playboy king should be refuted by his twenty years of faithful marriage to Katherine of Aragon, during which time he treated her with honour and affection, and had remarkably few mistresses by the standards of the time. He was not the libidinous predator he is often painted as. He did, however, live under the shadow of an old anxiety about the instability of the Crown, and he knew the importance of maintaining a strong line of succession. At his coronation, it was observed by Polydore Vergil that when the people acclaimed their new king 'their affections were not half-hearted, because the king on his father's side descended from Henry VI, and on his mother's from Edward IV'; but the first of these claims was not strictly true.[57] Dynastic policies were easy enough for even the simplest of his subjects to understand. Henry's rule, however bold, courageous and successful, would collapse into chaos if he could not produce a healthy male heir to secure the succession and perpetuate this union of Lancaster and York.

By the middle of the 1520s, this seemed unlikely. Henry VIII enjoyed every blessing as king – apart from that of a legitimate son to inherit his throne. But without that, he could have no peace, no confidence for the future. The king who so skilfully presented himself as sanctioned by divine acclamation was being undermined by this one very human weakness. Time after time he suffered the affliction, both personal and political, of watching his children die and his wife miscarry. As the years unfolded, Katherine went through at least seven pregnancies (and probably more), but her only healthy child was a girl. Henry was fond of his daughter Mary, and in 1525 declared her princess of Wales and sent her off to the Welsh borders as an off-shoot of his own royal person, to help enforce his authority there. Yet in the same year he ennobled his bastard son, Henry Fitzroy, making him duke of Richmond, and giving him similar responsibilities in the north. The title of duke was second only to that of prince, and was often given to those of royal blood; the title of Richmond, moreover, was that held by Henry VII before his accession and had been given to his chief palace. It was a name full of resonance. Henry was clearly considering whether he might make his illegitimate son his heir – a move so fraught with danger that it displays his desperation over the succession.

Sometime in 1526, Henry became enamoured of a young woman at court named Anne Boleyn. She was not the typical Tudor beauty, but pale-skinned, with long dark hair, beautiful dark eyes, and the kind of elegance and intelligence that set her apart. She had the manners and accomplishments of the French court, where she had been raised, and humanist and evangelical leanings which put her at the cutting edge of intellectual advance in the 1520s. Henry was soon deeply attached. His love letters to her were full of warmth; he seemed overwhelmed by his feelings for her. Alongside these emotions, however, lay complex legal and theological questions. Henry's reverence for what he perceived as the divine will, spurred on by his love for Anne, convinced him that the tragic fate of Katherine's many pregnancies was a form of divine chastisement. He had somehow offended against God, and he found an explanation in the Old Testament book of Leviticus, which contained a ban on marrying a brother's widow. All of Henry's doubts were compounded: he had broken divine law; Katherine had never truly been his wife; and by living with her, he was prolonging their sin, which was why his sons had died. Thus went the logic behind 'the King's Great Matter', which Henry came to see as incontrovertible. To those who found it less convincing, he responded with anger and vindictiveness.

This was not a man casting off his frumpy middle-aged wife to embrace a younger model. Katherine had lost her good looks and, being six years older than her husband, was beyond child-bearing; but she was still a queenly figure of immense dignity and erudition, a daughter of Spain's royal house and aunt to Charles V, Holy Roman Emperor. Anne Boleyn was not a nubile teenager, but a woman in her mid-twenties, mature by Tudor standards. Nor was it a question merely of alliances. Katherine stood for the Habsburg alliance of the past, whilst Anne had links to the French, whom Henry was assiduously wooing after 1525, but neither of these considerations was enough on its own to sway Henry. It was a human drama on a grand scale, with three highly intelligent and formidable people locked in a struggle that was both intensely private and glaringly public. It is clear that neither woman was solely interested in being queen: both of them seem to have loved Henry with real strength of feeling. Henry was appalled to discover that Katherine, previously the most dutiful of wives, would not accept his explanation and retire with dignity into a nunnery, keeping her title of princess dowager as Arthur's widow. Katherine was a woman of immense moral strength, and she would not falsely deny the validity of her marriage; more importantly, she loved her daughter, and would not declare her a bastard and deny her the chance of inheriting the throne. Her resistance to Henry was heroic. She marshalled behind her the best legal and clerical minds at her disposal. It was a good illustration of the limitations of kingship. Much as he might want to, Henry could not just repudiate her, or even execute her. He had to act within the law, or at least within the appearance of the law. He had to find a solution that was acceptable to as large a section of the ruling classes as possible, and which ideally also pleased the papacy, his foreign allies and, most importantly, God himself. It is an indication of Henry's immense confidence in his own exceptional abilities that he was not dismayed by the challenge.

It was characteristic of this oddly bookish king that this central crisis of his life was cast as an academic problem. Wolsey first gathered together a secret court at Westminster in May 1527 to consider the validity of the king's marriage to Katherine, and then proceeded to consult a selection of leading scholars, including men such as Robert Wakefield, Edward Foxe, John Stokesley, Richard Pace and Stephen Gardiner.[58] Other scholars laboured on Katherine's side of the argument: John Fisher wrote seven or eight books, so many that he himself lost count.[59] This level of intellectual engagement is crucial to understanding Henry's stance. He did not just want to get his own way: he wanted to present a case that was beyond reproach. What he needed, however, was a papal annulment; and with Clement VII the virtual prisoner of Katherine's nephew Charles V in the Castel Sant'Angelo in Rome, that was unlikely, despite the painstaking efforts of the English ambassadors there.

Kings had fought with popes before. One of the first books published in Henry's campaign against Rome was the *Disputation between a Clerk and a Knight*, which had originally been written in French in the 1290s, when Philip the Fair of France was quarrelling with Pope Boniface VIII. Henry had versions published in English and Latin, hoping to sway opinion both at home and abroad.[60] Yet there was also a contemporary feel to this campaign, founded on humanist learning. It used to be thought that Henry was the passive recipient of advice from Wolsey and other advisors, and that a succession of strategies was pursued in the attempt to rid himself of his first wife. On closer inspection, it is clear that Henry himself was the driving force, and that although various initiatives were tried, there was one underlying note of consistency, which was his appeal to the Bible. Leviticus said that if a man married his brother's wife, 'they shall be childless', which spoke with awful clarity to Henry in his predicament. The verse of Deuteronomy which instructed that a man *should* marry his brother's widow, a point underlined by the New Testament, was brushed aside as Jewish ceremonial law.[61] Jewish authorities were sought, but they unfortunately confirmed the view of Deuteronomy; they, too, were dismissed. If this all sounds ridiculously self-serving, there is still no doubt that Henry was in deadly earnest. He was helped by the humanist scholars whom he had promoted in easier days. Robert Wakefield, the Hebraist whom the king had appointed to Cambridge, rapidly became part of the king's team of scholars, arguing that a better translation of Leviticus would render its warning as 'he shall have no sons', which made the passage even more appropriate to Henry's situation.[62] It is an indication of the way this was being argued that Wakefield's work of 1534, the *Syntagma de Incorruptione Hebraeorum Codicum*, containing a treatise on divorce, also included Wakefield's inaugural lecture as king's reader of Hebrew at Oxford and a defence of the Hebrew text of the Old Testament.[63] If Henry was fighting to get the wife he wanted, he was also fighting for the moral high ground.

It is in this light that we should view one curious feature of these years: that Henry and Anne foreswore sexual relations until they were married.[64] They may even have been lovers already, but then chose chastity as a mark of their seriousness and in a bid to sanction the union. This was traditionally cast as Anne Boleyn playing hard to get, manipulating Henry; but it is difficult to see Henry as the dupe of faction, and it seems possible that he orchestrated this behaviour. It was quite clear where his affections lay. In July 1531, Henry left Windsor, without saying farewell to Katherine; he would never see her again, and instructed that she should be banished from public life and forbidden to see her daughter. For over a year, England was, to all intents and purposes, without a queen.

Henry's grim determination to conclude the divorce case on his own terms left several dead, many more frightened and some at least of his subjects appalled. His ire against the papacy expanded until it threatened the clergy as a whole. Thomas More resigned the chancellorship in 1532, after Henry pushed through the Submission of the Clergy, an attack on sacerdotal authority which seemed a fundamental challenge to existing notions of the Church. Even Stephen Gardiner, the consummate diplomat and career cleric, objected to this attack on the sanctity of priesthood, and was banished from court, probably missing his chance to be the next arch-bishop of Canterbury. John Fisher, who had steadfastly opposed the divorce from the beginning, and had already been briefly imprisoned by the king, spoke out against him in 1533 and was put under house arrest, then implicated in the affair of the Nun of Kent in 1535 and executed for treason on 22 June. Fisher was widely regarded as a martyr, and, with More, would eventually be canonized as a saint. St Thomas More, ironic-ally enough, is the patron saint of lawyers and politicians, although when alive he struggled to feel at ease with either role.

The Nun of Kent was a woman named Elizabeth Barton, who prophe-sied ruin as a consequence of Henry's actions. She was a threat, partly because she had links to many highly placed clerics, but mostly because she had obvious popular appeal as a religious visionary. Prophecy was a shadowy but powerful force in Tudor England, and from the attention paid to it by Henry's government, particularly during the 1530s, it was a force that they feared.[65] As the divorce crisis became a matter for public lament, Barton spread word that an angel had told her to warn the king against marrying Anne Boleyn or risk terrible consequences. As another mark of how seriously she was taken, we know she had at least two meet-ings with the king, and also spoke with Fisher, More and many other senior clerics. Henry denounced her as fraudulent. Another mark of how dangerous she was is the ferocity with which she was discredited, and ulti-mately both hanged and beheaded. Her head was put on a spike on London Bridge, her associates were also executed and there was a scramble by many to dissociate themselves from her.[66]

There were other signs of popular opposition at this time.[67] In 1533, two women, one of them heavily pregnant, were publicly beaten for upholding Katherine's claim to be the true queen of England. Such indica-tions of popular discontent underline the point that Henry was not just removing dissenting individuals: he was attacking convictions that ranged broad and deep, and to many he appeared to be undermining the divinely ordained composition of society. The papacy rarely impinged directly on early Tudor society, but the pope was still the symbolic head of Christendom and the representative of God on earth – and perhaps all the more mystical for being distant and unapproachable. Certainly, those who had actually visited the papal court and had witnessed its sometimes sordid realities tended to be a lot more sanguine about attacking papal authority, but to many his authority was beyond question. Given that Henry was also spurning his very popular queen, he was at a distinct disadvantage when it came to popular opinion. On personal, political and religious grounds, he was behaving contrary to all established expectations.

By 1532, it was no longer a campaign with a single focus, but a broad-based argument that the papacy had no right at all – whether by Scripture or by historical precedent – to decide English cases such as Henry's. Justifications were evolving at great speed to suggest that the pope was really the bishop of Rome, with no jurisdiction in England. With the Act in Conditional Restraint of Annates (1532) threatening to withhold the dues customarily paid to Rome, Henry was stepping up the level of threat. That autumn, he took Anne Boleyn with him on a state visit to France, as consort in all but name, having wrested the crown jewels away from Katherine of Aragon for Anne to wear. At some point around then they took the highly significant step of beginning, or at least resuming, sexual relations, and by the start of 1533 she was pregnant, and they were secretly married.[68] Henry began to implement the measures by which he would reject papal power and take into his own hands the supreme power over the Church. This was the beginning of the Henrician Reformation, with the king cast as a defender of biblical authority, a scourge of superstitious practice and corruption. This was a role which Henry adopted with relative ease, given that from the start of his reign he had carved out a role for himself as theologian and scholar, but the political ramifications were huge. Kingship, which had always claimed divine sanction, was now appropriating divine purpose, with Henry as God's deputy on earth. It was a beguiling, exciting prospect that seemed to promise Henry unparalleled authority. In search of a solution to dynastic instability, an alarming power had been unleashed.

Godly kingship

Henry stumbled into the role of supreme head of the Church almost accidentally; but having assumed the mantle, he wore it with an air. His fantasies concerning his newly minted power over Church as well as state are encapsulated in Holbein's painting of Henry as King Solomon, sprawled across his throne, as he lasciviously eyes up the queen of Sheba (see plate 7). The usual symbolism was that Solomon represented Christ and the queen of Sheba represented the Church, so Henry was perhaps implying a Christ-like role for himself. But Holbein managed to suggest, perhaps unwittingly, a more sinister meaning. To many horrified observers, Henry's rule after 1533 did indeed seem like the rape of the Church, as he stripped it of independence, wealth and spiritual authority. Henry had long played the part of Renaissance prince: magnificent, warlike, erudite, pious and sophisticated. He had also long had imperial pretensions. Now the idea of Henry as emperor took on a new emphasis, recalling the Emperor Constantine, who had ruled Church and state alike.[69] Henry added a new dimension to a sense of majesty which had always been strong. As supreme head of the Church he was, 'next under God', the sole focus of obedience. His royal play-acting had reached its apotheosis. It was around this time that Henry redrafted the coronation oath: the king was no longer to promise to 'do in his judgements equity and right justice', but to do equity 'according to his conscience'. The implication was that the king's own conscience could decide what was right and wrong.[70] The language of official pronouncements became triumphalist: the Act in Restraint of Appeals, which in 1533 severed England from Rome, declared 'that this realm of England is an empire'. The Submission of the Clergy described Henry's 'fervent zeal to the promotion of God's honour and Christian religion', alongside his 'learning, far exceeding, in our judgment, the learning of all other kings and princes that we have read of'.[71] With this document, which was signed into law, the clergy relinquished control over the Church into the hands of the king and his commissioners.

The naivety of describing Henry as cleverer than any other prince 'that we have read of', and the fact that his commission was never in fact appointed, indicates policies hurriedly constructed and hastily justified. Henry's claim to ecclesiastical authority, encompassing everything from control of the clergy to the definition of doctrine, was unprecedented and, to many observers, incomprehensible; it was also, in practical terms, enormously difficult to achieve. He was unpicking threads of authority that had been in place for centuries, challenging assumptions so deeply rooted as to have been almost unquestioned, and taking on responsibilities for which he was far from qualified. It is in this context that we might see the extension of the treason laws in 1534 as an attempt to shore up his authority, even as he tried to extend its reach.[72] His subjects were by turns baffled, alarmed and confused, whilst the small number who were enthusiastic about these developments largely misunderstood their significance.

It is easy to assume that Henry was motivated by ambition and greed to take over the power and wealth of the Church, but this was only part of the story. Some saw him moving towards Protestantism in his rejection of the papacy, but it is clear that Henry never felt attracted by Protestant ideas. He repeatedly criticized the core Protestant doctrine of 'salvation by faith alone', intensely disliked Luther, burned at the stake those who openly denied the Catholic doctrine of transubstantiation, and attended mass every day. And yet it would not be true to say that there was no ideological content to the king's motivation.[73] He clearly believed that he was following a path laid down by Scripture, that it was his moral duty to take up the reins of authority over the Church, and that he had the necessary sanction to decide questions of doctrine. This has been hard for many to conceptualize, then and since. Historians preoccupied with the workings of government have seen his formulations of religious doctrine as an exercise in political dominance. Those more interested in religion have argued over whether to categorize Henry as a slowly emerging Protestant or a wilfully disobedient Catholic. They have been reluctant to accept that neither category makes much sense in the context of the 1530s and 1540s. It should be clear, though, that Henry himself never separated his religious role from his political responsibilities. He represented his chief political duty as the cleansing of the realm from superstition – as the opening passages of his most important religious work, the 'King's Book' of 1543, made clear: 'Like as in the time of darkness and ignorance, finding our people seduced and drawn from the truth by hypocrisy and superstition, we by the help of God and his Word have travailed to purge and cleanse our realm from the apparent enormities of the same.'[74]

This message of a princely crusade against the forces of darkness colours all official rhetoric after 1533 to a wearisome extent. Sermons repeatedly drove the point home, from the cleverly constructed court sermons, which also frequently appeared in print, to the more homely offerings of parish priests, who were constantly being instructed to deliver homilies justifying the Royal Supremacy.[75] Royal iconography was adjusted to reflect the same line of argument and to depict Henry as an Old Testament king. In early portraits Henry had resembled his father and his Yorkist predecessors; in Holbein's presentation of his mature image, he was transformed into a colossus, devoid of all trappings of monarchy, his physical presence sufficient symbol of majesty in itself.[76] His purging of the Church was conveyed by images such as 'The Four Evangelists Stoning the Pope', which Girolamo da Treviso painted (see illustration 9) to symbolize the defeat of ignorance, corruption and superstition by the power of the Gospel.[77] For his private devotions, his Latin psalter, produced by Jean Maillart, depicted Henry in the guise of King David, confronting Goliath or composing the psalms. On the frontispiece of the English Bible which he commissioned, he appeared enthroned like Christ at the Last Judgement, handing down the word of God to his humble and grateful subjects (see illustration 10). At the trial of the sacramentarian John Lambert in 1537, the king presided, dressed all in white: Thomas Elyot thought the king's involvement was 'a thynge supernaturall',

9. Girolamo da Treviso, *The Four Evangelists Stoning the Pope*

10. Frontispiece of the 'Great Bible' of 1539

noting the 'divine influence or sparke of divinitie: whiche late appered to all them that behelde your grace syttyng in the Throne of your royal astate, as supreme head of the churche of Englande nexte under Christ'.[78] Elyot was also expressing his enormous gratitude at being allowed to use the royal library to get his dictionary finished; yet it is clear that some powerful political and religious theatre was being enacted on this occasion.

None of this makes sense from a later perspective, once Catholic and Protestant identities had become fixed; but if regarded from Henry's own viewpoint, a certain measure of consistency is apparent. Henry thought he had been rescued from both an illegitimate marriage and the usurped power of Rome by the Word of God, and his devotion to Scripture thereafter equalled that of any evangelical grateful for his conversion. Thomas Bilney related in 1527 how he had 'chanced upon' a single 'sweet and comfortable sentence' in the Bible that had changed his life; for Henry, it was the words of Leviticus that had brought light out of darkness.[79] His piety was idiosyncratic, but it was fervent.[80] For the rest of his reign, he would retain a sometimes naïve faith in the power of Scripture to bring about a solution to his problems. In the wake of the Pilgrimage of Grace, he thought that the distribution of English bibles in the north of England would help bring the people to a proper sense of obedience. His insistence on the purging of idols and his grave self-presentation in the guise of David or Solomon, was a continuation of the same biblical emphasis.[81]

The difficulty is that none of this was immediately intelligible to those around him. It is probable that the Henrician Reformation, as it is sometimes called, was only fully understood by Henry alone. Much of his justification was Erasmian, drawing on ideas of humanist reform. But the conclusions he drew from these ideas went much further than most humanists had envisaged: they mostly wanted to reform the papacy, not deny its authority entirely; and to purge the monasteries of superstition, not destroy them. Henry often spoke the language of evangelical awakening, but without arriving at any conviction of Protestant doctrine – somewhat to the mystification of those advisors and supporters who were becoming increasingly firm in their Protestant views as the 1530s unfolded. Henry's Reformation, therefore, was in large part the work of one man, implemented by an energetic array of ministers, churchmen and scholars, nearly all of whom were working – at least in part – at cross-purposes with their employer.

Alongside his faith in the Bible, Henry continued to have great faith in his own opinions. These did not constitute a complete theological system, however, which is why religious reform between 1533 and 1547 was patchy, gradual and often puzzling. On some points he felt confident: his loathing of Luther was sustained, as was his rejection of the central Protestant doctrine of 'justification by faith alone', which he saw as undermining the importance of good works. He considered the seven sacraments as inviolable, and indignantly defended the doctrine of the Real Presence against attack. And yet he was open to other ideas, if persuaded by his own conscience and the testimony of learned men. This was the formula that had served him so well with the divorce and the Supremacy, and he never lost his liking for it. He was particularly open to criticism of anything associated with the papacy, such as indulgences or the doctrine of purgatory. At one point, he even considered rewording the Lord's Prayer (although Cranmer managed to talk him down). Thus, he was not unwilling to consider radical changes, so long as they could fit within his own particular, and peculiar, frame of reference. The 'Ten Articles' issued in 1536, which were cast in reformist language, bore the imprint of his Protestant advisors; even more so did the 'Bishops' Book' of 1537, which most significantly embraced justification by faith alone, to the annoyance of the king, who does not seem to have reviewed it before publication. His response was chiefly expressed through the Act of Six Articles of 1539, which reaffirmed the traditional line on such things as clerical celibacy, confession to a priest and the physical presence of Christ in the eucharist; the 'King's Book' of 1543 was a statement of doctrine in similar vein. There was some exploration and experimentation, therefore, but the complexities and ambiguities of all these formulations do not fit neatly into a Protestant or Catholic agenda, neither of which had yet been clearly established.

Whilst churchmen and scholars agonized over the finer details, and bishops issued visitation articles for their diocese, the religious belief and practice of the country at large was rooted in custom and was not easily changed. When it did begin to change, it was not always along lines which Henry and his bishops might have considered acceptable. It left Henry both enraged and apprehensive when he realized that he could not in fact command the hearts and souls of his subjects. Many of them seem chiefly to have been confused, and even those who grasped the import of some of the changes tended to highlight inessentials. One troublemaker in Windsor in 1538 began by teasing two conservative acquaintances by proposing a 'dish of buttered eggs' in Lent, a recent proclamation having removed the traditional fasting laws. From this beginning escalated a row, which ended in a local priest accused of treason.[82] Henry was in danger of turning his subjects into a warring nest of religious pedants. Old enmities took on a religious flavour; heated arguments over dinner or in the tavern escalated until men and women found themselves in court, on trial for their lives.

The most immediate casualties of this were England's monasteries. Monasticism was troubling to Henry on several levels. He did not like the relative autonomy or the power of these different religious houses, which were the focus of much provincial loyalty. An abbey could be a safeguard and a refuge for a local community, a landlord and an employer, an infirmary, a school and a badge of regional pride all at once. Monastic houses could also be mausoleums where masses were said for the souls of benefactors, a practice that made Henry uneasy, because of its links to the papacy. Finally, many monasteries were pilgrimage sites, and retained relics for veneration by pilgrims, one of the many practices he had pledged to uproot and destroy. A reasonable case could be made that some monasteries were failing to prosper, or were troubled by corruption; a more cynical case could also be made that monastic wealth could perhaps be better directed elsewhere. Henry began with the least contentious approach, decreeing that the smaller houses should be closed down and their inhabitants moved to the larger houses, if they so wished. This could be cast as the reallocation of resources for the religious life, rather than an attack on religion in any way. The language of the 1536 Act of dissolution, however, spoke of the 'manifest sin, vicious, carnal and abominable living', which it said was 'daily used and committed' in these houses, in contrast to the 'great solemn monasteries of this realm wherein . . . religion is right well kept and observed'.[83] The campaign for dissolution expanded only gradually, therefore, and many monks and nuns from smaller monasteries took up the offer of a place in a larger house. In 1537, Henry even founded two new monasteries, an indication that he had not at that point wholly rejected the very principle of monasticism.[84] Yet in 1536, prompted in large part by the dissolution of monasteries in the north of England, the rebellion known as the Pilgrimage of Grace began. This would effectively sign the death warrant for England's monasteries. After the rebels had restored houses across the north of England, monasticism, which was already tainted with papistry, was further stained by association with sedition.

The Pilgrimage began with the Lincolnshire rebellion, at the start of October 1536. It emerged from a complicated tangle of grievances, in which the king's handling of the Church loomed large. As the rebels marched on Lincoln, Yorkshire began stirring. And in due course, the rebellion spread to County Durham, Northumberland, Westmorland, Cumberland and Lancashire.[85] From these seven counties, an army was raised which posed a serious challenge to the king's forces when the two sides encountered one another at Doncaster in December. The spokesperson for the pilgrims, Robert Aske, seems to have had hopes that the duke of Norfolk might carry their grievances to the king; but Norfolk had already written to Henry, promising that whatever he might guarantee the rebels, he had no intention of fulfilling it. He made sufficient promises that the pilgrims dispersed home; and while Henry stalled for time, Robert

Aske spent Christmas at Court as the king's guest, unaware of the fact that he was being manipulated. When none of Norfolk's promises showed any sign of being fulfilled, discontent began to grow again, and some isolated outbreaks of violence in the East Riding and in Cumberland gave Henry the pretext he needed. His vengeance was swift and vicious. Aske, who had ridden in Norfolk's entourage, was sent back to London with a letter to the king; on his arrival, he was arrested, imprisoned, tried and despatched to York to be hanged in chains, a slow and degrading death. Meanwhile Norfolk's retribution in the north was on a terrible scale. That Henry had been forced into subterfuge and guile to win out over the rebels was an appalling indignity, which he was determined to avenge. The monasteries thereafter had little chance of survival, and the last had closed its doors by the end of the summer in 1540.

This country has been so long without monasteries that the full impact of what Henry did is perhaps hard to realize. He attacked something so integral to society that it is little wonder rumours also circulated that he was intending to destroy parish churches as well. The abbeys and priories, even those that were run down or disliked, were testimony to the strength of a shared faith, and a place to run to in the face of danger. It was not just that they were the source of medicine, poor relief or education, a haven for travellers or a sanctuary for criminals. They were also the sentinels of centuries of Christian identity. It was an extraordinary act of vandalism. Yet Henry seems to have expected to carry popular opinion with him when it came to dissolution. It was a telling example of the dislocation between the views of the government and the views of the governed. It was also an indication that Henry's attempts to rule as a godly prince were failing miserably to convince his subjects.

Whilst 1536 saw rebellion and crisis on a grand scale, it also witnessed shocking developments at the heart of the regime. At the start of May, Queen Anne, for the love of whom Henry had reconfigured Church and state, was accused of treasonous adultery with five men, one of them her own brother. Within just three weeks, she was accused, convicted and executed, in a bewildering and brutal display of vengeance. Henry was clearly convinced of her culpability, but the case against her was deeply implausible. Nonetheless, she had been outspoken, forceful and jealous of Henry's attentions to other women; she had failed to produce a son; she had been both funny and flirtatious, at times outrageously so. Most of these characteristics Henry had, at one time, found beguiling; but they now laid her open to malicious gossip and the king's sudden conviction of her guilt. Four of the men found guilty of adultery with the queen, including her brother, Lord Rochford, and gentlemen of the Privy Chamber, Norris, Weston and Brereton, had been intimate friends of the king. It was perhaps the most chilling example of Henry's ability to suspect disloyalty among those closest to him, and to turn on them with fury at their perceived treachery. Thomas Wyatt – initially one of those under suspicion, though he narrowly escaped their fate – produced a poem of lamentation. 'These bloody days have broken my heart', he wrote. Truly the political stakes were higher than they had been in years, as Henry struggled to implement his flawed vision of the future, lashing out at all who opposed him.

The life and death of Queen Anne were part of the bigger picture of Henry's pursuit of godly kingship. In his heightened awareness of his role as God's deputy, it was unthinkable that he should continue much longer without the blessing of a son. His marriage to Anne had been confidently expected to culminate in the birth of a prince: the letters making the announcement had already been prepared before the birth of Elizabeth in September 1533, when 'prince' had to be hastily altered to 'princess'. The arrival of another daughter need not have been a problem, had a son followed swiftly afterwards. But in 1536, Anne had a miscarriage, possibly brought on by shock, after Henry's jousting accident left him insensible for several hours. This combination of elements was compounded by the fact that Katherine of Aragon had recently died. This meant that if Henry were to marry again, no possible accusation of bigamy could be levelled against him, as it had been over his marriage to Anne. It was also the case that he was already attracted by Jane Seymour. This intensely human drama can only be fully understood, however, in the light of Henry's role as supreme head of the Church. He purged Anne from his life in May 1536 with the same ferocity and dispatch with which he destroyed shrines and miraculous images.

Queen Anne and her brother were tried in the Tower before two thousand spectators and Anne was executed before a thousand onlookers. It is impossible to know what they might have been thinking, but the sight must at least have been thought-provoking. In attempting to make a show of strength, and ruthless justice, it could be argued that Henry had just proclaimed his cuckoldry to the world, as well as his vengefulness. Anne's speech from the scaffold was a model of dignified acceptance: 'I am come hither to accuse no man, nor to speak of that whereof I am accused.' But unusually, it contained no admission of guilt, and she said enigmatically 'if any person will meddle of my cause, I require them to judge the best'. Her death was a tragedy not only for her small daughter and the rest of her family, but also for Henry's pretensions to majesty, godly superiority and the detached administration of justice. He had been shown to be fallible, vengeful, perhaps impotent, and faintly ridiculous. It is little wonder that he sought to draw a line under the whole affair as swiftly as possible. On the day of Anne's execution, he was betrothed to Jane Seymour, and he married her on 20 May. One queen had been replaced by another within the space of a month. Henry's performance as God's anointed was proving to be not entirely convincing.

Consequences

Henry had taken to his new role as supreme head of the Church with enormous enthusiasm. His intention was to impart a new level of majesty to his kingship; indeed, it seems to be from the 1530s that the term 'the King's Majesty' became normal usage. This was given architectural expression in the new palace at Whitehall, which he and Anne planned together. It could perhaps be linked to other extensions of his power, including in 1536 the Act of Union with Wales. This served to integrate the Welsh gentry more closely within the administrative hierarchy of Tudor government, and had some success in building stronger ties between England and Wales.[86] On the whole, however, Henry's successes in these years were few and far between. And in his eagerness for his new role, Henry had expected God to be equally enthusiastic. Yet several years after the break with Rome, his situation showed none of the signs of divine approval. He still had no son; Anne Boleyn, for whom he had risked so much, was ignominiously and humiliatingly dead, and had been replaced with indecent haste; his subjects had risen in rebellion on an unprecedented scale; and his youthful vigour was long gone.[87] If the last ten years of Henry's reign were marked by increasingly defensive policies, the persecution of political enemies and religious offenders, and repeated domestic catastrophe, this was in large part due to his frustration at his continuing inability to command providential sanction. It was also a realization of the consequences of the policies he had unleashed. The campaign to implement the Royal Supremacy and reform England's religion was resulting in division and animosity at every level – from the Court to the village.

When the Lincolnshire rebellion broke out in 1536, there were three royal commissions then operating in the vicinity of Louth: one to collect the parliamentary subsidy; one to enquire into the abilities of the clergy; and one to dissolve the smaller monasteries.[88] This level of oversight and interference was profoundly unsettling. The rumours which abounded were all fearful of what the government might do next, conscious that the *Valor Ecclesiasticus* had enquired into all forms of church wealth, including that of the parishes. Others said that taxes would be levied on all baptisms, weddings and funerals; or on all horned cattle; or even on the consumption of goose, capon or white bread.[89] The levels of alarm here reflect the scale of Henry's innovations and meant that even his more reasonable reforms, such as the introduction of the subsidy, or the attempts to raise the educational standards of the clergy, had become tainted by association with the Supremacy and the Dissolution. Here was a king who was not afraid to break Christendom apart and to pull down monasteries that had stood for centuries; there was no telling what else he might do.

Closer to home, the king's domestic situation never truly recovered from the tragedy of Anne Boleyn's death. On one occasion when Jane Seymour annoyed Henry by pleading for the monasteries, he told her not to meddle, reminding his new queen that her predecessor had died because she had meddled too much.[90] Anne's small daughter Elizabeth was kept out of sight at Ewelme, but Anne's ghost still hovered in the background. And even those who praised Jane tended to do so by comparing her to the previous wife: one wrote of how the king 'hath come out of hell into heaven, for the gentleness in this, and the cursedness and unhappiness in the other'.[91] This idyll was short-lived. To the king's joy, Prince Edward was born at Hampton Court in October 1537. However, after complications in childbirth, within a fortnight Jane was dead. Even the triumph of securing a male heir, after nearly thirty years of waiting, was tainted by tragedy.

Henry lavished every possible attention on his tiny son, and ensured that he had the best of everything. He built the great palace of Nonsuch for him, a triumph of Renaissance architecture.[92] The security of the country now rested on the life of one small boy, however. Henry's grief at losing Jane was such that it was over two years before another match was made with Anne, daughter of the duke of Cleves. Henry's counsellors hoped anxiously for another son from this union, but Anne, who so regrettably appeared attractive in Holbein's portrait of her, in person proved repellent to the king. Henry was unable to consummate the match, apparently telling Cromwell on the day after the wedding that 'I liked her before not well, but now I like her much worse. For I have felt her belly and her breasts, and thereby, as I can judge, she should be no maid.' He confessed that 'I had neither will nor courage to proceed any further.'[93] After just a few months, an annulment was hastily contrived. Henry swiftly married his next wife, Katherine Howard. Yet Anne's shadow fell over this new match, too, since the match with Katherine, who was Anne's cousin, ended in catastrophe sixteen months later, when her sexual adventurism, both before and after her marriage, came to light. Katherine was a buxom teenager who clearly preferred illicit sex with a handsome young lover to dutiful sex with her bloated husband, thirty years her senior. Her liaison with Thomas Culpepper, a gentleman of the Privy Chamber, was facilitated by Jane, Lady Rochford, widow of George Boleyn. Lady Rochford went to the block immediately after Katherine Howard, in February 1542. It was six years on from the death of Anne Boleyn and her brother, but this disaster was strikingly reminiscent of the events of 1536. Henry's nightmares kept recurring.

The architect of the Cleves match, Thomas Cromwell, suffered his own catastrophic fall from grace in the wake of its failure, and was executed in July 1540. Henry's ability to identify men of political talent had never been more evident than in his recruitment of Thomas Cromwell; and his exploitative attitude to the people who served him was never more evident than in Cromwell's fall. Cromwell had done the king great service. Even if he did not quite revolutionize Tudor government in the way we once thought, he was a man of immense talent, whose attention to detail was extraordinary.[94] He shaped the break with Rome; he put the Supremacy into law and constructed the administrative machinery that enabled Henry to govern the Church; and he coordinated an exceptional team of scholars and writers to give the whole enterprise the aura of credibility that Henry craved. Unfortunately, however, he was – however discreetly – pro-Protestant; and equally unfortunately, his one attempt at royal match-making had proved a disaster. Henry VII had valued loyalty, but Henry VIII only valued the kind of loyalty which gave him what he wanted. Once Cromwell had failed, Henry's faith in him was shaken, and his opponents took the opportunity to reveal the extent of his heresy. This could be cast as a victory for the conservative faction, but that would be to overlook the role of Henry himself, whose furious disappointment was the driving force behind Cromwell's fall.[95]

That Cromwell, the architect of Henry's Royal Supremacy, should be convicted of both heresy and treason was a significant indictment of Henry's failed policies in the 1530s. The king had envisaged biblical authority as an adjunct to majesty, commanding loyalty and gratitude from the people, whilst reform proceeded in a decorous fashion, directed by the king's wisdom and that of his advisors. Instead, he discovered that biblical exegesis was a battlefield all of its own, that his advisors were bitterly divided and that those he had counted on for their help were unaccountably disposed to oppose him, even at the cost of their own lives. A war of words was under way. A proclamation of 1536 inveighed against the way rumours could 'stir up division, strife, commotion, contention and sedition.'[96] The king was outraged at the levels of resistance which his reforming policies engendered. Many individuals saw the danger he posed to their Catholic faith. Some, such as the London Carthusians, took a stand to defend their institution; others, such as John Fisher, tried to safeguard the sacred authority of the priesthood, whilst Thomas More seems to have gone to his death in defence of the principle of Christian community. Many of these acts of defiance Henry chose to take personally, and his retribution was terrifying. From the safe distance of Italy, his cousin Reginald Pole wrote a treatise on the unity of the Church, in which he denounced what Henry had done, thereby effectively signing the death warrants of several members of his family in England, including his elderly mother.[97]

Those of a more evangelical persuasion were also a thorn in Henry's side. They had no difficulty in embracing – and indeed fortifying – his anti-papal rhetoric, and they were immediate allies in the dissolution of the monasteries, pouring scorn and condemnation on monastic superstition and corruption, and eagerly assessing how the wealth of the abbeys could be redirected into Protestant educational initiatives. Henry had given Cromwell plenty of licence to implement the Supremacy, and if those he appointed to preach against the papacy were also promoting Protestant doctrine, this was not always immediately apparent to Henry. It helped, too, that the most influential of them, Archbishop Cranmer, was also careful not to alienate Henry, even if this required him to sit in judgement on men and women such as John Lambert or Anne Askew, whose views on the eucharist were remarkably close to his own.[98] Nevertheless, with the 'Bishops' Book' of 1537, and with the fiasco of Cromwell's fall from grace, Henry was forcibly reminded that here, too, was a source of resistance to his vision of godly reform. The Act of Six Articles of 1539 was a response to the 'great discord and variance' which had arisen in religion, 'as well amongst the clergy ... as amongst a great number of vulgar people'.[99] Reformers were appalled, and two of the more evangelical bishops resigned, whilst Cranmer had to hastily move his wife and children overseas.[100] Henry was alienating his subjects on all sides.

Some of these ambiguities shaped Henry's last marriage, to Katherine Parr. In many ways, this match was a success. Katherine was intelligent, animated, stylish and attractive. She was also deeply interested in theology and was highly educated, publishing a book of prayers in 1545. At their private wedding in July 1543 at Hampton Court, all three of the king's children were present, and over the coming years Katherine quietly did what she could to bring this most broken of families together. She shared Henry's regard for Scripture, and worked with a team of translators, including her stepdaughter Princess Mary, to render Erasmus's paraphrases or commentaries on the gospels into English. Her evangelical leanings were very nearly her downfall, however, as in 1546 Henry allowed the conservative faction at Court to draw up a list of articles against her, which he signed. This concern was related to the trial of Anne Askew, who was burned for heresy that summer, after a spell of torture, during which she was interrogated about her links to five of the women in the queen's household.[101] Katherine herself was warned, seemingly by Henry himself, of the accusations made against her; the king sent a message via the royal doctor. Katherine pleaded her case, and insisted that she had only debated with him about theology to take his mind off his ill-health – a plea which the king accepted. When Lord Chancellor Wriothesley, who had himself tortured Anne Askew, came to arrest Katherine, the king shouted at him 'Arrant knave, beast and fool!' and the queen was safe.[102] This was a striking example of how Henry could manipulate factions to frighten both them and their rivals into submission. But it was also an indication of how fragile his domestic peace was.

Henry's extravagant rhetoric concerning his role as supreme head of the Church should not be allowed to conceal the real consequences of what he had done. However loudly he might assert his claim to divinely sanctioned kingship, this was still an age in which politics relied on popular cooperation. Henry's dominion over the Church had brought him an increase in land, wealth and power, but it had not brought him popular acquiescence. Rather it had left communities divided and individual consciences deeply troubled. It had also provided those who opposed him with an ideological platform on which they could stand, something never before seen in English politics. By trying to make his kingly authority incontestable, Henry had, in fact, laid it open to question as never before, and had sown dissension among his subjects on an unprecedented scale. On Christmas Eve 1545, he came in person to parliament and made an extraordinary speech, in which he uttered a thinly veiled and largely impotent threat of his displeasure if its members did not 'take paines to amend one thing which surely is amisse, and far out of order ... which is, that charity and concord is not amongst you, but discord and dissention beareth rule in every place'. His words showed bitterness, as well as apprehension. 'Behold then what charity and love is amongst you when one calleth the other Heretick and Anabaptist, and hee calleth him againe Papist, Hypocrite and Pharisee, bee these tokens of charity amongst you?'[103] Henry's attempts to strengthen his authority, and to unite his country in a reformed and godly faith, had apparently had the opposite effect to that intended.

Meanwhile at parish level, the suffering was all the more acute on account of the confusion over what exactly Henry was asking of his subjects. The parishioners of Ashlower in Gloucestershire were not sure if their priest had committed treason or not, but reported him just to be on the safe side.[104] References to the papacy were diligently deleted from the liturgical texts, and the payment of Peter's Pence was no longer required. Some parish churches benefited from the Dissolution; at Halesowen in

Worcestershire, the rood screen, organ and other items were moved from abbey to parish church.[105] The royal injunctions of 1538 ordered a range of changes, however, including the removal of all lights in the church apart from those on the altar, the rood loft and before the Easter Sepulchre. Historians have pointed to the way in which bequests for intercessory masses and gifts to saints declined during the 1530s, suggesting there was a dwindling loyalty to traditional religion; but it is more likely that, bewildered by what was happening and observing how monastic wealth had been sequestered, Henry's subjects became cautious.[106] It is striking that as lights were extinguished in front of images, the funds that had kept those lights burning, in some cases for centuries, were redirected towards the altar and rood loft lights, the only ones still permitted. The injunction commanding each parish to buy an English Bible seems to have been widely ignored, which suggests that the key element of Henry's reforms was largely overlooked.

Not everyone regretted the loss of traditional religion. The plundering of the monastic houses for which the regime had set the example was enthusiastically taken up by some in the localities. In Warwickshire in 1538, it was recorded that 'the poor people ... be so greedy upon these houses when they be suppressed that by night and day ... they do continually resort as long as any door, window, iron or glass or loose lead remaineth in any of them'.[107] Respect for priests seems to have ebbed, too; but then the regime had set a powerful example here.[108] Given the ferocity of the official rhetoric, it is little wonder that some ordinary people were encouraged to attack their priests and plunder the local abbeys. In Croscombe in Somerset, the churchwardens reported their rector for maintaining a priest who was in favour of the Pilgrimage of Grace, but they were really getting their revenge because he had censured them for felling trees in the churchyard.[109] With those in authority giving voice to their religious animosities, it was hard to argue that the populace should remain peaceable. An attempt to oust Cranmer and his associates from Canterbury diocese in 1543, the so-called Prebendaries' Plot, not only caused tension at Court, but also divided popular opinion at the local level: as one of the plotters testified, 'schism did engender among the people, open disputation was in alehouses, and in household reasoning among servants, of the which did also arise much debate and strife'.[110]

In the years after the break with Rome, Henry's assertion of his sovereignty reached unparalleled levels of splendour. In his palaces at Whitehall, Nonsuch and St James, in the plundered monastic houses that he turned into royal houses, in the grandeur of his iconography, his literary patronage and his libraries, and above all in his self-presentation as supreme head of the Church and Christ's representative on earth, Henry trumpeted his authority, his godliness, the strength of his regime and the greatness of his dynasty.[111] It was an extraordinary exercise in dissimulation. In reality, the acquisition of four wives within ten years, the violent and disgraceful death of two of them and the fiasco of the Cleves match underlined his precarious hold on the succession, which rested on the one small son, born when Henry was already forty-six years old. Opposition to his religious policies came from every level of society, including from men he had admired and trusted, such as Thomas More and Reginald Pole. Religious conflict became endemic, from Court down to village level, while European powers derided his carefully sanctioned reforms as schismatic or heretical, and reviewed their options for making war on England. Henry had tested the potential of his royal authority, and to his fury had found it less than envisaged. He had deployed every tool at his disposal: parliamentary statutes, proclamations, show trials and judicial murders, sermons, publications, the power of magistrates and commissions, the sheer force of his personality. It had been enough to bring about the destruction of monasteries and shrines, the terrorizing of the north of England, the deaths of many powerful opponents, the sacrifice of ineffectual wives and ministers, the refiguring of political thought and religious doctrine. It had not, however, been enough to achieve what he wanted.

The closing years

The last years of Henry's reign were effectively an exercise in damage limitation. The regime never fully recovered from the blows dealt to it in the 1530s, which were further compounded by the ferocity of the king's response to his many critics. In a sense, Henry staked his all on his last military gamble, an invasion of northern France on an unprecedented scale in 1544. This succeeded in capturing Boulogne, but it very nearly bankrupted the country in consequence, and it engendered a fierce response from the

French. Their attempted invasion in 1545, on a scale greater than that of the Spanish Armada of 1588, required huge and costly military provision. At home, religious change and uncertainty continued to cause widespread conflict and grief, and Henry was repeatedly reminded that his vision of a princely reformation was shared by very few of his subjects. The king's health was also giving concern: he was prematurely aging in his early fifties, as he desperately tried to shore up the stability of the regime, with everything resting on the survival of his young son. Mary and Elizabeth remained illegitimate, but were returned to the line of succession in an act of 1544: Henry's willingness to even contemplate one of his bastard daughters on the throne is a measure of his desperate anxiety.

The concept of a united Catholic Christendom had been useful in the past, in justifying a military alliance of questionable integrity. Henry in 1513 had benefited from applying the rhetoric of godliness to his expansionist ambitions in France. In the later 1530s, he saw others deploy this kind of rhetoric. Both France and the Empire were willing to declare that Henry had turned his back on Christendom and descended into schism. To a king who had been used to playing off these two rivals one against the other, the prospect of them uniting against him was deeply troubling. After prolonged and strenuous diplomatic effort, the Anglo-Imperial alliance was revived in 1543, and plans were laid for a joint invasion of France in June 1544. Henry's Council asked the Imperial ambassador Chapuys to suggest to Charles V that he should decline to lead his troops in battle, hoping that this might persuade Henry to do likewise. But Henry, ill and aging, was resolved to pursue his last chance at military glory in person, with a determination that was almost pitiful. His arrival in Calais was a splendid occasion, but the king was too gross to mount his horse without help and too lame to walk without assistance. After the capture of Boulogne in September, the alliance with Charles V broke down, and by 1545 England was contending with a hostile France and Scotland, and an unpredictable Empire. In the summer of 1545, with the threat of a French invasion imminent, parish congregations went in procession to say special prayers for the king and for the realm's deliverance from the 'greate mallyce of his enemyes'.[112]

The 1540s involved a scale of military preparedness never before seen. In 1513, Henry had mobilized perhaps one in twelve adult men to fight; by

1545, it was more like one in six, representing perhaps one in three of those who were actually in a fit state to fight. The army in France numbered around 32,000 or more, and there were also thousands on the northern border facing the Scots.[113] This required a huge effort from the population at large. Towns and villages mustered resources to turn out soldiers equipped for battle; parish stores, which had been founded to pay for candles to burn in front of holy images, found themselves instead paying for armour. In Maldon, the town authorities also paid for a new nightcap and a haircut for each of the soldiers it was sending forth.[114] On the south coast, England's fortifications were brought up to date, and the navy was readied for action, described by the Privy Council as more powerful than any 'in the remembraunce of man'.[115] From the great ship *Mary Rose*, which sank in 1545, we have a good idea of the measure of preparation required by each vessel.[116] The capture of Boulogne imposed a still greater strain on the navy, which had to keep the garrison there supplied with food. In the middle of November 1544, Governor John Dudley was pointing out that his men had eaten nothing but biscuit for six days, but was told to keep 'a more wary eye to your victuals', given the difficulty of getting supplies across the Channel.[117] It was the end of the most abiding dream of Henry's reign, the reconquest of French territories held by his ancestors.

By the end of 1546, Henry's health had taken a turn for the worse. The drama of his last few weeks would take him back to the anxieties with which his reign had begun, and the problem of how to secure the succession. Edward was still a child, just nine years old in October 1546, and the political establishment he would need to draw on for a regency government was increasingly divided along confessional lines, in addition to the usual factional rivalries. Moreover, as Henry's own physical strength ebbed, his powers of coercion waned. His will, drawn up and signed at the end of December 1546, tried hard to put safeguards in place against some of the disasters he could foresee; in particular, its careful provision ensuring that none of his children married without conciliar approval reflected his fears that any of them might become the pawn of a domestic faction or foreign power. His regency council attempted to balance conservative against evangelical, leaving out such complicated characters as Stephen Gardiner, lest he make trouble for the young king. At the very last, the execution of the earl of Surrey – who had undoubtedly hoped to advance his family's cause at Court, and perhaps also to control the new king – was the final act of vengeance of a dying man; moreover, Surrey's father, the duke of Norfolk, was only spared because Henry died before he could sign the death warrant. Even before he died, however, Henry was losing his grip on the reins of power. The future king's uncle, Edward Seymour, and his coterie closed in around the deathbed and took steps to secure their future dominance.[118] Despite all his efforts, Henry's intentions would not exercise much sway beyond the grave.

Henry's will opened by trumpeting his titles – 'by the grace of god king of England France and Ireland defender of the faith and in earth immediately under god the Supreme head of the church of England and Ireland' – and by expressing gratitude for all the blessings he had received. As a document, however, it is full of apprehension – for his children, for his kingdom and indeed for the state of his soul: the king who had abolished belief in purgatory left instructions for 'all divine service accustomed for dead folk to be celebrated for us', as well as substantial sums of money to celebrate obits in St George's Chapel Windsor, and to give alms to the poor, in return for them praying 'heartily unto god for remission of our offences and the wealth of our soul'.[119] Henry's tomb, as originally conceived, was supposed to have been crowned by a huge triumphal arch and an equestrian statue.[120] In one last irony, this tomb had been planned as a gift by Pope Leo X, back in 1521, when Henry was the favoured son of the papacy; it would have rivalled Michelangelo's tomb for Julius II as one of the most splendid Renaissance tombs ever constructed.[121] The Italian tomb never got beyond a model, however, and the half-built version that was put together at Windsor was dismantled in the seventeenth century. Instead, Henry is interred at Windsor, alongside the bodies of Jane Seymour, Charles I and a nameless child of the Stuart Queen Anne, relics all of royal aspirations which ended in failure.

* * *

After Henry was dead, his memory lingered on as a powerful political force in its own right. All three of his children appealed to his authority, which still had traction from beyond the grave. Yet sixteenth-century judgements on his reign found it unusually difficult to sum up either the king or the consequences of his rule. A work published in Italy soon after his death reported what was allegedly a conversation held in Bologna about the king's achievements, in which the Italians denounced Henry as a tyrant, citing his treatment of Katherine of Aragon, the deaths of More, Fisher and others, the plunder of the Church and his unjustifiable wars. The English respondent defended Henry in language that he would have recognized, detailing the corruption of the monasteries, the vices of his enemies and the illegality of papal power, but even in a work bent on praising Henry's achievements, the author had to work hard to argue his case.[122] The Catholic priest and controversialist Nicholas Sander, in his account of what he called 'the Anglican schism', depicted a king tormented on his deathbed by what he had done in breaking the unity of the Church, consulting men too frightened to advise him. 'No man was found courageous enough to advise him honestly . . . they were all afraid because of his former cruelty.' And yet even Sander had to admit that Henry had qualities: 'we may say briefly that he was not unversed in learning, that he encouraged learned men'. He thought also that Henry's 'understanding was acute, and his judgement solid, whenever he applied himself to the serious discussion of any question'. Sander's last word, however, was a comment on how Henry's children never built the tomb he had so carefully devised, and how fitting it was 'that a man who scattered to the winds the ashes of so many saints, and who plundered the shrines of so many martyrs, should lie himself unhonoured in his grave'.[123] Dead kings were usually the subject of pious commemoration, not fierce debate; but in this, as in so many things, Henry was an exception to the rule.

John Foxe struggled to give an account of this man, who had almost inadvertently laid the foundations for English Protestantism, whilst remaining an implacable enemy of most of the central convictions of Protestant reformers. It was hard to frame succinctly a king who was responsible for defying and defeating the pope, publishing an English Bible and destroying the monasteries, and yet who defended the seven sacraments, burned Protestants at the stake and daily attended mass. Foxe took refuge in blaming the factions about him, describing a king who 'gave ear sometimes to one, sometimes to another'.[124] For the most part, later Tudor commentators avoided any detailed discussion of Henry's reign, seizing upon the obvious achievements and drawing a veil over the rest. The *Henry VIII* of Shakespeare and John Fletcher stops abruptly with the baptism of the future Elizabeth I in 1533, and a series of prophetic remarks about the 'thousand thousand blessings' which this 'high and mighty Princess of England' and her successors would bring to England.[125] The last fourteen years of Henry's rule were apparently too intractable even for Shakespeare.

Henry VIII was undoubtedly an extraordinary ruler, who brought about profound and disturbing changes in both politics and society. His expensive wars, his attack on religious tradition, his use of the Church as a vehicle for political propaganda and his ruthless repression of all who appeared to him to be opponents left scars upon landscape and psyche alike, a deep impression upon popular memory and a legacy of popular debate.[126] Henry's innovations cannot be fitted into any easy explanatory framework or model of progress. He reconfigured the notion of kingship, whilst yearning for the medieval past; he wrought destructive transformation of the Church, whilst defending traditional doctrine and rooting his claims in Scripture and history. In his unprecedented mobilizing of the kingdom's military potential, his most cherished ambition was to emulate the victories of Henry V and his Plantagenet ancestors. His novelty as a ruler was largely unintentional, and above all fiercely personal. His private passions, enthusiasms and his recurring sense of betrayal all had a disproportionate effect upon the political process.

Had Henry died in 1529, we might recall him in much the same way as we think of Henry V, and remember him as a valorous, gifted, beautiful warrior king, who defeated the Scots, raised diplomacy to new heights with the Field of Cloth of Gold and healed the age-old breach with France; who consolidated Tudor power at home and influence abroad; and who commanded the love and respect of his subjects. Concentrating on the first twenty years, rather than the final seventeen, helps explain why contemporaries viewed him with such reverence and followed him with such obedience. It also explains why some of them accepted (or even collaborated in) the remarkable transformations that followed after 1529. The first twenty years of stability and success also explain why Henry had the courage and conviction to do what he did in the 1530s, tearing apart family, Church and community, and launching himself into a world of unparalleled political ambition and risk. These were the bold initiatives of a king who was used to commanding the attention, respect and even the affection of his subjects, and who lived under the constant threat of dynastic collapse and with the abiding problem of inadequate finances.

Henry showed great ingenuity and intelligence at times in the way he governed, but he failed to internalize two of the lessons learned more painfully by his father. One of these was the limited nature of royal power, which depended for its effectiveness on the consensus and collaboration of his subjects. The other was the central importance of individual loyalty in an age of personal kingship. Henry aimed too high when it came to his reconfiguration of both Church and state, and in consequence left lasting fissures in both royal dignity and the national community. He commanded both love and devoted service from many of his wives, courtiers and ministers; but in making it clear that all of them were expendable, he sacrificed both his own integrity and the credibility of his kingship. Nevertheless, for all the damage that he wrought, he still achieved a great deal, and his reign demonstrates the extraordinary resilience and efficiency of Tudor government, which managed to effect such profound changes in the face of popular reluctance and opposition. Henry pushed the political system further than ever before, and stretched the boundaries of kingship to an unprecedented extent. If the end result was often violent, it still remains a remarkable testimony to the political and cultural potential of the age.

CHAPTER 6

AUTHORITY AND DISSENT
THE BALANCE OF POWER

The resplendent figures of the Tudor monarchs loom so large in the popular imagination that it is easy to assume that Tudor England laboured under despotic rule. Royal authority was at points brutally imposed, but in general the exercise of power was much more diffuse, negotiated and reciprocal than is often perceived. This dynamic at the heart of Tudor rule is frequently overlooked, or misinterpreted, but it remains essential to any real understanding of the age. It is the reason why Tudor monarchs behaved as they did. It lay beneath their magnificence, hovered behind their spoken and unspoken words, and governed their interactions with courtiers and subjects at home, and with friends or enemies abroad. They knew that their authority relied on the cooperation of those they ruled, and that political stability and social order required mutual effort. When Elizabeth I in 1601 told a parliamentary delegation that the 'glittering glory of a king's title' had not misled her into thinking 'all is lawful what we list', she was speaking the truth, just as when she went on to explain how her authority was distributed 'in sundry sorts to divers kinds'.[1] Government was a collaborative process, sustained as much by a sense of duty as by monetary reward. If the language of mutual obligation was widely used by the powerful, it was also deployed by those demanding their protection, for oaths of loyalty worked both ways. 'Ye that be of myght, Se that ye do right, Thynk on youre othe', warned a ballad from the 1490s.[2] The rhetoric of opposition was rooted, therefore, in the same ideology of communal responsibility as monarchical rule, and it was widely recognized that the participation of the ruled was just as necessary to governance as the initiative of the ruler.[3]

This symbiotic relationship made contemporary discussions of authority complicated. The contrasting rhetoric of paternalism and class antagonism can emerge side by side from the sources.[4] The Elizabethan MP who warned that if the 'ruder sort' were aware of 'their own strength and liberty allowed them by the law' then they would become like 'unbridled and untamed beasts' was simultaneously voicing both his fear of the multitude and his recognition of their legal rights.[5] Thomas More was only one of many who spoke out for those who committed crimes out of desperation and received 'terrible punishments', suggesting that it might be 'better to enable every man to earn his own living, instead of being driven to the awful necessity of stealing and then dying for it'.[6] Yet if More was here an advocate for the poor, he was also by profession a lawyer, charged with implementing the harsh penalties against such crimes. Those in authority never spoke with a single or a constant voice, just as those who wielded power for a span might find themselves in time disgraced or excluded: contemplation of the rise and fall of the great inspired many writers of the time.[7] Concepts of kingship and civic duty, honour and obedience were continually scrutinized and interrogated, and to balance justice with equity, and to exercise the rule of law in line with Christian compassion, was a far from straightforward task.

Whether at Court or within the household, in parliament or in the law courts, in towns or villages, there was recognition that the exercise of authority rested on reciprocal rights and duties. Those who expressed loyalty to their superiors also knew what they were entitled to expect in return. They might speak with emphatic condemnation if they saw their claims to common pasturage infringed, or were disallowed from gleaning after the harvest, or gathering firewood from common land. Even when driven to the extremity of rebellion, those involved would frame their grievances and petitions in formal, legalistic documents. In the uprising in East Anglia in 1549, rebels took over many of the processes of local government, protesting their loyalty to the king, and including in their list of demands a request for commissioners 'to redresse and refourme all suche good lawes, statutes, proclamacions, and all other your procedynges, whiche hath byn hydden by your Justices of your peace, Shreves, Escheatores, and other your officers, from your pore comons'. These commissioners were to be chosen by the 'pore comons', but ratified by king and Council.[8] The rebels here envisaged themselves working in concert with the Crown to restore good order in the provinces. They were in effect rebelling in order to reaffirm the workings of the social hierarchy. In concert with many other Tudor rebellions, this was a simultaneous expression of both popular resistance and deeply conservative notions of authority.

Contemporaries often described the political process in terms of a living organism, with many parts working in harmony with one another. Thomas Elyot, in 1531, defined the public weal as 'a body lyvyng, compact or made of sondry astates and degrees of men, whiche is dysposed by the order of equytye, and governed by the rule and moderation of reason'.[9] For him to describe the body politic as a thing ruled not first and foremost by a king, but by reason, should give pause for thought; his treatise has seemed to some an endorsement of royal authority, but the text contains some delicately phrased suggestions of limitations on that power.[10] Elyot described those who ruled as 'ministres for the onely profite and commoditee of them, whiche have not equal understanding', working for the benefit of others.[11] Edmund Dudley chose a different, but equally organic, metaphor, envisaging the commonwealth of England as a tree with five roots: namely, the love of God, justice, fidelity, unity and peace. Kings were born to protect the 'prosperous estate' of the country, and Dudley took a stark view of kings whose folly had eroded their power, such as Edward IV, whose sons had been murdered as a punishment, he argued, for licentious and lascivious living.[12] If a commonwealth was an organic entity, then diseased elements needed to be excised. The implications of these political ideas were striking: if authority was contingent on virtue and responsibility, then royal rule might readily be called to account.

Another organic model for society was that of the family. Kings were often described as fathers to their people, and the kingdom envisaged as a household writ large. Members of the nobility were, in this analogy, the king's offspring, and William Harrison surmised that the word 'baron' derived from the word 'bairn'.[13] Tudor government was expected not just to rule, therefore, but also to love and nourish its people. When the patriarchal head of state was a woman, as it was for the last half century of Tudor rule, the language of nurture became particularly striking. Mary I protested that 'if a Prince and Governour may as naturally and earnestly love her Subiectes as the Mother doth the Child, then assure your selves, that I being your Lady and Maistres, doe as earnestly and as tenderly love and favour you'. Both queens made profitable use of the idea that they were married to their country.[14] Mary drew attention to the 'spousall Ring' from her coronation, 'which never hetherto was, nor hereafter shall be left of', and reminded her subjects that they had 'promised your allegeaunce and obedience unto me'.[15] Elizabeth affirmed in a speech in 1559, that 'I am already bound unto an husband, which is the kingdom of England'.[16] The language of family ties was both strong and adaptable.

Those wielding power were called to account, perhaps haphazardly, but frequently. From debates in parliament, through legal judgements, to the varied moral voices of sermons or pamphlets or popular protest, different concepts of justice, responsibility and obligation were constantly under discussion. Many voices suggested that those who naturally possessed authority were not necessarily the best people to exercise it. John Rastell, the lawyer and MP who was Thomas More's brother-in-law, wrote a treatise on nobility, arguing that true gentility was based on virtue 'whych as well in pore men oft tymys we se / As in men of grete byrth of hye degre', noting also that those 'born to grete possessyons' could just as well prove 'vycious' and 'churlyssh'.[17] Those in authority might be reproached for failing in their duty to protect the people. In 1525, disaffected men in Kent, struggling to pay the so-called Amicable Grant, declared their willingness to give the king what they could, but declared that they 'woll in nowise geve at other mennys appointement whiche knowith not thaire neds'.[18] Their insistence that the demands made upon them needed to be considerate of their situation was a remarkable statement coming from the dispossessed. Equally striking was the fact that the king acknowledged the justice of their plea, and withdrew his demands.[19] In the same uprising, when the duke of Suffolk asked his tenants for help against those rebelling in Lavenham, they responded that 'they would defende hym from all perilles, if he hurte not their neighbors, but against their neighbors they would not fight'.[20] Society was layered with ties of obligation, and although the different limbs of the body politic were not always perfectly in harmony with one another, there was a rough and ready sense of where authorities exceeded the bounds of what was acceptable, and calls to bring them back into line.

It might be easy to assume that there was an inevitable gulf between rich and poor in Tudor England. A binary model of 'elite' and 'popular' is inadequate, however, to the task of analysing the social complexities of the age. It not only leaves out the middling sort central to so many interactions, but also overlooks considerations such as gender, age, kinship, occupation and local allegiance.[21] In particular, the assumption that relations between social groups must inevitably have been antagonistic has been shown to be deeply flawed.[22] Strong bonds of loyalty might bind together overlords and tenants. Shared religious and political convictions could cut across considerations of economic and social status, as the involvement of gentry and commons together in the Pilgrimage of Grace, or the Northern Rebellion of 1569, serves to demonstrate. Status depended on context: JPs powerful in the counties might still cringe when brought before the Privy Council.[23] At parish level, the subtle gradations of power were as significant as those between courtiers and ministers around the monarch.[24] In the last half century we have come to appreciate how Tudor politics were transacted at almost every layer of society, as much the business of the yeoman or peasant as the prelate or prince.[25]

The exercise of authority in the Tudor era was necessarily performative. It was not merely that kings and queens were expected to act out their majesty, their munificence and their piety. JPs and other office-holders were just as much required to act the right part.[26] For an alderman or a preacher, a lengthy beard and gown could be an important aspect of projecting the appropriate gravity; equally, the refusal to remove one's hat during a church court hearing could indicate a significant level of protest.[27] A badge of office was enough to render the office-holder a simulacrum of the authority he represented: in Thomas Middleton's 1602 play, *Blurt, Master-Constable*, the constable responds to a burglar's challenge by saying 'Do not you know this staff? I am sir, the duke's own image: at this time the duke's tongue . . . lies in my mouth.'[28] This reliance on performance will be discussed further in chapter 14, but it is important to see how it demonstrates the reciprocal nature of authority, and the limited coercive capabilities of those in power. Tudor authority was acted out precisely because it required audience participation to bring about its ends.

It was a far from straightforward matter to rule Tudor England; and it is not much easier to perceive how it was done across a gulf of several centuries. Confusion has often reigned precisely because so many aspects of Tudor government appear at first sight familiar. A monarch crowned in

Westminster Abbey; parliaments at Westminster, with a House of Lords, a House of Commons and a speaker; a legal system which relies on JPs at the local level and trial by jury for any case of importance: all these features survived to the modern age. Sheriffs, bailiffs, churchwardens; the universities of Oxford and Cambridge; the Inns of Court and the livery companies in the city of London: all these remain today. Yet these similarities are superficial at best, and frequently misleading. Tudor government was something distinct from its modern successors: far smaller, but often far tougher, and fracturing (when it did) along very different fault-lines. It was at the same time more violent and more religious, more ideological and more flexible, with inequalities of gender, wealth and status that would be anathema today, alongside a powerful sense of communal solidarity and responsibility that might put the modern world to shame.

Kingship and queenship

'The prince is the life, the head and the authority of all things that be done in the realm of England.'[29] This description by Thomas Smith, often cited to demonstrate the power of the Tudor monarchy, was in truth a double-edged observation, underlining how that power came with a heavy weight of responsibility. Thomas More emphasized the importance of giving good counsel to a ruler, on the grounds that 'a people's welfare or misery flows in a stream from their prince as from a never-failing spring'.[30] The knowledge that a kingdom's strength or weakness depended so directly on its ruler made the nature of kingship a keenly debated subject in the Tudor years. 'The breath of worldly men cannot depose / The deputy elected by the Lord', insists Shakespeare's Richard II, just before he is himself overthrown.[31] The strength, morality and extent of royal power was repeatedly brought under scrutiny, whilst the obligation of a ruler's subjects to advise and influence, criticize, or perhaps even challenge and subvert that power, was continually under discussion.

Edmund Dudley's treatise on commonwealth, written during imprisonment in the Tower in 1509, described the crowning moment of good kingship as the instant when God would say: 'I shall anoint thee a king eternall . . . and crown thee with the crown of mine own immortal glory and honour.'[32] This was an extraordinary vision, which demonstrates the laudatory capacities of early Tudor political thought. Divine sanction was confirmed by coronation, and signalled by royal crown-wearings at Christmas, Epiphany, Easter, Pentecost and All Saints.[33] It empowered kings as healers: at ritual points in the year, the monarch performed a ceremony of laying on of hands to cure the 'King's Evil', a scrofulous disease; at other points, including on Good Friday, he or she blessed rings for distribution to those suffering from what was probably epilepsy.[34] Elizabeth I seems to have discontinued this latter practice, but cramp rings would continue to be valued items: some were still in circulation in the 1790s.[35] Edward VI did not participate in touching for the 'King's Evil', possibly because of his youth, but both Mary I and Elizabeth I did. It may be that Elizabeth revived the practice after her excommunication by the papacy in 1570 to underline the fact that she still had divine approval, whatever the pope might say.[36] One of her surgeons, William Tooker, recorded several acts of healing by the queen, who declared how this was a direct gift from God, 'the greatest and best physician of all'.[37] This notion of the monarch channelling divine power would remain potent long after the Tudor dynasty had come to an end.

On the other hand, if divine sanction strengthened monarchical authority, it also imposed some stern obligations. Thomas Elyot warned that 'neither noble progeny, succession, nor election be of such force, that by them any estate or dignity may be so established, that god being stirred to vengeance, shall not shortly resume it'.[38] What God gave, he could also take away. The *Mirror for Magistrates*, a popular work first published in 1559, was based on the fifteenth-century text by John Lydgate, *The Fall of Princes* (itself based on a fourteenth-century work by Boccaccio).[39] In a series of verse tragedies, famous figures of the past recounted the reasons for their rise and fall; subsequent Elizabethan editions included additional lives, such as the sobering examples of Richard II, Henry VI and Richard III. Kingship which lacked virtue and providential blessing, it could be seen, might well end in usurpation and death. *The Education of a Christian Prince*, published by Erasmus in Latin in 1516, at first sight contains predictable admonitions about virtue, detachment and wise judgement; but in its insistence on the need to study good letters, rather than acquire military prowess, it struck at the heart of many assumptions about power. Its discussion of 'when a prince is born to office, not elected' could also be read as a tacit criticism of the very idea of rule by inheritance.[40] Erasmus's comparison of the king with the sun, put into the sky by God as a 'beautiful likeness of Himself', sounded like flattery; but here again was an implicit warning. 'The sun is freely shared by all and imparts its light to the rest of the heavenly bodies', and so, too, should a prince 'be readily accessible for all the needs of his people'.[41] Thomas Elyot's cautious translations of works by Plutarch and Isocrates contained carefully coded advice for Henry VIII. His *Pasquil the playne* of 1533 ostensibly discussed the nature of good counsel; but the classical notion of a 'pasquil' – a political comment or critique that could be submitted anonymously and therefore without fear – had inherently subversive undertones. Elyot's work encapsulated his fears about developments at Court in 1533, including what he perceived as the failure of good counsel, and the manipulation of a wilful and headstrong king by an evangelical faction.[42]

If advice to rulers was advanced cautiously, it was not just ambition or fear that stopped criticism from being too harsh. The monarch remained the linchpin of good order. As one obsequious Elizabethan minister observed to two eminent judges, 'so long as the Lord maintaineth the crowne upon the head of his annointed handmaid, and continueth our gracious Prince nurse royall of the Gospel, and mother of peace: we are to expect safely under such as you (Right worshipfull) being hir hands, and wings of defence'.[43] A more pragmatic statement of the same hierarchical idea was given by the Elizabethan JP and legal author William Lambarde to the juries of the quarter sessions at Maidstone in 1582: 'Our good Queen is the supreme executioner of all her laws. Between her Highness and you, in this part of the law, stand we that are justices of her peace. Between us and the offenders are you set chiefly that be sworn to inquire of offenses.'[44] Authority trickled down, through the social pyramid, layer by layer; but at the apex of that pyramid was the keystone, without which everything would fall apart. The Elizabethan homily 'Against Disobedience' reminded its audience that 'kings, queens, and other governors are specially appointed by the ordinance of God', and rejected justifications for rebellion against a bad ruler, observing 'what a perilous thing were it to commit unto the subjects the judgment which prince is wise and godly, and his government good, and which is otherwise'.[45] Yet subjects continued to make such judgements, and to remind monarchs of their duties. The opening sermon of Henry VII's first parliament in November 1485, given by John Alcock, bishop of Worcester and chancellor of England, discussed 'the loyalty which subjects continually and perseveringly owe to their kings', but equally noted 'the loyalty which kings and princes owe to their subjects'. Alcock likened them to bees, pointing out that 'the ruler of the bees is without a sharp sting', and drawing the conclusion that 'the ruler of rational men should exercise his authority with clemency, kindness and piety'.[46] In 1593, London leather-sellers, disputing the grant of a patent, reminded the lord treasurer that Henry VIII had declared 'that his mynde was never to ask anythinge of his comens that might sownde to his dishonor or to the breach of his Lawes'.[47]

It remained vital that rulers should secure the approval and coopera- tion of their subjects. Not only did they need popular consent to the voting and payment of taxes, but even more crucially, government depended upon the collaboration of a host of office-holders, many of them unpaid, serving on the basis of their sense of obligation. For those at Court filling advisory or administrative roles there might be substantial rewards; but for those in the villages acting as constables, jurors and churchwardens, there was little but the satisfaction of loyal service competently performed, and a measure of status within their small community. For everyone involved in the business of governance, it was necessary that the figure of the monarch should be convincing, commanding not only trust, but also affection, engendering a sense of godly protection and military security. The many public appearances of a monarch, therefore – from coronations to the opening of parliament, progresses, hunting trips, religious observ- ance, tournaments and touching for the 'King's Evil' – were all about rein- forcing the unwritten agreement between ruler and ruled. On the rare and therefore precious occasions when a monarch addressed the crowds direct, it was an indication of particularly strongly felt need for popular assent: Henry VIII more than once addressed a group of notables on the subject of his troubled conscience concerning his marriage to Katherine of Aragon, and made a speech on the day of Anne Boleyn's contentious coronation, trying to canvass his subjects' support.[48] Mary I, faced with the prospect of a rebel army advancing on London in 1554, appealed to the citizens at the Guildhall with extraordinary rhetorical skill; and in antici- pation of the Spanish Armada landing in 1588, Elizabeth I's speech at

Tilbury also went down in the annals. Public appearances usually involved popular engagement of some sort, from the aldermen invited to royal weddings and christenings, to the public bonfires and bell-ringing which celebrated royal victories, and the thousands of Londoners who attended court sermons, or tournaments.[49]

Much about the theory and practice of kingship was unchanging – indeed, self-consciously rooted in past tradition. And yet the Tudor era saw a fundamental change to kingship from the 1530s onwards. In his break with Rome, Henry VIII reconceptualized England as an empire, casting himself as God's foremost representative on English soil. His defence of the Supremacy was that it had returned 'his right and juste title of godly ministration and power over us, whereof he, and his moste noble progenytours, have ben unjustely, by usurpacion, longe deprived'. This was cast as an ideological revolution: 'Fantasies nor dremes, mens inventions do not nowe blynde or deceyve us any longer.'[50] England's independence from all foreign constraint was trumpeted: 'your Grace's realm, recognising no superior under God but only your Grace, hath been and is free from subjection to any man's laws but only to such as have been devised . . . within this realm.'[51] These claims were reiterated, with varying degrees of emphasis, by Henry's Protestant successors. Yet the long-term political consequences of Henry VIII's innovation might have given even him pause for thought. By welding his political authority so closely together with its godly sanction, he laid himself open to a kind of ideological challenge never previously envisaged. His claim to be both divinely sanctioned ruler and head of the English Church meant that anyone who questioned his right to be the second of those things might now have grounds for questioning the first. His legacy to his children was, on one level, an unprecedented measure of ideological confusion and the potential for a serious challenge to monarchical authority.

The complexities of contested political and religious loyalty became particularly intractable in the period 1540 to 1560. As Henry VIII persecuted both loyal Catholics and zealous Protestants, his authority was brought into question from both sides. When Edward VI began dismantling the old Church and replacing it with a Protestant settlement, many questioned not just whether he should do this, but also whether he could.[52] Mary I's reign saw the first coherent articulation of 'resistance theory', the idea that it was lawful to rebel against a monarch on religious grounds, initially advanced by Protestant authors, but later picked up and used by Catholics.[53] At its most extreme, opposition to a monarch involved talk of tyranny, perhaps using examples of tyrants from the classical past: the names of Nero or Caligula might easily be invoked as a byword for those who 'abound in wickednes'.[54] The putative tyrants of the sixteenth century, however, were more often viewed through the filter of religious division and conflict. When Pope Sixtus V accused Elizabeth I of 'exercysinge an absolute Tyrannie', his chief concern was not her style of rule, but her propagation of heresy.[55] If classical tyrants had been defined by the brutality of their methods, early modern tyrants were more often defined by the extent to which popular opinion cast them as heretics.

The second major challenge to Tudor kingship was the accession of a queen regnant for the first time in England's history, but how big a challenge this really was remains much debated.[56] It is often assumed that the authority of Mary I and Elizabeth I was compromised by their gender, and that their sovereignty was weakened by their inability to comply with the patriarchal expectations of the time.[57] The rhetoric deployed by John Knox in his *First Blast of the Trumpet Against the Monstruous Regiment of Women* suggested that female authority was a grotesque distortion of the natural order and that subjection to a woman's rule was akin to slavery. It should be remembered, however, that Knox was specifically attacking Catholic women in positions of power, and his condemnation was chiefly a reflection of his feelings about Catholicism. Women wielding power was not such an oddity: wealthy noblewomen customarily exercised authority as landowners, managed family concerns and acted as power-brokers at Court. Much of the criticism levelled at both Mary and Elizabeth reflected views about their religion, rather than their gender, even if their gender did give critics an added target for censure.[58] Although difficulties remained when it came to military leadership, these were not insuperable; male rulers, after all, did not always lead their troops into battle. Both queens showed ingenuity in developing their iconography to compensate for the difficulties caused by gender. Most of the challenges they faced in governing were not directly caused by the fact that they were women.

To exercise authority was one thing, however; to perpetuate a dynasty quite another. The real fragility of the Tudor queens was inseparably linked to their reproductive function. When one of the leading political minds of the age, Sir Thomas Smith, made a case for Elizabeth marrying, he did so in the form of a dialogue, putting both sides of the case. He dwelt at some length on the fact that women giving birth, 'be in such Danger of Death as at no time Men be more', noting that they prepared for it as other people prepared for death, and recalling former queens who had died as a result of childbirth.[59] Smith ultimately thought Elizabeth should marry, but he could see the risk, and so could Elizabeth, and Mary before her. When Mary told the London crowds that she would rather 'end her days in chastity', but felt duty bound to marry so that 'I might leave some fruit of my bodie behind me', she was probably speaking the truth.[60] Although this was particularly a problem for these female monarchs, it was a predicament that all early modern monarchs faced, as should be clear from the difficulties over the succession in the reigns of their father and brother, which had led one to break away from Christendom and the other to subvert the laws of inheritance, both of which were usually held sacred by Tudor society.

Shakespeare's *Julius Caesar* was written in the closing years of Elizabeth's reign. It depicted an aging and vainglorious ruler whose autocratic leadership renders the political classes deeply anxious. The contemporary resonance was guarded, but evident. The play interrogated the threat of tyranny and the alleged nobility of Brutus and Cassius, who assassinate Caesar to defend political freedom, with obvious significance for the political dilemmas of the time.[61] Yet the assassination of Julius Caesar in this play brings both personal morality and political stability into question, suggesting that however difficult, intractable or unjust a ruler might be, there was little alternative to monarchical rule. Ben Jonson's play, *Sejanus His Fall*, also written as Elizabeth's life drew to an end, depicted the aged and wayward Emperor Tiberius presiding over a corrupt court, and was full of echoes of Catholic resentment over persecution, and despair at political degeneracy. Yet it still contained a wistful idealization and defence of virtuous kingship, arguing that liberty 'Ne'er lovelier looks than under such a crown.'[62] The veneration of monarchical virtue and the longing for a wise, godly and fair-minded ruler was a constant in Tudor culture, perhaps felt all the more acutely at times when the reality was sadly far from the ideal.

'Skilful in all kind of martial feats': the Tudor nobility and gentry

No government would have been possible in Tudor England without the nobility and gentry, widely regarded as a linchpin of security and stability. The modern age views with hostility the idea of a caste distinguished by inherited wealth, privilege and power, but such animosity would have been incomprehensible to the Tudors. Both the principle and the practice of nobility were idealized in the sixteenth century, in terms of both private morality and public service.[63] The gentry, whose titles were less exalted than the nobles and whose lands were less extensive, nevertheless emulated them as much as possible in both military duty and civic responsibility.[64] Nobility and gentry alike remained essential to governance, deeply involved in the administration of justice, as well as in the management of the landed estates on which so many livelihoods depended. They were central to the provision of charity, education and artistic patronage; they helped to create provincial solidarity and prosperity; and, perhaps most important of all, they were the nation's chief line of defence in times of war or civil strife. In many of these activities, the role of women might be as important as that of men; and as courtiers, landowners, educators and scholars, Tudor noble-women exercised powerful influence over their families and localities, and often, too, over the workings of higher politics. For all that government may have centred upon the person of the monarch, in practice most people derived their most immediate experience of authority from their local lord and his family, turning to them for protection, support and a guarantee of their livelihood (see plate 13).

When Tudor theorists envisaged their polity as a body, then the nobility and gentry always had a substantial role to play: 'The knightes and the nobles holden the place of the hands and the armes. For lyke as the armes of a man ben stronge to meynteyne laboure and payne / so they ought to have the charge to defend the right of the prynce and the common wele.' These were the words of Christine de Pisan, the fourteenth-century feminist, published in translation in 1521.[65] She described them as 'the champyons that spende theyr blode / theyr body and theyr lyfe / for the honore of the prynce / and for the comon welthe'.[66] Christine could be cynical about the corrupting effects of power, but she respected the nobility. Many commentators of the age sounded the same notes of esteem, even veneration. Laurence Humfrey, president of Magdalen College Oxford, described in 1563 how the nobility 'flouryshe in all estates of honour, beare the sway in pryncely courtes' and were 'the piller and staye of all commen weales'.[67] In a dialogue between a knight, a merchant and a peasant published by John Rastell in 1536, the knight defended his importance to society, as one who had served as captain in 'every tyme of war', had put his life in jeopardy, kept a great house and punished the guilty, 'To the grete tranqaylyte of my contray'.[68] When William Thomas, in his 1549 *Historie of Italie*, described the return of the Medici to fifteenth-century Florence, he saw it as the salvation of the city that aristocratic rule had been restored.[69]

In Elizabeth I's reign, her chief minister Lord Burghley recorded his anxiety that she had not created more noblemen, leaving the realm 'disfurnished of principal persons to govern her people'.[70] Nobles and gentry were expected to serve in government. In 1536, the Lincolnshire rebels criticized Henry VIII's choice of ministers, deploring that 'yor grace takes of yor counsell and being a bowte you such persons as be of low byrth and small reputation'.[71] Those who joined the Pilgrimage of Grace vowed themselves 'to the purifying of the nobility, and to expulse all villain blood and evil councillors against the commonwealth from his grace and his privy council of the same'.[72] England's landowners were expected 'to take hede of the comon welthe . . . to kepe and mayntayne Iustyce after theyr degree as well as the prynce. And to be lyberall and piteous / and to love the wyse and good men / and governe them by good and sad counsayle'.[73] They were the connecting tissue between central authority and the populace at large.[74] Their standing at Court depended on their performance in the localities; the more useful they could be at home, the more valued they were by the monarch. Somewhere between 60 per cent and 90 per cent of Elizabethan courtiers were also MPs or JPs.[75] Their localities were their responsibility. With Spanish invasion imminent in the 1580s, the Council considered appointing one of their number, Lord Howard of Effingham, as lord lieutenant for the West Country, but Elizabeth vetoed the suggestion and instead appointed men of lesser standing who had strong local ties, such as Sir Walter Raleigh in Cornwall.[76] Even Catholic peers could still be required to serve Elizabeth: in Sussex, the five most important peers at the start of Elizabeth's reign were all Catholics, and even after the 1569 Northern Rebellion, leadership was shared between the Protestant Lord Buckhurst and the Catholic Lord Montague.[77]

Much of Tudor society might never set eyes upon the monarch; the local magnate represented authority to them. The Stanleys, influential in Cheshire and Lancashire since the fourteenth century, were further strengthened by the marriage of Thomas Stanley to Lady Margaret Beaufort and his subsequent ennoblement as the first earl of Derby. His successors led an army several thousand strong against the Pilgrimage of Grace in 1536, and served as ambassadors abroad, landlords and office-holders at home.[78] Returning home from London in 1597, the sixth earl was met at the county border by the sheriff of Cheshire and around five hundred horsemen; crossing into Lancashire the next day, he was welcomed by seven hundred horsemen and an open-air banquet.[79] The fourth duke of Norfolk, overlord of most of East Anglia between the late 1550s and 1572, lived in great splendour in mansions in Norwich and London, and in country seats at Kenninghall, Framlingham, Thetford, Castle Acre and Castle Rising, owning over 16,000 sheep and usually nominating the MPs for the region. He famously considered himself 'as good a prince at home in my bowling-alley at Norwich' as Mary Stuart was in the heart of Scotland. He was instrumental in the carving out of a new harbour at Yarmouth, which was essential to the region's prosperity; he gave liberally towards poor relief; and he persuaded the queen to allow 300 refugees from the Netherlands to settle in Norwich, boosting the city's economic resurgence. He also helped them to find a church building there that they could use.[80] He told William Cecil, 'I wold have bene sorye that my cuntrye mene schuld have hade cawse to have judged that enye matter concerning the Quenes Majestyes sarvys in Norfolke or Suffolke shulde rather thave bene committyd off first to others than to me.'[81] His disgrace and execution in 1572 left his locality seriously unsettled.

Noble households were in themselves a kind of commonwealth, with a series of officers including steward, comptroller, surveyor, receiver and auditor, as well as a host of minor functionaries from gentleman usher and gentleman of the horse, to cellarer, baker, brewer and slaughterman.[82] Many nobles also maintained or patronized companies of players and minstrels.[83] Henry Percy, fifth earl of Northumberland in the reigns of Henry VII and Henry VIII, maintained a household with 166 domestic servants. Seventeen carriages were required to move the household effects between properties.[84] The earl of Rutland in 1539 had a household including four chaplains, a secretary, a schoolmaster, two minstrels, five laundry-women, two joiners, two glaziers, a carpenter and a surgeon.[85] Even minor nobility or gentry were careful to assert their social status through domestic display: the plasterwork exhibiting the arms of the Wynn family in their Elizabethan house Plas Mawr, in Conwy, gives a vivid sense of their importance (see plate 14). Most peers and many knights also broadcast their status by maintaining a chapel, understood by contemporaries to mean not an ecclesiastical building, so much as a body of people to celebrate daily services.[86] Northumberland had a chapel of twenty-eight people, including nine adult singers and six choristers.[87] The patterns of worship in these chapels could be as elaborate as that in any parish church and were not just found in noble households: there were at least seventeen private chapels in the gentry houses of fifteenth-century Warwickshire.[88] The bible story of Dives and Lazarus, with the humble poor man in heaven and the selfish rich man in hell, was a frequently cited reminder of the duties of the rich to be charitable.[89] In 1586, the fourth earl of Derby was helping to support over eighty poor families in Prescot.[90]

Landowning families usually claimed illustrious heritage, but the social hierarchy was not nearly as fixed as we might assume. Nobility could be acquired in a single generation by those determined and talented enough. Of the sixty-two peers of the realm in 1560, only twenty-five had titles that went back before 1509.[91] In Norfolk, only 14 per cent of heraldic families in the early modern period could claim a fifteenth-century gentry forebear and at least 20 per cent were connected with trade.[92] John Russell came from a West Country family that had grown prosperous in the wine trade, but if the family story is to be believed, it was his linguistic ability that gave him his lucky break: when King Philip and Queen Juana of Castile were shipwrecked in Dorset, Russell was called upon to act as interpreter. He thus attracted the attention of Henry VII and came to Court, where he jousted, hunted and, in due course, fought in earnest alongside Henry VIII, losing an eye in 1522 to an arrow at the siege of Morlaix, and confirming his place among the great men of the day. His service under Edward VI earned him the earldom of Bedford in 1550. Despite all the grand claims to exalted ancestry, many nobles were new arrivals, rewarded for their military or political service.

The importance of the nobility was not being eroded by the 'new men' of the professional classes, although the expansion of government did bring many eager, talented, educated individuals into royal service. Those who achieved political or military success wanted nothing more than to join the ranks of the nobility, often creating a genealogy to support their claims, whilst in Wales, bardic tradition was deployed not only to preserve, but also to foster a sense of noble lineage.[93] Sir William Compton, who served Henry VIII as groom of the stool for nearly twenty years, was the son of a Warwickshire farmer worth £5 per year. By the end of his life, he had an annual income of around £1,500; and his descendants have continued as marquesses of Northampton to the present day.[94] Thomas Cromwell, the brewer's son from Putney who became Henry VIII's chief minister, arranged the marriage of his son Gregory to Jane Seymour's sister, and sought to endow his new-found dynasty with land and wealth. Cromwell himself died a traitor's death; but at Henry VIII's funeral, Gregory, now Baron Cromwell, was one of six noblemen who carried the canopy in procession above the king's coffin.[95] William Cecil was born into a minor gentry family, but his brilliance as Elizabeth's chief counsellor saw him ennobled as Lord Burghley: he built grand houses (see illustration 11) and commissioned genealogies to create the illusion of an illustrious heritage. His descendants still carry the titles of marquess of Exeter and marquess of Salisbury.[96] Talent had always been an acceptable route to nobility: the de la Pole family were originally wool merchants from Hull; the Spencers began as sheep farmers; and the Howards traced their descent back to a thirteenth-century lawyer in Lynn. Those who founded their careers on ability, rather than heredity, did not undermine the nobility; on the contrary, they revitalized it.

In 1524, there were about 200 knightly families and fewer than 5,000 lesser esquires and gentlemen; by 1600, there were roughly 500 knightly families and perhaps as many as 16,000 esquires and gentlemen.[97] In 1592, Richard Johnson's *Nine Worthies of London* celebrated nine great Londoners who had risen to wealth and influence: they included a fishmonger, two vintners, two grocers, a weaver, a tailor and a mercer.[98] The noble ideal was not being directly challenged here, but it was acquiring a new dimension, including a fresh emphasis on civility and manners.[99] Religious change also added something new. Philip Sidney's death after the battle of Zutphen left

11. Burghley House

onlookers mourning 'the loss of so rare a gentleman . . . so accomplished with all kind of virtue and true nobility'.[100] His nobility had an added dimension, however, for not only did his death represent the apotheosis of chivalric virtue, but it was also a perfect example of a godly Protestant demise, as he spent his last hours in prayer, repentance and thought for others.[101] Humfrey, in 1563, had propounded a Protestant agenda for the nobility, hoping to see 'this chosen order . . . seasoned wyth right and christian opinions'.[102] The concept of nobility was something that could be adapted to the changing circumstances of the sixteenth century. A striking Tudor evocation of chivalric values was found in Edmund Spenser's verse epic from the 1590s, *The Faerie Queene*, which the author declared was intended to 'fashion a gentleman or noble person in vertuous and gentle discipline'.[103] Yet Spenser himself was not born a gentleman, and his poetry was subtly critical of chivalric values.[104] Nobility, as an abstract concept encompassing virtue and strength, was to be interrogated, as well as cherished.

For all its traditions of service, nobility was not without the potential to cause difficulties at the centre of power. In the fifteenth century, Henry VII was not the only king risen from the ranks of the nobility to claim the throne. The first two Tudors worked hard to manage their nobility and Henry VIII was compelled to curb the ambitions of several great magnates, including the duke of Buckingham in 1521 and the duke of Norfolk and his son, the earl of Surrey, in 1546–47. In Wales, Rhys ap Gruffydd was executed in 1531 on arguably spurious grounds; but if he was not culpable of treason, he was definitely guilty of ambition.[105] At the end of the era, in 1601, Elizabeth I would face a serious threat from the earl of Essex that was in part founded on a sense of noble entitlement.[106] A high ideal of chivalric honour might be a necessary source of self-belief on the battle-field, but it could be a dangerous liability at other times. Privilege could also be misused, as demonstrated by the career of Edward de Vere, earl of Oxford, perpetually seeking funds to support his extravagance; scandal-ously estranged from his wife Anne, who was Cecil's daughter; suspiciously attached to a beautiful choirboy he brought back from Venice; killing a cook whilst practising fencing, but defending himself by claiming that the unfortunate man had committed suicide by impaling himself on the point of Oxford's sword; fathering an illegitimate child by Elizabeth's lady-in-waiting Anne Vavasour; and in consequence being imprisoned in the Tower. His saving graces were his outstanding gifts as a poet and his ability to charm Elizabeth.[107]

Power in the localities could also be abused at times. In the turbulent atmosphere of 1487, Sir Edmund Bedingfield wrote to John Paston to tell him how he had been coerced by the county elite – 'them that I myght not sey ney to' – into a meeting with those who looked to oppose the new king. He had been reluctant to agree with them, 'but they thought in asmoche as they ware the beste in the shere, that every man owghte to wayte and go with them'.[108] Those who failed in their duties to their tenants and to the poor, or in other ways fell short of the standards of noble behaviour, were widely recognized as breaking a moral, as well as a political code, however. In general, nobility and gentry sought to buttress government, rather than undermine it.

Underlying every other aspect of identity of the nobility was their military purpose, because at root, their social status was predicated upon their skill in warfare. The young noble must be 'norisshed and excersised in disciplines, doctrine, and usage of scole of armes', admonished the *Boke of noblesse*, spec-ifying that this should include the ability to joust, and fight with spear, axe, sword and dagger, as well as being adept at wrestling, leaping and running.[109] This emphasis was not lost even as the tide of Renaissance learning rose: a century later, when Sir Humphrey Gilbert designed an educational establish-ment for Elizabeth I's wards, he also emphasized the importance of martial skills: 'to teache noble men and gentlemen to ride, make, and handle a ready horse, exercizing them to runne at Ringe, Tilte, Towrney, and cowrse of the fielde, yf they shalbe armed. And also to skirmish on horsbacke with pistolles.' He saw mathematics as helpful in understanding fortifications and artillery, philosophy as useful in understanding military strategy.[110] His curriculum also included Greek and Latin grammar and literature, with an emphasis on learning oratory, which might be useful 'in preaching, in parliament, in Cownsell, in Commyssion, and other offices of Common Weale'. Civic duty and military skill were to go hand in hand.

Military history is too often studied separately from other developments; but the preparation, prosecution and impact of warfare were immensely influential in shaping the society of the time. Contemporaries talked ceaselessly about war, governments planned for it and society itself was organized in order to maximize the potential of the military orders.[111] The burden of responsibility rested upon the major landowners, who were expected to arm their tenants and, along with their retainers, lead their forces into battle as and when the king commanded.[112] John Aylmer reminded England's gentry in his work of 1559 that just as they had been blessed with property and privilege, so they were duty bound to defend their country: 'to serve the quene with your bodies, but help also with your goodes'.[113] Thomas Cromwell made sure that his London house was well stocked with weapons: 400 pikes, 759 bows, 459 bills, 272 handguns and armour for more than 600 men, all of which were shown off at the great London muster of 1539.[114] The epitome of virtue remained the noble and skilful warrior. Niccolo Machiavelli was best known to the Tudors as the author of *The Art of War*, published in English in 1562. The translator Peter Whitehorne explained that military skill 'cannot easely finde roote, but in the hartes of moste noble couragious and manlike personages'. Whitehorn, himself a professional soldier who had fought with Imperial forces in North Africa, hoped that 'our Englishemen', through reading this tome, 'might no lesse in knowledge of warres become incomperable', then in prowes also and exercise of the same, altogether invincible'.[115]

Every Tudor reign saw the aggrandizement of men who had rendered loyal service in battle – or, in the case of Thomas Wolsey, through the successful organization of the war of 1512–13: a man who could organize the transport of tons of beef and thousands of barrels of beer, as well as an army, across the Channel was a man Henry VIII knew he needed. When the fate of the Howard family hung in the balance after they backed the losing side at Bosworth in 1485, loyal service to Henry VII won back Thomas Howard his title of earl of Surrey; but it was by fighting the Scots and defeating them so convincingly at Flodden in 1513 that he regained the dukedom of Norfolk. The dukes of Somerset and Northumberland, who would rule England during Edward VI's reign, had both risen to prominence in Henry VIII's wars. The earl of Essex built his reputation in the later part of Elizabeth's reign on his military record, having fought in the Netherlands in 1585–86, taken part in the 'Portugal voyage' of 1589, commanded an army in Normandy in 1591–92 and led attacks on Spain in 1596–97, before leading the army to Ireland in 1599.[116] For all his erudition, classical learning and courtly sophistication, he was represented both by himself and by his followers as a soldier first and foremost.

Defence of the realm abroad could be complemented by defending the regime at home. A veteran of foreign wars (back in 1513, he had brought a retinue of 4,437 men to fight the French), the fourth earl of Shrewsbury was perturbed to hear news of the Pilgrimage of Grace on 4 October 1536. By 10 October, he had raised 3,659 men to fight the king's cause.[117] In 1549, the Council sent Sir John Russell to deal with a rebellion in the south-west, warning him that he was also to deal with any foreign invasions from the Scots or the French. In a series of letters, written in an increasingly agitated tone, he was told to keep the south-west 'in good order and quiet', rally the local JPs and gentry and co-opt their help, order masters and fathers to govern their children and servants better, and make sure that the notoriously dissident clothworkers were 'kept occupied'. He was also to marshal a military force to confront the rebels. This last point called for diplomacy, as well as military strength. He was warned 'before you shall attempt any enterprise agains them … lett them understand theyr dysobedyence' and was advised to persuade them to go home quietly, if he could. This was a well-nigh impossible brief. The fact that Russell succeeded, for the most part, in fulfilling the Council's expectations explains why he was subsequently able to found a noble dynasty.

Studies of the Tudor nobility have usually looked chiefly at men.[118] Only recently has research into the lives of noblewomen begun to give a fuller picture of how noble power was sustained and exercised at court and in the localities by female agency and by the workings of family networks more generally.[119] The rule of two Tudor queens underlined the point that wealthy, high-born women could exercise power. Four of Henry VIII's queen consorts had previously been ladies of the Court, and before they came to the throne, both Mary I and Elizabeth I were among the wealthiest and most influential of English landowners.[120] Women as land-owners and litigators are the easiest to see in the records; women as matri-archs, marriage-brokers and the builders of patronage networks are also visible. Broadly speaking, the alleged historical invisibility of women can have as much to do with the prejudice of the historian as with any inade-quacies in the historical archive.[121] Nor should it be assumed that women were restricted to traditional female roles: the activities of Tudor noble-women had as much political and economic importance as domestic, and legal and ideological inequalities were repeatedly rendered irrelevant by wealth and position – and often, too, by force of character.[122]

The life of a noblewoman could be subject to considerable strain – not least the all-important work of procreation. In the period 1450–1550, 94 per cent of the daughters of peers and knights married at least once, and 91 per cent of the wives of peers and knights bore at least one surviving child.[123] To consolidate alliances, girls of royal or noble birth were betrothed, and often married, while still very young, and attempts to protect them against falling pregnant at too early an age were sporadic. Margaret Beaufort gave birth at the age of thirteen; but in two subsequent marriages she had no more children, having probably been damaged by the experience. She intervened to protect her young granddaughter Margaret from a similar fate when, also aged thirteen, she married James IV of Scotland.[124] The necessity of building alliances and producing heirs meant that relatively few noble and gentry women entered the monastic life before the Reformation, and although some of them extended patronage to convents, they were more likely to endow chantries and give to their local parish churches or charitable causes.[125]

While men fought on the battlefield, women had to wage a different set of battles, and they were frequently the ones tasked with protecting the next generation. The earl of Surrey was imprisoned by Henry VII in 1485 for fighting on the side of Richard III at Bosworth, where his father John Howard, the duke of Norfolk, was killed. His wife Elizabeth swiftly took their children into sanctuary on the Isle of Sheppey, and wrote to the earl of Oxford to plead that her inheritance be secured, since her husband's lands were forfeit when he was attainted.[126] Women's political involvement frequently focused on the defence of their family interests. Mary Neville,

Lady Dacre, commissioned two portraits of herself from Hans Eworth, both celebrating her long campaign to win back the lands that were forfeited in 1541, when her husband was executed for murder. One depicts Lady Dacre wielding the pen with which she had fought her battle (see plate 15); the other shows her with her son and heir, for whom she had regained their estates.[127] Her identity and honour were inextricably bound up with those of her husband and son, but by no means eclipsed by either.

The importance of noble and gentry women within an array of overlapping circles of political authority, cultural influence and social agency demands clearer recognition; but so, too, does the realization that such women were defined by a great deal more than just their gender. Their experience was shaped by their place within their kinship networks, tied to the biological imperative of begetting the next generation and moulded by the demands of the household and locality. In this, they would locate themselves, by turns, in the contexts of family interests, communal preoccupations and religious observation. They might be influenced by independent study of humanist texts or of the Bible; they could be caught up in the drive for evangelical reform or the defence of a beleaguered faith; they could be inspired to write or to encourage other writers. And all the time they benefited alternately, according to what was required, from either their prominence in terms of social status or their relative invisibility as women. Tudor society may have had its constraints and restrictions, but for the women of the landowning classes, this was also an age of opportunity.

'Now cracks a noble heart', says Horatio over the dying Hamlet. The phantasm of true nobility, like the model of the chivalric knight, was something for which the Tudor imagination yearned. Despite the growth of the professional orders and the intermittent scorn of the dispossessed, the allure of heroic integrity, martial yet godly valour and fearless leadership never faded. The roles, symbols, rituals and demeanour of nobles and knights were universally recognizable on the battlefield, in parliament or in procession, in art, poetry and drama. Names such as Sir Philip Sidney, Sir Walter Raleigh and Robert Devereux, earl of Essex, were all still luminous as the Tudor era ended, and bitterness over the loss of Essex endured for years after his death.[128] Noblemen of repute could inspire passionate devotion in their followers. And yet the concept of nobility was fiercely debated, and the notion of what constituted true virtue was pulled back and forth by political commentators, poets and playwrights, lawyers and rebels. As the Tudor era drew to a close, a 1595 book translated from the Italian, and prefaced by sonnets from a formidable array of poets and scholars, asked whether noble birth or merit made a man 'greater in nobilitie'. It reached the conclusion that nobility of mind was far superior to that based on lineage and wealth.[129] Yet it was dedicated to the earl of Essex, fiercely proud of his ancient lineage, who then compounded the irony by falling dramatically from grace, demonstrating that the flower of chivalry might have a canker at its heart.[130] The debate was left unresolved. Nevertheless, the lustre of chivalric legend and reverence for knightly virtue reflected a very real and pragmatic longing for the combination of military protection, political skill and good lordship that the ruling orders of Tudor England were supposed to embody.

Parliaments and the law

The authority of the landed orders may have been reinforced by their formal representation in parliaments, but debates there also had to take account of the needs of the realm as a whole. Everyone's rights were underpinned, meanwhile, by a legal system extrapolated from royal justice and parliamentary judgement, but also from common custom. In large part, laws were implemented by the nobility and gentry, and yet the rights of the landowning classes were matched by an emphasis on their moral and legal obligations to those beneath them. The law did not just confirm the hegemony of the wealthy: it frequently provided a defence and a tool for the dispossessed.[131] In society at large, the potential of the legal system was widely acknowledged and deployed by those seeking redress; it could also be subverted or adapted in the course of its implementation at the parish level. Customary law in the localities might have even greater weight than any legal code handed down from Westminster, whilst Tudor society was highly attentive to questions of honour and reputation, and social expectations might prove as powerful as any statute. The complex web of constraints that sustained social order was thus shaped as much by informal assumptions as by formal legal process, and popular agency mattered.

Given the later history of parliament as an institution with a central role in government, it is hard to turn the clock back to a time when parliaments were more of an occasion than an institution, and when their authority was closely bound up with that of the king, the nobility and the higher clergy. The conundrum has been compared to reading a detective story from the beginning when you have already read the last chapter and discovered the perpetrator of the crime.[132] There was a long-held assumption that Tudor parliaments were a crucible for constitutional advance, and a place where popular resistance to monarchical power had begun to crystallize. Discerning the true role played by parliaments has proved all the more difficult, since much was claimed for them by certain commentators in the sixteenth century, and so much more by those embroiled in the political upheavals and conflicts of the seventeenth century. The innate conservatism of Tudor parliaments, and the extent to which they were fundamentally an extension of royal power, has only recently become more evident.[133] Henry VIII told the parliament of 1543 that 'we at no time stand so highly in our estate royal as in the time of parliament'.[134] Unlike modern parliaments, the Tudor versions had no automatic right of existence. They were called by the monarch when needed, dismissed when no longer useful, and it was quite usual for years to pass without one. When a parliament was called, the Crown was in a position to exercise influence over elections, which were, in any case, rarely contested.[135] Sheriffs would call together all the forty-shilling freeholders in a county town on the day when the county court usually sat, and they would shout out the name of the candidate they wanted – as far as we can tell, mostly with one voice. Those elected to represent the boroughs usually spoke for the established urban elite. MPs were, in any case, frequently the clients of courtiers or nobility: the duke of Norfolk generally directed the choice in at least eight local boroughs, and even minor gentry might influence the choice of a local candidate.[136] This was usually intended as a reward for a client, rather than as an incitement to action. Parliamentary procedures all indicated that parliaments were expected to be cooperative ventures. Successive Tudor monarchs expected their collaboration and expressed both surprise and indignation if it was not forthcoming. Meanwhile, the speaker of the Commons remained a crown appointee.[137] In the wake of Thomas Wyatt's rebellion in 1554, Mary I threatened to move the next parliament to Oxford, since London's loyalty had been called into question – a possible withdrawal of royal favour that was viewed with dismay.[138] The pageantry with which parliaments opened, meanwhile, with the monarch's procession to Westminster, was an echo of the coronation processions and reiterated how the majesty of the monarch was rooted in the consent of his subjects.[139]

Yet parliaments were far from servile. If Tudor MPs harboured no thoughts of constitutional opposition, they still had plenty to say on the issues they discussed. Records are patchy, but sufficient testimony has survived to show that parliaments in the period were the focus of heated expression and debate, and were viewed as important by observers, as well as participants. Many bills were proposed, although hundreds of them did not make it into law, failing to secure the consent of one house or the other, or being vetoed by the Crown. Much advice was addressed to the monarch and his or her Council. Elizabeth was particularly the target of recommendations concerning marriage, religion, the necessity of executing Mary Queen of Scots and the succession. It is noticeable, however, that Elizabeth almost never did what a parliament asked; and it is equally striking that parliaments did not attempt to coerce either her or her predecessors into any course of action by threatening to withhold their consent to taxation. Parliamentary debates were less a battle of wills than attempts to produce informed and useful agreement. Sir Thomas Smith, one of the more articulate MPs of Elizabeth's reign, wrote a dialogue in 1561 in which he put into the mouth of one of his disputants the words: 'What can a commonwealth desire more than peace, liberty, quietness, little taking of base money, few parliaments, their coin amended, friendship with their neighbours, war with no man?'[140] The absence of parliament signalled political tranquillity, not repression; and when parliament was called, it was usually because the realm faced a challenge for which the monarch needed to co-opt the help of his subjects. There could be an apologetic tone to the writs sent out by different monarchs to summon a parliament, and they frequently tried to give good reasons for all the trouble and expense a parliament would cause. In 1593, Elizabeth I was praised at the opening of parliament in the chancellor's speech for being a monarch 'most loth to call for the assembly of her people in parliament'.[141] Parliaments were therefore viewed more as an occasionally necessary evil, than as a chance to seize the political initiative.

Parliaments did undergo some important changes in the Tudor period, even if these alterations did not have the huge political and constitutional significance which once was claimed for them. At the most basic level, parliamentary record-keeping improved. From 1497, the clerk of the parliaments, who kept a register of all the acts passed, began to keep those records himself, rather than pass them on to the Chancery, thereby laying the basis for the parliament office. In addition, both Lords and Commons began to keep journals: that from the House of Lords survives from 1510 onwards; that from the Commons from 1547. A daily attendance register was begun in 1515.[142] The integration of Wales brought about a change in personnel, as did the Reformation.[143] Before the Dissolution, the House of Lords usually contained forty-eight spiritual peers, made up of twenty-one bishops and twenty-seven abbots, alongside just forty-three secular peers. The loss of the abbots left the bishops as a sometimes beleaguered minority in the Lords, just as the onset of religious change brought serious ideological conflict into play for the first time in England's history. The result was the emergence of a potentially dissident minority group within a body that historically had been expected to support and confirm the royal will. Those bishops who were brave enough to oppose Henry VIII's wishes in the 1530s and 1540s paved the way for the extraordinary spectacle in 1559 when all but one of the bench of bishops defied Elizabeth, in opposition to her religious settlement. From 1549, the spatial setting for parliaments altered, too. The House of Commons began meeting in St Stephen's Chapel at Westminster, whereas previously they had met in Westminster Abbey's chapter house, with occasional summons to the parliament chamber in Westminster Palace, where they were not permitted to pass beyond the bar. This is clear from the depiction of Henry VIII's parliament, where the Commons appear as temporary visitors to a gathering of which they form no integral part (see illustration 12). After 1549, with their own chamber, the Commons had a more permanent presence, although they still appeared in a subservient role at the opening or closing ceremonies.

More than anything else, it was Henry VIII's calculated decision to advance his claim to rule the English Church by co-opting parliament that brought about a change in the role of parliaments. The so-called 'Reformation Parliament' met first in November 1529 and – most unusually – was not

12. Henry VIII in parliament

finally dissolved until April 1536, by which time its members had been compelled and coerced to think the unthinkable.[144] At the same time, Henry was using language which emphatically located the king's legislative authority within the setting of parliament: in 1534, law-making power was described as belonging to 'your royal majesty and your Lords spiritual and temporal and Commons, representing the whole state of your realm in this your most High Court of Parliament'.[145] This was not Henry being constitutionally high-minded, but rather desperate for support, as he sought to render his newly fledged Supremacy credible. It did mean, however, that he was co-opting parliamentary power as never before, and from that time forward all major religious changes had to involve parliamentary consent. All three of Henry's children later faced significant opposition to their religious policies from their Lords and Commons. Before the parliament of 1584, the Privy Council was sending out missives like the one to Lord Cobham, which warned him that the queen wanted 'great care used in the choosing of the burgesses' and asked him to use his influence with the Cinque Ports, 'and to exhort them . . . to have an especial regard in their choice of burgesses, that they may be not only discreet and sufficient persons but known to be well affected in religion and towards the present state of this government'.[146] The most outspoken interventions in parliamentary debate all seem to have stemmed from religious zealots. In 1576, Peter Wentworth famously took a stand on freedom of speech, insisting that 'there is nothing so necessary for the preservation of the prince and state . . . and without it it is a scorn and mockery to call it a Parliament house, for in truth it is none, but a very school of flattery and dissimulation'. This apparently liberal intervention needs to be set in the context of his next comment: that without free speech, parliament would become 'a fit place to serve the Devil and his angels in, and not to glorify God and benefit the commonwealth'.[147] Wentworth's opinion, for which an indignant Commons sent him to prison, was founded on his desire to press openly for further Protestant reforms. He was protesting in particular at the 'doleful message', as he called it, that parliaments 'should not deal in any matters of religion'. To him, this was as bad as saying 'Sirs, ye shall not deal in God's causes, no, ye shall in no wise seek to advance His glory'.[148] What was at stake here was not incipient democracy, but Protestant ardour.

Thomas Smith wrote that the 'most high and absolute power of the realme of England is in the Parliament'.[149] This is easily misunderstood if parliaments are imagined as in any sense autonomous; Elizabethan commentators envisaged them as integral parts of a broader conjunction of authorities and the embodiment of mutual agreement. Richard Hooker described parliaments as 'the body of the whole Realm', explaining that 'it consisteth of the *King* and of all that within the *Land* are subject unto him for they all are there present either in person, or by such as they voluntarily have derived their very personal right unto'.[150] John Aylmer, defending female rule in 1559, painted a picture of the queen surrounded by lawyers, counsellors, parliaments, all of which simultaneously strengthened her power whilst directing her will. He insisted that 'it is not she that ruleth but the lawes, the executors whereof be her iudges, appoynted bi her', and that to avoid making mistakes in appointing them, rulers 'have theyr counsel at their elbow'.[151]

If parliaments embodied the consensual and collaborative workings of Tudor government, the laws they passed served to regulate the balance of society more broadly. The English legal system, which in the 1530s expanded to integrate Wales, too, was extraordinarily sophisticated and widely respected at every level.[152] It had the sanction of long tradition: trial by jury and the system of assizes dated back to the twelfth century. In all essentials, the legal system of England endured from the thirteenth century until the twentieth: the hall of Oakham Castle, for example, was the seat of the assize court from 1229 to 1970. The legal system was also the concentration of some deeply held convictions concerning morality, social order and social obligation.[153] The fact that the vast majority of disputes were resolved at an early stage by compromise solutions underlines the fact that law was widely understood as a means of healing conflict, rather than achieving domination.[154] The interweaving of legal and moral discourse in the 'charges' (which were the instructions addressed to most kinds of local courts) and the sermons (which preceded the holding of the assize courts) emphasizes how legal process was expected to underpin moral teaching. Legal process embraced a bewildering array of social problems. *The Boke of Justices of Peas*, published in 1505, contained a charge intended to be read aloud at the start of quarter sessions, reminding the JPs of their duties: these included tackling everything from murder and rape to the restrictions on playing football and the problem of lost falcons.[155] Finally, the enduring importance of the church courts in regulating society, dealing with questions of sexual morality, matrimony, defamation, heresy and the behaviour of the clergy, accentuates the extent to which law could permeate every aspect of human experience and attempt to regulate the day-to-day problems of ordinary people.[156]

The legal profession was an integral part of Tudor society, although not always a very popular one, gleefully satirized in plays and ballads.[157] Shakespeare made repeated references to the law in his plays; and if some of them were scathing, the triumph of true justice in *Measure for Measure* and the appeal to mercy by Portia in *The Merchant of Venice* demonstrate just how exalted a view might be taken of the workings of the legal system at its best.[158] The legal profession was also growing in this period. The century after 1550 has been seen as a 'watershed' in its history, embedding reverence for the law in English culture and enhancing the status of its practitioners.[159] The Inns of Court became what was effectively England's third university.[160] Lawyers were needed in increasing numbers because the amount of litigation, particularly from the 1560s onwards, was growing at a startling rate in every kind of court, including the local courts and the church courts.[161] A significant number of lawsuits were brought by women, particularly those anxious to clear their own or their husband's name of dishonour: by 1600, perhaps as many as half of the church court cases were brought by women.[162] Thomas Wilson, writing about rhetoric in 1585, observed that 'the Lawyer can never want living till the earth . . . be voyde', wryly testifying to the prominence of lawyers within Elizabethan society.[163] It has been suggested that the late sixteenth and early seventeenth centuries were more litigious than any other era of English history.[164]

The law might be crafted and wielded by the rich, but it could also be the refuge of the poor.[165] As other certainties were called into question during the sixteenth century, an already litigious nation turned more and more towards the law courts to settle their quarrels, defend their interests, protect their families and preserve their good name. It took thirty-one copyhold tenants of Wigston Magna in Leicestershire twenty years, but in the end, in 1588, they defeated their lord at law, and he was compelled to sell them their holdings.[166] Manorial courts testified to the need for legal redress at every level of society, but also to the involvement of local inhabitants in the presentment and judgement of offences.[167] Ordinary people might utilize the law for their own purposes, just as at other times they might consciously eschew formal legal process for the sake of maintaining communal harmony.[168] What a judge or puritan minister might deem a disorderly tavern could seem, at parish level, like good hospitality, better left unchecked. The population at large was just as likely to initiate legal process as to avoid it, however. One consequence of the proliferation of lawyers in this period was to make it all the more believable that the law could be utilized as a tool to be wielded by ordinary men and women.[169] It could also, of course, be used as a means to coerce and control dissident elements. Magistrates wielded significant influence, and many cases were decided on their sole authority. Bridewells were established to discipline the poor – in London in 1553 and thereafter in many different towns – and punishments there could be harsh.[170] Even so, the intention of the bridewell, however imperfectly realized, was to promote moral reform and industriousness, not solely to punish.[171]

Law was a refuge for kings and peasants alike. When monarchs destroyed their enemies, they tried to do so by due process of law; and when peasants sought retribution against their oppressors, it was again to the law that they appealed. In every legal record from this time, there is both an interrogation and an acknowledgement of authority, as the crime which transgressed the law is identified, investigated and judged by those upholding the law. Legal documents contain the historical records of relationships between husband and wife, landlord and tenant, ruler and subject, community and individual. The principles of law permeated Tudor society with a thoroughness matched only by the principles of Christian religion, with which they so often overlapped. It was understood that the one tribunal that everybody would have to face one day was that of Christ at the Last Judgement. And this gave moral resonance to every other encounter with the law.[172]

Vox populi, vox dei

The poor may have wielded less influence than their wealthier neighbours, but still they had agency, most particularly as part of the community to which they belonged, be it parish, guild, confraternity or town; meanwhile, the 'middling sort' were becoming increasingly important members of society, wielding authority in law, commerce and local government.[173] Honour was not solely the preserve of the wealthy and powerful. For poor

people, a good name was just as important and could make a big difference, not just to their chances of survival or prosperity, but also to their
standing in the neighbourhood. Those who were described as 'honest pore
men' or 'an honest poore woman', or who could say that they were 'countyd
for an honest poore fellow', had influence within the community in consequence.[174] Much effort was expended on maintaining that community and
keeping the peace. Thomas Egerton, complaining about the wealth of legal
business overwhelming Star Chamber in 1602, remarked pointedly how,
in times past, people had been 'so painful and careful as soon as they heard
of any differences or suits between any of their neighbours, that they
would interpose themselves and mediate an end'.[175] There was a point at
the intersection of national law and local custom where considerable
space could be found for popular initiative.[176] From the responsibilities
shouldered by parish constables and churchwardens, to the consensus of
the community as a whole, society could be shaped more immediately and
efficiently by local authority than by anything that trickled down from
Westminster; and those who lacked wealth or status might still hold sway
through their claims to godliness or respectability.

Popular agency was at its most striking when manifested in riot or rebellion. From the tax revolts and pretenders' campaigns of Henry VII's reign to
the Pilgrimage of Grace of 1536 and the rebellions of 1549, 1554 and 1569,
each Tudor ruler in turn saw challenges to their regime. These rebellions at
times involved thousands, and were frequently violent; and yet they, too,
were in their way a part of the recognized political process. Rebels did not
just randomly protest at perceived injustice: they also conveyed, often with
great formality, their suggestions for improving the situation. They might
appeal to the example of past custom, or to legislation, or to divine sanction,
or to a statement of what might broadly be called natural law. They were
often surprisingly deferential in their demands, again reflecting the shared
understanding of social obligation.[177] Rebellions were often motivated in
part by local issues and anxieties, but they also participated in large questions of national and international politics with surprising frequency,
demonstrating that the politicization of the populace was broad in scope. In
essence, Tudor rebellions were a form of political communication, from the
peripheries to the central authorities – sometimes crude, but sometimes
also surprisingly sophisticated – and sometimes effective.

At the root of every Tudor uprising was a point of principle. In Suffolk in 1525, some of the rebels against the Amicable Grant declared themselves ready to die in their quarrel, saying that the tax collectors were 'daily despoiling them of whatever God sent them for the labour of their hands'.[178] In popular resistance to authority there was frequently a strong sense of morality underpinning the protest. Even where threats were made against the gentry, actual violence was relatively rare; it was the unjust hedges and fences enclosing land, or other pieces of gentry property, that tended to be targeted.[179] In 1549, resentment against Sir William Cavendish for proposing to enclose common land in the village of Northaw in Hertfordshire resulted in the devastation of his rabbit warrens, in part with gunpowder, killing nearly two thousand rabbits. Rabbits were considered to be gentry fare, so violence against rabbits was symbolic of anger directed at the gentry. But still, it was the rabbits that suffered, rather than the landowners themselves.[180] When the recusant Rowland Eyre tried to enclose common land in Hassop in Derbyshire in 1589, it was the women who turned out to protect the villagers' sheep and intimidate Eyre's servants, who were trying to drive the sheep away. Eyre sued the women in Star Chamber. Their response was to condemn him as 'a man very covetous and extremelye impatient of their neighbourhood, thinking to engrosse their whole lyvinge unto his owne hands'.[181]

These underlying moral principles were frequently articulated. A ballad from around 1520 lamented the loss of past security: 'Our auncient customs bolde / More preciouser then golde / Be clene cast away'.[182] It was on the basis of this kind of nostalgia that the rebels of 1549 in East Anglia included in their demands a return to landholding patterns from the first year of Henry VII's reign. There was almost always an underlying rationale for disorderly conduct. The May Day riots of 1517 were described as stemming from the fact that 'the multitude of straungers was so great about London, that the pore Englishe artificers coulde skace get any living', and the uprising was prompted by a sermon about how 'alyens and straungers eate the bread from the poore fatherles chyldren, and take the livynge from all the artificers, and the entercourse from all merchauntes'.[183] The Northern Rebellion of 1569 only slowly took shape, needing the ideological justification of Elizabeth's excommunication to give it coherence.[184] Rebellions usually unfolded according to an established pattern, based on 'customs of disobedience'.[185] More than twelve people armed, or forty unarmed, assembled for an hour or more, constituted an offence, as defined by a statute of Mary I. In 105 cases of riot tried by the Elizabethan Star Chamber, only seven included more than thirty people; their objectives were to convince through a theatre of protest, and the presentation of a rational case, not to overwhelm by use of violence.[186]

By the second half of Elizabeth's reign, tensions were becoming more evident. The evolution of Tudor politics had perhaps brought about a loss of innocence. Where fifteenth-century commentators had grappled with the problems of inadequate kings, overmighty nobles and disobedient subjects, from the 1530s onwards the challenges to the political system became at once far more nebulous and far more frightening. The Royal Supremacy had ensured that monarchical rule would never again be free from the near-impossible obligation to appear as the embodiment of the divine will. This inspired levels of political disputation never before seen. Political commentary, advice and criticism appeared in a flurry of different guises, as pamphlets, broadsheets, woodcuts, ballads, prayers, prophecies, sermons, pageants, letters and libels.[187] Religious change and insecurity catalysed political questioning. In 1553, for example, the dilemma as to whether Lady Jane Grey or Princess Mary should inherit the throne summoned into existence what has been called 'an adjudicating public', to pass judgement on questions of succession law, legitimacy, female rule and the threat of foreign marriage, and the authority of parliament.[188] By the 1580s, exacerbated by war with Spain and conflict in Ireland, and by the increasing severity of religious conflict across mainland Europe, the exchange of opinions had reached a new pitch of fervour and sophistication.

Nevertheless, the ideal of the commonweal held firm, with the understanding that protection and patronage on the part of the monarch and landowning orders would be met with deference and service from the rest of society. The many spoken and written utterances on the subject have been conceived as a dialogue between rulers and ruled.[189] There were recurrent reminders of the obligations on both sides, and Sir Thomas Smith's *Discourse of the Commonweal*, written around 1549, was just as relevant when it was published over three decades later. Hugh Latimer was not afraid to offer advice to those in power, but even he trusted the power of mutual obligation, observing that 'covenants and contracts we remit to the godly wisdom of the high magistrates, who we pray God may take such order and direction in this, and all other, that the common people may be relieved and eased of many importable charges and injuries, which many of them, contrary to all equity and right, sustain.[190] Equity and right were a common possession, and a common point of appeal. The Elizabethan preacher Leonard Wright, who attacked the rich as 'great rich giants and covetous prowling cormorants of this land', thought that too much wealth had 'bewitched their insatiable mindes' and taken root 'in their flintie harts', so that they were left 'wallowing in welth', whilst the poor were left 'wrestling with neede, and like to sinke in miserie'.[191] Yet Wright was himself a member of the gentry, educated at Cambridge, and a defender of episcopacy.[192] He was not preaching revolution, so much as the Tudor understanding of responsibility.

*   *   *

Modern politics deal almost unthinkingly in conflict and opposition. Political parties compete ceaselessly and often savagely, and class differences are tied inextricably to class conflict. It is not often appreciated how much of a luxury this is. Adversarial politics are only possible in a country with a strong rule of law, institutions to lend stability and mechanisms to preserve security, so that political rhetoric can indulge in aggression without fear of the consequences. Tudor England had no experience of these levels of stability. It knew war and rebellion, famine and protest, and over it all stretched the long shadows of the Wars of the Roses. Its political orders knew that they needed to tread carefully, and their conservatism was far from unthinking. At the same time, Tudor rule was reliant upon popular acceptance and engagement, canvassed by libels, broadsheets, pamphlets, treatises, sermons and plays. If Tudor London, in particular, saw the development of something approximating to a 'public sphere', then the catalyst for this was surely religious change and the divisions that it engendered from the 1530s onwards. Henry VIII told parliament in 1545 how sorry he was to hear that 'the word of God is disputed, rimed, sung and jangled in every Alehouse and Taverne'.[193] A member of the King's Guard entering a shop in Bow Lane in 1546 was asked 'What news at court?', before becoming embroiled in an argument about an evangelical preacher.[194] In 1554, the London taverns were full of gossip and argument about Wyatt's rebellion, and the chancellor, Stephen Gardiner, warned the mayor that his city was 'a whirlpool and sink of evil rumours, where they be bred, and from thence spread to all parts of the realm'.[195] Executions for religion brought out huge crowds, for the burning of Protestant martyrs during Mary's reign, but equally for the Catholic priests put to death under Elizabeth: when Robert Southwell was hanged in 1595, the crowd would not allow him to be cut down and disembowelled. Instead, the onlookers were 'moved with great compassion' at his suffering and his scaffold speech, and it was 'throughe the crye of the people' that he was left to die without further torture.[196]

The word on the streets was just as much of a political intervention as debates in parliament or within the Privy Council chamber. Gossip and libel, no less than riot or rebellion, could be forms of political action.[197] Authority was always more than straightforward hegemony or coercion as far as the Tudors were concerned; it required validation, acceptance, cooperation and frequently collaboration to take effect. The wielding of power at this time was a relationship and a process, albeit a relationship that was under increasing strain and a process that was under growing scrutiny, as confessional division widened rifts on the international scale, as well as fissures within the social fabric. By the end of the century, Elizabeth I might be cast as goddess or tyrant, not just in the private exchanges of popes, princes and diplomats, but on the London stage and in taverns and alehouses, whilst the voice of the people was a recognized force that could be manipulated and undermined, but not silenced. And yet still, the exercise of authority rested on the consent and esteem of the governed, and in large part their approval and indeed affection for Tudor rule was maintained. It was this that would enable Elizabeth I to tell the parliamentary delegation in 1601: 'though God hath raised me high, yet this I count the glory of my crown: that I have reigned with your loves'.[198]

CHAPTER 7

FROM UTOPIA TO BABEL
THE BEGINNING OF REFORMATION

The single most significant transformation which Tudor England was to experience began in the most undramatic fashion possible. It drew its initial inspiration in part from a handful of scholars debating points of theology in a Cambridge pub, and in part from whispered conversations in the corridors of power about Henry VIII's marital problems. From these unlikely beginnings developed England's Protestant Reformation, which would shape the lives of every inhabitant of the country, and bring lasting changes to everything from the parameters of kingship to the games that children played in the streets. From the first stirrings in the 1520s to the consolidation of Protestant culture in the last decades of the century, the process of religious reform was slow, piecemeal, deeply contested and highly politicized, leaving a string of martyrs in its wake and engendering a flood of printed literature and a large amount of popular confusion and antagonism. It became one of the chief preoccupations of government, and the most divisive force in society at large. Five centuries on, large swathes of British society are still coming to terms with its legacy.

The story of England's Protestant Reformation was written by the winners. In particular, the polemicists of Elizabeth I's reign constructed a stirring account of a struggle for religious liberty which still resonates today. Foxe's *Actes and Monuments*, probably the most influential book of Elizabeth's reign, was, he told the queen, about 'suche godly Martyrs as suffered before youre reigne for the . . . testimonie of Christ and his truth'.[1] Protestants envisaged their Church as a militant body, founded on the blood of those martyrs, fervent in its condemnation of opponents, unyielding in its insistence on doctrinal rigour. William Tyndale in 1528 exhorted his co-religionists to 'be bold in the Lord'.[2] He and his brethren cast the Protestant Reformation as an encounter between humble believers doggedly committed to their faith in the face of terrible mistreatment and a tyrannical institution, which sought to enslave and indoctrinate the innocent and ignorant. At the time, and ever since, this made for a great story.

For centuries, much historical writing about the Reformation was based on the assumption that Protestantism was a better version of Christianity than Catholicism, an astonishing piece of prejudice which went largely overlooked in a majority Protestant culture. Tyndale's translation of the Bible into English was seen as a watershed moment, opening up 'a vast, rich sunlit territory, a land flowing with milk and honey of new images and metaphors'.[3] The notion of the 'individual Christian . . . finally able to read the Biblical text for him – or herself' was held to have important democratic implications, foreshadowing the developments of the seventeenth century.[4] The strong Lutheran bias of Tyndale's translation, and its inaccessibility to the illiterate majority of England's population, was mostly lost to view.[5] It was for many years taken for granted that Protestantism had an immediate and demotic appeal.[6] Only towards the end of the twentieth century, as religious diversity became more central to British culture, were these assumptions called into question.[7] The extent of popular loyalty to the old faith was uncovered, alongside an appreciation of the strengths of the pre-Reformation Church.[8] The early Reformation in England therefore began to look much more like a calculated political intervention than a spontaneous religious movement, and the extent to which early Protestants had appealed to royal sympathies became more evident. The Lutheran Simon Fish pointedly suggested to Henry VIII that bishops and abbots, all holding seats in the House of Lords, might be 'stronger in your owne parliament house then your silfe'. Meanwhile, Tyndale painted Catholicism as dangerously subversive: 'the bloody doctrine of the Pope which causeth disobedience, rebellion and insurrection'; at the same time, he temptingly described Protestantism as a creed in which 'the king is in this world without law and may at his lust do right or wrong and shall give accompts, but to God only'.[9] Henry, unsurprisingly, is supposed to have commented approvingly that Tyndale's book was one which every king should read.

It is clear that the arrival of Protestantism was not the straightforwardly revelatory experience its proponents liked to describe. On the other hand, an emphasis on Protestantism as the tool of princes, cynically deployed, ignores evidence of some genuine popular enthusiasm for Protestant ideas (although historians differ widely in their views of how widespread that might have been).[10] Politics clearly played a huge part in the religious changes of the 1530s and 1540s, but it was not politics alone that created an English Protestant movement, which before 1547 had to struggle for its existence in the face of fluctuating levels of official hostility. The pursuit of political ambitions by some was inextricably entangled with the religious idealism of others who were striving to build the kingdom of God on earth, and who were prepared to die in the attempt, if necessary.

There is still no single, coherent, convincing explanation of why England became a Protestant country. If older explanations have been broken into pieces, however, this is perhaps more helpful than it immediately appears. England's Reformation might be best understood as a history in fragments. Different individuals, different groups within society, had widely varying perceptions of both the old Church and the new. Some, such as William Tyndale, interpreted Luther's ideas as a spiritual awakening; others, such as John Fisher, saw them as the destruction of everything that was good and compassionate in European society. Many turned to new books, with no idea of what was in them; different people read the same texts and came away with wildly variant ideas of what they meant. Some of those in power were genuinely convinced by some of the ideas they promulgated; others used them to manipulate the political process to their own ends. And historians continue to debate which motivation was the stronger. Within a single family, there could be passionate endorsement of different religious viewpoints. Thomas More's beloved daughter Margaret married William Roper, who was in his youth 'a mervailous zealous Protestant' and who only got off on charges of heresy because Wolsey was fond of his father-in-law; later, however, he became a loyal Catholic and More's biographer. Thomas Harding, regius professor of Hebrew at Oxford, was converted by Protestant ideas through reading German commentaries on the Old Testament, before later returning to Catholicism: an outraged Lady Jane Grey, to whose parents he had been chaplain, condemned him as 'the deformed imp of the devil' and 'the unshameful paramour of Antichrist'.[11] Thomas Cranmer had a sister who was a devout Catholic nun and who petitioned Queen Mary on her brother's behalf when he was in prison.[12] There can be no easy answer as to why any of this happened.

The problem is complicated by the fact that those who stand out in the historical record are the zealots, the martyrs, the obdurate and the hyper-articulate: in other words, those who were probably least representative of the population as a whole. It is likely that those who are most visible in the sources represent those who were most unusual at the time. This would suggest that the shift to a broadly Protestant culture may not have happened until around the 1570s, when, as a great scholar once observed, the historian who cannot sleep starts counting recusant Catholics, rather than evangelical Protestants. It was at this time that Catholics became the intriguing minority, and therefore begin to stand out in the historical sources.[13] Delving into this question has brought a new historical awareness of religion as a social experience – an awareness shared by religious polemicists at the time: the Lutheran Simon Fish accused the Catholic clergy of bringing about 'the grevous shipwrak of the comon welth', by extorting money from the poor, corrupting the morals of the nation and turning good women into 'an hundreth thousand ydell hores'.[14] In attacking the old Church for what he perceived to be its social crimes, Fish was probably much closer to the heart of the problem than was Tyndale, when he wrote about salvation through faith. Religion in early modern society did not revolve first and foremost around considerations of doctrine, but around the hopes and fears, emotions and experiences of everyday life. The historical record has been distorted by lengthy testimonies left by churchmen, giving the impression of a conflict over religious ideas. But for the majority of the population, what made one person Protestant and another Catholic was probably not chiefly what they thought (if they did think) about transubstantiation, purgatory or salvation by faith alone, but rather what they felt about the patterns and relationships of their religious life. It probably had more to do with how much they liked their parish priest; whether they viewed their local monastery as an extortionate landowner or a source of charity; whether they perceived the new ideas preached from the pulpit as promising greater communal harmony or as threatening to break the bonds of mutual obligation. Reformation did not offer people a choice between two different intellectual propositions: it called upon them to protect what they held most dear and to choose which way of life might bring them closer to God. There may have been as many answers to this as there were people in Tudor England.

This kind of realization has engendered a new set of historical problems, as our focus has shifted from the copious writings of sixteenth-century theologians to the vast majority of sixteenth-century believers, who remain silent in the records, most of them unable to write even if they had had the opportunity. To get a picture of popular religion involves piecing together scraps of information from cheap print, ballads, inventories and wills; looking at churchwardens' accounts to see how the interiors of churches were altered; assessing the meaning of religious art, architecture or artefacts; interrogating the actions and declarations of rebels.[15] All of this has been done to extract a sense of how ordinary people understood and reacted to the religious changes preached, published or imposed from on high. Any conclusions drawn from this material have to be far more cautious than an assessment of the religious convictions of the educated and powerful.

That said, when we examine more closely the writings of the elite, we find no easy answers. We might, for example, look at the archbishops of Canterbury between 1533 and 1558, the Protestant Thomas Cranmer and the Catholic Reginald Pole.[16] Cranmer in his youth was a great deal more conservative than his future arch-rival Stephen Gardiner.[17] After 1533, in part transformed by his contact with German reformers, Cranmer probably did more than anyone to advance the Protestant cause in England; and yet, for fourteen years as Henry VIII's archbishop, he concealed his true allegiance, kept his wife and family secret, and celebrated the mass he had apparently ceased to believe was valid. Pole, exiled in Italy in the 1530s, wrote an eloquent denunciation of the Royal Supremacy that led Henry VIII to execute a large part of his family for treason, including his elderly mother; and yet, so heavily involved was he in Catholic reform circles in Italy that, after serving as Mary I's archbishop of Canterbury, towards the end of his life he was under recall to Rome to face charges of heresy.[18] Both these men believed in and energetically implemented reform of the Church: the decrees of Pole's reforming synod of 1555–56 were published after his death as *Reformatio Angliae*, the 'Reformation of England'. Both men had many ideas in common, even though they were also deeply opposed to one another's policies. Even among theologians, confessional identities were far from straightforward.

Protestantism in mainland Europe was itself at this time far from coherent, with divisions and animosities between Lutherans, Calvinists,

Zwinglians and the Anabaptists who were condemned from every side, whilst the ferocity of debates at the Council of Trent demonstrates the divisions within Catholic thought, too.[19] Reflecting this, the clear-cut historical certainties of the past have given way to something much more tentative, fractured and variegated. It might be argued that this is much more how we should expect the history of something so intensely personal as religion to look. A few things can be said with some certainty, however. It is clear that religion and politics were inextricably tied up: Henry VIII and all three of his children implemented policies on the basis of both genuine personal conviction and political viability, an approach shared by many of their key advisors. It is also clear that personal piety and personal gain could mutually reinforce one another: the spiritual attractions of Protestantism could be reinforced by the promise of monastic land and freedom from papal taxes or the cost of indulgences, just as the value of Catholic loyalism might be enhanced by the prospect of worldly reward. Personal animosities also had a part to play: existing antagonisms between different noble families, courtly factions or even rival groups of villagers were strengthened by the adoption of opposing religious views. This is not to suggest that the process of religious reform was fundamentally corrupt, but to emphasize that it was inescapably human.

At the same time, it must be recognized that the sixteenth century was an age of extraordinary religious commitment, and that many men and women were deeply involved in the task of sustaining, purifying and transmitting their faith. From the 1520s to the 1550s, there were many who were prepared to face death, rather than renounce their faith; and many more who went into exile or suffered imprisonment, rather than betray their ideals. It must also be recognized that England ultimately became a majority Protestant country, however halting, disputed and painful the progress was towards that end. Some historians have insisted that we should give greater weight to this achievement, even recognize England's Protestant Reformation as a 'howling success'.[20] It is clear, however, that it took many decades before Protestantism became established within popular culture, and that the consolidation of popular Protestant belief and practice had to wait until some years into Elizabeth's reign.[21] It is also clear that the process of popular assimilation had a profound effect upon Protestant ideology, and that both belief and practice were shaped and adapted by the parish communities which received them.[22] The Protestant culture that would emerge at the end of the Tudor period was markedly different from its fragmented, zealous, contentious origins.

On the most fundamental level, there was also a reforming impulse shared across the confessional spectrum, as both Catholics and Protestants sought to improve and revivify their faith, drawing on a wealth of reform ideas and initiatives from the fifteenth century.[23] One of the reasons there was not more opposition when religious change began in the 1530s was that the late medieval Church had already acclimatized people to reform initiatives and religious print culture. It took many people quite a while to realize that what was happening might qualify as a reformation. In effect, Catholic and Protestant reformations ran in parallel for much of the Tudor era, and it was hard to predict which individuals would be swayed one way or the other. John Laurence was a Dominican friar who converted to Protestantism and was burned at the stake for heresy in Colchester in March 1555. Anthony Browne was an Observant Franciscan friar who, when the Observants were closed down in 1534, transferred to a Conventual house; and then, when that house was dissolved in 1538, petitioned to be allowed to live as a hermit. He was executed for denying the Royal Supremacy in Norwich later that year. It is possible that the two men made their very different choices on very similar grounds.[24]

Even for those who did perceive that religious change was under way on an unprecedented scale, there was some confusion about how best to describe it. The terms 'Protestant' and 'Catholic', it should be noted, come with layers of modern accretions, but they are probably the best labels we have available. Many historians use the terms 'evangelical' and 'conservative' when discussing the earliest years of the Reformation. But this ignores the fact that many Protestants who were evangelical in their religious convictions were also conservative in much of their religious teaching regarding social and political issues, whilst many Catholics were not only radical in political terms, but also evangelical in their faith, if we understand 'evangelical' to mean a profound commitment to scriptural authority and inspiration.[25] It should be emphasized, though, that neither Protestant nor Catholic positions were clearly defined before around 1560, one of the reasons why many historians are reluctant to use the terms.[26] The word 'Protestant' was not used routinely until the 1560s, at the earliest; before that time, any reference to 'Protestants' was usually meant to refer to Germans, such as the representatives of the German Schmalkaldic League who attended Edward VI's coronation.[27] A Catholic treatise of 1556 called *The Displaying of the Protestantes* had to justify its use of such an outlandish term.[28] When it came to self-representation, religious believers of every hue laid claim to the term 'catholic' – in the sense of 'universal' – since everyone believed that their definition of the faith was the correct one. Others might refer to themselves as 'true believers' or 'the godly', and the two sides lambasted one another as 'schismatic' or 'heretic'.

The first moves towards religious reform in England were an intricate and sometimes contradictory combination of elements. Tyndale and Fish were Lutherans preaching radical ideas about salvation, whilst appealing to an absolutist notion of monarchy. Other more measured, but no less impassioned, calls for religious and social reform came from senior members of the clergy, who tried to defend the Church's independence from political control, or from scholars such as Thomas More, who went to the block rather than agree that the king had the right to rule the Church. Political and religious radicalism did not necessarily match up. Amidst much conflict, there were also many shared imperatives about the importance of education, the plight of the poor and the need to live in charity with one another. Reformation in England was not a single movement – and not even a movement towards Protestantism, for to begin with, it looked more likely that there would be a reformation within the existing Church, rather than a successful challenge from outside it. It was a many-layered and incremental set of changes, which began quite slowly and carefully, but would bring about a revolution in both politics and society.

Evangelical excitement

At some point around 1523, Thomas Bilney, a recently ordained Cambridge graduate from Norfolk, began reading the New Testament.[29] He read it in the Greek and Latin version published by Erasmus in 1516, and was especially struck by a passage in the first Epistle of Timothy, 'that Christ Jesus came into the world to save sinners, of whom I am the first'.[30] Bilney recorded the transformation which this had wrought within him: 'immediatly I semed unto my selfe inwardly, to feele such a comfort and quietnes, as I my self would not discerne and iudge, in so muche that my brused bones lepte for joye'. Inspired by this, he found that 'the scripture began to bee more pleasaunt unto me then the hony or the hony combe', and he discovered that all the fasting, masses, pardons and so on of his previous life were meaningless, if 'done without trust in Christ, which only saveth his people'.[31] Bilney began to preach against what he saw as institutional-ized error within the English Church. He did not attack the Church's authority, or its sacramental doctrine, but preached against pilgrimages and the veneration of saints and relics, which he saw as missing the point on a cosmic level. Salvation came through Christ, and Christ alone, not as a result of paying visits to a gilded statue or a collection of old bones. Bilney had reached these conclusions on his own, it seems.[32] His persist-ence in his views meant that he was eventually burned at the stake in 1531, for views which, to many, seemed barely even Protestant, and yet were undeniably reformed. Both John Foxe and Thomas More claimed him, at different points, as a fellow believer, giving some sense of the ambiguity of his position.[33]

Also in 1523, William Tyndale, an Oxford graduate from Gloucestershire, came to London to propose to its bishop, Cuthbert Tunstall, that he trans-late the Bible into English, bringing with him his translation of a Greek work by Isocrates to show his skills. Tunstall was himself a fine humanist scholar, who had helped his friend Erasmus with a second edition of his *Novum Instrumentum*: he seemed the obvious patron for Tyndale's proposed translation, which would mirror the work that was being done elsewhere in Europe in rendering the Scriptures into the vernacular.[34] Tyndale clearly expected Tunstall to agree. And if he had done, England might still be a Catholic country today.[35] But Tunstall, perhaps feeling harassed by some recent cases of heresy in his diocese, thought it wiser to wait. Tyndale, frustrated, went into exile, published his New Testament from Worms in the Holy Roman Empire, and was executed for heresy in 1536 near Brussels. Copies of his bible translations and theological works in English were smuggled into England, helping to fuel the growth of an underground Protestant movement. Alongside them were smuggled the works of George Joye, a Cambridge scholar from Bedfordshire exiled in Antwerp, who issued the first English psalter in 1529, and the first Protestant English Prayer Book, which replaced some of the traditional saints in the calendar with martyrs such as Thomas Hitton, who had been executed for heresy in February 1530.[36] In 1534, Joye helped with a revision of Tyndale's New Testament, but his correction of Tyndale's use of the word 'resurrection' to 'the life after this' (which was, in fact, in line with more mainstream Protestant theology) made Tyndale furious: he attacked Joye's 'spytfullest maner of provokynge' as being like 'the foxe when he hath pyssed in the grayes [badger's] hole chalengeth it for his awne'.[37] An unedifying exchange of insults followed.[38] Simon Fish, who entered Gray's Inn in 1525 and trained as a lawyer, first came to prominence towards the end of 1526, when he acted in a Christmas play that satirized Cardinal Wolsey. He spent time in exile, and then returned to form part of an early Protestant underground in London, smuggling in proscribed books and distributing them from his house near Whitefriars. His *Supplicacyon for the Beggers*, attacking the Church, was distributed in the London streets before the opening of the 1529 parliament – the so-called 'Reformation Parliament'. Fish died of the plague in 1531; his widow's new husband, his friend James Bainham, was burnt for heresy in 1532.[39]

Bilney, Tyndale, Joye and Fish are significant for several reasons. First, they make the emphatic point that England's Protestant Reformation was a highly intellectual movement, led in large part by university graduates. Cranmer, it is said, once tried to characterize the religious groupings in England promoting or resisting reform as the parties of Cambridge and Oxford, respectively.[40] This movement was heavily reliant on the printing press for the dissemination of its ideas, and was therefore targeted very specifically at the literate minority within Tudor society. Second, they suggest that quite varied strains of reform were stirring in England, with clear differences between the home-grown variety and the ideas fostered elsewhere on the continent, where men such as Tyndale, Joye and Fish acquired a more coherent set of theological propositions, and often a fiercely aggressive edge. This complex relationship with mainland Europe would continue to shape the road ahead.[41] Third, they suggest that the origins of English reform emerged less from the opposition to the existing Church than from the radical fringes of that Church, where many who would remain Catholic still had pronounced evangelical tendencies. Men such as William Tyndale, John Frith, Hugh Latimer and Thomas Cranmer were all Catholic clergy before they became Protestant leaders. Robert Barnes, Miles Coverdale and

John Bale all began as friars.[42] The Protestant emphasis on inspirational preaching, the reform of abuses, simplicity of life and the denunciation of church corruption resonated with many whose conception of their order had involved very similar preoccupations. Protestantism was less a rejection of late medieval religion than an intensification and development of certain ascetic, biblical, reforming strands within it, accompanied by a rejection of other more tangible, ritualistic or mystical elements.[43] It was not a reaction against the past, so much as a partial appropriation of it, with a newly antagonistic edge.[44] In this, Protestantism could be cast as the rebellious teenager who has been carefully raised by loving parents, but who stridently rejects that family, whilst continuing to rely on their inherited wealth.

Bilney was unusual, in that his conversion experience started with a bible passage. This was of course the idealized notion of conversion, since it reflected that of Luther, but in fact most Protestants were converted by other people. Hugh Latimer insisted that 'Master Bilney, or rather Saint Bilney . . . was the instrument whereby God called me to knowledge.'[45] Becon, as a student at Cambridge, was in turn overwhelmed by meeting Latimer, who tutored at Clare Hall, and George Stafford, professor at Pembroke College. He quoted a saying, apparently in circulation at the time, that 'When Maister Staforde read, and Mayster Latimer preached, than was Cambridge blessed.'[46] Other proto-Protestants in Cambridge in the 1520s included Thomas Cranmer, Matthew Parker, Nicholas Shaxton, Thomas Arthur, George Joye and John Lambert, alongside Robert Barnes, who was then prior of the Augustinian friary in the city, where he converted Miles Coverdale, another of his community. Eventually the Cambridge evangelical network expanded to include Edward Crome, John Skip, Simon Heynes, Nicholas Heath, Thomas Goodrich and others. Early Protestantism, then, was as much a group of friends as it was an intellectual construct. In mainland Europe, reformers were already tending to identify themselves in terms of the man they followed, as Lutherans or Zwinglians. In England, these personal ties were as much about sustaining one another under a hostile regime as they were about identity. Reformers looked back to the early years of the Church, where Christians had gathered in different cities, indicated by the titles of the Pauline Epistles which were addressed to those in Rome, Corinth, Ephesus and so on. England's equivalents were Cambridge, London, Colchester, Coventry and Ipswich.

Beneath the disputations about salvation or purgatory or the worship of saints ran a strong tide of human sympathy. Becon was drawn to Latimer by 'the puernes of his lyfe', and his generosity to the needy.[47] Barnes's famous Christmas Eve sermon of 1525 was prompted by the desire to protect a poor man being sued by a churchwarden in pursuit of a legacy to his church.[48] Fish's outrage focused on those who prolonged suffering within the existing order of society. Becon thought of himself as a prophet, surveying the sin and misery of the society to which he was sent by God with a message of repentance and renewal. Reformers wanted to change the society they lived in to something more charitable and compassionate. The old idea that the Reformation was about the defeat of over-emotional, and therefore gullibly superstitious, Catholic practice by an educated, text-based, intellectual Protestant movement now has little to support it.[49] Theirs was a passionate faith; indeed, one of the chief evils feared by Protestants was when emotion dried up, leaving a cold, dry, dull malaise, or hardness within the heart.[50] Cranmer's exhortation to the reading of Scripture in 1547 appealed to the emotions and the senses: 'These bokes . . . ought to be much in our handes, in our eyes, in our eares, in oure mouthes, but moste of all, in our hartes . . . the heavenly meate of our soules . . . a light lanterne to oure fete . . . more sweter then hony, or hony combe.'[51] The notion of 'sweetness' in devotional experience, another recurring theme from late medieval piety, was repeatedly applied to encounters with Scripture, and the revelations of Protestant doctrine.[52] The transformative power of Protestant understanding irradiated the lives of those who received it. They felt 'delivered from the hard, sharp . . . captivity of that Babylonical man of Rome, to the sweet and soft service, yea, rather liberty of the gospel'.[53]

Early Protestantism was fuelled by fervent conviction and often great courage. The sixteenth century would witness just how powerful and uncompromising the consequences of Protestant conversion could be, from the example of the martyrs who went to their death singing psalms, to those who suffered imprisonment, exile and condemnation. This zeal came in many guises, from the preoccupations of Cambridge scholars to the subversive anger of those who blamed the Church for institutionalized poverty and prejudice or the tribal loyalties of London lawyers, for whom the clergy were professional rivals. That zeal might often waver: Bilney twice recanted, as did many of his associates. More to the point, it might approach the question of religious reform from many different angles. Bilney was worried by image-worship and superstitious practices; Tyndale wanted everyone to read the Bible in English and to believe in salvation by faith alone; Joye wanted people to pray in English, and attacked the doctrine of the mass; Fish wanted Henry VIII to take action against the Church as an institution and undermine the authority of the clergy. The self-representation of early reformers was compounded by the efforts of propagandists to weave all this together into a single Protestant agenda, and label those who deviated as anomalies.[54] In 1547, John Bale published a work called *The Image of Both Churches*, which depicted a cosmic struggle between the true (Protestant) Church and the false (Catholic) Church of the pope, described as 'the proud church of hypocrites, the rose coloured whore, the paramour of Antichrist, and the sinfull sinagoge of Sathan.'[55] This polarized kind of view gave the illusion of clarity to what was actually a highly complicated religious situation, and was seized upon by those at the time and ever since who wanted to make sense of it. In reality, however, early Protestantism was a mutable, unpredictable, piebald and often fluctuating creed. England's Reformation would be built on broad foundations of popular piety, humanist learning, educational provision and biblical translation. Like the Tower of Babel, however, the work would remain unfinished, as the workers found themselves increasingly incapable of speaking one another's language.[56]

Building the godly kingdom

Conviction might come from within, but churches were expected to have walls and floors, not just inspiration. Early reformers could not conceive of more than one Church in a land, and like everyone else envisaged a Church universally accepted and directed by a clerical hierarchy. Tyndale therefore looked for reform at the hands of a godly king; but Henry VIII's religious policies were a long way away from the magisterial Lutheran Reformation that Tyndale and others might have hoped for. Here was an early indication that the Protestant method was not infallible. Reading the Bible had not made the king a Protestant. Henry rejected papal authority, only to put his own in its place; and although he emphasized the importance of scriptural authority, it was strictly according to his own idiosyncratic interpretation of the Bible text. Although he corrected some of the abuses identified by Protestants, he also upheld the sacramental doctrine which was to them the greatest abuse of all, and he steadfastly refused to see the merits of their doctrine of salvation. In the febrile atmosphere of the time, there were many opportunities for Protestants to find a foothold in the Church, and to advance their views; but their path ahead was far from straightforward, and there were many crushing reversals along the way.

The experiences of the 1530s and 1540s, until Henry died in 1547, were, from a Protestant viewpoint, a sobering lesson in the vagaries of royal will and the dangers of entrusting God's work to a secular ruler. Most of the main advances for Protestantism in these years were inadvertent. Henry's patronage of convincing anti-papal preachers and propagandists gave many a chance, most importantly Thomas Cranmer and Thomas Cromwell; but their Protestant views were not the reason why Henry employed them, and those views had to be kept at least partially concealed. Cranmer had declared his allegiance in 1532 on a visit to Nuremberg by marrying the niece of Andreas Osiander, a leading reformer in the city; for a priest to marry was an unequivocal declaration of Protestant convictions. Summoned home in 1533 to become archbishop of Canterbury, Cranmer then embarked on a fourteen-year stretch of deception and equivocation, concealing his Protestant tendencies, as well as his wife. Cromwell's evangelicalism also had to be channelled into serving the king's will, producing an impressive propaganda campaign for the Royal Supremacy. A series of negotiations with the German Protestant princes ended in frustration over points of Lutheran doctrine which the king could not stomach.[57] Cromwell's covert attempts to advance Protestantism left him open to attack and ultimately contributed to his downfall, when in 1540 he was executed for heresy, as well as treason.

From the outside, particularly from the viewpoint of Catholics in mainland Europe, Henry did appear to be advancing the Protestant cause. The reformers Hugh Latimer, Nicholas Shaxton, Thomas Goodrich, William Barlow, John Hilsey and Edward Foxe – nearly all part of the Cambridge group of scholars in the 1520s – were made bishops. Many lesser posts were quietly filled with Protestants in the dioceses that these men controlled. The universities saw some increased, if covert, interest in the new ideas, as did the Inns of Court in London; and in certain cities, including London, but also Ipswich, Colchester and Coventry, small

Protestant communities became established. The Ten Articles published by Convocation in 1536, and the 'Bishops' Book' in 1537, showed signs of Protestant influence, particularly in the latter case. These signs of apparent progress were largely deceptive, however. If the Ten Articles were in part inspired by negotiations with Lutheran envoys from Saxony, these were negotiations which had failed, and although the document contained reform emphases, these fell short of Protestant doctrine. The fifth article insisted on salvation through the merits of Christ, but without obviating the need for good works: 'by contrition and faith joined with charity'. This has been read with a Protestant slant, but it would appear that what was really intended was an insistence on justification through faith *and* works, a position put forward by Catholic theologians, particular those of an evangelical persuasion. Perhaps the most truly striking thing about the Ten Articles was that they were issued in the name of the king, asserting that the definition of doctrine was one of the matters 'appertaining unto this our princely office'.[58]

Protestants read into this what they wanted to see, but the reforms that Henry introduced were, in his own eyes, entirely consistent with a reformed Catholic position, and his consistent view that the core Protestant doctrine of 'salvation by faith alone' was wrong. This, augmented by his firm adherence to clerical chastity, the seven sacraments, the Real Presence in the eucharist and the importance of confession, suggests that he was never seriously tempted by Protestant doctrine. The high-point for Protestant hopes came with the doctrinal formulary of 1537, the 'Bishops' Book', which did put forward a Protestant view of salvation, whilst remaining conservative in other respects. Importantly, however, Henry VIII had not approved this work for publication, and insisted on its revision and reissue as the 'King's Book' in 1543. The clearest advance, in Protestant eyes, was the insistence in royal injunctions of 1536 that each parish church should have an English Bible. In 1536, this meant the Coverdale Bible, produced in 1535 under the auspices of Cromwell and licensed by the regime; ultimately, in 1539, the 'Great Bible' was published, an edition formally sponsored by the king and often seen as Cromwell's greatest achievement.[59] This put in place the single most important foundation for the advance of Protestantism, in the eyes of the reformers, though Henry viewed it rather differently. His first commitment to an English Bible had come in a proclamation of 1530 which promised a Catholic translation, whilst at the same time condemning Tyndale's 'evil translated' version. The king saw Scripture as a bulwark of royal power, not a challenge to traditional doctrine. Nor did he want his people to read it without the constraints imposed by deference to authority: he explained in a speech to parliament in 1545 that

> although you be permitted to read holy Scripture and to have the word of God in your mother tongue, you must understand that it is licensed you so to do, only to inform your own conscience, and to instruct your children and family; and not to dispute and make Scripture a railing and a taunting stock against priests and preachers, as many light persons do.[60]

Meanwhile, as it became clear that the break with Rome had raised the hopes of some Protestants both within and outside England, Henry hit back with a degree of savagery. Many Protestants were burnt alive for heresy by his regime. Those such as John Frith (executed in 1533), John Lambert (executed in 1538), Robert Barnes, Thomas Garrett and William Jerome (executed together in 1540) and Anne Askew (burnt in 1546) were among the roll-call of revered Protestant martyrs. The Act of Six Articles passed by parliament in 1539, which the Protestants called 'the bloody whip with six strings', reiterated core Catholic doctrine concerning the eucharist, vows of chastity, clerical celibacy and confession to a priest. As an indication, perhaps, of Henry's wish to be seen as detached from the Church of Rome, it avoided using the word 'transubstantiation' when describing the mass, but the doctrine it outlined was that in all but name. Bishops Latimer and Shaxton resigned their sees, and for many the hope held out by the Henrician Reformation was extinguished.

The problem of how to understand the reform process of the 1530s would not be satisfactorily resolved during Henry's lifetime. On the one hand, Henry was understood by nearly everyone to be divinely appointed, and in policies such as the introduction of the English Bible it was possible for Protestants to perceive divine providence at work; but on the other hand, he so obstinately refused to accept the truth of the Gospel on so many key points that it was hard to explain his failings. The usual way out of this dilemma was to blame ungodly influences, particularly those of staunch traditionalists such as Stephen Gardiner or Cuthbert Tunstall, bishops of Winchester and Durham, respectively. Blaming the king was both a risky path to take and something at odds with early modern attitudes. So the myth of Henry being swayed back and forth by different factions emerged, to be institutionalized by John Foxe. In reality, the king was firmly in control of most of the key religious policies of the time.[61] He wanted reform, but on his own terms; and when Protestant influence became too evident, he struck back, executing Cromwell in 1540, reiterating Catholic sacramental doctrine, forbidding Bible-reading in 1543 to the lower orders and all women, in the pointedly named Act for the Advancement of True Religion.[62] Henry's idea of true religion was sometimes hard to pin down, but it was not Protestantism.

Early Protestants in England were forced to live a parasitic existence, their ideas riding on the back of other agendas. They drew strength from antipathies towards the clergy, from the vestiges of Lollard opinions, and from the reform ideas of the humanists; and they sought to ride on the back of the king's attempts to demolish papal authority and purge the English Church of abuses. Slowly and unobtrusively, networks of fellow believers came into being, encouraged by those who held high church office, such as Cranmer, who were able quietly to place evangelicals as parish priests and ecclesiastical officials. The encouraging letters from reformers abroad were an important source of both strength and direction. Yet the problem remained that the doctrine of Henry's Church was, in all important essentials, still Catholic; and the king not only wanted it that way, but was also prepared ruthlessly to purge anyone he could find holding heretical opinions. If the 1530s and early 1540s saw some important Protestant advances, they also saw a distressingly high body count.

The 'godly imp'

The accession of Edward VI – whom Foxe would term the 'godly imp' – meant a sea-change in religious policy in England. Given that the king was a child, and the regime therefore far from confident, change was only gradual, but there was still a marked difference from the previous reign. Henry VIII had proceeded cautiously because his certainties were all about his authority over the Church, not doctrinal principle. Edward VI's regime proceeded cautiously because, despite more clear-cut aims, it was evident how difficult it was going to be to make England a Protestant country. At first, there were only hints, such as Cranmer's coronation sermon or the convictions of those employed as court preachers or chaplains. The *Injunctions* of 1547 and the *Book of Homilies* of that same year introduced a note of Protestant vigour, with their blunt instructions to 'take away, utterly extinct and destroy' all forms of imagery in homes, as well as churches.[63] Another significant advance was the 1548 Order of Communion, which turned the eucharistic section of the liturgy into English. Published as a ten-page booklet, this was seemingly an attempt to test the waters: the preface quite candidly asked Edward's subjects

> to receyve this oure ordinaunce, and most godly directyon, that we maye be encouraged from tyme to tyme, further to travell [travail] for the reformacion, and settyng furth of such godly ordres, as may be mooste to Gods glory, the edifiying of our subiectes, and for thad-vauncemente, of true relygyon.

This was advancing towards Protestantism one step at a time. The preface also contained a plea for those who wanted a faster pace of reform to remain patient and obedient, 'not enterprising to ronne afore, and so by their rashnes, become the greatest hinderers of such things'. It was evident from this very first endeavour that the Edwardian regime had a daunting task ahead.[64]

Perhaps the most profound difficulty lay within the nature of Protestantism itself. As the very name suggested, the movement had begun as a reaction against the established Church of the day. It was inherently critical, subversive and antagonistic by nature, and it had spent the last two decades in England struggling with a recalcitrant and often persecuting regime, channelling its evangelical energies into private networks, individual works of scholarship, the building of international connections and the godliness of isolated families or groupings. It was, in other words, ideally designed to advance the work of a covert religious underground movement; it was not well placed to run a national Church establishment. By its very nature, it distrusted the idea of compromise, was ill-equipped to promote consensus, and prided itself on stark loyalties and uncompromising principles. Even more frustratingly, the opportunity to bring together a godly people under a godly prince, for which so many Protestants had been longing, was confounded by the fact that the prince in question was a child, and in no position to take the kind of commanding role that his father had assumed.

From the first, then, the Edwardian Church found itself at a disadvantage. Elsewhere on mainland Europe, reformers faced with the challenge of establishing a Protestant Church had usually been able to draw on a measure of popular enthusiasm. England, by contrast, had a small, dedicated elite of churchmen and scholars, and a majority still largely traditional in its religious attitudes. The most successful attempts at reformation had been within individual European cities or small states: had Edward VI wanted to turn London into a version of Calvin's Geneva, he might have stood a better chance, but his objective was to transform the country as a whole. Inevitably, for a movement run by many opinionated, committed and highly cerebral individuals, there was a great deal of disagreement over what a Protestant Church should look like. Many reformers from abroad proffered advice, but their views were not always consistent. The negotiations for what eventually became the *Consensus Tigurinus* – the Zurich agreement on the eucharist that defused some of the tensions between Zwinglians and Calvinists – reached a settlement in 1549, which improved the situation somewhat, but differences remained.[65] A catechism published in 1548, translated from the German version authored by Andreas Osiander, uncle to Cranmer's wife, caused the archbishop severe embarrassment, since its Lutheran language concerning the eucharist in particular was widely condemned by Protestants holding different views.[66]

In 1549, after strenuous efforts of translation, consolidation and composition on the part of Cranmer, the first *Book of Common Prayer* was issued. This work, which was to be the foundation of English liturgy for the next four centuries and more, encompasses both the strengths and the weaknesses of the Edwardian Reformation. Cranmer had been at work on it for over ten years, and the draft versions had gone through more assertively Protestant and more conservative iterations.[67] It was a replacement for the Latin mass, in lucid, often beautiful, English prose, with passages from Scripture allotted to each day of the year. It was designed to lead the parish congregations of around nine thousand English churches through their daily or weekly worship, and step by step through almost the entirety of the Bible. It was an extraordinary achievement, and many of its phrases assumed a lasting place in the English language. To those wedded to traditional worship, however, the loss of the Latin liturgy was an affront and a betrayal, whilst at the other end of the spectrum, to those longing for a Protestant Church order, it seemed frustratingly tame. The title page even preserved the word 'mass', whilst in doctrinal terms it retained the Real Presence in the eucharist and prayers for the dead, and was arguably little more than the mass rendered into English. Stephen Gardiner, imprisoned in the Tower for his resistance to the regime's religious changes, sought to cause Cranmer and the duke of Somerset as much embarrassment as possible, by saying that he would be prepared to use it, were he not incarcerated.[68] Cranmer had declared to the Polish reformer Jan Łaski that he was 'desirous of setting forth in our churches the true doctrine of God, and have no wish to adapt it to all tastes, or to deal in ambiguities'; but the end result was deemed by many to be dangerously ambivalent.[69] John Hooper wrote that he was 'so much offended with that book' that he would not participate in the eucharist if it was not corrected.[70]

The 1549 Prayer Book was not only theologically divisive; it was also a major contributory factor to the outbreak of rebellion in Devon and Cornwall in the early summer of 1549, which in turn helped trigger a change at the highest levels of government. Somerset was replaced by the duke of Northumberland, who oversaw a revision of the Prayer Book, culminating in the new version of 1552. It is ironic that Somerset was probably the convinced Protestant, whilst Northumberland's Protestantism was very possibly just a career move intended to ingratiate him with Edward VI. And yet it was Northumberland's time in power that saw the most convincing advance towards unequivocally Protestant doctrine. The 1552 *Book of Common Prayer*, in particular, marked a clear shift in doctrine.[71] It insisted on bread for communion being 'such, as is usuall to bee eaten at the Table', in order to 'take away the supersticion' of previous practice.[72] At the same time, Cranmer was working on a reform of church law, faced by the anomaly of a Protestant Church still ruled by a medieval Catholic legal code. He also continued to work to interweave developments in England with their equivalents elsewhere in Europe. It was not enough that the leading Strasbourg reformers Martin Bucer and Peter Martyr Vermigli were in post at Cambridge and Oxford, respectively; Cranmer's ambition was to make England the location for a Protestant synod that would rival the Catholic Council of Trent, which had first met in 1545.[73] In this, as in so much, he was thwarted. In part, Cranmer, Northumberland and, most poignantly, Edward VI himself just ran out of time. In due course, the 1552 *Book of Common Prayer* would form the basis for the Elizabethan settlement, but the reform of canon law was left incomplete, and the great European reformers never did manage to make it to England. The ongoing divergence of views between those promoting reform also proved a frustration.[74] As Edward VI fell ill in the spring of 1553, the regime was still a long way from acquiring religious unity within Court and Council, let alone in the country at large.

The debate over Edward VI's religious achievements still rages. For some, this was the high-point of the Protestant Reformation in England, enacted with a rigour and enthusiasm that would leave Elizabeth I's more cautious enactment of Protestant reform looking feeble by comparison. For its detractors, this reign saw the ruthless destruction of the popular religious culture that had grown up over centuries, with the obliteration of an entire religious language of symbol and ritual, to be replaced by a wordy, intellectual form of religion that excluded the illiterate majority. If there were concrete advances made towards a national Protestant Church, they were made at the cost of much scholarly dismay, political animosity and popular discontent. Those who had served in the Edwardian Church would go on to provide many of the most famous martyrs who died for their Protestant faith under Mary I's regime, and those who survived would be instrumental in constructing a Protestant Church during Elizabeth I's reign. In the memory of churchmen and scholars, the Edwardian Reformation would retain its lustre and its integrity, despite all its flaws. In the memory of the populace at large, the years between 1547 and 1553 were frequently remembered, more than anything else, as years of destruction.

Reform in the parishes

The policies and preoccupations of kings, bishops and university scholars were a long way from the daily experience of religious life in rural England, where most of the population lived and worshipped. What seemed important, and comprehensible, at the highest level, might make little sense to those at grass-roots level, or be seen in an entirely different perspective. The break with Rome was of enormous political and ideological importance to those at the heart of government, and yet the repudiation of papal authority caused relatively few ripples in society at large. Surviving manuscripts demonstrate that many priests and churchwardens dutifully excised the name of the pope, and of discredited saints such as Thomas Becket, from liturgical texts.[75] Some showed gentle resistance, by crossing out the offending references with only the lightest of touches, or gluing small strips of paper over them, which could easily be removed when the rules changed.[76] The propagandist Richard Morison discovered that some conservative clergy refused to preach against the pope on the grounds that 'since your Majesty hath abolished him, the people need not talk of him'.[77] A printed picture of Christ as the 'image of pity', surrounded by the instruments of the Passion, has the indulgence rubric crossed out so lightly as to remain entirely legible, although the part relating to purgatory is more heavily erased (see illustration 13). Mostly, however, resistance was muted and acquiescence widespread. By contrast, the dissolution of the monasteries was not intended by those in authority to prove contentious. It was based on a comprehensive report into the supposed inadequacies of the religious houses, and was presented as being the kind of large-scale reallocation of resources, from abbeys to cathedrals, colleges and other worthy institutions, that had already been seen on a small scale in the late medieval period. It involved no real theological innovation, and yet it was perceived by many as an appalling act of violence. Similarly, the case for demolishing shrines and removing images to which supernatural powers had been attributed was quite defensible; indeed, Henry tried to present it to Catholic public opinion elsewhere in Europe as a laudable act of reform.[78] And yet it caused immense distress and outrage when beloved statues were taken away and smashed or burned.

There was also a measure of condescension in Henrician reforms. When, in 1538, the Catholic loyalist John Forest was burned at the stake for his papalism, the wood for his pyre was in part the broken-up image of Dderfel Gadarn, or St Derfel, brought from the small Welsh village of Llandderfel. This image had been believed to possess many supernatural properties, and there was a prophecy that one day it would set fire to a forest.[79] By using it to set fire to John Forest, the Henrician regime not only

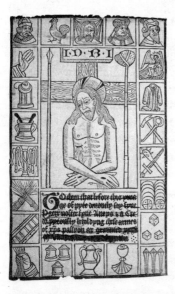

13. 'The image of pity': woodcut of Christ surrounded by instruments of the Passion and with an indulgence rubric

deployed an appalling pun, but used mockery of popular religiosity to make a propaganda point. Henry's own rhetoric, and that of Cromwell and his propagandists, drew a distinction between a time of darkness, error and folly and the brave new era of biblical rectitude and good order, which Henry was held to have ushered in. The reports from the commissioners visiting the monasteries dripped with scorn, gleefully recording the more outlandish relics, such as Thomas Becket's 'penneknyff and his bootes'.[80] This was not an age in which anyone felt embarrassed by their elitism: the radical Protestant William Turner, in 1545, briskly asserted that the 'learned men both of oxforde and cambrydge' were likely to perceive the true faith, where the ignorant and uneducated rural clerics continued to lead their ignorant flocks into error, being 'unlearned matten mumblynge sacrificers whiche can do nothyng ellis byt / play in ceremonies and / cast hallywater'.[81] At one level, this was an elite attack upon popular culture, and many resented it as such.

Much of the positive rhetoric accompanying reform was lost on Henry's subjects, who saw only destruction. As early as 1532, the prior of the London Crutched Friars was in trouble for calling the king 'Destructor Fidei'.[82] The more positive actions, arising from the Dissolution, such as the creation of six new bishoprics with former abbeys as their cathedrals, or the founding of Trinity College Cambridge and Christ Church Oxford, were not calculated to arouse popular enthusiasm. Evangelical reformers may have greeted the arrival of an English Bible with excitement, but two years after its publication, individual parishes had to be threatened with a fine (slightly larger than the cost of the book itself), in order to compel them to purchase it. Thomas Becon lamented that even when there was a bible in the church, it would very likely be thick with dust.[83] Gestures of resistance ranged from the upheaval of the Pilgrimage of Grace to smaller acts of defiance, as priests refused to deface their missals as instructed.[84] Robert Parkyn, curate in a small parish near Doncaster, wrote his account of the religious changes, noting how the loss of the monasteries came about 'thrughe cowncell of one wreatche and heretike Thomas Crumwell, and such other of his affinitie'. For him, the two biggest changes brought about by Henry were the Dissolution and the reduction in the number of holy days – attacks not on doctrine, but on the institutions and rhythms of religious life. Parkyn's conclusion was that 'in Kyng Henrie days began holly churche in Englande to be in greatt ruyne as it appearide daly'.[85]

There were also those who raced ahead of the regime's first steps in religious reform. In the early 1530s, there were acts of iconoclasm entirely unsanctioned by the regime, including the destruction of the Rood of Dovercourt, a highway cross at Coggeshall, and images in Ipswich and elsewhere, particularly London and East Anglia.[86] In 1536, Convocation drew up a list of sixty-eight common abuses, which it associated with 'light and lewd persons', including those who said the sacrament was nothing 'but a pece of bread', that the intoning of mass, matins and evensong was 'but roryng, howling, whistelyng, mummyng, conjuryng, and jogelyng', and playing the organ 'a folish vanitie'. Other recorded statements included the advice that holy water 'is a very good medicen for a horse with a gald back; yea, if ther be put an onyon therunto, it is a good sawce for a gygget of motton'. The list also included the saying that 'Godd never gave grace nor knowledge of holy Scripture to any great estate, or rich man'.[87] These were a potentially worrying mix of ribaldry, ignorance and subversion. The ten Dutch immigrants who were burned in 1535 for being Anabaptists bore testimony to the anxiety felt by the regime about the advance of radical ideas.[88]

For there to be effective resistance from any direction, Henry's subjects would have needed to know what they were facing. His reforms were not based on a single ideology that could be opposed; they were instead a series of steps – which sometimes faltered – along a path decided by principles which perhaps only Henry himself truly understood. Thousands were prepared to rebel in defence of the monasteries; but for the most part, it was harder to perceive what those uneasy about Henrician policy should choose to oppose. There was also a heavy official emphasis on the idea that Henry's approach was something balanced and moderate, compared to the extremes of religious conflict elsewhere in Europe. William Chedsey, in a Paul's Cross sermon of 1544 observed that the 'worlde (the more is the pity) is full of schysmes, full of diversite and contention: Some goyng to far on the one hande: somme to farre on the other'. He lamented that there were so few 'that kepe the kynges hye way and walke in the myddell path'.[89] Cranmer, in his 1540 preface to the Great Bible, had reiterated the idea of a middle way between 'those that be too slow and need the spur' and those who 'seem too quick, and need more of the bridle'; and Henry struck the same note in his speech to parliament in 1545, piously deploring those who hurled insults of 'papist' and 'heretic' at one another.[90] It was perhaps hard to appreciate this religious moderation, when the regime marked out its middle way by executing papists on the one hand and burning Protestants as heretics on the other. On the same day in July 1540, the Protestants Robert Barnes, Thomas Garrett and William Jerome were burned at the stake at Smithfield, even as three Catholics, Thomas Abell, Edward Powell and Richard Fetherstone, were being hanged, drawn and quartered as traitors. Henry's idea of balance was of an idiosyncratic variety.[91]

More clarity was achieved during Edward VI's reign, but also more devastation. The priest Richard Langrysh, anticipating what was about to happen, in 1547 jumped from the steeple of the church of St Magnus in London into the Thames and 'wilfully drowned', whilst the remaining Carthusians in London gathered up their relics and took them into exile.[92] To Robert Parkyn, it seemed like the Edwardian regime was merely bent on the annihilation of past practice. He described the loss of processions and other ceremonies, images and candles, chantries and hospitals, and the confiscation of 'all maner of jewells, chalesscis, boykes, bells vesti-

mentts, with all other ornamenttes'.[93] Parkyn is sometimes cast as an ignorant country vicar, but he was in fact highly educated: his commonplace
book contained several works by Richard Rolle, some prayers by Thomas
More, a survey of the Pauline Epistles and five letters of St Cyprian, which
seems to suggest that he had a copy of the edition by Erasmus, indicating
someone well versed in late medieval devotion and yet equally aware of
humanist texts.[94] On the new services in English being brought in, he had
nothing good to say. He observed that on Good Friday 1548, 'no sepulcre
was preparide nor any mention mayde thatt day in holly churche of Christ
Jesus bitter passion, death and beriall (as of longe tyme before was uside)
the passion only exceptt, wich was redde in Englishe'. The reading of the
Bible in his own tongue clearly left him completely underwhelmed.

One of the very first policy initiatives of Edward's reign went right to
the heart of traditional religion, with devastating effects. The dissolution of
the chantries was like the dissolution of the monasteries, but on a smaller,
more personal scale.[95] Some chantries took the form of a small chapel, and
larger churches might contain several of these; but most chantries were
merely an endowment of money to pay a priest to say masses for the souls
of the benefactor, usually in perpetuity. Chantry priests were useful
members of any parish community, often fulfilling the additional role of
local schoolmaster, whilst chantry bequests were an important form of
commemoration, which extended protection to the dead in purgatory.[96]
Chantries were abolished by act of parliament in 1547, alongside many
collegiate churches and guilds; the colleges of Oxford and Cambridge only
just survived.[97] This raised a considerable amount of money for the Crown,
but it was simultaneously an attack upon a belief system and an affront to
the families and communities of the founders.[98] In Seamer in Yorkshire,
the former mayor of York and two of the chantry commissioners were
dragged from their beds, one with his wife, and all four were murdered on
the moors by a mob of perhaps three thousand people.[99]

Whilst some lamented, others celebrated. For some, the arrival of the
Edwardian religious changes was the culmination of long years of hope
and longing, and a chance to shake off the superstitions of the past. In
1548, the church officers of Rye paid out over 33s 'for clensyng the
chaunsell from poperye'.[100] Some cast this in terms of the entire social
order renewed and inspired, and envisioned England as a godly kingdom

for the world to emulate. 'All the kings christened shall learn at you to reform their Churches', wrote Robert Crowley of Edward VI. 'You shall be even the light of the world.' Crowley was an Oxford graduate, a printer and a Protestant writer deeply concerned with social justice and the 'great oppression of the pore communes by the possessioners'.[101] His lofty view of Edward's vocation came with a sharp edge, however, as did his vitriolic condemnation of the rich who failed in their social duty. 'Ther is not one storie of the Bible that serveth to declare how readi God is to take vengeaunce for the oppression of his people, but the same hath ben declared unto you to the uttermoste', he warned Tudor property owners.[102] This was an abiding, and often uncomfortable, feature of Protestant rhetoric: that no matter how far the regime advanced, there were always those criticizing the lack of godly zeal and exhorting greater effort. Parliament was told in 1550 to pray for the king's zeal and strength to enact good laws, so that everywhere it would be 'reported how that we of thys realme have expelled all vayne tradicions of men, and receyved the true religion of Christ'.[103] Being held up to the rest of Europe as an exemplar of godly reform and virtue could not but impose a strain.

Early Protestantism possessed a close affinity with the cause of social reform, which could be both appealing to the populace at large and a source of worry for those in authority. The same work addressed to parliament noted that where once 'fatte priestes' had stood in the way, 'even so now at this daye there be many fatte marchauntes which wold have no reformation in the comon wealth'.[104] Some Protestant reformers were keen to cast the Gospel as 'the writynges of poore fysher men and symple creatures, even taken for the dregges of the worlde'.[105] Robert Crowley responded to the rebellions of 1549 by writing *The Waie to Wealth*, which began by deploring sedition, but then took the more unusual route of noting the plight of the dispossessed, and blaming those who so neglected true religion as to oppress the poor, rather than instructing them in their faith. He saw a combination of worldly greed and spiritual negligence at work, and he gave a passionate defence of the powerless and indigent, against the offences of the rich. 'You ungentle gentlemen! You churles chikens, I say! Geve me leve to make answere for the pore ideotes over whom ye triumphe in this sorte.'[106] This way of thinking promised to make the regime as anxious as it made the Protestant creed beguiling.

Protestantism had other forms of appeal. Freedom from fasting could prove popular: eating meat in Lent, while everyone else was denied it, offered an opportunity to feel both rebellious and sated. Convocation in 1536 had noted that some were teaching that 'it is no synne or offence to ete white metes, eggs, butter, chese, or flesh' during Lent or on other fasting days, and Catholic accusations that Protestants were libertines who opposed fasting and celibacy must have had some foundation.[107] There were more cerebral attractions, too: some apprentices clearly neglected their work to attend Protestant sermons, or dispute religious questions. Cuthbert Scot, fellow of Christ's College Cambridge, complained in 1544 about the kind of apprentice who was lured 'to stande in his owne conceyte, to disdayne his mayster, to neglecte his office, and dewtie'. Scot observed that 'these specially wyll have in their handes the new testament, and they wyll talke much of the scripture, and goddes word, and yet wyll not learne therof to be obedient, and gentle unto theyr maysters'.[108] A year later, Scot complained to Stephen Gardiner, as chancellor of the university, about a play performed at Christ's which questioned ceremonies of the Church, such as Lenten fasting.[109] London apprentices and Cambridge undergraduates did not have a great deal in common, apart from their youth, but both seemed to have appreciated the subversive potential of the Protestant message.

Not only could the radical edge of Protestantism prove troublesome for the authorities, but it might also bring the creed itself into disrepute. It was one thing for reformers to counsel against devotion to the saints, but in 1535 someone was preaching in London that the Virgin Mary was a 'maintainer of bawdery', and others had allegedly declared 'that Our Lady was no better than another woman, and like a bag of saffron or pepper, when the spice is out'.[110] Reformers could be sensitive to claims that they had preached such things: Miles Coverdale went to some trouble to defend Robert Barnes against the claim that he had compared the Virgin Mary to a saffron bag (saffron being a very precious and costly spice); and Latimer also tried to argue that Barnes had not used the analogy – and that if he had, it was not as rude as it sounded.[111] A year later, one William Collins was in trouble for firing arrows at sacred pictures and mocking the sacrament: during mass, when the priest elevated the host, Collins had lifted a dog up over his head.[112] Any radical message might find particularly willing listeners among the young. The 1543 Act for the Advancement of

True Religion noted with displeasure how people had perverted the Scriptures through books, ballads, 'playes, rymes songes and other fantasies', misleading the king's people 'and speciallye the youthe of this his Realme'.[113] The Dominican friar William Peryn published his sermons in 1546, because he was worried about heresy creeping 'secretly in to the hearts of many of the younger and carnal sort'.[114] Many Catholic commentators cast Protestantism as a creed with natural appeal to the young, licentious and unruly.[115] The Marian Catholic bishop, John Christopherson, described the young gospeller who complained that 'My father is an old doting fool . . . and my mother goeth always mumbling on her beads.'[116] It was certainly the case that the earliest Protestant groupings in England had begun as a student movement in Cambridge. It was also the case that the young were more likely to suffer the effects of poverty, which Protestantism also promised to address. The promise of both social and spiritual revolution could be a potent one.

If it was hard to convey a Protestant message to the less educated elements within society, it was also far from given that the views of humble converts would remain within the bounds of what might be considered orthodox Protestant belief. One group within mid-Tudor society was that of the 'freewillers', who, whilst upholding most of the tenets of Protestantism, believed in free will, rather than predestination.[117] A conventicle from Bocking in Essex was reported to the Privy Council in 1551, which included the most prolific of the group's authors, Henry Hart, who insisted that 'his faith was not grounded upon learned men, for all errors were brought in by learned men'.[118] There were other groups, too, in Kent and London, with a measure of internal coherence and discipline.[119] Yet just as they came under prosecution by the Edwardian Protestant establishment, they would later be all but expunged from the historical record by Elizabethan Protestants keen to play down fissures within England's Protestant community. But if the contribution of the freewillers to the tally of Marian martyrs was something that Foxe sought to gloss over, there were still divisions within England's Protestants at every social level.[120]

At its most radical, the Protestant creed could take the form of Anabaptism, which had produced alarmingly violent manifestations elsewhere in Europe. The only two people executed for heresy during Edward VI's reign were Anabaptists: Joan Bocher and the Dutch immigrant George van Paris, but Bocher boasted that 'a thousand in London were of her sect'.[121] It is extremely hard to assess whether there was indeed a substantial number of Anabaptists, not least because the alarm and anxiety of the authorities on this count tended to be wildly out of proportion to the actual threat they posed. Leading figures such as John Hooper published works decrying heterodox reform ideas, and the Privy Council took concerted action to uncover and destroy dissident groups. Roger Hutchinson, one of the theologians chosen to debate openly with Bocher, published a compendium of heresies to put people on their guard.[122] The existence of Protestant heresies was, at one level, an embarrassment to a Protestant movement already divided; but reformed writers worked hard to turn it into an advantage, since, by casting themselves as the scourge of heresy, they helped both to define and to justify their Church by taking the moral high ground.[123] How convincing this may have seemed can only be guessed at, although the quantity of writing against Anabaptism and its ilk suggests it may indeed have proved very useful to the Protestant cause to be able to denounce, rather than be held to embody, the threat of heterodoxy.

Not everyone in Tudor England was a religious zealot. Those who appear in the historical record are characterized by their outspoken commitment, their attempts to proselytize or resist, their sermons, books and speeches. Frustratingly, the majority of the population still remain silent. It seems probable that their religious faith was of a quieter, more prosaic sort. One of the most popular Protestant authors was Thomas Becon, who was adept at giving his religious advice a practical, domestic flavour. His work, A Christmas bankette, used tables, chairs and dishes as metaphors for encouraging household piety.[124] Propagandists for any version of the faith tended to see their belief system as something coherent, homogeneous and requiring total assent; but it is probable that ordinary individuals might not have comprehended, or accepted, a religious outlook in its entirety. In 1575, some of the citizens of Coventry complained to the queen about the suppression of their Hock Tuesday Play, a time-honoured celebration. They wrote that they could not understand why it had been discontinued, 'unless it were by the zeal of certain their preachers: men very commendable for their behaviour and learning, and sweet in their sermons, but somewhat too sour in preaching away their pastimes'.[125] Many who accepted aspects of Protestantism still held onto saying prayers for their dead, including, for a while, Hugh Latimer.[126] Others who believed themselves to be loyal Catholics nonetheless embraced aspects of the new faith, such as the emphasis upon scriptural authority, or the new ideas about salvation.[127] One man in Kent who crept to the cross on Good Friday 1543 admitted that he had done so 'more for company than for devotion'.[128] The practical application of religion was often a long way from the hopes of the reformers, and the notion of a godly, obedient, Bible-reading people was still more of a literary construct than a reality.

A religion of words

Histories of the Reformation, concerned with doctrinal change, have often overlooked the fact that some of the earliest steps towards Protestantism came through disagreements over form, not content. Early reformers liked to cast themselves as making a radical break with the past; but in fact, their levels of religious commitment were no different from those of the later middle ages, and many of their devotional patterns were very similar. They were, however, using a very different language much of the time. This was not about the gulf between Latin and English, but the fact that the pre-Reformation Church had communicated as much through ritual, drama, images and objects as through the written or spoken word, whereas the Protestant mentality repudiated material or visual embodiments of the sacred, and used texts and sermons to convey meaning.[129] Much of the early Reformation was preoccupied with this cultural shift, and much Protestant rhetoric poured scorn on the old ways, as when Thomas Cranmer denounced the pre-Reformation practice of seeing the elevation of the host, which 'made the people run from their seats to the altar, and from altar to altar, and from sacring (as they called it) to sacring, peeping, tooting and gazing at that thing which they saw'. He mocked those who said 'I cannot be quiet except I see my Maker once a day'.[130] To Cranmer, this was a shameful parody and a piece of idolatry. His God was mediated through words, and not through symbols. His faith rested upon printed or spoken words, not a wafer or a cup of wine. Nevertheless, he still moved with caution to reform the old ways. Hooper, writing to the Swiss reformer Heinrich Bullinger in 1550, noted the Protestant advances that were being made at the level of government, but recorded gloomily that 'the people . . .

that many-headed monster, is still wincing; partly through ignorance, and partly fascinated by the inveiglements of the bishops, and the malice and impiety of the mass-priests'.[131] Sacred materiality continued to exert a fascination over the populace at large.

Reformers were those who prioritized the religion of the word above all else, often to the complete exclusion of the symbolic, although, as disagreements among Protestants demonstrated, the extent to which symbolism was distrusted and expunged could vary a great deal between different branches of the Protestant cohort. To the many for whom symbol and ritual acted as a complement to the written or spoken word, the vicious denunciations of Protestant reformers were puzzling, as well as unpleasant, and much about the Protestant message remained unintelligible, or just unimpressive. In 1543, Cranmer's commissioners, investigating whether instructions about the use of the vernacular were being followed, discovered that some people were refusing to say the Lord's Prayer in English, because they did not think it would work unless recited in Latin.[132] At a time when important business was frequently transacted in Latin, it was perhaps not unreasonable to assume that God would also want to be addressed in formal and exalted language.

To make the matter still more complicated, views about materiality and the sacred could not be separated into two clearly opposing positions. Some had an absolute horror of any physical, visual or material expression of the divine. John Hooper not only disliked actual images, but was also worried about 'inward / and spirituall Idolatrie / of the mynd', which might be committed purely by the workings of the imagination. He argued that 'a man may lern / more of a live ape / then of a ded ymage'.[133] Nicholas Ridley, bishop of London, issued injunctions for his diocese in 1550 which gave stern warnings against such traditional practices as the priest kissing the altar or Lord's Table, ringing the sacring bell at the consecration or putting a light before the sacrament.[134] Other Protestants could see value in certain aspects of ceremony, however, such as kneeling, or lighting candles, or retaining clerical vestments in some form. Cranmer included an essay on ceremonies in the 1549 *Book of Common Prayer*. It carefully steered a middle course, defending the origins of church ritual as having been 'of godly intent', even if corruption had later set in, and distinguishing between those that had 'much blinded the people' and those that might continue to edify.[135] Such disagreements over church order, decoration, ritual and ceremony would continue to exercise English Protestants for centuries to come.

Books, however, were generally safe. It is unsurprising that Protestants tended to view the printing press as providentially sent by God for their purposes. Foxe asserted that the 'science of Printyng beyng found, immediately folowed the grace of God'.[136] Not only did Protestants found all their claims on the Bible text, but through long years of proscription and persecution under Henry VIII and Mary I, English Protestants also relied on books to tell their message when they, as individuals, were silenced. English Protestantism did not arrive on the same tidal wave of popular print as was witnessed in parts of mainland Europe, however. It has been calculated that England's presses accounted for just around 3 per cent of European output in this period. And for the first few decades of print, business was handled by just two printshops, whilst even in later decades English printing was limited to London and Westminster. None of Luther's works appeared in English before 1535, and it was only the break with Rome that facilitated the greater spread of Protestant texts in English – and even then with a heavy reliance on the printing industry in Antwerp and the work of certain key exiles there.[137] Nevertheless, books were at the heart of Protestant endeavour.

There was a problem in relying on the printed word, at a time when books were expensive and the majority of the population was illiterate. Sermons were therefore equally, if not more, important to Protestant culture; the best of them tended to end up in print as well. Nonetheless, the conundrum remained that Protestants were putting a great deal of effort into a medium that was inaccessible to many. The Bible was at the centre of these problems. In the late medieval Church, the Bible was a ritual object, as well as a text. It was carried in procession at mass and venerated in the same way as a holy relic. For those who could not read, Bible stories were mediated through sermons, plays, poems and pictures. In pre-Reformation religious culture, different modes of transmission sat very easily together; but for Protestants, they were diametrically opposed. This is why Cranmer, in his preface to the Great Bible, deliberately described the Bible as 'the woorde of God, the most preciouse juell, and most holye relyque that remayneth upon earth'.[138] He was consciously contrasting the Bible text of his own day with what he saw as the mistaken treasures of the past.

It was therefore essential to the Protestant cause to print bibles in great numbers, and to explain them to the populace at large. The Protestant cause thus remained closely tied to the development of popular print culture, in which it built on the foundations laid by Catholic print culture since the 1470s.[139] Rose Hickman had been converted by her mother, who in the 1530s herself discovered the 'light of the gospelle by meanes of some English books' which she kept in secret at home.[140] This did mean that Protestantism was inextricably bound up with literacy, which in turn would give it a very distinctive cultural shape. English religion was still the religion of the parish; but the balance of agency within the parish became more markedly tilted towards the educated, just as the book trade remained at the heart of reforming initiatives. In Henry's reign, heretics had been defined as 'a fewe particoler persons who carried in there bosomes certan bokes'.[141] Books became pivotal in the consolidation and expansion of English Protestantism.[142] This was a great blessing to its proponents, but it was also part of a broader transformation of religious culture – one that would affect all shades of opinion.[143] Religious life, which had always been so focused on the parish, the patterns of worship and the rhythms of the ritual year, was increasingly something with an added dimension that was personal and private, its chief truths contained within the pages of a book. This rendered religion more sustainable under persecution, more concerned with ideological definitions, more independent of communal expectation and more resistant to political control.

* * *

If there was a single point in time that separated the old world and the new, it would be 9 June 1549. This was Whitsunday, the feast of Pentecost, when the Church remembered how the Holy Spirit was sent down to a small bunch of terrified men locked in an upper room, converting them into the fearless apostles, saints and martyrs who went on to build the Christian Church. That Sunday in 1549 saw another kind of conversion, as in many churches, when the people gathered as usual, they found that the familiar hallowed ritual of the Latin mass had been replaced by something in English read out of a book. It was with the transformation of the liturgy that England's Reformation came of age, and the conflicts over religion began to form a gulf that would never again be bridged. From this point onwards, England was a divided nation. This was not because the new liturgy was particularly radical in its theology, or because the Edwardian regime had found any new means of coercing the populace into accepting religious change. This was, however, the first really convincing nexus between the ideals and aspirations of scholars and churchmen, the authority of the Crown and the patterns of popular worship at a local level. Nothing prior to this had connected the experience of these disparate pieces of society in such a noticeable departure from the past. Political power had engaged with theological innovation, and parish life would never be the same again.

The responses to the new service on Whitsunday 1549 were many and varied. In the south-west of England, a rebellion was triggered, amidst some passionate avowals of the strength of traditional religion. Elsewhere, others enthusiastically welcomed the new service. There would be many reversals ahead, but the idea of division was beginning to sink in as never before, with the Edwardian regime starting to institutionalize what had previously been unimaginable. Just before Whitsunday 1549, at a school in Bodmin, there had been a disturbance. Upon inquiry, it was discovered that the children had been divided into two playground gangs to fight; significantly, they had formed 'two factions, the one whereof they called the old religion, the other the new'.[144] It is perhaps the most incontrovertible testimony to social upheaval when children start enacting the conflicts of their elders. The reference to 'common prayer' in the new order of service was a gesture towards unity, towards a liturgy celebrated in common with the rest of the realm, using a common language. It was supposed to be a unifying experience. In reality, this was the moment when deep fissures began to appear within English society.

While divisions were widening, however, the authority of the state held firm. England's Reformation remained something first and foremost implemented by the Crown, through parliaments, royal injunctions, official publications and the authority of the magistrates, supported by the mechanisms of the church hierarchy. When royal commissioners were sent out to the provinces to ensure compliance, they frequently reported that they had found the people 'very quiet and conformable'.[145] Churchwardens' accounts from up and down the country show parishes dutifully removing statues, lights and ritual objects, and whitewashing over wall-paintings. Much of this was done not out of religious conviction, but out of obedience to the authorities.[146] William Paget commented in 1549 that 'what countenance so ever men make outwardly was to please them in whom they see the power resteth'.[147] Yet such obedience was in itself rooted in the religious conviction that a monarch was set over his or her people by God, and that to follow royal command was therefore to act in accordance with divine law. Even someone such as Robert Crowley, who was deeply sympathetic to the plight of the poor, accepted that it was wrong for them 'to take weapen in hand against Goddes chosen ministers', reminding his audience that 'be they good or bad, they are Goddes chosen, if they be good, to defende the innocente, if they be evell, to plage the wicked'.[148] On these grounds, the only moral choice was to submit. It was hard to distinguish between the will of the monarch and the will of God. Political stability was therefore preserved, but beneath the surface the religious ferment was growing all the time. The biblical narrative of Babel ends with a people confounded, unable to understand one another. The early years of Reformation in England were at least as much about the spread of confusion as the dawn of enlightenment.

CHAPTER 8

EDWARD VI AND THE TRIALS
OF THE YOUNG JOSIAH

Few children in any age can have carried a greater weight of expectation than Edward VI. Even before he was born, hope was already running high that he would help stabilize his father's reign, which in 1537 was in disarray, with rebellion and division at home, and threats from abroad. The news of Queen Jane's pregnancy was greeted with a 'Te Deum' at St Paul's Cathedral on Trinity Sunday, in May 1537, and the herald and chronicler Charles Wriothesley recorded that 'the same night was diverse greate fyers made in London, and a hogeshed of wine at everye fyer for poor people to drinke'. He added, 'I praye Jesue, and it be his will, send us a prince.'[1] The kingdom stood in need of reassurance. Less than two weeks previously, the leaders of the Pilgrimage of Grace had been found guilty of treason at Westminster, and just two days earlier, several had been hanged, disembowelled and beheaded, so that their heads could be set on London Bridge and their limbs above the gates of the city. In the weeks that followed the announcement of the pregnancy, the executions continued.

Henry VIII had been waiting nearly thirty years for a healthy son and heir. The day before Edward was born, a great array of friars, priests, the mayor, aldermen and livery companies processed through London, all praying for the queen, who had begun her long labour. The baby was born on the eve of St Edward the Confessor's day, 12 October, and that morning 'Te Deum was songe in everie parish church throughout London, with all the bells ringing in everie church, and great fiars made in everie streete.'[2] Two thousand volleys were fired from the Tower, and the bonfires and bells continued until late into the night. An elaborate christening at Hampton Court was an opportunity for a show of family solidarity: Edward's half-sister Mary was godmother, and four-year-old Elizabeth carried the chrism. She herself was carried in the arms of the queen's brother Edward Seymour. Archbishop Cranmer and the duke of Norfolk were godfathers, whilst Henry's brother-in-law Charles Brandon, duke of Suffolk, was godfather at the confirmation immediately afterwards.[3] Less than two weeks after the birth, however, Edward's mother was dead, perhaps killed by her privileged status, since the royal doctors who attended the birth had little midwifery experience, and may not have checked that she had expelled the placenta in full.[4] Her death underlined once more the fragility of royal succession.

Throughout Edward's childhood, the pressure remained intense to bring him up as the fulfilment of all Henry VIII's grandiose ambitions. Holbein's portrait of Edward as a very young child (see plate 9) drove home Edward's likeness to Henry VIII, and referenced his future kingship, with the baby holding his rattle as if it were a sceptre. The portrait bore a Latin inscription by the propagandist Richard Morison: 'Little one, emulate thy father and be the heir of his virtue; the world contains nothing greater.'[5] Other members of the political classes perhaps quietly hoped for qualities such as longevity and wisdom, without necessarily seeking a direct replacement for his often problematic father. But some had a more particular agenda. Protestant churchmen and courtiers, headed by Edward's godfather, Thomas Cranmer, and his uncle, Edward Seymour, envisaged a reformed future under a godly Protestant ruler.[6] Soon after his birth, Hugh Latimer was preaching on the necessity of him being brought up by men 'of ryght jugmentes'; since this admonition was addressed to Cromwell, it was clear that by 'right' he meant 'Protestant'.[7] This royal child, his character as yet unknown, was the vehicle for any number of aspirations.

Edward as a prince was also circled about with fears. Any childish ailment produced a flurry of anxiety, and the prospect of a royal minority made many apprehensive, most particularly his father. When this prospect became a reality in 1547, many will have thought back to the fates of previous child kings. Richard II's turbulent reign had remained unsteady even after he achieved adulthood, and ended in his deposition and murder; Henry VI's even more conflict-ridden years had seen him deposed twice and eventually murdered; whilst Edward V's brief time as king had ended with the murder of himself and his brother by Richard III, commonly depicted in Tudor culture as a twisted and ruthless tyrant. When, in 1549, the duke of Somerset was on the brink of being toppled as protector, he barricaded himself and the young king inside Hampton Court, tearing up the cobblestones to defend the gates, and delivered a speech in which he warned his listeners to remember Richard III and how his ambition had resulted in the death of the two young princes.[8] This was an unfortunate choice of historical example. Somerset may have been thinking of the potential threat from Mary, but arguably if anyone resembled Richard III at that point it was Somerset, who, like his younger brother, Thomas Seymour, had sought to use Edward as a pawn in his own political aspirations. 'Woe to thee O land, when thy king is a child', said the book of Ecclesiastes, although Protestant propagandists made strenuous efforts to counter the effects of this particular passage.[9] Contemporaries may have been wary of voicing this thought, but it was troubling a great many people in January 1547. Henry VIII in his will had recorded that 'our chief labour and study in this world is to establish him in the Crown imperial of this Realm after our decease in such sort as may be pleasing to god and to the wealth of this realm and to his own honour and quiet'.[10] He had foreseen the trouble ahead only too clearly.

If a bird's-eye view of Edward's accession looked less than promising, a grass-roots perspective was also not encouraging. It was in the 1540s that the evils of social disruption and economic travail had become particularly evident. In part, this was a consequence of a growing population. It has been suggested that between 1541 and 1551 England's population grew from 2.75 million to over 3 million; and certainly in this period London was growing at an alarming rate.[11] There were outbreaks of plague in the capital in 1548 and in the provinces in 1544–46 and 1549–51, and the sweating sickness would return as an epidemic in 1551.[12] The dissolution of the monasteries had been completed by 1540, but little had been put in place to supply the loss of charity that this had brought about. The systematic expropriation of church property had continued through the 1540s, causing much unease to those who wondered if their churches and chantries would be next: between 1538 and 1546, the church of St Laurence in Reading sold church plate to the value of £47, probably fearing that its possessions might soon be confiscated.[13] In 1545, the first Chantries Act had confirmed some of these fears, giving the Crown possession of all chantries, hospitals, fraternities and guilds, confiscation that would be consolidated by Edward's regime two years later.[14] Meanwhile, the economic impact of the wars of 1543–44, particularly the debasement of the coinage, had been shattering, and in 1547 war with Scotland showed no sign of abating.[15] Harvests failed in 1545 and between 1549 and 1551; even in the intervening years, when harvests were better, prices were still high because of inflation, 'most miserably oppressynge the poor', as the chronicles noted.[16] Harvest failure could be accepted as an act of God, but debasement was the government's work, and between 1544 and 1551 the silver content of the coinage was reduced by about five sixths, to much indignation. The poet John Heywood sardonically observed that the coins were turning red from all the base metal: 'they blushe for shame', he wrote.[17] The debasement of the smaller coins, in particular, was punishing for the poor, 'for theyr whole substaunce lay in that kind of money'.[18]

Edward VI's reign was from the start characterized by anxiety of many different sorts. Its history would later be appropriated by Protestant polemicists and rewritten as an era of triumphant religious advance, but the other side of rapid reformation was profound social disruption. The years after 1540 were the time when the impact of Dissolution, war and appropriation of church wealth, with all the disruption this caused to family and community life, was particularly severe. In this, Edward's reign blended to a certain extent with that of his father. Where it differed was in the pace of religious change, which accelerated markedly after 1547. Wriothesley began his account of Edward's first year with a report of how the rood screen and its images in St Paul's Cathedral were taken down, with one man killed when the great cross fell down upon him, and of how 'all images in everie parish church in London were pulled downe and broken'.[19] The iconoclasm, the erosion of the liturgy and the general transformation of religious life that accompanied it contributed to the general sense of unease. It is hard to separate out the effects of economic hardship from those of religious disruption. In 1548 and 1549, riot and rebellion swept across most of southern England, from Cornwall to East Anglia, and fears ran so high that probably only the bitter memory of repression after the Pilgrimage of Grace ten years earlier stopped the north of England from rising, too. These uprisings, however different their aspirations, were alike in looking back with longing to an era of greater stability. The western rebels in 1549 appealed to the 'holy decrees of our forfathers' and 'the Lawes of our Soverayne Lord Kyng Henry the viii'; those in Norfolk tried to return patterns of landholding and legal provision to the state they had been 'in the fyrst yere of the reign of Kyng henry the viith'.[20] Old certainties were being undermined; patterns of communal responsibility and the rhythms of the ritual year had been lastingly damaged; even those who welcomed religious change were painfully aware of the plight of the poor, and the damaged fabric of their society.

There was a terrible unease at being ruled by a child. Edward's vulnerability opened the door to ambitious courtiers with an eye on both personal aggrandizement, which was an expected development, and religious transformation, which was unprecedented. Protestants liked to cast Edward VI as the young King Josiah from the Old Testament, who became king of Judah at the age of eight, and who purged his realm of idols and restored the Temple. Viewed from another perspective, however, Edward's reign had plunged England into an Old Testament world of violence, upheaval and fear. In the six years of his short reign, these conditions would bring all sorts of social problems into painful relief, as the regime stirred up a maelstrom of religious change and conflict. It is a tribute to the strength of Tudor government, and to the sense of political responsibility and communal obligation among so many of its citizens, that England avoided civil war. Edward's reign showed both the worst and the best of the Tudor state.

Young Josiah

On 28 January 1547, Henry VIII died, aged only fifty-five. The 1559 version of Fabyan's *Chronicle* commented that under Henry 'his people of Englande lived long a joifull and peacable life'.[21] This was a charitable assessment of a reign that had seen its fair share of popular suffering; but in comparison to what followed, the previous reign did indeed come to look like a haven of sure government and social stability. The news of the old king's death was broken to his successor the following day by the new king's uncle, Edward Seymour, earl of Hertford, and Sir Anthony Browne, gentleman of the Privy Chamber. It would be another two days before the news of Henry's death was made public. As when Henry VII had died, the first instinct of those in authority was to proceed with caution – and with good reason. When, on the first day of February, the nobility came together to kiss the new king's hand, it was a nine-year-old boy who sat enthroned in the chair of state, an incongruous replacement for the king they had known, and who had imposed his will with such vigour for nearly forty years. When it was announced that the earl of Hertford had been chosen by Henry's executors to serve as protector, no dissenting voice was heard.[22] This has been described by many as a coup by the man who rapidly made himself duke of Somerset; but as the young king recorded in his diary, the Council 'thought best to choose the Duke of Somerset to be Protector', and everyone agreed to this, 'because he was the King's uncle on his mother's side'.[23] There was good precedent for having an uncle as protector; the prospect of a strong figure to head the regime was a welcome one; and Seymour had an impressive military record, as well as a long history of service at court. Yet for the king to be a child was plainly a misfortune. Despite all of Henry VIII's efforts, one of his worst nightmares had come true.

There is much debate about what Henry had intended for his son, in terms of both political management and religious aspirations. Some have argued that towards the end of his reign Henry was becoming more persuaded by aspects of Protestantism, as indicated by his tolerance of Queen Katherine Parr's evangelicalism, by his introduction of an English Litany and, above all, by the education that he gave his son, which, it is argued, had formed him as a Protestant.[24] Henry also appointed a council of sixteen men for his son, in which, it has been argued, evangelicals were the dominant force.[25] This line of argument is misleading – a composite of wishful thinking and a misunderstanding of Henry's religious objectives. Just as the English Litany should not be accorded too much significance, being a fairly minor addition to an otherwise unchanged reliance on Latin liturgy, so the significance of Edward's education can be distorted too readily.[26] It might be noted that throughout Henry's lifetime Edward had attended Latin mass, observed saints' days and performed all the rituals of the Catholic Church. He possessed a relic of the true cross, in a golden reliquary – even though, towards the end of his reign, he would be responsible for removing the Cross of Neith (*Croes Naid*) – the Welsh-owned fragment of the true cross taken by Edward I – from St George's Chapel Windsor, where it had been placed by Edward III.[27] He himself did not describe his tutors as having taught him the Protestant faith, but as having 'sought to bring him up in learning of tongues, of the scripture, of philosophy, and all liberal sciences'.[28]

Edward's tutors were not chosen because of their Protestant inclinations, but because of their academic excellence. The dominant religious emphasis of Henry's later years was that of theological moderation, combined with the forcible purging of extremists. Henry had some difficulty in recognizing the Protestant convictions of those around him, seemingly being unable to comprehend those who believed differently from their king, and was thus unlikely to spot more slowly burgeoning Protestant potential. He chose Richard Cox as Edward's tutor, because as headmaster of Eton and then later dean of Christ Church Oxford, he was the best educational authority available. Cox had also helped write 'The King's Book', which must have heightened Henry's impression that he was reliably of the king's views on religion.[29] John Cheke and Roger Ascham were leading intellectuals and pedagogues: Ascham's *The Scholemaster* would be perhaps the most famous book written on the subject of education in sixteenth-century England. John Cheke was already hinting at his Protestant views in the latter years of Henry's reign; but Henry was not disposed to take such a hint, and in all official pronouncements Cheke dissimulated to please the king.[30] Edward's education was first and foremost Erasmian: classical, sophisticated, evangelical and doctrinally conservative. Indeed, it was perhaps the most perfect example of a princely education on the Erasmian model.[31]

The council which Henry envisaged for Edward broadly comprised the most powerful and the most reasonable of the magnates and churchmen available. Henry's despair as he felt his strength ebbing, with his precious son only nine years old, must have been acute. He did everything he could to ensure that in the next reign there would be balance, order and consensus, the elusive virtues he had come to treasure so profoundly, since he had realized the disorder that he had unleashed by breaking with Rome. The regency council was predominantly composed of men he thought he could trust: it was headed by Thomas Cranmer and the prince's maternal uncle, and contained several long-serving members of the king's Privy Chamber. Alongside Protestants such as Cranmer and Sir Anthony Denny, it contained such leading Catholic voices as Cuthbert Tunstall, bishop of Durham, and staunch conservatives such as Anthony Browne, master of the horse; but it is probable that Henry selected them as much on grounds of proven loyalty as religious conservatism.[32] Foxe tells us that Gardiner, who had originally been on the list, was struck off because Henry judged him 'a wilful man . . . not meet to be about his son'; Henry believed that, while he himself 'could use him and rule him', others might not manage.[33] If Foxe could have told us that Henry excluded Gardiner on the grounds of religion, he would have done so; but even he put the decision down to Gardiner's intractability. Equally, Norfolk, who, together with his son, was disgraced just weeks before Henry's death, was in trouble not for any religious tendencies, but for his pride and ambition in aiming to control the future king. In any case, despite the staunch Catholic loyalties of Norfolk's descendants, the duke and his son, the earl of Surrey, showed few signs of Catholic loyalism in the 1540s; the duke had supported the break with Rome, and Surrey's leanings were, if anything, towards Protestantism.[34] Henry's will qualified his choice of counsellors: 'Not doubting but they will in all things deal so truly and uprightly as they shall have cause to think them well chosen for the charge committed unto them.' The old king included elaborate instructions to ensure that decisions were taken solely on the basis of their consensus. Yet there was a note of desperation, too, as he exhorted them to cooperate, 'because the variety and number of things affairs and matters are and may be such as we not knowing the certainty of them before cannot conveniently present a certain order or rule'.[35] Much as he might want to, Henry was not able to rule from beyond the grave.

Protestants had great hopes of this new reign. Earlier in the 1540s, many evangelicals – such as John Bale or Miles Coverdale – had thought it safer to stay in exile, but in 1547 such men came back full of optimism.[36] These were the only men for whom Edward VI's youth could appear as an advantage, because they could compare him to the young King Josiah in the Old Testament.[37] More quietly, they might have acknowledged that the king's age allowed religious policy to be left in the hands of Cranmer, Somerset and others. This suggested that reform might be able to progress without the kind of royal interference that had proved so frustrating to the Protestant cause during the later years of Henry VIII. Evangelicals had long been alive to the possibilities of moulding their future king. In 1545, one of the gentlemen of Edward's Privy Chamber, Philip Gerard, published a translation of a colloquy by Erasmus, with a lengthy preface full of exhortation. Dedicating the work to Edward, Gerard described him pointedly as someone who 'delecteth in nothyng more then too bee occupied in the holye Byble'. The book laid out the blessings in store for a godly prince. 'Blessed are you then if you obey unto hys word, and walke in his waies. Blessed are you, yf you supporte suche as preache Gospell.'[38] More ominously, he warned 'let your grace bee most fully perswaded in this, that ther was never Kyng nor Prince, that prospered whiche tooke parte against Goddes woord'.[39] In a 1549 reprint of the Bible, the editor Edmund Becke conveyed a similar message, reminding Edward that a king's prosperity 'dependeth upon the often and the reverent readyng of Gods boke'.[40] It is little wonder that this nine-year-old child swiftly learned to speak like a convinced Protestant.

Protestant exhortation often came with uncomfortable warnings for early modern rulers. Becke's preface to the 1549 Bible came with an ominous observation concerning a king's freedom of action. 'It lyeth not now in a kynges choyse to study or not study in Goddes boke. He muste not let the boke of this law departe out of hys mouth, but studie in it daye and nighte.'[41] The homilies issued in 1547 included a passage in the 'Exhortation to Obedience' which was critical of worldly authority, noting that 'Christ refused the office of a worldly Judge, and so he dyd the office of a worldly king.' It observed that 'Christ teacheth ... christen Emperours, Kynges and Princes, that they shoulde not rule their subiectes by will, and to their awne commoditie, and pleasure onely: But that they shoulde governe their subiectes, by good and Godly lawes.'[42] Such stern admonitions were potentially awkward politically. After appearing once, this passage was removed from all subsequent editions.[43] Protestant enthusiasm for the new regime was strong, but it was never going to be unconditional.

Despite the much-cherished depiction of Edward as a deeply pious child, it is hard to be sure whether his commitment to Protestantism was evident when he ascended the throne, or was the fruit of determined and sustained influence on the part of his uncle, his godfather Archbishop Cranmer and others who surrounded him. At Edward's coronation, which was in all other respects traditional (if slightly adapted to the needs of a small boy), Cranmer gave an astounding sermon.[44] It included a passionate denunciation of papal authority, and went on to compare Edward to King Josiah, in that he had a duty to see 'God truly worshipped, and idolatry destroyed, the tyranny of the bishops of Rome banished from your subjects, and images removed'. Cranmer dismissed the solemnities of the coronation as 'but a ceremony', noting that even without the anointing, 'that king is yet a perfect monarch notwithstanding'. Notably, he also stated explicitly that he had no power to depose Edward if the king failed in his godly duty: 'I openly declare before the living God, and before these nobles of the land, that I have no commission to denounce your majesty deprived.' This was seemingly an attempt to rebut the common accusation that Protestantism was a subversive creed, and at the same time to paint the papacy (which did claim deposing power) as an evil force.[45] After fifteen years of having to tailor his evangelicalism to Henry VIII's conservatism, it must have been liberation for Cranmer to be able to speak out; but the points he chose to highlight suggest that he envisaged a difficult path ahead for his contentious creed. If, fourteen years after the break with Rome, Cranmer was still having to argue its case, then he clearly perceived Catholic popular loyalties to be strong. He also seems to have been conscious of some possible political objections to Protestantism.

In the Protestant imagination, Edward VI would retain a glowing reputation. The woodcut from Foxe's *Actes and Monuments* (see illustration 14) of the young king at the heart of his court listening to a sermon by Bishop Latimer (in this picture centre-stage) has helped perpetuate the myth of the 'godly imp', as Foxe called him.[46] Given the flood of adulation that poured from the pens of both English and foreign Protestants, all desperate to confirm the young king in the role of Protestant reformer, it is little wonder that this has been the most lasting image of his reign. It is, however, important to realize that it was as much prescriptive as descriptive. And nor was the prescription just for Edward himself. A large part of his image was a product not of his Protestant reign, but of his sister's. Elizabeth was to prove a more unsatisfactory role model for many of her more committed evangelical subjects; and as her reign unfolded, and her dedication to the Protestant cause began to appear less zealous than many had hoped, the memory of Edward VI became a useful tool.[47] The woodcut of Edward's purified Church did not appear until the second edition of Foxe's *Actes and Monuments* (see illustration 16), in 1570, at a point when Foxe's own rhetoric was becoming increasingly pointed with regard to Elizabeth's failings.[48] Edward VI's fervent Protestantism is, then, to a certain extent an exercise in myth-building and a construct of later frustration at the slow progress of Protestant reform.

K.Edward.   M.Latimer.

14. Hugh Latimer preaching to Edward VI, from John Foxe,
Actes and Monuments

Even if we cannot be sure of his views in January 1547, however, it is undoubtedly true that the young king swiftly became Protestant in his convictions. Yet the propaganda of the reformers has skewed the historical record to make it appear that this was his most important objective. The easy portrayal of the mid-Tudor years is as an era of first Protestant zealotry under Edward and then Catholic bigotry under his half-sister Mary. The reality was a great deal more balanced and complex. If the young king increasingly supported the drive for religious reform, he also cared about many other things. He loved maps and was interested in the voyages of discovery; he spent large amounts on jewellery and enjoyed extravagant celebrations at Court; he was deeply engaged by questions of military organization and preparedness.[49] To judge from his own chronicle, it was military matters which, more than anything else, fired his enthusiasm. Above all, his concern for religion was never allowed to overwhelm his defence of his authority. Portraits repeatedly cast the young man in the guise of his father, and with good reason. It is significant that when Edward challenged Mary over her refusal to relinquish the Catholic mass, it was the affront to his authority that seems to have concerned him most.[50]

Edward VI was not the pious, pale, sickly child of legend. To read his chronicle is to discover a boy with a vivid sense of his own authority and importance, and a great liking for magnificence and display. His religious commitment was inextricably bound up with his understanding of monarchical supremacy: his lengthiest piece of writing on a religious subject was a condemnation of the papacy that had usurped the powers of kings. Other writings included memoranda on aspects of government, and some notes on the English occupation of France during Henry VI's reign which suggest an intelligent interest in the problems of financing an army.[51] He was undoubtedly a Protestant, but he was a king in his father's image – a Renaissance prince bejewelled and authoritative, more interested in war than in sermons. His memorandum for the Council concerning religion was more practical than pious, with an emphasis on uniformity reminiscent of Henrician reforms.[52] Like his father, he countered with fury any implied slights upon his majesty. Most importantly, it would seem that the young king had enough confidence in his own dominion that, when illness suddenly laid him low, he planned for the future, just as his father had done, proposing a radical subversion of the laws of succession in the interests of his Protestant polity. Edward was prepared not just to emulate the policies of the past, but also – just like his father – to attempt to control the future.

War, reformation and rebellion

The first two years of Edward VI's rule were particularly turbulent. It would be easier to look at them piece by piece, separately considering questions of military objectives, religious reforms and political control. However, the fact is that the young king, his ministers and his subjects had no choice but to face the tribulations of all three simultaneously. The balance of power at the centre was unsteady from the outset, and the strain of expensive and unsuccessful warfare on the one hand, and rapid religious change on the other, meant that doubt and unease percolated down through every layer of society. Furthermore, the fact that the man in power, Protector Somerset, had founded his reputation on his military achievements and was openly committed to the advance of Protestantism meant that the different challenges faced by the regime were all inextricably interwoven.

In Edward VI's own chronicle, his description of his coronation (see illustration 15) is immediately followed by a detailed account of a naval encounter, and then of the 'great preparation' that was made to go into Scotland, and the ensuing campaign, with details of troop numbers, castles burned, ambushes, skirmishes and enemies put to flight. This enthusiasm stands in marked contrast to the laconic accounts of other events and developments in the young king's narrative – for example, the record of Edward's first parliament, 'wherein all chantries were granted to the King and an extreme law made for vagabonds, and divers other things'.[53] If Edward shared his father's military leanings, it was perhaps his uncle who had the most direct influence on him in this regard. Edward Seymour was the son of a soldier, who had first fought in France in 1523, when he was knighted by the duke of Suffolk. He had benefited immensely from his sister's marriage to Henry VIII, and thereafter had prospered at Court; but most particularly, he had taken a leading role in military matters. He had demanded the unconditional surrender of the city of Edinburgh in 1544, and had sacked the city when it was refused. Later that year he joined the king in France, and helped capture the city of Boulogne. The following year, when the French attempted to retake the city, he repulsed an army three times the size of his own forces. His first campaign in Scotland under the new regime led to another victory over a larger force, when he defeated the Scottish army at the battle of Pinkie in September 1547. If he took pride in his military achievements, he had some reason for doing so.

For many years, Protector Somerset enjoyed a glowing historical reputation as the 'Good Duke', characterized by liberal policies and reforming intent, a man credited with 'no mean or selfish motives'.[54] The fact that Somerset had overseen several important steps towards a Protestant future was allowed to obscure his record as one of the more misguided and inept politicians of the sixteenth century. Leaving aside his religious policies – in themselves not without problems – his prosecution of wars (which had ruinous financial consequences), his high-handed style of ruling and his mismanagement of local government all ensured that his time as protector

15. Edward VI's coronation procession

was deservedly brief.[55] Even so, as the king's uncle, the former king's loyal servant and the officially recognized protector of the young king, his authority was preserved and respected for over two years by those who could see only too clearly the mistakes that he was making.

Edward Seymour (at that point still only earl of Hertford) had taken power before the old king had stopped breathing; famously, William Paget was later to remind him of promises made before 'the breathe was owt of the body of the king that dead ys'.[56] Certainly those who supported him in his appropriation of the protectorship were richly rewarded with titles and grants, mostly of lands confiscated from the duke of Norfolk and his son. Even this was not managed with complete success, however. Edward's younger uncle, Thomas Seymour, pointed out with some vigour, having researched Henry VI's minority, that where there were two uncles, 'if one were protector, the other should be governor'.[57] This younger Seymour brother owed his career to a combination of family connections and military prowess, and unwisely thought that these might be sufficient for him to seize at least some power from his brother. An early Elizabethan account noted 'the ambytion of the admirall and the envy he hadd that his brother should be more advaunced than he'.[58] He married Katherine Parr after Henry VIII's death with unseemly haste; as Edward VI noted drily in his chronicle, 'with which marriage the Lord Protector was much offended'.[59] Seymour also engaged in a dangerous flirtation with the young Princess Elizabeth while she was living with him and Katherine. In attempting to ingratiate himself with the young king, he gave him money and tried to persuade various nobles to side with him. All of this was done with more verve than sense, and it seems characteristic of his political ineptitude that when he made an attempt to abduct the king in January 1549, he began by killing Edward's pet dog when it barked at the intruders – an action hardly guaranteed to win the king's trust. After his execution for treason, Princess Elizabeth is said to have remarked judiciously, 'this day died a man of much wit, and very litle judgement'.[60] The episode underlines, yet again, the precariousness of minority rule; it also does not say much for the political acuity of the Seymour brothers.

If the younger brother lacked political sense, it could not be said that his older sibling was noticeably more capable. Somerset's military achievements did not, as it turned out, prepare him to be a particularly skilled ruler. His reputation for liberalism comes in part from his repeal of Henry's treason laws and his lifting of the controls on the printing trade; but neither of these moves was quite as impressive as we once thought. It was customary to begin a reign by repealing the more intractable features of the previous regime, and the treason laws were a part of this; meanwhile, removal of the constraints on publishing was done with a particular eye to encouraging Protestant evangelism. The printing trade certainly benefited: output peaked in 1548 and 1550, with over 250 books published in both years.[61] With this increase in publications, however, Somerset found himself facing worrying levels of religious disputation, and almost immediately restraints had to be put in place. A government letter of 1548 to all licensed preachers voiced concern for 'the conservacion of the quietnes and good ordre of the Kynges Maiesties subiectes'. It aimed to silence all unlicensed preachers, hoping 'that the devoute and Godly Homilies might the better in the meane whyle sincke into his subiectes hartes, and be learned the soner'. Despite the protestation that this was not meant 'to extinct the lively teachynge of the woorde of God', it was clear that the chief concern was that the people be taught deference and obedience, 'their duetie to their heddes and rulers, obedience to Lawes and ordres appointed by the superiors'.[62] The regime felt strongly enough about this to have the letter printed, one of a number of measures intended to moderate and control the pace of religious change.

Somerset's first objective, arguably even more important than godly reform, was to hammer the Scots. He had long experience of fighting on England's northern borders, and as protector he took the opportunity to build on that success. In September 1547, on the banks of the river Esk near Musselburgh, he won the battle of Pinkie. In military terms, this was a great achievement; politically, it was a disaster. The ostensible reason for the campaign was to secure the match between Edward VI and the young Mary Queen of Scots, who had been betrothed to each other back in 1543. Somerset's tactics, which included posting English garrisons across southern Scotland, in fact had the opposite effect of driving the Scots closer to their ancestral allies, the French. In the summer of 1548, Mary sailed for France and a future match with the dauphin.[63] This chain of events was symptomatic of Somerset's inability to see the bigger picture. It also gave him a very particular perspective on events which was shared by few. Back in London, the military campaigns in Scotland seemed a long way away. Wriothesley recorded the muster of the London troops, which were headed to Scotland, as 'the goodliest sight', but had little else to say on the subject.[64]

The Scottish campaign was not just a diplomatic catastrophe: it was also ruinously expensive. Between 1539 and 1552, military costs reached around £3.5 million, raised by various means, including six years of painfully heavy taxation from 1541 to 1547 and the debasement of the coinage, in which Somerset followed Henry VIII's lead. Debasement was always a damaging expedient, but perhaps particularly when pursued within the context of diminished royal authority. Tudor taxation worked best when it could make a clear claim to legitimacy.[65] Somerset's efforts, however, produced no obvious long-term gains. The French helped the Scots defeat the English garrisons one by one, and Mary was spirited away to the French Court.[66] There was not just a financial toll: the human costs of the war were also high. The loss of confidence in Somerset's authority was significant.[67] More worryingly, the resultant inflation was an evil that touched every layer of society.[68] Hugh Latimer, preaching before the king, was not afraid to mock the debased coinage. He found himself in trouble, but stoutly defended himself against the charge that he had been seditious by appealing to the prophet Isaiah, who had denounced Jerusalem, saying 'your silver has become dross'.[69] The prophet had indeed been a 'seditious varlet', he remarked sarcastically, for pointing out that it 'tended to the hurt of the poor people'.[70] Chronicles also recalled how the devaluing of coin had caused many to 'dayly inhaunse and encrease the prises both of wares and victualles, most miserably oppressynge the poore'.[71]

Social problems were at the centre of much Edwardian discourse. Harvest failures, epidemics and the loss of charitable foundations were compounded by the burden of inflation. War released disabled veterans to swell the ranks of vagrants. The debates of Edward's parliaments concerning tillage, dairy farming, purveyance and the depredations of middle-men in times of dearth underline the difficulties being faced, as do the discussions by writers of the period about the problems of poverty and vagabondage, and the moral necessity of discriminating between the deserving and the undeserving poor. It used to be thought that Somerset was a particular advocate for the poor and patron to a group of 'commonwealth' writers who preached social justice alongside evangelical inspiration.[72] There was indeed some powerful advocacy of the poor written both by those involved in administration and by some earnest Protestant clerics, for whom the preaching of God's word was intimately bound up with a defence of the indigent and oppressed.[73] More recently, however, the closeness of the ties between such writers, and of their links to Somerset himself, has been questioned. It appears that Somerset did feel some genuine compassion for the plight of the poor (as indeed paternalistic landowners quite frequently did, even without a Protestant spur); but his social radicalism can be overstated, whilst his social policies appear either largely ineffectual or actively disruptive. The Vagrancy Act of 1547 was unprecedented in its draconian provisions: even the young king described it as 'an extreme law'. It banned begging altogether and instituted enslavement of repeat offenders, in what proved to be an unworkable set of proposals.[74] Meanwhile Somerset's response to the issue of enclosures was both a deception and a disaster. Appointing the idealist John Hales to lead a commission to enquire into the practice of enclosure in the Midlands in June 1548 raised popular hopes that government solutions would be found to what was mistakenly viewed as a major cause of social distress. In reality, since the problems were chiefly caused by Somerset's tenacious prosecution of the war and the debasement of the coinage, Hales and his commission only caused further discontent.

In so far as Somerset and his associates had a clear view about the state of the commonwealth and the need for reform, they often did more harm than good, inflating expectations without offering workable solutions. Hugh Latimer, preaching before the king in March 1549, recalled his yeoman father, prosperous and loyal, whose harness he, as a lad, had helped buckle before his father rode off to join the king's troops suppressing the Cornish rebels in 1497. His father had farmed a good piece of land, Latimer reminisced, at a reasonable rent, and he compared this with the circumstances of the current tenant, whose rent was so high that he was 'not able to do any thing for his prince, for himself nor for his children, or give a cup of drink to the poor'.[75] Latimer was not seeking social revolution, however; he was attempting to harness indignation at social injustice for the Protestant cause, like many who framed their views on religious reform within the language of compassion for the poor.[76] This may have added considerably to the appeal of the new religion, but in political terms it caused disruption and disaffection.

In all of this, a constant problem was Somerset's style of rule. His sense of self-importance was obvious: he had made the dowager Queen Katherine Parr surrender her jewels for his wife to wear, and went in procession preceded by two gilt maces.[77] His house at Syon assumed the role of a royal palace.[78] He built Somerset House in the Strand on a grand scale, in the Italianate classical style, in the process demolishing the church of St Mary-le-Strand, as well as several other religious buildings. At his eventual trial for treason, he was accused of 'ambition and seeking of his own glory, as appeared by his building of most sumptuous and costly buildings, and specially in the time of the king's wars, and the king's soldiers unpaid'.[79] Yet for all his grandeur, Somerset lacked both the authority and the graciousness of majesty. Rather than work by conciliar process and mutual accord, he gave orders like a captain in the heat of battle. He seems to have been a good military leader: he knighted a great many men in the field, and was himself prepared to take up a spade to encourage his soldiers to dig in.[80] Military credibility was not enough, however, to secure the loyalty of his peers at Court. His close associate William Paget, who had all the political acumen that Somerset seemed to lack, repeatedly wrote to him, warning of the risks inherent in his foreign policy and of the damage caused by his demeanour; on one occasion, he pointed out how Somerset's rebuke had reduced Sir Richard Lee, a renowned soldier, to tears. Paget reminded the duke 'that yow supplie the place of a kinge', and pleaded with him to behave accordingly.[81] At times, Somerset was too harsh; at other times, he seemed to lack the necessary gravitas. As a New Year's gift for 1549, Paget offered him a 'mirror', or code of good conduct, in which the generic advice 'Be affable to the good, and sterne to the evell' was followed by the more pointed admonition 'Folowe advise in counsaile.'[82] To judge from the wealth of good advice that Paget poured forth, Somerset was not good at listening; a month later, Paget was pleading with the protector, 'make me not to be a Cassandra . . . one that told the trouthe of daungers before and was not beleved'.[83] It was an extraordinary attempt at a political education, but it did not work.

Somerset's most lasting achievement was that he undoubtedly had a measure of success in his pursuit of Protestant reform. He achieved this at a cost, and any evaluation of the wisdom of his policies must depend on an assessment of whether that cost was worth the result. Opinions vary as to how devout a Protestant he was. During Henry's reign, his religious inclinations were unclear, although he did have Hugh Latimer round to dinner in 1539.[84] During Edward's reign, he had several close Protestant associates (including the fiery John Hooper) and Thomas Becon as his chaplain, and an inventory of his possessions at Syon House shows that he possessed a range of Protestant theological works.[85] The prayer he wrote before his execution demonstrates a Bible-based piety; he wrote it in a small almanac.[86] He appropriated the lands of Glastonbury Abbey and planted a community of Flemish Protestant refugees there: this could be seen as a business venture, but the head of the community was a relation of John Hooper's by marriage.[87] The piety of his household owed much to his wife, Anne Stanhope, who had been a friend of Anne Askew and was a committed

Protestant: Thomas Becon observed with approval how she brought up her children 'in the knowledge of God's most holy laws'.[88]

The religious policies implemented between 1547 and 1549 had a measure of caution and moderation. This may suggest that Cranmer, a far better politician, exerted considerably more influence over them than Somerset; after fourteen years as Henry VIII's archbishop, Cranmer certainly knew a fair amount about the need to tread warily.[89] It also reflects the fact that any changes in religious policy needed the assent of parliament, which was not readily given, especially with a number of conservative bishops in the House of Lords.[90] In 1547, the *Book of Homilies* was published, a collection of simple sermons that were to be read aloud in parish churches week by week, in the hope of conveying the basic truths of the Protestant faith. Their emphasis on duty, charity, deference and quietness show an attempt to bring the transformative zeal of the Protestant faith into line with the needs of a national Church. Injunctions that year took a stern line on 'superstitious' practices, such as venerating or decorating images. Already iconoclasm of a more unofficial sort had begun in London.[91] Edward's reign would be remembered for its purging of the churches of the images and decorations of the past (see illustration 16).

It is perhaps a mark of how insecure and inchoate Edwardian Protestantism could seem, that so much energy was directed into anti-papal rhetoric. One cast-iron element of Protestant appeal was that it had such an excellent hate figure. From the ideological bankruptcy of papal sovereignty to the personal vices of a succession of historical popes, the evils of Rome formed the basis of much writing and preaching. Edward VI himself, as a French exercise, wrote a treatise against papal power, describing the pope as the Antichrist, and 'the source of all evil and the fountain of all abomination and the true son of the devil'.[92] Works such as John Ponet's translation of Bernardino Ochino, *A tragoedie or Dialoge of the unjust usurped primacie of the Bishop of Rome*, developed the subject of kings as Protestant champions against the Antichrist.[93] This theme was a rich source of both propaganda and entertainment. *The beginning and endynge of all popery*, another translated work (this time from German), had a series of woodcut illustrations to drive its point home, including one where the lamb of God was pierced by the papal sword, whilst the pope received his keys from a horned devil (see illustration 17).[94] With so much else about Protestantism in flux, the clarity of its antipapal message was satisfying and emphatic.

16. 'The Temple Well-Purged', from John Foxe, *Actes and Monuments*

By contrast, the reform of the liturgy proceeded slowly and warily. At the start of the reign, there were still evangelicals in prison under the Act of Six Articles for speaking out against the mass, and in April 1547 Bishop Bonner of London received a new commission to investigate and prosecute breaches of the Six Articles.[95] A careful transformation of the eucharist began in 1547, with permission for communion under both kinds (where the laity were given both the wafer, or bread, and the wine). This was something that was supported by certain conservatives, including Cuthbert Tunstall, bishop of Durham – perhaps because the bill also countered irreverent discussion of the sacrament, but perhaps also because Tunstall, like other Henrician Catholic bishops, was open to reform initiatives.[96] The 1548 Order of Communion, putting this part of the service into English, was another purposeful step towards a Protestant future, and the first edition of the *Book of Common Prayer* then appeared in 1549. This could be seen as a watershed

The beginning and endynge
¶ The pope thruſteth the lambe thorowe
with his ſworde. And therefore gy-
ueth him the deupll the keyes
that is, power and might.

Howe be it the pope boaſteth ₰ dap-
lye cryeth, his keyes to be of Chriſt,
though it be nothinge ſo. The olde
fathers perceaued the ſame righte
wel, and therfore haue they painted
here the deuil with the keyes by the
pope. Becauſe that all the auctoritie whiche he hath
here in earthe, commeth not from god, but from the
deupll. For howe coulde the power of god be with
the ſworde that kylleth the lambe.

The

17. The pope accepting the keys from the Devil, and piercing the lamb of
God: woodcut from *The beginning and endynge of all popery* (1548?)

moment, a triumphant statement of Protestantism and the successful destruction of the Latin mass.[97] Liturgy was the single most significant point of contact with religious experience for the population at large. Yet there were ambiguities to the new rite as well. Although it was in English, it retained the same structure as the old mass, and Cranmer had drawn on the Latin Breviary of Cardinal Quinones, the Catholic reformer, for some of the prefaces used in the book. For those who thought in theological terms, the *Book of Common Prayer* was a masterly exercise in caution: an adaptation, an echo, 'a kind of sacred parody' of what had gone before.[98]

Cranmer's beautifully modulated phrases and careful doctrinal formulations need to be set in the context of everything else that was happening in these years – from the despoliation of the churches and the confiscation of wealth from chantries and confraternities to the debasement of the coinage, rampant inflation and the disruption caused by the commission on enclosures. In the circumstances of Somerset's ruinous pursuit of the war with Scotland and France, and of the financial burden that this created, religious change proved even more disruptive than it might otherwise have been. Uprisings and rebellions spread across England: the two biggest would take place in the summer of 1549, but as early as 1547 there was insurrection in Cornwall against the changes in religion. And the man who implemented them, William Body, was killed by a Cornish mob at Helston in April 1548.[99] Not everyone was motivated chiefly by religion: the uprising in Northaw in May 1548 against the local landlord, Sir William Cavendish, may have been in large part about his enclosure of common land; but he was also a financial official, who would in due course begin the construction of Chatsworth House, and whose son would be the first earl of Devonshire.[100] In all, twenty-seven counties saw some kind of upheaval in 1548–49.[101] It was a damning indictment of Somerset's disastrous record and of the complicated mixture of social, religious and economic distress that he had engendered. The two great rebellions of 1549, the 'Prayer-Book Rebellion' in Devon and Cornwall, and 'Kett's Rebellion' in East Anglia, have been seen as quite different in tenor. Certainly, in the West Country there was outrage at the religious reforms and a vigorous attempt to restore the mass and the religious patterns of the past; while in East Anglia there was a measure of sympathy for reform ideas, and the main grievances seem to have been concerned with economic issues and matters of local politics. There was common ground, however, between the two, in that both were a response to the breakdown of good governance under Somerset's protec-torate. It is significant that the man who suppressed the East Anglian rising, John Dudley, earl of Warwick, would in due course take over from Somerset as the chief authority in the realm.

The 1549 rebellions testified to the lack of communication between the centre and the peripheries, an essential element of good government that was usually sustained by patronage relationships fuelled by royal favour. Somerset's ability to send people out of meetings in tears, and to alienate even loyal associates such as Paget, also weakened the chain of command and thereby damaged connections with the localities. In East Anglia, a measure of dislocation had been caused by the disgrace of the duke of Norfolk and the execution of his heir, the earl of Surrey, in 1547; in part, their role as local magnates had been assumed by Princess Mary, but her relations with the government were too frosty for her to serve as a useful conduit.[102] Local government became more precarious, and communication with the centre was weakened. In Devon, the marquess of Exeter and much of his family had been executed or imprisoned in 1538, after Henry VIII invented the 'Courtenay Conspiracy' in retribution for their Catholic leanings and their links to Cardinal Pole. One of the few non-religious requests made by the rebels in the south-west was to have Cardinal Pole pardoned, brought back from Rome and put on the Council.[103] There was a general sense not just that there were injustices at work in the provinces, but that something was out of kilter at the heart of the regime as well.

It was also the case that for a great many of Edward's subjects, the *Book of Common Prayer* was an abomination. It seemed a travesty of what had gone before; an empty form of words, with none of the mysticism, ceremony and ritual that had made the mass such a nexus of both social and supernatural forces. It was introduced in time for Whitsunday, which in 1547 fell on 9 June. The very next day, the rebellion began in Devon and Cornwall, with the villagers of Sampford Courtenay insisting that their priest put on his old vestments once more and celebrate mass in the proper fashion. From there it spread to Crediton, then to Clyst St Mary, and soon all of north Devon. Meanwhile, in Cornwall a separate band of rebels took Plymouth and marched to join their Devon compatriots in laying siege to Exeter. The demands of these rebels exist in several forms, but the most complete version was a manifesto drawn up outside Exeter. It was, on one level, an inchoate plea to return to the past, to 'have all the general counsell and holy decrees of our forfathers observed, kept and performed'. Yet it also contained a range of very precise demands concerning the return of the mass. The ceremonies of worshipping a reserved host, of holy bread and water, of prayers for the dead, palms on Palm Sunday and ashes on Ash Wednesday – all were specified. The new service was described as being 'but lyke a Christmas game'; these rebels demanded 'oure olde service of Mattens, masse, Evenson and procession in Latten not in English, as it was before'. In reinstituting Purgatory, they insisted that 'everye preacher in his sermon, and every Pryest at hys masse' would 'praye specially by name for the soules in purgatory, asoure forefathers dyd'.[104] They were protesting about the loss not just of a liturgy, but of an entire religious system.

Historians have pointed out that there were other concerns in south-west England in 1549, and not all of them had to do with religion. Some had to do with sheep. Somerset had passed a new law imposing a poll tax on sheep, with a higher rate for those kept on enclosed land. The aim was both to raise money for the war and to discourage large-scale enclosures. In this he showed a characteristic insensitivity to local custom, since most Devon farmers had a small number of sheep, kept in small enclosed fields.[105] The tiny village of Morebath had only thirty-three households, none of them wealthy, but all had a handful of sheep.[106] The different reasons for rebellion cannot be separated out into distinct categories of 'religious' and 'economic', however. In Morebath, it was partly money raised from the wool of certain designated sheep that paid to keep the lights burning in front of the statues of the saints in the parish church, including the local St Sidwell, after whom at least two children in the parish were named; recording the ear-marks of some of the sheep concerned, the priest would end with a pious flourish in Latin.[107] To those who spoke Cornish, the *Book of Common Prayer* was also an affront, since it was in English – another example of insensitivity towards local concerns, in which religious indignation was mingled with other considerations.[108] In East Anglia, the list of rebel demands included an insistence that common land be protected from the depredations of lords of the manor; but it also specified that any priest who was unable to preach should be sent away, and another chosen by either the parishioners or the local patron.[109] The rhythms and imperatives of day-to-day life rendered it hard to distinguish between sacred and secular concerns.

The rebellions of 1549 were the last straw for a political establishment already deeply worried by Somerset's policies. Frantic letters from the Privy Council to the different members of the nobility who were attempting to restore order in the provinces show the levels of tension at the heart of the regime. Somerset himself unnerved his colleagues even further by showing sympathy to the plight of the rebels, offering to grant them pardon and assuage their grievances (although some, if not all, of this may have been strategic).[110] It seems ironic that just when a hard-line military approach might, for once, have been appropriate, Somerset tried leniency instead. Paget warned him yet again, this time pointing out that his forbearance had 'given evil men a boldness', making the rebels 'think you dare not meddle with them but are glad to please them'.[111] It is not clear whether Somerset still had hopes of raising a popular Protestant movement, or whether he had just run out of alternatives. As his support among the nobility and gentry ebbed away, he issued a letter, using the king's signature, asking subjects to arm themselves to defend the king. Then he moved Edward to Windsor Castle and called for military support from Lord John Russell and Sir William Herbert. The Privy Council had already met to demand his abdication as protector, however, and Somerset was at least enough of a statesman not to risk civil war. He surrendered, resigned and was sent to the Tower. As the young king himself recorded, Somerset stood accused of 'faults, ambition, vainglory, entering into rash wars in mine youth ... enriching of himself of my treasure, following his own opinion and doing all by his own authority'.[112] This was a not unreasonable verdict.

Somerset's replacement was John Dudley, earl of Warwick, soon to become duke of Northumberland. The process has been described as a *coup d'état*, which rather casts Warwick (as he was then) in the role of political schemer. And indeed, some politicking and duplicity was involved.[113] In more general terms, it could be said that everyone benefited from having an undoubtedly competent individual take up the reins of power that Somerset had left in such a tangle – even if it did also make Warwick's own fortune.[114] Warwick had precisely that understanding of the political process which Paget had in vain struggled to teach Somerset. He was also a military man: his first step towards securing power was to put down Kett's Rebellion, defeating the rebel army at the battle of Dussindale with perhaps two thousand rebel casualties. Yet he was also someone who appreciated the value of clemency, and he stopped the local gentry from exacting brutal reprisals in the wake of this victory. This in itself was more kingly behaviour than Somerset had ever managed to muster. Most of all, Warwick was better at managing people, and knew the value of rule by consensus. After Somerset had been compelled to relinquish the protectorship in October 1549, the government was at first ostensibly headed by Thomas Wriothesley, earl of Southampton, who had served Henry VIII and had opposed Somerset's appointment as protector, losing his seat on the Council as a consequence.[115] Some outside observers assumed that this was the victory of a more conservative religious faction over an openly Protestant one, and some spoke of a Regency headed by

Princess Mary; but issues of political skill were as much at stake here as religious loyalties.[116] In December, after an alleged attempt by Southampton to accuse Somerset of treason and implicate Warwick, the Council rallied around Warwick – not necessarily for religious reasons, but because he inspired confidence as a potential head of government. Whether the threat to his position from Southampton had been real or was invented, Warwick used it to secure his hold on the Council.[117] The balance of power had shifted, but the idea of this as a *coup* has been overstated. It is striking how many people who had held office under Somerset remained in their posts; and Somerset himself was back on the Council and restored to the Privy Chamber by May 1550.[118] His eventual trial and execution for treason were brought about by his refusal to accept Warwick's authority and his obvious desire to regain his lost pre-eminence.[119]

Importantly, Warwick never sought the role of lord protector, and it was not until October 1551 that he became duke of Northumberland. He sought to exercise authority as lord president of the Council and as great master of the household to Edward VI; in both roles, he was the leader of a group, rather than a single voice of authority, as Somerset had been, and he consciously sought to differentiate his style of rule from the 'wylfull government of the late duke of Somerset'.[120] He was also deferential to the young king in a way that his predecessor had not been; and as Edward approached adulthood, Northumberland arranged for him to be tutored in political strategy and called Council meetings which enabled Edward to practise the art of government.[121] Northumberland also gave support to the more radical Protestant grouping at Court, probably reckoning that this was the best way to secure his role in government once the minority ended. He was a pragmatist, and as such realized the devastation wrought by Somerset's foreign policy objectives. Edward, in his chronicle, recorded how Somerset's release and return to Court followed on immediately from the proclamation of peace with the French in the Treaty of Boulogne and the thanksgiving celebrations in London. Once peace had been agreed, it was perhaps easier to forgive Somerset the damage he had caused.[122] Some moves were made to restore the coinage (albeit inept ones), but the fact that Northumberland managed to drive down food prices was a point in his favour.[123] Attempts were made to increase revenue elsewhere, and to review Crown finances.[124] The loss of Boulogne – surrendered to the

French after they had renewed hostilities in 1549 by attempting to retake the city – was mitigated by the money that was paid over at the same time. Edward recorded the details in his chronicle, down to the numbers of guns and other armaments due to be handed over, and the names of the twelve hostages – six on either side – due to be exchanged.[125] A similar treaty was signed with Scotland in 1551, and the country's regent, Mary of Guise, came to London to meet King Edward: 'she came like a friend', he recorded.[126]

Another mark of Northumberland's success was his pursuit of religious policies that were much less cautious than those of 1547–49, and yet which seem to have caused much less disruption. Northumberland was possibly not entirely genuine in his Protestantism: he certainly renounced his Protestant convictions on the scaffold before his death, making a moving avowal of his Catholic loyalties that would provide a propaganda point for the new regime. As a shrewd political operator serving under a king who was approaching adulthood and whose Protestantism was unquestioned, it was perhaps inevitable that he should have professed Protestant zeal during his time in power. Northumberland thus oversaw some significant advances in the implementation of religious changes, most particularly the 1552 Prayer Book, which was significantly more clear-cut in its Protestantism than its predecessor had been, and which determinedly excised all the remnants of Catholic practice that had been evident in the 1549 book.[127] In particular, any lingering sense of a Real Presence in the eucharist was expunged and the commemoration of the dead repressed. If late medieval worship had indeed revolved around the celebration of the mass, and the pious provision for souls in purgatory, then the 1552 service struck a calculated blow at the foundations of pre-Reformation devotion.

Northumberland's success in advancing a more openly Protestant agenda demonstrated his level of political control. This did not mean, however, that he was any more successful in converting the populace to the new faith. At the popular level there was a range of responses – from enthusiasm, through bewilderment and confusion, to outright opposition. Bishop Hooper in Gloucester was alive to the problem of those who 'refuse their own parish, and frequent and haunt other, wheras the communion is more like a mass than in his own'.[128] The areas of religious experience which touched the majority of the population had all been called into question. The time-honoured traditions of burial and commemoration had been abolished, and the deep-felt need to pray for the beloved dead had been declared ungodly. The baptism of babies had changed, and it was not clear that the words of the Prayer Book christening service would have enough strength to keep the Devil at bay, since the rituals of exorcism had been dropped from the rite. Making the sign of the cross to ward off evil or convey a blessing – a gesture that was instinctive to so many people – was now deemed to be an error. There was no holy water to bless the house, garden, animals and crops; there was no holy bread distributed at the end of mass (which was not even called mass any more). It was no longer clear if it was necessary to eat fish on Wednesdays and Fridays, and during Advent and Lent. It is little wonder that so many people complained that they were living in a world torn apart, and railed at those who repeatedly harangued them over their errors.

Others celebrated the fact that the English populace was turning its back on superstition, blind obedience, and forms of supplication or protection which had to be paid for, a practice that had enriched a corrupt clergy and left ordinary folk impoverished. Enthusiasm of this sort was particularly marked in London and the south-east.[129] Not all of it was helpful to the regime. Protestant teachings on marriage, including the marriage of clergy, sometimes included a defence of divorce, as in a work by Heinrich Bullinger translated into English in the 1540s; but this could bring the Protestant cause into disrepute.[130] The spectacle of Protestant clerical marriages which ended in disaster, such as Archbishop Holgate of York and Bishop Ponet of Rochester, provided rich opportunities for Catholic denunciation of Protestantism's carnal liberty.[131] Some zealots were so keen to expunge traces of the past that they made bonfires not just of images, but also of medieval books: much of Oxford University's library went up in flames.[132] The problem persisted that the Edwardian regime was a lot clearer about what it wanted to abolish than about what it hoped to put in its place. It also had to contend with the enthusiasm of those committed to reform, whose zeal very often carried them away. Injunctions for St George's Chapel Windsor issued in 1550 made elaborate provision for regular preaching; but at the same time they had to specify that the preachers 'shall in their sermons set forth the King's Majesty's godly proceedings, not swerving from the doctrine set forth in the Homilies and in the Book of Service'.[133] 'Swerving' was undoubtedly a problem, and not one that was easily corrected.

Whatever the complications of human experience, it remains clear that politically Edward VI's regime faced an exceptional challenge in trying to alter the religion of an entire country. It was not enough that the young king sought to implement godly reform, and that his advisors flocked to help him; it was not clear how best this was to be achieved. Preachers spoke stirring words about the fulfilment of God's work, to be achieved through the printing of the English Bible and other godly works: 'let us give thanks and rejoice that he hath sent us in these our days that science whereby all those who love the light might have the same for a little charge'.[134] Yet the fact remained that most of the populace could not read, and were generally considered to be both simple and ignorant. The instructions of 1548 to preachers had told them to have 'aspeciall regarde, to the weakenes of the people, what thei may beare, and what is most convenient for the tyme'.[135] It was not anticipated, however, by those who knew about such things, that the Holy Spirit was going to descend at a time 'convenient' for the regime. This tension was one that was never satisfactorily resolved during Edward's lifetime.

Dynasty and death

At the beginning of 1553, Edward VI was unwell. In March, the opening of parliament had to be moved to Whitehall Palace, as he was too weak to manage the usual procession. An apparent recovery in April was followed by a relapse, and by early June he was seriously ill. From early summer, therefore, the most pressing political question was what might happen next. By Henry VIII's Succession Act, the throne should pass to Edward's half-sister Mary, but that would inevitably mean the restoration of Catholicism. The steps that were taken to try to avoid this eventuality have been much debated, as have the insights they potentially provide into the political process.

When Edward eventually died in July, like many royal deaths it was shrouded in uncertainty and fearful rumour, including the suggestion that he had been poisoned.[136] The rumours might be taken as an indication of the political temperature in that hot and unhappy summer, when frenzied efforts were made to put Lady Jane Grey in the king's place. The notion that Edward suffered from a long wasting illness that allowed Northumberland to manipulate his way into power was a central feature of a persistent and popular set of rumours about the evil ambition of the Dudleys and how Northumberland had used the frail figure of the king as a shield, behind which he could spin webs with his own ambition.[137] Contrary to popular tradition, however, Edward VI was not a sickly child, any more than Dudley was an especially Machiavellian schemer. The king had been a robust infant, whom the French ambassador in 1541 had described as handsome, well-fed and big for his age; and although any ailment had thrown his father into abject terror, he had recovered quickly from illness.[138] As king, he enjoyed hunting, dancing, masques and all the other energetic diversions of life at Court. It was only in February 1553 that his health really came into question. By May, the Imperial ambassador was reporting that something was wrong with the king's lungs, that he was feverish, ulcerated, coughing and had a swollen belly. It soon became clear that he was dying. It seems likely that a persistent lung infection had, in the end, resulted in blood poisoning and kidney failure.[139]

It remains a significant fact about Edward's death that it was slow, which gave him and others in power time to plan. Yet it would be wrong to cast the king as a political irrelevance in this process, carried along by the scheming of Northumberland. Edward was nearly sixteen when he died, and had already begun to assume some of the powers of active kingship. It is clear that he shared with some of his closest advisors a dread of the throne passing to his older sister Mary, and this was more than a matter of self-interest among a ruthlessly greedy group of nobles. There were sound reasons for fearing Mary's rule, ranging from the fact that no queen regnant had ever ruled England to the likelihood that she would fall under Habsburg dominance and the strong probability that she would abandon the Royal Supremacy, which for twenty years had been a bulwark of royal authority and crown finances. The document entitled 'My devise for the succession' was almost certainly Edward's own inspiration, modelled as it was on his father's style of business, and taking liberties with the lines of royal inheritance which only a king would dare to attempt. His determination and courage in working on this, despite the extreme suffering caused by his final illness, was in itself a remarkable testimony to his sense of duty.

Edward sought to move both his half-sisters out of the line of succession and revert instead to the Grey family, the direct descendants of Henry VIII's younger sister Mary, dowager queen of France and later duchess of Suffolk. The legitimacy of the Grey claim would have reassured many of those complicit in Edward's planning; incidentally, this serves to underline the political worries at the time about the illegitimacy, still enshrined in law, of both Mary and Elizabeth. The intervention, however, bypassed Lady Frances Grey, duchess of Suffolk, in favour of her eldest daughter, Lady Jane Grey. This was clearly a reflection of the need for a committed Protestant claimant to safeguard the fledgling reformed Church that Edward had founded. The driving force behind the scheme was Edward himself, who seems personally to have altered the line in the document granting the crown first to the male heirs of Lady Frances and then to the male heirs of Lady Jane to 'the L. Frauncese heires masles, *if she have any* such issue *befor my death*' and then 'to the L. Jane *and her* heires masles'.[140] At the last moment, with the shades of death looming, it was imperative for the young king that Protestantism be sustained, for reasons of both the true faith and the strength and stability of the Crown, although in what combination we cannot be sure.

To subvert the lines of inheritance was a serious undertaking, and one that was, at best, morally dubious. In 1553, all that the Edwardian Reformation had achieved must have seemed unbearably fragile, however, as well as extraordinarily precious. This was surely why Cranmer and other committed Protestants were prepared to support the attempt to alter the succession. The reforms of canon law had not yet been enacted, leaving the Church – in legal terms – stuck in the pre-Reformation past. The bishops were having a difficult time promoting evangelical reform and conversion in the localities, and even at the heart of government there was a distressing lack of accord. This was one set of reasons to support the change to the succession. It was also perhaps the case that the authority of the king as he neared adulthood commanded more deference and obedience than we might expect. He may have been only fifteen years old, but Edward had spent his entire life preparing to be another Henry VIII. It would have taken a braver man than most to tell his king that his actions were wrong, and that he had no right to decide the succession as his father had done. The story of what happened next belongs in another chapter.

But the events of the summer of 1553 make the point that if anything could oppose the will of a Tudor monarch, it was a concern with issues of legitimacy and stability, sustained by custom. At the end of Edward's reign, just as at the beginning, the political establishment took the route suggested by past precedent, rather than the more innovative way forward suggested by the monarch. A king's ability to dictate was dependent on his ability to protect; and that left Edward's authority ebbing away, along with his life. He had sought for most of his short life to follow his father's example; it is a quiet irony that in nothing did he resemble Henry so much as in his failure to impose his will at the end.

* * *

The reign of Edward VI was brief, but it is of immense significance for our understanding of Tudor history. His rule has been taken as a shibboleth for true Protestant commitment, the nearest England ever came to a reformation on the 'proper' continental model.[141] From a political perspective, contemplating the rule of a child has led historians to ask searching questions about the stability of the Tudor state, and for a long time the concept of a 'mid-Tudor crisis' was a recognized, if not unquestioned, phenomenon.[142] More recently, both the coherence and the success of Protestant reform has been thrown into doubt. Historians like to compartmentalize; but in the years between 1547 and 1553 there was no easy separation between the religious destruction, which divided the ruling classes and broke communities apart, and the political commitment to a ruinous Scottish war, which sharpened the edges of faction-fighting at Court and placed a question mark over England's place in Europe. One difficulty spilled over into the other. Yet the idea of 'crisis' needs to be further interrogated, implying as it does an immature or inadequate political system struggling to cope with adversity. It might be better to concentrate on the resourcefulness of those who tried to deal with political and social difficulties; the courage and moral conviction of some of those who staged rebellions; the clear-sightedness of those who brought a halt to a futile and expensive conflict and sought to repair the economic damage it had caused; the sophistication of a political system which ousted an autocratic ruler in favour of one who ruled through collaboration; the civic virtue of individuals who worked to rescue colleges, schools and hospitals from the destructive impulses of a Protestant ruling cadre; and above all, the compassion and sense of those at the parish level who sought to mitigate the effects of punitive legislation and softened the damage done by religious reform to popular culture and communal cohesion. If the reign of Edward VI saw unprecedented levels of disruption and distress, it also demonstrated the capacity of Tudor society for coping with disaster and articulating forceful and reasoned responses to everything from political corruption to popular suffering.

CHAPTER 9

'THE VIGOUR OF INVENTION'
RENAISSANCE WORDS

When, in 1538, the palace of Nonsuch was built to house Prince Edward, Henry's precious son and heir, the inner courtyard was decorated with panels of figures from classical history and mythology, with explanatory labels in gilded text below to tell their story (see illustration 18). A stucco figure of Henry VIII crushing a lion beneath his feet, with Edward beside him, firmly located the Tudor dynasty amidst a constellation of Greek and Roman gods, goddesses, heroes and emperors.[1] Decades later, when Elizabeth I sought to embellish her image, she portrayed herself as the goddess Diana – chaste, militant, full of wisdom and, as a lunar deity, in control of the seas.[2] These monarchs were enacting, in elaborate detail, stories they had found in books. Tudor imagination was filled with the history, myth, drama and poetry of ancient Greece and Rome. As the decades unfolded, this brought forth an outpouring of printed works – from histories and chronicles, to treatises and plays – in which the classical world was translated, transmuted and reconfigured to answer the needs of sixteenth-century England.

There were many reasons for this. Scholars were studying and translating Greek and Roman texts and disseminating them with the help of an expanding printing industry. The founding of schools and colleges expanded educational provision, while the association of learning with political skill increasingly made scholarship a mark of status and a requirement for anyone seeking to hold office. Exploration overseas broadened the minds of those who pondered these voyages, and the growth of commerce fostered the trade in books. Yet it seems probable that the strongest influ-

18. Nonsuch Palace

ences, both inspirational and exacting, were felt closer to home, closer to the heart. Political and economic crisis, religious conflict and international instability all prompted a clamour of literary voices. Upheaval and antagonism shaped even those who wrote to beguile and entertain. The need to defend cherished beliefs provoked impassioned polemical writing, whilst the drive to make English literature the rival of its equivalents abroad inspired virtuoso performances from poets. This was the era of the Renaissance; but the 'rebirth' that it claimed to be was, in itself, a piece of artifice, with a more immediate agenda than simply the rediscovery of ancient wisdom. Classical literature may have provided the foundations on which they built, but in truth the chief concerns of Renaissance thinkers were contemporary, apprehensive and urgent. Many of the most eloquent voices of the era were voices raised in alarm.

Renaissance literary scholarship was a rare example of an academic development which genuinely brought about a broad cultural transformation. This was partly because it is hard, in any age, to read Plato, or Cicero, or Tacitus, and come away unchanged. Tudor translations were redolent with the excitement of encountering these great writers of antiquity and the sophistication and confidence with which they wrote. Classical authors commanded instinctive deference from their Tudor audiences. In 1600, translating Livy's history of Rome, the Coventry schoolmaster Philemon Holland declared such histories 'more durable and permanent . . . than either any monarchie been it never so great, or all those wonderfull Pyramides and Obeliskes, reared by most magnificent Kings, and mightie emperors, to immortalize their name and memorie'.[3] At a less exalted level, instant lustre could be added to pot-boilers or polemical rants by invoking classical authors, particularly Tully (which is what the Tudors tended to call Marcus Tullius Cicero), whom they considered 'the glorie of the ancient Rome'.[4] Even when writing a treatise on the abstruse subject of forest laws, John Manwood in 1598 felt compelled to begin with the views of 'the most famous Orator, Marcus Tullius Cicero'.[5] Almost any point could be effortlessly strengthened by adding 'as Tully saith', just as reputations might be instantly enhanced by the inclusion of Latin or Greek quotations. The shallowness of this approach was observed and reproached by the humanist scholar Roger Ascham, who compared it to sunburn: he noted how many 'seeming, and sunburnt ministers we have, whose learning is gotten in a summer heat, and washed away, with a Christmas snow again'.[6] Ascham's own scholarship, of course, was beyond reproach, and he was the tutor who guided the future Elizabeth I through 'translating of Demosthenes and Isocrates dailie' every morning, and 'som part of Tullie every afternone, for the space of a yeare or two'. His royal pupil attained 'soch a perfite understanding in both the tonges' that in his opinion, few even in the universities could match her.[7] A manuscript in her own hand of a translation from Tacitus's *Annales*, recently unearthed, supports this judgement.[8]

Renaissance ideas and influences were felt at every level. Classical myths coloured Tudor drama, and classical references crept into cheap print, whilst everything from tombs to coins to household decorations acquired elements of classical style.[9] Greek and Roman gods, heroes and villains were characters instantly recognizable. Achilles and Hector were symbols of martial valour, Odysseus of wisdom and Cassandra of doomed prophecy. Damon and Pythias, willing to die for one another, became model examples of friendship; an Elizabethan ballad deploring the unkindness of friends made its point by a comparison with 'true Damon and his friend'.[10] Another ballad warning London to beware the fate of the ransacked city of Antwerp made reference to the levelling of Troy, whilst yet another, bewailing the pains of love, used the example of King Solomon alongside those of Paris and Helen, Troilus and Cressida; references to Pyramus and Thisbe, Hercules and others were all drawn from Ovid's *Metamorphoses*.[11] Shakespeare deployed the story of Pyramus and Thisbe to comic effect in his *Midsummer Night's Dream*, in a bawdy scene clearly meant to have popular appeal, within a play that made riotous use of Ovid's highly sexualized stories.[12] If ancient Greece and Rome were supplying much of the mental furniture of the age, this was not just for the elite.

Classical learning did offer particular advantages, however, to the higher social orders. Many who studied in England were hoping for political preferment; those who travelled abroad to study were frequently equipping themselves for a career in politics and diplomacy. Renaissance learning, in all its manifestations, was much prized by princes, on whose patronage such learning frequently depended. Scholarship became the tool of propagandists, artistic display was used to channel royal ambition and a veneer of intellectual sophistication might be applied to a range of autocratic initiatives. Yet for every Greek or Roman archetype there was an alternative interpretation. Henry VIII might portray himself as Julius Caesar, and commission priceless tapestries to underline the resemblance, but the moral ambiguities of Shakespeare's *Julius Caesar* show the uneasy reputation of leaders in which greatness mingled with ambition.[13] 'As he was valiant, I honour him. But as he was ambitious, I slew him,' said Shakespeare's Brutus.[14] The subtleties of such judgements were a lasting legacy of the Renaissance in England.[15] Poetry and plays of exquisite beauty might enshrine social and political commentary no less lacerating for being couched in verse, or thinly disguised by classical imagery. For the harshest criticism, the protection afforded by writing a work of fiction could be a very necessary defence.[16] The playing out of different debates through works of literature became a central feature of Tudor culture, where the performance of a play might help launch a rebellion, and powerful political commentary could be embedded in poetry about fairies and monsters.

There was no single Renaissance mindset.[17] Tudor literary culture was protean, intricate, many-shaded and could be twisted to suit a range of often contradictory aims. It cannot even be said that Tudor thought divides readily into the conventional and the subversive, although modern commentators are often tempted to impose such a division.[18] Print was a precious medium, but it remained a highly unpredictable one. By the end of the sixteenth century, it was providing a conduit for a bewildering array of different voices, opinions and arguments. It could be both a prop for a regime and its scourge, could proffer both attack and defence in religious conflicts, and all of this while textbooks, primers, homilies, histories, chronicles, ballads, legends and poetry were keeping Tudor society informed, devout, beguiled and entertained by turn. This was first and foremost an age of debate, intellectual curiosity and imaginative expansion. It was the age of More, Wyatt, Marlowe, Shakespeare, Sidney, Spenser and many others, all of whom defy easy categorization, all of whose works contain questions, surmises and doubt. With the collapse of religious and political certainties at home and the escalation of conflicts abroad, the pace of censure, analysis and prescription quickened, but there were no easy answers. When Tudor writers and thinkers remembered the greatness of the Roman republic, they also recalled the corruption of Rome's emperors, and the devastation of Rome's fall. In poetry, plays and treatises, transactions of power were lauded by some, questioned and mocked by others. A chorus of voices from the past was echoed and refashioned by Tudor men and women in a flood of words that were to prove infinitely mutable, but impossible to stifle.

Castles in the air

Tudor literature comprised a rapidly growing array of genres, many of which had a quite mundane and practical purpose. Attempts at political consolidation by an unstable regime produced published proclamations and statutes; initiatives to engineer religious change prompted the publication of doctrinal tracts, prayer and service books, and officially sponsored homilies; professional needs called for books on the management of land, the ordering of households, the cultivation of crops, animal husbandry, gardening, and remedies against the plague and other diseases. Upon prosaic foundations, however, Tudor authors built extraordinary edifices of imagination and rhetoric, and blurred the distinctions between fact and fiction, instruction and poetry. Even works on military strategy, or 'the art of war', might combine useful advice about metallurgy and gunpowder with elements of chivalric romance, appeals to the classical past and a surprising amount of poetry.[19] A modern distinction between factual and fictional writing has limited use when applied to Tudor literature.

The writing of history matured especially rapidly under the pressures of the sixteenth century. Chronicles moved beyond their monastic past to embrace a wider array of concerns, as well as a wider audience, incorporating elements of medieval chivalric tradition alongside humanist classicism.[20] Polydore Vergil was commissioned to produce an Italianate humanist history of England; Thomas More modelled his history of Richard III on Tacitus. By the end of the century, John Hayward's *Life and Raigne of King Henrie the IIII*, and Camden's *Britannia* raised historical (and chorographical) writing in England to a new level of sophistication.[21] The Renaissance urge to delve into the past also brought to light histories from England's past written in Latin, Anglo-Saxon and Middle English.[22] The publication of Holinshed's *Chronicles* in 1577 (and in a longer edition totalling around 3.5 million words in 1587) showcased the range of historical scholarship engendered by Elizabethan culture.[23] Histories from elsewhere in Europe also proliferated: between 1560 and 1599, Guicciardini's history of Italy and Machiavelli's history of Florence were translated from Italian, Pedro Mexia's historical miscellany from Spanish and Johann Sleidan's history of the reign of Charles V from Latin.[24]

Religious literature also appeared in a great many varieties, from the polemic or didactic to the liturgical or devotional. The affective devotion that had been such a pronounced feature of late medieval devotional literature was partly suppressed by Protestant notions; but the presence of lyric verse in the Bible – in the form of the Book of Psalms and the Song of Songs – meant that religious poetry was a defensible medium, and one which rose to new heights in this period. Yet since religion was so highly politicized, religious works could also have serious political intent. Of the many attempts at psalm paraphrase, many contained thinly veiled political commentary, often alongside devotional expression that was no less fervent.[25] In this way, Thomas Wyatt in the 1530s simultaneously expressed both his faith in God and his deep unease at the rule of Henry VIII.[26] His friend Henry Howard, earl of Surrey, adapted Psalm 88 to make unfaithful friends the source of the author's desolation: his lament that 'faithfull frendes are fledd' was a reflection on the corruption of the Court.[27] In the 1580s, Philip Sidney translated the first forty-three psalms into English verse; and after his death, his sister Mary Sidney Herbert translated the rest and went on to revise her brother's work prior to publication in 1594. The Sidney psalms were both an exercise in devotion and a display of poetic brilliance in a selection of different verse forms.[28]

If much of this literature was for elite consumption, an increasing amount was also for a popular audience.[29] The history of Rome might be represented in Sir Henry Savile's translation of Tacitus in 1591, but it also appeared in doggerel verse in *Romes Monarchie* of 1596, which promised 'strange Tragedies, secret practises ... Ambition, hate and revenge' and took its readers at a brisk trot through the history of Rome, from Aeneas to Nero.[30] Accounts of British history, including those which dwelt on features of the local tradition, or the local landscape, helped foster civic pride and county loyalties.[31] Verse libels might be exchanged by literary giants such as Thomas Nashe and Gabriel Harvey, but they were also read voraciously by the wider public, who could produce more mundane versions of their own.[32] Anti-Spanish polemic could appear in popular broadsheets and ballads, just as much as in Sidney's exquisite verse, or Spenser's. Parish worship was sustained by the *Book of Common Prayer*; books of metrical psalms, the ancestor of the hymn book, were extremely popular, and sermons also sold well.[33] Household manuals gave guidance, usually with strong religious overtones, regarding the raising of children, the management of servants, and the maintenance of house and garden.[34] Since the rule of a family was taken as a direct parallel for the rule of the commonwealth, the moral probity of the householder was regarded as a matter of national importance.[35] Almanacs sold in huge numbers, and were a rich and eccentric compilation of detailed calendars, astrological, medical and agricultural advice, weather predictions, travel advice and histories of the world.[36] These texts were frequently personalized, as their owners used them to record family births and deaths, medicinal remedies, legal contracts and other important details which could be the precursors of autobiographical writings.[37] Bibles might be used to record genealogies, recipes or other important records of family life, from medicines to children's drawings.[38]

Quite a lot of popular literature was funny.[39] The more sophisticated authors of the time could be condescending about this. Sidney distinguished between true delight and shallow laughter: 'Delight has a joy in it either permanent or present; laughter has only a scornful tickling', he wrote severely. And he condemned works which showed 'nothing but scurrility, unworthy of any chaste ears, or some extreme show of doltishness'.[40] In the meantime, however, jest-books, broadsides, comic drama and satire did a brisk trade, and clearly had an appeal for the more educated elements of society, too, whatever their formal protestations.[41] Robert Armin's *Foole upon Foole* of 1600 was a collection of tales and verses about fools, written by an actor who played the part of fools on the stage, while in the same year his fellow fool Will Kemp published *Nine Days Wonder*, an entertaining account of how he danced to Norwich. If the literary merit of either work was open to question, it is clear that Armin in particular had a formative influence upon Shakespeare.[42] Armin was also well known as a writer of ballads, which were another highly popular form of literature.[43] As early as 1520, the Oxford bookseller John Dorne sold over two hundred ballads in a year, priced at a halfpenny per sheet. Ballads could be about many subjects, but the dominant theme was usually love, courtship and marriage.[44] They were viewed, and indeed often condemned, as being the entertainment of the lower orders: Mopsa, the shepherdess in Shakespeare's *Winter's Tale*, thought that if they were printed, 'then we are sure they are true'.[45] Ballad singers might also sometimes perform in great houses, and the educated might copy their favourite ballads into their commonplace books.[46] One godly Elizabethan commentator remarked sourly that in artisan cottages he was more likely to find 'one of these newe Ballades' than a copy of the psalms, and complained that the poor were 'cunninger in singing the one, than the other'.[47]

The role of print was immensely important in shaping Tudor culture, and yet some of the greatest works of the age never made it out of manuscript, at least in their author's lifetime.[48] Some of the most inflammatory works of the age remained in manuscript, since to be accused of rabble-rousing was a quick way to lose all credibility. The most outspoken denunciation of Henry VIII's break with Rome came in Cardinal Reginald Pole's 'De Unitate', written in manuscript and in Latin.[49] The political cynicism of Machiavelli was found in a manuscript treatise prepared for Philip II in Italian; for those who could not read Italian, the only works of Machiavelli published in English were his less obviously alarming *Art of Warre* and his *Florentine Historie*.[50] The decision to keep literary expression in manuscript form could also be, however, because the intended readership was an elite group of family, friends and close associates. Writers did not always want to reach the general public: they might prefer a select readership of like-minded individuals. Thomas Wyatt's poetry, which often contained elusive, many-layered political commentary, was meant for a small circle of courtiers, nobility and gentry. Sidney's *Arcadia*, in its first incarnation, was written for his sister and their circle; and with the possible exception of two sonnets, Sidney saw none of his work in print.[51] Letters were elaborately crafted according to strict rules of composition, and were often copied and circulated by both author and recipient.[52] This medium gave particular opportunities to women, who might want to avoid writing for a more public readership.[53] Printed texts were not the only medium for the circulation of ideas.

The difficulties of printing in the sixteenth century were legion.[54] The process involved a great deal of outlay in setting up a press, which like all new technologies was expensive; a prospective publisher also had to consider buying more than one press, so that his pressmen did not have to stand idly by whilst the compositor put the type in place. Even more expensive was the type, which had to be replaced regularly, as the soft metal wore down quickly. Paper and ink had to be bought up front. Ink was relatively cheap, but paper was costly: England's first paper mill supplying the printing trade would not be established until 1670.[55] Skilled workers were also expensive. Ideally a printworker should be fluent in several languages, including Latin, have excellent eyesight and be prepared for hard work; needless to say, such employees were difficult to find and tricky to keep. Henry Billingsley, whose translations of Euclid were published in 1570, pointed out to his readers that the complexities of the text had been beyond the understanding of the printers and observed in an aggrieved way: 'I was forced, to my great travaile and paine, to correcte the whole booke my selfe.'[56] Contemporary commentary suggests that printworkers, perhaps unsurprisingly, given the pressures of their trade, were inclined to drink too much, whilst several sixteenth-century printers seem to have been carried along by religious zeal, rather than the hope of profit. Patrons were often necessary: John Day, responsible for the colossal endeavour of producing John Foxe's *Actes and Monuments*, needed the protection of Leicester and Burghley, and the income derived from his monopoly on printing such works as the English metrical psalter and the primer.[57]

In recent decades a fascinating picture has emerged of the Tudor reader engaging with the text, often pen in hand, prompted by what he or she had read to a response that could be impassioned, angry, sceptical, devout or more besides. When Gabriel Harvey read his Livy, it was to prepare him and his patron to engage in political life.[58] Henry Savile, dedicating his translation to Elizabeth, urged his English readers to take Tacitus as a guide to understanding their own political world.[59] Their conclusions might be quite idiosyncratic. Thomas Bedingfield managed to view his translation of the history of Florence by the ardent republican Machiavelli as a plain demonstration of the superiority of monarchical rule.[60] It was also possible to read a polemical work and extract from it the exact opposite of what the author had intended: in the 1570s, Bishop Parkhurst of Norwich was worried that Catholics were reading the works of Protestant propagandists to extract the nuggets of Catholic text that the authors had included, in order to disprove them.[61] The rich and extraordinary array of comments and other marginalia which Tudor readers included in their books shows the range of reader responses.[62] At times, it appeared as if some readers were engaged in an ongoing dispute with the book before them.[63]

The English government was intensely interested in the workings of the printing trade. The propaganda potential of the printing press soon became clear: Henry VII used it in 1487 to publish the papal bull confirming his right to the English throne, and soon acquired a taste for printing his proclamations, whilst Henry VIII's regime was to take printed propaganda to a new level. The subversive potential of print was also evident early on: successive regimes battled with the challenge of censorship, and the attempted suppression of Protestantism in the 1520s was one of the first such interventions.[64] This was not just a question of book burning and repressive legislation, although both of these figured; perhaps the most significant element was official patronage of churchmen and scholars who were encouraged to write sermons and treatises responding to Luther's teaching.[65] It seems to have been accepted that the regime had an obligation to persuade, as much as to repress. The showpiece Paul's Cross sermon of 1521, delivered by John Fisher, was a *tour de force* built around metaphors of sunlight and storms, and the 'blak clowde of heresy', memorable and immediate.[66] It was swiftly printed in both English and Latin, and included the electrifying announcement that Henry VIII had written a book in refutation of Luther's heresies, and 'in his owne persone hath with his pen ... substauncyally foghten agaynst Martyn luther'.[67] Fisher backed up this public performance with the publication of theological treatises in Latin.[68] Already by the 1520s, then, the notion of a comprehensive media response was well understood.

The refutation of heresy might be a relatively straightforward matter, but the need to respond to political criticism posed a more complicated problem. It was one thing to pass a statute against 'fantastical prophecies' concerning the queen and nobility being set forth by 'writing, printing, singing or other open speech or word'.[69] Responding to more sophisticated criticism was another matter. After early failures to control the movement of books, the chief impulse seems to have been to channel, rather than try to block, the power of print. There was a continuous succession of royal printers from 1503 onwards, and in 1557 the Stationers' Company was given a royal charter. Edward VI's regime attempted the extraordinary feat of transforming the nation's religious allegiance: this was accompanied by a particularly vigorous printing campaign.[70] Mary I's regime faced a particular challenge from Protestant writers abroad, but attempts to suppress heretical literature were accompanied by an equally energetic campaign to defend and explain Catholicism in the press, whilst the justification for Thomas Wyatt's 1554 rebellion was thoroughly rebutted in print.[71] Such validations in print were not just for a domestic audience: considerable effort also went into producing accounts, generally in Latin, for European circulation.[72]

In this fertile literary landscape, a great deal of cross-pollination was at work. Philip Sidney's *Arcadia* was an intricate and fantastical blend of prose and verse telling the involved stories of imaginary characters in an idealized landscape, but was at the same time a veiled indictment of the failures of Elizabeth I's government. Edmund Spenser's *Faerie Queene* laid out an equally fabulous landscape of chivalric knights, mythical goddesses and wayward queens to suggest how the Elizabethan political classes might conceptualize their civic and moral duties. Pointed political criticism could be cast in poetic form, examples being Spenser's beast-fable, *Mother Hubberd's Tale*, and the *Mirror for Magistrates*, which in a series of editions endowed historical examples of political failure with a sharp contemporary edge. Military skill was taught in practical manuals; but military virtue might equally be commemorated in a Virgilian epitaph, as when Henry Howard, earl of Surrey, wrote on the death of his squire Thomas Clere, simultaneously advancing the development of English poetry and doing honour to Clere's bravery in the field.[73] Not only did the Tudor age see a multiplicity of literary genres, but it also saw no clear divisions between them. Poetry spilled over into politics, legend mingled with religion, and myth merged with history. Tudor men and women moved within a web of words, scribbled and printed, which shaped every aspect of their lives.

Borrowed wisdom

In terms of literary culture, Tudor intellectuals were all, in some measure, aping the sophistication of their counterparts abroad. The earliest manifestations of Renaissance literary culture in England had a pioneering flavour to them, a sense of exhilaration alongside a slightly defensive awareness of inadequacy. Whilst Europe was full of universities, England had just two: by the end of the sixteenth century even the much less populous Scotland had four. Almost every German city was equipped with printing presses, but in England there was little printing outside London.[74] The English borrowed heavily from their more cosmopolitan cousins abroad. The first book printed in English, *The History of Troy*, was translated from the French by William Caxton as he moved between Bruges, Ghent and Cologne, was printed abroad and was dedicated to Edward IV's sister Margaret, who, as duchess of Burgundy, presided over one of the most sophisticated courts in Europe. When Caxton took the plunge and relocated to Westminster, he continued to rely on books that had been successful when published in French. A nervous fledgling industry sought at first just to replicate established bestsellers, drawing on French and Burgundian courtly culture.[75] It also relied heavily on foreign expertise: Wynkyn de Worde was from the southern Rhineland, and Reyner (or Reginald) Wolfe, the printer responsible for Holinshed's *Chronicles*, was from Gelderland. The leading French printer Antoine Vérard made presentation copies of his works for Henry VII; liturgical books came from French presses for English use; and when, in 1539, Henry VIII gave his sanction to an official English translation of the Bible, the work was initially given to Parisian printers.[76] Caxton's output accounted for just a small fraction of the books circulated and sold in England during his lifetime. His innovation was to produce books in vernacular English: these comprised over 90 per cent of his output.[77] Books in French and Latin went on being printed across the Channel.[78] Later Reformation antagonisms were expressed through Protestant books printed in Emden or Geneva during Mary I's reign, and Catholic books printed in Louvain and Rheims during Elizabeth I's reign.[79]

By the second half of the sixteenth century, around a quarter of the books published in England were translations of works in other languages. Many of the most influential publications of the age were translations, from William Caxton's *Golden Legend* and William Tyndale's version of the Bible, to Arthur Golding's translation of Ovid's *Metamorphoses*, Thomas Hoby's translation of Castiglione's *The Book of the Courtier*, and the many versions of Thomas à Kempis's *The Imitation of Christ*, or the even greater number of translations and paraphrases of the psalms.[80] Yet translation was a complex and many-layered process; to translate a work was also to appropriate and often to reinvent it. The translator of the liturgy used by the nuns of Syon noted plaintively that 'Yt is not lyght for every man to drawe eny longe thyng from latyn in to oure Englyshe tongue. For there ys many wordes in Latyn that we have no propre englysshe accordynge therto. And then suche wordes muste be turnyd as the sentence may beste be understondyd.'[81] In Latin, the word for translation was *interpretatio*, which also implied elucidation and analysis.[82] When Roger Ascham wrote his celebrated treatise on education, *The Scholemaster*, he saw translation as the first rung on the educational ladder, from which the adept might mount to higher things.[83] Thomas North observed, in his 1579 translation of Plutarch's *Lives*, that 'the office of a fit translater, consisteth not onely in the faithfull expressing of his authors meaning, but also in a certain resembling and shadowing out of the forme of his style and the maner of his speaking', so the translator was also an impersonator.[84] Many of the translated works published in this century could be considered acts of ventriloquism, with the voices of contemporaries speaking under the guise of some ancient and venerable name. Contentious policies, or religious initiatives, could be softened and sanctioned by the apparent advocacy of some distant philosopher, historian or saint. Courtiers, counsellors and churchmen seeking to advise their monarch could do so more circumspectly through another man's words. Dissidents and critics could shelter behind the protection of another's authorship, and those who would not venture to publish under their own name could find expression by infusing a translated text with their own convictions. In this way, works in translation allowed the more contemporary voice of the translator to overlay much of the original work.

The printing press was a conduit for both reflection and protest regarding developments in the wider world, especially those that menaced peace within and between nations, or threatened to disrupt monarchical succession.[85] English authors and translators were painfully aware of the French wars of religion, the Portuguese succession crisis, the tensions within the Holy Roman Empire and the ambitions of the Counter-Reformation papacy, all of which had the potential to disrupt England's affairs.[86] A translation of Philippe de Commynes' history of France, 'treating of Princes secrets', was prepared for William Cecil in the 1560s; it was published in the 1590s, when concerns about the succession were raising interest in parallels abroad to fever pitch.[87] *The true history of the civil warres of France* appeared in 1591; *The historie of George Castriot* in 1596 recalled the Albanian hero Skanderbeg's rebellion against the Ottomans; and Richard Knolles' *General History of the Turks* was published in 1603. In the later part of Elizabeth's reign, Christopher Marlowe staged *The Massacre at Paris*, which recalled the gruesome events of the Massacre of St Bartholomew's Day in 1572, whilst George Peele's *The Battle of Alcazar* told the story of King Sebastian I of Portugal, who never returned from crusading in Morocco, thereby precipitating the succession crisis in Portugal, which could be held to mirror England's own.

By the end of the century, earlier diffidence about English as a literary language had almost dissipated. The great Elizabethan writers were quite aware that they were wielding a language of extraordinary subtlety, depth and beauty, although presumably they were also aware that they were often making it up as they went along. The Bible translators of the 1520s and 1530s had blazed this trail: Coverdale, for example, provided us with words including 'bloodthirsty', 'daytime', 'loving-kindness', 'slippery' and 'well-tuned'.[88] As the English began to engage more confidently with the outside world, they even began to conceive of their language as a commodity that might be exported:

> And who in time knowes whither we may vent
> The treasure of our tongue, to what strange shores
> This gaine of our best glorie shal be sent,
> T'inrich unknowing Nations with our stores?[89]

The dedicatory epistle to Edmund Spenser's *Shepheardes Calender* hailed him for restoring to 'theyr rightfull heritage such good and naturall English words, as have ben long time out of use and almost cleare disherited', and disparaged the practice of stopping the gaps in the English language with 'peeces and rags of other languages', creating 'a gallimaufray or hodgepodge of all other speaches'.[90] Spenser also deplored that the English in Ireland had abandoned their mother tongue to speak Irish.[91] The use of English had become something studied, self-conscious, competing with other languages and cultures in a way that was part celebratory, part defensive. England's Renaissance had passed beyond its apprenticeship.

A classical education

Education in the Tudor era was necessarily Renaissance education, requiring a close acquaintance with works written many centuries earlier in either Latin (which was spoken by a small fraction of society) or Greek (which was spoken by barely anyone at all). The works of Plato were already two millennia old by the time Tudor scholars encountered them, whilst the works of Cicero, Plutarch and Quintilian, three authors whose views on education were most commonly relied upon, were fifteen centuries old. This makes Renaissance intellectual culture sound rarefied, reactionary and potentially irrelevant, but the truth was quite the opposite. Age and cultural distance imparted precisely the kind of vigorous and even subversive inspiration which the modern age might associate with a thoroughly contemporary viewpoint. From the Tudor perspective, concepts such as revolution, republicanism, scepticism or democracy were classical ideas. Ancient wisdom came with a radical edge.

The literary works of classical Greece and Rome offered a vision of wisdom, erudition and cultural achievement unparalleled in any subsequent age, rendered both illuminating and exciting by the extent of the distance between the different eras.[92] Contemporary authors, such as the great Dutch humanist Desiderius Erasmus, were valued, too, but largely because Erasmus and his ilk were themselves so well versed in the classics and so adept at translating them. It is impossible to appreciate the depth and variety of Tudor culture without understanding not only how heavily indebted it was to the classical past, but also how scintillating, exquisite, varied and intermittently dissident these ancient voices could sound to their Tudor admirers.[93] The classical world became as familiar a cultural deposit as the Bible: a source of stories and examples that were instantly recognizable. Ancient Greece and Rome lived within Tudor imagination as a place of heroism and grandeur, a source of endless fascination, providing historical and literary paradigms for an array of Tudor experiences and preoccupations. Between 1500 and 1660, around a third of all the books translated into English had originally been in Latin, with sizeable numbers also coming from Greek and Hebrew.[94] Almost a hundred of the plays written in the Elizabethan and Jacobean periods had a Roman theme.[95] 'I am more an antique Roman than a Dane', says Horatio to Hamlet, as he proposes to take his own life alongside his dying friend. English translations of Plutarch, Appian, Polybius, Livy, Seneca, Virgil, Sallust and Tacitus were all available by the end of the century.[96] Virgil's *Aeneid* appeared in five English editions between 1553 and 1584; Heywood's translations of Seneca also went into multiple editions after 1560.[97] The study of the classics became established as a necessary prerequisite for public life. The earl of Essex advised the young earl of Rutland, 'Above all other books be conversant in the Histories . . . by which and in which you must ripen and settle your judgment.'[98] Essex, who was rumoured to have written a preface to Henry Savile's translation of Tacitus, was compared by his associates and admirers to Alexander the Great, Achilles, Scipio Aemilianus and Aeneas, with various shades of flattery and admonition.[99]

Classical learning was also increasingly essential in the exercise of authority. The extent to which royal or noble children were educated was quite startling. Since it was widely held that 'the main hope of getting a good ruler hangs on his proper education', serious effort was put into the task of educating a future monarch.[100] Even a moderate amount of schooling, however, might produce a promising acquaintance with antiquity.[101] Shakespeare's Roman plays were founded on nothing more exalted than a grammar-school education and a good grasp of Plutarch's *Lives*.[102] Knowledge of the classics was at the centre of the school syllabus and was strenuously enforced.[103] Erasmus, whose works *De ratione studii* and *De copia* became the basis for school curricula, advised pupils to read a text four times over, on the third occasion studying it for rhetorical technique and on the fourth 'seeking out what seems to relate to philosophy, especially ethics, to discover any example that may be applicable to morals'.[104] In schools where the working day began at five or six in the morning and lasted twelve hours, education was not something to be taken lightly. Nor did such schooling require a wealthy background. Shakespeare was educated in Stratford, Christopher Marlowe in Canterbury and Edmund Spenser in London; their fathers were all in trade as a glover, a shoesmith and a clothworker, respectively.

The proliferation of grammar schools during the sixteenth century meant that, by 1603, there were around 360 of them, a better provision per head of population than in Victorian times.[105] The fifteenth century had also seen a much wider provision of free schools than is often recognized, including those connected to Oxford or Cambridge colleges: Magdalen College School in Oxford, or Winchester with its link to New College Oxford, or Eton with its ties to King's College Cambridge. Many schools were linked to monastic foundations: the location of many post-Reformation schools suggests that they were preserved or refounded on the site of earlier monastery schools.[106] Educational patronage was expected of those with means. Edmund Grindal, archbishop of Canterbury in the 1570s, and his contemporary Edwin Sandys, archbishop of York, both came from the area known today as Cumbria; Grindal founded a grammar school in his home village of St Bees, where previously there had been a Benedictine priory, while Sandys founded the grammar school in the small town of Hawkshead, where William Wordsworth would later study. A wealthy patron was not always necessary: the school in the fen village of Willingham was founded by public subscription in 1593.[107] Bishop Richard Barnes of Durham issued instructions in 1577 that every clergyman not licensed to preach should teach every child in his parish to read and write, without charge, before encouraging their parents to send them for further schooling, or to learn some more humble craft.[108]

Basic education might be acquired at a 'dame school', or 'petty school', although their reputation was not strong. Erasmus was incredulous that 'some people send their sons to an incompetent, drunken female in order to learn their reading and writing'.[109] Francis Clement wrote a work in 1587 called *The Petie Schole*, which protested at children being taught by teachers 'altogether rude and utterly ignorant'. He sought, somewhat ambitiously, to provide instead 'a method to enable both a childe to reade perfectly within one moneth, and also the unperfect to write English aright'. In 1570, a pamphlet was published called *An ABC for children*, which promised lavishly that 'by this booke, a man that hath good capacitie, and can no letter in the book, may learne to read in the space of sixe weekes, both Latin and English, if he give thereto good diligence'.[110] This work was chiefly devoted to pronunciation and comprehension, but it also included prayers in both Latin and English, the Ten Commandments, and a list of short imperatives, such as 'Forgive gladly' and 'Use honest company', alongside 'Thrust downe pride' and 'Think of death', together with the more pragmatic 'Wash cleane' and 'Be no sluggard'.[111] There was much general insistence that educational methods should be thorough, which probably indicates how often they were not. Erasmus's advice when it came to letter-writing was that students 'should not at once have recourse to rules nor take refuge in books from which they may borrow elegant little words and sententious expression', but that they should reflect in depth, seek inspiration from the best authors and produce work of true excellence.[112] In reality, no doubt many took the easier route. Yet much of the advice given was eminently practical. In his handbook for students, *De copia*, Erasmus suggested 148 ways of saying 'your letter pleased me greatly', and 202 ways to express 'always, as long as I live, I shall remember you'.[113]

Literacy rates remain difficult to disentangle from fragmentary sources, but were obviously growing. Thomas More optimistically envisaged that over half the population could read, which perhaps describes his immediate acquaintances and the educated classes of early Tudor London, but not England generally.[114] For the population at large, there was probably closer to a 20–30 per cent literacy rate for men, lower for women; but this was linked to occupation, as much as to wealth or status. It has been estimated that by 1600, 97 per cent of goldsmiths were literate, but only 54 per cent of brewers.[115] These literacy rates indicate that although education was not universal, it was available to many. Much thought was certainly given to pedagogical technique. Thomas Elyot, in *The Boke Named the Governour*, which went through many different editions from the 1530s onwards, suggested that young children should not be burdened with the 'tedyous labours' of grammar learning, but that after 'a fewe and quicke rules of grammar' the child should be read Aesop's fables in Greek, in which 'children moch delyte' and which had the advantage of being both 'elegante and brefe', yet also containing 'moche morall and polytyke wysedome'.[116] John Holte learned how to teach whilst serving as usher at Magdalen College School in the 1490s.[117] His textbook, *Lac Puerorum or Mylke for Children*, was unusual in employing visual aids to help children memorize the rules of Latin grammar, and went into several editions, whilst Holte succeeded John Skelton as tutor to the future Henry VIII.

Renaissance education was therefore a curious combination of elements. Founded on the wisdom of the ancients, it nevertheless had a pointed contemporary application.[118] The precise status of innovative thinking in the Tudor years was always doubtful: the word '*ingenium*' was only just beginning to take on connotations of inventiveness, and although it gave rise to the word 'engine', mechanical inventions could be viewed with alarm, as a threat to the natural order.[119] One oddity of the Renaissance was that it deployed enormous ingenuity in pursuit of a state of mind which, whilst startlingly innovative, rejected all accusations of novelty. Any novel initiatives in education, politics or religion were justified by appeals to the classical or Christian past. Another obvious peculiarity of Renaissance thought was that it blended together pagan and Christian wisdom in this way. An array of pagan authors was used to support and extend Christian piety, and Aristotle was matched with St Augustine, Cicero with St Paul, in the pursuit of true understanding. When Roger Ascham wrote his famous description of how he had educated Elizabeth I, he spoke of her reading Cicero and Livy alongside the New Testament in Greek, and studying the orations of Isocrates and the tragedies of Sophocles at the same time as the works of St Cyprian and the Lutheran reformer Philipp Melanchthon.[120] Erasmus's work *De Copia* was viewed not just as a guide to mastering classical Latin, but also as a path to spiritual development.[121]

Intense, eclectic, demanding and multi-lingual, Tudor education was overwhelming in its effects, but unpredictable in its consequences. Protestant and Catholic polemicists would draw equally upon the works of Augustine; political rivals would argue from the same texts by Livy, Aristotle or Plutarch; moralists and Machiavellians would appeal with equal vehemence to Cicero. There were some certainties, however: Latin, and to a much lesser extent Greek, was widely accepted as a means to unlocking both the storehouses of wisdom and the chances of political and social influence. The political process, no less than the experience of education, necessarily involved repeated encounters with the ancient civilizations of Greece and Rome, and established them as parallel worlds with which Tudor statesmen and commentators found themselves constantly in dialogue. It imparted a distinctive quality to the culture of the age that so much of it rested on characters, events, prose and poetry created entirely in the imagination, and captured between the covers of books.

Dialogue and debate

Thomas More's *Utopia*, perhaps the most arresting work of the early Tudor period, sums up much about England's complicated relationship with Renaissance literary culture. It is to this day hailed as one of the most important works by any English author, and yet it was written in Latin, and published in Louvain, Paris, Basel and Florence between 1516 and 1519, only appearing in English translation in 1551, sixteen years after its author had been executed for treason. It was a work defined by its ambiguity, where each place name or proper name is open to multiple interpretations: while 'Utopia' might be translated as 'No-place', it can also have overtones of the Greek '*eudaimonia*', and thus indicate 'place of happiness'. The protagonist 'Hythlodaeus' might be translated as 'peddler of nonsense', but the character's first name is Raphael, the name of the archangel; and since his name seems to include an appeal to 'Deus', it could also be the 'voice of God'.[122]

More's work described a remote island whose pagan society was organized on the basis of ruthless equality and the communal sharing of all work and wealth alike. It could have been meant as an attempt to shame Catholic Europe into a realization of its own transgressions; it might have been meant as an attempt to communicate the essence of the Christian ideal, freed from all association with the contemporary Church; it could equally have been intended as a criticism of his fellow humanists and the complacency of their claims to understanding. It might have been that More himself was not sure of his own mind, and did not know whether to side with Hythlodaeus the visionary, or with Morus, the character purporting to be More himself, who was the voice of caution and compromise. International in scope, multivalent in meaning, full of humour as well as tragedy and ultimately impossible to pin down, More's work characterized all that was best and yet most baffling about the English Renaissance.

One striking aspect of *Utopia* is the extent to which, having displayed its mastery of Renaissance language, rhetoric and culture, it then departs in unexpected directions. Disquisitions on 'the best state of the commonwealth' were common, yet most left the social hierarchy unchallenged. More's vision of a commonwealth, by contrast, was based on radical egalitarianism; he attacked the rich in vivid prose, which all but snarled as it described their idleness and their corrupting effect upon society. His fury at a society which left the poor subject to the 'awful necessity of stealing and then dying for it' was a thread running throughout the book.[123] The satirical edge of proposals that gold should be reserved for chamber pots and children's toys, or that foreign conflicts should be resolved by the covert assassination of foreign leaders, were indictment more than solution; little wonder that a succession of later interpretations hailed the work's 'modernity', and chattered foolishly about its links to modern communism. A particularly important aspect of *Utopia* is its unwillingness to reach a conclusion. At the end of the book, the character who bears More's name notes wistfully that 'there are many things in the commonwealth of Utopia that I rather wish, than hope, to see followed in our governments'.[124] The characters agree that it would be good to talk further at some other time, and the work closes, leaving behind a host of silent questions. Was this More's lament for the political idealism he knew was doomed, or his own personal elegy for the life of virtuous contemplation from which he had walked away? Shortly after *Utopia* was published, More joined Henry VIII's Privy Council. He would rise to the office of lord chancellor, only to fall six years later to disgrace, imprisonment and a traitor's death, as if fulfilling one of his own fables about the dangers of political life. His most famous work would remain a series of unanswered questions, a debate never concluded.

Books frequently make reference to 'Renaissance ideals' or 'Renaissance thought'; but this gives a false impression of consensus, or shared values. Not only was there no single set of Renaissance values, but Renaissance thinkers and writers prioritized debate, celebrated the ebb and flow of argument, and found virtue in a variety of viewpoints. Just as grammarschool children were taught to argue *in utramque partem*, presenting the case both for and against a given proposition, so writers wove skeins of contrasting ideas and claims. A large amount of Tudor literature was therefore in the form of dialogues, in direct imitation of many classical works. When More was trying to defeat William Tyndale's heresies, he wrote *A Dialogue Concerning Heresies*; in the Tower facing execution, he wrote *A Dialogue of Comfort against Tribulation*. Henry VIII, in *A glasse of the truth*, explored the reasons behind his break from Katherine of Aragon by means of two disputants. Almost any crucial question might be addressed in dialogue form. Those striving to inculcate religious doctrine discovered that the catechism form of question and answer was by far the most profitable route to take.[125] In 1592, Thomas Hood, instructing his readers in the use of the celestial and terrestrial globes, gave his views 'most plainly delivered in forme of a dialogue.'[126] In this fever of debate, many dialogues did present a dominant point of view that pushed the reader to a single answer; but they still espoused the exchange of different ideas. Some of the greatest works genuinely left the reader still thinking the question through.

Successful debate required oratorical skill, and the ability to speak well was an important Renaissance accomplishment. An educational guide by the humanist Johannes Sturm averred that although half of his attention would be given to 'the knowledge of things which polisheth the minde', the other half would be devoted to 'the exercise of the tongue and practise of speeche, which is to be uttred discretely and eligantly, and being represented to the eares of the hearers, it doth shewe a sweete and sugred consent of the minde'.[127] Above all, the gift of eloquence was sought after as a powerful political tool. If some Tudor debates were civil exchanges over abstruse points of philosophy, others were more combative; yet political debate, always an essential part of parliamentary or conciliar proceedings, was seen as a virtue. Such debates were not just restricted to courtiers and scholars. Particularly from the mid-century onwards, political tracts and polemics might appeal to a popular audience. Libel came of age, too, under the Tudors: the word itself comes from the Latin *libellus*, or 'little book'. In 1566, a libellous set of verses giving malicious descriptions of over forty MPs in the House of Commons was written half in English, half in Latin.[128] A version of this was the 'pasquil', named after a statue unearthed in Rome in 1501, on which it became fashionable to affix verses commenting (trenchantly) on contemporary themes. In 1533, Sir Thomas Elyot's *Pasquil the playne* compared straight-talking and flattery, explaining that 'Pasquillus . . . is an image of stone, sittinge in the citie of Rome openly: on whome ones in the yere, it is leful to every man, to set in verse or prose any taunte that he will / agayne whom he list, howe great an astate so ever he be.'[129] In 1559, the *Mirror for Magistrates* first appeared. It purported to be a continuation of John Lydgate's fifteenth-century work *The Fall of*

Princes, but in fact incorporated a much broader critical analysis of the political process, including a set of characters from Roman history in its 1587 edition.[130] It encouraged its readers to anatomize the sins of past leaders, whilst echoing contemporary anxiety about the political follies and instabilities of the day.

Literary persuasion might also be applied to the most pressing social problems of the age. There were many fierce and eloquent pleas on behalf of the poor. Poverty was an ugly and unavoidable blight upon Tudor society, and it became all the more painful every time the harvest failed or the plague struck, or when the conclusion of a war brought the maimed survivors back onto England's highways. More in *Utopia* was not afraid to contrast the nobility, 'who live idly like drones off the labour of others', with those who lived in poverty and misery.[131] He was frustrated by the senseless ordering of society, where so many people were idle, while others were broken by labour and want; in his idealized communities, everyone would work, but nobody would need to work for longer than six hours each day. More wrote in elegant and satirical Latin, and envisaged that his ideas would only be discussed by the educated; indeed, in 1533, at a time of much greater political tension, he said he would rather burn *Utopia* than allow it to be translated into English, if it was to cause social unrest.[132] Yet his contemporaries, particularly those spurred on by the new Protestant creed, were not so cautious. In the mid-century in particular, poems and dialogues, sermons and treatises, all put forward biting criticism of social inequality and suffering. *A Supplication of the Poore Commons*, published in 1546, reproached Henry VIII for promising to help 'the lame and impotent creatures of this realm' and failing to deliver.[133] Its anonymous author blamed the clergy, as many other Protestant writers did; but criticism could be levelled at the rich laity, too. Thomas Becon also attacked the wool trade and the 'gredy woulves and comberous cormerauntes' who pastured their sheep on common lands, so that 'poore people are not able to kepe a cow for the confort of them, and of their pore familie, but are like to starve and perish for honger'.[134] Robert Crowley, writing during Edward VI's reign, when evangelicals cherished great hope of social reform, castigated the gentry for their oppression of the poor, and exhorted the parliament to bring about change.[135]

Literature did not just identify the corruption and failings of the age: it also suggested solutions. What the modern world might regard as fiction was expected to offer moral and political guidance. Prefaces to works such as Marlowe's *Tamburlaine*, Mary Sidney Herbert's *Antonie* or Shakespeare's *Rape of Lucrece* showed how they should be read, making note of the historical sources on which they were based to demonstrate how they should be understood as pieces of historical analysis.[136] In particular, literature – both classical and contemporary – was regarded as a guide to the political process. Francis Walsingham, when trying to construct intelligent foreign policy, turned to Livy for guidance.[137] He noted how 'in these the reading of histories, as you have principally to mark how matters have passed in government in those days, so have you to apply them to these our times and states and see how they may be made serviceable to our age'.[138] Philip Sidney, preparing for a life of public service, also read Livy. So deeply steeped were these Tudor statesmen in the works of classical authors that they saw no incongruity in taking the example of ancient Rome as a basis for policy formation in Elizabethan England. Their French contemporary Michel de Montaigne thought that Tacitus was 'most useful for a troubled sick age like our own; you would often say that it is us he is describing and us he is criticizing'.[139] Advice channelled through literature in this way could be quite uncompromising. In 1570, the first English translation of Demosthenes by Thomas Wilson was also a stern critique of Elizabeth's foreign policy and a vigorous piece of anti-Spanish propaganda. The ancient Greek orator's warnings against Philip II of Macedon were commuted neatly into warnings against Philip II of Spain. Pagan gods were consolidated into the single 'God' of the sixteenth century, and the gibe against 'all these in our dayes that are common traytors and open Rebels to their natural soyle and Countrie' was directed at Elizabethan Catholics.[140] Wilson may have been unusual in aiming a translation of a classical text so specifically at a particular contemporary debate, but he was building on the accumulated usage of many years. He had himself spent nine months in a Roman prison after arrest by the Inquisition, so his loathing of Catholicism was understandable.

Political criticism in the guise of literature could be hard to suppress. Elizabethan censors might be on fairly firm ground when it came to the suppression of Catholic books published abroad or the scandalous

Presbyterianism of the 'Martin Marprelate' tracts, which lambasted episcopacy with all the scabrous force of Elizabethan invective; but more
subtle reproaches were harder to combat. Authors frequently adopted a
measure of restraint precisely in order to give themselves a voice that
could be heard, becoming masters of ambiguity, as they crafted political
commentary which could evade open condemnation.[141] The potential
risks were illustrated by the number of writers called before the Privy
Council to explain themselves. Some authors, such as Philip Sidney, might
demonstrate anxiety that their chosen medium could be so cautiously
framed as to render its message blunted or lost altogether. His pastoral
fable of irresponsible kingship and the dangers of human emotion, the
Arcadia, was full of pointed messages for the Elizabethan ruling classes,
should they be perceptive enough to read them.[142] Sidney, however, had
already tried the direct approach, writing a letter to Elizabeth to warn
her off marrying a French Catholic which so enraged her that he was
compelled to explore instead the labyrinths of his own imagination.[143]
There was little that was openly challenging to the Tudor regime. The
most defiant works to emerge in print were those of the Protestant resistance theorists of the 1550s, and when John Ponet put his case for tyrannicide, it was of necessity printed abroad.[144] It is striking, however, that
many books published overseas might still adopt a fairly deferential tone
towards the Tudor government, if only as an intelligent polemical strategy:
many of the books published by Catholic exiles during Elizabeth's reign,
for example, were notably polite towards the queen.[145]

If few works threatened the existence of the monarchy itself, however,
plenty of them were prepared to criticize the actions of individual
monarchs. Criticism was particularly outspoken in the later years of
Elizabeth, when the combination of international instability, religious
conflict and the rule of an aging childless queen ratcheted up political
anxieties to breaking point.[146] By the end of the 1570s, the outpouring
of political advice and agitation had also begun to interlink different kinds
of literary expression. Opposition to the Anjou match produced everything from the exquisite intricacies of Sidney's *Arcadia* to the brutal
censure of John Stubbs' *The Discovery of a Gaping Gulph* (which led to the
author's hand being cut off) and the ballad of 'The Frog He Would
A-wooing Go'.[147] The disastrous war in Ireland, and the political tensions

which it engendered, alongside a looming succession crisis in the 1590s, left its imprint on everything from Spenser's *Faerie Queene* and Shakespeare's *Julius Caesar* to Hayward's history of Henry IV (which landed him in the Tower) and Henry Savile's translations of Tacitus.[148] Government attempts at censorship in the 1590s, including the 1599 Bishops' Ban on satire, epigrams and the use of English history in plays, demonstrates just how powerful criticism could be when couched in a play, a poem or a work of history.[149]

The study of letters became for the Tudors the basis for both personal morality and political competence: as Francis Walsingham observed, the aim of learning was 'to serve the commonwealth'.[150] Tudor commentators placed enormous faith in the regenerative and inspirational powers of good literature. In Stephen Hawes' *The Example of Vertu*, composed around 1503–04, it was even claimed that the salvation of souls after death might depend on their 'instruccyon' or 'informacyon' when alive.[151] Thomas Elyot, who thought that the 'end of all doctrine and studie is good counsayle', himself embodied the idea that education, virtue, political wisdom and civic duty were inextricably bound up with one another, writing books on all these subjects, as well as on the preservation of health and preparation for a good death, whilst himself serving as an MP. In all these endeavours, the classical past was the richest source of sagacity. In a letter to Fulke Greville, which may have been authored by Essex, or perhaps by Francis Bacon, the writer recommended Tacitus as 'simply the best' guide to politics, followed by Livy, while Thucydides was the best Greek authority.[152] The study of good letters, therefore, was intended to have a very practical application, starting with the moral regeneration of the individual, but ending in the greater good of society.

Did women have a Renaissance?

This question was asked in the 1970s, at a time when women's history was fighting to achieve proper recognition. It was raised in an essay which bluntly pointed out how 'events that further the historical development of men' might have 'quite different, even opposite, effects upon women'.[153] This helped to reconfigure historical debate about women, although the conclusion that the status of women had suffered a blow during the

Renaissance was less convincing.[154] Tracing one particular kind of inequality was always going to be tricky in an age when inequalities were not only rife, but also broadly considered to be the natural order. Similarly, categorizing human experience primarily according to gender arguably remained problematic with regard to a society with such pronounced divisions of status, wealth and occupation. More recent research has uncovered a more complicated and variegated picture.[155] It may be that women did have a Renaissance after all.

Where women exercised influence in the early modern period, it was usually as a consequence of their social status, although sheer force of character could also prove remarkably enabling. Yet exposure to the radical and astonishing ideas of classical authors could not fail to have an effect on thinking both by and about women. In particular, the Renaissance emphasis on education was extended to include certain groups of women, with some startling effects. The first book published by a woman in Tudor England appeared in 1526, when Thomas More's daughter, Margaret Roper, described as 'a yong vertuous and well lerned gentylwoman of xix yere of age', printed her translation of Erasmus's treatise on the Paternoster. The preface defended the principle of classical education for women.[156] If its author's name was not included on the frontispiece, the preface nevertheless made some piercing remarks about how superior the erudition of women could be to that of the clergy. More himself was emphatic that he regarded women as rational creatures who had intellectual as well as spiritual potential. He said of men and women, 'If they are worthy of being ranked with the human race, if they are distinguished by reason from beasts; that learning, by which the reason is cultivated, is equally suitable to both.'[157]

Education was not, of course, open to very many Tudor women, but those who benefited from it made the most of the opportunity. Knowledge of languages brought a very particular kind of empowerment; Latin and Greek, in particular, enabled women to take their place within scholarly networks, as well as facilitating their political engagement. William Harrison, in his description of England, was inclined to be censorious about the Court; but in his praise of the women who waited upon Elizabeth, he noted that 'there are very few of them which have not the use and skill of sundry speeches, besides an excellent vein of writing beforetime not regarded'. And he observed that many 'besides sound knowledge of the

Greek and Latin tongues are thereto no less skilful in the Spanish, Italian, and French, or in some one of them'.[158] Literary works in the 1590s were chiefly dedicated to men such as the earl of Essex or Lord Burghley, but an appreciable number were dedicated to Mary Sidney Herbert as well as to the queen herself.[159] The extraordinary scholarship of the Cooke sisters brought them the respect of literary circles, and their place at the heart of Elizabethan politics was as much facilitated by their intellectual training as by their marriages to leading statesmen and diplomats.[160]

This knowledge of languages was very frequently deployed in the service of religion; and here, too, was a potential source of liberation. Many male commentators might have felt uneasy when women produced religious works, but it was hard to argue with anyone who might plausibly be said to be channelling divine instruction. The outspokenness of female witnesses and martyrs is reflected in the tendency for their detractors to accuse them of sexual licentiousness.[161] Such women drew on scriptural justification. The description in Proverbs of the good wife whose value was 'far above rubies' delineated a woman of resilience and resourcefulness, who 'girdeth her loins with strength, and strengtheneth her arms'.[162] The replies of Anne Askew under interrogation, as recorded by John Bale, demonstrate the confidence which knowledge of Scripture might impart to a feisty woman defending her faith. When she was charged with having said that 'God was not in temples made with hands', Askew responded by demonstrating the relevant passages of the New Testament which supported her; and when asked for further clarification, answered dismissively 'that I would not throw pearls among swine, for acorns were good enough'.[163]

The question of whether the example set by two female rulers of England changed perceptions of women more broadly is much debated, and largely inconclusive. The extent of their learning, however, definitely had an impact, with ramifications for their exercise of authority. They also brought about practical opportunities. The female households of the Tudor queens created a new role for educated women, their intellectual aspirations heightened by humanist notions of erudition. Anne Boleyn's copy of the New Testament (in French), which she made available for consultation in her chambers, was akin to Katherine Parr's publication of her book of prayers and meditations. Royal women had long felt their obligation to exert a pious influence; but as print culture expanded, their piety used books as a conduit. The literary circle fostered by Katherine Parr generated two books by the queen herself – the first to be published in English by a named female author – endeavours echoed by the authorship and patronage of Anne Seymour, Katherine Brandon and Mary Fitzroy. This scholarly grouping also contained two future queens: under Parr's tutelage, the future Mary I translated some of Erasmus's *Paraphrases* and the future Elizabeth I produced her *Mirror of a Sinful Soul*, translated from the French work by Marguerite de Navarre.[164] Following this example, noble and gentry families increasingly provided education for their daughters; and if this was aimed primarily at enhancing their social status and marriageability, it also had the fortunate effect of releasing some of their intellectual and creative potential.

The influence of the Renaissance on less privileged women is perhaps more questionable; and yet the predominance of classical themes in popular print culture demonstrates the accessibility of some of this culture at every level. In the proto-feminist tract of 1589, *Jane Anger, Her Protection for Women*, the defence of women against slander drew its examples from Greek and Roman literature and mythology. 'But let us graunt that Cletemnestra, Ariadna, Dalila, and Jesabell were spotted with crimes: shal not Nero with others innumerable, and therefore unnameable joine handes with them and lead the daunce?'[165] Anger's tract showed an awareness of different categories of reader and had two prefaces, one more courteously worded and addressed to gentlewomen, and a second 'To all Women in generall' which was more trenchant: 'Fie on the falshoode of men, whose minds goe oft a madding, and whose tongues can not so soone bee wagging, but straight they fal a railing.' This readership was expected to be familiar with the legends of Troy, the virtues of King Cyrus and Xenocrates, the wisdom of Plato. If the classical past was more often the preserve of male scholars, it could still be contested territory.

Isabella Whitney was the first woman to write and publish secular verse in England, and the first to declare herself a professional poet. In 1567, she published *The copy of a letter, lately written in metre by a young gentlewoman to her unconstant lover. With an admonition to all young gentlewomen, and to all other maids in general, to beware of men's flattery*. It turned the tables on the many male poets who had written bewailing women's inconstancy. The poem is candid, heartfelt, yet dignified in its reproaches. It is striking how the author's voice is strengthened by the traditions of Renaissance writing. An array of classical and mythological figures appear in the poem: Dido abandoned by Aeneas, Medea abandoned by Jason, Oenone deserted by her husband Paris. The author, in the role of abandoned lover, expresses her resignation in words that have been taken by some as an indication of female 'forced passivity', but that might equally well be seen as women occupying the higher moral ground of forgiveness.[166] In the warning to maids which was also included in this work, Whitney did not lack edge:

> Trust not a man at the fyrst sight,
> But trye him well before:
> I wish al Maids within their brests
> To kepe this thing in store.[167]

Whitney fashioned herself through her work – how accurately we cannot be sure – as a woman poor, sick, childless and alone, a dismissed maid-servant now left reliant on her writing.[168] In *A Sweet Nosgay* of 1573, she described her quest for knowledge leading her through Scripture, histories, classical and neo-classical literature, until finally she found solace in the fragrant nosegay of flowers which is her own verse.[169] Her work betrayed her distinctiveness, and defiance, at being a female author; but it also showed her familiarity with both the Renaissance tropes and authors of the time, as well as the more practical aspects of the London book trade.[170] Like other female authors of the time, she wrote within a Renaissance tradition, whilst at the same time presenting a subtle challenge to many of that tradition's assumptions.[171]

Renaissance women writers faced many discouraging prospects: from the risk that female authorship might be linked to sexual licence, to the possibility that their work, if it was commended, might be given the back-handed compliment of having been written by someone who had overcome the limitations of being female.[172] When Juan Luis Vives wrote *The Education of a Christian Woman*, he devoted a chapter to outlining the classical works that he thought women should read; but he also devoted another chapter to the works that they should not read. In his preface, Vives took issue with a host of authorities for neglecting the upbringing of women, but he still considered that a woman should aim to learn 'for her selfe alone and her yonge children or her sisters', since 'it neither becometh a woman to rule a schole / nor to lyve amonge men / or speke abrode . . . if she be good / it were better to be at home within / and unknowen to other folkes'.[173] Whitney made her work *A Sweet Nosgay* more defensible by including letters from friends and kin, in order to cast it in the form of a manuscript text privately circulated.[174] When Mary Sidney Herbert completed the Sidney Psalter, her friend John Harington insisted that she must have had the help of her chaplain to translate from the Hebrew, 'for the translation . . . was more than a woman's skill to express the sense so right as she hath done in her verse, and more than the English or Latin translation could give her'.[175] And yet this seemingly patronizing comment did at least signal that Harington accepted without question that Mary Sidney Herbert was fluent in Latin, and may in fact have been chiefly a reflection on the rarity of Hebrew proficiency.[176]

Richard Hyrde, who translated Vives' work into English, was more outspoken in endorsing the education of women: 'what is more frutefull than the good education and ordre of women, the one half of all mankynde?' He also attacked the 'unreasonable oversyght of men' who ceaselessly complained about women, yet who not only failed to teach them, but 'purposely with drawe them fro lernynge / by whiche they myghte have occasyons to waxe better by them selfe'.[177] Translation, in particular, offered an unparalleled opportunity for women authors, constrained by the expectation that 'the highest ornament of woman is silence'.[178] Many women during this period professed their unworthiness precisely in order to facilitate their self-expression in print, for which the work of translation was the perfect metaphor. Anne Locke, who translated Jean Taffin's *Markes of the Children of God*, wrote in her preface:

> Because great things by reason of my sexe, I may not doe, and that which I may, I ought to doe, I have according to my duety, brought my poore basket of stones to the strengthening of the wals of that Jerusalme, whereof (by Grace) we are all both Citizens and members.

Her apparent self-abasement here was balanced by the boldness of her claim to spiritual equality, and the potentially subversive nature of her chosen text, a Dutch Calvinist work on affliction and persecution.[179] The defence of the fledgling Elizabethan Church by John Jewel, bishop of Salisbury, was printed in Latin in 1562; its appearance in English in 1563 as *The Apology of the Church of England* was the work of Anne Cooke Bacon. Matthew Parker claimed in the preface that it had been published without the knowledge of the 'right honorable learned and vertuous Ladie A. B.', in order 'to prevent suche excuses as your modestie woulde have made instaye of publishing it'.[180] Nevertheless, Bacon's work became one of the most significant texts of Elizabeth's reign. In 1578, Margaret Tyler published the first prose romance to be translated by a woman, downplaying her own role by describing it in terms of 'giving entertainment to a straunger' by translating another's words.[181] Mary Sidney Herbert, in 1592, published a joint translation of a Huguenot moral tract by Philippe du Plessis-Mornay and Robert Garnier's *Antonius*, a retelling of the story of Antony and Cleopatra, which together made a subtle but powerful offering to Elizabeth I in the year that the Herberts hosted a royal visit. The latter work, about the passionate Egyptian queen, warned how a monarch, by indulging her own emotions, could unleash civil war, whilst the former suggested Mary Sidney Herbert herself in the role of dispassionate counsellor.[182] By cautious, sometimes covert, means, intelligent and educated women were finding their literary voice.

* * *

The concept of the Renaissance has a long and venerable history, rooted in early modern self-fashioning and in nineteenth-century self-satisfaction. But to the English men and women who lived through the Renaissance, it was something raw, sharp-edged, invigorating and disputed. The introduction of Greek, for example, into the universities was seen as something excitingly innovative, and prompted stern opposition from conservatives, who were quickly characterized as 'Trojans'.[183] The ideas of Tacitus about tyranny, or Lucian's use of satire, or Cicero's characterization of political virtue could all be applied in arresting ways. When the earl of Essex sought to stage a political demonstration in his own defence, he and his friends were inspired by Livy and Tacitus to seek political agency, reprove tyranny and secure the succession.[184] Essex recruited as his advisor Henry Cuffe, regius professor of Greek at Oxford, who on the scaffold would break with usual practice to protest against his conviction, angrily declaring that 'Schollars and Martialists (thoughe learning and vallour should have the prehemynence yet) in England must dye like doggs and be hanged.'[185] Learning was not just a conservative force.

Literature was, to the Tudors, more than diversion and entertainment: it was moral instruction, preparation for government, and spiritual education. Philip Sidney, writing in defence of poetry, argued that it was more influential than either history or philosophy. The philosopher might teach, but he was so obscure that only those already learned could understand him, whilst the historian, 'loaden with old mouse-eaten records', was hindered from laying down true moral guidance by being 'captived to the truth of a foolish world'. Only the poet could truly inspire, by presenting ideals, by showing 'virtue exalted and vice punished', whilst at the same time entrancing the reader.[186] Poetry, said Sidney, was 'full of virtue-breeding delightfulness', and this was why Scripture 'hath whole parts in it poeticall' and was even used by Christ, as when he inspired through parables. Sidney recalled the bible story of the prodigal son, confessing, 'Truly, for myself, me seems I see before my eyes the lost child's disdainful prodigality, turned to envy a swine's dinner'. In literature, 'a feigned example hath as much force to teach as a true example', but the poet did not only show the way, but he also 'giveth so sweet a prospect into the way, as will entice any man to enter into it'.[187]

The seductiveness of language, particularly when combined with the other attractions of the theatre, was deemed powerful by both defenders and detractors. Stephen Gosson had himself failed as both poet and playwright before he forged an alternative career as a critic. In his work *The Schoole of Abuse*, aimed at 'poets, plaiers, jesters, and such like caterpillers', he described poetry as honey mixed with poison.[188] 'Cookes did never shewe more crafte in their junckets to vanquish the taste, nor Painters in shadowes to allure the eye, then Poets in Theaters to wounde the conscience', he asserted. Poets, he thought, 'by the privie entries of the eare, slip downe into the hart, and with gunshotte of affection gaule the minde, where reason and vertue should rule the roste'.[189] This may well have been sour grapes on his part; it was certainly testimony to the power of words. This was a debate with no easy answer. In *A Midsummer Night's Dream*, Theseus is critical of the tale the lovers tell: 'The lunatic, the lover and the poet / Are of imagination all compact'.' Yet his wife, Hippolyta, is not so sure, thinking it grown 'to something of great constancy . . . strange and admirable'.[190] Despite the dissenting voices of some sceptics, the majority of Tudor writers and readers tended to see the written word as possessing and reviving the wisdom of the ancients, with the potential of alchemy to transform all into gold. The unprecedented breadth, depth and brilliance of English literature in these years opened new ways into the 'infinite space' of the imagination.[191]

CHAPTER 10

THE PROBLEM OF QUEENSHIP
THE REIGN OF MARY I

The history of Mary I's reign is a case study in the temperamental nature of historical writing. For centuries, 'Bloody Mary' was the black sheep of the Tudor family, her reign viewed as an exercise in religious bigotry and political ineptitude. Only in recent years have we come to realize that we may have been almost completely wrong about Mary. This change of heart is in large part because we are no longer in thrall to decades of Protestant tradition, and can no longer condemn Mary purely because she sought to bring back Catholicism. It is also because we have begun to pay closer attention to the views of ordinary men and women. The traditional view of Mary I was largely constructed by the educated Protestant elite, for whom Mary's accession was a disaster that shattered all their hopes. Many of them went into exile, from where they wrote spirited treatises decrying Mary's rule, especially the execution for heresy of almost three hundred of their co-believers. It was their narrative of the 1550s that set the tone for what followed, and produced an account of Mary's reign which was colourful, highly partisan and largely unrepresentative, it seems, of popular opinion.

One eyewitness account of how Mary rallied her supporters in East Anglia in 1553 remarked on 'how much excitement there was among the countryfolk'; and how 'every day they flocked to their rightful queen ready to lay out for her in this worthy cause their wealth, their effort, and life itself'.[1] Robert Parkyn, a curate in a village near Doncaster, recorded in his commonplace book how the nobles were divided in their loyalties, 'butt tholle Comonalltie (certayne heretikes exceptt) dyd applye unto the saide Lady Marie'; and he described the celebrations in the north, where the people 'grettlie reiocide, makynge grett fyers, drynkinge wyne and aylle, prayssing God'.[2] On her first journey towards London as queen, greeted by crowds in Ipswich, some little children gave her a golden heart, which was inscribed 'the heart of the people'.[3] Mary herself thought she had secured the throne by popular acclaim; threatened by Wyatt's rebellion in 1554, she gave a speech at the Guildhall to rally London to her side, and spoke of how she was not only a consecrated monarch, but also one whose claim had been reinforced by the 'unanimous acclamations and votes' of her people. She also spoke of how 'at my coronation . . . I was wedded to the realme'.[4] Later that year, some Norfolk yeomen would remind Mary how they had stood up for her, and how her opponents 'had not us your said subjects and commonalty at their commandments'.[5] It was noted that at her coronation, 'such a multitude of people resorted out of all partes of the realme, to see the same, that the lyke have not bene seen tofore'.[6]

In one other crucial respect, Mary's reign was pivotal. As England's first queen regnant, she forged a new political language and, in the process, demonstrated the resilience of the Tudor polity.[7] In a century deeply uncomfortable with innovation, she pioneered female rule; and in an age which generally assumed religious authority to be the preserve of men, she oversaw a programme of religious reconstruction which was, in part, the blueprint for the Counter-Reformation. It was during her reign that John Knox wrote his famous diatribe against female rule, *The First Blast of the Trumpet Against the Monstruous Regiment of Women*, which was aimed chiefly at Mary, although also at other European royals. Knox's motivations were shaped more by his fear of Catholicism than by straightforward misogyny.[8] Nevertheless, his work has often been woven into a narrative about the oppression of women in the sixteenth century.[9] Knox was not attacking these queens for their weakness, however; on the contrary, he was furious at beholding their evident strength. Mary's experiment in female rule, so much of which Elizabeth was to emulate, brought a new consciousness to debates about sovereignty, new urgency to discussions about gender and new clarity to conceptions of religious division. The significance of her queenship would long outlive the five short years of her rule.

'More than a monster'

In the four centuries and more since the death of Mary I, she has been condemned fiercely, lavishly and not very logically, for everything from demonic brutality to feminine frailty. There is often a nauseating, visceral quality to this historical condemnation, as if permeated by the stench of burning Protestant flesh. Historical accounts have dwelt with unpleasant emphasis on the bloating of her barren body, heavy with what she thought was England's next Catholic king, but in fact swollen with the illness that killed her; whilst portrayals of Mary in television and film almost always have a menacing, hysterical edge to them.[10] 'Obstinacy, bigotry, violence, cruelty, malignity, revenge, tyranny; every circumstance of her character took a tincture from her bad temper', wrote David Hume in the eighteenth century.[11] The language became more moderate in the twentieth century, but no less disapproving, and still redolent of misogyny: perhaps the most famous modern judgement was that 'sterility was the keynote of her reign'.[12] She did not just fail as a monarch; she failed as a woman.

The explanation behind such startling levels of animosity lies chiefly in what happened after Mary had died, shaped in particular by how Foxe's 'Book of Martyrs' dwelt at length not only on the persecutions of 'the horrible and bloudye tyme of queene Marye', but also on her other failures. Foxe asked 'when was the Realme of England more barren of all Gods blessinges? what Prince euer raigned here more shorter time, or lesse to his owne hartes ease then didde Queene Mary?'[13] Foxe's book, however, was the work of a partisan in the ideological guerrilla warfare of the late sixteenth century, not a final historical verdict on Mary and her reign. What is often still forgotten is that whilst Mary lived, her religion was only a problem for a fairly small, if outspoken, minority of her subjects. No one then could predict that thirty years after her death, representatives of that same minority would find themselves running the country, even as the Spanish Armada set sail. Her reign is a perfect example of history written by the winners. She became a bad queen after she was dead, because she had been a Catholic and the power-brokers of the next four centuries were nearly all Protestants.

In 1553, the significance of Mary's rule appeared very different from the way in which it was later portrayed. Mary acceded to the throne with the solid backing of many from the nobility and gentry, and with popular enthusiasm for both her religion and her claim to the throne. It has been argued that she kept quiet about her Catholicism during the tense weeks when the accession hung in the balance, but this seems implausible.[14] Her Catholic loyalties were widely known: during the reign of Edward VI, she had repeatedly refused to conform to Protestant worship; and when her household retinue, around 130 strong, had ridden through London, each person had openly displayed a rosary.[15] It is hard to judge the respective weights of her claim as Henry VIII's oldest surviving child under the terms of his will, and of her obvious commitment to the traditional faith; but clearly, both could command significant allegiance. In the eyes of observers such as Henry Machyn, a London chronicler with clear Catholic loyalties, the attempt to put Lady Jane Grey on the throne seemed a shabby and disgraceful affair, firmly linked in his mind with the suspicious death of Edward VI, who 'was poyssoned, as evere body says'.[16] Mary, by contrast, was the legitimate heir to the throne.

The events of the summer of 1553 showed just how far political control depended on popular loyalty. Lady Jane Grey's cause appeared strong and enjoyed the backing of the Privy Council, and therefore had control of the Armoury, the Mint, the Tower and many more resources of the central government. Yet Mary prevailed, on the basis of a groundswell of popular feeling and a strong sense of the need to see rights of inheritance observed. Sailors on the five ships sent to apprehend her mutinied in her favour. The common folk in the streets of Ipswich and London murmured against the attempt to impose Queen Jane.[17] The earl of Oxford's household servants pressured him into joining Mary, even though his relatives urged him to support Jane.[18] In London, Machyn recorded how one Gilbert Potter was put in the pillory and had his ears cropped by Lady Jane Grey's supporters, 'for spykyng of serten wordes of qwen Mare, that she had the ryght tytle'.[19] Within days, an anonymous pamphlet had been printed purporting to be a letter to this unfortunate youth from a friend described as 'Poor Pratt', suggesting the idea that Mary could command support from lowly but loyal Londoners, casting Northumberland as 'the ragged beare most rancke' and praising the valiant young man who 'did offer thy bodye to be slayne in her quarell' and 'in the defence of thy countrey'.[20] Perhaps the work of an educated supporter of Mary's claim, masquerading as a commoner, it was still an intelligent appeal to the strength of popular opinion, which would help secure Mary the throne.

The pamphlet attributed to 'Poor Pratt' also demonstrates how Mary's claim to the throne was closely tied to questions of religious loyalty. The Latin quotation on the title page, *Si deus nobiscum, quis contra nos* ('If God is with us, who can be against us'), underlined the sense that this was a struggle not just for the true queen, but for the true religion. Gilbert Potter was compared to Daniel in the lions' den. That said, some Protestants supported Mary, despite her religion. Most of her household and patronage network were Catholic, but Anne Bacon, a committed Protestant, remained in her service, despite her own and her family's Protestant loyalties.[21] Richard Taverner, one of Cromwell's more eloquent propagandists during Henry VIII's reign, published in 1553 *An oration gratulatory made upon the joyfull proclayming of the moste noble Princes Quene Mary Quene of England*, containing the polite hope that she would retain 'the true religion of Christe' (by which he probably meant Protestantism), but also emphasizing that Mary was 'the true and undoubted heir to the Crowne imperiall'.[22] A work in verse by the cleric Richard Beard, although it too expressed the hope that Mary would 'strongly buyld upon / Her brothers good fondacion' in the matter of religion, also rejoiced at length at the accession of the 'lawful, iust and rightuouse' queen, pointedly contrasting Mary's legitimacy with the deceitful schemes of Lady Jane's supporters.[23]

The backing of committed Protestants suggests that Mary's claim to the throne seemed good, and certainly several key members of the Edwardian government quietly adjusted to the new order and continued to serve faithfully and competently under her authority. For many of her subjects, meanwhile, Mary was the embodiment of the true faith and the past that they had lost, the brave daughter of a much-loved queen, whose banishment and lonely death had been seen as an outrage. Fifty years later, Shakespeare would cast Katherine of Aragon in his play *Henry VIII* as the only unambiguously virtuous character in the whole drama.[24] As Mary made her first entry into London, many Londoners brought out the statues of the Virgin and the saints that they had hidden away during Edward's reign, and displayed them prominently in their windows.[25] The new reign seemed to offer the chance of returning to an older, less confusing world.

'Very true owner of the Crown and government'[26]

Mary Tudor was the granddaughter of two exceptional monarchs: Henry VII of England and Isabella of Castile. Both had begun with only a dubious right to the throne; both had made a bold play for power; and both had seized it against the odds, in large part through military skill. Their grand-daughter followed their example. She was also herself an experienced politician. This had become evident during the previous reign, when, despite the regime's antagonism, she had maintained her household and, to a large extent, protected her supporters, whilst at the same time preserving diplomatic connections with her Habsburg relations. During the tense weeks of July 1553, she demonstrated her political acumen still further. Consciously or not, she was following the example of Isabella, who, on receiving news of her half-brother's death, and with the prospect of a contested succession, had acted swiftly to secure the throne of Castile.[27] By the time Mary arrived at Kenninghall to rally her supporters on 9 July, the news of Edward's death had been confirmed. That evening she spoke to her assembled household, proclaiming herself as their queen. 'Roused by their mistress's words, everyone, both the gently-born and the humbler servants, cheered her to the rafters', recorded Robert Wingfield.[28]

A peremptory letter to the Privy Council in London asserted her right to the throne, 'provided by act of parliament, and the testament and last will of our dearest father'; she went on to observe pointedly that the whole world knew her claim to be legitimate, and that 'there is no good true subject that is, can, or would pretend to be ignorant thereof'.[29] She advised them to think carefully, promising that if they submitted, and proclaimed her in London, she was willing to be gracious. At the same time, she was sending out letters to the gentry requiring them to raise their localities in her support, and contacting the Imperial ambassadors.[30] In addition to her own landholdings in East Anglia, she had been able to call on loyal connections in the Thames Valley: within the week, much of Oxfordshire, Buckinghamshire, Berkshire, Northamptonshire and Bedfordshire had declared for her.[31]

The Council wrote back professing its allegiance to Queen Jane, and twenty-one brave individuals signed this letter. They seem to have expected Mary to flee to the Netherlands, because they sent Lord Robert Dudley to intercept her. Mary was often much tougher, however, than some of the men around her expected. It soon became clear that she was not going anywhere, and that the country was rising in her support. Even the Imperial ambassadors, who were inclined to assume gloomily that England was full of heretics and traitors, perceived that there were popular uprisings in her favour.[32] Northumberland went after Mary with an army: Henry Machyn noted how, just two days after Jane had been proclaimed queen, carts full of ordinance were carried to the Tower by night, accompanied by 'a grett nombur of men of armes'. Machyn described disapprovingly how Northumberland went with a great company 'toward my lade Mare Grace, to destroye here grace'.[33]

As the tide began to turn in her favour, Mary moved to the castle of Framlingham in Suffolk. William Cecil quietly began to back away from Jane's cause; the treasurer of the Mint went to join Mary, helpfully taking some of the Crown's money with him; and the Council issued a reward for the capture of the duke of Northumberland. The hunter had become the hunted. Leaving the Tower, where Jane was, the earl of Arundel called together the core of the Privy Council at Baynard's Castle, and the decision was taken to proclaim Mary. It was Wednesday, 19 July. Heralds at Cheapside Cross issued the proclamation amid cries of acclamation; the Spanish merchant Antonio de Guaras noted how 'all who had money in their purses threw it to the people' and 'men of authority and years, could not refrain from casting away their garments, leaping and dancing'.[34] When the news reached Northumberland in Cambridge a day later, he realized he had lost. He tried to find a herald and trumpeters, but finding none, went out into the street and proclaimed Mary as queen, throwing his cap in the air in a rather pathetic attempt to regain lost ground. As one chronicler commented, 'his attempt, for asmuch as it was not of God, colde not come to no good successe', noting how 'part of the nobilitie, and al the common people fel from him', so that 'he wyth hys sonnes, and a few more wer left alone'.[35]

Mary's triumph was hailed by many as a providential gift. As her archbishop of Canterbury, Reginald Pole, described it, 'when numbers conspyred agaynste her, and pollicies were devised to disherit hir, and armed power prepared to destroy hir', her victory was a sign of 'the almighty greate goodnes and providence of God'.[36] Like many of his contemporaries, Pole could underrate female agency, and he did not give Mary herself enough credit for strengthening her own position. In particular, Mary had been quite prepared to face Northumberland in battle, reviewing her troops at Framlingham just as Isabella might have done, walking among them for three hours. She also trusted to popular support. Once she had been proclaimed queen in London, she progressed to the capital to popular acclaim, optimistic enough to dismiss many of her troops long before she had even reached London. At Beaulieu Palace (also called New Hall), so many people came to see her that nobody could find lodgings within 3 miles of the house.[37] When Northumberland and his retinue were brought into the Tower, Guaras noted that 'since the people were evilly disposed towards them, it was needful for the Queen to proclaim that under pain of punishment they should allow the prisoners to pass peaceably'.[38] Mary's merciful gesture indicated the confidence she felt; this was echoed by the fact that of the forty-eight men excluded from her coronation pardon, twenty-six were later pardoned anyway.[39] In her coronation pageants, she was compared to the goddess Athena, the biblical heroine Judith who had slain Holofernes, and Queen Tomyris, who had defeated Cyrus and the Persians.[40] Both Judith and Tomyris had beheaded their enemies, which imparted a martial flavour to this iconography, and perhaps evoked the execution of Northumberland a month before the coronation.[41] There was nothing faint-hearted in the way Mary seized power.

The queen was prepared to command even her former enemies. In due course, when they had eaten their words, several of those who had opposed her would go on to serve with loyalty and distinction in her government, including the marquess of Winchester and the earls of Shrewsbury, Pembroke and Arundel. When a Court of Claims was set up to prepare for the coronation, two of the four commissioners appointed – Richard Rich and William Paget – had barely six weeks earlier signed the Council letter professing their allegiance to Queen Jane.[42] Mary showed good sense in choosing men qualified by long years of faithful service. William Paulet, marquess of Winchester, had held office since the 1530s and would go on to serve Elizabeth until 1570, when he was in his nineties.[43] Many more of Mary's counsellors had served her father: John Russell, earl of Bedford; Francis Talbot, earl of Shrewsbury; William Herbert, earl of Pembroke; Sir John Baker; Lord Clinton.[44] Many of them had also served her brother, and some had supported Lady Jane Grey. It was a mark of Mary's success that two of these, Pembroke and Clinton, would later be instrumental in opposing Wyatt's rebellion. Mary also made extensive use of her household, much as her father had done before her. Robert Rochester, Henry Jerningham and Edward Waldegrave, all imprisoned during Edward VI's reign for their loyalty to Mary and the Catholic faith, became, respectively, comptroller and vice-chamberlain of her household, and master of the horse – as well as important conduits of Mary's authority.[45]

At Mary's funeral, the bishop of Winchester would declare that she had been 'a queen and by the same title a king also'.[46] In the royal pageantry so essential to Tudor rule, Mary played the part of ruler without hesitation or apology.[47] In her first royal entry into London, she put on a magnificent display, with an entourage around three thousand strong. Her velvet and satin robes in the royal colour purple were thick with jewels and gold, and her horse was draped in cloth-of-gold trappings, which reached down to the ground.[48] She was attended by a 'flock of peeresses, gentlewomen and ladies in waiting, never before seen in such numbers'.[49] At her coronation, Mary assumed the role of king, with some added rituals from the order for a queen consort, drawing validation from both gender roles. She was anointed with chrism just as a king would be: on the hands, breast, shoulders, elbows and head. She had spurs put on her feet, a sword girded about her, and she was crowned with three crowns in turn, before receiving the homage of the peers of the realm. According to the papal envoy, she was invested with two sceptres, 'the one of the King, the other bearing a dove which, by custom, is given to the Queen'.[50] Everything hammered home the idea that the kingdom had been put back to rights.[51] Some small adjustments were necessary: when creating new knights of the bath, as was traditional before a coronation, she deputed to some of her courtiers the task of administering the oath to the new knights sitting naked in the bathwater. Where a male monarch would have ridden on horseback under a canopy to his coronation, Mary was carried in a litter, although her canopy of white cloth of gold was similar to the one her brother had used. She was 'appareled with a mantel and kirtle of cloth of gould furred with minnever and powdred ermines . . . having on her head a circlet of gould sett with rich stones and pearles'.[52] Just over five years later, Elizabeth would reproduce this piece of pageantry; she would even wear the same mantle and kirtle of cloth of gold, in a tacit compliment to her sister's mastery of political theatre.[53]

Mary's regime vigorously contested the notion that her gender was in any way a difficulty (see plate 10). The first parliament of her reign passed an act declaring that royal power 'is in the Queenes Majestie as fully and absolutely as ever it was in any of her moste noble Progenitours Kinges of this Realme', and stating that she wielded her authority 'without Doubte, Ambiguitie, Scruple or Question'.[54] The Imperial ambassadors informed Charles V that some of her counsellors felt it was safer to call a parliament before the coronation, 'the better to establish and confirm the reign' – in particular to reverse Mary's illegitimacy and to 'avoid the likelihood of trouble'.[55] Mary's insistence that the coronation proceed in the traditional way indicates her confidence; and although the Imperial envoys took credit for this, having advised her accordingly, it was all of a piece with Mary's other decisions.[56] She also used divine sanction to good effect, although she seems genuinely to have regarded her royal office as a sacred vocation. She was compared to the Virgin Mary, viewed by Catholics as the queen of heaven: a broadside ballad printed in 1553 was entitled 'An Ave Maria, in commendation of our Most virtuous Queene', and also recalled Judith's victory over Holofernes.[57] The theme of Judith, in particular, would be one evoked repeatedly by printed literature of the reign.[58] Mary frequently held services of touching for the 'King's Evil', underlining her semi-sacred ability to heal with the laying on of hands, and in the process doing what no woman had ever done before. She also participated in the Royal Maundy, kneeling to wash and kiss the feet of poor women, a ceremony which cast her in the role of Christ before the Last Supper. One description of the ceremony of 1556 noted how she ministered to forty-one women (reflecting her age), going the length of the hall on her knees, and kissing their feet 'so fervently that it seemed as if she were embracing something very precious'.[59]

There was one particularly crucial moment in Mary's reign, when she was called to account. In February 1554, about three thousand rebels, led by Thomas Wyatt, advanced on London to protest against her proposed marriage to Philip of Spain. Some of them were secretly intending to depose her, and many were hoping for the restoration of Protestantism. Some advisors, including the Imperial ambassador, urged her to flee the capital and take refuge behind the thick walls of Windsor Castle. Mary refused, and instead rode to the Guildhall to rally the city. Her courageous response to the threat, and her inspirational speech to the citizens of London, were among the high-points of her reign. 'More than marvell it was to see that daie, the invincible heart and constancie of the queene hir selfe, who being by nature a woman, and therefore commonlie more fearefull than men be, shewed hir selfe in that case more stout than is credible', wrote one chronicler.[60] The speech she gave was not just brave: it was also exceedingly shrewd. She reiterated the notion of the marriage between queen and subjects, reminding her hearers of the fact that monarchs were divinely ordained: 'God did marrye her (sayd she) to this region, when she was anointed and crowned our Quene.'[61] She reminded them whose daughter she was, and said that she expected the same level of obedience that they had shown him. She also reminded them that they had made a promise: 'I am your queene, to whom at my coronation . . . ye promised your allegiance and obedience.' Finally, she told them that she was their mother, and that she loved them just as a mother loves her child. It was Tudor theatricality at its most forceful and effective. When the rebels clamoured at the city gates, the citizens refused to let them in. Mary had won.

In popular memory, Mary I is the antithesis of the half-sister who succeeded her. Yet since 1606, they have lain entombed together in Westminster Abbey, with the caption: 'Partners both in throne and grave, here rest we two sisters Elizabeth and Mary, in the hope of one resurrection.'[62] Despite their very different objectives as rulers, they shared a common challenge of being queens regnant, reinforced by the questionable legitimacy of both – both having been bastardized by their father when young and restored to the succession in 1544 without ever having been declared legitimate. Nonetheless, Mary's first proclamation emphasized the sense of continuity with the long line of kings before her, 'assuring all our good and faithful subjects that . . . they shall find us their benign and gracious sovereign lady, as others our most notable progenitors have heretofore been'. Other proclamations also referred to these 'noble progenitors'.[63] Shoring up her authority took some effort and ingenuity, but was successfully achieved, securing her support at home and earning her a glowing reputation across Catholic Europe. If Elizabeth made a success of being a queen regnant, it was in large part by building on the solid foundations laid down by her sister.

The pursuit of godliness

Mary's religious convictions were never in any doubt. As she told the Council in 1550, 'I would rather refuse the friendship of all the world . . . than forsake any point of my faith.'[64] She was known to attend mass daily, and had thereby infuriated the Edwardian regime. On Whitsunday 1549, the day the new Prayer Book service was introduced, Mary had ensured that mass was celebrated at Kenninghall with particular pomp.[65] Her household portrayed itself as a model Catholic community, and Catholic nobility and gentry sought places for their daughters there.[66] The comment of a diplomat – that 'where she had the power to do it she had Mass celebrated' – perhaps suggests that her reach extended to nearby parish churches, too; in 1548 she appointed the brother of one of her chaplains to be priest at Holy Trinity Church, Long Melford, in Suffolk.[67] When she took power, priests in some places began saying mass again, even before any official instructions had been issued. Robert Parkyn noted how 'in many places of the realme preastes was commandyde by lordes and knyghttes catholique to say masse in Lattin with consecration and elevation of the bodie and bloode of Christ under forme of breade and wyne with a decentt ordre as haithe ben uside beforne tyme.'[68] At Melton Mowbray, the altar was replaced in the church in time to sing a requiem mass for the dead king who had ordered the abolition of both altars and masses.[69]

Wingfield recorded that, once she had arrived at the Tower, 'the queen suddenly turned her whole attention to religion and godliness, the excellence of which she had learnt from her childhood under the guidance of that most sacred princess her mother'.[70] One of Mary's first acts at the Tower was to release some of her co-religionists imprisoned there. These included the duke of Norfolk, now aged eighty, Stephen Gardiner, the former bishop of Winchester, and Cuthbert Tunstall, former bishop of Durham. All these men, it might be noted, had been key figures supporting and propounding the highly idiosyncratic Catholicism of Henry VIII's reign, and all three had supported the Royal Supremacy. Such ambiguities continued to impinge on Mary's restoration of religion. Many viewed her accession as providential deliverance for the faith that, for the last six years, had been so ruinously undermined, and which, even during her father's reign, had been badly damaged, particularly through the loss of over eight hundred religious houses. The queen's piety was evident, and her resolve was strong. Yet quite what constituted Catholic orthodoxy in 1553 was not completely clear, and the best way to pursue a Catholic restoration was not entirely obvious. Questions remained over the viability of restoring the monasteries, and whether landowners holding former monastic lands could be recompensed. In ideological terms, the problem was illustrated by the anomaly that the churchmen performing the coronation rituals were all officially still in schism, and that before parliament met, the masses being celebrated up and down the land were technically illegal. Mary was concerned that the holy oil customarily used at coronations might have been tainted, and requested a replacement: Cardinal Granvelle, Charles V's secretary of state, sent three phials from Brussels, accompanied by a wild boar – a gift from Charles V's sister.[71]

In many matters, however, Mary did not feel compelled to appeal to European authorities, and took an independent view of the religious question. Imperial envoys were apprehensive, but Mary seems to have had the firm conviction that, bar a few troublemakers, she was essentially ruling a Catholic country with the support of its people. Mary's understanding of Catholic identity was arguably more broad-minded than has generally been assumed. She frequently referred to Henry VIII as her 'most dear father of famous memory'.[72] She never questioned her half-brother Edward VI's legitimacy, even though he had been born with the realm in schism and when Henry VIII was excommunicate.[73] In the proclamation of October 1553 announcing her regnal style, she was described as 'of the Church of England and Ireland Supreme Head', and she continued to manage religious matters even after November 1554, when she abolished the Supremacy and returned the realm to Roman obedience.[74] Three of her bishops, Bonner, Heath and Day, had been consecrated when the realm was in schism, and Gardiner, Bonner and Tunstall were among many who had preached sermons and written books demoting the pope to 'bishop of Rome' and denying his authority in the realm. Gardiner's *De Vera Obedientia* was published with scurrilous intent in English translation by Protestants, with annotations gleefully relishing the embarrassment this would cause to Mary's new lord chancellor.[75] Mary did not seem to feel this, however, and Gardiner presided at both her coronation and her wedding. Her reign began, moreover, with a quite extraordinary act of religious toleration. Despite some reluctance, she allowed her brother to be buried using the Protestant funeral service, as he would have wished.

We think of Roman Catholicism as a fixed, unchanging entity, partly because it is painted that way by both its loyal defenders and its fierce opponents. Yet sixteenth-century Catholicism went through many upheavals and was full of both conflict and variegation. Challenged from the outside by Protestants, the Catholic Church in Europe had also been questioned from within by reformers, including Reginald Pole, Mary's cousin and, from 1554, her archbishop of Canterbury. Pole was one of many Catholic churchmen who sought to revive, as well as defend, their faith: indeed, his involvement with the *spirituali* who promoted such renewal would later bring him under suspicion of heresy.[76] Catholicism was also undergoing a reformation, therefore, and Mary and her senior churchmen had themselves been shaped by reforming ideas. Mary's humanist education had been devised by one of Europe's foremost scholars, Juan Luis Vives, and in the 1540s she had been part of the team of translators, which included Katherine Parr, that produced an English version of Erasmus's *Paraphrases on the New Testament*. This guide to understanding the Bible became one of the key texts of the Edwardian Reformation, placed alongside the Bible in every parish church.[77] In the preface, the editor Nicholas Udall, the Protestant humanist scholar, praised Mary for 'furthering both us and our posterity in the knowledge of God's Word'.[78] Mary's association with the project put her at the more reforming end of the Catholic spectrum.

Like the rest of England, Mary had lived for twenty years without the pope, and with the strong Henrician emphasis on biblical authority and the rooting out of superstition. It is probable that this had some influence on her religious attitudes. It is notable that she never went on pilgrimage, and nor did she restore the shrines of St Thomas Becket at Canterbury, St Cuthbert at Durham or the Virgin Mary at Walsingham. Many of her leading churchmen had been key figures in Henry's Church, and most had had a humanist education. The queen's first attempts to set religious affairs in order saw her returning the Church to how it had been in 1547, before Edward's changes, rather than 1533 before the break with Rome. Many who wrote in support of her Catholic restoration did so drawing on their experience during her father's reign: Roger Edgeworth, for example, published a book of sermons in 1557 which were, he explained in the preface, the fruit of over forty years' preaching. He lamented the heresies of Luther, but he also spoke approvingly of how Henry VIII had sought to combat them, casting the king as a bastion of Catholic belief. His definition of the Catholic Church was a universalist, rather than a papalist one: 'universall or whole over all the world, not muttering in sundry corners of countryes, as heretikes have imagined theyr Churches'.[79]

Mary's Catholic restoration was therefore, on the one hand, reflective of reforming emphases, while on the other it was mindful of the need to strengthen the Church as an institution with the added security of papal headship, since it was becoming increasingly clear across Europe that the papacy, however flawed, was essential to the unity of Catholicism. This meant that attempts to justify the reconciliation with Rome were balanced by an emphasis on biblical authority, and some vigorous use of the printing press and the vernacular. Many Marian churchmen, for example, tended to take a positive view of having the Bible in English: as Edgeworth wrote, 'I have ever bene of this minde, that I have thought it no harme, but rather good and profitable that holie Scripture shoulde be hadde in the mother tong.'[80] On the other hand, John Standish took a more cautious view, arguing that 'if all men were good and catholike, then were it lawefull, yea, and verye profitable also, that the scripture should be in Englishe, so that the translation were trew and faythfull', but opining that in reality 'neither all the people be good and catholyke, nor the translations trewe and faythfull'.[81] The English Bible was never banned by Mary's Church, even though some Protestant translations were burned, and Pole's legatine synod commissioned a Catholic translation of the New Testament into English. Still, people were beginning to envisage a world where 'Catholic' faced 'Protestant' in a world of two competing faiths. John Christopherson, Mary's future bishop of Chichester, wrote that the 'religion that the Queenes grace maynteyneth, is fiftenne hundreth yeare olde: thys new religion is scarcelye twoo hundreth yeares olde' (he must have been thinking back to the Lollards).[82] Increasingly, the Tudor populace was being required to choose between alternatives.

The restoration of Catholicism in England was an exemplar for the rest of Europe. A monarch rescuing her realm from the spreading disease of Protestantism was an inspirational sight to many onlookers in the

Netherlands, the Holy Roman Empire and further afield. When Pole was dispatched to reconcile England to Rome in November 1554, observers in Brussels waited impatiently for news: one cleric wrote to a colleague in Germany that 'letters are anticipated hourly' confirming his success, and when news of the reconciliation arrived, Mary of Hungary commanded thanksgiving services across the Netherlands.[83] Mary I communicated closely with her mother's nephew, Charles V, although she did not always listen to the pessimistic warnings of the Imperial envoys in England.[84] In Mary's self-fashioning of herself and her regime, European opinion remained important, with key documents translated into Latin and other languages for circulation abroad – from Northumberland's scaffold speech of 1553 to accounts of reunion with the papacy.[85] Many of the challenges for her religious policy were specific to the English situation, however, and the highly idiosyncratic Catholicism of her father and his policies continued to exert an influence. When Bishop Bonner of London brought out a book summarizing Catholic doctrine in 1555, he based it on the 'King's Book' of 1543, and several of the homilies that accompanied it were only slightly modified versions of those published by Edward VI's regime in 1547. The Catholic primers published under Mary were in English, rather than Latin, and contained a range of prayers, including some by Protestant authors such as Wolfgang Capito and Thomas Becon.[86] Mary's devotion to the mass was well attested, and her determination to return England to the papal fold was clear; but her religious policies were far from unthinkingly reactionary.

King Philip and Queen Mary

Being a woman was no obstacle to wielding power, but it was problematic when it came to securing the succession. For a woman ruler, the uncertainties and dangers of procreation became a direct threat to the sacred body of the monarch, whilst power-brokerage between husband and wife became a matter of national importance. No matter how successful Mary's statecraft might be, she needed an heir; and the presence of Elizabeth, the focus now of Protestant hopes, made that realization all the more painful. Marriage would be a gamble: at thirty-seven, Mary was old to be a first-time mother, but she had to try. The alternative was to abandon her country to the heresy espoused by her half-sister. Another reason why Mary was expected to marry was that ruling a country was a difficult job, and one in which close family could be an invaluable support. The epistle of 'Poor Pratt' in 1553 expressed the hope 'to live to se the day her grace to mary such one, as knoweth what adversity meaneth, so shal we have both a merciful quene and king', as well as 'frute to inherite the kingdome after her'.[87] Mary's choice of Philip of Spain has traditionally been decried as the worst possible decision, plunging England into war with France, opening the way to Spanish domination and tainting Mary's rule by association with this most feared of monarchs. Most of this is based on hindsight, recalling Philip as the evil genius behind the Armada of 1588; and Philip was not even king of Spain when Mary married him in 1554 – although on his wedding day, his father, Charles V, created him king of Naples to give him equal status with his new wife. More importantly, Spain and the Netherlands were England's natural allies, linked by a shared hostility to France, a shared interest in trade between London and Antwerp, and long years of Tudor diplomacy stretching back to the reign of Henry VII. In marrying Philip, Mary was achieving considerable status for herself and her kingdom.

Although the novelty of a queen regnant seeking a husband caused some anxiety, the match between Mary and Philip was still widely acknowledged at the time as a great achievement. European commentary, of which there was a great deal, sounded this note of success.[88] Robert Wingfield called it 'the most splendid royal match since the Norman Conquest', emphasizing that Philip was 'the eldest son of the most powerful monarch in the whole world'. He also added that by way of dowry 'he most munificently offered all Burgundy and Lower Germany, that thus he might entice the queen's tender affections into love'.[89] To many, the alliance appeared chiefly as an Anglo-Burgundian match, with the negotiations ratified in the Low Countries; the Greyfriars chronicler described the envoys coming to London 'in the name of the hole howse of Bowrgone [Burgundy]'.[90] In a proclamation of 1554, which sought to regenerate the wool trade between the two countries, Mary expressed her 'great commiseration and pity of the afflictions and miseries of the subjects of those parts', already showing a proprietary interest in them, whilst her marriage treaty recalled the match of 'Lady Margaret of England' to Charles the

Bold of Burgundy, suggesting that Mary's regime was anxious to empha-size the precedents for this match.[91] Charles V's poet laureate, Nicolaus Mameranus, envisaged the marriage as a key step in the campaign to rein-vigorate Catholicism in northern Europe, with Mary providing religious inspiration and Philip, as a warrior, poised to defend the Catholic cause.[92] In his first speech to parliament, Pole compared Charles V to King David, and Philip to his son Solomon, builder of the Temple, envisaging that Philip 'shal perfourme the buildyng that his father hath begun'.[93] The marriage treaty emphasized how the union built upon earlier treaties made in 1542 and 1546 by Henry VIII.[94]

Others were more alarmed at the prospect. A deputation from parlia-ment in November 1553 warned the queen of the risks of marrying a foreigner.[95] Some of the anxiety was clearly the product of a generalized fear of strangers: a Cornishman reported a rumour that 'before New Year's Day outlandish men will come upon our lands, for there be some at Plymouth already'.[96] One MP during a Commons debate in December 1553 asked what would happen if 'the Bands should be broken between the Husband and the Wife, either of them being Princes in their own Country, who shall sue the Bands? Who shall take the Forfeit? Who shall be their Judges?' Some of Mary's own counsellors were apprehensive, too, and suggested an English alternative in the form of Edward Courtenay, the great-grandson of Edward IV. Courtenay had been imprisoned by Henry VIII aged twelve, and as an obvious dynastic threat had not been pardoned by Edward VI; but he had now been released and made earl of Devon and a knight of the bath.[97] Mary was close friends with his mother, and Gardiner was fond of the young man, whom he had tutored in the Tower when they were fellow prisoners there. Even Noailles, the French ambassador, who was backing the match, had to admit, however, that Courtenay was volatile and untrustworthy. Mary clearly favoured the idea of marrying Philip of Spain.

The strategic planning of the wedding was skilfully done. Mary knew the complexities of what she was attempting, and had told the London crowds at the Guildhall, that 'should it not be recognized' that her reasons for the marriage were 'to the advantage of my Kingdom and of the welfare of you all, I shall willingly refrain from pursuing it'.[98] She had a marriage treaty drawn up, which limited Philip's role within the realm to little more than the purely ornamental. He was not to exercise power, or command the Council; he had to have Englishmen in his household, not just Spaniards; he was not to attempt to change the laws in any way, or appoint his henchmen to office. England was not to be involved in any wars because of the alliance. Philip was so appalled by this treaty that he made a private vow that he would not be bound by it, but the value of the document in any case lay in its ability to calm popular fears. Mary made sure it was twice validated by parliament, and she also sent copies to be published in the provinces. The accepted rhetoric thus became that Philip was sacrificing a great deal to support Mary and the Catholic cause. Pole, speaking to parliament in November, described the way Philip had come to England, 'leaving behind him his sworde and kingly aucthoretye for no interest or comodetye of himselfe but to serve the Realme and to help to restore into the same the feare and love of almighty Godd'.[99]

Some at least of this careful framing was in response to the rebellion of January 1554. Wyatt's rebellion, as it is generally known, was in fact intended to be an uprising from four distinct locations. Lady Jane Grey's father, the duke of Suffolk, was supposed to raise the Midlands; Sir James Croft was meant to rally troops in Herefordshire; Sir Peter Carew tried to gather a following in the West Country; and Sir Thomas Wyatt mobilized support in Kent.[100] Their proclaimed cause was to oppose the marriage, defend the realm against Spanish interference and free their queen from evil counsel. They drew on anti-Spanish sentiment, sustained by the French, whose agreed role was to send ships to protect the ports of the south-west against the Spanish, whilst Wyatt in Kent guarded against any Imperial intervention from the Netherlands.[101] Yet Wyatt's cause was also that of Protestantism, although allegedly he warned a follower not to breathe a word of this, 'for that will withdraw from us the hearts of many'.[102] Suffolk was also a convinced Protestant, and Croft, as Edward VI's lord deputy of Ireland, had made strenuous efforts to enforce the *Book of Common Prayer* there.[103] Carew's Protestantism was perhaps more contingent; he was quoted in his later indictment as having said, 'If the quene wold forebeare this marriage wyth the Spanyard, and use a moderation in matters of relygion, I wold dye at her foote, but otherwise I will do the best to place the Lady Elizabeth in here stede.'[104] Carew had served with distinction in the wars of the 1540s, and was an adventurer known for his forthright character; he had travelled

Europe and seen the court of Suleiman the Magnificent in Constantinople. These were men who were used to taking a leading role in politics, with a measure of self-belief in their own competence.

The rebellions were a failure. Planned for Palm Sunday 1554, they were triggered in haste in January, when rumours of an uprising began to circulate and Edward Courtenay confessed to Gardiner what was being planned. Courtenay was now envisaged by some as a husband for Elizabeth, with the mostly unspoken intent that they might then together replace Mary on the throne. None of this plotting proved realistic. Suffolk could not raise Leicestershire beyond his own retainers, and Croft made no attempt to raise Herefordshire. In Devon, too, many remembered Carew's brutal suppression of the 1549 rebellions; finding that he could not raise a force, he fled to France. Only Wyatt had moderate success, raising a body of perhaps two thousand men from some of the more Protestant areas of Kent. John Ponet, the former Edwardian bishop of Winchester, was his advisor; the only real damage done by the rebels was when they arrived in Southwark and sacked the bishop's palace, now belonging to Ponet's replacement, Stephen Gardiner. The rebels had some success, when a body of Londoners raised by the duke of Norfolk to defend the queen defected to Wyatt's camp, However, when the rebels got to London, the city barred London Bridge against them, compelling them to re-route to Kingston in order to cross the river. As they arrived in London, the mood of the crowd seemed uncertain, perhaps because of the rumour that the queen had granted their requests and pardoned them.[105] But at Ludgate the gate was closed, and after a brief skirmish, with perhaps forty casualties, Wyatt's march ended in defeat. This was hardly a widespread popular uprising: its chief actors were Protestant gentry and their immediate followers, although there was some popular feeling in the south-east, in particular. Maidstone in Kent was responsible for the greatest number of volunteers, seconded by Tonbridge and Sevenoaks – all areas with a significant number of Protestants. Elsewhere, the citizens of Coventry armed themselves to defend Mary; in Leicester 'few there were that would willingly hearken' to the rebels' call; whilst in the West Country, the sheriff Sir Thomas Denys prepared Exeter to withstand attack. Mary herself declared this the work of a minority of zealous Protestants, and the official account of the rebellion lamented that in Wyatt 'so manye good and commendable qualities were abused in the service of cursed heresie'.[106] Mary pardoned most of the rank and file involved. The luckless Courtenay was again imprisoned, and later banished to Italy, where he became the focus for various conspiracies and a Spanish assassination plot; eventually, he saved them the trouble by going hawking in the rain and dying of a chill. Wyatt and Suffolk were executed, but Croft was eventually pardoned, as was Carew, when he returned from exile in 1556. Carew later served under Philip II in the military campaign against the French in 1557. If Wyatt's rebellion was a test of Mary's authority, then she passed fairly well.

The arrangements for Philip's arrival were still undertaken very carefully. The marriage was celebrated in Winchester, where the cathedral was provided with a high walkway so that all could behold the spectacle of bride and groom, both dressed in white, sparkling with jewels. Stephen Gardiner, reinstated bishop of Winchester, displayed the marriage treaty and made a short speech about how it was 'confirmed by Parliament', remarkably reinforcing the message even as the wedding ceremony was about to begin.[107] The ceremony was conducted, unusually, in both English and Latin, enacted in a setting which still bore the scars of Protestant iconoclasm, since the niches stood empty of their saints in Bishop Waynflete's great fifteenth-century reredos behind the altar. It appears that the couple did not take communion at the mass which followed the marriage: this would have been awkward for Philip, since Gardiner was still technically in schism. The Spaniards and the English eyed one another warily; the Spaniards commented disparagingly on Mary's waiting-women, noting 'few attractive and many ugly ones'. There were problems over court etiquette: Philip did not know to remove his hat when he met the bishop.[108] The English custom was to give a kiss of greeting on the mouth: Mary had a tussle with the duchess of Alba, who stubbornly grabbed and kissed her hands in the Spanish fashion instead, and then sat on the floor to be lower than Mary, who had tried to seat her on a stool beside her. Yet Mary eventually prevailed (in this case, she sat on the floor, too).[109] To reassure the English, Mary was careful to take precedence over her husband, eating from gold plate at the wedding banquet, whilst Philip was served from silver dishes; but they sat together under a single cloth of estate, perhaps to placate Spanish opinion.[110] It was a delicate balancing act, in which the symbolic language of court ritual was noted by observers from all sides. For the wedding jousts, Philip was able to take the leading role among the nobility, an important demonstration of his worth as an adjunct to Mary's queenship.[111] At his first royal entry into London, 'the most excellent pageant of al', according to one eyewitness, was that which emphasized Mary and Philip's common descent from Edward III.[112] This was a point made, too, by the royal chaplain John Christopherson, when he wrote: 'As for their muttering that they make for her marriage, yf they knewe, how the Prince of Spayne is unto us no straunger, but one of the bloude royall of Englande . . . they wolde perhappes . . . lay it aparte, and . . . thanke god hartelye.'[113]

Much of the apprehension felt about Mary's marriage seems to have dissipated once Philip's presence had become established in England. One of his entourage wrote that on Philip's first public appearance after his arrival in Southampton, he 'gave great satisfaction to the English, to whom he had been depicted as of a very different disposition and manner by the French and some others'.[114] The fact that all royal pronouncements were issued in the name of 'Philip and Mary' caused some to protest that Isabella of Castile 'signed alone after she was married'; on the other hand, it was agreed that Philip should never sign his name alone, and indeed he never did, even when Mary was in seclusion expecting the birth of their child.[115] Depictions of the two of them usually accorded Mary the edge in terms of authority, as in the portrait by Hans Eworth, where Mary sat enthroned whilst Philip was standing.[116] On one side of their joint seal Mary and Philip were enthroned co-equal, but on the other Mary took the higher position (see illustration 19). Meanwhile, as an extension of Mary's sovereignty, Philip as her spouse could be extremely useful. On St George's Day in 1554, Mary had presided alone over the Order of the Garter ceremonies, delaying the feast itself until the summer, when she could bestow the order on her new husband, who then shared the monarch's stall with her during the chapel service. On St George's Day in 1555, Mary, now in confinement, made a ceremonial appearance at the window of her chamber, but it was Philip who presided alone over the celebrations.[117] Meanwhile, the glamour of this Habsburg match was hard to overlook. Philip presented the queen with vastly expensive jewels, and the twelve great tapestries commemorating his father's victory at Tunis, which were hung in Whitehall, were the most exquisite tapestries that England had ever seen.[118] John Elder commented that 'none in the worlde maye excell

19. The joint seal of Mary I and Philip II

them'. He noted that they arrived along with a pair of organs from the queen of Poland, 'so curiouslye made of golde and silver, and so set with precious stones, as lyke or none suche have bene seldome sene'.[119] Titian's *Venus and Adonis* also arrived in London.[120] The message was clear: England was now part of a partnership linking a formerly second-rate power to a political player of formidable magnitude.

The patterns of the past

Where Edward VI's reformation had wrestled with the problems of defining theology and converting the populace, Mary's reformation sought to give the populace back what it had lost. Rather than define and defend a new doctrine, she was seeking to explain a traditional doctrine already understood, which imparted to her religious endeavours a less polemical and more pastoral edge. Mary's first parliament sought to bring back 'the olde divine service and administration of Sacramentes' as it had been 'in the laste yeare of the raygne of our late Soveraigne Lord, kynge Henry the eight'. It contrasted the religion of 'our forefathers', sanctioned by antiquity, with the novelty of the Edwardian formulations, which were 'such as a feaw of singularitie have of them selves devised'.[121] The significance of Mary putting the clock back to 1547, rather than before the break with Rome in 1533, can be overstated. It was in part a procedural matter, being the best that parliament could manage before such time as the country was formally reconciled to the papacy. However, it also indicated that much about Henrician Catholicism was acceptable to Mary. Her first proclamation on religion used language reminiscent of her father's, as it urged her subjects to 'live together in quiet sort and Christian charity, leaving those new-found devilish terms of papist or heretic'.[122] Above all else, Mary looked to restore the devotional patterns of everyday life lost during Edward's reign. She focused on the needs of the parish community, and in particular the restoration of the mass – not only because it was the most important sacrament, but also because 'of late yeres it hath most of all other, bene assaulted, and impugned', and had become a symbol of Catholic loyalty.[123] It was also, crucially, a widely recognized symbol of unity, 'the misticall body of Chryst, sygnified and represented in the fourmes of breade and wyne'.[124]

Mary and her churchmen strove to rebuild the disoriented and divided people of England into a unified Catholic Church once more. A large part of this involved putting the parish churches back to rights, restoring or replacing the altars, statues, vestments and vessels that had been sold or smashed or hidden. Preaching in Whitehall on St Andrew's Day 1557, on a day of solemn celebrations commemorating England's reconciliation with Rome, Pole reminded the city fathers of their obligation to maintain the churches, 'the whyche you maye yn no wyse fayle to doo, excepte you wyll have your people wax brutyshe and wylde, and your commonwealthe wythout foundacyon'.[125] The parish church was the guarantor of good order, as well as right faith. When Pole issued injunctions for the visitation of the diocese of Canterbury in 1557, he enquired whether the sacraments were being duly administered, and the church maintained; but out of fifty-four questions, ten concerned basic morality, such as 'drunkenness, ribaldry, evil living and lewd pastimes', whilst another seven dealt with the maintenance of church buildings and registers, and another nine with care of the poor, the sick and children.[126] The returns from this visitation show that churches were still being commanded to make repairs and to restore church ornaments; but on the whole, the items missing were of a relatively minor sort, comprising altar frontals, vestments, candlesticks and side altars, suggesting that the main altar had been successfully restored in most churches, even in Kent, which had been a Protestant heartland.[127]

Mary was also dedicated to the task of reforming and strengthening her Church. She was highly educated, as well as deeply devout, and in Pole she had an archbishop who was known throughout Europe for his reforming ideals. Mary's directions to her Council ordered them to cooperate with Pole, and to pay particular attention to 'good preaching I wish that may supplie and overcome the evill preaching in tyme past'. She also wrote 'I verelye beleeve that manye benefices should not be in one mans hands but after such sort as every Preist might looke to his owne chardge and remayne resident there, whereby they should have but one bond to discharge towards God'. She intended her priests to bring about change, 'not only by their preaching, but alsoe by their good example without which, in myne opinion their sermons shall not soe much profit as I wish'. This is the same document which talked about heretics being punished, but 'without rashnes', a phrase often quoted: it is equally important that Mary was here laying out a very personal vision of a church reformed.[128] Her instructions to Pole included the desire for bishops and their chaplains 'and as menie as be learned and good men within there dioces to travaile contynually in preaching'.[129]

Sermons were a central concern of the Marian restoration. Official books of homilies were published in 1555 and 1558 by Edmund Bonner, bishop of London, and Thomas Watson, bishop of Lincoln. Those wishing to take degrees at the universities were required to preach either in Oxford or at Paul's Cross in London.[130] By synodal decree, seminaries were to be attached to every cathedral to educate the next generation of priests: the statutes of the one established in York in 1557 spoke of producing 'militant shepherds . . . who with the sword of the spirit . . . may be able to drive away and put to flight the rapacious wolves, that is devilish men ill understanding the catholic faith, from the sheepfolds of the sheep intrusted to them'.[131] It was once alleged that Pole was distrustful of preaching – an allegation that drew on a poorly translated statement from a letter to Carranza in 1558.[132] In reality, the letter in question detailed the regular weekly sermons at Paul's Cross, the provision of sermons in the London parishes and the preparation of printed homilies, as well as Pole's own preaching. It noted, however, that in the particular circumstances of London, still so 'corrupt and diseased' in matters of faith, sermons could sometimes be 'more of a hindrance than a help' if viewed purely as entertainment by 'carnal men'. For all that, there was no question of 'the necessity of preaching the Word'.[133] Pole was also criticized for failing to draw on the expertise of the Jesuit order, explained by the Spanish ambassador, Count Feria, in a letter to the Jesuit Pedro Ribadeneira, in terms of Pole's 'lukewarm' religion.[134] In fact, as the letter makes clear, it was Mary's decision as much as Pole's; and given that there were no English-speaking Jesuits at this point in time, and that the order was still very new, independent of all episcopal authority and closely linked to the papacy, the decision was sensible enough.[135] Pole was happy to ask for help from the Benedictine mother house at Monte Cassino when it came to refounding the monastery at Westminster Abbey.[136] There were also some formidable Spanish theologians and churchmen helping with the work of restoration: the Dominicans Bartolomé Carranza and Juan de Villagarcía and the Observant Franciscans Alfonso de Castro and Bernardo de Fresnada were churchmen and scholars of international repute, and they were joined later by the Dominican Pedro de Soto, founder of the Catholic University of Dillingen, near Augsburg.[137] Mary's restoration was thereby connected with the Counter-Reformation currents circulating elsewhere in Europe.

There were many aspects to Europe's Counter-Reformation, however, and some were more reformist in intent than others. Mary's Church was more open to reform initiatives than some. When Feria observed that 'I do not believe the lukewarm go to Paradise, even if they are called moderates', this was probably a veiled criticism of Pole's reforming ideals. Relations with Rome were not defined by the slavish obedience once ascribed to Mary where the papacy was concerned. In particular, once Gian Pietro Carafa was made pope in 1555, his strong anti-Spanish sentiments rendered relations with Rome decidedly frosty. When Philip II went to war with the Papal States in 1556, Mary had no difficulty at all in siding with her husband. She also continued to make policy decisions for the Church in England throughout her reign. The royal visitations of March 1554 were carried out under her authority as supreme head of the Church, even though later that year she would renounce this title. She also appointed eleven bishops on her own authority, eight of them before Pole had even set foot in England.[138] And when, in April 1557, Pope Paul IV cancelled Pole's legation and recalled him to Rome to face charges of heresy, Mary commanded Pole to ignore the summons, and threatened

1 *The Whitehall Mural*, painted by Remigius van Leemput in 1667, is a copy of the one on the wall of the Privy Chamber in Whitehall Palace, lost when the palace burned down in 1698. Henry VIII is depicted with his parents and Queen Jane Seymour, who may already have been dead by the time the mural was completed.

INITIVM SANC-
TI EVANGELII
SECVNDVM MAT-
THÆVM.

The Gos-
pell by Saint
Matthew.

Matthew. 1. Chapter.

Matt. Chap. 1.

Efteꞃ Matheuꞃ ᵹe receonyꞃꞃe. heꞃ iꞃ
on cneoꞃiꞃꞃe boc. Hælendeꞃ Cꞃiꞃteꞃ
Dauiðeꞃ ꞃuna. Abꞃahameꞃ ꞃuna; 2. Soð-
lice Abꞃahã ᵹeꞇꞃynðe Iꞃaac. Iꞃaac ᵹeꞇꞃynðe Iacob ; Iacob ᵹeꞇꞃynðe Iuðã. ꞇ hiꞃ ᵹebꞃo-
ðꞃa. 3. Iuðaꞃ ᵹeꞇꞃynðe Phaꞃeꞃ. ꞇ Zaram oꝼ
þã piꝼe þe pæꞃ ᵹenemneð Thamaꞃ ; Phaꞃeꞃ ᵹeꞇꞃynðe Eꞃꞃõ. Eꞃꞃõ ᵹeꞇꞃynðe Aꞃã. 4. Aꞃã
ᵹeꞇꞃynðe Aminaðab. Aminaðab ᵹeꞇꞃynðe
Naaꞃon ; Naaꞃon ᵹeꞇꞃynðe Salmon. 5. Salmon ᵹeꞇꞃynðe Booꝛ oꝼ þã piꝼe Raab ; Booꝛ
ᵹeꞇꞃynðe Obeꞇh oꝼ þã piꝼe Ruꞇh. Obeꞇh
ᵹeꞇꞃynðe Ieꞃꞃe ; 6. Ieꞃꞃe ᵹeꞇꞃynðe þone
cyninᵹ Dauið. Dauið cyninᵹ ᵹeꞇꞃynðe Salomon oꝼ þã piꝼe þe pæꞃ Vꞃiaꞃ piꝼe. 7. Salomon
ᵹeꞇꞃynðe Roboã. Roboaꞃ ᵹeꞇꞃynðe Abiã.
Abia ᵹeꞇꞃynðe Aꞃa. 8. Aꞃa ᵹeꞇꞃynðe Io-
ꞃaphaꞇh ; Ioꞃaphaꞇ ᵹeꞇꞃynðe Ioꞃã. Ioꞃaꞃ ᵹeꞇꞃynðe Oꞃiam ; 9. Oꞃiaꞃ ᵹeꞇꞃynðe Ioaꞇhã.
Ioaꞇhã ᵹeꞇꞃynðe Achaꞃ. Achaꞃ ᵹeꞇꞃynðe
Eꞃechiã. 10. Eꞃechiaꞃ ᵹeꞇꞃynðe Mannaꞃen ;
Mannaꞃeꞃ ᵹeꞇꞃynðe Amon, Amon ᵹe-

B.i.

ꞇꞃynðe

1 This is the booke
of the generation
of Iesus Christ,
the sonne of Dauid the
sonne of Abraham.

2 Abraham begat Isa-
hac, Isahac begat Iacob,
Iacob begat Iudas, and
his brethren.

3 Iudas begat Pha-
res & Zara of Thamar,
Phares begat Esrom,
Esrom begat Aram.

4 Aram begat Amina-
dab, Aminadab begatte
Naasson, Naasson be-
gatte Salmon.

5 Salmon begat Boos
of Rachab, Boos be-
gatte Obed of Ruth,
Obed begat Iesse.

6 Iesse begatte Dauid
the king. Dauid the king
begatte Solomon, of
her that was (the wife)
of Vrie.

7 Solomon begatte
Roboam, Roboam be-
gat Abia, Abia begat
Asa.

8 Asa begatte Iosa-
phat, Iosaphat begatte
Ioram, Ioram begatte
Ozias.

9 Ozias begatte Ioa-
than, Ioathan begatte
Achas, Achas begatte
Ezchias.

10 Ezchias begat Ma-
nasses, Manasses be-
gatte Amon, Amon be-
gat

---

2 *The Gospels of the fower Evangelistes translated in the olde Saxons tyme out of Latin into the vulgare toung of the Saxons, newly collected out of auncient monuments of the sayd Saxons, and now published for testimonie of the same,* printed by John Day in London, 1571. This book contained the Gospels in Anglo-Saxon and English in parallel columns, with an introduction by John Foxe. It was a piece of Protestant propaganda masquerading as an antiquarian work.

3 The ruins of Fountains Abbey in Yorkshire. The great Cistercian house was founded in the twelfth century and dissolved by Henry VIII in 1539. The great tower is still visible, built by Abbot Marmaduke Huby (in office 1495–1526), suggesting the vigour of monasticism even on the brink of the Dissolution.

4 Fifteenth-century wall-paintings of the *Seven Corporal Works of Mercy*, from the church of St Peter and St Paul in Pickering, North Yorkshire. We see the faithful feeding and clothing (a bit awkwardly) those in need, visiting those in prison, comforting the sick and burying the dead.

5 Portrait of King Henry VII, c.1505, by an unknown Netherlandish artist. It may have been intended for use in marriage negotiations after the death of Elizabeth, his queen. Although unimposing by comparison with later Tudor portraits, it was an impressive piece of work at the time, when a head and shoulders pose was the usual format.

6 Henry VIII depicted on the 1511 Westminster Tournament Roll. This tournament celebrated the birth of Prince Henry on New Year's Day 1511, although within weeks the young prince would be dead. The monograms on Henry VIII's costume proclaim his affection for his queen and he is depicted shattering his lance on his opponent's helmet, a particularly skilful feat of arms.

7 *Solomon and the Queen of Sheba*, by Hans Holbein the Younger, c.1534. Henry VIII, as Solomon, sprawled in a lascivious pose, contemplates the beauty of the Queen of Sheba. The picture evokes the relationship between Christ and the Church, underlining the extraordinary nature of Henry's claims to ecclesiastical supremacy.

8 *Henry VIII and the Barber Surgeons*, attributed to Hans Holbein the Younger and his workshop, c.1541. This group portrait was commissioned to celebrate the joining of the Barbers' Company with that of the Surgeons, and therefore glorifies the members of the livery company as well as the king himself.

9 *Edward Prince of Wales*, by Hans Holbein the Younger, c.1538. The pose of the young prince evokes his future majesty and emphasizes his likeness to his father, even in the choice of headgear. Latin verses by Richard Morison sycophantically praise Henry VIII as the greatest of kings, whom his son might emulate but can never outdo.

10 *Mary I*, painted by Hans Eworth, 1554. It is thought that this was the first major portrait painted after Mary's coronation. She wears her mother's jewelled cross and a reliquary hangs from her girdle, while her left hand bears the coronation ring with which she proclaimed herself married to her country.

11 *Elizabeth I*, by Quentin Metsys the Younger, c.1583. This was one of several portraits of Elizabeth painted holding a sieve, a classical symbol of virginity and wisdom. The visual emphasis on chastity and restraint was probably a response by those who commissioned these portraits to the threat of her proposed marriage to the French duke of Anjou.

12 Queen Elizabeth's locket ring, c.1575. This ring has Elizabeth's monogram, 'ER', on the bezel, fashioned from table-cut diamonds and blue enamel. It opens to reveal portraits of the queen (in profile) and her mother, Anne Boleyn, wearing a French hood. It perhaps suggests that Elizabeth cherished the memory of her mother.

13 The Dacre Beasts, c.1520. These large heraldic ornaments represent different members of the Dacre family and stood for centuries in the Great Hall of Naworth Castle in Cumbria. The Red Bull represents Thomas, Lord Dacre (d.1525) who commissioned the beasts. The Dolphin represents his wife, Elizabeth de Greystoke (d.1516).

14 The plasterwork fireplace from Plas Mawr, the house of the rich merchant and traveller Robert Wynn in Conwy, Wales. The symbolism proclaims both the distinguished ancestry of the Wynn family, which claimed descent from the princes of Gwynedd, and their loyalty to the Tudor dynasty.

15 A portrait of Mary Neville Fiennes, Baroness Dacre, by Hans Eworth, c.1555. Mary Fiennes's first husband, Baron Dacre, was executed for murdering a gamekeeper in 1541. She campaigned vigorously to have the family property restored, succeeding when Elizabeth I restored the title of Baron Dacre to Mary's son Gregory.

16 John Blanke, royal trumpeter at the courts of Henry VII and Henry VIII, and perhaps the only Black Tudor for whom we have an identifiable image. He is depicted here on the Tournament Roll of 1511. Documentary evidence suggests that he was a valued musician with a measure of social status.

17 *The Ambassadors,* by Hans Holbein the Younger, 1533. Holbein's portrait of Jean de Dinteville, the French ambassador, and Georges de Selve, bishop of Lavaur, who visited England in 1533, is thronged with expensive artefacts and rich with symbolism. The broken lute-string and the mathematical treatise open at a page on division, for example, hint at the religious discord of the age.

18 This *Armada Portrait*, c.1588, is one of three versions of the painting which proclaimed Elizabeth's victory over the Spanish Armada. The triumph of the English navy and the ruin of the Spanish fleet is echoed by Elizabeth's proprietorial gesture towards Virginia, where England's colony was intended to defy the Spanish monopoly over the New World.

19 The late medieval screen from All Saints church in Morston in Norfolk. The four Fathers of the Church have survived in their pre-Reformation incarnation, but the cardinal's hat worn by St Jerome and the papal tiara worn by St Gregory the Great have been carefully scraped away to remove any suggestion of popery.

20 The Triangular Lodge at Rushton in Northamptonshire was designed by the recusant Catholic Sir Thomas Tresham and is an architectural encapsulation of Trinitarian doctrine, built as a demonstration of Tresham's Catholic faith and laden with allegorical meaning. Tresham's son Francis was one of those complicit in the Gunpowder Plot of 1605.

21 The Banner of the Five Wounds of Christ, as used in the Pilgrimage of Grace in 1536–37, in the Prayer Book Rebellion in the south-west of England in 1549 and again in the Northern Rebellion of 1569. It is suggestive of both fierce nostalgia for the lost religion of pre-Reformation England and the subversive potential of post-Reformation Catholicism.

22 *The Family of Henry VIII*, c.1545, by an unknown artist. Henry is flanked by his third wife, Jane Seymour, who died in 1537, and his children. Through the arches we see the garden of Whitehall Palace, with heraldic beasts on columns. The king's fool, Will Somers, is also depicted; the woman in the other archway is possibly Princess Mary's fool, Jane.

23 *A Fête at Bermondsey*, by Marcus Gheeraerts the Elder, c.1571. This is one of the earliest depictions of a landscape in British art. It gives a vivid sense of the diversity of Tudor society, from those on horseback, richly dressed, to the woman nursing a baby, the man in the stocks and the dog-fight breaking out in the foreground. The variety and movement in this scene contrast with the rigid formality of the depiction of royalty; a reminder of how authority strove constantly to impose order on a changeable and unpredictable society.

24 Interior of the Globe Theatre, which originally opened in Southwark in 1599. It burned down in 1613, set alight after cannons were fired in a production of Shakespeare's *Henry VIII*. This reconstructed version, built very close to the original site, was opened in 1997.

25 *Elizabeth I with Time and Death*, artist unknown, c.1610, from Corsham Court, Wiltshire. The defiantly ageless portrayals of Elizabeth during her lifetime have given way to this more candid portrayal of a queen still majestic but weighed down by the passage of time and her unavoidable mortality.

the pope with the prospect that she might 'regret our piety toward the apostolic see'. In effect, she warned Paul IV that she might behave as her father had before her. Like her father over his divorce case, she refused to have Pole's case recalled to Rome, and insisted that any trial would need to take place in England.[139]

Mary's Church was not the bigoted, zealous and reactionary institution of legend. Its reformist vision was, in part, enshrined in the published works of her reign, most of which were in English. The Council of Trent, which had first convened in 1545, and which would finally conclude in 1563, would enforce the rule that Latin was the proper language for religious publications; but in England, the importance of vernacular religious works was long established, and Mary's reign reflected this. Education was also a priority: Trinity College and St John's College Oxford were founded during her reign, as was Gonville and Caius in Cambridge; meanwhile, Mary effectively refounded Trinity College Cambridge, which her father had first established. The queen made generous provision for the universities, tripling Oxford's income with a major grant in 1554.[140] The consequence was that in 1558 there was a striking show of resistance to Elizabeth.[141] Twenty-five heads of college would be removed in the next reign, and Marian Oxford in particular would provide the nucleus of the Catholic exile community.[142] Mary's episcopate was also distinguished for its academic credentials. Several had studied and taught abroad: Ralph Baynes, bishop of Coventry and Lichfield, had been professor of Hebrew at Paris, while John Hopton, bishop of Norwich and a former Dominican, had a doctorate in theology from Bologna. James Brooks, bishop of Gloucester, had formerly been master of Balliol College Oxford, whilst Cuthbert Scot, bishop of Chester, had been master of Christ's College Cambridge.[143] The reign also saw seventeen new schools established, including Oundle, Brentwood and Repton, with the refoundation of Ripon Grammar School and three schools established by the priest Thomas Alleyne.[144]

Mary also promoted the revival of monasticism. The impetus for restoring Westminster Abbey was given by sixteen monks who arrived at Court wearing their monastic habits to petition for refoundation. Under the abbacy of John Feckenham, Westminster displayed marked reformist features, echoed by the classical lines of the restored shrine of Edward the Confessor at the heart of the abbey.[145] Of the other restored houses, the

Carthusians at Sheen, the Observant Franciscans at Greenwich and Southampton, and the Brigittines at Syon had been the orders most known for asceticism and learning before the Dissolution. The Dominicans returned to Smithfield, Dartford and Oxford, the Knights Hospitaller to Clerkenwell and the Franciscans to Guernsey, whilst plans were made to restore the Benedictine abbeys at Glastonbury and St Albans.[146] Mary was not an indiscriminate advocate for monasticism: in 1555 her new statutes for Durham Cathedral confirmed it as a secular cathedral, but she gave encouragement to those houses she thought had the potential to strengthen her restoration.[147] The refounded houses would again suffer dissolution at the start of Elizabeth's reign, but many would preserve their communities in exile, some of them for centuries, eventually returning to England in the late nineteenth and early twentieth centuries.[148]

Pole's innate conciliarism resulted in him calling a reforming synod to Lambeth in 1555, which drew up a list of decrees to revitalize the Church, echoing his work in Rome in the 1530s, but also anticipating the language Trent would use in its decrees in 1564. It took a stern line with absentee bishops and priests, insisting that they must live among those for whom God would hold them accountable; they were to 'show their flock the presence that is due, and watch over their guardianship without any worldly distractions, and according to the precept of the Apostles'.[149] The importance of preaching, teaching children and caring for orphans and widows was underlined; priests were also not to dress in silk or have expensive furniture, and at meals 'should not be served more than three, or at the most four . . . kinds of meat, besides fruit and confectionary'.[150] Above all they were to educate the next generation: in establishing the idea of seminaries, the Lambeth Synod anticipated the Council of Trent in suggesting one of the most fundamental reforms of the era. These decrees would be published in 1562, after both Pole and Mary were dead, as *Reformatio Angliae*, the 'Reformation of England', a blueprint for Catholic Reformation across Europe. The emphasis was on harmony, 'lyke as in musycke when tharmony in stringes, pipes, and tunes, do well agree together . . . even so it is with us the membres of Christes misticall bodye'.[151] The clergy were to be 'the fathers of the poor, the refuge and defence of the orphans, widows and oppressed . . . assiduously employed in the study of the Holy Scriptures', whilst the realm as a whole was envisaged as united 'in an indivisible bonde or knotte of concorde, and unytye'.[152] In just five years, the realm saw an extraordinary amount of progress towards these objectives.

The problem of heresy

Unity needed to be built upon consensus, and the less appealing side of Mary's church policy concerned the elimination of the threat from heresy. Between 1555 and 1558, nearly three hundred Protestants of various sorts suffered execution by being burnt at the stake. This was to shape the reputation of the regime from 1558 onwards, and it is still a deeply contested question in modern historical debate. The Marian martyrs were the heroes of England's Protestant future. They included the very old, the very young, and some so simple-minded it is doubtful how well they understood the accusations they faced. Many were of humble origin: weavers, fishermen, butchers, barbers, carpenters and bricklayers. A few were leading churchmen of the previous reign, most famously Archbishop Cranmer and Bishops Latimer, Ridley and Hooper (see illustration 20). The stories of how they were brought to trial and execution were told in indignant, loving and scrupulous detail by Foxe, who left us such a series of court-room dramas and heroic, pitiful deaths, as would continue to shape the English imagination for centuries to come. It has to be remembered, however, that Foxe was so determined to give a compelling portrayal of Protestantism that he edited out some of the awkward details that might challenge his picture.[153] It has been suggested that some of those who died might equally have been executed under Edward VI, such was the oddity of their beliefs; that they upheld not Protestant views but older heresies, such as the denial of the Trinity, or rejection of the divinity of Christ – views that were anathema to Protestants, as much as Catholics. Foxe smoothed these wrinkles out, and wrote a book that would define English Protestantism.

The executions detailed by Foxe were heart-breaking. One of the worst was the execution of Perotine Massey in July 1556, executed alongside her mother and sister in St Peter Port in Guernsey. She had reported a neighbour for stealing a cup; in the consequent investigation, the matter of her church attendance had come to light, and she was convicted of heresy. Amidst the flames, she gave birth to a baby boy, who was rescued by a bystander; but the bailiff in attendance thrust him back into the fire to

Lord Jesu receiue my soul

20. The execution of Bishop Hooper at Gloucester in 1555, from John Foxe, *Actes and Monuments*

perish with his mother. We know this was not Foxe's invention, for the bailiff was found guilty of murder during Elizabeth's reign. This is by far the most arresting of many dreadful stories, but Foxe was very good at tales that stay in the memory. At Laxfield in Suffolk, in 1557, the shoe-maker John Noyes was sentenced to be burned; but in silent solidarity, his neighbours put out their hearth fires, so that there would be no way of lighting his pyre (although the executioners found a way in the end). These deaths were symptomatic of the cruel punishments of this era, when a man could be hanged for stealing a sheep. Mary was not alone in targeting religious dissent: after the Northern Rebellion of 1569, Elizabeth I ordered that even the rank and file of the rebellion be executed under martial law, with perhaps seven hundred people or more put to death for their Catholic loyalties. Thus, if Mary's regime was harsh, it was not uniquely so. It may, however, have been unusually efficient – a mark of Mary's determination to put her country to rights and restore the age-old faith.[154] It is also important to remember that the reason these prosecutions for heresy were able to take place is that so many ordinary citizens were actively involved in searching out Protestants. This was not the work of a vindictive queen and a handful of callous bishops, but the judgement of a society.[155]

Even so, to burn a heretic was to have failed. More than anything, the regime wanted people to recant their errors. Sometimes this was achieved. The duke of Northumberland, sentenced to death for his very obvious treason in trying to supplant Mary with his daughter-in-law, Lady Jane Grey, converted back to Catholicism and proclaimed as much from the scaffold, warning against 'these factious preachers and teachers of the new creed, who pretend to preach the word of God, but in truth . . . preach only their own fancies' and who showed 'no consistency in their testament, or teaching, nor wisdom'.[156] His speech was published by John Cawood, and swiftly translated into Latin, Italian and German.[157] Most startling of all, Mary's government even managed to secure a recantation from Thomas Cranmer, who had done more than anyone to draw up a Protestant blueprint for the English Church. In the end, he was to think better of it, but long hours of persuasion from the best Catholic minds of the age had clearly had a profound effect. Cranmer struggled with the conundrum that any number of his contemporaries would face after the Reformation was in train: namely, how to obey both God and king. Badgered by the English clerics who had once been his colleagues, such as John Harpsfield, and by the Spanish theologians Villagarcía and de Soto, in February 1556 a highly emotional Cranmer admitted that he had seen the error of his ways. He confessed, was absolved and was given Thomas More's *Dialogue of Comfort* to read – written by another prisoner under sentence of execution, to guard other souls against despair and desolation. He would soon have needed comforting, for his recantation did not save his life, which was irredeemably forfeit in Mary's eyes, so badly had he offended. Instead, he had to prepare for the horrible death that he had already seen consume his friends, for his jailers had made sure that he watched from the prison window as Latimer and Ridley burned.

Cranmer's last day was an exercise in political theatre. He was brought before a crowd of dignitaries in the University Church and directed to read aloud to them his recantation. Little knowing what was in store, the throng listened as he spoke, bowing as he made reference to the king and queen, referring to one particular sin that weighed upon his conscience. His audience must have presumed he meant his adherence to the Protestant faith; but as he reached his peroration, it dawned on them that Cranmer was actually condemning his own recantation and proclaiming himself a steadfast Protestant once more. Uproar ensued, and the last thing Cranmer was heard to shout above the noise was that in the matter of the eucharist, he held by what he had written in his book against Stephen Gardiner. He was taken to Broad Street, where – so the story goes – he held in the flames the hand that had signed the recantation. The place where he perished is marked to this day with a cross made out of cobblestones, a quiet witness in a sea of tarmacadam.

The story of Cranmer's end would become famous, and at the time was discussed across Europe. Yet Mary was regarded by many in her lifetime as being merciful. Northumberland, for example, may have gone to his death in 1553, but only two of his henchmen, Thomas Palmer and John Gates, died with him.[158] His sons Ambrose, Robert, Henry and John, and his brother Andrew were all spared, as was the marquess of Northampton, despite being convicted of treason.[159] Most notably, Lady Jane Grey and her husband Guildford Dudley were allowed to live – until the renewed threat engendered by Wyatt's rebellion made it prudent to execute them. Nevertheless, Mary's vision of a prosperous society and a united realm had no place for religious division. This was in part expressed in the funeral sermon given for her by Bishop White of Winchester:

> To be born in Christ's church, and not to abide therein; to promise, and not to perform; to promise penance here, and not to practise; to hear the truth, and not to believe; to be daily taught, and never to learn; ever to be warned, and never to beware; that is horrible execrable, cursed, and damnable. I am born into this world to this end, to serve God, and to be saved. I shal be dampned, not because I was born, but because I served not . . .[160]

This uncompromising view of Catholic fidelity is a memorial that Mary probably would have appreciated.

The state of the commonwealth

When Cranmer delivered his final speech, he exhorted his listeners to have love of three sorts: love of God, love of the monarch and love of one's neighbour. As he spoke of the plight of the poor, he broke down and cried, for in England in 1556 the poorest members of society were suffering terrible hardship. The middle years of the sixteenth century saw a series of bad harvests, floods and epidemics among both animals and humans: typhus, and then influenza, caused the worst mortality crisis of the century.[161] These practical problems have usually been woven into the condemnation of Mary's reign; but without subscribing to a belief in the workings of providence and the righteousness of the Protestant cause, it is hard to hold her responsible for natural disaster. On the other hand, the response from the Marian regime to the slew of social problems in the 1550s gives an impression of some competence in Mary's government, including its willingness to build on Edwardian initiatives. The notion that poverty was a problem requiring a political solution had been growing in strength since the 1530s, leading to such measures as the licensing of beggars and the founding of the London hospitals. These built on initiatives by individual city authorities, including the regulation of begging in Norwich, Southampton, Cambridge, Chester, Lincoln and other cities, and hospitals such as St Thomas' in London, which was the result of collaboration between the city and the Crown.[162]

The sense that poverty and suffering required a centralized response is one borne out by the initiatives of 1553–58. The government had an eye for detail: in 1556, it was regulating the price of sweet and barrelled butter and cheese from Essex; and the following year it issued a proclamation against swords and rapiers being made 'of a much greater length than heretofore hath been accustomed', which was apparently facilitating riots and affrays, particularly in churchyards. It was even prepared to tackle the 'shameful deceit' of those who drove up the price of their wool by not washing or clipping their sheep adequately, and thereby making their pelts weightier 'by means of their sweating . . . and partly also through other filth'.[163] In 1555, a parliamentary statute prohibited the export from the realm of 'Corne Butter Chese or other Victuall', and also wood, blaming 'many and sundrye covertous and unsatiable persons' for transporting large amounts of these commodities for the sake of their own profit. 'By reason whereof', the act continued severely, 'the sayd Corne Vyctuall and Wood arre growen unto a wonderfull dearthe and extreame pryses, to the greate detryment of the Common wealthe'.[164] A proclamation of 1555 reinforced the importance of statutes covering a slew of social issues; and if the laws it was seeking to enforce also touched on heresy, Lollardy and rumour, those that targeted sturdy vagabonds, the counterfeiting of coin and the excess of apparel, as well as those that governed the duties of sheriffs, the role of journeymen and the regulation of alehouses, were all intended 'for the good government, order, and commonweal of this realm'.[165]

The Marian regime showed some sympathy for the needs of townsfolk: one of Mary's earliest proclamations was to enable the sale of firewood in London, since the influx of people for her coronation and first parliament had used up so much fuel that there were fears of a shortage that winter.[166] The regime was, in general, disposed to protect urban manufacturers and traders. A proclamation of August 1553, barely a month after Mary took the throne, proposed reform of the coinage, although in the end it would be Elizabeth who would achieve this.[167] Another, early in 1554, sought to revive the wool trade with the Low Countries.[168] Parliamentary statutes concerning retail trade confirmed the sense of a gradual shift from isolated attempts at assistance by local authorities to a more national solution.[169] Mary's concern for urban issues was in part born of her gratitude for the support many towns had shown her in 1553.[170] It also showed a keen awareness of the distress being experienced by many.[171] Marian charters were still providing the basis of urban governance in nine English towns as late as 1835.[172] Mary's most distinctive contribution in London was the Savoy hospital on the Strand, intended for paupers, which promised each supplicant food, alms and a bed for the night. There was a distinctive Catholic gloss to this, since no attempt was made to distinguish between the idle and the deserving poor, and the same attitude was reflected in the revision of the 1552 Act 'for the relief of poor and impotent persons' in 1555: although otherwise almost totally echoing the Edwardian Act, the Marian revision showed a greater acceptance of indiscriminate charity.[173] Civic charity was a key element of Protestant philanthropy, but it was also a theme in contemporary Catholic thinking. In a sermon, Pole compared London with the Italian cities, pointing out how many more hospitals they had, and suggesting that those who had acquired former monastic wealth might want to use some of it to correct this imbalance.[174] The Franciscans petitioned for the return of the London Greyfriars, which had been turned into Christ's Hospital for foundling children, but

Philip's Franciscan confessor Alfonso de Castro and the Dominican scholar Villagarcía had dined there and had been profoundly moved by the sight of the children. Villagarcía said that he would rather serve the orphans than be steward to the king, and so the hospital, founded by Edward VI as an example of Protestant charity, remained.[175] If the Marian regime was again connecting with the agenda of the broader European Catholic Reformation, it was also capable of building on Edwardian achievements.[176]

It was the destructiveness of the previous Protestant regime that was emphasized by preachers and writers, however. Edward's reign was cast in popular memory not just as 'the tyme that lights wer put downe', but as an era which saw 'all good order broken'.[177] Viewed from the perspective of many Marian writers, the effect of Edward's rule had been to produce complete social breakdown. One treatise spoke of the damage done to normal social relationships. 'No man durst trust hys nexte neyghboure. Amitie and frendshyp was fled the realme, truth exyled.' The loss of the true faith and the loss of social harmony were perceived as inextricably combined. 'The clergye ashamed of chastitie, the pryestes and mynysters of prayer, the aged of devocion, and as our mayster Christe saythe, where wyckednesse wexed plentyfull, there charitye wexed colde.'[178] What historians are minded to term social and economic policy was, to Mary I's government, a reaction to a moral and religious problem also. In this, Catholic commentators shared a view propounded by other European writers. Gardiner's chaplain, John Bullingham, translated a work by the Parisian John Venaeus which delineated how heresy could render 'all things ... foule disordered' and described how 'charitie is exiled and banished every where, that true and faithful hartes with the loving concord of Turtle doves can not be founde amonge men'. He lamented the discord between princes, between commons and magistrate, servant and master, 'even under one roufe and in one house (O miserable and pitifull case) the father dissenteth from the sonne, the mother from the doughter'.[179] Social dislocation was the inevitable consequence of religious division and error. Marian initiatives to harmonize society, encourage trade, strengthen urban communities and restore the traditional rhythms of life in the parishes were all closely connected to attempts to rebuild the true faith.

Warfare

Restoration of Catholicism at home was closely linked to defence of the Catholic cause abroad; but neither was a question of straightforward loyalties, particularly after the election of Gian Pietro Carafa as Pope Paul IV in 1555. Carafa, a Neapolitan, loathed the Habsburgs who ruled his native kingdom, so Mary's commitment to the Habsburg alliance put her at odds with the papacy, even as she was engaged in the work of Catholic renewal. Philip II had not married for love, but for the clear strategic reasons that formed the basis of most royal matches. He is recorded as having told a servant, 'I'm not going for a wedding, but to fight.'[180] England's command of the Channel was key to this vital communication link between Spain and the Netherlands, whilst from England's point of view, links to the Netherlands were integral to financial and commercial interests. Thus, the union between Mary and Philip repeated a pattern of dynastic alliance which was long established.[181] Mary's marriage, from a European perspective, established a vital new axis that would build a bulwark against the rising tide of heresy. An atlas which Mary commissioned as a present for her husband, although never completed, was a powerful political statement about the union they had constructed, and the territories under their combined control.[182]

The Protestant narrative of Mary's reign, constructed after her demise, lamented the way that England was drawn into conflicts in Europe as a consequence of the Anglo-Habsburg alliance. This was no different, however, to how Elizabethan England was later drawn into conflict in the Netherlands, in France and in Ireland. As the Reformation became ever more entrenched, confessional divisions exacerbated international tensions, and the necessity of having foreign allies ineluctably involved others in hostilities. Mary was repeating the logical patterns set by her father and grandfather in prioritizing diplomatic and trading links with the Netherlands and combating the ambitions of the French, whose hostility towards their Burgundian neighbours also dated back to medieval times. The fact that she did this in concert with her Spanish husband has sometimes obscured the otherwise obvious truth that her foreign policy was entirely in keeping with the strategy developed by her predecessors, and reflected England's most important strategic and economic interests. A radical departure in terms of foreign policy would have to wait until her sister's reign.

Nonetheless, if supporting the Habsburg cause in the Netherlands could be read, at least in part, as a defence of the Catholic faith, the Habsburg cause further afield brought complications. Philip II may have championed Catholicism, but in 1556 he oversaw an invasion of the Papal States by Spanish forces, as part of a long-running conflict that had seen the Habsburgs' opponent, Henry II of France, form alliances with both Suleiman the Magnificent and the German Protestant princes. In the febrile international climate of the time, strategic alliances did not always follow religious imperatives. The tensions in Italy provoked French aggression on the borders of the Netherlands, and by the end of January 1557 France and Spain were involved in a war that Philip II had neither wanted nor sought. Mary's government was wary of involvement at first, probably because the country was reeling from the effects of atrocious harvests in 1555 and 1556. The French had been encouraging piracy in the Channel, however, and provided backing for Thomas Stafford, who captured Scarborough Castle from the sea in April 1557, in an eccentric and futile attempt to raise a rebellion against Mary. This helped focus conciliar opinion, and by June England had joined the war.[183]

It was in December 1557 that rumours of a French attack on Calais began to circulate: one of the duke of Guise's Italian officers had been seen investigating the state of Calais and its defences. When word of this reached Lord Grey, he sent word of it back to London, not giving the rumour much credibility, but observing that he had neither the men nor the armaments to repel any kind of serious assault. When rumour turned into the reality of a French assault in preparation, it was too late to organize an effective response, and in the last cold days of December, the rivers and waterways that usually helped defend the Pale had frozen over. Philip II in Brussels was doing his best to galvanize the English into action, but on 7 January 1558 the French bombarded the town and it surrendered. Wentworth, the lord deputy, was taken prisoner, along with about two thousand of his men. The English vacillated, perhaps intending to wait until spring to send a force to recapture the lost territory, since campaigning in winter was highly unusual. Philip took more concrete steps to assess the situation; but when his envoy, Count Feria, arrived in London, he soon came to the conclusion that Mary's government was not prepared to fight in order to recover Calais.[184]

This could be read as lassitude or military inexperience; but it could also be read as common sense. At the time, the loss of Calais was a blow, and it has since given rise to various historical laments at the passing of medieval England – including the entirely invented story that Mary said she would be found, when dead, to have 'Calais' engraved upon her heart. Calais has been cast as the last remnant of that chivalric dream of recapturing ancestral lands in France which had so animated the Plantagenets, and which had brought about the victories of Crécy, Poitiers and Agincourt. It has to be remembered, however, that in 1557 these victories were centuries old, and that Calais had, for many years, been an expensive anomaly. Boulogne, the other fragment of English land in France, had been sold back to the French by Edward VI's government in 1550 for 100,000 crowns. Elizabeth's government after 1558 was equally reluctant to engage with the task of trying to get Calais back. Strategically, this French outpost had outlived its usefulness, since England's greatest hope of strength now lay in the English Channel and the guarantee of links to the Netherlands, not the chance of an offensive war in France. To preserve the Anglo-Habsburg connection, Philip II was willing to do everything he could think of to keep England friendly; having married Mary, it is clear he had hopes of marrying her half-sister Elizabeth, too, after Mary died. England's best chances of keeping the ancestral French enemy at bay lay not in a garrison at Calais, but in its diplomatic links with Spain. The loss of Calais does not deserve the prominence which it later acquired in historical legend.

The military involvement of 1557–58 also had the effect of justifying Mary's choice of husband. War was one of the more difficult challenges for a female ruler, and being able to entrust military command to her husband was a great help to her authority. It gave former rebels, such as the sons of the duke of Northumberland, a chance to redeem their reputation through a display of loyalty; and it gave Philip the allegiance of the English soldiers who fought with him, and who came to hold him in respect as their military leader. Two of the would-be leaders of rebellion in 1554, James Croft and Peter Carew, served as commanders, and the more disaffected elements of the nobility and gentry were thereby reconciled and included in this shared military endeavour.[185] The war was also the first opportunity to deploy the navy, which Mary's government had been refurbishing and expanding to such effect. The three great warships of these years – the *Philip and Mary*, the second *Mary Rose* and the *Golden Lion* – would all still be in service in the 1580s. It was one of the ironies of Mary's reign that she was responsible for constructing the navy, now based in Portsmouth at her husband's suggestion, which would eventually withstand Philip's Armada in 1588.[186]

The death of Catholic England

The common narrative of Mary's reign used to portray her last year as sunk in gloom and despair, with the loss of Calais, another failed pregnancy and the persecution of Protestants drying up in the face of popular hostility. From the viewpoint of many contemporaries, however, England in 1557 had acquired a new level of stability, as Philip II's leadership energized the loyalties of the ruling classes and the queen's apparent pregnancy offered the hope of dynastic continuance, whilst the declining number of executions for heresy suggested that the campaign against Protestantism was achieving the desired end. In the summer of 1558, Pole told Carranza that religion in England was 'beginning to recover its pure form'.[187] Had Mary lived, 1558 might have been viewed as the year in which her authority was finally consolidated, as the country recovered from famine, the work of Catholic restoration neared completion and the Anglo-Spanish union made its presence felt within a European arena. When Mary made her will in March 1558, a common practice for a woman approaching childbirth, she clearly envisaged leaving the country to an heir of her body. Philip, informed of Mary's hopes, recorded his 'joy and contentment' at the news, describing it as 'the thing that I have most wanted in the world . . . so important for the good of Religion and of our Kingdoms'.[188]

As the summer of 1558 wore on, however, another epidemic was raging. At the end of 1557, a 'new ague' or 'new disease' had begun to spread through the country. In the parish of St Margaret's Westminster, the impact was so bad that the parish records broke down between November 1557 and October 1558.[189] This was clearly a virulent viral infection, usually assumed to have been influenza, and it took a particular toll of the more affluent, who were generally more resilient in the face of epidemic disease. By October, it was clear that Mary was seriously ill, with high fevers and periods of delirium. By the time Philip was informed, he was in the midst of planning the obsequies in Brussels for his father Charles V and Charles's sister Mary of Hungary, both of whom had just died. He was also needed at a peace conference that sought to end the war with France. It was Count Feria whom he dispatched to Mary's deathbed. On 28 October, she added a codicil to her will, asking 'my next heire and Successour' to enact the terms of her will. It was the nearest she ever got to naming Elizabeth as her heir.[190]

On 17 November, early in the morning, as mass was being said, Queen Mary died. The news was taken to Pole, himself desperately ill in Lambeth Palace. He wept as he spoke of the close bond between them, where their shared kinship had been reinforced by 'a great conformity of spirit'.[191] Pole himself died later that same day. Elizabeth would allow his lying in state at Lambeth Palace for forty days before his funeral at Canterbury, where he was buried, at his own request, in the chapel where Becket's relics had once been kept.[192] Count Feria's brusque communication of the news to Philip II suggested that his death was not viewed as a great loss, presumably because of the accusations of heresy that had been levelled against him. At the time Pole died, his friend and fellow humanist Cardinal Morone was undergoing trial in Rome, the unwritten intention being to prevent any chance of his acceding to the papal throne.[193] Not long before he died, Pole had written to Paul IV, expressing his frustration and grief at Morone's treatment by the Holy See, and noting that a pope was never beyond reproach. He observed that 'it is clear not only that it is proper for cardinals to admonish a supreme pontiff freely, should they know that his actions are not of God but of men; in truth they must do this and use clear words, because if they do nothing, they will have to give Christ a good reason for it'.[194] Pole's own life had been devoted to the service of God and the regeneration of his Church. There were two funeral orations for him: the Latin one noted how he had so very nearly been made pope himself, but observed that God had been saving him for England and compared him to a second Augustine, sent to convert the English.[195]

Mary was accorded a lavish funeral by her half-sister, who asked Lord Treasurer Winchester to organize the ceremony, just as he had organized the funeral of Katherine of Aragon in Peterborough Abbey in 1536. The sermon was preached by John White, bishop of Winchester, and it was a *tour de force* which led to the bishop being imprisoned immediately afterwards, and within weeks deprived of his see by a furious Elizabeth. It set the tone for the events of 1558–59, which would see the new queen struggling against the implacability of the fervent Catholicism which Mary had done so much to revive and strengthen. In parliament, in the Church and in the universities, as well as more tacitly in the country as a whole, the scale of the resistance to Elizabeth's religious policies was a tribute to Mary's achievements. White praised her piety and her humanity: 'She used singular mercy towards offenders. She used much pity and compassion towards the poor and oppressed.' He also unleashed the full force of his scorn and condemnation of those who were traitors to the truth she had defended, and spoke to his noble audience in Westminster Abbey of

> this vertuous and gracious lady, this innocent and unspotted Queen: whose body lyeth there in your lap, whose livery is on your back, whose memory is or ought to be printed in your hearts: whose fame is spred throughout the world, whose praise the stones wil speak, if we do not; and whose soul I verily believe, without prejudice of God's judgement be it spoken, is now in heaven.

He sneered at those, 'men, perhaps, of great dignity and vocation, who dare not open their mouths and bark; but suffereth, while al goeth to ruin, the decay of Christian religion, and the subversion of the public wealth'. He knew only too well what was around the corner: 'the wolves be coming out of Geneva, and other places of Germany, and hath sent their books before, ful of pestilent doctrines, blasphemy, and heresy, to infect the people'; and he warned that a terrible fate awaited bishops and clergy if they 'should not give warning, neither withstand and resist, but for fear or flattery with the world, forsake their places, and therby give occasion to the wolf to enter, and devour the flock'.[196] It was a sermon almost entirely devoid of subtlety, flattery or political sense. White could see what was about to happen, and he was going to go down fighting.

Posterity may have mangled her reputation, but to a great many of her contemporaries, Mary was a ruler worthy of her ancestry. In her five years as queen, she worked to ensure that the kingdom was purged and inspired; her attempts to strengthen the social order were as much a part of her religion as the restoration of the mass. She was trying to put back together an entire way of life, and rebuild a community from without and from within. Her reign saw the last convincing embodiment of the ideal of Catholic Church and commonwealth. From this point onwards, the chance of a reunified society would fade away. Tudor England was looking towards a future of division, conflict and confusion.

CHAPTER 11

IMAGINING THE OTHER
EUROPE AND THE WIDER WORLD

In June 1553, as Edward VI lay dying and Mary was preparing to take the throne, three ships set sail for the Arctic, in search of a passage to the east. Richard Chancellor, captain of the *Edward Bonaventure*, reached the Russian port of St Nicholas on the White Sea, near what would eventually be Arkhangelsk, from where he decided to travel by land to the court of the tsar. He reached Moscow in the winter, secured a letter from Ivan IV granting permission for the English to trade in Muscovy, and returned home to present it to Queen Mary in 1554. The consequence was the creation of the Muscovy Company in 1555, and a return voyage by Chancellor to the Russian capital. He was not to return from this second expedition, drowning with most of his crew as he worked to save the life of the Russian ambassador, just off the Scottish coast, on his way back home in November 1556.[1] Chancellor left detailed accounts, however, of the Russian cities he had visited, the strange rules and rituals of the tsar's court, and the manner of warfare in Russia, notes carefully guarded by the Muscovy Company as an invaluable source of information until Hakluyt printed them in his *Principall Navigations* of 1589. The combination of ambition, danger, commercial aspiration and geographical miscalculation which shaped Chancellor's experiences is characteristic of Tudor attempts at exploration.

England's relationship with the wider world altered irrevocably from the 1550s onwards. Fluctuations in trade, which had up until then been mostly focused on northern Europe, necessitated reaching out for new connections, and trading networks were extended not just to Muscovy, but also to the Ottoman Empire, Persia, West Africa and Newfoundland.

Christendom itself was being pulled apart, as growing religious differences put pressure on international alliances, and England became involved in a succession of conflicts, prompting new developments in both diplomacy and espionage. The problem of Ireland, always complicated, took on new and alarming dimensions in the wake of the Reformation, as the largely Catholic Irish discovered a new reason to oppose English Protestant rule and settlement. There were shifts in perceptions of the wider world, as voyages of discovery encountered previously unknown lands, firing both imagination and ambition. Travel itself became a form of education: travellers' tales circulated widely and the English tried harder to learn foreign tongues.[2] European upheavals brought successive waves of immigrants to settle in England, as well as establishing English exile networks abroad. England's black community began to be more visible in the historical records, while the first lamentable steps were taken towards England's participation in the slave trade. As Europe slid ever further into religious conflict, issues of identity acquired a new level of urgency and England's interactions with the rest of the world were brought under intense scrutiny.

When Henry VIII came to the throne in 1509, he was content to draw on patterns from the past to configure England's place in Europe. In search of military glory, he made war on France, England's medieval foe, and tried to emulate the achievements of Henry V a century earlier. The chivalric aspirations of the past still seemed credible, and when the king proclaimed his imperial status, he was not thinking in terms of overseas conquest, but was seeking to emulate the Roman Emperor Constantine. By the end of the century, Spanish and Portuguese conquests overseas were modelling a very different pattern of empire, and England had begun taking tentative steps towards colonial competition with the Spanish, based more, however, on trade and Protestant values, than on colonization and Counter-Reformation zeal. These attempts remained fraught with difficulties and largely characterized by failure, but they laid the foundations for future developments. Most astonishing of all, between 1577 and 1580, Francis Drake sailed around the world, an achievement no less impressive for being unintended (see illustration 21).[3] By 1603, it was clear that England's place in the wider world was more complicated than ever before.

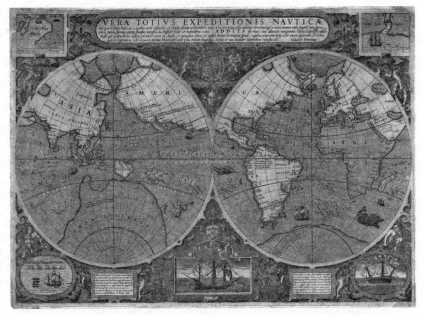

21. Map of the world showing Francis Drake's circumnavigation of the globe, by Jodocus Hondius, c.1590.

Perceptions and peoples

Tudor imagination grappled at some length with the dimensions of a wider world which was far out of reach of most people at the time. William Harrison noted that, where once the world had been divided into the three continents of Asia, Europe and Africa, as bequeathed by Noah to his three sons, nowadays it was necessary to take account of the newly discovered lands 'now called America'.[4] He argued for seeing Britain as part of Europe, although others would see it as more set apart. Holinshed's *Chronicle* had originally been conceived as a 'universall Cosmographie', although in the end it managed to encompass only the British Isles.[5] Thomas Smith described scholars studying other realms, as if 'we might flie from one countrie to another like byrdes, and yet with lesse travayle and daunger. Maye we not by cosmographie see the situation, temperature and qualities of everie countrie in the world?'[6] The first world atlas was published in Antwerp in 1579, Abraham Ortelius's *Theatrum Orbis Terrarum*.[7] Its English translator of 1601 described the world as a manifestation of the Almighty, 'surely a mirrour of moste great admyration, wherein the unsearchable scyence of the all-surpassing Artizan is to bee seene.'[8]

By the second half of the century, travel literature was supplementing the imaginative flights of cosmographers.[9] In 1589, Richard Hakluyt's *Principall Navigations, Voiages and Discoveries of the English nation* comprised three volumes: the first concerned the Middle East, India and Africa; the second looked north to Lapland, the Baltic and Russia; and the third concerned America, north and south.[10] Fynes Moryson, leaving Cambridge to travel in the 1590s, spent four years encountering Germany, Prague, Switzerland, the Netherlands, Denmark, Poland, Moravia, Austria and Italy, returning via France. A second journey to Jerusalem and Constantinople was undertaken with his younger brother Henry, who died in the Holy Land. Fynes Moryson's accounts of his travels, a wealth of knowledge, observation and prejudice, were published in 1617.[11] In 1599, George Abbot, the future archbishop of Canterbury, published *A Briefe Description of the whole worlde* – testimony to the intellectual optimism of a time when describing the whole world was seen as something that could be achieved briefly. For Abbot, America was a distant realm just opening up. Commenting on inland seas, he described the Dead Sea and the Caspian Sea, and then said 'and such a one is said to be in the North part of America'.[12] Much was still a mystery, but over the course of the sixteenth century, the world seemed to come a little closer.

Comparisons with other countries generally worked in favour of the English: 'in the lectorne of cosmography / The gyfte of nature in none more opulent / Than in Englande of noble memory', wrote Robert Saltwood, a Benedictine monk, in 1533.[13] The Venetian visitor noted waspishly in 1500 that 'the English are great lovers of themselves, and of everything belonging to them . . . whenever they see a handsome foreigner, they say that "he looks like an Englishman" and that "it is a great pity that he should not be an Englishman" and when they partake of any delicacy with a foreigner, they ask him, "whether such a thing is made in *their* country?" '[14] John Aylmer, the Elizabethan bishop who famously insisted that 'God is English', drew an impassioned comparison between the life of the English peasant and his counterparts in Italy, in the process rather failing to see the attractions of a Mediterranean diet:

We live in paradise. England is the paradise and not Italy, as commonlye they call it. For they have figges, Orenges, Pomgranates, Grapes, Pepons, Oyle, and herbes: and we have Shepe, Oxen, Kine, Calves, Conies, Fish, woll, Leade, Clothe, Tinne, Leather, and infinite treasures more, which they lacke.

Aylmer declared to his countrymen, 'if thou knewest thou Englishe man in what welth thou livest, and in how plentifull a Countrye: Thou wouldest vii times of the day fall flat on they face before God, and geve him thanks, that thou wart born an English man'.[15] This extravagant outburst of patriotism was a calculated plea to Aylmer's compatriots to fund the fortification and administration of the country by paying their taxes; it is hard to gauge how persuasive it might have seemed.

Comparisons were not always biased: the surgeon John Banister, writing in 1578, observed that Asians were 'fairer, greater, more gentle, fearful', compared with Europeans who were by contrast 'cruell, of hauty courage, bold, upright or honest, and given to warre'.[16] Moryson thought England could learn from German, Italian and Dutch examples. Reginald Pole, preaching in London in 1557, thought England compared poorly to Italy where 'there is more almes given to monasteryes and poore folks in one monthe, than yn this realme in a hole yeare'.[17] Elizabeth I was fluent in French, Italian and Spanish, as well as Latin and Greek, and enjoyed talking to her Italian musicians or welcoming foreign ambassadors in their own language.[18] Shakespeare set his plays in a range of Italian cities, and also in Ephesus, Navarre, Athens, Illyria, Sicily, Bohemia and Denmark, whilst Marlowe's *Tamburlaine* ranged widely across the East; several Elizabethan plays were set in Ottoman lands.[19] The wider world, it was clear to many, offered an abundance of imaginative possibilities. Despite this, xenophobia, or at least a wariness of foreigners, was frequently encountered in both theory and practice.[20] John Alcock, bishop of Ely, preaching in London in 1498, saw the vanities of youth as a cosmopolitan problem, observing gloomily that

ther is no vanyte in no partye of the worlde but we ben redy to bye it. Long heres and shorte collers of Almayns [Germans]. Evyll fasshened garmentes / and devyllysshe shoon and slyppers of Frensmen. Powches and paynted gyrdels of Spaynardes / newe founde hattes of Romayns.

Alcock was even-handed in his reproaches, however; he thought that the fickleness in fashion of the English should be a warning 'to all wyse straungers. That Englysshmen be as chaungable in theyr maners and wyttes as they be in outwarde garmentes'.[21] On the other hand, Ranulf Higden regarded it as a mark of England's greatness that it provided a haven for foreigners: 'that londe releveth straunge men that hath nede therto. And whan honger greveth other londes that londe fedeth them'.[22]

Myths and legends could also be reconfigured to fit new constructs of meaning. The legend of Prester John, a Christian emperor whose Eastern kingdom lay somewhere beyond the Muslim world, had had a place in European thought since the twelfth century.[23] Whilst he was once held to rule somewhere in India, by the sixteenth century Portuguese explorers were insisting that he ruled Ethiopia. The idea that he might espouse an ancient brand of Christianity that pre-dated the Roman Church was peculiarly attractive to Elizabethan Protestants. Abbot wrote of the 'dominion of Prester John' and of how his subjects were Christians 'in no sorte acknowledging any supreme prerogative of the Bishop of Rome. It is thought that they have retayned christianitie, even from the time of our Saviour'.[24] When Benedick in *Much Ado About Nothing* is desperate to escape Beatrice, he pleads with his prince to send him on a mission to the world's end, to bring a toothpick from the farthest reaches of Asia, or 'the length of Prester John's foot'.[25] The oddities and mysteries of foreign lands were an accepted phenomenon. In a work on horse-breeding, the author declared his intention to talk only of the horses known to him, demanding rhetorically

> what wold it availe you to heare (onles it were for noveltyes sake) that in some contreys there be horses no bigger than Rammes, and in some Countreis horses be made like Unicornes, in some Country agayne Mares do conceyve with the westerne wynde, without the helpe of any Stallion, whose Coltes do not live above three yeares.[26]

Some of the spectacles were man-made: William Thomas thought 'the mervailouse Situacion of the citee of Venice' a thing to wonder at, since in such an inhospitable marsh men had raised up a city not only populous, and 'riche of treasure and buildynges', but so wholesome 'that I thynke none other citte hable to shewe so many olde men'.[27] Lewis Lewkenor agreed, asking 'what ever hath the worlde brought forth more monstrously strange, then that so great and glorious a Citie should bee seated in the middle of the sea . . . such pallaces, monasteries, temples, towers, turrets and pinacles reaching up unto the cloudes, founded upon Quagmires'.[28]

The Reformation called all England's relationships with other countries into question in new ways. Hostility developed towards former allies, and xenophobic rhetoric took on a new edge in a climate of religious conflict. Roger Ascham, despite his debt to Renaissance learning, found it necessary in his book *The Scholemaster* of 1570 to condemn the corrupting effect of Italian culture upon the English.[29] He was quick to explain that he did not condemn 'the knowledge of strange and diuerse tonges', nor did he 'despise, the learning that is gotten, or the experience that is gathered in strange contries' and noted that Italy and Rome 'I haue always speciallie honored'. But Italy had turned sour for this particular humanist. 'Vertue once made that contrie Mistres ouer all the worlde. Vice now maketh that contrie slave to them, that before, were glad to serue it'.[30] He feared that a young man was likely to bring back from Italy papistry, ignorance, 'a factious hart' and 'plentie of new mischieves neuer knowne in England before'.[31] Much of this was caused by an excess of freedom, in cities 'where a man may freely discourse against what he will, against whom he lust – against any prince, against any government, yea, against God himself and his whole religion'.[32] Lewis Lewkenor, in 1595, gave similar treatment to the Spanish, depicting their cruelty and treachery, sodomy, blasphemy and murder.[33]

The circumstances of the sixteenth century drove many to encounter the wider world against their will, as significant numbers of English men and women were forced into exile for the sake of religion. If the Reformation broke old ties, therefore, it also formed new ones, and the inherent wariness of early Tudor society towards foreigners was modified by the realization of a common identity with Protestants or Catholics abroad. Protestant exiles from Henrician or Marian persecution found safety in German or Swiss cities such as Frankfurt and Geneva; Catholic exiles fled to Louvain, Douai or Rome. Many of the ties formed abroad were academic, but mercantile networks also helped sustain the movement of religious refugees. The Italian merchant banker Antonio Buonvisi had moved to England aged seventeen to work in the London branch of the family business, and had become a close friend of men such as Thomas More, Thomas Cromwell and a network of other humanist thinkers.[34] Finding Edward VI's reforms uncongenial, he left England, and his house in Louvain became a refuge for Catholic exiles and, in particular, home to Thomas More's extended family.[35] Rose Hickman, the Londoner whose Protestant faith was sustained by the import of books, alongside the other commodities that her father and husband traded, was able to take refuge in Antwerp because her family already owned property there.[36]

The experience of exile could be formative in many ways. It could be a time of loneliness and estrangement. Maurice Chauncy, formerly of the Carthusian house in London, wrote that finding co-religionists abroad was small consolation for the loss of his homeland. 'My soul refuses to be comforted in this manner', he avowed.[37] Richard Pate, formerly Henry VIII's ambassador to the Imperial Court, fled to Italy to escape the Henrician Reformation: he wrote to his friend Reginald Pole of their shared 'banishment' and compared it to 'the depths of hell'.[38] Such experiences could have a powerful radicalizing effect, and might impart particular rigour to doctrinal views.[39] At the same time, exiles found themselves putting down roots in foreign communities.[40] To mark the first clothing of English nuns at the Benedictine convent in Brussels, the Archdukes Albert and Isabella gave a grand feast in celebration.[41] Those who learned at first hand the rules of cohabitation with foreigners often, as a result, moved towards a more collaborative, even eirenical position. It has recently been argued that, rather than view exiles as passive victims of circumstance, we should appreciate the 'confessional mobility' of those who sought to build new lives and establish new networks abroad.[42] The ability to draw parallels between exile for religious causes and the wanderings of the Jewish people in the Old Testament could even make the experience of exile a positive asset in the construction of a religious identity.[43] Friendships were made, as well as broken, as a consequence of religious exile.

The movement of religious exiles could, of course, go in both directions. In England, the regime of Edward VI welcomed the influx of foreign Protestants as a potential source of religious inspiration.[44] Interest in religious developments abroad was intense; it was in 1549 that the term 'News' first appeared in a book title, in *Newes concernynge the general councell, holden at Trydent*; what was happening at the Council of Trent was of consequence to Protestant and Catholic alike.[45] The thought that Protestantism might prove usefully infectious led to substantial encouragement from the

Edwardian regime for the exiles, who in 1549 were given the church formerly belonging to the Austin Friars, under the superintendence of the Polish reformer Jan Łaski, sometimes called John a Lasco, who was given a generous stipend.[46] Religious connections helped establish ties of fraternity with these strangers from overseas.[47]

There would always be those who viewed foreigners with suspicion and latent hostility; and particularly in times of economic hardship or political instability, this might be roused to active animosity. This was the case with the 'Evil May Day' riots of 1517, caused chiefly by apprentices fired up by a preacher's suggestion that foreigners were taking their jobs, although no foreigner was killed on this occasion.[48] In general, however, foreign merchants, craftsmen, artisans and servants were accepted as a necessary and usually fruitful element within society.[49] The alien subsidy of 1485 was paid by around 1,600 resident foreigners, and by 1541 the number had risen to 2,500. Since this was a subsidy paid only by adult males, and many of those evaded it, the estimate is that there were over twice as many foreigners resident in England as paid the tax. These numbers were swelled by the tide of religious refugees, perhaps as many as 50,000 in the sixteenth century.[50] In the 1520s, foreigners came under the control of the London livery companies, with privileges for those prepared to formally register as 'denizens', which enabled them to ply their craft in London and lease property. In 1544, under the shadow of war with France, a proclamation was issued commanding all Frenchmen who were not yet denizens to either register or leave. Of the three thousand or so who registered at this point, many had been resident in England for many years.[51] In a pattern that would be recognizable in later centuries, most of the immigrant population was concentrated in the eastern parts of London and by the waterfront, with only wealthy foreign goldsmiths and a handful of merchants settled in the more prosperous areas. Immigrants, especially from France and the Netherlands – mostly Protestants fleeing persecution – settled in Norwich, Canterbury, Colchester and Sandwich, in particular. A petition in 1599 described them as having 'abandoned and left all together with their native Countries, and betaken themselves to handy labours according to Gods word, under the wings of her Majesties most gracious protection'.[52] In 1583, apart from four thousand living in the city of London, there were 'great nombers of Strangers' in the suburbs of Westminster, Southwark, Newington and Lambeth.[53]

Norwich in 1571, according to the census, had 868 Dutchmen, 203 Walloons, 1,173 women of both and 1,681 children, of whom 666 had been born in England.[54] Colchester had two Dutchmen serving as town counsellors during Elizabeth's reign; and in Great Yarmouth, where the Dutch immigrants were fishermen, they were said to 'live godly and orderly . . . behave themselves quietly' and 'apply their fishing to the benefit of that town'.[55]

Some immigrants came from as far away as Africa. Contrary to easy assumptions, black people in England during the Tudor years were not slaves: contact between England and West Africa at this point was predominantly concerned with trade in gold, spices and ivory.[56] The black trumpeter John Blanke (or Blak) is pictured on the manuscript roll that recorded the 1511 tournament to celebrate Henry VIII's first-born, but short-lived son (see plate 16).[57] The diver Jacques Francis was one of a chiefly Venetian team hired to salvage valuable articles from the *Mary Rose* after she sank in 1545, and was prized and well paid for his skills. When cited as a witness in a court case of 1549, his Italian detractors tried to dismiss his words on the grounds that he was an infidel and a slave, but his testimony was accepted by the English court as that of a free man.[58] The number of 'black Tudors' was small, but the way in which they were discussed by contemporaries shows early modern society grappling with the issue of racial difference. Before 1558, the archival traces are minimal, but there was a small black community near the Court in Westminster.[59] These were not necessarily people of low status: Peter Negro, a Spanish mercenary whom some historians have identified as black, was knighted on the battlefield in 1547, and it is possible that he may have been in part the inspiration for Othello.[60]

Some reactions to black people were hostile. Thomas More wrote to a friend in 1501, commenting on the Spanish escort that had arrived with Katherine of Aragon, which included people of colour. 'Except for three, or at most the four of them, they were just too much to look at: hunchbacked, undersized, barefoot Pygmies from Ethiopia. If you had been there, you would have thought they were refugees from hell.'[61] On the whole, however, there seems to have been a measure of acceptance and toleration of racial difference.[62] Tax records from the 1580s show a possible black Dutch shoemaker, Charles Negroe, living as a professional artisan in London. Meanwhile, parish registers suggest several possible inter-racial marriages, and record the black family of Resonabell Blackman.[63] Mary Fillis from Morocco lived in London for thirteen or more years, before being baptized a Christian at St Botolph's, Aldgate. Bristol and the West Country, with their mercantile interests, seem to have been home to several people of colour: the legacy of the Hawkins family, and its activities in Africa, seems to have been a number of black people living in Devon, and a black man in charge of Sir John Young's garden in Bristol was referenced in a court case in 1560.[64]

Giles Fletcher, ambassador to Moscow in 1588, wrote an account of the 'Tyrannical state' he had encountered there.[65] Dedicating his book to Elizabeth I, he deplored Russia as a land 'most unlike to your own', being 'without true knowledge of GOD, without written Lawe, without common iustice'. He piously observed that seeing 'the poore oppressed people, that liue within those Countreyes' made him all the more grateful that Elizabeth was 'a Prince of subiectes, not of slaues, that are kept within duetie by loue, not by feare'.[66] As his work unfolded, however, his discussions of commonwealth and corruption showed how the Elizabethan mind might use descriptions of other polities to reflect on their own political challenges.[67] Roger Ascham, reflecting on the torrid political scene in the Holy Roman Empire in the early 1550s, congratulated himself on living 'under such a Prince, as kyng *Edward* is, and in such a countrey as England is'.[68] Encounters with other lands could sometimes, however, provide food for more constructive thought. The Polish–Lithuanian Commonwealth, for example, provided a fascinating example of both elective monarchy and religious toleration.[69] A treatise by a Polish bishop and statesman supportive of a mixed constitution was published in English as *The Counsellor* in 1598, at a time when ideas about a mingling of monarchist and republican ideas were of great interest to some among the political classes.[70] Conversely, the difficulties caused by Henry, duke of Anjou, elected king of Poland in 1573, only to desert Poland to become king of France, were a warning of the volatility that elective monarchy might bring.[71] Meanwhile alongside the Jews, Armenians and Muslims within Poland–Lithuania were Catholic exiles from England, as well as Anabaptists, Mennonites, Hussites and others fleeing persecution in other parts of Europe. The Polish–Lithuanian Commonwealth had six official languages: Polish, Latin, Ruthenian, Hebrew, Armenian and German.[72] These were examples which gave pause for thought.

Venice proved a particular inspiration to many Tudor commentators. Prosperous, civilized and above all stable, the republic of Venice 'hath contynuyd above a thousand yerys in one ordur and state', and its people were 'as helthy and welthy as any pepul now I thynke lyvyng', wrote Thomas Starkey, in his imaginary dialogue between Thomas Lupset and Reginald Pole.[73] Starkey's work was not published in his lifetime, but others echoed his approval. The model of a working republic that managed to sustain the dignity of its oligarchs alongside its fabled prosperity was a thought-provoking example, particularly to those already enthused by republican ideals, which were influential in England from early in the sixteenth century.[74] A 1543 account by the Venetian Cardinal Gasparo Contarini was published in translation in 1599 by Lewis Lewkenor as *The Commonwealth and Government of Venice*, praising a state where the ruler is 'wholy subiected to the lawes'.[75] The attractions of a polity that was ruled on the basis of a consensus between rich nobles might not, for the modern observer, imme-diately evoke the 'Democrasie or popular estate' which Tudor commentators commended, but they were an immediate draw for the educated men of the sixteenth century.[76] William Thomas, in his *Historie of Italie*, described Venice's Great Council in approving terms, as akin to the English parlia-ment. In the process, he rather overstated the role of that parliament, but then Thomas's strong Protestant convictions inclined him towards repub-lican notions; he was eventually executed for involvement in Wyatt's rebel-lion.[77] Lewkenor's translation of Contarini rejoiced in how Venice's monarchical government was 'so curbed and restrained with lawes, that all dangerous inconveniences, whereby the commonwealth might sustain harme, are thereby removed', leaving it 'enjoying a true libertie and freedome, and yet neverthelesse as it were a king for our governour'.[78] This might have significant undertones in the closing years of Elizabeth's reign.

Encounters with strange lands could breed some cautious acceptance of cultural difference. Moryson was even able to register that Catholic art might be appreciated for its own sake, albeit with some wariness; he noted that the images of the Virgin Mary and the Crucifixion in one of the churches in Lübeck 'are thought workes of singular art', although he was not entirely persuaded by the former.[79] Roger Ascham, despite his Protestant zeal, was able to record a conversation with the Venetian ambas-sador, who told me that the great Turke him selfe (Religion excepted) is a good and mercyfull, just and liberall Prince, wise in makyng and true in performyng any covenant, and as sore a revenger of troth not kept. He prayed God to kepe him long alive: for his eldest sonne Mustapha is cleane contrary.[80]

Moryson also thought little of Wittenberg, despite its Lutheran connections, recording the proverb that a man should meet nothing there 'but whores, students, and swine ... Whence may be gathered that the Citizens have small trafficke, living only upon the Schollers, and that the streets must needs be filthy'. Luther's house was open to view, and Moryson noted the fraudulent inscription which claimed that Luther had died there. He related the Jesuit slanders about Luther having died when drunk, but he also listed the fictions told by the townsfolk about their most famous citizen, deriding the tale of 'an aspersion of inke, cast by the Divell when he tempted Luther', which he thought far-fetched.[81] At a time when Europe was riven with religious conflict, interactions with the wider world could produce the tentative conclusion that what lay at the root of all this enmity was not doctrinal error, so much as an inclination towards aggression more generally. Erasmus, who had lived in the Netherlands, Paris, Italy, England and various parts of the Empire, deplored Protestantism for its belligerence, but Roger Ascham, reflecting on European conflict in the early 1550s, thought that the primary cause of it was unkindness: 'Religion and libertie were sayd to be of many men the very causes of all these sturres: yet in myne opinion and as the matter it selfe shall well proue it, vnkyndnes was the very sede, whereof all these troubles dyd grow'.[82]

To foreign observers, events in England proved fascinating and foreboding by turns, and foreign opinion was important enough for different regimes to invest in propaganda to be spread abroad.[83] Johannes Opicius produced a Latin verse account of Henry VII's invasion of France in 1492 (his brother Benedictus crafted a presentation manuscript of music for Henry VIII and Katherine of Aragon).[84] Within a short period of the break with Rome, it became a commonplace to view England as a land of heretics.[85] Pole asked rhetorically of Henry VIII, 'Should I tell you that no word is mentioned more frequently in conversation than your tyranny and impiety? Should I tell you that not only in barber shops but in every gathering of men you are reproached in the words of men of high and low rank?'[86] The brief reunion with Rome during Mary I's reign was a cause for rejoicing across the continent, with publications in Latin, Italian, Spanish, Dutch and German celebrating the event.[87] After 1558, the English were once more viewed with alarm and hostility in Catholic Europe; Fynes Moryson learned to avoid eye contact, act with deference and keep his money out of sight; perhaps wise precautions for any traveller, but he also kept his religious convictions hidden. Print shops across the continent sold accounts of the Tudor succession crises and the upheavals of religious change and persecution. The challenges, as well as the technologies, of the sixteenth century had taught England and its foreign counterparts to be increasingly attentive to both the similarities and differences between them.

Tudor men and women tended to share the view that the natural world was a theatre in which humankind might discern the mind of God at work. To encounter the wider world and explore the globe, therefore, was not just a route to commercial profit or political dominion, it was also an encounter with the divine. As one influential work describing the new world explained on its title page, here was an account in which

> the diligent reader may not only consyder what commoditie may hereby chaunce to the hole christian world in tyme to come, but also learne many secreates touchynge the lande, the sea, and the starres, very necessarie to be knowen to al such as shal attempte any navigations, or otherwise have delite to beholde the strange and woonderfull woorkes of God and nature.[88]

The exploration of the globe raised questions of divine providence, human morality and self-knowledge. By the Elizabethan period, when commentators at home were grappling with issues of political stability and succession, discussions of other countries became a way of judging problems closer to home. To this end, the blurring of the boundary between fact and fiction was relatively unimportant. The first English book to mention the New World was a translation in 1509 of Sebastian Brandt's *Das Narrenschiff*, in English *The Ship of Fools*, which was largely a moral fable; seven years later, Thomas More's *Utopia* was a fiction which drew inspiration from the voyages of discovery to discuss the immediate and pressing difficulties and moral dilemmas of the early Tudor state.[89] The examples of other lands and cultures allowed singular and significant insights into England's own issues.

Trade and empire

When Tudor ships set sail to encounter the world outside England, it was not colonies they sought, but commerce. When encountering a new country, one of the first questions asked would be about the products that might conceivably be exported to England or traded elsewhere. Giles Fletcher, giving an account of Russia, put 'furres of all sortes' at the top of his list of the country's 'commodities', with the pious observation that here 'the providence of God is to be noted, that provideth a naturall remedie' for the Russians to counter 'the colde of the Clymat'. He then listed wax, honey, tallow, leather, seal oil, flax, hemp, salt, tar and a kind of thin stone good for lanterns.[90] John Browne's *The marchants aviso* in 1589 gave scrupulously exact descriptions of different commodities, for the benefit of Bristol merchants: he wrote of pepper, for example, that if it was 'very black of colour and the dust of it moist and sticking to your fingers then hath it taken wet and is not so good'.[91] It was not dreams of empire, but the troubles of the cloth trade and the increasing market for luxury goods that encouraged London merchants to reach out into the Eastern Mediterranean and that drove Bristol merchants to invest in speculative expeditions to Morocco, Guinea and Benin.[92] In 1553, as the three English ships set sail for the Arctic sea in search of a passage to Asia, another three ships set out from Portsmouth bound for the west coast of Africa to find gold, ivory and pepper. These voyages would later be invested with significance for the expansion of England's political interests overseas; but at the time, what they sought, with the backing of the mercantile community, was profit. Even those most beguiled by notions of conquest were still at root entrepreneurs.[93] This was not so much empire-building as fortune-hunting.

At the start of the period, trading activity was already energetic. Ranulf Higden in the mid-fourteenth century had described England in terms of her trading links, in a work printed by William Caxton in the early Tudor period. 'Flaundres loveth well the wulle of this londe. And holand the skynnes and felles of alle maner of bestes / Guyan [Guienne] the yron and the leed / Irlonde the oor and the salte / Alle Europe loveth and desireth the whyte metall of this londe.'[94] One of the first books ever published in England was Caxton's 1480 phrasebook in French and English. Among the essentials of both languages was all the vocabulary a merchant might need, concerning cloth and wool, towns and fairs, promising that 'who this booke shall wylle lerne / May well entreprise or take on honde / Marchandises fro one land to anothir'.[95] Caxton, who had himself lived in Bruges and learned the printing trade in Cologne, knew what life was like for England's merchants. His book was full of shrewd and pithy phrases with which to do business; it also provided the necessary words for merchants who had long-standing acquaintances in foreign lands, to which they returned regularly.

Trade in this period was highly variable in its patterns, moving from one city to another in response to trade disputes or political tensions. Moryson found the citizens of Hamburg 'unmeasurably ill affected to the English', to the extent that 'it is unsafe to walke out of the gates after noone, for when the common people are once warmed with drinke, they are apt to doe them iniury'.[96] Their grievance was that the English had relocated their trade from Hamburg to the nearby city of Stade. Perhaps the single most significant turning point was the closure of Antwerp to English merchants at two different points in the 1560s. Antwerp had long been the pivot on which the English cloth trade turned, and the realization that it could no longer be relied upon was a formative influence in directing English trading activities elsewhere.[97] By the 1570s, England was trading with long-standing partners in the Low Countries, France, Germany and the Baltic, and further afield in the Mediterranean. It had established new trading links with Russia and Persia, and from 1581 the new English Turkey Company was trading with the Ottoman Empire, which at this point was the world's largest empire, stretching from Hungary to Saudi Arabia, from Egypt to Iraq. The Muscovy Company was given its first charter in 1555, and in 1592 the Levant Company was set up to regulate trade with the Ottoman Empire and the Levant. On the last day of the century, 31 December 1600, the East India Company was founded, which would in time account for half the world's trade. A merchant could have some extraordinary experiences: Anthony Jenkinson, born and brought up in Market Harborough, saw Suleiman the Magnificent ride into Aleppo at the head of his conquering armies, travelled to the Caspian Sea and to Persia, and was acquainted with Ivan the Terrible, ruler of Muscovy.[98]

Africa saw an increasing number of expeditionary forays during Elizabeth's reign. This led to Tudor England's first encounter with the slave trade. In 1597, Abraham Hartwell published *A Reporte of the Kingdome of Congo*, a translation from the Portuguese work by Edoardo Lopez. This work spoke of trade with the Cape Verde islands, noting in a matter-of-fact way how the Portuguese traded various products, such as cloth, caps and knives, and how in 'exchaunge whereof they bringe back again, slaves, wax, hony, with other kind of food, and cotton-cloth of sundry colours'.[99] Portuguese merchants were also trading slaves from West Africa, and had been doing so since the fifteenth century; by 1539, over ten thousand Africans were trafficked each year through Lisbon.[100] It was here, lured by the profits made by the Portuguese, that England's slave trade had its origins, for in 1562 John Hawkins, from a well-established Bristol mercantile family, decided on a venture to ship enslaved Africans to the Caribbean.[101]

The Tudor involvement in the trading of slaves remained small. It was not until a century later that Britain would see any large-scale involvement, and British trade in slaves would not reach its heights until the eighteenth century. There were fewer than thirty voyages to Guinea in the sixteenth century, and the vast majority of these did not deal in slaves.[102] Nevertheless, John Hawkins was responsible for several hundred slaves trafficked in three voyages in the 1560s. The trade was fuelled by the speed of expansion in the New World, where Spanish and Portuguese colonists sought cheap labour to establish their settlements and work in their mines. Hispaniola, Cuba and Jamaica were some of the destinations for those enslaved and shipped. The profits were such that Hawkins conceived the ambition of emulating their ventures. In this he was evading the law, since Spanish licences were needed to trade with the New World; but much of this business was, in any case, of dubious legality even by the laws of the time.[103] In 1562, he landed in Sierra Leone, captured three hundred inhabitants and sailed for Hispaniola. He traded the slaves for hides, ginger, sugar and pearls, and returned having made a substantial profit. A second voyage also yielded profit, sufficient to win him an invitation to Court and a knighthood; his coat of arms displayed a golden lion walking over the waves, with a crest of a black man bound and captive. Hawkins' ships included one named the *Jesus* and another the *Angel*, and his sailing orders for the second voyage included the injunction, 'Serve God daily; love one another, and keep good company'; he seems to have had no conception that what he was doing might be regarded as morally wrong.[104] He returned to other forms of trade only because his third voyage failed, owing to a combination of storms and Spanish aggression.

The conception of slavery as an evil was present in the minds of some of his contemporaries. William Harrison declared that England had no 'slaves and bondmen', since 'if any come hither from other realms, so soon as they set foot on land they become so free of condition as their masters'. Slavery also could not be overt, because the papacy had granted a monopoly on trading in slaves to the Portuguese, and the Elizabethan regime did not want either to challenge this openly or to compromise its claim to moral superiority over the Catholic powers.[105] Nevertheless, Hawkins commanded significant backing from the queen and others, and in his first two voyages made considerable profit. When his near-contemporary Fynes Moryson encountered the slave trade in the Ottoman Empire, by contrast, he was sickened. He described the merchants who bought and sold slaves 'using no Compassion to noble, or aged persons, or to tender women and children', and wrote with disgust of how 'faire women and boyes suffer fowle prostitutions, the strong men are used to grinde in mills, to beare heavy burthens and to doe all base and laborious woorkes'. He also wrote with horror of the merchants 'forcing the sick and weake with whips to march as fast as the rest, or els cutt their throates if they be not able to goe'.[106] These appeals to humanity and decency circulated during the same period as Hawkins was seeking profit through the selling of slaves.

The translator and alchemist Richard Eden's most famous work was a 1555 translation of a work by Pietro Martire d'Anghiera, rendered in English as *The Decades of the newe worlde of west India*, which compared the achievements of the Spanish explorers to those of the classical heroes of old.[107] At this point Philip II of Spain was also king of England, and Eden's lavish admiration of the Spanish was probably largely sycophancy; but his enthusiasm for the work of exploration was unfeigned.[108] Eden praised the Spaniards for the good they had done to the natives of the newly discovered lands, implausibly suggesting that 'theyr mercyfull warres ageynst these naked people' had actually benefited those defeated more than they had the victors. This was an early statement of the self-serving idea that colonial subjugation of indigenous people could have a civilizing effect. 'Theyr bondage is suche as is much rather to be desired then theyr former libertie which was to the cruell Canibales rather a horrible licenciousnesse then a libertie.' He thought the Spaniards had improved things immeasurably, 'partely by the slaughter of suche as coulde by no meanes be brought to civilitie, and partly by reservynge such as were overcome in the warres, and confertynge them to a better mynde'.[109] Such rhetoric sat uncomfortably with the views of other commentators seeking to denigrate the Spanish. Hakluyt, for instance, dwelt on their 'moste outragious and more than Turkishe cruelties in all the west Indies', while Raleigh noted them acting 'contrarie to all naturall humanitie'.[110] Notions of what constituted humane behaviour could vary wildly according to ulterior motive, and racial stereotypes remained inchoate. Some treated people of colour with the same kindly condescension as they used towards all foreigners. Some thought black skin was caused by climate; George Best argued that it must result from some infection, on the basis that he had seen 'an Ethiopian as blacke as a cole broughte into Englande, who taking a faire Englishe woman to Wife, begatte a Sonnee in all respects as blacke as the Father was'; it is notable that he made no further comment on this inter-racial match.[111] Probably the most dangerous ideas of the age were not the theoretical, but the practical ones. Hawkins launched his slave voyages on the back of the proven profitability of such a trade, rather than on any notion of racial superiority, but that in no way lessened the impact of his activities.

Not until the reign of James VI and I would the first permanent English settlement overseas be established at Jamestown, Virginia. England's earliest attempts at colonization all ended in failure. Indeed, most of England's overseas ventures before 1603 were unsuccessful.[112] Still, it is impossible to separate the history of trade from the early history of empire, because the two were so closely interwoven. The primary impetus was the thought of financial profit and commercial interest, which is why the backers for such ventures were predominantly drawn from the mercantile community.[113] Many of the earliest foundations for overseas colonies were based on the activities of adventurers or 'privateers', whom it was difficult to differentiate from pirates.[114] In so far as limited investment was forthcoming from different regimes, this was usually with a view to financial profit also, and the major spur to exploration remained the difficulties experienced by the cloth trade in the middle years of the century. When Anthony Jenkinson of the Muscovy Company voyaged to Lebanon and the Holy Land, to Persia, Syria and Norway, as well as to visit Ivan IV, it was not because he had grown up in Leicestershire full of ambition to see the world; rather, he felt he owed it to his backers to develop new commercial opportunities for their trading company.

The monarchy did, from time to time, supply encouragement and funds. Henry VII made a modest contribution to John Cabot's voyage in 1497, which was intended to reach China, but in fact landed in Newfoundland.[115] Cabot had been building a harbour in Valencia in 1493 when Columbus passed through, and perhaps was fired by his achievements; but more pragmatically, he knew that Bristol merchants were interested in exploration as a way of defending their fishing trade against the domination of northern European waters by the Hanseatic League. Henry VII gave a gift of £10 'to hym that founde the new Isle', and a pension of £20 per year – significant sums, but still not huge, and the pension was to come out of Bristol's customs revenues.[116] Bristol continued to invest in voyages to Newfoundland, but for a voyage of exploration to engender serious excitement, and therefore investment, it needed to promise the discovery of precious metals, not just cod.[117] Cabot's twelve-year-old son Sebastian went with him on his first voyage to Newfoundland, but in so far as he followed in his father's rather unsuccessful footsteps, it was under Spanish patronage. That said, he always claimed to be an English citizen, and in 1547 the Privy Council paid him £100 to return to England, and granted him a yearly pension of £166.[118] This flicker of enthusiasm under Edward VI was short-lived, however. Elizabethan backing also remained fairly minimal. Hawkins' voyage of 1567 to exploit the possibilities of the Caribbean had two out of its six ships supplied by Elizabeth I; but, like everything Hawkins did, it was teetering on the edge of piracy, and the government was quick to draw back and issue denials when it became diplomatically awkward.[119] Nor did royal backing necessarily signal imperial ambition: the political benefits for the Elizabethan regime were largely understood to be the needling of the Spanish, and the main hope was some kind of financial windfall. The gold and silver which Spanish ships were bringing back across the Atlantic exerted a fascination for seafarers and their backers to a disproportionate extent.

England's efforts in this direction were frequently disastrous. Frobisher's voyage in pursuit of the North-West Passage resulted in him bringing home vast quantities of ore, which was ultimately – after significant efforts regarding smelting – discovered to be valueless. In other words, his spoils consisted of ships full of useless rock – plus three Inuits, who died disconsolate in Bristol. On the other hand, Drake's expedition of 1577, another combination of exploration and outright piracy, led to him capturing gold, silver, jewels, Chinese silks and porcelain, buying 6 tons of cloves from the sultan of the Philippines, and returning home after three years, having inadvertently sailed around the world.[120] Elizabeth I may have knighted him, but she also had to smooth over the diplomatic incident he had caused with the Spanish, who were requiring restitution for their plundered gold. The queen countered by demanding restitution for the Spanish troops who had been sent to Ireland: given that the troops had been massacred by the English at Smerwick in 1580, this showed considerable cheek. She rejected Spanish claims to the New World, commenting dismissively that: 'The Spaniards have no claims to property there except that they have established a few settlements and named rivers and capes.'[121]

A few went beyond just the profit motive and dreamt of empire in terms of conquest and glory.[122] Eden thought the overseas expansion of the Spaniards 'shewed a good example to all Christian nations to follow', and compared the less intrepid English to sheep.[123] Hakluyt, in 1582, deplored England's lack of initiative as he addressed Philip Sidney, marvelling

that since the discovery of America (which is now full fourscore and ten years), after so great conquests and plantings of the Spaniards and Portingales there, that we of England could never have the grace to set fast footing in such fertile and temperate places as are left as yet unpossessed of them.[124]

Such enthusiasts were clear that when England did establish a colony of its own, it would be on loftier principles than those of the gold-hungry and papist Spanish. The strongest voices raised in support of expansion were zealous Protestant ones, although William Cecil's vision got no further than encompassing Scotland and Ireland, in order to build a Protestant Britain.[125] His ideas were echoed in *Toxophilus* by Roger Ascham, who noted how

England and Scotland shared 'one God, one faythe, one compasse of the see, one land and countrie, one tunge in speakynge, one maner in trade in lyvynge, lyke courage and stomake in war'.[126] Abraham Hartwell, describing the Congo in 1597, told the dedicatee, Archbishop John Whitgift, that he had published his book to admonish

> such valiant english, as do earnestly thirst and desire to atchieve the conquest of rude and barbarous Nations, that they doo not attempt those actions for commodity of Gold and Silver, and for other transitorie or worldly respectes, but that they woulde first seeke the Kingdome of God, and the salvation of many thousand soules.[127]

Most of these ideas remained intensely impractical. John Dee's writings in support of empire have long been considered to presage later imperial expansion; but he was, in fact, envisaging the creation of an apocalyptic empire, in part achieved by magical means and inspired by Arthurian legend, which would be ecumenical and absolute, and which bore only superficial resemblance to the commercial and libertarian empire envisaged by later commentators.[128]

The history of the colony of Roanoke in North Carolina is particularly symptomatic of the failures of early English colonialism.[129] When Elizabeth I granted a charter to Sir Humphrey Gilbert in 1578 – and, after his death, bestowed it jointly on his brother Adrian Gilbert and Walter Raleigh – it was more a speculative move than a strategic one.[130] Raleigh's instructions were vague in their exhortation to him to seek out 'remote heathen and barbarous Lands', and it was envisaged that his efforts might establish a privateering base, but not a colonial settlement. It was only after the successful return of the first exploratory voyage, with its description of fertile land and friendly natives, that Elizabeth knighted Raleigh and despatched him to found Virginia. But even then, Raleigh had to find his own investors to provide financial backing. The chief financial gain from the expedition was tangential, coming from a Spanish galleon which the maritime adventurer Sir Richard Grenville captured near Bermuda on his way home from Roanoke. A second attempt to establish a colony – this time at Chesapeake Bay – saw the settlement struggle to remain viable. The governor John White, who was also an artist and cartographer, sailed back to England to seek help in 1587. However, the threat of the Spanish Armada led to a ban on any shipping leaving the country, in order to avoid weakening England's defences. When a relief party finally arrived at the settlement three years later, there were no colonists to be found. This sad story indicates how little priority the government accorded to laying the foundations of empire.

'The state of the world is marvellously changed'

International relations in the early modern period were as fragile, divisive and changeable as they have proved to be ever since. It would be hard to assert that there were any clear rules governing Tudor foreign policy, although certain continuities remained visible throughout the period. Commercial links with the Netherlands were vital to England's trade, and centuries of animosity between England and Scotland meant the borders were frequently a site of conflict. The strategic significance of the English Channel for communications between the Habsburg lands in Spain and those in the Netherlands gave Spain a good reason for preserving the alliance with England, while the long history of Anglo-French conflict and the ancient English claims to territory in France meant that it was easy to find justifications for aggression against France. There was also a broader principle underlying all military and diplomatic endeavours: successful kingship appealed to a code of honour rooted in chivalry, and both status and wealth were frequently based on military achievement and skill. Nevertheless, between 1485 and 1603, England's relations with its neighbours underwent some significant alterations. In 1485, Henry VII's fortunes were closely tied to the politics of northern Europe, and his immediate concerns were to maintain profitable ties with Burgundy, a defensive position against Scotland and an advantageous relationship with France, whether through peace or war. It was a delicate balancing act, which aimed at minimizing the threat of any foreign-backed pretender, whilst maximizing trading links – and seizing the opportunity for successful military action whenever it fleetingly presented itself. It was, however, clearly conceived and allowed Henry to pursue fairly consistent objectives. A century later, the map of Europe had been redrawn by war, dynastic marriage, trade and the fruits of seaborne exploration, but above all by religious conflict and the hardening of confessional hostilities. Henry VII's greatest international success lay in securing an alliance with Ferdinand and Isabella, the rulers of Aragon and Castile; his granddaughter's most significant international moment would be the defeat of the Spanish Armada despatched by Ferdinand and Isabella's great-grandson, Philip II of Spain.

In 1485, Henry VII owed his own personal survival to his ability to play off Breton and French interests against one another, and his subsequent foreign policy traded on the long-standing tension between France and Burgundy. At this point, Europe had many autonomous or semi-autonomous duchies and principalities to complicate the international balance of power. Brittany was joined to France by marriage in 1491, however, and was gradually absorbed into the kingdom of France. The duchy of Burgundy was connected with the wider Habsburg cause when Charles of Burgundy also became king of Spain in 1516, and then Holy Roman Emperor in 1519. The kingdoms of Castile and Aragon, linked only by dynastic union during Henry VII's reign, would emerge as the kingdom of Spain in the sixteenth century, and in the 1580s would absorb Portugal, too, into the growing Iberian Empire. Across Europe, configurations were changing, and in many places kingdoms were coalescing into larger and more assertive polities. Not only did this prompt a rearrangement of old alliances, but it also raised the stakes of international warfare. A major complicating factor came in the 1530s, when Henry VIII broke away from the papacy, presenting any Catholic power with an unassailable justification for making war on England. In the reign of Elizabeth, activities by various Protestant groupings in Scotland, the Netherlands and France established a common cause between them and the fledgling Church of England. English interventions helped secure regime change in Scotland in the 1560s; they also made a significant contribution to the revolt of the Netherlands, which would end in Dutch independence, partly declared in 1581 and partly secured by 1609. In France, the situation was even more complicated, and the plight of the Huguenots was keenly felt by the English, but without conclusive intervention.

If the religious wars of the sixteenth century were a cause of deep anxiety, also troubling were the encounters with an Ottoman Empire bent on expansion, which swept up and down the Mediterranean and, on land, reached as far as the gates of Vienna in 1529. The successful defence of Malta against the Ottomans in 1565 by the Knights Hospitaller was celebrated in England: the letter announcing the victory was translated into

English and printed, and special prayers of thanksgiving were ordered to be said for six weeks, on Sundays, Wednesdays and Fridays, throughout the archdiocese of Canterbury.[131] The drama of this defeat of a great army by a much smaller band of defenders was underlined by the writer of the letter listing his terrible injuries, as well as the list of those who died. The Knights Hospitaller had been evicted from their home on Rhodes in 1522; they would henceforth be known as the Knights of Malta, and they were Catholics. Yet in the prayer commanded by the archbishop of Canterbury, they were described as 'our christian bretherne' and 'the afflycted and distressed christians in the Isle of Malta'. The divisions left by the Reformation were here eroded by the greater threat posed by those 'most deadly and cruell enemies, Turkes, and Infidels'.[132]

In 1541, Suleiman the Magnificent renewed his campaign against the Habsburgs and attacked Hungary, capturing Buda and aiming to conquer the rest of the country. Henry VIII agreed to send £10,000 to assist, and sought to raise the money from his subjects by means of parish collections. It was, in effect, a call to support a crusade. The archbishop of Canterbury suggested to the bishop of London that the churchwardens of each parish should make an appeal every Sunday and holy day, 'in the tyme of service when the number of the people ys greatteste'.[133] Despite the oddity that Henry was here allying with Charles V, who had so roundly condemned his break with Rome, and the added peculiarity that the Ottomans were in alliance with the French, the official exhortation to be read aloud in the parishes was a model of indignant Christian solidarity, warning that 'the barbarous and cruell enemye of Chrystendome, the Turke' not only intended pillage and slaughter, but also 'to subverte and extynguysshe the true relygion of Chryste, and brynge in the false and dyvylyshe persuasion of Mahomet, his fantastycall prophecte'.[134] By the end of the century, however, the logic of shifting alliances would prompt Elizabeth to reach out the hand of friendship to the Ottomans, as fellow antagonists of the Spanish: when the English ambassador to Istanbul William Harborne proposed a united effort, he cast it as an attempt to defeat Philip II 'and all the other idolators'.[135] The relationship between religious identity and national interest was always a complex one.

An older view of Tudor foreign policy trumpeted some vainglorious and largely inaccurate assertions, namely that it was in the sixteenth century that the foundations of future imperial power were established, as maritime strength was consolidated and a sense of 'British' identity was forged. It was suggested that Tudor England began to stand apart from the rest of Europe, in an intimation of future greatness. Subsequent study pointed out how often Tudor foreign policy was nothing more than a series of *ad hoc* responses to often unforeseen developments, with few underlying principles. If there was ideology at work, it revolved less around nationalistic or expansionist ideas, and more around religious identity. If England did become more isolated from Europe in the sixteenth century, it was because Henry VIII's break with Rome put it at odds with the great Catholic powers (which might otherwise have remained its natural allies), whilst the peculiarities of English Protestantism did not help it build connections with other Protestant nations strategically ill-placed to be English allies. By the end of the sixteenth century, there was a clear sense of how far international relations had been transformed. William Cecil observed in 1589:

> The state of the world is marvellously changed, when we true Englishmen have cause for our own quietness to wish good success to a French King and a King of Scots; and yet they both differ one from the other, in profession of religion; but seeing both are enemies to our enemies, we have cause to join with them in their actions against our enemies.[136]

Certainly, at the start of Elizabeth's reign in 1559 the age-old threat from France and Scotland had predominated, such that one commentator could describe England as 'a bone thrown between two dogs'.[137] Religious upheaval was to change this, as strategic concerns warred with confessional identities. In a final irony, as Elizabeth lay dying in 1603, it was Scotland, the age-old enemy, that proffered the most likely heir to the throne.

Foreign policy is a slippery subject for the historian. Alliances changed so fast that it can be hard to draw any broader conclusions from the kaleidoscope of events. It is even harder to ascribe any sincerity to the words of rulers, ministers and diplomats, who could celebrate the signing of a treaty with every excess of hyperbolic eloquence, and then go to war with their co-signatories only months later. The most grandiose diplomatic summit of the age was undoubtedly the Field of Cloth of Gold in 1520, when Henry VIII met his former rival Francis I of France for several days of elaborately displayed amity, only to go to war with him again two years later. There is also the problem of contingency. Carefully constructed alliances could be shattered by a single unforeseen event. In 1487, Henry VII was poised to build an alliance with Scotland, consolidated by three royal marriages, most notably that of the dowager queen, Elizabeth Woodville, to James III of Scotland. But James III was killed and the plan collapsed. Ten years later, in 1497, Henry VII was poised to make war on Scotland, which had in the meantime given substantial help to the pretender Perkin Warbeck. The outbreak of rebellion in south-west England scuppered that campaign, and the eventual consequence was the Treaty of Ayton of 1497. The Treaty of Perpetual Peace signed by England and Scotland in 1502 had a title which suggested grandiose expectations – although it did last for ten years, which was better than most. It was sealed by the marriage between James IV and Henry VII's eldest daughter Margaret, a union that would result, a century later, in the union of the crowns, with the accession of James VI as James I of England. The hurried recalibration of foreign policy could be rendered necessary by events, such as the unexpected sack of Rome by Imperial troops in 1527, or the revolt of the Netherlands in the 1560s, whilst the Massacre of St Bartholomew's Day in Paris in 1572 had a psychological impact that would endure for decades.

In 1568, an English ambassador was sent to Moscow and in 1583 an English ambassador was installed in Constantinople. This was an extension of an existing diplomatic network that already stretched across Europe, with resources for espionage, where necessary.[138] Tudor diplomats were often men of high social status and great learning, and their network was a valuable source of both knowledge and influence (although much diplomatic business was still carried out by temporary envoys, or merchants).[139] The task of acting as a foreign envoy was expensive, often frustrating and sometimes dangerous. Francis Walsingham, in Paris in 1572, had to hide his Protestant compatriots within the embassy, along with his small daughter and pregnant wife, to protect them from the fury of the St Bartholomew's Day Massacre.[140] Many more mundane difficulties were involved, too: the luckless Jerome Horsey, ambassador to the court of Muscovy – quite apart from any unease caused by having to encounter Ivan IV, or 'Ivan the Terrible', on his mission in 1584 – had to convey a bull, twelve large dogs and two lions to Moscow. At least it was someone else's job to make them go in procession before the emperor and get the bull to kneel. Gift-giving was a necessary but tense business: if the tribute was deemed inadequate, offence might be taken and the gifts returned.[141] Elizabeth I received camels from the French in 1565, but was displeased by the loan from the French of an elephant in 1591, in consequence according it no formal procession.[142] One of the most famous portraits of the sixteenth century, Holbein's *Ambassadors* (see plate 17), was painted for the French ambassador to London in 1533, Jean de Dinteville, and depicted him alongside his fellow emissary Georges de Selve. This picture referenced both the cosmopolitan nature of diplomacy, with its range of luxury artefacts, and the European competition for overseas influence on the terrestrial globe, where the route of Magellan's circumnavigation is absent, and the line of the Treaty of Tordesillas is curtailed in a tacit rebuttal of Habsburg influence.[143] It also underlines the human cost of a life spent in diplomacy: Dinteville's home town of Polisy is labelled.

Foreign diplomats had a privileged status in England, and a unique perspective on English affairs. This was often mistaken, sometimes the result of manipulation by an English informant, but was frequently colourful. Raimondo de Soncino, envoy from the Sforza dukes of Milan to the Court of Henry VII, gave it as his opinion of the king that 'I fancy he will always wish to have peace with France, though I think if he saw her up to the neck in the water, he would put his foot on her head to drown her, but not otherwise.'[144] Many of our impressions of the Tudor Court in particular come through the eyes of foreign ambassadors: Eustace Chapuys, Charles V's ambassador to Henry VIII, who was vitriolic in his criticism of 'the concubine', as he called Anne Boleyn; Simon Renard, Charles V's ambassador to Mary I, who thought England a nest of heretics and took a gloomy view of the regime's chances; Guerau de Spes, Philip II's ambassador to Elizabeth I, who was highly unpopular with the English and dismissed William Cecil as 'a man of mean sort . . . very astute, false, lying, and full of artifice'.[145] These personal insights, vivid, fascinating and often misleading, are both valuable and problematic sources for understanding the international connections of the age.

'A barbarous people'

Arguably the most persistent foreign policy problem faced by the Tudors was that posed by Ireland, and it was a problem which successive Tudor regimes failed to solve.[146] It could be said that Ireland, nominally under direct English rule, should be discussed under the heading of domestic policy, but every Tudor commentator on Ireland made it clear that this was an alien land, and most were ready to term it a land of barbarians. When Henry Sidney, chief governor of Ireland in 1565–71 and again in 1575–78, finally departed, he was said to have boarded his ship quoting Psalm 114, which, in the words of the Geneva Bible, referred to departing from 'a barbarous people'.[147] When Elizabeth was commenting on the transgressions of yet another lord deputy, Sir William Russell, she observed that such things were all 'too common in foreign service', underlining how Ireland was viewed as a place apart.[148] From the start of the Tudor era, when Ireland was still a Yorkist stronghold and a safe haven for pretenders, to the later stages, when it was a Catholic stronghold and the obvious base for any French or Spanish invasion, Ireland was an expensive, unfathomable and volatile territory, which repeatedly evaded attempts by the English to establish control.

Tudor encounters with the Irish were a particularly complicated blend of suspicion, antagonism, ineptitude, ambition and violence. Francis Bacon in 1621 wrote that the Tudors always knew about Ireland 'that it was a ticklish and unsettled state, more easy to receive distempers and mutations than England was'.[149] Part of the problem was the fact that Ireland remained such an unknown and almost uncharted land to the English. Henry VII never visited it, and few of his advisors had ever set foot there.[150] When Polydore Vergil wanted to write about Ireland, he had to borrow from Jean Froissart, the French chronicler who had written a century earlier, or from Gerald of Wales, who wrote in the twelfth century.[151] Gerald of Wales was one of the first to cast the Irish as a barbarian race.[152] One of the most memorable achievements of medieval English overlordship in Ireland was the Statutes of Kilkenny, which had deplored Irish culture and established a kind of apartheid mentality, where the English were warned off Irish language, dress and customs.[153] Contemporary knowledge was harder to find. A number of Tudor manuscripts survive in which anxious officials attempted to get to grips with the features of this mysterious island, and several show a preoccupation with Ireland's harbours, or 'havens'.[154] The island was porous, open to enemies as well as merchants, a potential source of wealth, but also a likely source of trouble. The way the Tudors wrote about Ireland was akin at times to their discussions of more far-flung territories inhabited by savages; they noted how the Irish lived in forests, and were thus wild and uncivilized. Henry VIII described them as '*sylvestrium*', or 'of the forest', in a letter to the Knights of St John explaining why an English-born cleric was a better choice for a benefice in their gift.[155] Edmund Spenser would describe a woman drinking blood from the severed head of an executed criminal, and smearing her face and breast with it, and he was not the only writer to accuse the Irish of cannibalism.[156] The soldier Sir John Dowdall, writing to Burghley in 1596, described the Irish as 'these cannibals'; and Fynes Moryson, secretary to Lord Mountjoy as he campaigned in Ireland, recorded what were purportedly first-hand accounts of three Irish children eating their dead mother, and of women killing and eating children.[157]

Tudor attitudes to Ireland were never straightforward, however, and these condemnatory accounts were balanced by some more hopeful descriptions. After Henry VIII had declared himself king of Ireland in 1541, the Irish strictly speaking were fellow subjects of the English, and nominally at least under the same rule of law. Sir William Herbert, in his Latin treatise on Ireland in 1591, blamed the carelessness of English magistrates for allowing the Irish to slide back into their former savagery, and recommended the translation of the Bible and liturgy into Irish to improve their 'minds and wills . . . by the instructing them in true religion . . . which in a strange tongue could be to them but altogether unprofitable'.[158] Even Spenser, who deplored its crudities, could also see the beauties of Ireland.[159] The country was itself divided, with the English ruling the Pale directly, and attempting to control the rest through relations with a series of great lordships.[160] The Pale comprised the coastal plain between Dublin and Dundalk, the four counties of Dublin, Kildare, Louth and Meath, and in addition the English had a presence in the towns of Cork, Limerick, Galway, Wexford, Waterford and Carrickfergus, all of which were ports, and so could be sustained from the sea. Inside the 'English' towns there was a strong sense of Anglo-Irish identity and civility, contrasted with the customs and culture of the Gaelic hinterland.[161] Uneasy alliances between Irish lords and the English authorities might break down with the symbolic rejection of English dress: the earl and countess of Desmond, before their rebellion in 1574, adopted Gaelic dress and reinstated Brehon law, although in this they were ignoring their own Anglo-Norman ancestry and the complexities of Irish and Anglo-Irish identity.[162]

Part of the difficulty was encountering a society in which none of the usual laws seemed to apply. English expectations regarding family structures and inheritance were confounded by a land where no particular distinction was made between legitimate and illegitimate progeny, and where titles and land were passed down to the heir who looked most likely, frequently with accompanying violence. In 1493, the chief of the O'Neills was murdered by his half-brother, Henry Óg, who took on the role of chieftain only to be murdered himself by the sons of his former victim.[163] One of those sons, Conn Bacach, having killed his uncle, later became chief of the O'Neills.[164] He rebelled against Henry VIII, was defeated, visited England and became a Protestant, whereupon the king made him earl of Tyrone, no doubt hoping to exert influence through him over his lands and clan in Ireland. This closeness to the Crown, and his change of religion, only exacerbated existing family feuds, however; his son Shane O'Neill murdered the chosen heir, Matthew Feardorcha, before assuming the role of chieftain; he, too, visited the English Court, this time of Elizabeth I, to be confirmed as earl of Tyrone, but he caused nothing but trouble for the English in Ireland. If violence marked native Irish politics, however, it was no less a feature of English rule. Humphrey Gilbert was military governor of Munster in 1569; having suppressed the Fitzgerald uprising, he forced the Irish lords who had surrendered to approach through an array of severed heads on poles.[165]

Some of the worst excesses of English rule in Ireland followed on from the failure of the Reformation to take root there. Before the Reformation, English descriptions of Ireland tended to be milder. Ranulf Higden's fourteenth-century account, published in 1480, thought it 'worthy and semely to prayse that londe with larger praysing', and described a country 'full of montayns of hilles of wodes of mareys and of mores' which was 'softe rayny wyndy' and where the beasts had to be driven out of their pasture lest they overeat. Even so, his depiction was of a place tinged with strangeness, where visitors sickened: 'men of that londe have communely their helth and strangers have ofte a perilous flux because of the moisture of the mete'. It was a place with 'grete plente of samon / of lamprayes / of Eelis and of othir see fissh / Of egles of cranes / of pecokes / of curlewes / of sperhaukes / of goshaukes and of gentill fawcons / Of wolves and right shrewd myse [mice].'[166] The failure of the Reformation in Ireland only made its strangeness more alien. It also came to justify appalling levels of violence. Edmund Spenser, himself a Protestant settler in Ireland, defended the brutality of English rule in Ireland in his *Faerie Queene*, including the Smerwick massacre of 1580, when Spenser's patron Lord Grey orchestrated the killing of around six hundred papal and Spanish troops and their Irish accomplices, an action justified in apocalyptic terms as a blow struck against the Antichrist.[167] Elizabeth I wrote to Grey claiming to have seen the 'mighty hand of the Almightiest power' at work, and rejoicing 'that you have been chosen the instrument of His glory'.[168] Time after time, a new lord deputy took up his office, determined to civilize Ireland, promote Protestantism and make Irish rule self-financing.[169] Almost inevitably, this would end in frustration and violence. Walsingham wrote to Burghley in 1571, opining that victory in Ireland 'is in the hands of God, who many times disposeth the same contrary to man's judgement'.[170] If Protestant zeal made English policy in Ireland more brutal, it also made it more unrealistic.

It might be argued that Ireland saw the earliest example of English colonialism at work. Richard Eden, Cambridge graduate, alchemist and cosmographer, and the translator of half a dozen works on navigation and exploration, was the protégé of Sir Thomas Smith, whose enthusiasm for colonial projects sent his illegitimate son and heir (also called Thomas Smith) with grand designs to found a colony in northern Ireland.[171] This Thomas Smith was of the opinion that nothing 'maketh men more civil . . . than the plough', and wrote to Elizabeth recommending farming in Ireland as 'a helper and a mainteyner of civilitie'.[172] The project promised extensive commercial benefits to its backers, and much booty to those participating, with the pamphlet aimed at securing financial backing promising unconvincingly that the Ards Peninsula would become 'another Eutopia'.[173] The attempt ended in ignominious failure and the assassination of Thomas Smith the younger, whose body was then boiled and fed to dogs by his killers.[174]

From 1541 onwards, successive Tudor regimes sought to subjugate Ireland and bring it convincingly under English control. This shift from an earlier policy of more distant overlordship had, in large part, been triggered by the rebellion of 1534, when a disastrous uprising led by the over-confident earl of Kildare wrecked the delicate balance of power previously maintained in Ireland.[175] Henry VIII's army had defeated Kildare and his allies, but trying to extend English law and institutions in Ireland was always going to be difficult; and when combined with an attempt to extend

English Protestantism after 1547, it became even more problematic. The small body of troops sent across in 1534 had, by the 1550s, quadrupled in size to something like two thousand men.[176] Perhaps the most worrying element of Ireland's recalcitrance was the opportunity it offered to Catholic powers elsewhere in Europe. The French were swift to see the potential for launching an invasion via Ireland.[177] The scale of the Spanish threat was even greater, particularly from the 1580s onwards, which was why the Nine Years' War, or 'Tyrone's Rebellion', proved such a challenge for the Elizabethan regime, and why it cost such a huge amount of money – over £200,000 each year between 1594 and 1603.[178]

The Nine Years' War was, in the end, a victory for the English forces. But it came at a terrible price – not just in terms of the financial cost, but also the numbers of casualties, ruined reputations and damaged trust. The final success of Lord Mountjoy, sent over in 1600 as lord deputy, came from a policy of maintaining garrisons, combined with devastation of the countryside, which reduced much of the population to starvation. Somewhere between 50,000 and 100,000 soldiers and civilians died during the Elizabethan tenure of Ireland, from violence and famine, at a time when the population of Ireland was around half a million.[179] By this point, the conflict had become starkly confessionalized, as signalled by Tyrone's rhetoric of 'the extirpation of heresy, the planting of the Catholic religion, the delivery of our country'. He characterized English rule as 'nourished in obscurity and ignorance, maintained in barbarity and incivility' and responsible for 'infinite evils which are too lamentable to be rehearsed'.[180] The conflict had also become an international one, as indicated by the landing of Spanish troops at Kinsale, where, in the last major battle of the Nine Years' War, Mountjoy defeated both Spanish and Irish alike. In 1599, a London JP sent Robert Cecil a libel which he had found in the street, purporting to be a letter from the earl of Desmond to the king of Spain, asserting that Elizabeth's tyranny in Ireland exceeded that of the Emperor Nero.[181] If this was England's first attempt at colonial rule, as indeed the attempted plantation of Munster from the 1580s seemed to suggest, it was both bloody and inept, and would leave a lasting legacy of division and conflict.[182]

* * *

John Speed, who began compiling maps of the counties of England in the 1590s, publishing them as *The Theatre of the empire of Great Britaine*, described his labours, which here I offer upon the altar of love to my country, and wherein I have held it no sacrilege to rob others of their richest jewels to adorn this my beautifull Nurse, whose wombe was my conception, whose breasts were my nourishment, whose bosome my cradle, and lap (I doubt not) shall be my bed of sweete rest, till Christ by his trumpet raise me thence.[183]

He was following in the footsteps of his friend William Camden, who in 1586 had published *Britannia*, and for whom love of his country was necessarily rooted in an appreciation of its history. He looked for the approval of 'well bred and well meaning men which tender the glory of their native Country'.[184] For all their ideas of incipient nationhood, however, England depended on its European neighbours for prosperity, intellectual stimulus, military standing and religious credibility. Trade, education, war and religious conflict were the four things that propelled Tudor men and women overseas, so their perceptions of the wider world were strongly coloured by the very precise circumstances in which they travelled. For some, the boundary lines were clear. To the waves of exiles fleeing Edwardian or Elizabethan Protestantism, or Marian Catholicism, the churches abroad offered sanctuary and solidarity, and the religious map of Europe was imagined in terms of clear identities and unshakeable hostilities. Diplomacy offered much less certainty, as alliances shifted constantly, and by the end of the sixteenth century, debates at home about foreign policy were proving deeply divisive of the political classes. In the dreams of explorers and the scholarly quest for knowledge lay a fascination with difference, uncertainty and shifting identities. Fynes Moryson could pose as German or Dutch in Italy, or Polish when entering France, and disguised himself as a poor Bohemian servant in Friesland to evade the attention of Spanish troops. His Protestantism had to be dissembled on several occasions, and speaking German, Italian, Dutch and French he could cross many different borders. Scholars moved relatively freely between universities in Oxford, Cambridge, Padua, Bologna, Louvain, Paris and Kraków, among many others. Their language was Latin, and therefore universal. England's place within the wider world was therefore changeable and contingent.

The story is told that the soldier and adventurer Humphrey Gilbert, who drowned when his ship was wrecked on a voyage in 1583, went down clutching a copy of More's *Utopia*.[185] On the face of it a book about a harmonious settlement in a faraway land, More's book was, in fact, a subtle questioning of every value it seemed at first sight to be upholding. It makes an appropriate symbol for England's encounters with the wider world in the Tudor era, where the triumphalism of some of its imperial and Protestant rhetoric needs to be contrasted with the fantasies, failures and underlying weakness of overseas exploration. A more concrete development was the changing pattern of European alliances, in which England's place underwent a striking transformation under the pressure of increasingly confessionalized politics. The most notable happening of the Tudor years, however, was the expansion of overseas trade and the founding of the many new trading companies, in particular the East India Company in 1600, which was destined to overshadow them all.[186] When Elizabeth died, England was still a small country on the edge of Europe, its language spoken by only a few foreigners, its connections with the wider world either tenuous or speculative. The scale of its involvement in later centuries was barely envisaged, except by a few Protestant zealots, a few hard-nosed businessmen, and one alchemist and sorcerer. In two of the three surviving versions of the 'Armada' portrait (see plate 18), Elizabeth is depicted resting her bejewelled hand upon Virginia, while English ships bask in providential sunshine and the Spanish ships are consumed by stormy waters; but the visual claims of the picture are almost all fraudulent. Maritime greatness, colonial conquest and Spanish decline all lay in the future. Like most Tudor iconography, this portrayal of Elizabeth was an exercise in embellishment and misdirection.

CHAPTER 12

THE INVENTION OF GLORIANA
THE REIGN OF ELIZABETH I

'The eyes of many behold our actions; a spot is soon spied in our garments; a blemish quickly noted in our doings. It behooveth us therefore to be careful that our proceedings be just and honorable.'[1] Elizabeth I spoke these words in 1586, responding to a parliamentary appeal to execute Mary Queen of Scots, her Catholic cousin and rival for the throne, then under house arrest in England. Elizabeth was protesting that her behaviour, scrutinized across Europe, must be beyond reproach. On one level, this seems the stuff of the Elizabethan legend, demonstrating the integrity of the queen who would at the last assure her subjects, 'though you have had and may have many mightier and wiser princes sitting in this seat, yet you never had nor shall have any that will love you better.'[2] Such words help sustain the image of 'Gloriana', presiding for nearly half a century over an England grown to greatness. But it should be remembered that these fine words on the higher calling of princes were not a private comment which, by rare chance, survived: Elizabeth had this speech written out by her secretary, carefully corrected it with her own hand and then had it published. Moreover, despite these protestations, three months later Mary Queen of Scots was beheaded at Fotheringhay Castle, although the queen immediately denied that she had intended the execution to take place, and in a fury imprisoned the secretary who had conveyed the warrant. Here is another side to the story of Elizabeth's reign, the assiduous crafting of a virtuous image for public consumption to conceal the true extent of political anxiety beneath. The legend of Elizabeth is beguiling, heroic and inspirational, and some pieces of it may even be true. But not everything was what it seemed in Elizabethan England.

The reign of Elizabeth saw key elements of England's identity called into question as never before. The fragility of the queen's hold on power, compounded by her refusal to marry or name a successor, prompted an extraordinarily intense examination of the political process. These discussions became all the more feverish during the long years of war in Ireland and against Spain, during which martial law was intermittently deployed at home.[3] At the heart of this debate lay questions not just of political responsibility, but of religious conviction and ecclesiastical authority, as England was transformed slowly, messily, acrimoniously, into a more Protestant state. Nearly every exchange about religion might have ramifications for the way in which England was ruled. Conversations about republicanism, for example, were indissolubly linked to conversations about Presbyterianism.[4] Between Catholics asserting the ultimate authority of the pope, and zealous Protestants asserting the superior authority of the Bible, Elizabeth had to fight to hold on to her prerogatives as head of the English Church. In this struggle, she was constantly misunderstood, as well as criticized, by those for whom the dictates of their religion overrode all other considerations. The queen was never allowed this luxury of obedience to a higher power: every decision she made had to be weighed anxiously to assess how far it might affect stability at home and abroad. The narrower vision of those who threatened her with 'the heavy displeasure of God' if she neglected divine imperatives seemingly exasperated her, just as much as her apparent lukewarmness in religion, her hesitations and contradictions infuriated those godly critics in return.[5] These arguments were played out against a backdrop of international tension, and the country repeatedly faced the threat of invasion, usurpation and foreign-backed rebellion. Much of Elizabeth's reign was spent in that state of exacerbated self-scrutiny that results from an existential threat.

Elizabeth was a consummate performer, a woman of extraordinary intellect and education, as skilled at playing on popular sentiment and the emotions of courtiers and ambassadors as she reputedly was at playing music.[6] Despite being bastardized and repudiated as a child, then marginalized and threatened as a young woman, she took the throne and held on to it tenaciously for nearly forty-five years. She survived disease, rebellion, the threat of usurpation and long years of war. Most startling of all, she contrived to quell religious dissent and conflict to a level where it was containable, and passed the throne on at her death, without civil strife, to an experienced and plausible successor. If some of these achievements owed more to luck than judgement, she was still an outstanding ruler. In particular, the fact that Elizabeth was a woman, and ruled as such with flair and conviction in a society deeply unsure about female authority, is no less impressive today than it was at the time.[7] It is an irony that after all the fuss about a male heir in her father's reign, this rejected female came to be the most famous member of the dynasty, and to give her name to an era.[8] Some authors have commented disparagingly on how Elizabeth's behaviour seemed only to reinforce patriarchy, and as a feminist icon she is certainly a far from straightforward proposition.[9] She was not beyond exploiting the idea of female weakness when it proved a useful stratagem.[10] Nonetheless, in her letters, and particularly in her public addresses – unusual for a female monarch – she displayed precisely the kind of authoritative and sophisticated rhetoric and oratory that was the focus of the humanist educational system for statesmen at the time.[11] She ruled with conviction and commanded obedience, despite her gender; and looking back from the second Elizabethan age to the first, it is hard not to cheer for this brilliant and indomitable woman, who battled so untiringly to do an extraordinarily difficult job, and managed to do it reasonably well. The icon of 'Gloriana', however, was a mask intended to deceive: it was a composite of early modern sycophancy and the highly charged anxieties of a regime continually on the defensive. Elizabeth's authority was never without serious challenge, and her image was fashioned to keep at bay both those who claimed the right to influence her and those who plotted to destroy her.

Elizabeth was the focus of much attention, but hers is not the only story worth telling from these years; it is a point worth celebrating that recent histories have become 'less Queen-fixated'.[12] Elizabethan England was a country of over four million people struggling to make a living, feeling the unease of female rule and an uncertain succession, and trying to frame the correct response as the government attempted to impose a Protestant faith on a previously Catholic population. The day-to-day concerns of most Elizabethans centred on how best to survive in an age of recurring plague and famine; how to maximize the harvest and foster trade; how to build stronger communities in the face of poverty, vagrancy and religious division; how to answer the calls for money and men to fight in Scotland,

France, the Netherlands and Ireland, and to man a navy against the Spanish threat. If the 1580s and 1590s saw the production of some of the most sublime drama and poetry ever known, it was not the efflorescence of a triumphal Elizabethan epoch. At the most basic level, it was the outgrowth of urban culture in one of the largest cities in Europe; on another level, it was a manifestation of popular attitudes, in part agonized and in part inflamed by the challenges of those difficult and unstable times. It makes Elizabeth's achievements all the more striking that they were attained against a backdrop of such uncertainty and strife; but it also makes the point that they were never easy. Elizabeth often referred to her own survival and rule as miraculous, and gave thanks for such 'wonderful works and graces, which to me have been so many, so diversely folded and embroidered one upon another, as in no sort am I able to express them'.[13] These were not just pious platitudes: Elizabeth was right to acknowledge just how remarkable it was that she was able to rule with even a measure of success. For all that she glittered, the background for the long years of Elizabeth's reign was always dark and stormy.

'Much suspected by me, nothing proved can be'

The myth-making that marked Elizabeth's life has continued in every century since her death.[14] Her image was evoked in the wake of the French Revolution and under the shadow of Nazism, as a rallying point for English national sentiment.[15] Yet Elizabeth was the target of fierce criticism in her lifetime, beginning even before her birth, when Anne Boleyn's coronation during the sixth month of pregnancy brought her unborn child under scrutiny.[16] During the reign of Edward VI, Elizabeth was cast by some as the devout and learned princess true to the Protestant cause; but others spoke of her alleged adulterous relationship with her stepmother's husband, Thomas Seymour. Imprisoned during Mary I's reign after her implication in Wyatt's rebellion, her survival was cast by some – including Elizabeth herself – as providential; but others would point out how she had collaborated with the regime and prevaricated over religion. John Knox would later remind her with characteristic bluntness that 'for fear of your life, you did decline from God, and bow in idolatry'.[17] Protestant champion or dissembling Nicodemite; skilled politician or vacillating and contradictory ruler; rational or emotional, merciful or vindictive: such characterizations were bitterly contested at the time. Even William Camden, perhaps her greatest historian, remained ambivalent about many aspects of her reign.[18]

The story is all the more complicated because Elizabeth took care to render her own character unfathomable. Throughout her life, she would have a reputation for being opaque and elusive in her utterances, or for making pointed use of silence.[19] It seems to have been her defence mechanism to take refuge in ambiguity. Many literary works which she is held to have authored still survive, from letters and speeches to prayers and classical translations; and yet barely any are in her own handwriting, leaving it open to question how far they might have expressed her true convictions.[20] In 1555, imprisoned in the royal lodge at Woodstock under suspicion of treason, Elizabeth was questioned again and again, but evaded compromising herself. It is said that at this time she scratched two lines of verse on a window with a diamond: 'Much suspected by me / Nothing proved can be' – lines characteristic of her frequent evasions.[21] Under pressure regarding Mary Queen of Scots in 1586, she gave a long and equivocating speech, observing that 'she never had a greater strife within herself than she had that day, whether she should speak or be silent', and concluding by admonishing the parliamentary delegates that they 'must take an answer without an answer at my hands', asking them to be satisfied with 'this answer answerless'.[22] It was one of her more candid admissions of a strategy central to her queenship.

Elizabeth's motto was *Semper Eadem*, 'always the same', suggesting a conscious attempt to counter the changeability of her fortunes and her policies. It also evokes the shadowy presence of Anne Boleyn, the mother rarely mentioned, perhaps never forgotten, who is said to have used this motto, and whose portrait was hidden inside one of Elizabeth's rings (see plate 12).[23] The hidden shame of having a mother executed for multiple adulteries was just the first of many weaknesses for which Elizabeth had to compensate; it is not known if anyone ever made a convincing case to her for her mother's innocence, but she insisted on a parliamentary statute which reversed every ruling that had been 'contrary or repugnant' to the queen's mother. Some of her subjects hung portraits of Queen Anne as a mark of loyalty to Elizabeth, and Anne's former chaplain wrote an account of her life which attempted to restore her reputation, presenting the manuscript to Elizabeth as a gift.[24]

By the later years of her reign, Elizabeth had become a gilded and bejewelled construct, an image of virtue and constancy, a symbol whose attributes were woven into countless poems and proclaimed through pageantry and ritual, concealing only imperfectly the instability of her regime.[25] Much upheaval was caused by her religious policies, which brought about a complete transformation of Church, society and culture; however, it was not just private inclination which determined Elizabeth's Protestant allegiance, but political necessity, since, from a Catholic perspective, she was the illegitimate child of Henry VIII's concubine, and the true queen of England was Mary, queen of Scotland and, in 1558, the future queen of France. Elizabeth's Protestant settlement of religion was implemented on the one hand in the face of considerable popular resentment; whilst on the other, more fervent expressions of Protestant zeal threatened to weaken her authority. Her religious policy was, by definition, incapable of satisfying everyone, and it made her reign a perpetual struggle to find both religious credibility and comparative calm. The continual presence of the Catholic threat could only confirm the impression that the Elizabethan regime was like a house of cards, ready to topple if Catholic winds from Europe blew hard enough. Though Elizabeth herself was temperamentally conservative, the logic of her position required her to commit to policies of religious upheaval, as the price of remaining in power; little wonder that, in response, she painted herself as the embodiment of constancy.

'Determined to be governed by no one'

Elizabeth's early life was unusually fraught, even by the standards of the time, and the story of her sad childhood and turbulent adolescence is well known. She lost her mother, her father's approval and her status before she was three years old: after her mother was executed and she herself was demoted, the little girl noticed the change immediately, demanding of her governess, 'How haps it, yesterday my Lady princess, today but my Lady Elizabeth?'[26] From her mother's death in 1536 to her own accession in 1558, Elizabeth lived through twenty-two years of instability and often acute danger. Her view of her father can only be guessed at, but in a letter to Queen Katherine Parr in 1544, she asked her stepmother 'to recommend me to him', confessing that 'I have not dared to write to him.'[27] Her only known letter to Henry was written a year later and accompanied a trilingual translation, in Latin, French and Italian, of Katherine Parr's *Prayers or Meditations*, a singular achievement for a twelve-year-old. In it, she acknowledged Henry's threefold power over her: 'I am bound unto you as lord by the law of royal authority, as lord and father by the law of nature, and as greatest lord and matchless and most benevolent father by the divine law.'[28] If this was an admission of her dependency, it was also an early expression of her view of monarchy as sanctioned by human, natural and divine law.

In Edward's reign, Elizabeth found a home with Katherine Parr and her new husband, Thomas Seymour, only to be banished after Seymour's ostentatious attempts at flirtation became too flagrant. Elizabeth's servants were arrested and interrogated, Katherine died painfully in childbirth, whilst Seymour was found guilty of various crimes, most notably with regard to the royal children, for he had also tried to bribe his way into the young king's favours.[29] Elizabeth wrote to the lord protector, aghast that 'there goeth rumors abroad which be greatly both against mine honor and honesty, which above all other things I esteem, which be these: that I am in the Tower and with child by my lord admiral'.[30] She pleaded to be allowed to come to Court and show herself. Yet she remained in seclusion at Hatfield, where news reached her of Seymour's execution for treason. In Mary's reign, too, Elizabeth struggled to survive with her reputation intact. She could not hide her former Protestantism, even if she did dutifully attend mass under the new regime, and she was implicated in the plotting of Wyatt and others. In February 1554, as she responded unwillingly to her summons to Court, her cousin Lady Jane Grey was beheaded; and in March, Elizabeth was taken to the Tower by river, entering through Traitors' Gate, where, twenty years before, her mother had passed in to her death. She was even incarcerated in the same royal apartments where her mother had been lodged before her execution. Twenty-five years later, a published collection of prayers by eminent women would contain this supplication, supposedly composed by Elizabeth in the Tower: 'Help me now, O God, for I have none other friends but Thee alone.'[31] After two months' imprisonment, Elizabeth was released, probably in part through Philip II's advocacy, and a year's incarceration at

Woodstock began, from which she was set free only because Mary believed herself pregnant. Philip II's intervention saved her from open implication in subsequent plots, but he also put pressure on her to marry his vassal, the prince of Piedmont, Duke Emmanuel of Savoy, which required skilful evasion on her part.[32]

These early years provided some stern lessons in politics. She saw the price her brother paid – in faction-fighting at Court and in tumultuous popular rebellion – for the attempted imposition by an insecure regime of an inflexible Protestant settlement. She also witnessed the vigour of the Catholic reaction under Mary, on the one hand backed by Habsburg strength, but on the other warmly welcomed by much of the populace at large. She observed her sister's statecraft, and the way in which she fashioned herself as queen regnant. She also learned what it was like to be the heir to the throne, and to carry the weight of every malcontent's expectations. She managed the vast estates left to her in her father's will; under interrogation she commented that she could not remember where all her houses were.[33] She became acquainted with people she could trust, and in the management of her landholdings discovered the dependability and skill of William Cecil, former secretary to her brother, who acted as agent for her, initiating a relationship that would last half a century and define the politics of her reign. All these lessons would shape her experience as a monarch. In the months before Mary's death, Elizabeth was increasing the size of her retinue, negotiating support in different parts of the country; very probably she was preparing to fight for her life, as well as for the crown. In the first twenty-five years of her life, then, she had comprehended the dangers that came from personal relationships, the threat posed by any known successor to the throne, the potential of the Anglo-Spanish alliance, and the art of deploying religious, classical and military symbolism to strengthen the authority of a queen regnant. She had, in short, learned the importance of artifice and the value of caution.

When, in the autumn of 1558, it became clear that Mary I was dying, Philip II despatched his ambassador, Count Feria, to visit Elizabeth. England and Spain were still partnered in a war against France, in an important strategic alliance that Philip was anxious to retain. Feria seems to have appreciated the experience of dining with Elizabeth, reporting that 'we laughed and enjoyed ourselves a great deal'. His judgement of her character raised several uneasy possibilities, however; he described her as 'a very vain and clever woman' and commented that 'I am very much afraid that she will not be well-disposed in matters of religion', noting that 'there is not a heretic or a traitor in the kingdom who has not joyfully raised himself from the grave in order to come to her side'. In particular, he noted grimly that Elizabeth was 'determined to be governed by no one'.[34]

Elizabeth had every reason to sound a defensive note. She was only twenty-five; she was Protestant, which put her at odds with much of the population and nearly all those who were in office at that time, as well as her major allies abroad; she was illegitimate, not just by the laws of the Catholic Church, but by the laws of common decency, since she had been born to her father's second wife when his first was very much alive. She inherited a throne which few had envisaged she would ever occupy, on the questionable grounds of her father's Act of Succession from 1544, which had restored her standing as an heir to the throne, but made no attempt to reverse her bastardy. Moreover, there was a powerful alternative available in the form of Mary Queen of Scots, who had married the dauphin in a splendid ceremony in Notre Dame Cathedral in April 1558, and who, within seven months of Elizabeth's accession, also became queen of France. She had every reason to tread carefully. A contemporary historian described the tense atmosphere. 'Every report was greedily both inquired and received, all truthes suspected, diverse tales beleeved, many improbable conjectures hatched and nourished. Invasione of strangeres, civill dissentione, the doubtfull dispositione of the succeeding Prince, were cast in every man's conceite as present perills.'[35] Elizabeth's first speech, to the lords assembled at Hatfield, was in many ways an apparent admission of her own weakness and a plea for help:

> And as I am but one body naturally considered, though by His permission a body politic to govern, so I shall desire you all, my lords . . . to be assistant to me, that I with my ruling and you with your service may make a good account to almighty God and leave some comfort to our posterity on earth.[36]

It is probable that Elizabeth was using the rhetoric of feminine weakness here as a political tool, just as Mary I had done when necessary.[37] Nevertheless, her very real vulnerability is clear from the tentative steps taken by the new regime. An early position paper warned of threats from Rome, France, Scotland and Ireland; it anticipated discontent among the population at home, including privy counsellors, magistrates and the universities, as well as the clergy.[38] Watched by foreign envoys for the slightest indication of how she intended to proceed, she was adept at giving hints and impressions and confirming nothing. To tell the Spanish ambassador that she was 'resolved to restore religion as her father left it', given the ambiguities of Henry VIII's religious policies, was to commit herself to nothing.[39]

Elizabeth had much to do, and swiftly. An early memorandum from Sir Nicholas Throckmorton began by advising that she keep Cecil on as secretary from the previous regime, and be sparing of any grants; both safe decisions. He then sketched out an agenda for her, which included 'appointing a meet officer in the Tower of London for the time of your coronation ... summoning your parliament ... creating noblemen and Knights of the Bath', and dealing with prisoners, officers, the House of Lords and Commons, the Privy Chamber, the keeper of the seal, the speaker of the Commons, as well as 'nominating apt Commissioners to take a view of your whole revenue, debts, jewels, apparel, munition, navy, mints and sundry other things'. Throckmorton was right to describe this as 'the beginning of your weightie and comberous charge'.[40] His letter also underlines another potential difficulty, however. Throckmorton clearly thought he had the right to dispense this advice, and for all his fulsome apologies for proffering his 'poore opinion', his memorandum has a distinctly proprietary tone. Like many others, Throckmorton seems to have assumed that a woman would need to be told what to do; even Feria, who clearly appreciated her strength of purpose, spoke of her being 'inclined to govern through men who are believed to be heretics', as though government by a woman must necessarily be conducted 'through men'.[41] Elizabeth found herself on the receiving end of copious quantities of political advice, all of it from men, much of it tactless.[42] John Hales, an ambitious administrator and returning Protestant exile, presented Elizabeth with an oration he had written soon after his return.[43] Having laid down a programme of Protestant reform, he concluded peremptorily: 'Thus must your Grace do, if you mind the advancement of God's glory, your own quietness and safety, and the wealth of this your body politic'.[44] It is questionable whether anyone would have tried to tell Henry VIII what he 'must' do in the same way.

It would be wrong to call Tudor England chauvinist; the term is too modern to fit. Women occupied important roles in Tudor society, and not just within the home. They could own property, run businesses, litigate, manage estates; they could inspire as saints or scholars. But the Tudor age delineated fairly sharply those areas of male and of female expertise, and the business of ruling was generally located firmly in the male sphere. This was particularly true of those theorists with strong Protestant convictions. John Knox's damning conclusion was that, 'To promote a woman to beare rule, superioritie, dominion or empire aboue any realme, nation, or citie, is repugnant to nature, contumelie to God, a thing most contrarious to his reueled will and approued ordinance, and finallie it is the subuersion of good order, of all equitie and iustice.'[45] A response was very swiftly published by John Aylmer, Lady Jane Grey's former tutor and another Protestant exile who had escaped from Mary I's regime, at one point hiding in a wine barrel as his ship was searched.[46] This work exhorted obedience to Elizabeth, but in the process still managed tacitly to concede many of the points his opponent had made. He characterized Knox's argument as being equivalent to saying that 'Chalke is whyter than cheese, ergo cheese is black'; this may have reproved Knox's extremism, but still admitted that men and women were as different as chalk and cheese.[47] Aylmer argued that Elizabeth might be the figurehead for the regime, but that sober and judicious men would in fact be taking the decisions.

Neither Knox nor Aylmer should be regarded as wholly representative of views of the time. This was emphatically an argument between zealous Protestant clerics. Aylmer was a Protestant exile in Strasbourg, and his work had been organized by the exile community there; he would later be bishop of London.[48] Knox, meanwhile, was fired by anti-Catholic sentiment; when he wrote 'how abominable before God, is the Empire or Rule of a wicked woman, yea of a traiteresse and bastard', he was specifically talking about Mary I.[49] Regrettably for him, by the time his work began to circulate in print, Elizabeth was England's queen, and she never forgave him.[50] Her fury was not just personal (although it was also that): it was fuelled by the recognition that from a Protestant theological point of view, it was hard to argue a case for a queen's authority, especially when that queen was also expected to be head of the English Church. Right from the start, what modern commentators have assumed was misogyny was usually a more precise set of difficulties rooted in Protestant theology. Luckily for Elizabeth, most of her subjects were not Protestant zealots. She managed fairly skilfully to navigate the challenges of being a female ruler, and many of her subjects were happy to accept her self-justification. Like her sister before her, she appropriated classical and biblical imagery of all types to build a composite image, in which she could draw just as much on male as female typology.[51] Even the Geneva Bible of 1560, in its dedicatory epistle, compared her to Zerubbabel and Josiah.[52] Preachers compared her to Judith and Deborah, but also to Moses, David and Solomon. Elizabeth herself, before her coronation procession left the Tower where she had formerly been a prisoner, addressed God in a prayer that compared her situation to that of the prophet Daniel, 'whom Thou deliveredst out of the den from the cruelty of the greedy and raging lions'.[53]

It was a political imperative that Elizabeth had to be Protestant if she wanted to be queen, but her own convictions are much harder to read. They were indisputably Protestant, but of a distinctive variety. Some would argue that she was merely idiosyncratic in her religious beliefs and practices: an 'odd sort of Protestant', upholding biblical authority and a Protestant doctrine of salvation by faith, yet deploring excessive zeal and sermonizing, retaining a belief in the Real Presence and a devotion to the symbol of the cross.[54] A better description of her, it has been argued, might be as an 'old sort of Protestant', a creature shaped by the emphases of her father's reign, with a firm commitment to the Bible and the Royal Supremacy, alongside a wariness regarding too much innovation, too much strident evangelizing or too much irreverence towards the sacraments.[55] In other words, Elizabeth was less an eccentric Protestant in the context of the 1560s, than an evangelical Protestant on the model of the 1540s. It has been taken as a sign of her Protestant commitment that of the Marian counsellors she retained in her own Privy Council, nine had served under Edward VI; it might equally be noted that most of the nine new counsellors appointed – all of them Protestants – had also served Edward. Only two had been in exile.[56] Elizabeth's kind of Protestantism had been shaped in Cambridge and Westminster, not Frankfurt or Geneva.

There were very practical reasons for Elizabeth to hold on to the religious outlook of her younger days. English Protestantism had emerged alongside the expansion of royal control over the English Church, and that control promised a way to consolidate the new queen's otherwise tenuous authority. Like her first archbishop of Canterbury, Matthew Parker, and her chief minister, William Cecil, Elizabeth had endured the uncertainties of Mary I's reign without leaving England. She was not influenced by the experience of reformed Protestantism abroad, and nor was she persuaded by its propaganda. It could be argued that she wanted stability as much as she wanted Protestantism; certainly, she would always put a pragmatic, unifying, cautiously reforming notion of religion before an idealized and ruthlessly reforming alternative. How far this was spiritual conviction and how far it was political sense is hard to determine. For a woman who understood that she had been appointed by God to protect her realm from division or conquest, whilst at the same time promoting the true faith, it is possible that there was no separation between these two motivations.

Elizabeth began her reign under very strong pressure from those whose Protestant zeal was not tempered by either doctrinal moderation or political skill. Hales had warned her that the reform of her realm 'may not be done with piecing and patching, cobbling and botching, as was used in time past, whilst your most noble father and brother reigned'.[57] Another self-appointed advisor was Richard Mulcaster, whose account of the queen's coronation procession attempted to force her image into the mould of the providential Protestant ruler.[58] He reminded his audience that 'forasmuch as god hath so wonderfully placed her in the seate of government over this realme', it was necessary that Elizabeth should 'in all doinges ... shew her selfe most myndfull of his goodnes and mercie shewed unto her'.[59] The language of such commentators was buoyed up by a conviction of their own godly inspiration to deliver imperious instruction. From the very start of her reign, therefore, Elizabeth was under pressure from a very particular interest group, whose vehemence would only increase as the years went by, and whose political sense was perpetually blunted by their religious bias. With an astonishing lack of political acuity, some exiles in Geneva apparently lamented that the queen had been crowned according to the customary rites, seemingly little appreciating how vital it was that her coronation should be sanctioned by tradition.[60]

This kind of rhetoric would be an enduring feature of her reign. As the early position paper, the 'Device for the alteration of religion', had presciently warned, 'Many people of our own will be very much discontented ...

when they shall see peradventure that some old ceremonies shall be left still or that their doctrine which they embrace is not allowed and commanded only.' And the author predicted that many 'shall be discontented and call the alteration cloaked Papistry or a mingle mangle'.[61] Amid conflicting expectations, Elizabeth moved carefully. To begin with, she continued hearing mass in her Chapel Royal, although, as many noted, on Christmas Day 1558 she walked out before the elevation of the host. There were marked Protestant overtones to her coronation, and possibly a new line in the coronation oath, where the queen vowed herself to 'the true profession of the Gospel'.[62] An initial Paul's Cross sermon delighted Protestant observers; but the following week, from the same pulpit, John Christopherson, bishop of Chichester, launched a ferocious attack on Protestantism as 'not the gospel, but a new invention of new men and heretics'.[63] The pulpits were silenced in December 1558 until the religious settlement was resolved: the clergy were told they could read the Gospel, Epistle and the Ten Commandments in English, but without 'any maner of doctrine or preachyng'.[64] As the 'Device' had commented regarding the more fervent Protestants, 'better it were that they did suffer than her Highness or commonwealth should shake or be in danger'.[65] An even greater danger came from Catholic opposition, which nearly prevented Elizabeth from passing her Protestant settlement at all. The religious settlement was a battle that she won by only the narrowest of margins. Initially wrecked in the House of Lords, in large part by the bishops whom Elizabeth had inherited from Mary, a second attempt in the same parliament involved two separate bills. The Supremacy Bill ensured that Elizabeth was to be 'Supreme Governor of the Church', a slightly easier title to swallow than 'Supreme Head'; it also repealed the heresy laws, allowed freedom of worship for Protestants in a Catholic realm and provided for communion in both kinds. These were presumably the minimum requirements for making Elizabeth's position tenable. This bill suggests that the queen was by no means sure that she could actually get rid of Catholicism. She then put forward the Uniformity Bill, which abolished the mass and brought in the *Book of Common Prayer*. With several of the bishops who had formerly opposed her either dead or imprisoned, the bill passed by just three votes. It was Elizabeth's first political victory, but it showed how fragile was her hold on power.

It was once thought that Elizabeth aimed at a moderate settlement which echoed that of her father and was curiously suggestive of a particular brand of modern Anglicanism; but this idea is highly anachronistic and ignores the tensions of the late 1550s, when it was evident that there could be no compromise between Catholic and Protestant viewpoints. It was also once thought that Elizabeth was pressurized into a more openly Protestant settlement by her MPs and the views of those Protestants returning from exile who had experienced a truly reformed church order and were enthusiastic to see it duplicated in England.[66] In reality, it seems that Elizabeth was clear-sighted in her pursuit of a Protestant settlement, albeit one with some cautious features, but that she faced considerable opposition from the Catholic episcopacy and nobility.[67] It is also evident that once she had achieved her settlement, she authorized the systematic evaluation and, where necessary, expulsion of parish priests resistant to the changes. Whilst the Marian bishops were swiftly removed from office, however, the parish clergy were weeded out more gradually.[68] The much-vaunted Elizabethan *via media* was not a theological compromise, so much as a piece of Protestant pragmatism. The settlement was quite clear in its rejection of Catholicism, but it was also emphatic in its attempts to stir up as little popular disruption and dismay as possible.

Elizabeth's preachers continually struggled with the task of addressing a ruler who was both a sovereign and a sinner, compounded by the fact that, as a woman, they regarded her as especially subject to their authority.[69] There were not enough available Protestant clerics for Elizabeth to be too selective: at least eight of the bishops promoted in the early years of the reign were of the zealous Protestant variety.[70] Such men, and their friends abroad, were swift to criticize Elizabeth, albeit sometimes from a safe distance: Rodolph Gualter warned Elizabeth against adopting 'a form of religion which is an unhappy compound of popery and the gospel, and from which there may at length be an easy passage to the ancient superstition', but he wrote from Zurich to say this.[71] Plenty of observers, then and since, seem to have missed the point of Elizabeth's objections to admonitions such as this. The frequent repetition, for example, by those who served her of the plea 'God open her Majesty's Eyes' has generally left historians with the impression that Elizabeth was rather lukewarm about her religion.[72] The frustration felt by those uttering this petition to the Almighty was based not on workplace politics, but on a disagreement over the vision of England's Protestant future. Elizabeth wanted her country to be Protestant, but she wanted to remain at its helm, not surrender to a bench of bishops and a chorus of theologians, all convinced that they were acting in the Lord's name when they told her to back off and let them make the decisions. This would be summed up by Edmund Grindal in 1576, when he told her she should 'refer all these ecclesiastical matters which touch religion, or the doctrine and discipline of the church, to the bishops or divines of your realm, according to the example of all godly Christian emperors and princes of all ages'.[73] Grindal was far from being the only one, although he was possibly the bravest, or the most unwise.

Arguments about church reform, therefore, ineluctably became arguments about the extent of Elizabeth's monarchical authority, which is why she reacted to them so trenchantly, at times with outright fury. This was made evident in the mid-1560s, when Elizabeth's insistence on clerical dress was being painfully implemented by Archbishop Parker, to the outrage of those Protestants who felt that any kind of vestment, no matter how plain, was a popish legacy.[74] The question was not just whether a clergyman should dress in a particular fashion, but also whether the queen had the power to command him to do so. Some of the more vehement clerical critics were academics, and when the queen visited Oxford in 1566, she made some acerbic comments about their defiance, now curbed.[75] The university, outwardly enraptured by the queen's visit, nonetheless staged disputations for entertainment that discussed questions of princely power, justified resistance and elective monarchy. They asked, among other things, whether a bad leader had to be obeyed. It was a startling display of academic presumption, to address in this way some of the most sensitive issues of Elizabeth's reign. It is little wonder that she responded by saying of the issues under discussion, 'I do not approve them by my authority as Queen, nor by my judgement as a Christian.'[76]

Elizabeth was determined to be ruled by no one, as Feria had correctly observed back in 1558. Nor was this a question of self-aggrandizement, or arrogance: to understand her stance properly, it is necessary to look beyond the clamour of her bishops and divines to the policies she implemented at parish level. The Elizabethan Injunctions of 1559 had marked notes of continuity with those of Elizabeth's predecessors. Instead of provision for an impassioned preaching campaign, which some had expected, the queen's commissioners were to enquire whether the clergy were resident and doing their duty, keeping the church in good repair, educating the children of the parish and staying out of taverns. Significantly, they were instructed to make sure that the communion table was 'decently made, and set in the place where the altar stood, and there commonly covered'. Instructions were also given for the use of communion wafers, slightly larger and plainer than the Catholic variety, but still not common bread, as in the Edwardian Church. It was clearly stated that this was 'ordered for the more reverence to be given to these holy mysteries, being the Sacraments of the Body and Blood of our Saviour Jesus Christ'.[77] There is no doubt that these Injunctions were intended to establish a Protestant Church: images, ornaments and vestments were to be taken away, the congregation was to be warned off superstitious practices and enjoined to listen quietly to readings from the Bible. Yet Elizabeth's paramount concern was not for the zealous spreading of the Gospel, so much as to avoid 'discord among the people, and thereupon slanderous words and railings', which so commonly accompanied 'all alterations, and specially in rites and ceremonies': the instructions stated that the queen was 'most desirous of all other earthly things, that her people should live in charity both towards God and man, and therein abound in good works'.[78] This emphasis upon both charity and good works at this time was, in the eyes of the more dedicated Protestants, at best misguided and at worst offensive. It was clear that to Elizabeth, however, 'the love and due reverence of God's true religion' could only be 'truly set forth by public authority'.[79]

In early June 1561, on the eve of what would formerly have been the feast of Corpus Christi, the great church of St Paul's Cathedral was struck by lightning, and its steeple, bells and roof were all destroyed. It was not hard for Catholics to interpret this as a sign of God's view of the Elizabethan Church 'as a newe fangled doctrine and scismaticall'. John Morwen, formerly chaplain to Bishop Bonner, distributed manuscript copies of his thoughts on the subject in the streets of Chester. That England had moved away from the true faith, he opined, 'I thinke there is no man so simple but he may easely perceive'.[80] Protestants indignantly rebutted such a view, and Morwen's tract was printed in a refutation by the Protestant bishop of Durham, James Pilkington, who tried to frame the lightning strike as a comment on human sinfulness more generally, and defensively provided a list of calamities that had formerly struck Catholic churches.[81] This argument rumbled on for several years, but it is striking that Morwen appealed to the queen's example in his attack upon the Protestants. He spoke of how 'where the Quene hais geven streyght commaundement to abstayne from flesh in Lent ... these new Preachers and Protestantes have eaten flesh openly to the great sclaunder of other: so they obey neither the Quene nor the churche'.[82] Morwen was, of course, seeking to score points, but that he could appeal to Elizabeth's conservatism in this way suggests that her caution was holding out hope to a broader section of society than just those wedded to Protestant zeal, and blunting the edge of their evangelical message precisely in order to minimize its divisive effect upon the realm.

The marriage game

Elizabeth's approach to one of the most contentious issues of her reign, namely the question of her marriage, was also characterized by caution. Parliaments of 1559, 1563, 1566 and 1576 all petitioned her to marry.[83] The chief anxiety was not about female rule as such, but about the need for the queen to produce an heir, a question that had been every bit as urgent during the reigns of her predecessors and that had prompted some of her father's most striking political interventions. If Elizabeth's subjects wanted her to marry, it was less as a defence against female incompetence than to prevent a disputed succession, with the attendant risk of civil war and foreign invasion.[84] The window of opportunity for Elizabeth to produce children was a smaller one than that faced by her father. Tudor noblewomen usually gave birth for the first time in their teens, not their late twenties. When Elizabeth's very first parliament petitioned her on the subject, she gave a delicate reproof, commenting that since the request was simply cast, she was prepared to take it in good part; but if 'it had been otherwise, I must needs have misliked it very much, and thought it in you a very great presumption'.[85] Subsequent parliaments continued still to press the necessity of marriage. Cecil prayed, 'God send our mistress a husband, and by him a son, that we may hope our posterity shall have a masculine succession'.[86]

The problem of marriage was bound up with the problem of the international balance of power and how that might be affected by the queen's

Protestantism, rendering her remarkably cagey about her faith with foreign envoys. Anthony Cooke, writing to the Swiss reformer Heinrich Bullinger in December 1559, saw the marriage question as an immediate one: 'for if that should take place under favourable auspices, every thing else will go on far more happily and with greater security'. He opined, however, that the queen 'would not now, I think, marry a foreigner if she could; nor do I see how, if she were so inclined, she could do it without the greatest danger'.[87] Yet Elizabeth continued to hold out the possibility of marriage when speaking to foreign envoys, although she may have been honest when she told the Spanish ambassador Guzmán de Silva: 'If I could appoint such a successor to the Crown as would please me and the country, I would not marry, as it is a thing for which I have never had an inclination.' In the same conversation, she also remarked: 'There is a strong idea in the world that a woman cannot live unless she is married, or at all events that if she refrains from marriage she does so for some bad reason.'[88] This may have been a genuine expression of exasperation.

Foreign princes brought their wars with them; marriages at home might create civil strife and risk tarnishing the royalty of a queen who, in the eyes of many, was already a bastard. These were gloomy considerations, compounded by the fact that the marriage market was not looking very promising when Elizabeth came to the throne. Catholic princes came with severe complications, and even those who recommended them did so with the optimistic forecast that the prince in question would be converted to Protestantism. It was hard to see how a Catholic could marry a Protestant, when no marriage service existed that would be amenable to both. Protestant princes, meantime, were in short supply: Eric XIV of Sweden was the most plausible, but he was the son of a usurper. In her reign as a whole, Elizabeth seems to have only twice considered marriage very seriously: to Robert Dudley in the early 1560s and to the duke of Anjou in the late 1570s.[89] But Dudley's wife had died in mysterious circumstances, found dead at the bottom of a flight of stairs in 1560. Cecil campaigned vigorously against the Dudley match, but Elizabeth was herself already capable of seeing the dangers. Dudley's lineage was not only relatively undistinguished, but both his father and grandfather had been executed for treason. His ambitious family was a positive disadvantage, whilst as an Englishman he brought none of the strategic and financial benefits of a foreign match: as Cecil put it, 'Nothing is increased by Marriadg of hym either in Riches, Estimation, Power.'[90] It seems that Elizabeth loved him: she must have done, for his eligibility even to have been under consideration. Significantly, when there was a risk of her dying of smallpox in 1562, she directed that he be made lord protector. The following year she suggested that he marry Mary Queen of Scots – to solve the Scottish problem through the man whose loyalty she clearly did not doubt, but perhaps also to give the man she loved a crown, even though she could not give him a share in hers. In the first years of her reign, they were constantly together, hunting, riding, dancing; and even when she travelled on more official business, as her master of the horse he went with her everywhere (see illustration 22). The death of his wife, although most probably through suicide, heightened the stakes on both sides. In November 1560, Elizabeth was on the point of ennobling him, which would have given him sufficient status to become her husband; at the last moment she thought better of it, and taking up a knife, cut the prepared patent in pieces.[91] Dudley's last affectionate letter to his 'gracious lady', told her 'the chiefest thing in the world I do pray for, for her to have good health and long life'; it was written from 'your old lodging at Rycote', perhaps a reminder of their visit there together in 1566. The letter was labelled solemnly by Elizabeth, 'His last letter'. She kept it with her until her own death.

That Elizabeth never did marry caused several decades of anxiety for all those involved in politics, and brought a very real risk of war, both civil and international, when she died in 1603. Suggestions that she had a deep-seated psychological fear of any sexual encounter are probably wide of the mark.[92] The idea that her early life had established a frightening correlation between sex and danger works quite well in the modern mind, but looks less plausible from a Tudor perspective, where the fear of sex was probably a lot less immediately relevant than the fear of death. Marriage always included a significant chance of death for women through childbearing, and Elizabeth's counsellors noted the chances of her dying in childbirth, or from grief at an unhappy match.[93] The nexus between procreation and violent death was a stark fact of Tudor life, not the stuff of neurosis. The idea of an aversion to sex and marriage looks even less plausible, given Elizabeth's own character. Although she was always secretive about her emotions, it is evident that she was extremely tough, and capable of keeping her feelings under control. Nor was

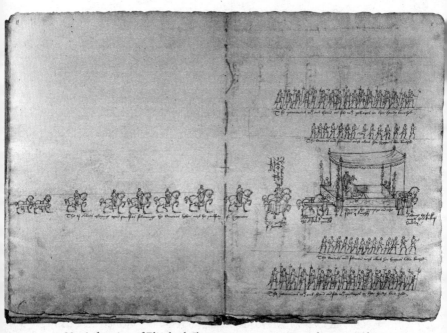

22. A drawing of Elizabeth I's coronation procession, showing Robert
Dudley as Master of the Horse riding directly behind the queen

she vowed to virginity from the first, as some have claimed. In her first
speech to parliament, responding to their petition that she should marry, she
famously remarked that she would be content at the end of her life to have a
tombstone which declared 'that a queen, having reigned such a time, lived
and died a virgin'. Yet in that same speech, she also declared her openness to
marriage, 'whensoever it may please God to incline my heart to another kind
of life'.[94] It would be another nineteen years before she openly referred to
herself in public again as a virgin queen.[95] It makes better sense to consider
more pragmatic political explanations.[96] For Elizabeth to marry would have
been a political gamble, and she was not fond of gambling. If she won the
gamble, it would produce a male heir and an advantageous foreign alliance.
If she lost, she might lose everything. She had before her the examples of her
sister Mary I and her cousin Mary Queen of Scots, who had both faced
rebellion as a result of an unpopular marriage. Mary I had married a foreign

prince, and thereby stirred up opposition: Elizabeth had remarked bluntly to the Spanish ambassador, regarding her half-sister, 'that the Queen had lost the affection of the people of this realm because she had married a foreigner'.[97] Mary Queen of Scots had married from among her subjects, and thereby lost the respect of the rest of them, and in due course her throne. Marriage was not an impossible challenge: Mary I had done a reasonable job of ring-fencing her authority. Indeed, Elizabeth's Privy Council agreed that her marriage treaty could be a useful blueprint if Elizabeth married.[98] But there had been no child for Mary, and so her gamble had not been worth it in the end. In her first speech to parliament on the subject, Elizabeth gave the assurance that 'I will never in that matter conclude anything that shall be prejudicial to the realm, for the weal, good, and safety whereof I will never shame to spend my life.'[99] What lay at the forefront of her mind was the potential political risk.

In 1582, when Elizabeth's last real chance of marriage had been defeated, she wrote a poem.

> I grieve and dare not show my discontent
> I love, and yet am forced to seem to hate;
> I do, yet dare not say I ever meant;
> I seem stark mute, but inwardly do prate.
> I am, and not; I freeze and yet am burned,
> Since from myself another self I turned.[100]

Like so many of Elizabeth's utterances, this was open to several interpretations. It could have been an elegant diplomatic gesture, explaining her rejection of her French suitor in such a way as to cause no offence – even keeping alive the possibility of another chance. It was probably at least partly that, for Elizabeth was always too shrewd to turn down a possible diplomatic advantage, especially one which could be bought solely with words. Yet it might, in addition, have contained some echo of Elizabeth's real feelings about her lonely existence as queen. The second stanza began, 'My care is like my shadow in the sun / Follows me flying, flies when I pursue it.' These words might express Elizabeth's sadness at the failure of her proposed marriage to the duke of Anjou; they might equally express her life-long weariness at the burden of office she could never escape, and the always unresolved conflict between her womanhood and her states-manship.

The construction of authority

If the first decade of Elizabeth's reign saw her tackle the questions of reli-gion and marriage, it also saw her broker peace with France, tackle a foreign policy dilemma regarding Scotland, visit the universities, enforce her rules on church decorations and clerical vestments, and keep the normal busi-ness of government running as smoothly as possible. As Cecil had fore-seen, this required some scrutiny of personnel, since government in the localities depended on the JPs, and the implementation of a Protestant settlement was always going to be difficult with convinced Catholics in positions of local authority. Cecil had opined that this would need 'gentle and dulce handling, by the commissioners', coupled with 'the readiness and goodwill of the lieutenants and captains to repress them if any should begin a tumult, murmur or provide any assembly, or stoutness to the contrary'.[101] Like so much Elizabethan policy, a careful balancing act was required, in order to advance the regime's objectives without engendering active resistance.

Religious zealots disdained political pragmatism. John Jewel, eventually the Elizabethan bishop of Salisbury, had said at the start of the reign that 'I only wish that our party may not act with too much worldly prudence and policy in the cause of God'.[102] It would appear he got his wish: the lack of prudence and political sense on the part of the 'hotter sort of Protestant' was a continual irritation to Elizabeth. The majority of the political classes had a more practical approach, and were less prepared to antagonize either the queen or those who were used to wielding authority in the provinces. Elizabeth was largely successful in securing the cooperation of her courtiers and counsellors. Certain key topics regarding foreign policy, religion and the intractable issue of Mary Queen of Scots could lead to marked diver-gences in opinion, but these were usually manageable. The Elizabethan Privy Council was not the hot-bed of faction which some have assumed it to be, and nor did Elizabeth's gender make business unworkable, as some have claimed.[103] Under duress, her counsellors were capable of making occasional disparaging comments about the unreliability of women, but mostly they spoke of their monarch with respect, and often affectionate admiration. The earl of Sussex was of noble descent, and might therefore have had reason to think well of his own authority, but he said of Elizabeth in 1579 that 'her heart is to be guided by God's direction and her own because no man can know the inward direction of her heart', nor 'can any man give counsel therein'.[104] Robert Beale, as clerk of the Privy Council, knew one or two things about Elizabeth's vagaries, but could write simply to his son, 'I have no dealing with the queen but as with the image of God.'[105] Burghley, explaining to the MP James Morrice the limits of what counsel could achieve (in this instance concerning reform of the church courts), told him: 'if it please hir to reforme it, it was well; if not, wee were to praie to God to move hir harte thereunto, and so to leave the matter to God and hir Majestie'.[106]

Elizabeth was wise enough to promote continuity in government where she could. She held on to some of the lords assembled at Hatfield, 'of long experience in governance and enabled by my father of noble memory, my brother, and my late sister to bear office', as she described them, ensuring that she had privy counsellors with relevant experience.[107] Later historical debates about the workings of the Elizabethan Privy Council were influenced by twentieth-century ideas about the institutional importance of different aspects of government, most particularly the Council.[108] More recent research has demonstrated that the bureaucratic elements of Tudor government were not their determining feature; personal connections, and the more informal conduits of power which flowed from the person of the monarch, were more important than institutions.[109] Court and Council overlapped, or flowed into one another, and Elizabeth would, when she desired, summon groups of counsellors or courtiers to discuss a specific issue quite independently of any formal Privy Council meetings, which she in general preferred not to attend personally.[110]

The most important player in the regime was undoubtedly Elizabeth's chief minister, William Cecil. His career was an example of the Elizabethan political system at its best, and in his loyalty and longevity he recalled some of the men who had served Henry VII. Cecil's father and grandfather had been minor royal officials, and Cecil had proved his worth in the service of Edward VI, when he had been a close advisor to the duke of

Somerset; after being imprisoned at the time of Somerset's fall, he had risen again to the post of secretary of state under Northumberland. Despite his Protestantism, he was suggested as a possible successor to William Petre as secretary of state during Mary I's reign. He was efficient in a manner reminiscent of Thomas Cromwell, an assiduous collector of detailed information, an inveterate networker, and a sage and loyal counsellor.[111] He was also – as Elizabeth well knew – a man of exceptional integrity. It was said that he never went anywhere without his copy of Cicero's *De Officiis*, the handbook of the Renaissance statesman, which urged a life of civic duty and moral probity. His working partnership with Elizabeth was, in many ways, the foundation stone for what stability the regime was able to achieve. When Cecil was sworn in as privy counsellor on 20 November 1559, Elizabeth famously said to him: 'This judgement I have of you, that you will not be corrupted with any manner of gift, and that you will be faithful to the state, and that without respect of my private will you will give me that counsel that you think best.' It should also be noted that Elizabeth continued by saying: 'And if you know anything necessary to be declared to me of secrecy, you shall show it to myself only, and assure yourself I will not fail to keep taciturnity therein.'[112] Elizabeth could recognize his statesmanlike qualities, but needed sometimes to remind him that he was answerable to her alone. These were the terms of an exclusive partnership that was to last through countless vicissitudes for the next forty years. Cecil worked night and day, often in indifferent health. Writing to his son in 1595, he asked: 'I pray yow gyve my most humble thanks to hir Ma[jes]ty for hir offer sendyng to know of my head and neck which on Satyrday, semed to be made of lead and yesterday somewhat lighter as of Iron.'[113] In his last illness Elizabeth visited him, and sitting on his bed fed him with a spoon. She must have known just how much she owed him.

For all that the two worked together so closely, Cecil and Elizabeth did not see the world alike.[114] Cecil's reputation as a grave bureaucrat and statesman was one he took care to present to posterity, but his driving force was as much to do with the furtherance of his religion as with the security of the realm.[115] He had sat as MP for Stamford in the first parliament of Edward VI's reign, and helped usher in the dawn of a Protestant era.[116] His marriages – to the sister of John Cheke, and later to Mildred Cooke, one of the highly educated Protestant daughters of Sir Anthony Cooke – indicated his religious commitment, as well as his social ambition.[117] He has been described as a man on a mission, his vision one of 'light against dark, truth against lies, Christ against Antichrist'.[118] He sympathized, however circumspectly, with some of the religious opinions that Elizabeth viewed with both personal distaste and political caution. For this reason, he was more willing to countenance foreign intervention in the face of a Catholic threat, and he always viewed Mary Queen of Scots as villainous, where Elizabeth was more willing to grant her the respect owing to an anointed ruler.[119] Cecil darkly observed in 1565 that Mary Queen of Scots knew the English crown 'to depend only upon the breath of one person, our sovereign lady', and was disposed to take her as a threat very seriously indeed.[120] He was exasperated that Elizabeth was so reluctant to countenance war and the expense it brought.[121] He wrote to Leicester that 'If Her Majesty will continue her delays in providing for her own surety, by just means given to her by God, she and we all shall vainly call upon God when calamity shall fall upon us.'[122]

Early in the reign, Cecil and Elizabeth disagreed profoundly over whether to intervene in Scotland, where the uprising by the Protestant Lords of the Congregation in 1559 raised the possibility that the Catholic regime of Mary Queen of Scots might be undermined, or at least eroded. Elizabeth did not want to be openly involved; as Cecil gloomily wrote to Throckmorton, 'The Queen's Majesty never liketh this matter of Scotland.'[123] Cecil was pushed to the brink of resignation in his determination to insist on aiding the Scots Protestant lords, couching what was in effect an ultimatum in the language of self-abasement and respectful counsel:

> With a sorrowful heart and watery eyes, I your poor servant and most lowly subject . . . beseech your Majesty to pardon this my lowly suit, that considering the proceeding in this matter for removing the French out of Scotland doth not content your Majesty, and that I cannot with conscience give any contrary advice, I may, with your Majesty's favour and clemency, be spared to entermeddle therein.[124]

In the end, Cecil prevailed, although it was one of the very few occasions when he managed to persuade Elizabeth out of her chosen course of action. It is possible that the experience deepened their respect for one another and illustrates how Elizabethan politics could be deeply divisive without at the same time being adversarial.

In dealing with the business of government, Elizabeth I borrowed heavily from Mary I where she could, using everything from her sister's coronation robes to her rhetoric of being married to her country. Where Mary had always intended to marry, however, Elizabeth had to rule alone, and she needed to evolve her own distinctive style of wielding authority and commanding obedience and respect. Most immediately, she had to rule over the Court. This was a community of around 1,700 people, perhaps a thousand of whom worked 'below stairs'. However, several hundred had access to the public rooms, and a group of eighty or a hundred – nobles, counsellors, courtiers and intimate servants – were allowed access to the privy apartments.[125] She had to fulfil the roles of both king and queen, with all their attendant expectations; and she also had to defy popular expectations about womanly behaviour, at least in part, in order to stop her ministers from making her decisions for her and attempting – from what they considered the worthiest of motives – to take business out of her hands. There would always be those who expressed sentiments similar to those of Sir Francis Knollys in 1578, who said heatedly 'if her Majesty does not suppress and subject her own will and her own affections unto sound advice of open counsel, in matters touching the preventing of her danger, then her Majesty will be utterly over-thrown'.[126] Every head of state is subject to advisors who think they know best what to do; in Elizabeth's case, this was compounded by her gender.

With both flair and originality, Elizabeth devised a response which turned her gender into an asset, rather than a disadvantage, deploying the traditions of courtly love in support of her personal rule, and turning the potential constraints of being a woman into an incisive political tool. Her father had made political capital out of his masculinity, hunting, jousting and campaigning alongside his nobility and courtiers, and thereby empha-sizing the extent to which they were a band of brothers. Elizabeth, in anal-ogous fashion, deployed her femininity as a means of dispensing or withholding royal favour, to manipulate those around her. Her godson Sir John Harington recalled Sir Christopher Hatton observing that: 'The

Queen did fish for men's souls, and had so sweet a bait that no one could escape her network.'[127] She invented nicknames for her closest courtiers, engaged in flirtatious wordplay, and at banquets or dances, on hunting trips or royal progresses, she spun ties of friendship that fostered loyalty, or issued reproaches that stung like reprimands. The worst rebuke was to be banished from her presence. Courtiers and petitioners used poetry, music or other courtly arts to try to please her. Writing not long after her death, Francis Bacon recorded more critically how she had expected to be 'wooed and courted' by her subjects; but his conclusion was that it detracted 'but little from her fame and nothing at all from her majesty'.[128]

Gift-giving was an important aspect of this piece of political and social drama.[129] A costly gift was at the same time a tribute to the queen, an embodiment of the subject's obedience, and an ongoing reminder of that subject's loyalty and expectation of future favours. Thomas Gresham is believed to have given Elizabeth a gold bowl that was decorated with the queen's coat of arms, but also with the Greshams' symbol of grasshoppers – a constant, if tacit, reminder of his family's loyalty.[130] In the tense years of 1599 and 1600, the earl of Essex, his wife and his mother all presented Elizabeth with gifts which, wary of Essex's intentions, she evaded accepting.[131] Many of these exchanges and much of the courtly play-acting took place during celebrations or whilst hunting, or at jousts – in particular, the Accession Day tilts, which involved elaborate skeins of symbolism and where the example set by the queen's father's Court was echoed.[132] On a visit to Bristol in 1574 she received a salamander-and-phoenix jewel from Sir John Young and a dolphin made of gold and mother of pearl from Sir John Sherington.[133] In return, the queen was inclined to give such gifts as knighthoods, which did not require expenditure, but the benediction of royal favour.

These feminine wiles were not always gentle. Elizabeth was famous for her rages: her eloquent speeches were matched by the earthiness of her profanity, and she was also notorious for her unpredictability. Her mode of interaction with her closest advisors was never predictable. Her courtiers and counsellors (two groups which frequently overlapped) often gave expression to exasperation at what they saw as dithering, or excessive emotion. It was easy for contemporaries to overlook the deeper significance of Elizabeth's behaviour. Her reputation for being both passionate and volatile may have undermined her reputation, but it allowed her to keep the initiative in the personal interactions that were so central to the business of government. And if Elizabeth could be quick to take offence, this was in part because she was also often provoked. In a court sermon of 1596, Anthony Rudd, bishop of St David's, advised (perhaps maliciously) by Archbishop Whitgift to deliver some plain-speaking admonitions, rather than something overly clever, made the disastrous choice of preaching on the text 'Teach us to number our days', and reminded the sixty-three-year-old monarch of her mortality with some observations concerning mystical arithmetic. The queen commented that Rudd should have kept his arithmetic to himself; clearly stung by his comments, she made some pointed remarks about the excellence of her eyesight, hearing and dexterity as a musician.[134] Her response was nonetheless still a measured one. She was said to have commented that 'you have made me a good funerall sermon: I may dye when I will', which shows more wit than wayward emotion.[135]

Historical discussions of Elizabeth's idiosyncratic approach to wielding authority demonstrate a recurring usage in the writings of (chiefly male) historians of facile gender stereotypes. Her management of her courtiers has been dismissed as vain and hysterical; her furious reactions to unsanctioned marriages have been ascribed to sexual jealousy, as has her loathing of married clergy; her comments to ambassadors have been read as expressing conceitedness; and it is still widely alleged that her fury in 1599, when Essex returned from Ireland and strode unannounced into her bedchamber, was because he saw her without her wig and make-up.[136] It is astonishing that reputable historians have accepted such judgements so unquestioningly. Some are pure exaggeration: Elizabeth does seem to have felt a certain dislike of married clergy, but this has been inflated out of all proportion, and certainly did not affect her patronage of married bishops.[137] All betray a fundamental misunderstanding of Elizabeth's intentions. Whatever the personal emotions of the queen in these events, there were always sound political explanations for her reactions. When, for example, Lady Katherine Grey married Edward Seymour, earl of Hertford in 1560, the couple were committing treason, since Grey was the granddaughter of Henry VIII's sister and in direct line of succession, so only allowed to marry with royal approval; she was duly imprisoned. It might be noted that the fathers of both Grey and Seymour had themselves been executed for treason, and that Grey's sister had attempted to usurp the throne and also died as a traitor. The fact that Katherine's younger sister also contracted a secret marriage to Thomas Keyes, effectively the head of security at Court, made the matter much worse, but Elizabeth was charitable enough to have Katherine and her children transferred out of London when plague hit in the summer of 1563.[138] Their imprisonment was analogous to that of John Hales, who, in 1563, wrote a tract defending Grey's place in the succession; it is hard to see how his punishment could be ascribed to sexual resentment on Elizabeth's part. Similarly, when the queen objected to the unsanctioned marriages of her gentlewomen of the Privy Chamber, it was because they performed an important role which, through their marriages, became open to outside influence: it was this that made Walter Raleigh's seduction of Elizabeth Throckmorton, and their clandestine marriage in 1591, the cause of their disgrace. The queen's flirtatious or feminized comments to ambassadors were, like all such interactions, a way of extracting useful information through informal encounters. As for Essex, his assumption that he had the right of entry to the queen's private chambers was an extraordinary act of hubris characteristic of his self-belief and political misjudgement. The affront to Elizabeth's feelings as a woman was as nothing to the affront to her majesty.

Just as Elizabeth kept the attention of her Court through the exercise of her forceful personality, so she extended her scope periodically by going on progress during the summer months. This was, of course, about showing herself to her more humble subjects, but it could also be a very useful stratagem in terms of power-brokering at the higher levels. Her visits to her loyal subjects were complicated for those tasked with organizing them, and ruinously expensive to those who hosted her and her Court, but they were also precious opportunities to strengthen ties and reinforce royal authority. She deployed the same waywardness about her movements as she often showed at Court: commenting on the queen's plan for her summer progress in 1576, Gilbert Talbot told his father, the earl of Shrewsbury, 'For these two or three days it has changed every five hours.'[139] Arguably, this was a tried-and-tested means of reasserting her authority over men disposed to make trial of their own power where they could.[140] The exchange of pleasantries and gifts, as well as the all-important access to the queen, worked to buttress her relationships with the nobility and gentry within their localities. Progresses could also be opportunities for counsel, reified or enacted. In both 1591 and 1594, when Burghley entertained the queen at his great house of Theobalds, he wove into her reception the message that he would like to retire and see his son Robert succeed him as secretary of state.[141] The royal visits to Leicester's castle at Kenilworth involved some heavy hinting as to Dudley's matrimonial ambitions. There was also the opportunity for politicking: in the progress to East Anglia in 1578, the intention was in part to consolidate royal authority in an area still painfully conscious of the execution of its leading noble, the duke of Norfolk, just six years earlier. Elizabeth's privy counsellors took the opportunity to implement some stricter curbs on local recusants than the bishop of Norwich, Edmund Freke, had been able to manage, with a stringency that is unlikely to have emanated from the queen herself.[142]

Progresses were also about meeting the populace at large, and Elizabeth's histrionic talents were particularly suited to her encounters with her more humble subjects. Stories circulated of how affably she dealt with people on her many summer progresses. The Spanish ambassador recorded how she 'was received everywhere with great acclamations and signs of joy, as is customary in this country, whereat she was extremely pleased and told me so, giving me to understand how beloved she was by her subjects'. He also commented that she 'ordered her carriage sometimes to be taken where the crowd seemed thickest, and stood up and thanked the people'.[143] When Feria had tried to suggest that Elizabeth owed her survival to Philip II's protection, she responded very firmly that in fact she owed it to the support of her future subjects: 'She declares that it was the people who put her in her present position and she will not acknowledge that your Majesty or the nobility of the realm had any part in it'.[144] She had been visibly protective of her popular reputation ever since the Seymour affair, when she had suggested to Protector Somerset that he issue a proclamation declaring her innocence.[145] The people often responded in kind: visiting Coventry on the progress of 1565, she was greeted with an oration which hailed her as 'a mother to your kingdom'.[146]

In the eyes of her subjects, Elizabeth's gender could make her a symbol of adoration, the mother of her people, 'good queen Bess'. It could also prove a liability. When the disaffected spread rumours about her, they were often gendered, and scurrilous allegations were usually sexualized ones. Some suggested that when the queen went on progress, it was to give birth away from the capital. One Henry Hawkins said scathingly in 1581 that 'She never goethe in progress but to be delivered.'[147] In the 1590s, two Essex peasants alleged that the queen had had children by Leicester, who had stuffed them up a chimney. Such rumours were not confined to the lower orders: the papal nuncio in 1578 also made reference to her illegitimate children by Leicester.[148] The example of female rule was not necessarily something other women appreciated: Joan Lyster from Cobham argued in 1586 that 'bycause she is but a wooman she owght not to be governor of a Realme'.[149] As Elizabeth's gender became compounded with old age, some have discerned the emergence within later Elizabethan poetry of sexualized imagery that channelled hostility to the regime of the 1590s.[150] To her supporters, her gender might even have seemed an advantage at times; to her detractors, it made her an easier target.

In the first decade of her reign, Elizabeth achieved more than anyone might have anticipated, but these years saw her tread with caution for any number of good reasons. Her country was still predominantly Catholic in conviction and tradition, and even those who shared her Protestant faith were predisposed to defy her authority in their excess of zeal. Her unmarried state was unnerving to her counsellors, and her refusal to declare a successor speaks eloquently to her anxieties concerning possible usurpation. She nearly died in 1562. The man she almost certainly loved was the man her counsellors were largely adamant she should not marry – and her own political sense told her that they were right. At every turn there was someone exhorting her to do something she thought unwise, whether it was to marry an unsuitable husband, embark on a more radical Reformation or declare a successor. If the 1560s appear on the surface to have been a relatively peaceful era, this is probably a direct reflection of the levels of anxiety experienced by the political elite, who came together in a remarkable show of solidarity to defend and support their queen. Solidarity is by no means the same thing as security, however; if she could usually count on the former, it is probable that Elizabeth never knew anything even approaching the latter.

'One firm and loyal society', 1568–85

The storm clouds that had never been far away since Elizabeth's accession came together threateningly in the second decade of her reign. If any more justification were needed for the cautious policies of Elizabeth's first decade, it was provided by the crisis which erupted from 1568 onwards. Mary Queen of Scots, having stirred up in Scotland precisely the kind of religious and political opposition that Elizabeth on her own account worked so strenuously to avoid, fled from Scotland to seek sanctuary in England, creating overnight a huge political problem. Rebellion broke out in Ireland and the north of England, in both cases with a strong confessional edge and, in the latter case, directly prompted by the presence of Mary Queen of Scots in the realm. In 1570, the publication of the papal bull *Regnans in excelsis*, which excommunicated Elizabeth and called on her Catholic subjects to resist her authority, compounded all these difficulties.[151] The bull asserted that the pope had power 'over all peoples and kingdoms, to pull up, destroy, scatter, disperse, plant and build'; it also detailed Elizabeth's 'impieties and crimes' and noted 'the persecution of the faithful and afflictions of religion daily growing more severe'. It was a deeply influential document, vigorously translated and disseminated by Catholics, and woven into the resistance theories of Nicholas Sander and others.[152]

In the background to these political developments, the suspension of Anglo-Spanish trade between 1568 and 1574 dealt a heavy blow to the commerce on which England's prosperity was founded. The escalation of civil unrest in the Netherlands, in which resistance to Habsburg rule increasingly melded with the assertion of Protestantism, left Elizabeth with a headache never to be resolved in her lifetime, as she sought, simultaneously and unsuccessfully, to support her co-religionists, whilst still protecting English commercial interests and attempting to retain the goodwill of an important ally. On one level, England was being caught up in a maelstrom that was affecting half of Europe, as pre-existing social and political tensions and conflicts were brought to breaking point by the weight of religious division and animosity. Rebellion and resistance spread across the continent like an untidy game of dominoes. The Protestant Reformation in Scotland had contributed to Mary's expulsion, which then compounded existing Catholic discontent in England. The risk of Mary replacing

Elizabeth, and thereby consolidating the power of the French, initially kept Philip II friendly; but English sympathies for the Protestant rebels in the Netherlands, combined with trading difficulties and English privateering, damaged relations to the point where the duke of Alba ordered the seizure of all English shipping and merchandise in the Netherlands in December 1568. The repressive regime which Alva had instituted there caused great unease, and when viewed in the context of Elizabeth's excommunication, the Ridolfi Plot and the Massacre of St Bartholomew's Day in 1572, it could appear that the persecutory violence and political aggression of European Catholicism was reaching a new level of threat. When news of the massacre in Paris reached London, the government issued special prayers to be said throughout the realm, and Elizabeth put the Court into mourning.[153]

This level of animosity at the international level translated into unease in society at large. Here there were already other strains. In 1570, the plague was so bad in London that the queen adjourned the Michaelmas term law courts.[154] In 1572, the government issued a proclamation prohibiting the export of grain, which had seen a rapid increase in price since 'the unseasonableness of the late harvest time'.[155] When, in 1569, a servant woman from Market Harborough allegedly gave birth to a cat, it was considered an ominous enough portent for the case to be referred from the archdeacon's court to the earl of Huntingdon, who in turn relayed it to Cecil, who in turn asked advice of the archbishop of Canterbury.[156] Monstrous births might be taken as signs of the monster that was rebellion, or just as divine commentary on the lamentable state of the kingdom.[157] Through the 1560s, there were frequent reports of such occurrences: the birth of conjoined twins in Kent in 1565 and in Buckinghamshire in 1566 was taken as divine reproach for 'the great decay of hearty love and charity', symbolized by the position of the babies, who appeared to be embracing.[158]

A constant and worrying theme throughout these years was the strength of Catholic loyalism, which in 1569 bubbled over into the Revolt of the Northern Earls. In many ways this was the disaster for which Elizabeth had been bracing herself for over a decade. Around six thousand men rose up, led by the earls of Westmorland and Northumberland; they captured various key locations in the north, and reinstated the mass, marching behind banners of the Five Wounds of Christ, just as the rebels had done during the Pilgrimage of Grace. Durham Cathedral was violently purged of all traces of

Protestantism, and mass was sung; so many people came that there was barely room to stand. The Protestant bishop of Durham, James Pilkington, fled south with some of his more zealous co-religionists. This was a rebellion which historians once used to ascribe to disaffected remnants of the old nobility, angry at being marginalized, but that is to underestimate the antagonistic religious atmosphere of the 1560s.[159] If it was a combination of elements that prompted the uprising, the foundational role was played by Catholic allegiances, compounded by the presence of Mary Queen of Scots on English soil. It could be said, too, that Elizabeth, defensive of her authority in the north, had provoked a reaction by the strictness of the curbs she had imposed on the earls of Northumberland and Westmorland.[160] Sir George Bowes, loyal to the queen, sent a stream of letters to the earl of Sussex, lord president of the Council of the North; it was his contention that, at least in part, the earls had risen up 'for ther owne garde, beynge in greate feare to be apprehendid'.[161]

For Elizabeth, the rebellion portended potential disaster. It was not just a menace to her religious settlement, but a threat to her authority as queen and her legitimacy as monarch, and she hastily raised a formidable army of around fourteen thousand men. The retribution was violent, and over seven hundred men were hanged under martial law in an extraordinary display of state-sponsored vengeance, which also involved the widespread seizure of lands and assets.[162] This far greater number would never compete in Tudor mythology with the three hundred (or fewer) who died for their religion under Mary I's rule, but it was a devastating riposte and betrays the level of anguish and anxiety felt by the regime.[163] The proclamation which Elizabeth issued declaring the treason of the two earls went into some detail to explain their perfidy, and to justify the queen's actions in demanding their presence. It was curiously rude about the earls' poverty and about how they 'do go about through the persuasion of a number of desperate persons associated as parasites with them to satisfy their private lack and ambition'. Notably, this proclamation made no mention of religion, other than accusing the rebels of having 'invaded houses and churches'; it is probable that the threat from Catholic sentiment was too great for the regime to mention it by name. The proclamation appealed for popular support, declaring that 'her majesty chargeth all her good subjects to employ their whole powers to the preservation of common peace'.[164]

Perhaps the most significant consequence of the rebellion was the publication of the papal bull excommunicating Elizabeth, although – owing in part to the difficulties of circulating a forbidden text – it was not distributed in England until after the uprising had been quelled.[165] It exacerbated the concerns of an already agitated society. Thomas Drant, preaching at Court, compared Elizabeth unfavourably with the Old Testament King David, bluntly observing 'David destroyed all Gods enemies: her Maiestie hath destroyed none of Gods enemies.'[166] To the more zealous of Elizabeth's subjects, it appeared that all their forebodings had been proved right, and God was punishing her lukewarmness. The queen was not unmindful of the Catholic threat, however. Twice in 1570, proclamations ordered the arrest of those who smuggled and circulated seditious books, specifically because they were thought to be seeking 'to engender in the heads of the simple ignorant multitude a misliking or murmuring against the quiet government of the realm'.[167] One of the proclamations referred in particular to the 'fugitives and rebels being fled now and remaining out of the realm', who were stirring up trouble by means of 'seditious messages and false reports'.[168] Elizabeth's persecution of Catholics increased markedly in the years following the 1569 rebellion. One thread running through the events of these years was the idea that the duke of Norfolk should marry Mary Queen of Scots and thereby help her to usurp Elizabeth. This is what lay at the heart of the Ridolfi Plot of 1571, and the notion behind it attracted considerable interest and support abroad. The proposal was that the duke of Alva would invade from the Netherlands with a large army, prompting a Catholic uprising among the nobility and those loyal to the old faith that would ensure the assassination of Elizabeth. Norfolk had already been imprisoned once; in tense language, a warrant of 1571 from Elizabeth allowed – indeed commanded – the torturing of two of his adherents.[169] The level of threat can be gauged from the draconian response that the failed plot called forth. In 1572, at the trial of the duke of Norfolk, there could be little doubt that he was guilty of conspiring against the queen, but he was refused legal counsel and representation, and only one witness spoke in person, whilst all other testimonies against him were read aloud by the prosecution, leaving no room for their evidence to be weighed or cross-questioned.[170]

The threat from Norfolk, Ridolfi and others was soon neutralized, but Mary Queen of Scots remained alive, despite the many urgings to the contrary. Penal laws against Catholics became harsher. Recusants could be imprisoned without any form of trial, merely on the word of the Privy Council; and from 1570 onwards, the use of torture, particularly against Catholic priests, became increasingly common.[171] The parliament of 1571 passed a new Treason Act making it an offence to deny that Elizabeth was the rightful queen, or cause her harm, 'by any printing, writing, ciphering, speech, words, or sayings', or to call her 'heretic, schismatic, tyrant, infidel or an usurper of the crown', a clear indication that all these things were being said and done. The act gave as its justification the fear of many 'whether the laws and statutes of this realm remaining at this present in force are vailable and sufficient enough for the surety and preservation of the Quen's most royal person, in which consisteth all the happines and comfort of the whole state'.[172] Much ink has been spilt over the parliamentary attempts to safeguard Elizabeth in the 1580s, but the level of the threat, and the regime's defensive response, were already vividly apparent in 1571.

The 1570s were also the decade in which the frustrations of many of Elizabeth's more Protestant subjects began to find strident expression. For the godly, the way forward was clear, and one key element in their programme was an increased emphasis on sermons. It was therefore a shock to discover that their queen thought 'three or four sermons a year should suffice', and chiefly wanted a ministry of those who could read aloud the Bible and the official homilies to the people, without adding any interpretation of their own.[173] Such a stance on preaching appalled nearly all Elizabeth's bishops and senior Protestant clergy, to whom sermons were the chief conduit for the voice of God. Elizabeth would never overcome her distaste for the strident Calvinism and authoritarian churchmanship of much of her own Protestant establishment, compounded by the insistence of so many Protestant commentators on the extent to which her authority was limited and circumscribed by the will of God. The Elizabethan Londoner Thomas Bentley published *The Monument of matrones* in 1582, in part in celebration of Elizabeth's piety and that of other devout women; but it was accompanied by the warning (in which Bentley ventriloquized his Creator) to 'beware therefore that yee abuse not this authoritie given unto you by me . . . For be ye sure that I have placed you in this seate upon this condition'.[174] The minatory tone of Protestant zealots, alongside their slowly deteriorating faith in Elizabeth as an exemplary Protestant ruler, can be seen in the subtle shifts within Foxe's *Actes and Monuments* or 'Book of Martyrs', as the optimism of the first edition in 1563 gave way to the more critical or reproachful observations of later editions in 1570, 1576 and 1583.[175]

Protestant campaigns for further reform were often channelled through parliament. Elizabeth's parliaments were for a long time assumed to be an arena in which constitutional progress was slowly being made, as the Commons found a newly assertive voice and began to take the initiative on important national questions, acquiring the confidence to criticize not only government policy, but even the prerogative powers that lay behind that policy. Only more recently has the idea of opposition between Crown and parliament been replaced by a recognition that these were different arms of a single system of ruling, in which all aimed at collaboration rather than confrontation, even if some disagreement was unavoidable.[176] If anything, it would seem that Elizabethan parliaments had less power than formerly, since Elizabeth was sufficiently defensive of her authority to keep them on a very tight rein, and repeatedly forbade any discussion by parliament of questions which she felt were none of its business, including her marriage, the question of the succession and the fate of Mary Queen of Scots. On all of these points, it is true, successive parliaments repeatedly petitioned the queen; but it is equally important to note that at no point were their petitions very effective.

Just because Elizabethan parliaments were not a breeding-ground for republican ideology or for the emergence of proto-democratic forces, that did not mean they caused Elizabeth and her regime no trouble. In particular, issues of religious reform often posed a challenge. It is true that MPs were often at least as interested – if not more so – in local matters than in large national issues. It has been pointed out that the second reading of the Act of Uniformity was held on the same day as the second reading of a bill which revived the Act for the Killing of Rooks and Crows.[177] However, MPs could also feel strongly about questions of national importance, and they had a clear sense of responsibility, albeit sporadically expressed, when it came to advising the queen. At times, this could cross the line between concerned advocacy and impudent reproof. Peter Wentworth was, with his brother Paul, particularly known for his outspoken interventions concerning the succession, Mary Queen of Scots, freedom of speech and parliamentary privilege more generally. He was a brother-in-law of

Walsingham and a zealous Protestant, both of which may have given extra edge to his remarks. It is also possible that he was one of the hot-heads whom Elizabeth's privy counsellors found useful in voicing what they themselves dared not say, but his intemperateness won him few allies.[178]

One of the things Elizabeth feared most from her more zealous Protestant subjects was their capacity for independent expression. The queen preferred any criticisms to be conveyed privately, not proclaimed publicly.[179] When James Morrice made a proposal in parliament concerning the activities of the church courts, he was put under house arrest for a time; Burghley explained to him that he should not have broadcast his views to the 'common people', but quietly advised the queen in private.[180] Protestants, however, were supposed to preach the Word of God from the roof-tops, and reticence was not a virtue they recognized. As Elizabeth's reign wore on, and no promises of further reform were made, their efforts were increasingly focused on independent efforts to evangelize. In large part this came through building the godly community. In market towns all over England, ministers were in the habit of coming together for confer-ence, followed by dinner at an inn, to strengthen the ties of fellowship and at the same time develop their preaching skills. These gatherings took various forms, but were often referred to as 'prophesyings' – from St Paul's first letter to the Corinthians, in which he enjoined his followers to 'prophesy one by one, that all may learn, and all may be comforted'. The end result was a cross between an academic disputation and a sermon workshop held (at least in part) in public.[181] Elizabeth disliked events such as these, and in 1576 issued instructions that they were to cease: these public clerical gatherings had, in her eyes, strong overtones of presbyte-rian forms of church government, where the secular authorities exercised only minimal influence over the religious institutions. She was at least partially correct: these pious gatherings were in part intended as a show of strength by the godly, who regarded the queen's interventions as 'a service to Satan'.[182] The fight which ensued demonstrates some of the divisions that were present in Elizabethan society. This was not just a squabble between queen and bishops: it was something on which many local communities were divided. Elizabeth was able to take action precisely because information about such gatherings was being relayed by those in the localities who were hostile.

In December 1576, Grindal, now archbishop of Canterbury, composed a letter to Elizabeth that was breath-taking in its presumption.[183] He declared himself grieved at her offence against divine will, and threatened her with the 'famine, war and pestilence' that afflicted disobedient rulers in the Old Testament. At the heart of his message was a blunt accusation of delinquency. 'Alas, Madam!', he wrote, 'is the scripture more plain in any one thing, than that the gospel of Christ should be plentifully preached?' Moving from the particular issue to the more general question, he told her that concerning religious matters she should 'not use to pronounce so resolutely and peremptorily, as from authority, as you may do in civil and extern[al] matters; but always remember, that in God's causes the will of God, and not the will of any earthly creature, is to take place'. This letter was long, and its author may have been more correct than he really intended when he described it as 'tedious'; it was unmistakably an attempt to tell Elizabeth off, once and for all. For this reason, it was also, as it transpired, the end of Grindal's career. When he warned the queen that 'although ye are a mighty prince, yet remember that He which dwelleth in heaven is mightier', he might as well have signed a letter of resignation. His sympathizers on the Council tried to save him, but Grindal was obdurate, and so was Elizabeth: for the next six years, the archbishop was effectively in limbo. It was probably a relief to all concerned when, after years of ill health, and all but blind, Grindal died in 1583.[184] The queen had needed to battle to assert herself, but her authority had triumphed over Grindal's reproaches.[185]

Tensions at the heart of government were echoed by stresses and strains at the parish level. In 1578, when a servant woman called Mercy Gould delivered an illegitimate baby that was either born dead or died soon after birth, it seemed just another example of a tragedy that befell many vulnerable women. The subsequent row over whether Mercy had attempted to abort her child, possibly helped by her former mistress, divided the village of Cuckfield in Sussex with consequences that were to reach the Privy Council and the Court. The reason for this escalation was that the village, caught up in the scandal, divided along lines of religious loyalty. On the one side was a zealous, puritan ironmaster, whose will specified that he be buried with 'no manner of pomps and glory' and charged his son to 'embrace the gospel of Christ'. On the other was the parish minister, brother to the zealous but conformist bishop of Chichester. Both men were attacked by having their wives traduced; and three years on there was an altercation, during which the rival factions actually fought for control of the pulpit.[186] The repercussions of this torrid affair reached the desk of Francis Walsingham, and drew in several higher authorities on the way. Fault-lines could run all the way through the social hierarchy.

These fissures were not to be found everywhere; but after 1570, they were always possible, as every Catholic in the realm was under a moral obligation to dislodge Elizabeth from the throne. Towards the end of the 1570s, with an eye to shoring up a degree of autonomy in the Netherlands, the queen contemplated marriage with Francis, duke of Anjou, thereby alarming many of her closest advisors, as well as her subjects. The strength of popular outrage is an indication of just how divided Elizabethan society had become. Elizabeth had briefly considered a match with Henry, the then duke of Anjou, in 1570; but by 1578 Henry was ruling France, and it was his brother – formerly the duke of Alençon, but duke of Anjou after 1576 – who became a serious contender for Elizabeth's hand. Short, bandy-legged, pock-marked and twenty-two years her junior, Francis still seems to have touched Elizabeth's heart: the courtship, unusually, was conducted in person, when Anjou visited the English Court. Like all the people close to her, he was given a nickname: 'her Frog'. This match, first discussed in 1572, was dropped as a consequence of the St Bartholomew's Day Massacre, but then revived with particular intensity in the period 1578–81. This was not a reflection of Elizabeth's wayward emotions, however, despite the ink that has been spilt on such speculations. It was a much more pragmatic and unemotional response to the international situation: with the strife in the Netherlands worsening, Anjou offered a possible counterweight to Habsburg domination. It is important to realize that the question of Elizabeth's marriage was always a political matter.

Elizabeth, raised to consider royal matches as a tool of political strategy, must have been drawn by the prospect of Anjou as the ruler of the United Provinces of the Netherlands, since in 1579 William the Silent had invited him to assume the sovereignty of this newly fledged state, created out of opposition to Spanish Habsburg rule. There were therefore sound political reasons for considering the match; but the popular reaction to the prospect of a Catholic king was a fearful and often angry one, and the response from those in positions of authority was not much better.[187] There may even have been an assassination attempt made against the French envoy: certainly, in July 1579 a boatman fired on the barge in which Simier, Anjou's envoy, and the queen were travelling, although Elizabeth insisted it was an accident and pardoned the man involved, possibly to avoid making a martyr of him.[188] More articulate opposition engendered more vengeful retribution. John Stubbs, who in 1579 wrote *The Discoverie of a Gaping Gulf*, lost his right hand (as did his publisher) for maligning the proposed match. Stubbs's pamphlet, which prophesied conflict on an international scale, as well as domestic disaster, was printed in London just a day after Anjou's arrival. One Londoner sent fifty copies to a friend in Cornwall for distribution.[189] Elizabeth was furious, and her reprisals were harsh. She could perhaps tell that Stubbs's arguments mirrored with suspicious closeness the objections that had been raised by her privy counsellors.[190] The boundary between popular culture and aristocratic counsel was a decidedly porous one.

The prospect of the Anjou match caused such a stir because there was, by the 1570s, a sizeable constituency among the ruling classes – strongly supported by popular opinion more generally – that saw questions of international politics in starkly confessional terms. To them, French Catholics were irretrievably tainted by their complicity in the mass slaughter of French Protestants in the Massacre of St Bartholomew's Day, and for Elizabeth to be proposing marriage to one of them was offensive to the point of obscenity. Elizabeth was neither giddy with emotion nor foolishly irresponsible in her consideration of this marriage, however. The single most pressing threat in Europe after 1567 was the army of seasoned Spanish veterans who had arrived with the duke of Alva in the Netherlands. Elizabeth wanted to return to an older balance of power, where Spanish rule in the Low Countries was exercised at a distance. This would enable English commerce through Antwerp to continue as it always had, and would promote Anglo-Spanish trade more generally. The duke of Anjou, as putative ruler of the United Provinces, promised a valuable alliance for England, as well as a defence against further Habsburg encroachments on England's back doorstep. For this reason, even some of her more Protestant counsellors were, at certain points, persuaded that the marriage might be good policy.[191]

From a purely political point of view, there was a good case to be made; placed in the context of popular religious culture, however, the proposal was a disaster. The notion of the 'Virgin Queen' was in large part a consequence of the negotiations for the Anjou match, and it demonstrates some of the polarities emerging within Elizabethan society. The 'sieve portraits' (see plate 11) were painted in this era, and provide in microcosm an illustration of how historical understanding of Elizabeth has changed. They were once taken as straightforward Elizabethan propaganda, with the sieve evoking the legend of the Roman vestal virgin, who proved her virginity in the face of slander by carrying water from the River Tiber in a sieve. The fact that these propaganda pieces, which were expensive artefacts, relied on a knowledge of Roman mythology underlines the point that the pictures were destined for an elite audience. More tellingly still, it would appear that these ostensibly flattering portraits of the queen were not painted at her behest, but were instead intended as a warning. They might be read as an exhortation from subjects who wanted to see their queen dressed in severely puritanical black and white, with pearls to signify her chastity, in stark contrast to the flamboyance of a dissolute and depraved French Court.

As the Catholic threat at home and abroad became ever more menacing, the political classes came together in 1584 to sign a document declaring that they would bind themselves 'in the bond of one firm and loyal society' for Elizabeth's defence.[192] It is an indication of just how worrying the political situation was that the nobility and gentry were proposing what was, in essence, vigilante justice to protect their queen and country. It was in effect a declaration of a state of emergency.[193] That stability was sustained during these years attests not just to Elizabeth's political acumen and determination, but to the profound sense of civic responsibility felt by so many among the political classes. The Bond of Association was an extraordinary manifestation of this.[194] The assassination of William the Silent in July 1584, the first head of state ever to be shot with a handgun, was carried out by a Catholic subject of Philip II, who had put a bounty on William's head.[195] Protestant Europe mourned; Catholic Europe rejoiced. In this febrile atmosphere, fears for Elizabeth's own safety escalated. To this end, almost all elements of the political nation came together solemnly to add their names to a document in which they promised to exterminate any who attempted to harm Elizabeth and vowed to prevent that person succeeding to the throne. The document did not need to mention Mary by name.

The Bond was an unprecedented attempt to build political consensus and defend the regime. In an age which generally looked with disfavour on the concept of innovation, the circumstances of Elizabeth's reign forced some intense political introspection. In 1562, when Elizabeth contracted smallpox and nearly died, the fledgling Protestant Church had hung by a thread, and the queen could do no more than instruct that Lord Robert Dudley should act as protector in the event of her death. Cecil's thoughts – and those of many others – must have raced ahead to the possible consequences of her demise. He probably concluded that the takeover of the throne by Mary Queen of Scots, backed by her Guise uncles, would mean the restoration of Catholicism and the loss of English autonomy. That was emphatically the worst nightmare of a great number of the ruling elite. At the time, Cecil had outlined to himself a plan, which he would revive (in modified form) two decades later, when a state of emergency again threatened. Strictly speaking, on the death of a monarch the entire structure of government vanished overnight, as Privy Council, Court and parliament were all disbanded, to await a new monarch and fresh summons to constitute their own advisory and executive bodies. Cecil imagined an alternative: he envisaged that the Privy Council could prolong its existence through an interregnum, and that parliament would stay in session; between them, they would decide on the next monarch. He was one step away from suggesting an elective monarchy, a constitutional innovation that – in the context of the times – was an extraordinary thing to be contemplating. His plans have famously been described as reflecting the 'monarchical republic' of Elizabeth – a regime that was indisputably centred on the person of the monarch, and yet where there was a republican sense of both obligation and entitlement among office-holders and men of authority to preserve the state.[196]

The Elizabethan regime was indeed an intricate construct of prerogative powers and civic obligation, and it is true that republicanism was a well-established intellectual influence on generations of statesmen who had received a humanist education.[197] The case for a monarchical republic should not be overstated, however. First, and most crucially, few of these ideas ever got much beyond the drawing-board: Cecil's jottings remained speculative, and his Act for the Security of the Queen's Person did not go as far as he envisaged, and perhaps wanted. Second, if this was republicanism, it was of a very particular and not very secular sort: it came with a very marked Protestant identity. Republican liberty was not perhaps nearly as central to the political anxieties of the time as the 'liberty of the gospel'.[198] This is partly why Elizabeth remained wary of such ideas: she regarded arguments about a 'mixed polity', where the power of the monarch was tempered by that of Council and parliaments, as increasingly suspect, especially as they were put forward by religious radicals. It was central to the presbyterian convictions of Thomas Cartwright (perhaps the most outspoken presbyterian sympathizer) and his ilk, but it could also be deployed by Catholics. From whichever direction, it promised in particular a measure of religious autonomy that completely undermined the Royal Supremacy – and with it Elizabeth's own sovereignty.[199]

By 1585, the articulation of the threats against Elizabeth and the eloquence of those coming to her defence were both problematic in their different ways. This was also the year when events in Europe reached crisis pitch, so that the regime could no longer hold back from direct involvement. By the Treaty of Nonsuch, Elizabeth finally committed herself to overt support for the Protestant rebels in the Netherlands, whose cause she had been informally encouraging for years. The European balance of power demanded it, but the queen was fearful of the consequences of this level of involvement. She was right to be apprehensive.

'These threatning daies of sword and famine': 1585–1603

The last eighteen years of Elizabeth's reign saw the elaboration of the iconography of Gloriana, the Virgin Queen, as never before. If this cult of Elizabeth reached a new pitch of fervour in the late 1580s and 1590s, however, it was because there was even more reason than before to fashion an iconography of greatness in the face of war, suffering, religious animosity and political tension. The phrase 'these threatning daies of sword and famine' appeared in a book containing remedies to stave off starvation in a third successive year of harvest failure.[200] At all levels of society the strain could be felt: from those on the poverty line, who could be devastated by food shortages, to those in positions of authority, who were obliged to respond to this crisis, whilst at the same time raising money for the defence of the realm and fighting in the Low Countries and Ireland to protect both faith and kingdom.[201] All this unfolded as Elizabeth aged, her chances of a child now long gone, and the prospect of a disputed succession all too immediate. Spain, once England's most treasured ally, had become her enemy, and after the Treaty of Joinville in 1584 was in partnership with the powerful Guise faction in France – an alliance which threatened to have devastating consequences for Protestants across Europe. Already the Throckmorton plot had envisaged that the duke of Guise might invade England with Spanish support. The last two decades of Elizabeth's reign posed all these problems, without proposing any solutions. If the government response to these challenges has been viewed as autocratic, this is less because of any shift in political strategy than because of the need for defensive policies at home, as well as abroad. From 1585 until she died, Elizabeth would remain at war.[202]

Elizabeth had foiled parliamentary attempts to have the Bond of Association's provisions written into statute law, uneasy at being managed in this way, but the Privy Council still had to respond to the manifold threats at home and abroad. In part, it did so by reviving the institution of lords lieutenant, effectively introducing martial law in the provinces.[203] The Council also became much more draconian in the handling of recusant Catholics, who were now excluded from the militia and the magistracy as never before. At the same time, John Whitgift, archbishop of Canterbury since 1583, was determined to pursue the heterodox thinkers in his own Church, and the animosity between conformist and reformist Protestants was a pronounced and painful feature of these years. The enduringly problematic figure of Mary Queen of Scots remained under house arrest, but she was never politically inactive.[204] Cast by most of her supporters as a symbol of the true Catholic faith, she in fact remained broad-minded about religion, sometimes attending Protestant services, whilst some of her close servants were Protestants. In political terms, however, she was the focus of Catholic ambitions. She never stopped working towards a return to power, and in the early 1580s had proposed that she be rehabilitated in joint sovereignty with her son James. At the same time, she continued to plot to overthrow Elizabeth by violent means, generally with Spanish aid, although her status as dowager queen of France and her son's Protestant religion were both problematic for Philip II.

When it came to patterns of alliance, however, the map of Europe was being redrawn in the 1580s. Mary's survival had, in one sense, been an asset for Elizabeth: it kept Philip II at bay, since he feared her accession would create an axis of England, Scotland and France under Guise influence, which he would be hard pressed to withstand. But after 1584, there was a sea-change, as the Guises became Philip II's allies. This meant there was no longer any strategic purpose in keeping Mary alive. There were, however, some very powerful scruples on Elizabeth's part. Her counsellors seemed to struggle to comprehend why she was so reluctant to see Mary executed, but they could have looked more closely at the parallels between the two queens. If Mary could prove so fragile as to succumb to political and religious pressures and have her anointed head struck from her shoulders, then Elizabeth's equally fragile position might seem all the more worrying. Nevertheless, the political elite in England was determined to be rid of the menace that was Mary. The Babington Plot of 1586 was her downfall, and although she was entirely complicit in it, the plot was equally the result of Walsingham's careful manufacture. His double agents were aware of every step, encouraging the plotters in the hope of incriminating Mary beyond all doubt. Mary herself, in the course of hatching the plot, promised that she would declare Philip II her heir, given her son's Protestantism, which was perhaps the most powerful bid for Spanish support she could have made. Once uncovered, there was little difficulty in establishing Mary's treasonous intent. Though her guilt was not in question, her punishment was, for part of Elizabeth remained horrified at the prospect of executing an anointed ruler. She was also profoundly indignant at the pressure she was experiencing from the political classes, and also at the idea that having 'in my time pardoned so many rebels' she should now 'be forced to this proceeding'.[205] When Elizabeth, having signed the death warrant, was foiled in her attempt to forbid its despatch, she was furious – perhaps not so much over Mary's death, as about her perceived responsibility for it.

Even as the last scene in the drama of Mary Queen of Scots was being played out, the Armada was under construction in Spain, and in 1588 it sailed. Popular literature might hail the defeat of the Armada as providential, but this was to put a reassuring, godly gloss on a much more unpredictable and frightening experience. The Armada of 1588 may have been defeated, but it was as much a casualty of unfavourable weather and Spanish disorganization as of English naval skill. Philip II subsequently rebuilt the Spanish navy to be even bigger and more powerful, sending further armadas in 1596 and 1597, as well as a force to Ireland in 1601.[206] Meanwhile, the most that can be said of England's preparedness to face invasion is that it was not quite as bad as we used to think.[207] Elizabeth was at her most vulnerable during time of war, when the constraints of her gender became most painfully apparent, as she was unable to lead her troops into battle.

The international situation exacerbated religious animosities that were already well established, and after the menace from abroad in 1588 came a further challenge from within the country, with the publication in October of a tract by 'Martin Marprelate'. This was the first in a series of scurrilous and clandestinely printed pamphlets that attacked the bishops (and indeed the whole system of episcopacy), prompting an indignant rebuttal by the regime.[208] The full brilliance of Elizabethan satirical wit was deployed in mockery of the episcopate.[209] It was powerful ecclesiological argument in the most entertaining of guises, as Francis Bacon would later describe it, 'whereby matter of religion is handled in the style of the stage'.[210] Ridicule aside, its purpose was to display 'the goodnes of the cause of reformation, and the poore, poore, poore nakednes of your government'.[211] This pamphlet war shows many things at work: the animosities between different elements of English Protestantism, for one, but also the power of the popular press not only to unnerve the regime, but also to serve it, for this episode witnessed the Privy Council covertly engendering responses in like manner.[212] The retribution for nonconformist tendencies was severe. Under John Whitgift's leadership as archbishop of Canterbury, the prosecution and expulsion of overly zealous Protestants was so vigorous that Burghley compared it to the Spanish Inquisition.

Whilst godly Protestants were voicing their discontent, and while Elizabeth's closest counsellors were struggling to maintain stability, the persecution of Catholics increased. For many recusant Catholics, the Elizabethan administration was a persecuting state riddled with corruption. There was deep resentment, as well as fear, that the authorities labelled Catholic loyalism as treasonous; priests who faced a traitor's death protested loudly at being convicted of treason when what was really at stake was their religion. From a Catholic point of view, it should be possible to be a loyal servant to the queen without violation of religious conscience. Indeed, the Privy Council distinguished – in a very haphazard way – between Catholics who were deemed a threat and those who were tolerated, and over the years many Catholics moved back and forth across the line of what was considered permissible. The Catholic recusant Thomas Tresham served as sheriff in his locality for many years, although he was in the end imprisoned.[213] Priests trained abroad were the chief target of the penal laws, but those who helped them also ran a terrible risk. A new and volatile element had been introduced by the entrenchment of the Reformation across Europe. This made it possible, as never before, for loyalty to a prince to be at odds with a subject's loyalty to God. William Allen, writing in 1584, declared that 'Ther is no warre in the world so just or honorable be it civil or forraine, as that which is waged for Religion.' He argued that 'the armes taken for defence of Godlie honor' were 'commendable and glorious', and that 'no crime in the world deserveth more sharpe and zealous pursuite of extreme revenge ... then revolting from the Faith to strange religions'.[214] In particular, he firmly asserted the right of priests and religious authorities to challenge the ungodly actions of princes.

> Princes being not subject to superiours temporal, nor patient of correction or controlment by their inferiours, may easelie fal to greeuous disorders, which must tend to the danger and ruine of whole countries. In respect wherof, great spirite, power, courage, & freedome of speech haue bene from the beginning graunted by God, as wel ordinarie to Priestes, as extraordinarie to some Prophets and religious persons, in al ages and times, both of the new & old testament.[215]

Allen's assertion of the principles of resistance theory would, of course, have been entirely recognizable to his Protestant opponents, particularly those who, like Grindal, felt emboldened to reprove and instruct their secular prince. Thomas Bilson, writing a reply to Allen a year later, made an almost identical assertion concerning men who held religious office: 'God hath placed them in his church to teach, reprove, instruct and reforme as wel Princes as others.'[216] The issue of holy war had never been more central to European politics.

The intellectual and religious debates of the 1590s had an energy and fury never seen before. They spilled over into rancorous pamphlet wars, found more subtle outlet through public and private theatre, and engaged the hearts and minds of many. This was the beginning of the politics of 'popularity', as Archbishop Whitgift termed it, which he saw as rooted in religious division, but which spread to the point where political theory was anatomized and extended as never before.[217] Historians have long since noted the change of tone in the politics of the 1590s. In part, this was just a change of personnel. Between 1588 and 1590, some of Elizabeth's closest advisors died: the earl of Leicester; his brother, the earl of Warwick; Sir Walter Mildmay, who had served the Crown since the last years of Henry VIII; Sir Francis Walsingham, who had controlled Elizabeth's diplomatic networks and deployed her spies. The period has also been seen as a time of political calcification, as the Privy Council shrank in size, patronage dried up and the regime adopted a more authoritarian tone, perhaps particularly in the drive to defeat Puritanism as a political and ecclesiastical force. The corruption of those in power has also been noted: Burghley, despite his reputation for integrity, as head of the Court of Wards made three times as much profit as that made by the Crown, and recorded these financial benefits on a paper labelled, 'This note to be burned'.[218] There was increasing use of the Court of High Commission to target puritan ministers. In 1591, in a case brought by one of those puritan ministers, Robert Cawdrey, this practice was challenged. However, the judgement went in favour of the Crown, thus reinforcing the Royal Supremacy. In 1596, after the Oxfordshire rising – an initiative barely worthy of the name of rebellion – two men were tortured to uncover what was, in fact, a non-existent conspiracy.[219]

The case for a *fin de siècle* slide into repressive authoritarian government and greater religious conservatism can be overstated, however. The practice of torture, the dislike of religious radicalism and the use of repressive policies can be found long before the 1590s, provided the threat loomed large enough. Evidence of financial corruption can be found in every decade of the century, and was a normal part of life at Court, where minimal remuneration for office-holding was expected to be augmented by gifts, which a more modern observer might call bribes. Leicester and Walsingham were dead, but Burghley lived on, albeit complaining bitterly of ill health at times; he was determinedly instructing his son Robert to take over from him when he died, as he did in 1598. Most importantly, it needs to be remembered that the country at this point was deeply embroiled in an expensive and distressing war with the greatest power in Europe, and with its own subjects in Ireland. Rather than start with the political response, and assume that there was a shift in the political approach, it makes more sense to look to society at large, and to the deprivation and destruction caused by conflict and dearth. It would then be reasonable to conclude that if the government response was markedly more defensive and autocratic, that was probably a direct response to the political, social and economic strains of the time. And if Elizabeth seems to have been more wary, at times slow to trust those around her, and vehement in her criticism of any failings, she was perhaps recalling her grandfather a century before, battening down the hatches in the 1490s, when he was faced with both threats abroad and treason within the royal household.

In the 1590s, England's dilemmas should also be seen within the broader context of European upheaval. The threat of dynastic failure was not unique to England: it had been experienced by the Polish Jagiellonian house in 1572, by the Joanine dynasty of Portugal in 1580 and by the Valois line in France in 1589. The English ruling classes paid close attention to what was happening in these other lands, but the lessons from each were unclear. Poland responded by broadening the franchise; Portugal was sublimated into the Spanish Empire; and France descended into yet further civil war. In England's case, the threat of both Spanish conquest and civil war was keenly felt. It was hard to see how the latter could be avoided. Robert Persons identified over a dozen possible claimants to the throne in his highly contentious tracts concerning the succession in 1593 and 1595.[220]

Meanwhile, other Elizabethans had less cerebral concerns. In the mid-1590s the harvest failed three years in succession, and the population, which had already shouldered the costs of war, was now faced with a heightened risk of starvation. There were plague outbreaks of particular intensity in London in 1593 and 1603. The suffering was intense, and responses were fearful. There was also a concern that dearth might breed rebellion. The Privy Council warned the archbishops in 1596 to ensure that the people were 'taught to indure this scarsety with patyence' and not to listen to those who tried to make them 'swerve from the humble dutyes of good subjectes'.[221] The providential mindset of the age meant that catastrophe was usually interpreted in terms of divine judgement, and in the 1590s this tendency was particularly marked. The Privy Council issued instructions to the archbishops on Christmas Day 1596 to respond to the crisis by instituting public prayers and fasting every Wednesday and Friday, 'according to her Majesty's desire to the releif of her poore people, who no doubt do lamentably suffer want of sustenance in theis tymes'.[222] This automatic assumption that any kind of disaster must be a punishment for sin was characteristic of the age, but it was here cast in unusually weighty terms. Popular rumours suggest that others were drawing their own conclusions. In Hampshire, a young girl in 1593 awoke after spending fifteen days and nights asleep to report that she had seen both Mary Tudor and Mary Queen of Scots in heaven, and Henry VIII and the earl of Leicester in hell. She predicted that Elizabeth I would die before Michaelmas, and was imprisoned in Winchester amid rumours that she was a witch.[223]

Out of this state of emergency emerged the Elizabethan Poor Laws of 1598 and 1601. At first sight, this makes it look as though the issue of poverty was becoming the responsibility of central government, and indeed the provisions of the statutes did lay the foundations for what would become a more bureaucratic system.[224] But the underlying dynamic was much as it had been earlier in the century: the poor were the responsibility of the wealthy and of the parish. In London, in 1596, householders were urged to contribute to collections for poor relief, 'for that it is a woorke of Charitie for those whom almightie god has blessed in more plentifull measure to releeve their poor and neadie breathern'.[225] The burdens of the time may have been shouldered haphazardly and inequitably, but they affected all parts of society.

The many tensions of the age were made manifest in 1601, in the earl of Essex's rebellion. This demonstrated the corrosive effects of warfare on the ties between those in power, breaking trust and souring relationships between the queen and many of her counsellors and courtiers. Since it was on these ties that political stability depended, the uprising was both a consequence and a cause of much alarm and reproach from both the ruling classes and the people at large, among whom Essex had been very popular: when he was dangerously ill at the end of 1599, several churches in London had offered special prayers for him. It was alleged that Essex had attempted a *coup d'état* on Sunday, 8 February 1601, but the truth was rather more messy and complicated. In effect, Essex had lashed out at his political fate, which – after failure in Ireland and arrogance at Court – had seen him disgraced, excluded from the circles of power which he felt to be his rightful arena, and deprived of income. Elizabeth had, in fact, safeguarded him against charges of treason, but he had been examined for his insubordination in Ireland and prohibited from Court; the factional ructions he had caused reached as far as Denbighshire.[226] His house in London became a nest of disillusioned nobles, radical scholars and Protestant zealots, fired by rumours that Essex's enemies intended to assassinate him. His rebellion, therefore, was meant to be a pre-emptive attempt to force an audience with the queen and defeat his enemies by revealing their designs. He had refused to obey a summons to appear before the Privy Council the day before, and had seized the four men, including the earl of Worcester, who arrived at Essex House seeking an explanation. Essex then led a march through London of perhaps three hundred men, only lightly armed, who appealed for the support of Londoners as they went. When London proved obdurate, Essex retreated in confusion, and when his house was besieged later that day, he surrendered. It seems clear that he had not intended much more than a political gesture. Nevertheless, one of his henchmen subsequently attempted to apprehend the queen and force her to grant Essex an audience. It was not hard to convict him of treason.

It could be said that Essex's offence was essentially a thought-crime. He was consumed by his understanding of the international situation and its imperatives, which demanded aggressive intervention in the Protestant cause. He was also convinced of his own obligation to act: as a member of the high nobility, as a scholar and statesman, as a valiant warrior in a godly cause. This level of self-belief was lethal. It had earlier led him, during a Council meeting of 1598, to respond to a put-down by the queen by turning his back on her. An infuriated Elizabeth had struck him on the head; he had instinctively reached for his sword and had to be restrained. According to Camden, he had protested that 'he neither could nor would put up so great an afront and indignity', although he had the wit to add that 'neither would he have taken it at King Henry the Eighth his hands'.[227] His apparent unawareness of how grievously he had offended Elizabeth's sense of majesty indicates the extent to which he dwelt within a separate and imagined world, where he had not only the freedom, but the obligation, as a member of the nobility and a military commander, to seize the initiative.[228]

Deeply imbued with the classics – and in particular inspired by Tacitus, his accounts of corrupt emperors and his appeal to the virtues and valour of the senatorial class – Essex envisaged himself as embracing that noble destiny. That his secretaries included Oxford's regius professor of Greek and a logician from King's College Cambridge indicates just how far the life of the mind informed his political strategies.[229] When, in 1579, Leonard Digges' posthumously published work had described the requisite virtues of a general, he could have been providing Essex with a blueprint: 'he must be Religious, Temperate, Sober, Wise, Valiaunte, Liberal, Curtous, Eloquent, of good Fame and Reputation: learned in Histories, and in those Sciences and Artes that may enhable him of himselfe, without directions from others, readily to conceyve and iudge of Militaire Actions of all sortes'.[230] Not only did Essex read himself into the role of military and civic leader, but a great many of his friends and followers also saw him as a valiant figure from the Roman past – and so did a great many commentators, once he was dead.[231] 'Sweet Englands pride is gone', lamented a seventeenth-century ballad, which hailed him as a 'vertuous Peere' of whom it could be said 'For valour there was none / like him before.'[232] He had come to stand for the values of republican honour, political entitlement and Protestant zeal, all of which Elizabeth regarded as a potential threat to her authority.

Elizabeth mourned the loss of Essex. In a last private conversation with her godson, Sir John Harington, in December 1602, she cried at the mention of him. Whether it was the loss of his friendship and affection that she minded most, or the loss of trust, is hard to tell. She may also have felt lonely at the thought that Essex, despite his intellect and professed affection for her, had failed to understand the project on which she was engaged. He had delved into classical history to cast her as a weak and tyrannical ruler, easily swayed by the flattery of evil counsellors and her own emotions (incidentally setting a pattern for later commentators to follow). He had also cast himself in the role of the loyal senator, standing alone against the corruption of her government.[233] That Elizabeth used her passions as a tool of statecraft and a shield; that she could see only too well the artifice of courtly flattery; that she perceived how radical Protestantism contained the seeds of ruinous political instability; that she did not trust Essex because he was not, ultimately, to be trusted – all this had escaped him, just as it has often been overlooked by historians in every century since that time.

The end of an era

At the start of the seventeenth century, Elizabeth was approaching the age of seventy, although her wits were unclouded and her resilience was still evident. In the summer of 1602, she was still able to ride 10 miles a day on horseback, and she was talking of a possible progress to the West Country. She could not, however, acknowledge that most of the planning for the future that was being done at Court was revolving around James VI of Scotland, and she resolutely refused, as she always had, to make any declaration about the succession. Elizabeth was nothing if not responsible as a monarch; this almost criminal act of irresponsibility, which potentially endangered her entire realm, must be an indication of just how precarious she felt her position to be, right until her last days. Henry VIII, faced with untimely death and an uncertain succession, had produced a will and testament that laid down detailed instructions for the way ahead. Elizabeth did nothing, fearful to the last that any mention of her successor would be her own undoing, and unable to relinquish the control she had struggled for so many years to maintain. Her godson, Sir John Harington, who visited her in her last months, wrote of how she paced her chamber, at times driving a dagger through the tapestries which hung on the wall, as if to apprehend a hidden assassin.

When Elizabeth felt death approaching, she fought it to the last, refusing to take to her bed and lying instead on cushions on her chamber floor. She had had to fight every inch of the way to assert her legitimacy and her authority, to survive as a princess and as a queen, as a Protestant and as a Tudor, and she did not weaken her stance even as she died. To the last, she preserved her silence on the question of who should inherit the throne – although it was later said that at her final Privy Council meeting, held the day before she died, she had raised her hand at the mention of James VI. Her advisors had to make do with this as their best chance of a stable succession. Despite her bravery – or perhaps obstinacy – it was in many ways an ignominious death. Her courtiers raced to express their undying loyalty to the king of Scotland, and to laud him for being everything that Elizabeth had not been – a man, married with two healthy sons, and with a habit of command that came easily to a king with years of experience as a ruler.

The reign of Elizabeth has been fitted into several larger historical narratives over the centuries. From the establishment of Protestantism to the beginnings of empire, many of these have sounded a triumphalist note that is clearly simplistic, as well as anachronistic. A biography first published in 1936 confidently asserted that Elizabeth transformed England: 'She inspired its patriotism, its pageantry, its heroisms, stimulated its poetry and shaped its destiny. And when she died she left behind her a kingdom that had won a commanding position among the great powers of Europe.'[234] None of those statements can pass unchallenged today, and most can be flatly contradicted. And yet Elizabeth was undoubtedly touched by greatness. Her determination, her political expertise, her intellectual acuity, her steady religious devotion – all these made her legendary in her own time, as well as since. To stay in power had required a delicate balancing act at all times. The government needed to pursue its policy of turning England Protestant with sufficient rigour to produce the desired effect, and yet without propelling its initially largely Catholic populace into rebellion. In international affairs, it needed to strengthen its ties with emerging Protestant polities without openly antagonizing the Catholic behemoths that threatened to invade the country and depose its queen. In the localities, it could not function without the assistance of the nobility and gentry, but many of them had played key roles in Mary I's reign and the restoration of Catholicism, and were not entirely to be relied upon. For all these reasons, the Elizabethan regime had to tread carefully, and each major intervention abroad was preceded by a great deal of agonizing, as the potential risks and opportunities were carefully weighed. There were always those who wanted to push a more reckless and partisan Protestant line in international affairs, but Elizabeth was cautious, weighing up the expense, the human cost, the political risk and the threat of reputational damage.

All Tudor monarchs depended on their credibility to command the allegiance and cooperation of their subjects, but the challenge for a young, unmarried, childless woman to sustain the appearance of majesty, strength and competence was sometimes overwhelming. As a young woman, she had written to her brother: 'Nothing is so uncertain or less enduring than the life of man, who truly . . . is nothing else than a dream of shadows.'[235] Her frequent acknowledgements of the providential nature of her own survival were probably not just the self-fashioning of the godly Protestant queen: it is likely that she did indeed marvel at her own survival through her turbulent childhood and adolescence, and for forty-five years as queen. In her last speech to parliament in 1601, she told its members:

> Though it hath pleased God ... by many hard escapes and hazards both of divers and strange natures, to make me an instrument of His holy will in delivering the state from danger and myself from dishonor, all that I challenge to myself is that I have been studious and industrious ... as a careful head to defend the body.[236]

She could at least say that she had tried hard to keep everyone safe.

CHAPTER 13

A WORLD DIVIDED

In the summer of 1549, when violence and upheaval were widespread across southern England, one man died a particularly terrible death. Robert Welsh was a parish priest in his early forties, described as 'of no great stature, but well sett and mightelie compacte', known for his skill at wrestling, hunting and archery. He was executed for his role in the Prayer-Book Rebellion, hanged in chains from a gallows erected on the tower of his parish church in Cowick, just outside Exeter, so that all could see his slow, painful end. Most significantly of all, he was garbed in what the chronicler of these events called 'his popishe apparell' – in other words, he was clothed in the sacred and symbolic vestments that priests had worn for centuries to celebrate mass. The chronicler also noted that he had 'a holye water bucket, a sprinkle, a sacringe bell, a payre of beddes, and such other lyke popyshe trashe hangued aboute him'.[1] This execution was not just a punishment for Welsh's own crime, but a theatrical attempt to discredit the faith for which he had fought and a visual denunciation of what so many regarded as sacred. Welsh's body would hang there for the next four years, until the reign of Mary I. In due course, the church itself, dedicated to St Thomas the Martyr, would be renamed St Thomas the Apostle, as the medieval saint was replaced by one of the apostles from the Bible, and an ancient faith was rebranded.

John Hooker, who chronicled Welsh's hideous end, was a loyal citizen of Exeter, a scholar, antiquary and civil servant. He thought Welsh had the makings of a good person, 'had not the weedes overgrowne the good corne'. But Hooker had no time for Welsh's convictions. He himself was a convinced Protestant, having studied theology in Strasbourg, where he had stayed with Peter Martyr, the reformer who, by 1549, was vigorously enacting Protestant reforms in Oxford. Hooker saw the rebellion in the south-west as misguided loyalty to 'the Idoll of Rome'. In his contribution to Holinshed's *Chronicles*, he would describe the pope as

> the sonne of sathan, and the manne of sinne, and the enimie unto the crosse of Christ, whose bloodthirstiness will never be quenched, but in the blood of the saints . . . whose ravening guts be never satisfied, but with the death of such as doo serve the Lord in all godliness . . . as it dooth appere by the infinit and most horrible massacres, and bloodie persecutions, which he dailie exerciseth throughout all christian lands.[2]

This uncompromising view allowed of no concessions. Hooker had been born around 1527, just as Henry VIII was having misgivings about his marriage to Katherine of Aragon; he died in 1601, as the Tudor era was coming to a close, having fathered seventeen Protestant children. His lifetime saw his country's deepest convictions transformed, that which was formerly sacrosanct reviled or destroyed, and a new understanding of religious truth brought into existence. This would be one of the most profound alterations that England would ever experience. For some, it brought a transformative experience of religion that was revelatory and exhilarating; for others, it meant the loss of much that was sacred, familiar and sustaining. For society as a whole, it meant deep and painful divisions, and a legacy of fear, suspicion, bewilderment and sadness. It created a culture in which the kind of ritualized violence that led to Welsh's death seemed justifiable.[3] The Kentishman in the 1570s who said 'if I knew him that would go to mass I would thrust my dagger in him' was expressing the generalized religious animosity which, by the end of Elizabeth's reign, had become normative for many.[4]

The instigators of religious reform in England had never intended to tear their society apart. There was no conceptual framework in the early modern imagination for anything but a single unified Church. Religious life centred around community, from the parish community through the monastic brotherhood or sisterhood to the godly kingdom headed by a divinely appointed monarch, and Christendom itself, united against the threat from the East. The defining feature of all these groupings was their corporate identity, and a shared sense of Christian unity. The idea of rival Christian churches in Europe was almost impossible to envisage, and it would take long years of bitter religious conflict before Europeans even began, reluctantly, to accept the practical necessity of Protestant and Catholic co-existence; even longer to understand toleration in anything like the modern sense of the word.[5] The burning of heretics at the stake was not intended to be a weapon in an ongoing struggle; it was supposed to remove the pollution of heresy from the world once and for all, restoring consensus and harmony. As Tudor authorities soon realized, however, these attempts to extinguish religious error did not have the intended effect. They could create martyrs, whose dedication and self-sacrifice gave lustre to whichever interpretation of the Christian faith they espoused (see illustration 23).[6] The very nature of Christianity itself complicated the problem, since it spoke in about equal measure of a Church unified throughout world and time, but also envisaged a small body of God's chosen people at odds with a hostile environment. Protestants who strove to follow the Bible's prescriptions to the letter often did not know whether to see themselves as builders of a godly nation or as a small persecuted flock of true believers, at odds with the worldly values of society at large.

The sixteenth century saw a slow unravelling of a religious unity that everyone believed in, but nobody could sustain. Society was ineluctably and painfully pulled apart by the intensity of diverging views on doctrine, and by the way in which religion swiftly became an element of statecraft and a defining feature of each regime. The country sank unwillingly into a state of suspicion, apprehension and sometimes open hostility. In Elizabeth's reign, the poet Philip Sidney corresponded with his Huguenot friend Hubert Languet, who feared that divisions within Europe might facilitate Turkish invasion; Sidney, however, welcomed the prospect as something likely to destroy the papacy.[7] Many commentators aspired to Christian values of forgiveness and neighbourly love, even as preachers hammered home their vision of the one, true faith, almost always defined in contradistinction to its enemies. The two most basic imperatives of the Christian faith – to love God and to love one's neighbour – increasingly appeared irreconcilable, as religious divisions widened. Families were torn apart and communities polarized, while existing animosities – whether at Court, in the universities, in the marketplace or the village square – took

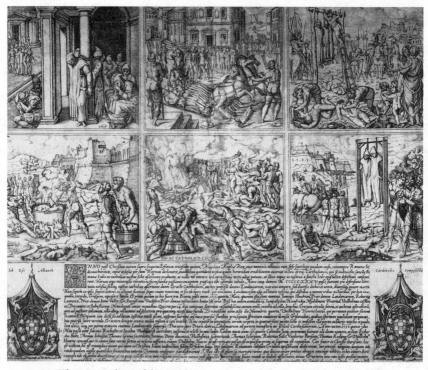

23. The Martyrdom of the Carthusians in an Italian woodcut from the 1550s

on the added vicious edge of religious hostility. The conflict is easy to read in the sources. Less immediately obvious is the bewilderment, which was also widespread. Confusion was rife, as the uneducated struggled to understand the theological imperatives that were shaping their lives. Many were apprehensive about heresy, without fully understanding what exactly it consisted of; others appealed to older ideas of religious obligation, only to find themselves condemned. Fear spread more swiftly than ideology, and by the reign of Elizabeth communal tensions were producing accusations of witchcraft, as well as heresy. Those accused of witchcraft were sometimes said to have muttered incantations in Latin or to have railed against a neighbour who refused them charity – tattered remnants of a Catholic past now demonized by a new and nervous Protestant culture.

Yet animosity and division were not the only course open to Tudor men and women. Many continued to cling to Christian values of love and charity, even as more rancorous souls exchanged insults. Quietly, but insistently, older ties were sustained between families and friends, scholars and courtiers, and even occasionally between churchmen with different loyalties. Many took a more detached view of religion, such as the Axminster cobbler who said he 'would never go to the church for devotion, or holiness of the place, but because other men did such, to keep them company'.[8] Human love, loyalty and compassion were still capable of cutting across the harsher divisions imposed by confessional difference. The perennial rhythms of community life also made a difference, as villages and towns sustained patterns of religious worship. There was likewise a recognition by some of the many similarities that underlay starkly opposed theological formulations. While scholars wrestled over the doctrines of predestination or transubstantiation, the daily experience of religious devotion involving prayer, sermons, the reading of devotional books and charitable works was common to Christians of any persuasion. Books about theology may have drawn lines in the sand; but books about devotion borrowed from one another across the religious divide, and Protestants and Catholics, at times unknowingly, prayed the same prayers.

Many of those in government saw religion as a potential source of stability. Official injunctions, formulations and homilies which attempted to regulate religion in the localities put forward a vision of quiet and orderly faithfulness: responsible clergy who stayed away from the tavern and educated the children of the parish; loyal parishioners who provided generously for the poor and kept the church building in good repair; a community which dutifully followed the order of service prescribed by the government and lived together in harmony. The Elizabethan regime in particular consciously steered around some of the more contentious doctrinal issues to focus on good order at the parish level. Yet most aspects of religious experience in the second half of the sixteenth century were caught in a conundrum they could not escape, striving for consensus and Christian unity on the basis of convictions that could not fail to divide them from others. Protestant and Catholic alike insisted that only through their understanding of the faith could peace and unity be regained. Their most central beliefs revolved around notions of unity. This was how Catholics described the mass, their most important sacrament: 'For this meate is the strength of our soule, the synewes of our minde, the knot of our trust, the foundation of our hope, our health, our light, our lyfe.'[9] For Protestants, the doctrine of election bound them together in a select company of the godly, brothers and sisters together in Christ. With high-minded motives, churchmen, scholars and statesmen often wrought havoc pitiful to behold, even while, in society at large, the steady currents of religious devotion and worship continued to flow around the immovable obstacles of dogmatic conviction, like water around rocks set in the riverbed. This combination of zeal and quietness, of admonition and gentle evasion, made the later Reformation in Tudor England a complicated mixture of beliefs, loyalties, enmities and emotions.

Protestant zeal

English Protestantism was a curious agglomeration of elements: scholarly, parochial, foreign and official. The model of men and women fired with passion for a new understanding of their faith, rejecting all the corrupt traditions of the past and loyal to a single sacred text was the Protestant ideal, but the truth was much more complicated. To judge from the published output of early Protestants, many were motivated by their hatred of the institutional Catholic Church, pouring vitriol on the papacy and priesthood. Others took a more political view, envisaging a godly kingdom and seeking to advise magistrates and monarchs how this might be achieved. Another group seemed deeply concerned with the plight of the poor, inveighing against social injustice, whilst yet another set considered the needs of individuals, writing and preaching chiefly about personal devotion and the life of faith. These four elements – polemical, political, social and devotional – were found in different combinations in different thinkers, reformers, communities and conventicles, and they made the emerging Protestant Church in England an oddly variegated entity that was frequently at war with itself.

In the mid-Tudor period, English Protestants had undergone the intensity and upheaval of Edward VI's reign and the reversals and persecutions of Mary I's, both deeply formative experiences. Many key players in the Edwardian regime returned to office under Elizabeth, and sought to regain what they had lost: an English service book, churches purged of altars and saints, leading foreign scholars installed in the universities, schools founded and books published. What had at the time seemed a hasty and sometimes ill-assorted array of Edwardian reforms, variously implemented across thousands of parishes, took on a new lustre in the light of the Marian persecutions. What figures such as Thomas Cranmer, Hugh Latimer and Nicholas Ridley, the most famous of the Marian martyrs, had failed to achieve in life, they came some way towards reaching in death: namely, a unified sense of Protestant identity. Those who had fled abroad, however, had encountered the Protestant communities in Frankfurt, Strasbourg, Geneva and Zurich, among other cities, and had their notions of what constituted Protestant Church order and worship shaped accordingly. English Protestantism at the start of Elizabeth's reign in 1558 was therefore many things: wounded, inspired and complicated. Many of the more zealous had been shaped by their time in exile, and continued to correspond with their foreign Protestant mentors, rejoicing when they perceived that Elizabeth had 'taken good Christians into her service in the room of papists', and anxiously watching events at the heart of power.[10] They had no hesitation in advising the queen of what they considered to be her religious duty: Rodolph Gualter in Zurich wrote to congratulate Elizabeth on her accession, rather spoiling the effect by adding that 'we should rather congratulate the church of Christ herself'.[11] Their constant reiteration of how much Elizabeth owed to God, their persistence in identifying her as an instrument of Protestant Reformation, and the freedom and confidence with which they were moved to advise her that 'by the activity and zeal of your majesty might be happily completed what the most godly king your brother had piously and success-fully begun', go some way to explaining Elizabeth's frequent irritation with them.[12]

Correspondence between Protestant reformers shows how far some of them were at odds with the Church that Elizabeth seems to have envis-aged. Thomas Sampson wrote to Peter Martyr in Strasbourg in December 1558, agonizing about the queen's putative title of 'Supreme Head of the Church of England' (this was before it was altered to 'Supreme Governor') and wondering whether he could 'with a safe conscience' accept any church post under her. He was concerned that the episcopal system in England was so far declined 'from the primitive institution' that there was no election, only appointment, 'for there is required neither the consent of the clergy, nor of the people'; in the end, he refused the offer of a bishopric.[13] Briefly dean of Christ Church Oxford, he caused further trouble by his uncompromising refusal to wear clerical dress, and became the first minister of the Protestant Church of England to be deprived for nonconformity.[14] This kind of Protestant was not just insensitive, overbearing and inclined to be dismissive of royal authority, but could also be unnervingly antagonistic towards the 'papists, anabaptists, and very many gospellers, who are enemies both to learning and a godly reformation'.[15]

This kind of attitude was strongly contested by other, more conservative voices within the Protestant Church. Those who located their Protestantism within a more local frame of reference were less strident in their statements and more moderate in their objectives, although no less committed. They were not attempting a *via media* between Catholicism and Protestantism, something that was in any case unthinkable in the context of the 1550s; their moderation was not compromise, but an emphatic championing of the course they thought most likely to achieve a lasting Protestantism.[16] Matthew Parker, Elizabeth's first archbishop of Canterbury, was one of these more cautious voices.[17] This established a foundation for a less radical tradition, which would, in due course, find a voice with which to answer its more intemperate critics. By 1588, Richard Bancroft, the future Jacobean archbishop of Canterbury, could be just as loud in his denunciation of the more radical branches of his Church as they were in return. Preaching at Paul's Cross, he attacked Presbyterians and other Protestant radicals as schismatics and false prophets, who 'murder the Scriptures to serve their owne purpose'.[18] In particular, he noted their political subversiveness: 'they despise government and feare not to speake evill of them that are in dignitie and authoritie'.[19] Theories put forward by Bancroft, Richard Hooker and others towards the end of the century embodied a view of the Church crafted from a distinctive blend of Elizabethan Protestant practices and political pragmatism. It has been suggested that the Tudor regime tended to proclaim its moderation at precisely those moments when it was being most vicious.[20] This may be an exaggerated claim, but certainly moderation was frequently deployed in the interests of maintaining political control over otherwise wayward ideological forces.

The challenge for Protestantism since its inception had been how to take what was effectively a protest movement, and from its inflexible set of attitudes construct a stable institutional Church. Those who had a better idea of political realities, and a more immediate set of political responsibilities, often proceeded more cautiously in the matter of religious reform. This was particularly true of Elizabeth herself, whose wariness of the 'hotter sort of Protestant' was clear to see. It is probable that she feared the kind of political disruption that could result from uncompromising religious zeal; she could remember the upheavals of 1548–49, when she was living at Hatfield, close to Northaw, Tyttenhanger and St Albans, all centres of rebellion.[21] Protestant commentators pondered the reasons why she seemed so 'wonderfully afraid of allowing any innovations'; but then, they were more interested in the kingdom of God than the stability of the kingdom of England.[22] Elizabeth's caution was not all political pragmatism, however. She seems to have upheld a more restrained understanding of Protestantism, of a kind shaped by English experiences more than by European example. In particular, she seems to have had a more reverent conception of the eucharist than those who dismissed it as purely symbolic. The Elizabethan Prayer Book, or *Book of Common Prayer*, reinstituted the communion sentences from the 1549 version, where the minister reminded those receiving that what they were being given was 'The bodie of our lord Jesu Christ' and 'The bloude of our lorde Jesu Christ'.[23] The second Edwardian Prayer Book had merely said 'Take and eate this, in remembraunce that Christ dyed for thee', and this very particular amendment opened the way to those Protestants who still believed, as Luther had, that the bread and wine of the eucharist truly contained the body and blood of Christ.

This single point of doctrine was one of the most hotly contested issues between different shades of Protestantism, reflecting broader sentiments. To the 'hotter sort' of Protestant, faith was a largely interior matter, stirred up by sermons and based on long hours of bible study and prayer, whilst the church building was of secondary importance, merely a convenient place to hold communal worship and hear sermons. More conservative Protestants could still feel, however, that the place in which the sacraments of baptism and the eucharist were performed should be a place set apart. Their willingness to embrace the notion that things and places could still be sacred appeared to their more ardent co-religionists a potentially disastrous survival from the superstitious practices of the past. The whole question of what could be perceived by the human eye, or touched by the human hand, and its relationship with the divine, was one of the most painfully contested of the period.[24] It was a question that would continue to trouble Protestant scholars for many years to come.[25]

Historians debate the issue of when it becomes possible to identify the Protestant grouping commonly called 'puritan'. This is hampered by the fact that 'puritan' was, at the time, a term of abuse, rather than a label consciously adopted. It gradually became apparent to many over the 1560s and 1570s that Elizabeth was refusing to alter her Church settlement, not out of political caution alone, but on the basis of principle. This was when a puritan voice became more easily identifiable; but from the start of the reign it is possible to identify those impatient for further reform, critical of conservative elements and, above all, inclined to trumpet the authority of Scripture and the judgement of Protestant churchmen over the authority and judgement of the monarch. At its most defiant, Protestantism held the explicit promise of political subversion, framed by religious exiles during Mary's reign. In the work of Christopher Goodman, John Ponet and John Knox, the suggestion was made that a true believing Protestant might have the right – perhaps even the obligation – to resist the authority of a misguided monarch. Carefully justified by appeals to biblical precedent, this point of view was nonetheless inflammatory. Many of their concerns were rendered redundant by the accession of a Protestant queen, but their basic assumptions also helped shape the more assertive Protestant criticisms of the Elizabethan regime.[26] Several key works embellishing this theme were published during Elizabeth's reign, including those of Francois Hotman, Philippe du Plessis-Mornay and George Buchanan. Even if Elizabethan Protestants were wary of openly espousing the idea that the authority of God trumped that of the monarch, they implied as much on numerous occasions, and the marginalia of the Geneva Bible gave support to such a view.[27]

A few Protestants separated altogether from the national Church, of which they initially had such high hopes.[28] The Family of Love was one such movement: it took the principle of Protestant interiority to its furthest extreme, following the mystical teaching of the Dutchman Hendrik Niclaes, referred to by his followers simply as H.N.[29] It was denounced by other Protestants as being a form of heresy, and (ironically) even accused of having Catholic tendencies.[30] Like many religious sects under attack, it was charged with allowing women an inappropriate measure of religious agency.[31] Yet its shadowy existence reached into the royal Court, and Elizabeth may have been aware that some of her yeomen of the guard belonged to the Family of Love.[32] Familists in England belonged to a wider European network, which reached into the Low Countries, the Holy Roman Empire and France.[33] Their piety was simple, dedicated and mystical, with at times shades of Anabaptist influence: one group in Surrey in 1561 confessed to a repudiation of infant baptism, the doctrine of the Trinity and the taking of oaths.[34] On the whole, however, Familist belief seems to have been less dogmatic than this, more peaceable, and intensely private, to the extent that equivocating about their beliefs was considered entirely acceptable practice.

Between outspoken zealots and hidden separatists were many more moderate Protestants. The overriding tone of the Elizabethan Injunctions tended towards good order, reverent and charitable behaviour, and obedience. People were to 'forbear all vain and contentious disputations in matters of religion, and not to use in despite or rebuke of any person these convicious words, papist, or papistical heretic, schismatic or sacramentary, or any suchlike words of reproach'.[35] This was a vision of orderly parish worship at odds with the vision of the Gospel cherished by the more zealous. Aghast, John Jewel wrote to Peter Martyr that 'those very things which you and I have so often laughed at, are now seriously and solemnly entertained by certain persons ... as if the christian religion could not exist without something tawdry'.[36] It is likely, however, that parish worship, with its more gentle rhythms, was where Protestant strength and stability were chiefly located. The history of the English Reformation as a whole suggests that compliance with the monarch's intentions and the government's policies usually won out in the end.[37] Imperatives produced by different theological formulations may have consumed the minds and energies of some, but were of less relevance to the majority of the laity. By 1600, around 40 per cent of clergy were university graduates; but even so, they were still in the minority, and the more educated tended to gravitate to the more lucrative posts, rather than serving in country parishes.[38] Popular zeal, where evident, seems to have more easily embraced psalm-singing than sermon attendance, when even the committed among the congregation had to bite down on garlic or cloves to prevent themselves from falling asleep.[39]

From the beginning of Elizabeth's reign, therefore, there was variega-tion, and some unease, within English Protestantism. Some longed to cleanse the kingdom of idolatry and to preach the Word of God with vigour. Others, including Elizabeth, aimed to build a stable and godly Church, in which every one of her subjects might worship on the basis of Protestant consensus. The Protestant doctrines of predestination and election, which held that only a small and select number of the godly had been chosen for everlasting life, and that the rest of humanity was unre-generate and destined for damnation, underlay the vision of the first of these groupings, and tended to make the second uncomfortable. This was set out in the Thirty-Nine Articles, the definition of doctrine ratified by the Elizabethan Church in 1571, which noted that the doctrine of election was 'full of sweet, pleasant, and unspeakable comfort to godly persons', but that for 'curious and carnal persons, lacking the Spirit of Christ, to have continually before their eyes the sentence of God's Predestination, is a most dangerous downfall, whereby the Devil doth thrust them either into desperation, or into wretchlessness of most unclean living'. In other words, the key doctrine, which made the more zealous Protestants convinced of their special status and relationship with God, was liable to undermine the efforts of the more conservative Protestants to build a godly national Church for everyone. It is little wonder that the history of later sixteenth-century Protestantism was so fraught with difficulties. If the majority of Elizabethans by about 1580 would self-identify as Protestant, they meant by that a great range of different beliefs and practices. Allegiance was chiefly what mattered, not dogma.

Catholicism

Before the break with Rome, there had been no such thing as Catholicism – just the religion of England's population, practised with different degrees of zeal, indifference or ignorance. It required no label, because there existed no viable alternative. Heresy had existed, but it was defined by its otherness, its nonconformity; it was an act of defiance or separation, not an alternative world-view. The word 'catholic' was used in its sense of 'universal', and religion was more about belief and practice, than about identity. It was the Reformation that created Catholicism in the sense of Roman Catholicism, an alternative to Protestantism, and – in the minds of its opponents – a Church defined by its association with a foreign authority, in the form of the pope. The traditional religious practice of the pre-Reformation period may have formed the foundation for Catholic loyalism, but the experiences of the sixteenth century, ranging from biblical revival to persecution and exile, and the impact of Protestant condemnation, produced a more complicated and diverse form of English Catholicism.[40] Some clung to age-old formularies and customs; some practised their faith in secret; others developed a fiery intellectual justification for their beliefs and made common cause with foreign Catholic powers. Many died for their faith. It is possible that many English Catholics were united by little more than their loyalty to the mass – and even that could be interpreted in different ways.[41]

Catholics from the mid-century onwards struggled with a complicated legacy. Henry VIII had confused almost everyone by consistently asserting his Catholic identity, even as he transformed religious life a piece at a time. His idiosyncratic approach to Church reform had required those churchmen desperate to salvage the essentials of their faith to sacrifice obedience to the pope in exchange for the sacraments and notions of salvation. Early disputes revolved around particular points of doctrine, rather than coherent confessional alternatives. Stephen Gardiner, bishop of Winchester, the most intelligent and provocative of the traditionalists, had preached before Edward VI in 1548, arguing that whilst he could accept the dissolution of the abbeys and chantries, the removal of images and even communion in both kinds, he could not accept any criticism or reform of the mass, and would continue to condemn any priest who had broken his vows of chastity to marry. When he said 'I will playnly declare what I thinke of the state of the Church of England at this day, how I like it, and what I thinke of it', it was one of the last declarations of the early Reformation.[42] Gardiner at this point was still describing a single Church, and the shifts taking place within it. He was soon imprisoned by the Edwardian regime, and when he emerged from the Tower of London after the accession of Mary I, it was to a future in which there was less and less a sense of a single Church in turmoil, and more and more a sense of two Churches in opposition to one another.

In the reign of Mary Tudor, an older and less doctrinaire form of Catholicism encountered a heavier and more precise emphasis on papal authority as the guarantor and identifier of Catholic identity. Fostered in part by Reginald Pole, cardinal archbishop of Canterbury, whose loyalty to the pope was forged out of much personal anguish, and encouraged by the example of a Spanish Catholicism strong and autonomous enough to accept papal authority without feeling threatened by it, a new level of commitment to Rome began to emerge. The success of Mary's endeavours was shown by the reaction in 1559 to Elizabeth's attempts at a Protestant settlement. The virtually unanimous opposition of the bishops created an almost insuperable obstacle for Elizabeth; and when she insisted on forcing through her settlement, she was compelled to imprison many of those bishops, whilst many other leading Catholic scholars and churchmen fled into exile, and hundreds of parish and cathedral clergy were deprived.[43] It seems likely that the majority of the English population in 1558 was still attached to traditional or Catholic forms of belief and worship, and visitation returns suggest that many people would go on clinging to the old ways. Thomas Bentham, bishop of Lichfield and Coventry, was still struggling in 1565 to get the people in his diocese to 'cast away their beads with all their superstitions that they do use', and to get his clergy to dispense with their mass books and the Catholic rituals surrounding burial.[44] Yet there was also a strain of more educated, austere Catholicism, in part fostered by the Marian restoration, which was perpetuated by the university scholars who had left England after 1558 and moved to Louvain or Douai. There they continued to write in passionate defence of their faith and in opposition to the public utterances of the newly fledged Elizabethan Church. In 1559, the new bishop of Salisbury, John Jewel, preached his 'Challenge sermon' at Paul's Cross, defying the Catholics to prove a set of their core beliefs from Scripture or the early Church.[45] English and Welsh Catholics in exile rose to this challenge, led in particular by Thomas Harding, formerly regius professor of Hebrew at Oxford and fellow of New

College.[46] The 1560s and 1570s saw a great many of their books printed abroad and smuggled across the Channel: in 1571, Bishop Guest's visitation articles for Rochester diocese asked if 'any within your parish have in their hands or have delivered to others any English books set forth of late by Harding Dorman Allen Sanders Stapleton Marshall or any of them or by any other English papist', a roll-call of Catholic scholars in exile.[47] Harding's colleague from New College, Owen Lewis, became vicar-general to Carlo Borromeo, the reforming archbishop of Milan, in the 1580s; had the Spanish Armada succeeded, he was being considered for the archbishopric of York, although there was a view that a see in his native Wales would suit him better.[48]

Many Catholics during the first years of Elizabeth's reign clearly expected that her rule would be as short-lived as that of her siblings, or that marriage to a Catholic prince would compel her either to convert, or at least to allow Catholic worship within the realm.[49] In the 1560s, many Catholics remained in positions of influence in local government, and there were different shades of opinion as to how much of a threat they might pose. This would change after the Northern Rebellion of 1569 and the papal bull of 1570 excommunicating Elizabeth and instructing her Catholic subjects to procure her death or deposition. Such developments confirmed the more hard-line opinion held by many that most Catholics were not to be trusted. From the 1570s onwards, the laws against Catholic worship became more draconian, and in particular the open expression of Catholic loyalties through non-attendance at church became expensive. Recusancy fines brought about the phenomenon of 'seigneurial' Catholicism, where only nobility and gentry were able openly to espouse their faith.[50] In the case of Thomas Tresham, he planted his identity upon the landscape, in the form of the Triangular Lodge, resonant with Catholic symbolism (see plate 20).[51] Meanwhile, many exiled Catholics began to put down roots abroad in their host communities.[52] This could lead to a more defiant political stance, and it certainly wove English Catholicism more closely together with Counter-Reformation trends.[53] In 1566, Laurence Vaux, formerly rector of Manchester College, was despatched to England to explain that attendance at a Church of England service was unacceptable – a message not always welcome to those struggling to survive in England.[54] Separation from parish communities at home combined with the influence of foreign Catholicism to create an interesting hybrid, rein-forced by the number of English children being sent to be educated abroad. It has been suggested that 'exile' is an inadequate term in this context: many went abroad not because they were forced to, but because they wanted to seek new connections, experiences and education.[55]

From 1572, Catholic priests trained abroad started to return to England to minister to the underground Catholic congregations there, and frequently to face imprisonment, torture and a terrible death.[56] During Elizabeth's reign, nearly two hundred Catholics died a traitor's death: hanged, disembowelled and cut into quarters for what the regime insisted was their treason, but Catholics insisted was their faith. One of Elizabeth's chief interrogators was Richard Topcliffe, who was personally responsible for sadistically torturing and raping many prisoners. Published accounts dwelt on the terrible details of their suffering: William Allen described, for example, how Father Alexander Brian 'was even to the dismembring of his body rent and torne upon the rack', and how Father John Nelson, 'cut downe before he was halfe dead, dismembred and ripped up', had, as the hangman plucked out his heart, 'lifted him self up a litle, and . . . spake these wordes, I forgeve the Q[ueen] and al that were causes of my death'. Allen noted, 'thus he changed this mortal life with immortalitie'.[57] These experiences put martyrdom at the heart of English Catholic culture, just as Foxe's 'Book of Martyrs' had accorded martyrdom a central place within Protestant culture. In both cases, they heightened anxiety and exacerbated antagonism between the two confessions, even as they provided believers with a source of strength; and they made the theme of exile and martyrdom a central part of Elizabethan culture more gener-ally.[58] Robert Persons asked: 'What greter matter of comfort can there be to us that ar Catholikes then to see God worke these strange wonders in our days . . . that is to geve suche rare grace of zeale, austerytie of lyef and constancy of martirdom unto yonge men.'[59] These experiences imparted a new intensity to Catholic religious culture, which developed many new devotions to cope with the challenges of proscription and persecution.[60]

The Elizabethan regime was not entirely wrong about Catholics: there was a small number of determined plotters, including the Jesuit Robert Persons, whose collaboration with Philip II contributed to several invasion plans, and whose propaganda campaign against Burghley caused considerable concern.[61] There were many others about whom the regime, and subsequent historians, were never sure, such as Edward Stafford, ambassador to France from 1583, whose loyalty remained questionable.[62] Some engaged in conspiracies, of which the Ridolfi, Throckmorton and Babington plots were the most famous, but by no means the only ones. In particular, as Elizabeth aged and the succession remained uncertain, the involvement of Catholics in real or imagined assassination attempts, and their very concrete contributions to the cause of the leading Catholic claimant, the Infanta Isabella, posed a genuine risk to stability.[63]

By the end of the century, Elizabethan Catholicism had developed many facets, embracing everything from the parishioners who still preserved elements of past practice, through the exile communities whose scholarship helped define Counter-Reformation theology, to those who plotted Elizabeth's assassination. Some localities had particularly strong recusant populations: Lancashire retained a strong Catholic presence; and in 1603 a fifth of residents of Monmouthshire were still deemed recusants, despite the limitations of the Catholic mission in Wales.[64] A single family might contain a broad range of views: the Throckmorton family (which gave its name to the Throckmorton plot of 1583), contained both zealot and moderate Catholics, as well as outspoken Protestants such as Job Throckmorton, partially responsible for the 'Martin Marprelate' tracts.[65] Catholic identity and activism were far from static phenomena, and people might move from opposition to conformity and back again many times in a lifetime. Just as the regime found the Catholic threat amorphous and hard to counter, so Catholic identity remained shifting and unpredictable.

Religion in the parish

Scholars and churchmen may have spent long hours grappling with theological propositions, but for the vast majority of Tudor men and women religion was something lived, not something disputed. At parish level, religion dictated the rhythms of the working week and marked out the different stages of the year in feast days and fast days; it provided the rites of birth and baptism, betrothal and marriage, death and burial (see plate 23). It brought each family and community together in common worship, provided comfort in times of trouble and protection against danger. All this was hallowed by appeal to ancient tradition and entrenched in society by long usage. The religious changes of the sixteenth century were therefore not just a challenge to a belief system; they were a disruption to daily life, and a threat to communal harmony and identity. Despite the many antagonisms engendered by religious change, the ideal of Christian solidarity endured. Tudor commentators continued to express an overwhelming yearning for fellowship, for concord, for neighbours living together in charity.[66] 'Of all thinges that be good to bee taught unto christian people, there is nothinge more necessarie to bee spoke of, and daiely called upon, then charitye.' This observation, in one of the Protestant homilies issued by Edward VI's regime in 1547, was repeated eight years later in the book of Catholic homilies issued during Mary I's reign.[67] The charitable ideal was too central to religious experience to be jettisoned. It was not just an abstract notion expressed in sermons and treatises, but a practical tool applied repeatedly through both formal and informal conduits of authority.[68] In civil and church courts, in the interactions of constables and churchwardens with their villages, towns and parishes, and in the judgements of manorial lords, aldermen of the city or the clergy, the principle of living in charity was applied as a tool of judgement and reconciliation. One London parish clerk inscribed in his parish records a quite atrocious poem to underline how 'neighbours being ioyned in love together can never be severed'.[69]

John Mirk had said in his *Festial*, 'he that loveth god loveth his neyghboure' and – in the sermon for Quinquagesima Sunday, just before Lent, when the need for all men to be in a state of charity was emphasized – he insisted 'thus must a man have full charyte that wyll be saved'.[70] A fourteenth-century Quinquagesima sermon by Thomas Wimbledon had instructed its listeners that 'all men is as one body, whose kyndlye or naturall hearte is charitie, that is love to god, and love to thy neighboure'; Wimbledon's sermon had a long afterlife, being reprinted twenty times or more in the sixteenth and early seventeenth centuries.[71] So, too, the collect, or prayer, for Quinquagesima Sunday in the *Book of Common Prayer* retained the emphasis on charity at the start of Lent: it noted that 'al our doinges without charitie are nothyng worthe' and asked for 'that most excellent gyft of charitie, the very bond of peace'. In the post-Reformation communion order, ministers exhorted their congregations to 'Amende your lyves, and be in perfect charitie with all men', only admitting those to communion who were 'in love and charitie with your neighbours', a point reiterated by visitation articles and injunctions.[72] Protestant catechisms continued to insist that anyone preparing for communion must be penitent of past sins, 'purposing to leave them, and to live godly, endeavouring himselfe to be in brotherly love and charitie with all men'.[73]

The pursuit of charity was not just a pious intention, but a practical response to the problems that beset any community. Its absence was universally recognized as an obstacle to Christian fulfilment.[74] In London in the 1520s, one woman had tugged at the sleeve of another as she knelt to receive communion, telling her she could not continue until she had asked forgiveness for offending her.[75] Cranmer's preface to the communion service in the 1549 Prayer Book enjoined the curate to ban from communion those 'betwixt whom he shall perceive malice and hatred to reign', until they had made their peace.[76] This important point of continuity with pre-Reformation practice became all the more important from the mid-century onwards, precisely because societies were becoming so divided. Henry VIII, in his speech to parliament on Christmas Eve 1545, had demanded 'what charity and love is amongst you when one calleth the other Heretick and Anabaptist, and hee calleth him againe Papist, Hypocrite and Pharisee, bee these tokens of charity amongst you?'[77] Refusing communion to anyone who had 'maliciously and open contended with his neighbor' remained a key part of Protestant teaching, alongside the belief that communicants were 'spiritually tourned into the body of Christ, and be so joined unto Christ, and also togither among themselves, that they do make but one mystical body of Christe'.[78] Catholics said the same, that people were 'tied and joined togither by the communion', which brought about 'conjunction in bodie and soule of them to Christe, and of Christe to them, with a mutuall conjunction also in love and charitie, of eche good man in Christ to other'.[79] To this end, forgiveness between neighbours was of fundamental importance. If a neighbour asked forgiveness, Latimer observed, 'if I then be sturdy and proud, my heart flinty, and my stomach bent against him', then it was 'a sure token that I am not of the number of the children of God'.[80]

Unsurprisingly, the frequent religious reversals since the 1530s had left many people concerned that charity had suffered and 'waxed cold', a biblical phrase that often recurred as commentators mourned the antagonisms within their communities. 'As for charitie howe colde it is, would god it were not so manifest and open before our eyes', wrote one Catholic author in 1555.[81] A Catholic homily from 1558 stated bluntly that those out of charity with their neighbour could have no forgiveness from God: 'Because God is charitie, and the God of peace and not of discension . . . therefore no man can be reconciled to God . . . that is not reconciled to his brother or neighboure.'[82] At parish level, the definition of doctrine might be unimportant, compared with the maintenance of neighbourliness. The Essex preacher George Gifford wrote a work in 1582 in which a dialogue between the godly Zelotes and the country bumpkin Atheos exposed the errors and misconceptions of the simple country folk.[83] Atheos, asked to describe his parish minister, spoke approvingly of his ability to make peace between his parishioners: 'if there bee anye that doe not agree, hee will seeke for too make them friendes: for hee will gette them too playe a game or two at Bowles or Cardes, and too drynke together at the Alehouse'. Gifford clearly disagreed, but Atheos thought this 'a Godlye waye, to make Charitie: hee is none of these busie Countroulers: for if hee were, hee coulde not be so well liked of some'.[84] Atheos also doubted whether godly reproaches were really based in charitable intent: 'If they woulde doe it in charitie, I could like of it: but men have no love, they doe it because they are precise and captious.'[85] Gifford was trying to argue for the godly point of view, but he did almost too good a job of making Atheos's case. His work gave a candid account of the cultural division between the learned and the illiterate, underlined by the way in which Zelotes' contributions were printed in the Roman type of the educated, and Atheos's in the black letter type associated with cheap print. As the appeal of a simple faith rooted in good fellowship came through loud and clear, so too did the gulf between the zealous Protestant and the well-meaning parishioner. Where one was concerned with the frequency and quality of sermons, Bible-reading, education of both ministry and laity, and a true understanding of election, the other was focused on peace, stability, the generosity of the clergy, the hospitality of all and the marking of the church year with festivities.

The range of attitudes is nowhere so evident as in the approach to sermons, which were the jewel in the crown of puritan religiosity, but less rapturously welcomed by many ordinary listeners. The charge of being known to sleep through sermons, and even services, was a fairly common one; Hugh Latimer told the story of the insomniac who sought out sermons as a cure.[86] The purchase of hourglasses by churchwardens became a common item in church accounts from the 1560s onwards, presumably both a spur to the preacher's endeavour and a reminder not to go on too long.[87] Not every parish would have had easy access to sermons: finding a licensed preacher willing to take on a country parish was one challenge, and frequently those who did would be responsible for several churches or chapels.[88] Leading churchmen prided themselves on their preaching: Tobie Matthew recorded in his preaching diary 720 sermons he gave as dean of Durham from 1584 to 1595, and 550 as bishop of Durham for the eleven years that followed.[89] It is probable, however, that the majority of clergy resorted to reading aloud one of the official homilies; the increase in university-educated clergy from the 1590s onwards was matched by new editions of the homilies being printed at the same time.[90] Some of the laity left bequests to fund sermons, such as Agnes Spylman of Thaxted in Essex who left 6s 8d to her vicar in the 1570s to make an 'honest and learned sermon at the time of my burial when the people may be taught . . . the way to salvation'.[91] These bequests were nothing like on the same scale as pre-Reformation bequests for masses, however, and it is likely that many congregations found long sermons on the approved Protestant model something of a trial. As Gifford observed: 'If the Preacher doe passe his houre but a little, your buttokes beginne for to ake, and yee wishe in your hearte that the Pulpit woulde fall.'[92]

Where there was a gifted preacher who managed to strike a chord with his congregation, however, the sermon became a medium for precisely the kind of emotional encounter that had given pre-Reformation religion its popular appeal. Hugh Latimer could keep his congregation enthralled even as they stood in the rain, and Henry Smith in Elizabethan London earned himself the sobriquet 'silver-tongued'.[93] Puritan culture has often been characterized as something sober, book-centred and cerebral, but in the right hands the zeal of the godly could engender untrammelled enthusiasm and command a vigorous response. Although some encouraged their congregations to bring their Bibles with them to church, others were concerned it might detract from the spiritual encounter; yet others advised against note-taking, lest it hinder the impression the sermon might make upon the hearts of the congregation.[94] It is clear that those who have assumed that Elizabethan sermons led only to 'sheer uncomprehending boredom' have not appreciated the complexities of post-Reformation Protestant culture.[95] When Gifford and others described the ignorance of the 'common sort', they were not reproaching them, so much as issuing a call to arms.[96] There was a strong sense among the more zealous Protestants that they needed to respond with vigour to the challenge posed by popular lack of knowledge. The brilliance of Gifford's depiction of the humble villager was only accidentally sympathetic; it was intended to be a believable portrait of a well-meaning but uninformed villager endangering his immortal soul through sheer lack of awareness, and was therefore supposed to work as a spur to action.

The scale of popular ignorance was often noted. With all the disputations over theology that crowd the books of the time, it is easy to forget that many people were still unaware of the basic truths of the Christian faith. In 1552, Bernard Gilpin had expostulated over the fact that 'boyes and girles of xiiii or xv yeares olde cannot say the Lords prayer', and asked: 'Shall suche injury to Christ and his gospel be suffred in a christian realme?'[97] These churchmen could appreciate that in many ways the Reformation had had precisely the opposite effect to that intended. Amid the rapid changes, the confusion over true doctrine, and the fear engendered by conflict and persecution, the routine pastoral provision of the Church had suffered. The loss of the monasteries, the preaching friars and the chantry priests had dealt a significant blow to the personnel of the Church. Even a Protestant such as Bernard Gilpin noted the loss: in his sermon of 1552, he recorded sadly how 'a thousand pulpets in England are covered with dust, some have not had four sermons these xv or xvi yeares, since Friers left their limitations'.[98]

If some reformers and churchmen sought to enlighten the 'simple and unlearned', others sought to discipline them. The homily of 1547 on 'Christian love and Charity' underlined the fact that charity had two offices, and where one was to 'cherishe and reward them that be good and innocent', the other was 'to rebuke, correct, and punish vice'.[99] This high-minded ideal could in practice have a disruptive effect upon communities. The impact of religious change in the sixteenth century is usually cast in terms of the division it created between Catholic and Protestant; but it could equally involve division between the authorities of Church and state and the people they were trying to command, instruct and control.[100] To complicate the picture still further, there was often tension between different authorities over the extent to which this 'reformation of manners' should be attempted. Many zealous Protestant voices within both Church and parliament received only a lukewarm reception. Attempts to legislate against adultery, for example, were constantly frustrated, and would only succeed in 1650; the closest the Tudor proponents of sterner punishment got was the 1576 statute dealing with illegitimacy, which punished the parents and required the father to provide for the child's maintenance, rather than leaving the parish to bear the costs.[101] It is significant that this piece of legislation had a more practical than moral impact.

The conundrum that has puzzled so many historians of the Reformation is how some Tudor men and women were so completely persuaded by the message of the reformers, whilst others held with equal passion to the faith of their fathers and forefathers.[102] There were many reasons behind any choice of religious loyalties. Some religious conservatives may have been motivated just as much by the potential for troublemaking as by reverence for past practice. One William Akers, repeatedly in trouble with the Ely Consistory Court in the 1580s, had denounced his puritan minister for his preachings, threatening that he would be 'pulled out of the pulpit like a rascall'; Akers was accused of ringing the bells 'superstitiouslye', but also of being drunk and disorderly.[103] He was not the only person to ring bells in defiance: in a case from Bilsthorpe in Nottinghamshire in 1602, a malefactor was accused of 'setting others to ringe in contempte of the minister'. Those who did this were not necessarily aiming at the clergy, however: when, in 1594, someone in Cassington in Oxfordshire locked the church door and smeared its handle with dung to prevent those who rang bells in the night, it looked more like a dispute between neighbours.[104]

It seems probable that the character and behaviour of the parish priest or minister made a considerable difference to how people experienced the Reformation. A good vicar could command extraordinary levels of loyalty, both personal and confessional; a bad one was the quickest way to turn hearts and minds towards the reformed faith, whose most immediate characteristic was its emphatic anticlericalism. The churchmen of the age were only too aware of this. In 1510, William Melton, archbishop of York, had warned in a sermon about the dangers of 'oafish and boorish priests' who were 'completely ignorant of good literature'; there was a well-established rhetoric in pre-Reformation England criticizing the clergy and exhorting them to bible study.[105] Priests were perceived as carrying a heavy burden of responsibility, and even after they changed from priests in the Catholic Church to ministers of the Protestant religion, expressions of anxiety continued. Where a priest or minister served his parish faithfully, the ties between them were strong. Christopher Trychay, the parish priest of Morebath in Devon, cared for his flock for decades, and despite his obvious Catholic sympathies, went on serving them under Elizabeth.[106] Bernard Gilpin, who served in the north of England, turned down a bishopric and an Oxford college headship to stay ministering to the needs of his congregations. He was famous for his compassion for the poor, the ignorant and those in prison.[107] John Rogers of Chacombe in Northamptonshire was a Puritan who put great care into the construction of his sermons; despite his hostility to Catholicism, he preached special sermons on holy days, as in 1588, when he described Pentecost as 'beautified with a notable mark and wonderful work above other days'. This was accompanied by a strong emphasis on the importance of the sacraments – an openness to elements of past practice that probably helped encourage his flock into Protestant loyalties.[108]

The experience of parish religion was closely involved with the sacred space in which formal worship took place, which meant that the arrangement and decoration of the parish church was central to Reformation disputes.[109] It is very possible that the changes to the churches may have had a greater impact than many of the doctrinal changes. John Stow in his chronicles said comparatively little about liturgical change, but noticed the removal of altars and the changes in ecclesiastical vestments. He also noted with approval how, in 1553, the singing of anthems returned to St Paul's, which was illuminated with cresset lights (oil lamps), 'after the old custom'. Following the accession of Elizabeth, he gave little attention to the parliamentary settlement, but noted the burning of images in St Paul's churchyard and elsewhere across the city.[110] Actions sometimes spoke louder than words, and objects often conveyed meaning more successfully than text. In the godly household of the Puritan John Bruen, the servant known as 'Old Robert' had acquired an impressive knowledge of Scripture with the help of an intricate leather girdle, which was divided to represent the different books of the Bible and had knotted laces to represent each chapter.[111] Mnemonic devices and Protestant images in the domestic sphere, such as bible verses on cushion covers, used the materiality that had been central to pre-Reformation religion to expound the teachings of its Protestant successor.[112]

Across England's nine thousand or so parishes there was a high degree of variation in the implementation of Protestant changes to church interiors. In the parish church of Ludham in Norfolk, the rood screen had been taken down during Edward's reign, then restored under Mary. Faced with the injunction to remove it once more, the parish prudently decided to stretch a length of canvas over the Marian painting of the crucifixion, and had the royal coat of arms painted upon it, presumably unconvinced that Elizabeth's reign would last any longer than her brother's. In the church of Morston in Norfolk, the rood screen was taken down, leaving only the lower screen, on which were painted images of the four Evangelists and the four Fathers of the Church: Jerome, Augustine, Gregory and Ambrose. These were left largely untouched, except for the papal attributes, which were scratched out: the cardinal's hat worn by Jerome and Gregory's papal tiara (see plate 19). Accommodation to the new order was slow, patchy, often reluctant and sometimes bemused. On the other hand, change could be reified through church decoration: the reformed understanding of the Ten Commandments and their place in Protestant belief was driven home by the paintings and inscriptions that became commonplace in the Elizabethan Church.[113]

Within the walls of the parish churches, the most important rites of passage took place, as babies were baptized, marriages solemnized and the dead consigned to the afterlife, whilst the yearly ritual of taking communion was a reassurance of salvation and an individual encounter with the divine. These were some of the most disputed elements in post-Reformation religious practice, precisely because they were so important to popular religious understanding. They were physical encounters, in which the experience of the sacred took material form. The water, oil and salt used in baptism, the ring in marriage, the candles that burned around the coffin,

and the wafer and wine of the eucharistic service were all of huge significance in popular understanding and custom. And for the same reason,
they were the target for attack by zealous Protestant critics, to whom the
whole idea of a sacred object was anathema. Popular religious practice
stubbornly clung on to these reified elements of the divine in many places
up and down the country. Altars which were supposed to have been taken
down remained in place, as did the rood lofts above them, with their
reminder of what the eucharist symbolized. For the visitation of the prov-
ince of York in 1571, Archbishop Grindal's articles enquired whether 'all
altars be utterly taken down and clean removed ... And whether your
rood-lofts be taken down and altered.' The same articles also gave a lengthy
list of all the holy objects which, after twelve years of Protestant rule, were
still apparently lingering in the churches: 'antiphoners, mass-book, grailes,
portesses, processionals, manuals, legendaries' were all books, but there
was equal concern with 'vestments, albs, tunicles, stoles, fanons, pixes,
paxes, handbells, sacring bells, censers, chrismatories, crosses, candlesticks,
holy water stocks, images and such other relics and monuments of superstition', which Grindal wanted 'utterly defaced, broken, and destroyed'.[114]

Grindal's visitation articles also asked about the ringing of the passing
bell for those who had died, and the ringing of bells 'on All Saints' day after
Evening Prayer', an evasive way of asking about bell-ringing for the eve of
All Souls' Day, the yearly commemoration of the dead which was so important in pre-Reformation worship, but which was repellent to Protestants.
He was intent on weeding out all 'superstitious ceremony ... tending to
the maintenance of popish purgatory, or of prayer for the dead'.[115] The
centuries-old commemoration of the dead had been too central a part of
religious practice for it to be easily lost, however. Only in 1552 were prayers
for the dead expunged from the liturgy, alongside a dramatic reform of the
burial service. The Elizabethan Prayer Book contained no prayers for the
dead, but its Latin equivalent, for use in cathedrals and colleges, retained an
order for a burial eucharist.[116] Meanwhile, the 1559 Elizabethan Injunctions
brought back prayers of thanksgiving 'for all those that are departed out of
this life in the faith of Christ', arguably an attempt to include the dead,
without giving obvious offence to Protestant theologians. This did not
prevent puritan criticism of the dead being laid to rest with the words, 'in
sure and certain hope of resurrection to eternal life', which seemed to offend

against the doctrine of election.[117] Whatever the dogma, many people still wanted reassurance that their loved ones were safe in the hands of God: the habit of engraving on tombstones the prayer 'to whose soul God graunte a joyfull resurrection' was a vernacular echo of the pre-Reformation inscriptions, '*cuius animae propicietur Deus*'.[118] Some post-Reformation tombs still included the words '*ora pro nobis*', as if Protestantism had never happened.[119]

Whilst it is probable that every parish in England responded slightly differently to the religious changes of the era, there are widespread examples of elements of traditional religion being subtly transformed. Church bells were retained, partly for the practical reason that they were too huge and heavy to destroy easily, and partly because they were a useful form of communication. In some places they went on being used in the old way: in the early 1560s, the sexton at Benenden in Kent was still tolling a bell during thunderstorms, and bells continued to be made with holy names and inscriptions.[120] Change-ringing took on a new impetus, however, towards the end of the sixteenth and the beginning of the seventeenth century, as part of the new Protestant culture. Perhaps, like psalm-singing, it was an element of the reformed Church that helped congregations adjust to the new order. If the prayer-book service was surrounded by what looked to some like accretions from the past, it was still an English liturgy.

Witchcraft

By the second half of the sixteenth century, England's population had seen definitions of true belief and heresy questioned, inverted, restored and then again contradicted, as the religious policies of Henry VIII and his three children successively refashioned religious practice. As religious unity splintered, fears about moral decay and the strains of divided communities fostered dark imaginings about the forces of evil, and the intersection of popular fears and elite concern expressed in parliament produced new laws regulating society. The desire to live in unity and fellowship was in no way eclipsed by the travails of the sixteenth century – indeed, it was heightened by the painful experience of religious and political division. But by 1600, it appeared to many that the bonds of charity had been badly damaged, perhaps even irretrievably broken, which is one reason why, in the next century, so many people would set sail for America, in the hope of recreating 'a model of

Christian charity' there.[121] For those with nowhere to go, the lack of clarity as to what constituted truth, and what was error, opened the way for vengeful or frightened neighbours to bring accusations against those they distrusted or believed capable of doing them harm. This poisonous combination of uncertainty and fears about both social difference and spiritual error was exacerbated by the perceived and actual poverty of many communities, and by a willingness on the part of some of the more educated to believe that Satanic forces threatened their society.[122] Communal tensions and long-standing disagreements between neighbours could then escalate into one of the most peculiar and abhorrent manifestations of Tudor concerns about the social order: namely, the accusation, trial and execution of witches.[123]

The history of witchcraft sheds light on many different aspects of Tudor society.[124] It demonstrates the workings of village communities, and what could happen when things went wrong there.[125] It offers a way into understanding popular beliefs about magic, disaster, neighbourliness and domestic order.[126] It illustrates contemporary expectations of the woman's role within the family and the parish – and, since some witches were men, it gives a sense of contrasting attitudes towards the different genders.[127] It shows the legal system in action, its potential for brutality, but also its capacity for detachment and common sense: from fear of perpetrating injustice, the conviction rate for witchcraft remained low, at around 22 per cent in south-east England.[128] It also provides an example of how religious reformers capitalized on aspects of popular culture to push their own message, since the horrors of witchcraft made a profitable subject for ministers condemning the lax morals which they perceived in the communities around them. Scandalous accounts of diabolical crimes were also profitable in a more straightforward sense for printers and booksellers: many pamphlets from the time record the stories of witches brought to judgement. These publications seem to have been motivated by both pious and commercial intent at the same time, and they condemned witchcraft whilst simultaneously spreading ideas about it.[129] Above all, witchcraft cases reveal the dynamics of Tudor society at work, when very different elements just occasionally came together to reach a consensus about the dark forces which they feared.[130] The majority who did not bring accusations of witchcraft tell us just as much as the minority who did, illustrating the contrary impulses of fear and security, malevolence and compassion, which sprang from the disrupted religious culture of post-Reformation society. Each witch-trial was founded on a seemingly unique tangle of neighbourly animosity, religious anxiety, social unease and legal process, offering a cross-section of Tudor society at its most febrile and convulsed.[131]

The history of witchcraft is often studied as an aspect of social, rather than religious history; but beliefs about witchcraft offer an unparalleled insight into the history of religion, since accusations of witchcraft were inextricably bound up with fears of religious error. In 1583, a couple in Romford in Essex were condemned by their neighbours for 'using of their talk something savouring of false doctrine; and she something of witchery'.[132] Witchcraft beliefs occupied the contested space between elite and popular religion, between a scholarly view of faith and the lived experience of good and evil, charity and neglect, where so many of the uneducated located their religious understanding. Most of those who wrote about witchcraft in this period were Protestant ministers troubled by the gulf between official Protestant formulations of faith and the complex and intractable nature of popular religion at parish level. George Gifford had explored this gulf in his *Countrie Divinitie*, but in 1593 he used another dialogue to tackle the same problem specifically with regard to witchcraft, about which he had already written one long treatise.[133] He had to tread a delicate line, because to impute real power to witches was to undermine the omnipotence of God, so Gifford argued that witches were in fact powerless, and were only made to seem as if they had powers through the connivance of the Devil, just as cunning men and wise women were taught remedies by the Devil 'so that he may be sought unto and honoured as God'.[134] Not all discussions of witchcraft managed to achieve the subtlety of Gifford's explanations; for many, the malevolent power of witches was real and alarming. Nonetheless, it was only during the upheavals of the Reformation that this was given statutory form, as anxieties about heresy fed into concerns about immorality in all its guises.

Witchcraft had first been made a criminal offence by a statute of 1542, in legislation that was probably a reflection of Henry VIII's anxieties about public order. This first witchcraft statute was also the most vengeful, making all the practices which it listed punishable by death.[135] These included what would become the dominant feature of later witchcraft accusations – namely the use of magic 'to the destruction of their neighbours' persons and goods'; but the act was equally concerned with the use of magic to find buried treasure, or lost and stolen goods.[136] Love charms and the conjuring of spirits were also a concern, as was the digging up or pulling down of crosses, which seems to suggest some overlap with the religious confusion of the times. This statute was repealed five years later, and it was rather an act from 1563 that formed the basis for the Elizabethan prosecutions. In its earliest draft form, this legislation targeted a broad array of social ills that linked witchcraft and conjuration with prophecies, male homosexuality and bestiality, as well as the threat from Catholics; thus, the initial impulse seems to have been part of a general effort to reform society.[137] The initial proposals were then separated into individual bills, and the statute 'agaynst Conjuracions Inchantments and Witchecraftes' came into being, whilst the idea of witchcraft as a threat started to become a commonplace in Elizabethan moral commentary.[138]

Alongside official concern in parliament lay popular expressions of anxiety, intermingled with salacious interest. A pamphlet of 1579 saw the threat as part of a more general scourge for sin: 'Among the punishementes which the Lorde GOD hath laied uppon us, for the manifest impietie and carelesse contempt of his woorde, aboundying in these our desperate daies, the swarmes of Witches, and Inchaunters are not the laste nor the leaste.' This author thought that Satan, 'hath of late yeares, greatly multi-plyed the broude of them, and muche encreased their malice'.[139] This apocalyptic opening gave way to a narrative of how one man and five women from Berkshire had between them killed six people and afflicted several others by their use of magic. Many of the details of this story were characteristic of other witchcraft stories. The accused all kept 'familiars', small animals which acted as intermediaries between the witch and the Devil, and did their evil bidding: one had a rat named Philip, another a toad which lived in a bed of herbs in her garden, a third a black cat which she fed with milk mixed with blood.[140] The six accused conspired together, and four of their victims were despatched by making images of them and driving a hawthorn spike into their hearts. All the accused were poor, but believed they had special powers: the male witch, it was alleged, had the ability to turn himself into an ape or a horse. They had used these powers to take revenge on those whom they perceived as enemies, in particular those who had failed to give them food out of charity. Their victims were not entirely powerless: one had fought back, scratching one of the witches and making her bleed, which was acknowledged to be effective counter-magic. Yet in the end, it was the more formal legal process that brought them down: four of the women were hanged for their crimes.

This pamphlet sought to convey more than just news. It was intended also to edify, partly by recording the confession of one of the women, Elizabeth Stile, after her religious conversion in Reading gaol. Moral warnings were aimed at both the educated and the more lowly. The preface warned against laxity in the prosecution of offenders, and it blamed the 'foolishe pitie, or slackenes' of the public and lower officers, which allowed many such crimes to be 'winked at, and so escape unpunished'. The author also criticized those who actually sought out witches to ask their help and 'have recourse to them for the health of themselves or others, and for thinges loste, callyng them by the honorable name of wise women. Wherin they know not what honour they doe to the devil.'[141] The pamphlet was probably intended to titillate, as well as instruct, and might therefore be expected to have sold well. This combination of legal narrative, moral exhortation and commercial strategy shows just how intricate, tangled and fascinating a subject Tudor witchcraft can be, and how discussions of witchcraft were central to the moralizing attempts of Protestant reformers and their attacks upon popular superstition and error.

A belief in magic and the supernatural was accepted by the educated, just as much as the unlearned. Many of the nobility consulted astrologers on a regular basis, just as Elizabeth I would rely on the advice of Dr John Dee.[142] Popular beliefs about magic, however, were often condemned by the more educated – both by those who thought witchcraft should be prosecuted and by those who thought that witchcraft trials were in themselves an indefensible, disreputable and superstitious process. A shared distrust of popular mentalities led to the strong conviction that the simple and uneducated were too ignorant to grasp the subtleties of the subject. From a village perspective, however, magic was an accepted part of life, and the practitioners of magic were largely benign members of the community – 'cunning folk' who could be a valuable asset within the parish, providing medicine or skilled assistance in solving a range of common problems.[143] Repeated warnings about the inadvisability of consulting cunning men and women shows just how widespread the practice was. One of the characters in

George Gifford's book about witchcraft declared of cunning folk that: 'There be divers things which have persuaded me to thinke marveilous well of them, and even as of such as God hath given wisedome and skill unto, even for to doe much good. For we see many receive help by them, and are delivered from the plagues which come by devils.'[144] Gifford was clearly ventriloquizing here a commonly held view.

Witchcraft accusations were usually a sign that something in the community had gone badly wrong. They nearly always originated in damage to property or some personal affliction that defied easy explanation, leading to the suspicion that there were supernatural forces at work. Those accused of witchcraft were often poor, dependent upon alms and living precarious lives. In some cases, it would seem that they were easy scapegoats for the misfortunes of others. In other cases, so-called witches might be more proud than downtrodden: they may have sought to empower themselves, believing that their rats, cats, toads or ferrets were little fiends or 'familiars' sent by the Devil to help them, or else convincing themselves that they had seen Satan or his minions in bodily form (see illustration 24).[145] Those who felt threatened by them generally invoked the power of the law to crush them only when more homely counter-charms failed. Minor incidents of *maleficium* (harm done to an individual or their property) could be resolved by scratching the witch and drawing blood, or cutting the witch's hair, or by using a hot nail or penny to cure bewitched milk that would not churn or beer that was sour. Both accusers and accused were drawing on a common fund of beliefs about magic, therefore, which in most cases might be expected to resolve the difficulty. In other words, witchcraft accusations only reached the law courts when the usual reconciliatory mechanisms of local society had broken down. These mechanisms worked particularly well in Wales, where alleged witches were dealt with in line with customary Welsh law, and so were very rarely punished. Instead they were brought to admit their guilt and make restitution, with the ultimate goal of all concerned being the reconciliation of the disparate elements within the community.[146] It was normal practice for those who believed themselves bewitched to address the witch directly, and often to seek their blessing, which again was customarily given, thereby ending the bewitchment; equally, the witch was usually believed to be acting in response to some slight received at the hands of the victim.[147] Witchcraft beliefs

¶ And firste concernyng those persones that practice the damnable arte of Witchecraft, Sorcerie, or Inchauntement of her owne certaine knowledge, and voluntare motion, she vttered to this effect ensuyng.

IN Primis that one father Rosimonde, dwellyng in Farneham Parishe, beyng a widower, and also a daughter of his, are both Witches or Inchanters, which Rosimōd she saith hath and can transforme hymselfe by Dueliſhe meanes, into the shape and likenesse of any beaste whatsoeuer he will.

2 Item, that one Mother Dutten dwellyng A.v. within

24. *A Rehearsall both straung and true* (1579) showing a witch and her familiars

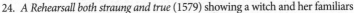

therefore enabled both the enactment and the resolution of social tensions, with an appeal to law used as a last resort. In other words, studies of witch-trials may be less about the history of magic than about the history of neighbourliness, and what could go wrong with it.

Elsewhere in Europe there were profound concerns about diabolism and witches who had sexual relations with the Devil; but English witchcraft beliefs were more likely to revolve around the question of *maleficium*, or harm done to an individual or their property. This imparted a slightly more matter-of-fact quality to English discussions, as distinct from some of the more hysterical denunciations of diabolism found in Scotland or elsewhere. Indeed, many of the popular pamphlets concerning witchcraft cases seem to have been struggling to convince their readership to take the threat of witchcraft more seriously. The 1582 account of the St Osyth witch-trials in Essex called for witches and so-called 'wisewomen' to be 'rygorously punished', adding 'I should rather have sayd most cruelly executed: for that no punishment can bee thought upon be it in never so high a degree of torment, which may be deemed sufficient for such a divelish and damnable practise.' The anonymous author was laying heavy emphasis on the awfulness of the crime of witchcraft, and making a case for 'a death so much the more horrible' than just ordinary hanging for those convicted.[148] He seems to have been working hard to persuade his target audience. Popular doubt is one of several reasons why it is not really appropriate to talk about a 'witch-craze' in Tudor England. Not only did the legal system operate with ponderous detachment (which much of the time militated against the levels of persecution seen elsewhere in Europe), but there was also routine acceptance of magic as part of everyday life. Nevertheless, for a witchcraft prosecution to come to court, there had to be more than just tension between neighbours. Just as the law rested on a foundation of popular belief, so too the legislative process required the collaboration of magistrates and assize judges, as well as the countenance, if not the proactive involvement, of the ruling classes more generally. It would be easy to characterize Tudor beliefs in witchcraft as the superstitious ideas of the uneducated and credulous; but in fact, the preoccupation with witchcraft was partly the creation of those members of the educated elite responsible for introducing the laws and for enforcing them in the localities. Concerns about the malevolent workings of witches were probably closely linked to the fears of political instability and religious heterodoxy that increasingly assailed the ruling classes of the mid-Tudor period.

Not everyone believed in witches. In 1584, Reginald Scot published *The Discoverie of Witchcraft*, which eloquently attacked the practice of prosecuting witches. Scot was a minor gentry figure from Kent; his previous work had been a book on how to cultivate hops, and he is also remembered for the detailed account of the rebuilding of Dover harbour included in Holinshed's *Chronicle*.[149] The 1886 edition of Scot's work described him as a man 'whose honesty, intelligence, and compassion fought against the cruel superstition and ignorance of his age', but the truth was more complicated than that.[150] Scot was certainly impatient with much of the dominant discourse concerning witchcraft; he had been prompted to write after attending a witch-trial in Rochester, where the chief witness was a minister with puritanical tendencies. Scot sought to uncover a whole range of offences, 'the lewde dealing of witches and witchmongers . . . the knaverie of conjurors, the impietie of inchantors, the follie of soothsaier', but also 'the infidelitie of atheists'. His main objection to both those who claimed to be witches and those who claimed to be extirpating witchcraft was that in both cases they were arrogating to themselves 'that power which onelie apperteineth to God'.[151] In Scot's view, unearthly power was only too real, but it belonged in the hands of the Creator, not his creatures. Witches, he argued, were either pitiful and innocent victims, or fraudulent deceivers seeking to 'amase or abuse the people' with their tricks.[152] Scot's work was in part seeking to counter some of the ideas current in the European-wide debate about magic. He consulted works by 212 Latin and 23 English authors, and included a list of these to emphasize his academic credentials.[153] He was also motivated by a wish to defend the poor and helpless, a desire that had been evident in his work on hop-farming.[154] Scot was dismayed by the socially divisive consequences of zealous puritan belief, and struck by how 'in truth, that commonwealth remaineth in wofull state, where fetters and halters beare more swaie than mercie and due compassion'.[155] His dedication of his work to Sir Roger Manwood, alongside two others, was because 'I know that your Lordship is by nature whollie inclined, and in purpose earnestly bent to relieve the poore', and because he thought Manwood had 'a speciall care for the supporting of their right, and redressing of their wrongs'. Scot envisaged his work as being 'in the behalfe of the poore, the aged, and the simple'.[156] So both those who accused their neighbours of being witches and those, such as Scot, who sought to halt what he saw as persecution were moved by a sense that the world was out of kilter, that charity had been eroded. He also dedicated his work to Manwood because he was a JP, for 'a discreet and mercifull magistrate, and a happie commonwealth cannot be separated asunder'.[157] Scot's objections were those not of the modern sceptic, but of the committed Protestant. He condemned his contemporaries because, by ascribing powers to witches, they were denigrating the omnipotence of God. So those who urged the prosecution of witches and those who protested against it had something else in common, namely a desire to protect and to evangelize the 'simple and unlearned' element of the population.

Witchcraft accusations were what happened when the usual tenor of life in the village was disrupted, and quotidian belief in the supernatural became distorted, or alarmed, or vengeful. The problem was caused not by popular beliefs about magic, which were usually taken as a part of life, but by beliefs concerning witchcraft that had got out of control, that could not be restrained by counter-magic or religion, and that seemed to demand a more vigorous response. A telling feature is that many of the people accused of witchcraft seem to have been witches by reputation for years, sometimes decades, before their cases came to court. Many had mothers or grandmothers who had also been known to be witches The history of witchcraft prosecutions is a way of taking the pulse of post-Reformation society and of judging the levels of anxiety being mapped onto ideological constructs and finding expression through the legal process. It was all too easy not only to believe that there were dark forces at work, but also to feel a compulsion to fight back against them.

Legacies

'What is the world?' asked John Jewel, leading apologist of the Elizabethan Church of England:

> Some think it to be a place full of all delights and pleasures, a goodly, strong and gorgeous palace and a paradise of joy. Let no man deceive us, nay, rather let us not deceive ourselves: the world is a shop of vanities, it is a dungeon of darkness, a pot full of poison, a ship full of leaks, a way full of snares. It blindeth our eyes, beguileth our senses, and helpeth us forward into all dangers.[158]

Jewel, like many other Elizabethan writers, was partial to describing the world in terms of binary oppositions: light and dark, good and evil, the kingdom of God and the kingdom of man. It was an approach that could readily be applied to many aspects of post-Reformation culture, especially the opposition of Protestant and Catholic, represented on the cover of Foxe's *Actes and Monuments*, which gave a visual comparison of the true and false churches (see illustration 25).[159] Ironically, however, this attachment to binary thinking was in itself a point of similarity between the two sides. There were many such similarities, as some inadvertent remarks often suggested – a reminder that these were, after all, different aspects of the same

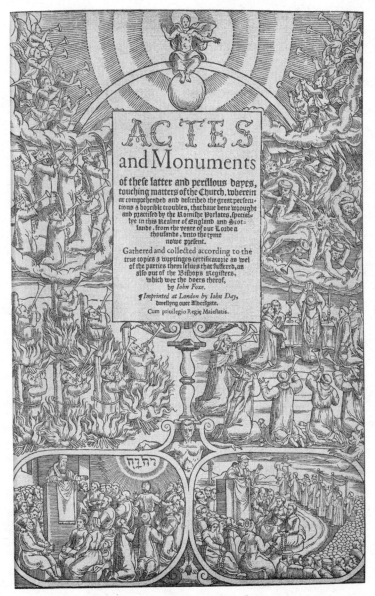

25. Frontispiece to John Foxe's *Actes and Monuments*

faith, heated up in the same crucible of reforming fervour and political instability. When Jewel wrote about the importance of the Bible to the Protestant
cause, and the dilemmas of a believer seeking religious truth, he made the
religious disputations of his age sound oddly like reflections in a mirror:

> If he make reckoning of learning, there are learned men on both sides;
> if he make reckoning of virtue and godly life, there be virtuous men
> and of godly life on both sides; if he make reckoning of zeal, either side
> is zealous in the religion they hold; if he make reckoning of the name
> of the church, they take it as well to the one side as to the other; if he
> make reckoning of the multitude, there are many on either side, but
> neither side hath so many as hath the Turk. Whither then may a man
> turn himself, and to which side may he safely join?[160]

The answer to this question was, for Jewel, 'the word of God', since he was
making an argument for the supremacy of biblical authority. Unwittingly,
however, he had given a telling illustration of the resemblance between the
two traditions. A work by his Catholic contemporary Cardinal Stanislaus
Hosius, translated into English by the former Oxford don and Elizabethan
exile Thomas Stapleton, also bore unintended testimony to the parallels
between the two sides.[161] This work commented: 'But seeme they not on
bothe sydes armed with the woordes of the lawe of godd? Truly both
partes glory of his expresse woorde. Bothe crye, the woorde of the lord.
The mouthe of the lord hath spoken it. Thus sayeth the lord.'[162] Hosius and
Stapleton were, like Jewel, trying to make a case for the ultimate authority
which cut across these resemblances, in this case the Catholic Church.
Both sides were intent upon proving the superiority of their respective
religious authorities, and yet they could not conceal the fact that they
seemed strangely to resemble one another.

At the start of the century, there had been many voices urging Church
reform, seeking to endow educational institutions for both laity and clergy,
expressing concern about the morality of those in authority and the superstitious credulity of the ordinary people. These concerns may have been
overtaken by more theologically driven controversies, but the desire for
reform remained constant, as did the yearning of many for a more profound
personal experience of God. Historical attention has always been drawn

first and foremost to the antagonism between Protestant and Catholic and the many points of difference between them; but the points of similarity may have been just as important. Both groupings sought to promote education, founding schools and colleges. Both made extensive use of the printing press, not just for polemical exchanges, but for works of instruction and devotion. Both sought a closer acquaintance with the Bible, and both advocated a more ascetic, less politicized, more educated clergy. Finally, both were engaged in the work of proselytization, seeking to counter popular ignorance and error with simple, moral, Christian teaching. Between them, they spurred the development of Tudor society towards an increasingly self-aware, literary, intellectualized and moralistic understanding of the religious life, forming a religious culture with shared elements that may not have been open to all, but that touched the lives of many.

Two books could be said to epitomize this paradoxical aspect of the Reformation. One was the late medieval bestseller *The Imitation of Christ*, first composed by Thomas à Kempis in the Netherlands in the 1420s. Between 1500 and 1700, there would be sixteen editions of this work in English translation; nine were Catholic, but seven were Protestant.[163] The emphasis on the love of God and the human striving to emulate Christ won out over other more divisive considerations. Similarly, the great work of Catholic spirituality by Robert Persons, *The First Booke of Christian Exercise*, published in 1582, was recast two years later by the Puritan Edmund Bunny as *A Book of Christian Exercise*. There was close correlation between the two versions of this text, and a remarkable level of agreement on the demands of the religious life.[164] This shared territory was reflected in other patterns of life. Protestantism is often vaunted as being the 'religion of the book', but Catholics could be just as reliant on the printed word, and just as energetic in their deployment of print. Towards the end of the century, indeed, Catholicism was forced to rely more and more on printed literature, as it lacked church buildings or a clerical hierarchy to provide support.[165] As the preface to an Elizabethan edition of the *Imitation of Christ* observed, 'good and holie bookes are as ladders to climbe up to heaven; as sparks to kindle the heate of the spirit, when it is quenched or waxed colde in them; and as proppes to staie up their faith, that it may increase'.[166]

Few sentiments inspired quite such energetic engagement as the confessionalized exchanges between Catholic and Protestants in this era.

Yet if this level of strenuous hostility was a stimulus to some, to others it was a tragedy – or at least a diversion from matters of weightier importance. Sir John Harington, author, godson to Elizabeth I, wayward courtier and inventor of the flush lavatory, described himself as a 'protesting Catholic Puritan'; his religion had a highly individual flavour which opposed persecution, equated Protestant communion with Catholic mass and was of the opinion that 'tis pity we should fall out about them'. He perhaps wrote at least partly to provoke, and yet his understanding of faith as rooted in friendship found many quiet echoes elsewhere among his contemporaries.[167] Harington stands out in the historical record, given his status and connections; but there must have been many more who silently upheld a faith that defied easy categorization, in which no point of doctrine was worth a price paid in hatred.

So much of the history of the Reformation was written by churchmen who knew their theology that we have forgotten how many Tudor men and women had only the haziest grasp of religious doctrine in all its precision. William Cecil, Lord Burghley, was said to have only discovered the details of the Protestant doctrine of predestination aged seventy-five and to have been appalled by what he discovered, considering that it 'charged God with cruelty'.[168] Historians have tried to argue that there was a Calvinist consensus emerging by the last decade of the sixteenth century, and that the doctrine of predestination could even be a rallying point for popular believers.[169] For some, a belief in election was clearly a source of strength (although for many it was a source of anguish).[170] Like the Elizabethan homilies, however, many religious works of the time thought it better to skirt around the proposition that the majority of the population were damned by God to eternal punishment, regardless of what they might think or do. What the homilies did hammer home was the necessity of Christian virtue and godly obedience, and this was a message more widely shared, as well as more generally amenable.

The Catholic controversialist Thomas Stapleton claimed that, for all the wrangling between theologians, the true definition of God's teaching was a single word: 'And that is this worde. *Love*, or *Charyte*: The only scope of al scriptures. The ende of all the Commaundementes: The consummation and accomplishement of the whole lawe.' He was, of course, attacking the Protestants for not being loving and charitable at all, but seditious and aggressive; and yet his words appealed to a higher truth which was widely agreed to be important – that love or charity 'dothe not dissolve, but unyte, not mangle, but amende: not rente and wounde, but ioyne and heale, and is ever occupied, in doing good'.[171] Stapleton's colleague Thomas Harding echoed the words of St Augustine, and wished that 'these hote talkers of gods worde, had lesse of that knowledge, which maketh a man to swell, and to be proude in his owne conceite'. His plea was heartfelt:

> God graunt all our knowledge be so joyned with meekenesse, humilitie and charitie, as that be not justly sayd of us . . . The unlearned and simple aryse up, and catche heaven awaie from us, and we with all our great learning voyed of heart, lo where are we wallowing in fleshe and bloude?[172]

Tudor religion went far deeper than the arguments of theologians. It was the stuff of life, the stay of all strength and goodness within society. The Elizabethan vicar of Ormesby in Yorkshire, who was known for his orchards, wrote a treatise on gardening which summed up forty-eight years of labour and contemplation. He insisted that a gardener must not only be skilful and hardworking, but religious:

> By religious, I meane . . . maintaining, and cherishing things religious: as Schooles of Learning, Churches, Tythes, Church-goods, and rights; and above all thinges, Gods word, and the Preachers thereof, so much as hee is able, practising prayers, comfortable conference, mutuall instruction to edifie, almes, and other workes of Charity, and all out of a good conscience.

This breadth of vision and activity would preserve and protect the common-weal; it was also needed in order to make trees grow.[173] Such underlying hopes of Christian harmony bore a strong resemblance to those expressed at the start of the Tudor era. Pre-Reformation parishes had also contained the zealous alongside the lukewarm believers, and known corrupt priests as well as godly preachers. The difference was that, by 1600, religious variation had become problematized to the point where the wrong set of beliefs could be categorized at best in terms of neighbourly annoyance, and at worst in terms of disobedience, diabolism or treason.

CHAPTER 14

THE DRAMA OF LIFE AND THE POLITICS OF PERFORMANCE

In Tudor England, power was ritually enacted; shame was a matter for public show; political allegiance and religious devotion alike were acted out for all to see. Structures of authority were sustained by demonstrations of good lordship, from the rituals of the coronation, through the swearing of feudal oaths, to the parish constables and night-watchmen processing through the streets with their staves of office.[1] Meetings of assize courts began with a solemn sermon and saw robed judges in procession with trumpeters.[2] Punishment was acted out in the theatre of the marketplace, with offenders pilloried or placed in the stocks; when the Marian regime wanted to demonstrate the fate of London's heretics, it was in Smithfield market that it built the bonfires.[3] Those infected with the plague had to carry a white rod if they walked abroad.[4] In the churches before the Reformation, the Last Supper and the death of Christ on the cross were re-enacted on a daily basis, and even after the arrival of Protestantism, church services still retained significant ritual elements, to the alarm of many Protestant zealots. Mystery plays had already spilled out of the church and onto the streets by the fifteenth century, and they lingered on after the Reformation, despite official condemnation, only to be replaced by the extraordinary dramatic output of the later Elizabethan period. Social crimes were punished by public humiliation, with adulterers and cuckolds paraded with 'rough music'.[5] In 1548, when the prostitute Elizabeth Whytehed, also known as 'Flouncing Bess', was taken to the pillory to have her hair chopped short and to be displayed with a paper listing her offences, she was accompanied 'with basones and other instrumentes and melodie ryngyng and playing before her'.[6] Authority and justice were not just dispensed; they were performed.

As the tensions of the later sixteenth century, both religious and polit-ical, became more acute, Tudor drama itself became more sophisticated, and more heavily freighted with meaning. Elizabethan plays might have a dangerously polemical edge, or a blunt propaganda purpose. Where fifteenth-century plays had often conveyed a religious message, later Tudor drama continued to explore moral dilemmas, albeit with a level of self-conscious wariness that earlier dramas had lacked. Solely religious plays became a thing of the past in the fraught confessional climate of the 1580s and 1590s, but drama became, if anything, more pervasive.[7] Plays, or 'playings', took place at Court, in private households, in the universities and Inns of Court, in taverns and inns, in the market square or through the streets of a city on May Day or to celebrate midsummer. By the end of the sixteenth century, there were also commercial theatrical spaces akin to the modern theatre; the first of these was built by James Burbage in Shoreditch in 1576, and called simply the Theatre.[8] South of the river, Philip Henslowe built the Rose on Bankside in 1587, and it was joined in 1595 by the Swan and in 1599 by the Globe (see plate 24). Yet even in the age of Shakespeare, theatre still belonged as much in the street or the household as upon a stage.

Drama was not just a source of entertainment or moral commentary: it was proactive in the shaping of affairs and attitudes. In an age when insti-tutions were still flimsy, and politics were intensely personal, power could be confirmed or qualified through magnificence and display. The common-wealth, or state, was something imagined, but still it elicited an emotional investment given immediacy through symbolism.[9] Each display of power required a response, and each enactment of authority called for an answer, so drama was also a site for negotiation and the exchange of ideas in this 'theatre state'.[10] Royal processions, progresses and tournaments encapsu-lated important transactions between ruler and ruled; in council meetings, parliaments and royal audiences, confrontations were enacted in which policy was shaped by participants on both sides. Deaths on the scaffold required the speeches of those about to die to reinforce codes of honour and obedience, while subtle alterations to the formulaic expressions of penitence and obedience might equally convey protestations of innocence, or even defiance. The drive for religious conformity made martyrs of many whose extraordinary commitment led them willingly to play their parts in a terrible drama of death. In their sufferings could be seen either the moral might of a government staunchly opposing heresy, or conversely, a testimony to religious truth serving as a powerful reproach to a persecutory regime; it was for the audience to choose.

This was an age in which men and women often found it easiest to express their own identity by acting a part. Elizabeth I in her lifetime was cast by both herself and others in roles as various as the Old Testament heroine Deborah or the goddess Diana; as the mythical King Arthur or the historical Emperor Constantine. When she famously remarked to William Lambarde, keeper of the Tower, 'know ye not I am Richard II?', she was acknowledging her own questionable reputation as ruler in her twilight years; she was also signalling the broader principle that political meaning could be readily conveyed by mimesis.[11] Badgered by parliament to execute Mary Queen of Scots, she reminded them of the dangers of public scrutiny: 'Princes, you know, stand upon stages so that their actions are viewed and beheld of all men; and I am sure my doings will come to the scanning of many fine wits, not only within the realm, but in foreign countries.'[12] Henry VII, in just a single royal progress in 1486, had been variously depicted as Solomon, Noah, Jason, Isaac, Jacob, David, Scipio and Arthur – legendary figures, invoked at a time of dangerous political instability, when the sanction of past rulers, generals and prophets was badly needed.[13]

Such characterizations might be open to question, and appeals to mythical, legendary, biblical and classical figures could encapsulate devastating political criticism. Whilst Henry VIII aped the role of the biblical King David, the great king who slew Goliath and purged his realm of idolatry, other voices spoke obliquely but fiercely of David's sins, in subtle but potent censure of Henry's incipient despotism. When Thomas Wyatt wrote his paraphrase of the penitential psalms, his David appeared not only as the sinner stained by adultery, but as the corrupted king abusing his power.[14] Wyatt's work offered no obvious indication that this was a reflection on his own king, but his friend the earl of Surrey would describe it as a place 'Where rulers may see in a mirror clear / The bitter fruit of false concupiscence.'[15] Much Tudor commentary was concerned with mirrors that might reflect truth. When assize judges came out to the provinces, they were understood to carry the 'two glasses or mirrors of the

State', displaying the king's 'graces and care' to the people, but equally presenting the 'distastes and griefs of the people' to their king.[16] The Bible was described as a text 'wherein the simple and ignoraunt may plainly and clearly see as it were in a Glasse, what syde holdeth of Christe most truly'.[17] The *Mirror for Magistrates* used the lives of historical figures as a moral lesson, a 'rude myrrour' in which political probity might be assessed.[18] Plays provided a particularly vivid and immediate reflection of Tudor society. Shakespeare's *Hamlet,* written as the century drew to a close, used the 'play within the play' of *The Murder of Gonzago* as Hamlet's device for uncovering the possible murderous guilt of his uncle, since 'guilty creatures sitting at a play' can, he knows, be prompted to confess 'by the very cunning of the scene' (see illustration 26).[19] This trope of the 'play within the play' was repeated in many other works of the time; whether it served to challenge or amuse the audience, it underlined Tudor fascination with the power of performance and the porous boundaries between theatre and real life.

The performance of power

In Tudor England, the written word was already prominent in certain transactions, but the survival of such written records is in danger of obscuring how almost all such interactions had an equally important performative element. When regimes issued proclamations, they may have been published; but it was the act of them being proclaimed and affixed to market cross or church door which transmitted their message. In courts of law, sentences were pronounced; in parliament, consent was verbal; in marriage, from 1538 onwards the contract was recorded in the parish register, but what mattered to contemporaries was the public exchange of vows and the declaration of the priest or minister that the rite had been solemnized. Some of the greatest statements of political power were enacted rather than written. The power of a prince or magnate was embodied by his or her retinue, cloth of estate and the symbols of authority carried in procession, and sanctioned above all by the performance of a coronation. When Cardinal Wolsey went in procession, he had 'two great crosses of silver' carried before him – one to represent his archbishopric, the other his legatine powers – and he made sure that they were borne 'by

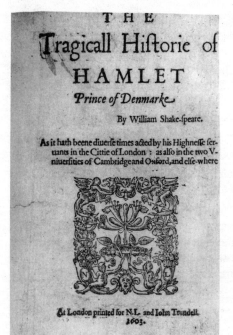

26. The title page of William Shakespeare's *Hamlet*, published 1603

two of the most tallest and comeliest priests that he could get within all this realm'. When his cardinal's hat was sent from the pope by messenger, and Wolsey heard that 'the people's opinion and rumour' was that this messenger was 'but a person of small estimation', he had him stopped and arrayed in 'costly silks, which seemed decent for such an high ambassador', before he could complete his mission. Cavendish, who observed the final reception of this hat, thought the occasion as grand as a coronation.[20]

The enactment of power could also be subversive and disruptive. The first act of any rebellion or riot was to gather, and the second was often to march. The Pilgrimage of Grace, the largest rebellion of the era, was acted out at many places in the northern counties. Rebels made a symbolic progress to the nearest city, be it Lincoln, York or Carlisle, like pilgrims coming to make offering in the cathedrals. Their proceedings were solemnized by oath-taking, their legitimacy displayed by the banners of the Five Wounds of Christ which they carried (see plate 21).[21] Popular uprisings have been interpreted by some as disorganized and unprincipled, but in general they paid careful attention to the good of the commonwealth and the obligations of every member of society.[22] The politics of household, community and parish were also all acted out on the village green, in the streets, the marketplace, the village church and in procession.[23] Rogationtide processions marked out parish boundaries, reaffirming communal space and solidarity, condemning those who would encroach upon their neighbours' territory, and asking for divine blessing upon land and settlement.[24] In more difficult times, they provided a model for enclosure riots, which sought also to affirm traditional boundaries and asked for divine sanction for the enterprise.[25] This was a political language which anyone could speak, regardless of background or education.

Monarchs may have stood at the centre of the political stage, but they could not always expect to command applause. From the moment Henry VII landed near Milford Haven and kissed the sand, Tudor kingship was a performance played to an emotional, often enthusiastic, but frequently also sceptical audience. 'I can counterfeit the deep tragedian', said Shakespeare's Buckingham to Richard III, mocking the melodramas of kingship.[26] The weakness of the initial Tudor claim to the throne necessitated repeated demonstrations of royal authority in the first fifty years of Tudor rule. Thereafter, Henry VIII's break with Rome called for even greater histrionic display to justify the extraordinary and disturbing claims he was making to sovereignty over Church as well as kingdom. The triumphalism of the Royal Supremacy was enacted in parliament, at Court, at public executions and in pulpits across the land, and the complicated legacy he bequeathed to his children required them to deploy similar tactics. For a great many subjects, however, the performance of the Supremacy was an act which failed to persuade or convince. Every piece of royal pageantry was, on one level, an answer to implied scepticism or tacit challenge.

A great deal of historical writing has revolved around the magnificence of the Tudor monarchs.[27] Some of it suffers from an unhelpful tendency to equate Tudor display with modern propaganda, casting 'art as power'.[28] This ignores the extent to which Tudor pageantry exploited an already established shared language of symbolic meaning and was constrained to work within the parameters of that language; it also ignores the targeted nature of much of the message towards those who shared in the exercise of power, rather than those expected to submit to it. And above all, it ignores the extent to which the performance of power required audience participation and approval in order to be effective. There is also too little attention paid to the rituals of authority performed at every level of society, right down to the petty officialdom at village level. The solemnity with which churchwardens signed off their accounts equalled that of any lord treasurer, just as the rituals of the parish church echoed the grander displays within England's cathedrals. It was not that power was imposed through performance and display, but that it was constructed and brokered in visual, material and performative terms, between power-brokers of many different sorts. When royalty or other dignitaries arrived in a city or town, the civic elite amassed to meet them would be ordered according to hierarchy, with mayor and aldermen to the fore. Hall's chronicle described Henry VIII's coronation procession entering the city, 'where every occupacion stode, in their liveries in ordre, beginnyng with base and meane occupacions, and so assendyng to the worshippfull craftes: highest and lastly stode the Maior, with the Aldermen'.[29] It was an encounter between all the different orders in society.[30]

The reign of a Tudor monarch began with the ultimate piece of theatre, whereby the coronation ritual turned the monarch into a sacred figure, anointed with holy oil, garbed in special vestments, endowed with powers of healing.[31] The newly crowned monarch was presented to his or her people as a holy icon, an amalgam of ruler and saint, priest and king. At the heart of the coronation, however, was the affirmation by those present of their acceptance of the new monarch, and the monarch's oath by which he or she vowed to uphold the law and protect the realm. It was a contractual ceremony, where royal power was simultaneously celebrated and limited.[32] This was affirmed, too, in the spectacle of the coronation procession and festivities outside the abbey walls. Royalty, nobility, royal household, city dignitaries, foreign envoys and the people of London and Westminster all collaborated in a demonstration of mutual support. The Court of Claims, which decided who should take which role in the proceedings, also agreed what they were entitled to in exchange. For Henry VIII's coronation, the earl of Surrey was made earl marshal, which entitled him to keep the horses that the king and queen had used in the procession, as well as the cloths on and above the royal table at the coronation banquet. The earl of Arundel was the hereditary butler at the banquet, and in return his benefits included all the wine that was not used (this may not have been a large item) and the king's best cup. Whilst the grander roles were decided, it was also decreed who would carry the king's salt cellar to the table and who would be falconer for the occasion.[33] Parts were being assigned for a drama in which many different people had a role to play, and from which all concerned would derive benefits.

The sixteenth century saw huge upheavals in terms of religious ritual, and yet significantly the coronation order seems hardly to have varied in its essentials from Henry VII to Elizabeth I.[34] But behind the fixity of traditional ritual there were anxieties, compounded by religious division and the fact that the last four Tudor coronations were of three contentious women (including Anne Boleyn) and one young boy.[35] In 1559, a glowing account of Elizabeth's coronation procession, and in particular the loving exchanges between queen and subjects, was written and printed in the space of just nine days. Richard Mulcaster, the author, made a conscious appeal to the theatricality of the occasion: 'So that if a man shoulde say well, he could not better tearme the citie of London that time, than a stage wherin was shewed the wonderfull spectacle, of a noble hearted princesse toward her most loving people.'[36] But Mulcaster wrote at a time of great unease, when in particular the future direction of religious policy was unclear, and his work was pushing the agenda of the Protestant elite in the city: his emphasis on the godliness of both queen and citizens was barbed. So, too, were some of the pageants: one in which virtue and vice were compared meant, Mulcaster explained, that the queen was only secure so long as she 'embraced vertue and helde vice under foote. For if vice once gotte up the head, it would put the seate of governement in peryll of falling.'[37] This was stern warning under the guise of adulation.

The foundation of royal authority was military might, although modern commentators sometimes forget this; and here, too, display was essential. Military men took a prominent role in politics, partly on the basis of their achievements in the field.[38] Chronicles contained descriptions of militias being mustered, or troops being readied for battle, with what might seem tedious detail and elaboration; but contemporaries had a better sense that these were key elements in the construction of authority. Edward Hall recorded the activities of Henry VIII on his French campaign of 1513, noting both how the 'kyng prepared all thinges necessarie to mete with the [e]mperour in triumphe' and how the 'noble men of the kynges campe were gorgeously apparelled, ther coursers barded of cloth of gold, of damaske and broderie, theire apparelle all tissue cloth of gold and sylver, and gold smithes woorke, great cheynes of balderickes of gold, and belles of bullion'.[39] The description of this magnificence was closely linked to the accounts of military action and the capture of Tournai. Hall also described the muster of 1539, when the fields from Whitechapel to Mile End, and from Bethnal Green to Stepney, were 'all covered with harness, men and weapons, and in especial the battle of pikes seemed to be a great forest'.[40] Nearly fifty years later, the forces assembled at Tilbury were intended to achieve a similar effect; the propaganda regarding Elizabeth's own role there seems to have been greatly exaggerated after the event, but there were around eight thousand troops assembled for her to review.[41] This was an emphatic statement of political competence. Henry VIII's reputation was, in large part, bolstered by the fact that he sent armies overseas on twelve separate occasions, as well as waging three wars with Scotland; his army sent to France in 1544 was of a size not equalled until the expeditions of the duke of Marlborough at the end of the seventeenth century.[42] Military grandeur was more persuasive, however, if it was accompanied by success; here again, audience reaction was key to the drama being enacted. The splendour of Henry VIII's arrival in France in 1513 and again in 1544 book-ended his reign with military display on a grand scale; but the gains made by the two campaigns remained meagre when set against the victories of previous centuries. And the expense of military display without the glory would contribute to the uprisings of 1548–49.

Performances of power could function as a helpful smokescreen in time of trouble. As Edward VI lay dying, the Council reassured the Court that his health was improving, and ceremonies such as playing trumpets to announce the arrival of new courses at dinner were revived, just as if the king was himself present.[43] Elizabeth I's Accession Day tilts became more and more elaborate celebrations of the queen's ageless beauty, chastity and power at the very time when her physical health was deteriorating, and her aging and childless state was threatening both her authority and the future security of the realm.[44] The political process could also make strategic use out of theatrical performances. In 1527, in a bid to help seal an alliance with France, the boys of St Paul's School enacted a Latin play for the French ambassadors in which the kings of England and France together set the captured pope at liberty. In an emotional ploy, two boys played the parts of the French king's own sons, at that time hostages of Charles V. In the play, the two young princes were freed by the intervention of Cardinal Wolsey; by these means, the glories of the cardinal, the king and the proposed treaty were all simultaneously enhanced.[45] Other political plays might be a lot less subtle: in 1539, a mock battle on the Thames between a barge representing the papacy and another representing the king culminated in the pope and his cardinals being thrown into the river.[46]

At the level of town and parish, both the exercise of power and challenges to that power had strong performative elements. Marketplaces and the principal streets of the town or city were the spaces where news was proclaimed, or civic rituals and other dramas played out.[47] The credibility of administrative acts rested on the reception they could command from their audience, and often that reception was a critical one.[48] The social standing of any individual was in large part decided by public opinion. At a time when most people's lives were largely lived in sight of their neighbours, and privacy was not only unusual but generally considered undesirable, the bedchamber could be as much of a shared space as the street outside, so there was nearly always an audience for any domestic drama.[49] In local disputes, which might come before the church courts or form the basis of civil suits at law, the question of 'common fame' was key. In 1586, the churchwardens of Gainford in County Durham reported that 'there is a verie great talke and common fame in the parish' that their minister was living 'very ungodlie and naughtilie' with another man's wife.[50] It was highly significant for anything to be kept secret: in 1579, the court of London bridewell decided not to name a 'sodometicall synne not mete to be wryten'.[51] In a defamation case arising from a slanging match between two women in London in 1590, witnesses testified to the rich and varied insults exchanged, but one stopped short of repeating 'other words past womanhood to name'.[52]

Responses to authority might appear to follow a script. Paupers were more likely to secure poor relief by enacting deference to their social superiors than by voicing complaint or defiance.[53] When pushed to extremes, however, riot and rebellion might follow. Riots in the Tudor era were not spontaneous and untrammelled acts of violence, but something choreo-graphed and performed within frames of reference, which were widely understood. Rioters felt themselves to be justified in their defence of tradi-tional rights and customs.[54] This kind of political performance frequently included a high level of female participation.[55] Women were very protec-tive of their public reputation, and lawsuits concerning slander and defa-mation were more often brought by women than by men.[56] Where insults against men were as likely to be 'knave' or 'rogue' as 'cuckold', the defama-tion of women was usually more sexualized, and 'whore' or 'queane' was the most common slur.[57] The drama of public denunciation was played out in the marketplace or street, just as the drama of retribution was then played out in the church courts. Women were particularly strident in protests about enclosure, or any other agrarian grievance that restricted their ability to provide for their families, although men might also complain: the rioting Gloucestershire clothworkers asserted in 1586 that 'they were dryven to feede their Children with Catts, doggs and rootes of nettles'.[58] Women could also be violent, threatening workers who were erecting fences that they would chop the men up 'as small as herbs to the pot'.[59]

Acting a part required, of course, the right costumes and props. Magnates clothed their followers in their heraldic colours and badges; at the Field of Cloth of Gold the displays were so dazzling that the chroni-clers spent half their time just recording the colours, fabrics, jewels and devices.[60] The ornate clothes worn by Tudor kings were so extensive, and so labour intensive to produce, that the king's wardrobe was not an article of furniture, but a collection of buildings in the heart of London, which is why the local church was called St Andrew-by-the-Wardrobe. In 1521, Henry VIII had sixty gowns – the uppermost garment worn by men at the time, something like a loose-fitting, wide-sleeved dressing gown – which together were worth £6,140. The most expensive of them was made of purple velvet trimmed with sable fur, and was valued at £430.[61] Charles Brandon, duke of Suffolk, signalled his closeness to Henry VIII by dressing in identical outfits at jousts and court masques.[62] In 1522, Henry VIII and Emperor Charles V rode into London together in matching costumes of cloth of gold embroidered with silver; ten years later, Henry VIII and Francis I both wore white and silver to meet one another.[63] The effect was intended to be overwhelming. The Venetian ambassador recorded that in

Elizabeth's coronation procession, the 'whole court so sparkled with jewels and gold collars' that 'they cleared the air, though it snowed a little'.[64]

The relevance of dress worked at every level.[65] John More, a leading Protestant in Norwich, 'was said to have grown the longest and largest beard of his time so that no act of his life would be unworthy of the gravity of his appearance'.[66] Elizabethan Catholic priests were viewed with suspicion by many, not only because of their faith, but also because they were often in disguise; it caused additional comment if their clothes were inappropriate to their social status, or made them look like ruffians, encouraging the authorities to note down details such as 'red breeches and yellow stockings' or 'gold or silver lace'.[67] The lower orders were not expected to dress above their station. One Elizabethan proclamation took a dim view of padded breeches and commanded no man 'under the degree of baron to wear within his hose any velvet, satin, or any other stuff above the estimation of sarcenet or taffeta'.[68] Overlords were expected to give annual or biannual gifts of cloth or clothing to their servants and retainers, and this 'livery of cloth' obligation was fiercely upheld by successive parliaments. Some yeomen seem to have hopefully, but illegally, donned appropriate colours or badges in the hope of enhancing their status or securing the relevant lord's patronage.[69] Since power and status could seep into fabric and fur, and be found concentrated in badges and devices, the temptation to seize on such status symbols and 'dress up' was a powerful one.[70] One of the Elizabethan homilies was specifically directed 'Against excess of apparel', putting it in company with the idolatry, rebellion, gluttony and drunkenness to which other homilies were addressed. It was also a view commonly held that wearing inappropriate clothes could warp the mind and morals of the wearer.

With fixed notions concerning male and female attire, cross-dressing was a ready means of making a statement.[71] Often this was just an aspect of carnivalesque celebration, although some of those brought before the church courts for their behaviour seem to have aimed at something more subversive, such as the woman from Essex who, in 1596, 'came into our church in manes apparell upon the Sabaoth daie in the servyce time'.[72] It could also be a means of protection: male rioters borrowed female apparel, in the knowledge that women might be less severely punished; although equally, some women participating in riots would dress as men to enhance the significance of their protests.[73] Some costumes might transcend gender differences, however: in the reign of Mary Tudor, some Protestants donned long white shirts for their execution, acting the part of the white-robed martyrs from the book of Revelation.[74]

Play-acting is meaningless without an audience, and the essence of performative politics was one of reciprocity. Even at the lowest level of society, there was still an expectation of involvement. In part, this was expressed by sheer noise: the shouting of the populace, accompanied by the pealing of church bells, led commentators to compare Mary I's coronation procession to an earthquake, and Elizabeth's to the end of the world.[75] The humbler folk also brought tributes, and there was an exchange of guarantees implicit (and sometimes explicit) in these encounters. The description of Elizabeth's coronation procession noted that 'To al that wyshed her grace wel, she gave heartie thankes, and to suche as bade God save her grace, she sayd agayne god save them all, and thanked them with all her heart.' As the commentary notes, 'on eyther syde ther was nothing but gladnes'.[76] Authority and obedience, rebuke and avowal, commentary and criticism, all were a matter of public performance.

Theatres of punishment

The maintenance of justice in the early modern period was of crucial importance in sustaining some level of social stability. With only limited literacy, and few channels of direct communication, central lessons about morality, crime and punishment had to be acted out for all to see.[77] The scaffold was the visible embodiment of the authority of law, and the public display of the dismembered body parts of traitors, preserved in pitch and hung over town and city gates, or on spikes on London Bridge, was a stark warning against breaking the law.[78] Those about to be executed reinforced both legal and moral codes, with a pattern of behaviour that included the confession of their crimes, professions of loyalty to the ruler, pardon of the executioner and anyone else deemed to have offended them, and a plea for forgiveness. These scaffold speeches were an extraordinary example of social conformity. They were usually directed at the public, who gathered in large numbers to watch these spectacles; indeed, these theatrical last speeches seem to have been, in large part, a Tudor innovation.[79] William

Harrison saw this kind of honourable death as a mark of England's moral superiority: 'one cause wherefore our condemned persons do go so cheerfully to their deaths, for our nation is free, stout, haughty, prodigal of life and blood', he wrote optimistically.[80] Such executions seem to have lingered long in popular memory: in the 1590s, a Kentishman was prosecuted for saying that if the queen outlawed begging, she would be 'worse than Nan Bennett, which forssoke God and all the world'; he was recalling a member of his parish hanged for witchcraft twenty years earlier.[81]

These public confessions of guilt must, in part, have been made to protect family and friends; indeed, one study of them in the 1950s drew direct parallels with the show trials of Stalinist Russia.[82] The levels of prosecution illustrated the extent of official anxiety in Tudor England, particularly after the break with Rome, which prompted the 1534 redefinition of treason to include the written or spoken word. One contemporary, Anthony Waite, commented ironically to Lady Lisle a year after the new statute that 'it is rumored that a person should be committed to the Tower for saying that this month will be rainy'.[83] On notable occasions, even words were not necessary to convict someone, if the judge was convinced that their mere intention was malicious. The attorney general at Thomas More's trial in 1535 said, 'though we should have no word or deed to charge upon you, yet we have your silence, and that is a sign of your evil intention and a sure proof of malice'.[84] The pronouncements of the condemned almost universally declared acceptance of their fate. George Boleyn, convicted of incestuous adultery with his sister Queen Anne, said on the scaffold: 'I was born under the law, I am judged under the law and I must die under the law, for the law has condemned me.'[85] He did not, however, admit that he deserved death for his crimes; arguably this was as close as he might come to a declaration of innocence. Yet he also acknowledged that he was a sinner who had deserved death a thousand times over, and with this Christian truism warned his hearers not to fall into the same kind of error.[86] It remains fairly certain that the men accused of adultery with Anne Boleyn were not guilty of the crime of which they stood accused.[87] Still, the most outspoken declaration, that of William Brereton, remained shrouded in deferential ambiguity: 'the cause whereof I die, judge not. But if ye judge, judge the best.' Onlookers concluded that he had died 'charitably'.[88] Outright defiance was not an option.

This kind of performative justice was not solely about toadying to the power of the state, however. It was also an affirmation of a moral code which benefited every member of the commonwealth.[89] Crucially, it also slotted into a world view where each and every member of the human race stood convicted of original sin. Thomas More, imprisoned in the Tower and expecting imminent execution, faced the stark truths of human existence: 'we think that we are lords at large, whereas we are indeed, if we would consider, even poor wretches in prison. For, of very truth, our very prison this earth is.'[90] The duke of Somerset, on the scaffold, told onlookers that 'it is the ordinance of God thus to die, wherewith we must be content'.[91] The earl of Essex, to whom humility did not come easily, even so admitted at his trial that 'I do not speak to save my life, for that I see were vain: I owe God a death.'[92] Essex's death was a drama played out with particular intensity. His initial conception of his own actions seems to have been that he was acting in self-defence, and at his trial he was openly defiant. But after his trial, he discovered that his confederates had confessed to conspiracy, and he seems to have been persuaded whilst in prison that he was indeed guilty. His final drama of repentance was, significantly enough, played out on Ash Wednesday, a day more powerfully associated with penitence than any other. It was reported that on the scaffold, having recited the Creed, he spoke the opening verses of Psalm 51, the *Miserere Mei* central to the Ash Wednesday liturgy; he then laid his head on the block and pronounced that 'in humility and obedience I prostrate myself to my deserved punishment'.[93] And yet other accounts recorded that he had in fact recited either Psalm 54, which promised vengeance upon enemies, or Psalm 94, which threatened the defeat of evildoers; and that at the last he removed his black doublet to reveal a scarlet waistcoat underneath, perhaps consciously displaying the colour of martyrdom. These ambiguities, and the contested account of Essex's end, were an eloquent testimony both to the complexity of his political motivation and to how far his death had divided the political nation.[94] It also showed just how far such symbolic actions were regarded as conduits of political meaning.

As the Tudor era approached its end, criminal prosecutions reached unprecedented heights. At least 2,928 individuals were sentenced to death on the home circuit of the assizes alone between 1559 and 1624; this was almost a quarter of those who had been indicted for a capital crime, and 41 per cent of those convicted.[95] This speaks perhaps less to the expanding competence of the judicial system, than to a rising population, a time of war, disease and inflation, and a highly apprehensive government. It is notable that the crime of homicide seems, if anything, to have been in decline by the end of the sixteenth century, yet its popularity as a subject for cheap print shows that levels of alarm and moral outrage could be inversely proportional to the incidence of crime.[96] The increasing severity of Elizabethan penal statutes against Catholics similarly indicates not a growing number of Catholic recusants (since there was every indication that these had dwindled to a very small percentage of the population), but a growing anxiety on the part of the Elizabethan regime about potential Catholic threats. Simultaneously, a host of lesser penalties indicated the concerns of state and Church regarding other political, social and economic offences.

Most types of legal penalty were highly theatrical. Criminals were paraded through public thoroughfares, whether on their way to the scaffold to face death, or through the streets to be shamed as prostitutes, slanderers, bawds or perjurers. The young man who spoke out in favour of Mary I during the attempted coup of Lady Jane Grey had his ears cropped as punishment, in a carefully staged drama of disgrace: Henry Machyn recorded how 'ther was a harold, and a trompeter blohyng'.[97] A display of clemency could also make a powerful impression. After the May Day riots of 1517, several of the ringleaders were condemned to death, some of them described by the chronicler as 'poore yongelinges'. Those under sentence of execution were dragged on hurdles to Cheapside, and the chief instigator John Lincoln was the first to hang. Then 'as the other had the rope about their neckes, there came a commaundement from the kyng to respite execucion'. In this moment of dramatic tension, 'the people cried, God save the kyng'.[98] Even among the elite, a performance was expected. Katherine Howard asked to be able to rehearse with the execution block the night before her death, so that 'she might know how to place herself'.[99]

Such displays were choreographed to have as great an impact as possible. Elizabethan men or women who had used witchcraft or sorcery to harm someone, for example, were not only to be imprisoned for a year for their first offence, but 'once in every Quarter of the said Yere, shall in some Market Towne, upon the Market Daye or at such tyme as any Fayer shalbee kepte there, stande openly upon the Pillorie by the Space of Syxe Houres, and there shall openly confesse his or her Erroure and Offence'.[100] Public shaming was clearly a powerful ploy. In 1602, Sir Henry Winston was prosecuted in the Star Chamber for having attacked a bailiff trying to arrest one of his servants, but he pleaded to be let off a public confession of his offence at Gloucester assizes. He asked to remain in prison, rather than 'receive open disgrace in my county'.[101] In Mary I's reign, Bishop Bonner tried to persuade a Protestant apprentice William Hunter to recant by promising him some clemency from public display: 'I thinke thou art ashamed to beare a fagot and recant openly,' he said, 'but if thou wilt recante they sayinges, I will promise thee, that thou shalt not be putte to open shame'.[102]

Localized punishments were frequently aimed at localized offences: assaults, drunkenness, domestic abuse, fornication and so forth, which were often punished by whipping, or with the pillory or the stocks, would see the perpetrator humiliated in front of their community.[103] The punishment of 'carting', where the offender was taken through the town either in a cart or tied to the end of one, was to achieve the greatest possible exposure for this type of moral lesson. Where popular indignation might have been expected to be particularly strong, the performance tended to be the more elaborate. An unmarried woman convicted in 1543 not just of lechery, but of abandoning her illegitimate child, was paraded 'upon a bare horsebak wyth her face turned towarde the tayll ... her bodye being garnysshed wyth the ymages of yong infantes and a paper stonding upon her hedde declaring the cause of her ponyshement'.[104] An apprentice caught in bed with a maidservant in London in 1534 was whipped with particular severity by order of his livery company's court, because he had not only committed a crime, but also boasted about it afterwards, 'gevyng verey yll ensample to other yong men apprentices'.[105] The Protestants executed at Colchester during the reign of Mary I were taken there precisely because the town had such a strong Protestant presence.[106] The execution of John Hooper, the first English bishop to be burned for heresy, was carefully staged in the city of Gloucester, where he had served as bishop, 'for the example and terror of suche as he hath there seduced and mistaught'.[107]

The educational potential of such display frequently took on a religious edge. At the height of Protestant reform under Edward VI, the new Protestant mayor of London, Rowland Hill, and the aldermen attempted a purge of immoral behaviour within the city, partly in response to a letter from John Calvin to Protector Somerset, which Somerset arranged to be translated and printed even after he had fallen from power.[108] Calvin's letter impressed upon its readers that the godly needed 'to shewe that our christianitie causeth not dissipacion in the humain lyfe' and that they were not 'men unruled and without a brydle'.[109] This resulted in a campaign against vice; extra carts had to be hired to deal with the traffic of offenders and reports were taken from local clergy.[110] Men, as well as women, were targeted, including some who were quite well connected: one William Archer, a yeoman of the king's guard, had to make formal guarantee to evict his concubine and not replace her with another.[111]

Such performative justice was not the preserve of state and civil authorities alone; government rested upon delegation and cooperation, and therefore justice could be as powerful a tool in the hands of neighbours and communities as in the hands of privy counsellors and magistrates.[112] The 'charivari', a demonstration of public mockery, was a form of coercion which aimed at the reimposition of social order. Frequently a response to a wife who had assaulted her husband, a 'riding' was a public display of either the victims themselves or their representative or effigy. 'Rough music', either played raucously on instruments or banged out on bells, pots and pans, accompanied the display, which often included cross-dressing, filth, obscenity or other forms of inversion.[113] Gentler and more light-hearted versions of this kind of demonstration were also common, but riots, too, might incorporate elements of charivari. The displays which accompanied 'ridings' were, however, close cousins to the popular celebrations with which communities celebrated festivals of May Day, or Midsummer, Christmas, New Year and their own particular parish feast days. In both their festive and repressive forms, this kind of communal action underlined the fragility of the social order and its dependence on popular collaboration, with laughter underpinning both the celebration and the fear.[114] Yet they also reinforced a sense of shared social values communally sustained. Social harmony was celebrated, as well as mended, by rituals that brought communities together in common performative action.[115]

Religion and drama

Plays had originally been the preserve of the Church, enacted in the nave before moving out into the churchyard and thence further abroad.[116] The act of worship was itself a re-enactment of Christ's life and death, demanding both audience participation and response. At Easter, the story of the Passion was read aloud in its entirety from the Gospel, and at least some of the time this was semi-staged. Audience response also had a performative element. The practice of praying on one's knees with hands held together, formerly a gesture used when swearing allegiance to an overlord, was encouraged by the Franciscans and became an integral feature of worship in the fifteenth century. The elevation of the host by the priest was increasingly accompanied by prayers and gestures from the congregation.[117] Climactic moments in the year were marked by religious processions, as were times of crisis, when famine, plague or the threat of invasion prompted special prayers of supplication, accompanied by procession. The feast of Corpus Christi was widely described and understood as a symbol of unity and was celebrated in early summer with sermons, processions, the formation of special fraternities and often also with plays. Corpus Christi plays have survived from York, Chester and Wakefield, and in a play often called *Ludus Coventriae* (though it seems not, in fact, to have come from Coventry, but from East Anglia), whilst fragments also exist from the plays of Norwich and Newcastle.[118] These plays contained a sequence of biblical stories, beginning with the Creation and ending with the Last Judgement. The core beliefs of Christianity were turned into a saga and enacted one by one in a tableau of sin, sacrifice and salvation.

In the earliest years of Protestant reform, it came naturally to several leading reformers to use theatre as a medium for their message. John Bale, a former Carthusian, appropriated the model of the pre-Reformation morality play to spread the evangelical message.[119] John Foxe in 1556 did something similar with his Latin drama about the apocalypse, *Christus Triumphans*. Such plays could intermingle a hefty dose of Protestant doctrine with the bawdiness of the theatrical tradition.[120] Lewis Wager's play about Mary Magdalen gave a comprehensive account of 'justification by faith alone', but it also included some lively *double entendre* on the subject of the 'prick of conscience'.[121] Most Protestant commentators feared the seductive powers of drama, 'daungerous on the day time, more daungerous on the night', as Gervase Babington commented darkly in 1583, as 'an occasion of adulterie and uncleanenesse'.[122] Matthew Hutton, the future archbishop of York, opined uneasily that such plays were 'plausible 40 yeares agoe, and wold now also of the ignorant sort be well liked: yet now in this happie time of the gospell, I knowe the learned will mislike it and how the state will beare with it I knowe not'.[123] Philip Stubbes in 1583 was far more decided in his views, feeling that Christian truths 'were not given to be derided and jested at, as they be in their filthie playes and enterluds on stages and scaffolds, or to be mixt and interlaced with bawdry, wanton shewes, and uncomely gestures, as is used (every man knoweth) in these playes and enterludes'.[124] A dialogue between Youth and Age in John Northbrooke's anti-theatrical work of 1577 portrayed Youth as puzzled at Age's opposition to plays, 'seeing that many times they play histories out of the Scriptures'. Age's ferocious response to this was that it was a great evil to see theatre and the Bible mingled: 'will God suffer them unpunished, that with impure and wicked maners and doings, doe use and handle upon scaffoldes, Gods divine mysteries, with such unreverentnesse and irreligiousnesse?', he asked ominously. 'What fellowship hath righteousnesse with unrighteousnes? What communion hath light with darknesse?'[125] To Northbrooke, the matter was black and white, but to his contemporaries more generally it was less certain.

Religious theatricality found other outlets which survived the arrival of Protestantism rather better. The city fathers, who periodically tried to impose restrictions on the London theatres, were acting, ironically enough, under strong pressure from the godly histrionics of the city's preachers. As well as Paul's Cross, other prominent stages for sermons included St Mary Spital, the Chapel Royal, the Inns of Court and the universities. In 1569, a 'sermon house' was built by the lord mayor to shelter his wife and the wives of the aldermen as they listened at Paul's Cross, and a clever preacher such as Lancelot Andrewes could weave an elaborate pun into the text of his sermon which contrasted the ranks of the aldermen seated before him with the courts of heaven.[126] When Henry VIII constructed his new Palace of Whitehall, he included a 'preaching place' at the centre in a courtyard facing the Council chamber, where the monarch could listen to the sermon through a window, as lesser individuals milled in the courtyard below.[127] Every new parliament opened with a sermon, even though Elizabeth quelled an initiative to have additional regular sermons for MPs; she felt they could spend their time better.[128] A wealth of pre-Reformation foundations and endowments had been aimed at training good preachers, and the homely metaphors and cautionary tales of sermons such as John Mirk's *Festial* suggest a shrewd awareness of how to hold the audience's attention. Pulpits were intricately carved and coloured to catch the eye of the congregation; outdoor pulpits were constructed near cathedrals, hospitals or priories.[129] After the Reformation, churches which followed reforming guidelines – and many did not – had pulpits even more prominently placed. Considerable thought went into the crafting of a successful sermon. Thomas Wilson's *Arte of Rhetorique* spoke sagely of the need to 'quicken these heavie loden wittes of ours, and muche to cherishe these our lompishe and unweldie natures, for excepte menne finde delight, thei will not long abide'. This, he observed, was why 'even these auncient preachers, must now and then plaie the fooles in the pulpite, to serve the tickle eares of their fleetyng audience, or els thei are like some tymes to preache to the bare walles'.[130] He advised the use of pathos, and warned against digressions. 'I knew a preacher, that was a whole houre out of his matter, and at length remembryng hymself, saied, well, now to the purpose ... whereat many laughed, and some for starke wearinesse wer fain to go awaie.'[131]

Contemporaries described a good sermon in emotional terms, 'sweet' or 'powerful'.[132] Sermons were acknowledged to be an effective tool to mobilize an audience: when John Lincoln was trying to stir up opposition to foreigners in the run-up to the May Day riots of 1517, he tried to persuade the preacher of that year's Spital sermons 'too move the Mayre and Aldermen to take parte with the comminaltie agaynste the straungers'.[133] Sermons, just like plays, did not always reflect opinions which those in authority found agreeable. Religious zeal might inspire a preacher to speak out against the limitations or errors of the powerful. The Easter sermon of 1532, in which Friar Peto, preaching to the Court at Greenwich, compared Henry VIII to the wicked King Ahab, was an extreme example; retribution against Peto's order of Observant Franciscans followed.[134] The Lenten sermons at Court in 1553 were a famously bitter attack by a series of preachers on the failures of those in power, who declared in some indignation that 'they would hear no more of their sermons'.[135] Dedicated Protestants often took as their model the prophets of the Old Testament, whose role it was to utter warnings about the consequences of ungodly living. It is little wonder that preachers, like plays, had to be licensed, and that unlicensed preaching was viewed with alarm and despondency by the authorities; the power of the word was clearly formidable.[136]

The response of a congregation to a sermon was not always encouraging. In Gifford's *Countrie Divinitie*, the opinion of the lax parishioner regarding preaching was that 'a man may have overmuch of any thing, and ynough is as good as a feast'. Gifford also noted sadly those whose drowsiness might reduce a sermon to 'onely a sound and a confused humming'.[137] Conversely, an overly enthusiastic audience might prove problematic. A hostile Catholic account described how Puritans attending sermons would look up the Bible texts cited by the preacher and discuss 'whether they had quoted them to the point, and accurately, and in harmony with their tenets', leading to arguments about Scripture which often ended 'in violence and fisticuffs'.[138] Puritans liked their sermons a great deal, and frequently endowed additional lectureships to provide extra sermons in parishes where the minister did not preach, or on Sunday afternoons or weekdays.[139] Even for those who paid attention, however, comprehension might be an issue. George Gifford commented wearily on the number of hearers 'which carry away almost nothing which is to any purpose'; people could remember a good story, he remarked bitterly, but 'let the Preacher speake never so plaine, although they sit and looke him in the face, yet if ye enquire of them so soone as they be out at the Church dores, ye shal easely perceive that (as the common saieng is) it went in at the one eare, and out at the other'.[140] Advice literature dwelt severely on the necessity of paying attention and of people playing their part.[141] One work from 1599 pictured listeners as if they themselves were on show, 'as it were upon the Theater, or into the open view and sight of the Church'.[142] Here, this work insisted, they should be prepared to enact their role, in part by knowing how to sing the psalms, but also in knowing the Bible more broadly. Other responses emphasized the efficacy of theatrical strategies on the part of the preacher. Dramatic emphasis remained a staple element of Tudor sermons. Even on their funeral monuments, Protestant preachers were frequently depicted with one hand raised in exhortation.[143]

Public disputations over religion were not uncommon: in 1549, at Oxford, the Italian Protestant reformer Peter Martyr Vermigli debated the doctrine of transubstantiation with William Chedsey, William Tresham and Morgan Phillips. Martyr had government backing, but the disputation was not the clear win for the Protestants that the regime had hoped.[144] In 1559, in the uncertain climate of Elizabeth's first year as queen, a religious debate was staged in Westminster Abbey to discredit the Catholics; again, the victory was far from clear.[145] By the 1580s, religious disputation had taken on a wider dimension. Thwarted in their efforts to persuade and pressurize the government into more zealous Protestant reform, critics of the Church found a voice in print. John Udall published *The State of the Church of Englande laide open*, in which a bishop, a papist, a usurer, an innkeeper and a preacher all debated the vices of the bishops who 'stop the mouth of the sheepeheardes, and set at liberty the ravening wolves'. He intended it as a warning against Satan's attempts 'to subvert and utterly overturn the course of the Gospell here in England'.[146] Attempts to shut down the printing press of Robert Waldegrave, the puritan sympathizer who had published such works, drove him underground and prompted the publication of a series of clandestine and scandalous pamphlets by 'Martin Marprelate'.[147] These attacked the bishops who 'will lye like dogs' but 'were never yet well beaten for their lying', accusing them of greed, corruption, simony and neglect of their flocks.[148] Perhaps the most striking thing about the 'Marprelate' tracts, however, is that they prompted a reply from every bishop they attacked, and that these responses were 'after their own vein' (as Archbishop Whitgift described it), using everything from sermons and proclamations to pamphlets and stage burlesques.[149] It was no accident that one of the authors co-opted to the task of rebuffing the 'Marprelate' tracts was the playwright Thomas Nashe, and that so many of the responses were themselves staged. The ribald mockery of the 'anti-Martinists' may even account for Shakespeare's Falstaff, who was originally given the name of the infamous Lollard Sir John Oldcastle.[150]

Popular religious discourse and debate might also be highly theatrical. In March 1554, a voice was heard to issue from the wall of a house in Aldersgate Street in London. It attacked Catholic practice and denounced Queen Mary and King Philip, but when the onlookers said 'God save the Lady Elizabeth', it replied 'So be it.' This 'bird in the wall', as the audience took to calling it, attracted crowds many thousands strong, before it was discovered that some leading Protestants had persuaded a young woman named Elizabeth Crofts to be walled up in the house with a whistle to play her part. Here one piece of theatre was answered by another, as Crofts was, in due course, compelled to appear at Paul's Cross to make a confession of her offences, and publicly to accuse her handlers, although it appears she received no further punishment, since she had so obviously been the dupe of others.[151] The most striking religious theatre of the Tudor century, however, was provided by the execution of religious dissidents. Martyrdom was perhaps the most heartbreaking manifestation of the Renaissance principle of appealing to the past. The trials and persecutions of the first Christian martyrs were re-enacted by both Protestants and Catholics reliving the experience of the early Church. It was a bitter irony that Catholic and Protestant alike were prepared to die horribly for the same God; but the same zeal which gave the martyrs their courage also convinced their persecutors that they were right to condemn and execute heretics. It was a piece of composite theatre, in which both persecutors and martyrs were laying claim to a role of moral sanctity and superiority. The repeat patterning of these dramas was thus something vitally important to their successful performance.[152]

These dramas of religious and political obedience, and the terrible judicial violence which they could prompt, were increasingly reflected in the theatre of the later Elizabethan period. It comes as no surprise to find the language of dismemberment rife in the drama of the age. In Marlowe's *Massacre at Paris*, the rituals of violence and display are applied to the corpse of the murdered Coligny, as Anjou says 'Cut off his head and hands / And send them for a present to the Pope.'[153] Later, as murderers anticipate their killing of the duke of Guise, one exclaims 'O that his heart were leaping in my hand!', a clear evocation of the ritual where the executioner removed the victim's beating heart.[154] Marlowe's play was probably responsible for the word 'massacre' entering the English language at this time.[155] The levels of violence in revenge tragedies from Thomas Kyd's *The Spanish Tragedy* of 1587 onwards echoed the savagery of the martyrs' deaths. From the meditative sanctity of the Lord's Supper, to the starkness of the Crucifixion and the brutality of martyrdom, the drama of religion shaped the imagination of the age.

Tudor theatre

Tudor theatre had medieval ancestry. Since the fourteenth century, wandering groups of professional players, as well as more amateur groups, had acted out folk drama in towns and villages. Craft and religious guilds performed plays regularly, as did students in the universities. Some companies of players were sponsored by their towns, such as those of High Wycombe, Coventry, Kingston and St Albans.[156] It was common for the nobility to maintain companies of players, too.[157] The preoccupations of noble households can be found reflected in early Tudor drama, such as *The Interlude of Youth*, written about 1513, which raised the problem of a noble heir reluctant to assume his adult responsibilities and making merry with Riot.[158] Henry VII set up his own band of players in the 1490s, as did Prince Arthur, whose troupe was inherited after his death by his brother. Henry VIII as king had two companies, as well as the Gentlemen and Children of the Chapel Royal, who frequently performed plays, masques and interludes. Henry's queens had their own actors, and so did his children, including his illegitimate son Henry Fitzroy.[159] Plays or 'interludes' kept company with other dramatic genres, such as mummings, disguisings, pageants and tournaments in great households or the Inns of Court. From the scripts of early Tudor plays, it is possible to deduce that some were intended to take place in banqueting halls or other convenient spaces; when, in 1569, the City tried to prevent innkeepers from allowing 'any mannour of stage play, enterlude, or other disguising whatsoever' in houses, courtyards or gardens, it demonstrates that any kind of space might serve.[160] An Elizabethan proclamation of 1559 seeking to ban unlicensed plays noted how 'common interludes in the English tongue' were usually played between All Hallowtide (at the start of November) and early summer. It also warned the nobility and gentry to keep an eye on any of 'their servants being players'.[161]

Theatre was to escape its domestic setting in the most remarkable fashion during the reign of Elizabeth I. In the 1570s, nine new commercial theatre spaces were opened in the City of London in which the plays of Shakespeare, Marlowe, Jonson and their contemporaries were performed. Some of these playhouses could seat up to three thousand people at a time, it has been estimated, and in the period 1560–1642 around three thousands plays were written, of which perhaps a sixth survive.[162] The arrival of new theatrical space led to larger theatre companies than had previously been the case with the touring companies (which had typically comprised only two to six players), and this widened the range of dramatic possibilities.[163] Even so, the life of a playwright or actor remained precarious.

Since income was directly dependent on performances, which varied according to season and could be cancelled at short notice, theatre companies cut costs to a minimum, which meant no understudies, no directors and probably few, if any, group rehearsals. The 'gatherers' who collected ticket money at the start probably doubled up as 'mutes' who could fill out a crowd scene in the later parts of a play; it has been argued that this is why Shakespeare's plays tended not to have crowd scenes at the very beginning. There was no guild of professional actors, so those who wanted to take apprentices had to do so in their capacity as a member of a guild such as that of the grocers.[164] An actor might hope to earn between 5s and 10s a week, but this was halved if they were not performing, and playhouses were susceptible to closure by plague, official condemnation or disasters, such as fire.[165]

Household drama did not disappear, however, so much as develop new dimensions. In particular, there was a close relationship between the theatres in the City and plays at Court, since, from the start of Elizabeth's reign, the Privy Council had encouraged the development of drama in the City, so that players might acquire 'the more dexteritie and perfection in that profession, the better to content her maiestie'.[166] It would be a mistake to think that theatrical affairs were driven solely by popular demand: the role of the Court was immensely important, not only in terms of financial reward (each play earned the company £10, as a rule) but perhaps even more importantly in terms of political backing.[167] The 1572 Act against Vagabonds made it clear that actors were meant to belong to noble households, or else be specially licensed by JPs, and the Court was merely the biggest of these households. During the 1590s, the two companies that played most at Court were those of the lord chamberlain and the lord admiral, and since both were cousins of the queen, this reinforced the sense that this was a family affair. Between 1594 and 1603, the Chamberlain's Men performed at court thirty-three times.[168] Many of the variations within different versions of certain plays probably reflect the modifications that were made when performing a play at Court.[169]

The city fathers, many of whom upheld a stern set of Protestant ideals, were unenthusiastic about public theatres, although more tolerant of private performances. Debates on this issue were frequent, and bans were imposed intermittently, sometimes in an attempt to limit the spread of plague, which caused particularly long closures in 1581–82, 1592–93 and 1603–04.[170] The closures of the 1590s were partly responsible for turning Shakespeare into a poet, because it was in 1592 that he turned to writing *Venus and Adonis* and *The Rape of Lucrece*. In a sobering display of pragmatism, if mortality rates in the city were below fifty per week, the theatres were often allowed to reopen.[171] Drama might have been morally, as well as medically, questionable, but it was also good business. The troubles of the 1590s were such that the theatres were finally expunged from the city; but since they settled in the suburbs, out of reach of aldermen and their regulations, the theatres of the south bank and the west end continued to flourish after 1600, under the more tolerant jurisdiction of the Privy Council.[172] Civic authorities elsewhere could also sometimes perceive players as a nuisance: in Chester in 1596, it was noted that 'by daylie experience it has fallen out what great inconveniences there have Arrysen by playes and bearebeates'.[173] It was not always discernible whether the chief concern was with popular morals or civic order: in 1600, plays were banned on Sundays, in Lent and during times of plague; but whether the last consideration concerned public hygiene or the belief that plague was a consequence of sin is unclear.[174]

The pace and intensity of life in the Elizabethan theatre was extraordinary. Companies of players were called upon to perform dozens of plays in any one season. The Admiral's Men in 1594–95 offered thirty-eight plays, twenty-one of them new, and performed six days a week. Actors were not given a full script, but instead a 'cue-script' containing only their part and the necessary cues, which must have demanded immense concentration.[175] It did, however, mean that an actor with a tragic part could play it unaffected by the fact that the play as a whole was deemed to be a comedy.[176] The diary of Philip Henslowe, who was both actor and manager, suggests that writers took between four and six weeks to finish a play, with perhaps two further weeks to prepare for the performance.[177] This combination of fervour and unpredictability in the life of an Elizabethan actor may, in part, explain the quarrels and the duels. Marlowe was killed in a pub brawl in 1593 (although some have seen it as a political assassination) and Ben Jonson went to prison in 1598 for manslaughter, after killing a fellow actor.[178] The many references in the plays of the time to the volatility of players, theatres and the world of illusion generally show some of the emotional intensity and social fragility of an actor's life.

The range and scope of late Tudor drama was breathtaking. From revenge tragedy to comedy, epic to satire, within a space of about twenty years Elizabethan playwrights were expanding, problematizing and complicating dramatic tradition as never before. Play-going was clearly immensely popular. Puritan authors, railing against the lewd behaviour among theatregoers, inadvertently made it sound like enormous fun:

> Marke the flocking and running to theaters and curtens, daylie and hourely, night and daye, tyme and tyde, to see playes and enterludes; where such wanton gestures, such bawdie speaches, such laughing . . . such kissing . . . suche winckinge and glancinge of wanton eyes, and the like is used as is wonderful to behold.[179]

At Court, plays became the preferred form of entertainment. They could also be a form of advice. The play *Gorboduc*, performed in the Inner Temple at Christmas 1561, and then at Court in January 1562, was clearly framed as an encouragement to the queen to marry, warning against the dangers of a disputed succession. A rare piece of testimony from an eyewitness shows that when first enacted at Court and accompanied by a masque, the drama was even more pointed in its message, enjoining the queen to reject the suit of King Eric of Sweden and marry Lord Robert Dudley.[180] Essex, bitterly lamenting in Ireland the way his enemies were blackening his reputation at home, wrote that 'the frantic libeller writes of me what he lists; already they print me and make me speak to the world, and shortly they will play me in what forms they list upon the stage'.[181]

Elizabethan drama could also be appallingly gruesome. In *Titus Andronicus*, the heroine is raped and then mutilated, and her attackers are killed and served up in a pie at dinner to be 'daintily' eaten by their mother. In the midst of extraordinary levels of violence, when Titus cuts off his own hand to provide what he mistakenly thinks is the price of his sons' freedom, only to have it returned to him along with their heads, the truly shocking thing is his response: he breaks into laughter. It needs to be remembered that in Tudor London the playhouses on the south bank were only a short walk from London Bridge, where the dismembered heads of traitors were stuck on pikes for all to see. Wars of religion abroad gave rise to atrocities that were echoed in contemporary drama, and few people could have been unaware of these traumatic events: the government had ordered special prayers to be said on Sundays, Wednesdays and Fridays, 'specially in Cities and great Townes, duryng this daungerous and perillous tymes of the troubles in Christendome'.[182] In Marlowe's *Tamburlaine*, the virgins killed outside Damascus are 'hoisted up' as 'slaughtered carcasses' on the city walls, and later Tamburlaine tells a traitorous servant to execute judgement on himself, instructing him to 'rip thy bowels and rend out thy heart'.[183]

Humour and horror of necessity existed in stark juxtaposition. The theatres in which sublime dramas were enacted stood close to the Beargarden on the south bank, where animals were encouraged to rip one another to pieces for the audience's entertainment.[184] Elizabethan drama was just one of many popular entertainments; in plague years, when all forms of attraction that might engender crowds were banned, plays were listed together with bear-baiting, dancing schools, fencing matches, football games, bowling, puppet shows and cockfighting. The sharp contrast in so many plays of the time between bawdy humour and tormented tragedy could be cast as a commercial choice, as playwrights aimed to please as wide an audience as possible; but it could also be taken as a reflection of the many paradoxical elements in Elizabethan society.

Plays could also be subversive. The proclamation of 1559 warned against unlicensed plays, but particularly those 'wherein either matters of religion or of the governance of the estate of the commonweal shall be handled', rather pointedly observing that such subjects should be the preserve instead of 'men of authority, learning, and wisdom, nor to be handled before any audience but of grave and discreet persons'.[185] When the city fathers were trying to pressurize the Privy Council into policing the theatres more closely in 1589, they warned that 'the players do take upon them to handle in their plays certain matters of divinity and of state unfit to be suffered'.[186] In part, those who were suspicious of drama were being practical about the potentially slanderous messages that they might contain. In the 1590s, the Privy Council was writing to the JPs of Middlesex about the actors at the Curtain Theatre in Shoreditch, who 'represent upon the stage . . . the persons of some gentlemen of desert and quality that are yet alive, under obscure manner but yet in such sort as all the hearers may take notice both of the matter and of the persons that are meant thereby'.[187]

There was also the risk of commentary on controversial subjects: the Act of Uniformity of 1559 had warned against anyone who might 'in any interludes, plays, songs, rhymes, or by other open words, declare or speak anything in the derogation, depraving or despising' of the *Book of Common Prayer*, suggesting that drama was firmly fixed in the popular imagination as a conduit for criticism and protest.[188]

The extent to which playwrights were often in trouble is also indicative of their potential to disturb and disrupt.[189] It was acknowledged that plays could in themselves be political interventions. The earl of Essex was so adored by Londoners that Shakespeare made mention of it in *Henry V*, noting how 'London doth pour out her citizens' to cheer him, in the only direct reference to a living figure in any of his plays; but Essex's fall from grace made such literary tributes dangerous.[190] Samuel Daniel's play, *The tragedy of Philotas*, written as the drama of Essex's final months was unfolding, saw the playwright brought before the Privy Council to explain himself, while Ben Jonson's *Sejanus* of 1603 was also censored: both evoked Essex as a virtuous, honourable and dynamic military leader overwhelmed by the corruption of the political process.[191] Some literary critics have seen Elizabethan drama as played out in theatres such as the Globe as unavoidably weakening structures of authority, as kingship was reduced to a form of mummery on stage.[192] Others have suggested that the acting-out of political fallibility served only to reinforce authority structures, by managing 'to contain the radical doubts' which such drama 'continually provokes'.[193] The fact that so many Elizabethan plays were also performed at Court adds a new layer of complexity. It seems implausible that any direct challenge to Elizabeth I's authority would be contained in a play staged for her entertainment.[194] Nevertheless, Elizabethan playwrights – and, we may assume, their audiences – were fascinated by the rise and fall of rulers and their regimes, and by the symbols and strategies of power, and commented accordingly.

Tudor attempts at censorship were frequent, but somewhat erratic. Plays for the stage were supposed to be heard by the master of the revels at Court before they were licensed, while printed plays had to be authorized by an ecclesiastical licenser before being entered into the Stationers' Register. A 1581 commission to Master of the Revels Edmund Tilney made it clear that the players were supposed to recite their parts in front of him; but by the 1590s it appears that he was instead reading and anno-tating a draft of the play.[195] *The Book of Sir Thomas More* was censored both for its depiction of xenophobic riots, which Tilney tried to tone down, and for its portrayal of More's defiance of the king, which he indi-cated should be removed altogether; in consequence, the play never made it to the stage.[196] Just occasionally, there could be a more severe backlash, as in 1597, when for reasons unknown, a play called *The Isle of Dogs* was deemed dangerously seditious. Its writers, Thomas Nashe and Ben Jonson, were apprehended, and Jonson and two other actors were imprisoned; the company responsible, Pembroke's Men, was disbanded and the Privy Council instructed that all playhouses should be demolished.[197] In a particularly sinister development, the notorious torturer and inquisitor Richard Topcliffe was brought in to make enquiries.[198] Yet Jonson and his companions were soon released, and the playhouses survived. Nashe compared the perils of being a writer or printer to that of men at a Persian banquet: 'if they rowle they eye never so little at one side, there stands an Eunuch before them with his hart full of jealousie, and his Bowe readie to shoote them through, because they looke father then the Lawes of the Countrey suffer them.'[199] Yet he wrote this in a play in 1598; both Nashe and Jonson continued to write plays after *The Isle of Dogs* disaster. The incident suggests that state censorship of the theatre could just occasion-ally be quite brutal, but was never systematic.

In the sophistication of Elizabethan theatre, the moral messages of the early Tudor dramatic tradition were not lost to view.[200] In Kyd's *Spanish Tragedy*, the character called 'Revenge' echoed the personified virtues and vices of the medieval mystery plays. 'Rumour' – in a costume painted with tongues – featured in *Henry IV, Part II*; and 'Time' appeared with an hour-glass in *The Winter's Tale*. Indeed, the expectation that on one level plays were also supposed to preach imparted extra weight to the dramatic force of those works that explored human dilemmas and questions of ethics in such depth and detail. There were also plays such as *A Looking Glasse for London and England*, written by Thomas Lodge and Robert Greene and staged in the 1590s, which retold the bible story of the prophet Jonah and the fall of Nineveh, warning those who ignored the plight of the poor of the retribution they might expect, and cautioning 'London awake, for feare the Lord do frowne.'[201] Moral messages had acquired new elements, too, in the course of the Reformation: in Nathaniel Woodes' play of 1581, *The Conflict of Conscience*, Satan fondly describes the pope as 'My eldest boy, in whom I doo delight'.[202] The dramatic character of Hick Scorner, who in early Tudor plays was equated with vice and courtly corruption, became increasingly associated with Catholic vice. Thomas Becon denounced Catholic priests 'as men well harnessed for an interlude', coming forth 'to play hickscorner's part with your shameless, smooth, smirking faces, and with your lusty, broad, bald shaven crowns, antichrist's brood of Rome'.[203]

Many debated over whether plays were themselves, by their very nature, a corrupting force. Stephen Gosson, himself a former playwright, emerged in the 1570s as one who deplored the vulgarity, duplicity and sensuality of drama, in his *Schoole of Abuse, containing a pleasant invective against Poets, Pipers, Plaiers, Jesters and such like Caterpillars of the Commonwealth*.[204] Interestingly he excluded from his criticisms those plays that had an obvious moral standpoint, such as his own *Catiline's Conspiracies*, although he alleged that his eyes were full of 'teares of sorrow' to behold his own plays still being performed. Otherwise, in his *School of Abuse* he marshalled an array of classical authorities to warn of the dangers of this 'Poetrie in the lowest forme'.[205] Plays were to him a composite of 'straunge consortes of melody, to tickle the eare: costly apparell, to flatter the sight: effeminate gesture, to ravishe the sense: and wantone speache, to whet desire too inordinate lust'.[206] The valour and skill of the rugged, athletic and courageous English race of old, Gosson asserted, had been corrupted by 'banqueting, playing, pipyng, and dauncing, and all such delightes as may win us to pleasure, or rocke us a sleepe'.[207]

Plenty of voices put the contrary view, however, and the theatre business continued to flourish. London was undoubtedly the epicentre of Elizabethan theatre, but touring was also an essential element in the life of most theatre companies. The Queen's Men travelled as far as Edinburgh, and in 1588–89 even Dublin.[208] Touring companies were occasionally turned away, as when Leicester's Men were dismissed from Oxford in 1587–88; they were given 20s to depart 'without greater trouble to the University'.[209] On the whole, however, companies seem to have been welcomed enthusiastically. There was occasional mockery of these provincial performances: Ben Jonson's *Poetaster* of 1601 made derisive comments about those who 'stalke upon boords, and barrell heads, to an olde cract trumpet'. The same companies that performed in the city and at Court, however, seem to have toured on an annual basis, often visiting those parts of the country where their patron had particular influence, performing in the larger towns and in private households. Records show plays being staged in guildhalls in Bristol, Leicester and Barnstaple, in the Bear Inn in Cambridge, the Red Lion Inn in Norwich, the church in Dartmouth, the vicarage in Plymouth, Dover Castle and the Moot Hall in Kendal.[210]

Tudor drama is an unparalleled source for historians who want to get close to the experience of life for broad swathes of society. Legal records tell us about lawsuits; parliamentary records tell us about parliamentary debates; theological treatises tell us about doctrinal disputes. All such sources can be read across the grain to discover other things, but they still retain a primary focus. Plays had no single focus, and in trying to appeal to their audiences, drawn from every layer of the social hierarchy, they gave rich and complex insights into love and violence, madness and grief, moral dilemmas and dirty jokes, poverty and power. Some of the audience paid only a penny for admission (at a time when a journeyman might earn 5d or 6d a day), and formed the mass of 'groundlings' or 'penny stinkards', who might find themselves incorporated into some of the crowd scenes, which both mocked their vulgarity and appealed to their humour with crude jokes.[211] Yet much of the audience was drawn from the nobility and gentry, and many of the plays of the time were performed at Court. Their appeal encompassed every aspect of the social order, as well as nearly every aspect of human experience. Arguably, Elizabethan plays give a more integrated and substantial picture of the fabric of society than anything else we possess.

The Taming of the Shrew

Tudor performance clearly demonstrated the gap between theory and practice in many fields, from kingship to justice; but it gave particularly trenchant illustration to the relationship between the sexes. Plays, ballads and jests offer a strong corrective to the historical assumption that early modern patriarchal ideas left women silenced and oppressed. Sermons may have lauded the chaste and obedient wife; laws may have denied women equality; and medical treatises may have classified women as incomplete men. But in the theatre, bold, inventive, witty and morally superior women suggested another set of realities. From books of merry tales and jests (which were intended to be read aloud), women emerge as 'bawdy storytellers . . . witty answerers, and keen satirists'.[212] The quick-fire repartee between Benedick and Beatrice in *Much Ado About Nothing*, or the use of neighbourly solidarity to confound a sexual aggressor and censure a violently jealous husband in *The Merry Wives of Windsor* show a level of female agency and confidence that is hard to discern in other sources.[213]

This level of female assertiveness was not just found on the stage, but was acted out in the community at large. Hocktide celebrations, increasingly prevalent in England since the fifteenth century, were held on the second Monday and Tuesday after Easter, and involved (with some variants) one day when the women of the parish captured and tied up the men, releasing them only on the payment of a fine; on the second day, the men did the same to the women.[214] By the later part of the century, Hocktide had become a source of parish funds, and so easier to trace through the records.[215] The participants tended to be not riotous youths, but married men and women.[216] Like charivari, the ritual involved a subversion of common gender roles, and might therefore best be seen as a way of exploring, understanding and reaffirming social order. The striking aspect of Hocktide, however, was the balance between the sexes, who seemingly participated on equal terms in the celebrations.[217] In organizing these fund-raisers, women also showed the extent of their agency within the parish.[218] That Hocktide was perceived as celebrating the strength of womankind is demonstrated by the city of Coventry reviving the Hock play in 1573 to entertain Elizabeth I: 'becauz the matter mencioneth how valiantly our English women for loove of their cuntree behaved themselves'.[219] Ballads were sung by women as much as by men, and the celebrated Romany ballad singer Alyce Boyce performed for Elizabeth I.[220] A great many ballads had as their chief focus the question of gender roles, and debated the rights and wrongs of marital relations in particular.[221] The 1590s ballad 'The Valorous Acts performed at Gaunt, by the brave bonne Lasse Mary Ambre' told a tale of a female warrior that was popular enough to be a talking point in Ben Jonson's drama.[222]

At the other end of the social spectrum could be found female playwrights. They wrote not for the public stage, but for the household, in what is termed 'closet drama'. Even then, they might take refuge in translation, rather than original authorship: the earliest surviving drama by a Tudor woman is Lady Jane Lumley's translation of Euripides' *The Tragedy of Iphigenia*.[223] The decorum of this approach might bely its subject matter, however. Mary Sidney Herbert's translation of a French play by Robert Garnier, *The Tragedy of Antony*, dealt with challenging themes of female rule and sexual passion.[224] Lady Elizabeth Cary's *Tragedy of Mariam*, written around 1602, concerned the conflicted feelings of King Herod's wife, torn between love and hatred, obedience and rebellion. It contained a passionate advocacy of divorce for women – voiced by Salome – which asked 'Why should such priviledge to man be given?' and vowed to 'be the custome-breaker and beginner / To shew my Sexe the way to freedomes doore'.[225]

The dramatic tensions of Elizabethan plays were often created by the games they played with gender, reinforced by the fact that female roles were played by boys. Puritans were appalled by this convention: 'if anie man doe put on Womans raiment, hee is dishonested and defiled, because he transgresseth the boundes of modestie and comelinesse, and weareth that which Gods lawe forbiddeth him to weare', wrote the Oxford scholar and cleric John Rainolds in 1599.[226] Rainolds would, within the decade, be one of the translators of the King James Bible, so he knew his Scripture; he perhaps also knew the perils of cross-dressing, since in 1566 he had (to his later embarrassment) acted a female role in the play *Palamon and Arcite*, staged to entertain Elizabeth I on her visit to Oxford. The puritan mind retreated in horror from the notion of cross-dressing, but playwrights embraced the idea with interest.[227] Shakespeare included cross-dressing heroines in five of his plays, each of them raising a different set of questions – from the grave legal expertise of Portia in *The Merchant of Venice*, whose moral and intellectual stature eclipses that of the men that surround her, to the flirtatious Rosalind in *As You Like It*, who takes the name Ganymede in evocation of Jove's boy lover, a name which was also common slang for a boy prostitute.[228]

Shakespeare's most famous treatment of the relationship between the sexes came in *The Taming of the Shrew* from the early 1590s. This notoriously controversial play could be taken as a work which reinforced patriarchal power, or as a sophisticated denunciation of patriarchal precepts and a tribute to clever, forceful, funny women. The story of the forced marriage of volatile and defiant Kate, and her subjection by her cruel husband, to the point where she submits completely to his dominance, looks at first sight like the fulfilment of every sober admonition about the subjugation of women. The fact that this is a play within a play, put on to trick a drunken tinker, begs the question of whether it is in fact a clever satire. Kate's final speech in which she admonishes her fellow women to accept that 'Thy husband is thy lord, thy life, thy keeper' looks, on the face of it, submissive; and yet it is by far the longest speech in the play, and could be read as fiercely sarcastic.[229] There is reason to think that Shakespeare was taking an older play, *The Taming of a Shrew*, which was much more straightforwardly misogynous, and inverting and complicating it for both comic and moral effect.[230] Contemporaries certainly upheld the view that Kate had not really been 'tamed'.[231] Tudor drama clearly demonstrated that when it came to the relationship between the sexes, there was no single accepted view, but a level of debate just as energetic and acrimonious as it is today. Elizabethan playhouse audiences contained women as well as men, as the plays themselves suggest.[232] When Benedick and Beatrice sparred with one another in *Much Ado About Nothing*, they were tapping into established traditions of both misogynous criticism of women and anti-masculinist criticism of men.[233] John Rainolds deplored the gentlewoman who defended theatre by saying 'that she was as much edified at a play as ever she was at any sermon', but there were probably supporters on both sides of this question.[234] Some literary critics have read Shakespeare and his contemporaries as compounding the patriarchal notions of many of their peers.[235] Others, perhaps more immediately in tune with the audiences of the time, have seen it differently.[236] Orderly unions sat alongside disorderly desires.[237]

The power of persuasion

If the Tudor century saw an unprecedented intensification of political and religious theatricality, this was in part because the ruling classes had discovered Cicero, and 'the might and power of Eloqution'.[238] Politics became inseparable from rhetoric, and those who sought public office strove to acquire the skills of oratory. In 1553, Thomas Wilson published *The Arte of Rhetorique*, which ran to eight editions before 1585, and which aimed to teach the Tudor intelligentsia the oratorical skills of Cicero and

Quintilian.[239] Paraphrasing Cicero's *De inventione*, Wilson commented that 'Soche force hath the tongue and soche is the power of eloquence and reason, that most men are forced even to yelde in that, whiche most standeth against their will.'[240] He recalled the legend of the Gallic Hercules, who was so eloquent that he held men chained by the ears through his oratory, to direct them wherever he wanted.[241] Rhetoric, so Cicero had written, must be able 'to prove, to please and to sway or persuade' (*ut probet, ut delectet, ut flectat*).[242] Wilson's rendering of this as 'to teach. To delight. And to perswade' was to be echoed by many later commentators.[243] Speech had acquired power as never before.

Drama was acknowledged to be powerful; for the same reason, it was also feared. Richard Morison in the 1530s advocated the use of plays as a valuable tool to reinforce the regime's rejection of papal power, commenting that 'into the common people things sooner enter by the eyes than by the ears'.[244] Fifty years later, poetry was an acknowledged force: 'the Poets were . . . from the beginning the best perswaders and their eloquence the first Rethoricke of the world', wrote George Puttenham.[245] The same agency was acknowledged by others as something to beware. 'There commeth much evil in at the ears, but more at the eies, by these two open windowes death breaketh into the soul', wrote Anthony Munday in his tract criticizing the theatre.[246] Munday is best known for the plays he wrote, yet in this work of 1580 he poured out all the fears of his age about the ability of plays to twist, deceive, seduce and corrupt.[247] 'Manie have ben intangled with the webs of these Spiders, who would gladlie have bene at libertie when they could not.'[248] Throughout the Tudor era, there were fluctuating anxieties about representation and the potentially dangerous impact of something acted. Some Protestant commentators thought plays might safely be read, but should not be seen on the stage, for risk of corruption or idolatry.[249] The irony here was that Protestantism itself was such an intensely theatrical religion, with a culture of preaching that was a showcase of oratory.[250] There was no straightforward transition from the ebullient theatricality of the early Tudor period to the puritan criticisms of the later sixteenth century; rather it was an ongoing anxiety about the power of representation, which had troubled some fifteenth-century observers just as much as their Elizabethan successors.[251]

Contemporary concerns about Tudor drama need to be taken out of the debates about Puritanism and idolatry and set in a broader context, and the impact of Protestant criticism should not be overstated.[252] Theatre was dangerous because it was powerful. It is true that by the end of the sixteenth century debates over representation were particularly febrile; but the early Tudor period had not lacked self-consciousness in its performance of either plays or politics. The first play ever to be printed in England was Henry Medwall's *Fulgens and Lucrece*, which begins with an unexpected piece of meta-theatre.[253] Two unnamed characters introduce the play about to be performed, and stand aside to watch it unfold, only for one of these preliminary characters to decide to plunge into the drama he has just introduced, seeking employment with one of the chief characters.[254] The uncertainty here over where the boundaries lie between drama and reality shows a startlingly sophisticated appreciation of theatrical ambiguity in a play from the 1490s. Throughout the Tudor century, the theatricality of politics and religion, justice and morality, was appreciated and feared alike. Thomas More in *Utopia* in 1516 was in part posing the question of whether the performance of humanist virtue was merely a hollow act, where, as in his imaginary country, apparent integrity concealed a more savage dynamic underneath.[255] Disillusion regarding Elizabeth's Accession Day tilts made their political message no less significant, and the self-awareness of Elizabethan actors rendered their plays no less telling. Envisioning human life as a series of parts played upon a stage made the dilemmas of human existence no less important. Walter Raleigh even envisaged the Last Judgement as a drama, where 'Heaven the judicious sharp spectator is, That sits and marks still who doth act amiss.'[256]

It is unquestionable that, as the century drew to a close, the performative nature of English religion and politics had reached fever pitch. By the 1590s, religious and political divisions had become dangerously antagonistic over the threat of an uncertain succession and the risk that rival Protestant and Catholic candidates might drag the nation into civil war. More and more voices entered into the debate, and rivalries were played out through a succession of pamphlets, plays, libels, sermons and speeches. Taking the route of 'popularity' became an acknowledged political tactic.[257] Francis Bacon, writing to the earl of Essex in 1596, warned him that his popular reputation needed to be 'handled tenderly', and that he should (hypocritically) speak out to the queen 'against popularity and popular courses', whilst at the same time continuing to promote his popular following, as before.[258]

It has been argued that this is the point where a 'public sphere' first began clearly to emerge.[259] Certainly, the enactment of conflict on both the theatrical stage and the broader political stage had become an established feature of Tudor culture, and a significant legacy for the seventeenth century.

'What is our life? A play of passion', wrote Sir Walter Raleigh.[260] Tudor performance was not just an exercise in artifice: it conveys real and urgent truths about the patterns of human emotion and endeavour, the moral and religious realms, and the workings of power at every level. It gives a more intricate, varied and complete picture of Tudor society than perhaps any other source we might use. It shows that there were no laws that went unexamined, no powers that were not questioned, no gender roles that could not be subverted – nothing so sacred that it could not be the subject of derision. It also gives us the stuff of life which escapes other kinds of historical record – in particular, the loves and loyalties, the fear and jealousy, the violence and vengeance of this turbulent era.

AFTERWORD

One last portrait of Elizabeth I exists, painted a few years after her death, in which some of the artifice of earlier depictions is put aside (see plate 25). Elizabeth is old and weary, her head resting on her hand, her elbow propped up on a velvet cushion – perhaps not unlike the ones on which she was said to have rested as she lay dying. Behind her, Death grimaces over one shoulder and Father Time slumbers wearily by the other. Her clothes are magnificent as ever, stiff with jewels, roped with pearls, her surcoat trimmed with ermine. Her crown, however, is being lifted away by cherubs, hers but for a brief span of one human life. From a pale, lined face, the queen's eyes look straight at the viewer, as if in tacit admission of the fact that all pretence is at an end. It is a striking visual statement of the burdens of ruling – at once exhausting and ephemeral – and of the transient nature of dynastic power.

To end with the death of the last Tudor monarch would be a neat way to conclude this book. But it was not just one old woman who died in the spring of 1603, resisting to the last the pull of mortality. Almost as soon as James VI and I had taken control, the plague arrived. The regime issued orders, instructing the over-worked magistrates in each area to assess the numbers of those diseased and to raise money for the poor 'that are or shall be infected', exhorting the sick not to 'resort into the company of others that are sound' and placing households in isolation for up to six weeks if someone was taken ill there.[1] The playwright Thomas Dekker published his account of the plague and the suffering it had brought, in *The Wonderfull Yeare*, painting in stark words a picture of the human anguish that swept through London.[2] 'Sorrow and Truth, sit you on each side of me, whilst I am delivered of this deadly burden', wrote the poet, as he described the horrors his city was living through, invoking

> you desolate hand-wringing widowes . . . you wofully distracted mothers . . . kissing the insensible cold lips of your breathlesse Infants: you out-cast and downe-troden Orphanes, that shall many a yeare hence remember more freshly to mourne, when your mourning garments shall looke olde and be forgotten.[3]

It was a vivid evocation of a community in crisis, and the complexities of human grief.

Yet Dekker, painfully alive to the misery around him, also mourned the loss of his queen. He wrote that the news of her death

> tooke away hearts from millions: for having brought up (even under her wing) a nation that was almost begotten and born under her; that never shouted any other *Ave* than for her name, never saw the face of any Prince but her selfe . . . how was it possible, but that her sicknes should throw abroad an universall feare, and her death an astonishment?

He understood the symbiotic relationship between a monarch and the people, in which the notion of the Crown remained a moral force even to those who never set eyes upon their king or queen. He was also aware of what a shock it was when that monarch passed away. 'What an Earth-quake is the alteration of a State!', he wrote. 'Looke from the Chamber of Presence, to the Farmers cottage, and you shall finde nothing but distraction.'[4] Tudor society had lived through several such upheavals. Its communities – in city, town or village – were still in thrall to the ideals of justice and sanctity, protection and preservation, with which the ruler was invested in the popular understanding.

Five consecutive Tudor regimes had overseen decades of war and poverty, disease and destruction. Successive generations had witnessed a subtle but strong transformation in the nature of government, and complex shifts within economy and society. Communities had been put to the test, time after time, and had patiently rallied to the task of maintaining the peace, providing for the poor, mustering troops for military campaigns and educating the next generation. Tudor men and women had witnessed an outpouring of words – in sermons, plays, poetry and devotions, as well as in political instruction, polemic, controversy and condemnation – and had learned as never before to debate, appraise and critique the authorities to which they were subject. Perhaps more striking than anything else, they had lived through an ideological revolution in religious belief and practice, which left late Elizabethan society caught between rival views of Christian truth. This was not just the conflict between Catholic loyalism and Protestant dedication; there was just as much tension between the zealots of every type and the quieter expectations of quotidian religious life. William Perkins wrote disparagingly in 1591 of the faith of the ignorant, whose opinions encompassed the view that 'it is the safest, to doo in Religion as most doo' and that 'it was a good world when the old Religion was, because all things were cheap'.[5] His own vision was more exacting, austere, inspirational, judgemental. There had always been variation, even enmity, within pre-Reformation religion, but this was something new. The legacy of the Tudors was a religious world that was painfully self-conscious, troubled, ardent and defensive by turns, and a source of strife which tore at government and community alike.

Millions of people lived and died in Tudor England. It is easy to remember the few who ruled or rebelled; those who preached, or died, for their faith, or who wrote books and plays; the people who made a name for themselves. We sometimes also remember those whose names we will never know, but who built the great houses, carved the wooden pew-ends in the parish church, painted pictures on the walls of taverns, cast silver altar vessels or patiently sewed together the pages of books. From bills of mortality and the records of churchwardens, we learn the names of those who were baptized, married and buried, but about whom we will never know any more than that. And from the comments of others, the marks on the landscape, the mute witness of ruined walls or illegible tombstones, we know that there were many thousands whose lives lie beyond our reach. Writing the history of any era is an exercise in humility, as we realize the depths of our own ignorance, the banality of our modern assumptions and the levels of challenge faced by those who lived and died so many centuries ago. With the Tudor era, there is much that will forever lie out of sight, but this book has tried to give a voice to those whose experiences are so often overlooked, and to bring to life some of the richness, intricacy, eloquence and vision of this extraordinary epoch.

At about the same time as the portrait of Elizabeth with Time and Death was being painted, in 1609, William Shakespeare published his book of sonnets. In Sonnet 60, he wrote about the passage of time:

> Like as the waves make towards the pebbled shore,
> So do our minutes hasten to their end;
> Each changing place with that which goes before,
> In sequent toil all forwards do contend.

Tudor England saw over a hundred years pass by, as its people contended – valiantly, angrily, compassionately, resourcefully – with all the trials of human existence. We cannot do more than trace the lines left in the sand, and turn over a few of the pebbles left on the beach. But for all that, they still tell an enthralling and astonishing story.

NOTES

Abbreviations used in the notes

APC	*Acts of the Privy Council*, ed. J. R. Dasent, 46 vols. (1890–1964)
BCH	*British Catholic History*
BIHR	*Bulletin of the Institute of Historical Research*
BL	British Library
Chronicle of Edward VI	*The Chronicle and Political Papers of King Edward VI*, ed. W.K. Jordan (1966)
Chronicle of Queen Jane and Queen Mary	*The Chronicle of Queen Jane, and of two years of Queen Mary*, ed. J.G. Nichols, CS first series, 48 (London, 1850)
CRS	Catholic Record Society
CS	Camden Society
CSP Sp.	*Calendar of State Papers, Spanish*, ed. G.A. Bergenroth et al., 13 vols (1862–1964)
CSP Ven.	*Calendar of State Papers, Venetian*, ed. Rawdon Brown et al., 9 vols (1864–98)
EBBA	English Broadside Ballad Archive, at http://ebba.english.ucsb.edu/
EconHR	*Economic History Review*
EETS	Early English Text Society
EHD V(A)	*English Historical Documents. Volume V(A): 1558–1603*, ed. Ian W. Archer and F. Douglas Price (London, 2011)
EHR	*English Historical Review*
Elizabeth I: Collected Works	Leah S. Marcus, Janel Mueller and Mary Beth Rose (eds.), *Elizabeth I: Collected Works* (Chicago, IL, 2000)
Elton, *Tudor Constitution*	Geoffrey R. Elton, *The Tudor Constitution: Documents and commentary* (Cambridge, 1960)
Fabyan, *Chronicles*	Robert Fabyan, *The New Chronicles of England and France in Two Parts*, ed. Henry Ellis (1811)
Foxe, *A&M*	John Foxe, *The Actes and Monuments*, at The Acts and Monuments Online (TAMO), at: http//www.dhi.ac.uk/foxe
Hall, *Chronicle*	*The Union of the Two Noble and Illustre Famelies of Lancastre and Yorke* (1548), ed. Henry Ellis (London, 1809)
HJ	*Historical Journal*
HLQ	*Huntingdon Library Quarterly*
Holinshed, *Chronicles*	Raphael Holinshed et al., *Chronicles of England, Scotland and Ireland* (1577; second edition 1587), at http://english.nsms.ox.ac.uk/holinshed/

HR	*Historical Research* (see also BIHR)
HWJ	*History Workshop Journal*
JBS	*Journal of British Studies*
JEcclesH	*Journal of Ecclesiastical History*
Latimer, *Sermons*	*Sermons by Hugh Latimer*, ed. G.E. Corrie, Parker Society, 2 vols (Cambridge, 1844–45)
Leland, *De rebus Brittanicis*	John Leland, *De rebus Brittanicis collectanea*, 10 vols
Lisle Letters	*The Lisle Letters*, ed. Muriel St Claire Byrne, 6 vols (Chicago, IL, and London, 1981)
L&P	*Letters and Papers, Foreign and Domestic, of the Reign of Henry VIII*, ed. J.S. Brewer, J. Gairdner and R.S. Brodie, 21 vols (1862–1932)
Machyn's *Diary*	*The Diary of Henry Machyn, Citizen and Merchant Taylor of London, 1550–1563*, ed. J.G. Nichols, CS first series, 42 (London, 1848)
Narratives of the Reformation	*Narratives of the Days of the Reformation*, ed. J.G. Nichols, CS first series, 77 (1859)
ODNB	*Oxford Dictionary of National Biography*
P&P	*Past and Present*
RH	*Recusant History*
RQ	*Renaissance Quarterly*
RS	*Renaissance Studies*
SCH	*Studies in Church History*
SCJ	*Sixteenth Century Journal*
STC	*Short-Title Catalogue of Books Printed in England, Scotland and Ireland and of English Books Printed Abroad, 1475–1640* (revised), ed. W.A. Jackson, J.F. Ferguson and K.F. Pantzer (London, 1986)
TED	*Tudor Economic Documents*, ed. R.H. Tawney and Eileen Power, 3 vols (1924)
TLS	*Times Literary Supplement*
TNA	The National Archives
TRHS	*Transactions of the Royal Historical Society*
TRP	*Tudor Royal Proclamations*, ed. P.L. Hughes and J.F. Larkin, 3 vols (1964–69)
VAI	*Visitation Articles and Injunctions of the Period of the Reformation*, ed. W.H. Frere and W.M. Kennedy, 3 vols, Alcuin Club Collections, xiv, xv, xvi (1910)
VCH	*Victoria County History*
Vergil, *Anglica Historia*	*The Anglica Historia of Polydore Vergil, A.D. 1485–1537*, ed. Denys Hay (London, 1950)
Wriothesley, *Chronicle*	Charles Wriothesley, *A Chronicle of England*, ed. William D. Hamilton, 2 vols (London, 1875)

Introduction

1. *The Gospels of the fower Evangelistes translated in the olde Saxons tyme* (London, 1571), STC 2961, dedication by John Foxe. For Foxe's limited role in the production of this volume, see Michael Murphy, 'John Foxe, martyrologist and "editor" of Old English', *English Studies* 49 (1968), 516–23.
2. C.S.L. Davies, ' "A rose by any other name": Why we are wrong to talk about "The Tudors" ', *TLS* 5489, 13 June 2008; Patrick Collinson, 'Through several glasses darkly: Historical and sectarian perceptions of the Tudor Church', in Tatiana C. String and

Marcus Bull (eds), *Tudorism: Historical imagination and the appropriation of the sixteenth century* (Oxford, 2011), 97–113.

3. String and Bull (eds), *Tudorism*; Mark Rankin, Christopher Highley and John N. King (eds), *Henry VIII and his Afterlives: Literature, politics and art* (Cambridge, 2009); Estelle Paranque (ed.), *Remembering Queens and Kings of Early Modern England and France: Reputation, reinterpretation and reincarnation* (Basingstoke, 2019); Carole Levin, 'Elizabeth's ghost: The afterlife of the queen in Stuart England', *Royal Studies Journal* 1 (2014), 1–17.

4. Susan Doran and Thomas S. Freeman (eds), *Tudors and Stuarts on Film: Historical perspectives* (Basingstoke, 2009).

5. C.S.L. Davies, 'Tudor: What's in a name?', *History* 97 (2012), 24–42.

6. C.S.L. Davies, 'Information, disinformation and political knowledge under Henry VII and early Henry VIII', *HR* 85 (2012), 228.

7. Steven Gunn and Linda Monckton, 'Introduction: Arthur Tudor, the forgotten prince', in Gunn and Monckton (eds), *Arthur Tudor, Prince of Wales: Life, death and commemoration* (Woodbridge, 2009), 1; see also Martin Biddle and Sally Badham, *King Arthur's Round Table: An archaeological investigation* (Woodbridge, 2001); John N. King, *Tudor Royal Iconography: Literature and art in an age of religious crisis* (Princeton, NJ, 1989), 38–40; Roy Strong, 'Queen Elizabeth I and the Order of the Garter', *Archaeological Journal* 119 (1964), 245–69; Raymond B. Waddington, 'Elizabeth I and the Order of the Garter', *SCJ* 24 (1993), 97–113.

8. Christopher Maginn and Steven Ellis, *The Tudor Discovery of Ireland* (Dublin, 2015); Brendan Kane, 'Ordinary violence? Ireland as emergency in the Tudor state', *History* 99 (2014), 444–67; Brian Mac Cuarta (ed.), *Reshaping Ireland 1550–1700: Colonization and its consequences* (Dublin, 2011); William Palmer, *The Problem of Ireland in Tudor Foreign Policy, 1485–1603* (Woodbridge, 1994), l; Peter Roberts, 'Tudor Wales, national identity and the British inheritance', in Brendan Bradshaw and Peter Roberts (eds), *British Consciousness and Identity: The making of Britain, 1533–1707* (Cambridge, 1998), 8–42; Brendan Bradshaw, 'The Tudor reformation and revolution in Wales and Ireland: The origins of the British problem', in Brendan Bradshaw and John Morrill (eds), *The British Problem, c.1534–1707: State formation in the Atlantic archipelago* (London, 1996), 39–65; J. Gwynfor Jones (ed.), *Class, Community and Culture in Tudor Wales* (Cardiff, 1989); Peter Roberts, 'Wales and England after the Tudor 'union': Crown, principality and parliament 1543–1624', in C. Cross, D.M. Loades and J.J. Scarisbrick (eds), *Law and Government under the Tudors: Essays presented to Sir Geoffrey Elton* (Cambridge, 1988), 111–38.

9. Some authors have risen to this challenge. See, in particular, Alec Ryrie, *The Age of Reformation: The Tudor and Stewart realms, 1485–1603* (second edition, London, 2017).

10. Peter Roberts, 'The English crown, the principality of Wales and the Council in the Marches, 1534–1641', in Bradshaw and Morrill (eds), *The British Problem*, 118–37. See also J. Gwynfor Jones, *Early Modern Wales, c.1525–1640* (Basingstoke, 1994).

11. *The State of England, Anno Dom. 1600*, ed. F.J. Fisher, *Camden Miscellany XVI*, CS third series, 52 (London, 1936), pp. 2, 5; see also Susan Doran and Paulina Kewes (eds), *Doubtful and Dangerous: The question of succession in late Elizabethan England* (Manchester, 2014), 4.

12. Elizabeth Evendon Kenyon, 'The impact of print', in Elaine Treharne and Greg Walker (eds), *The Oxford Handbook of Medieval Literature in English* (Oxford, 2010), 90–108; Lotte Hellinga, *William Caxton and Early Printing in England* (London, 2010); William Blades, *The Life and Typography of William Caxton, England's First Printer*, 2 vols (original edition, 1861–63; reprinted Cambridge, 2014).

13. Lucy Wooding, *Henry VIII* (second edition, Abingdon, 2015), 278.

14. Suzanne Cole, *Thomas Tallis and his Music in Victorian England* (Woodbridge, 2008), 97–98.

15. F.J. Levy, *Tudor Historical Thought* (San Marino, CA, 1967); Arthur B. Ferguson, *Clio Unbound: Perceptions of the social and cultural past in renaissance England* (Durham,

NC, 1979); Donald R. Kelley and David H. Sacks (eds), *The Historical Imagination in Early Modern Britain: History, rhetoric and fiction, 1500–1800* (Cambridge, 1997); Daniel R. Woolf, *The Social Circulation of the Past: English historical culture, 1500–1730* (Oxford, 2003); Paulina Kewes (ed.), *The Uses of History in Early Modern England* (San Marino, CA, 2006).

16. Richard Carew, *The Survey of Cornwall* (1602), STC 4615, fo. 2^r.

17. Thomas Blundeville, *The true order and methode of wryting and reading hystories* (1574), STC 3161, Sig. Aij^r.

18. Cited in D.R. Woolf, *Reading History in Early Modern England* (Cambridge, 2000), 22.

19. *The Gospels of the fower Evangelistes*, dedication.

20. Patrick Collinson, 'William Camden and the anti-myth of Elizabeth: Setting the mould?', in Susan Doran and Thomas S. Freeman (eds), *The Myth of Elizabeth* (Basingstoke, 2003), 79–98; Collinson, 'One of us? William Camden and the making of history', *TRHS* sixth series, 8 (1998), 139–63; Wyman Herendeen, *William Camden: A life in context* (Woodbridge, 2007).

21. Cited in Hugh Trevor-Roper, 'Queen Elizabeth's first historian: William Camden', in Hugh Trevor-Roper, *Renaissance Essays* (London, 1986), 136.

22. See, for example, Keith Thomas, 'History and anthropology', *P&P* 24 (1963), 145–64; E.P. Thompson, 'History and anthropology', in *Making History* (New York, NY, 1994), 201–22; Ronald Hutton, 'Anthropological and historical approaches to witchcraft: Potential for a new collaboration?', *HJ* 47 (2004), 413–34; Peter Burke, *History and Social Theory* (Cambridge, 1992); Stuart Hall, 'Race, the floating signifier: What more is there to say about "race"?', in Paul Gilroy and Ruth Wilson (ed.), *Stuart Hall: Selected writings on race and difference* (Durham, 2021), 359–73.

23. See, for example, Joan W. Scott, 'Gender: A useful category of historical analysis', *American Historical Review*, 91 (1986), 1053–75; Alexandra Shepherd and Karen Harvey, 'What have historians done with masculinity? Reflections on five centuries of British history, c.1500–1950', *JBS* 44 (2005), 274–80; Jim Sharpe, 'History from below', and Joan W. Scott, 'Women's history', in Peter Burke (ed.), *New Perspectives on Historical Writing* (second edition, Cambridge, 2001), 25–42, 43–70; Garthine Walker (ed.), *Writing Early Modern History* (London, 2005); Brodie Waddell, 'Writing history from below: Chronicling and record-keeping in early modern England', *HWJ* 85 (2018), 239–64; Jacques Le Goff, 'Mentalities: A history of ambiguities', in Jacques Le Goff and Pierre Nora (eds), *Constructing the Past: Essays in historical methodology* (Cambridge, 1974), 166–80; Peter Burke, 'Strengths and weaknesses of the history of mentalities', *History of European Ideas* 7 (1986), 439–51.

24. See, for example, Peter Burke, *Eye Witnessing: The use of images as historical evidence* (London, 2001); Ulinka Rublack, *Dressing Up: Cultural identity in renaissance Europe* (Oxford, 2010); David Freedberg, *The Power of Images: Studies in the history and theory of response* (London, 1989); Tara Hamling and Richard L. Williams, (eds), *Art Re-formed? Reassessing the impact of the Reformation on the visual arts* (Cambridge, 2007); Tara Hamling, *Decorating the Godly Household: Religious art in post-Reformation Britain* (New Haven, CT, and London, 2010); David J. Davis, *Seeing Faith, Printing Pictures: Religious identity during the English Reformation* (Turnhout, 2013); Tara Hamling and C. Richardson (eds), *Everyday Objects: Medieval and early modern material culture and its meanings* (Abingdon, 2010); Tara Hamling and Catherine Richardson, *A Day at Home in Early Modern England: Material culture and domestic life, 1500–1700* (New Haven, CT, 2017); Anne Gerritsen and Giorgio Riello (eds), *Writing Material Culture History* (London, 2014), chapters 3 and 12; Paula Findlen, *Early Modern Things: Objects and their histories, 1500–1800* (Abingdon, 2013); Dan Hicks and Mary Beaudry (eds), *The Oxford Handbook of Material Culture Studies* (Oxford, 2010).

25. On revisionist views of the Reformation, see J.J. Scarisbrick, *The Reformation and the English People* (Oxford, 1984); Christopher Haigh, *English Reformations: Religion, politics and society under the Tudors* (Oxford, 1993); Eamon Duffy, *The Stripping of the*

Altars: Traditional religion in England, 1400–1580 (New Haven, CT, and London, 1992). On Catholic history, see, for example, Alexandra Walsham, *Church Papists: Catholicism, conformity and confessional polemic in early modern England* (Woodbridge, 1993); Michael Questier, *Catholicism and Community in Early Modern England: Politics, aristocratic patronage and religion, c.1550–1640* (Cambridge, 2006); Peter Lake and Michael Questier, *The Trials of Margaret Clitherow: Persecution, martyrdom and the politics of sanctity in Elizabethan England* (London, 2011); Ethan H. Shagan (ed.), *Catholics and the 'Protestant Nation': Religious politics and identity in early modern England* (Manchester, 2005); Victor Houliston, *Catholic Resistance in Elizabethan England: Robert Person's Jesuit polemic, 1580–1610* (Aldershot, 2007); Alexandra Walsham, *Catholic Reformation in Protestant Britain* (Farnham, 2014).

26. Richard Ovenden, *Burning the Books: A history of the deliberate destruction of knowledge* (Cambridge, MA, 2020), 55–62.
27. Jonathan Lamb, *Shakespeare in the Marketplace of Words* (Cambridge, 2017).
28. Francis Meres, *Palladis Tamia Wits Treasury* (London, 1598), *STC* 17834, 279–87. See also Jason Scott-Warren, 'Commonplacing and Originality: Reading Francis Meres', *Review of English Studies* 68 (2017), 902–23.
29. Naomi Tadmor, *The Social Universe of the English Bible: Scripture, society, and culture in early modern England* (Cambridge, 2010), 17–22; Peter Lake, *How Shakespeare Put Politics on the Stage: Power and succession in the history plays* (New Haven, CT, 2016), 12–14; Lisa Jardine and Anthony Grafton, ' "Studied for action": How Gabriel Harvey read his Livy', *P&P* 129 (1990), 30–78; Paul Hammer, 'The earl of Essex, Fulke Greville, and the employment of scholars', *Studies in Philology* 91 (1994), 167–80. See also Kevin Sharpe, *Reading Revolutions: The politics of reading in early modern England* (New Haven, CT, and London, 2000).
30. Alexandra Gillespie, 'The history of the book', *New Medieval Literatures* 9 (2007), 254.
31. Krista J. Kesselring, *Mercy and Authority in the Tudor State* (Cambridge, 2003).

1 Landscape and Seascape

1. This is Psalm 42 in the Vulgate; in the King James Version it is Psalm 43.
2. Andy Wood, *Faith, Hope and Charity: English neighbourhoods, 1500–1640* (Cambridge, 2020), 106; Nicola Whyte, *Inhabiting the Landscape: Place, custom and memory, 1500–1800* (Oxford, 2009), 1–2, 9, 61, 66–68.
3. Andy Wood, *The Memory of the People: Custom and popular senses of the past in early modern England* (Cambridge, 2013); Nicola Whyte, 'Remembering Mousehold Heath', and Heather Falvey, 'Relating early modern depositions', in Carl J. Griffin and Briony McDonagh (eds), *Remembering Protest in Britain since 1500: Memory, materiality and the landscape* (Cham, 2018), 25–52, 81–106; Steve Hindle, 'Beating the bounds of the parish: Order, memory and identity in the English local community, c.1500–1700', in Michael Halvorson and Karen E. Spierling (eds), *Defining Community in Early Modern Europe* (Aldershot, 2008), 205–28.
4. Andrew McRae, *God Speed the Plough: The representation of agrarian England, 1500–1660* (Cambridge, 1996), 8.
5. Denis Cosgrove, *Social Formation and Symbolic Landscape* (London, 1984); Denis Cosgrove and Stephen Daniels (eds), *The Iconography of Landscape: Essays on the symbolic representation, design and use of past environments* (Cambridge, 1988).
6. Joan Thirsk, 'Forest, field and garden: Landscapes and economies in Shakespeare's England', in John F. Andrews (ed.), *William Shakespeare: His world, his work, his influence* (New York, 1985), 257–67.
7. Thomas Wyatt, 'Mine own John Poyntz', in R.A. Rebholz (ed.), *Sir Thomas Wyatt: The complete poems* (London, 1997), 186–89.
8. Cynthia Herrup, *The Common Peace: Participation and the criminal law in seventeenth-century England* (Cambridge, 1987), 11.

9. *Sir Gawain and the Green Knight*, trans. Simon Armitage (2012), ll.701–02. I am grateful to Ebrahim Hanifehpour for suggesting this example. See also Michael J. Bennett, 'Sir Gawain and the Green Knight and the literary achievement of the north-west Midlands: The historical background', *Journal of Medieval History* 5 (1979), 67.

10. William Harrison, *The Description of England*, ed. G. Edelen (Washington, DC, and London, 1994), 333–39. In 1577, Harrison published *An Historical Description of the Island of Britain* as an introduction, in three books, to Holinshed's *Chronicles*; the second edition of Holinshed in 1587 contained a revised version of Harrison's work, which kept the original title for the first book, but rechristened the second and third in the running title as *The Description of England*. See Glyn Parry, 'Harrison's chronology and descriptions of Britain', in Felicity Heal, Ian W. Archer and Paulina Kewes (eds), *The Oxford Handbook of Holinshed's Chronicles* (Oxford, 2013), 93–110; Parry, 'William Harrison and Holinshed's Chronicles', *HJ* 27 (1984), 789–810.

11. Harrison, *Description of England*, xv.

12. Robert Wyer, *The cronycle, begynnynge at the vii ages of the worlde with the commynge of Brute* (London, 1532), STC 9984, Sig. bv^v.

13. Ranulf Higden, *Here endeth the discripcion of Britayne* . . . (1480), STC 13440a, ca. iii. Further editions were published in 1498 and 1528.

14. Nicholas Orme, 'Church and chapel in medieval England', *TRHS* sixth series, 6 (1996), 84–85; Alexandra Walsham, *The Reformation of the Landscape: Religion, identity, and memory in early modern England and Ireland* (Oxford, 2011), 23, 441, 445–46.

15. Alexandra Walsham, 'Holywell: Contesting sacred space in early modern Wales', in Will Coster and Andrew Spicer (eds), *Sacred Space in Early Modern Europe* (Cambridge, 2005), 213–14.

16. Walsham, *Reformation of the Landscape*, 41–42.

17. ibid., 49–66, 89–90.

18. Naomi Tadmor, *The Social Universe of the English Bible: Scripture, society, and culture in early modern England* (Cambridge, 2010), 19–20.

19. James Clark, *The Dissolution of the Monasteries* (New Haven, CT, and London, 2021).

20. See Harriet Lyon, *Memory and the Dissolution of the Monasteries in Early Modern England* (Cambridge, 2021), for an account of the previously neglected subject of the conversion of monastic buildings.

21. Henry French, ' "Gentlemen": Remaking the English ruling class', in Keith Wrightson (ed.), *A Social History of England, 1500–1750* (Cambridge, 2017), 274.

22. Margaret Aston, 'English ruins and English history: The Dissolution and the sense of the past', *Journal of the Warburg and Courtauld Institutes* 36 (1973), 231–55; Maurice Howard, 'Recycling the monastic fabric: Beyond the act of dissolution', in David Gaimster and Roberta Gilchrist (eds), *The Archaeology of the Reformation, 1480–1580* (Leeds, 2003), 221–35.

23. John Speed, *The Theatre of the empire of Great Britaine* (1611), STC 23041, 17.

24. Michael W. Thompson, *The Decline of the Castle* (Cambridge, 1987), 18.

25. John Leland, *The Itinerary of John Leland*, 5 vols, ed. Lucy Toulmin Smith (1906–10), V, 47; II, 64–65.

26. George Owen, *The Description of Pembrokeshire*, ed. Henry Owen (1906), III, 57.

27. Thompson, *Decline of the Castle*, Appendix 2, 171–78; Penry Williams, *The Later Tudors: England 1547–1603* (Oxford, 1995), 109; Michael Hicks, 'Thomas Stafford', *ODNB*.

28. Warren Chernaik, *The Myth of Rome in Shakespeare and his Contemporaries* (Cambridge, 2011), 16; Harrison, *Description of England*, 225.

29. Diarmaid MacCulloch, *Thomas Cromwell: A life* (London, 2018), 15, 356.

30. Steven Gunn, *Henry VII's New Men and the Making of Tudor England* (Oxford, 2016), 259.

31. Edward A. Wrigley, *People, Cities and Wealth: The transformation of traditional society* (Oxford, 1987), 170. Wrigley's definition of a larger town was a population of 5,000 or more, which is probably too inflated by Tudor standards.

32. C.G.A. Clay, *Economic Expansion and Social Change: England 1500–1700*, vol. 1: *People, Land and Towns* (Cambridge, 1984), 1–2, 67.

33. Regional variation was marked in Wales, as well as England: see Matthew Griffiths, 'Country and town: Agrarian change and urban fortunes', in Trevor Herbert and Gareth Elwyn Jones (eds), *Tudor Wales* (Cardiff, 1988), 72–73.

34. Marjorie K. McIntosh, *A Community Transformed: The manor and liberty of Havering, 1500–1620* (Cambridge, 1991), 7, 113, 402–11.

35. Thomas Smith, *A Discourse of the Commonweal of the Realm of England*, ed. Elizabeth Lamond (1893; reissued Cambridge, 1929), 19. For the authorship of this work, see Lamond, 'Introduction'; Mary Dewar, 'The authorship of the "Discourse of the Commonweal"', *Economic History Review* 19 (1966), 388–400.

36. *TED*, iii, 56.

37. Harrison, *Description of England*, 256.

38. *TED*, i, 4–5.

39. McRae, *God Speed the Plough*, 2, 58–79.

40. Thomas More, *Utopia*, ed. George M. Logan (third edition, Cambridge, 2016), 19.

41. Albert F. Pollard and Marjorie Blatcher (eds), 'Hayward Townshend's journals', in *BIHR* 12 (1934–35), 10.

42. *TED*, iii, 62–63.

43. Harrison, *Description of England*, 276.

44. Clay, *Economic Expansion*, 1: 29–31.

45. ibid., 31.

46. F.J. Fisher, 'Tawney's century', in F.J. Fisher (ed.), *Essays in the Social and Economic History of Tudor and Stuart England* (Cambridge, 1961), 3–4. On Londoners' use of coal, see Derek Keene, 'Material London in time and space', in Lena Cowen Orlin (ed.), *Material London, ca. 1600* (Philadelphia, PA, 2000), 68.

47. W.G. Hoskins, *The Making of the English Landscape* (London, 1955), 14; Oliver Rackham, *The History of the Countryside* (second edition, London, 1995), 29–30.

48. Bell pits can be seen at Strelley in Nottinghamshire, Louth in Leicestershire and Nostell in West Yorkshire.

49. William Lawson, *A New Orchard and Garden* (1618), *STC* 15329, 54. Lawson's work was the fruit of forty-eight years' experience and had been circulated in manuscript before its publication during James I's reign.

50. William Camden, *Britain, or A chorographicall description of the most flourishing kingdomes, England, Scotland and Ireland, and the ilands adjoyning, out of the depth of antiquitie*, trans. Philemon Holland (1610), *STC* 4509, 4. The original Latin edition of the work, *Britannia*, was published in 1586. See also Joan Evans, *A History of the Society of Antiquaries* (Oxford, 1956); Graham Parry, *The Triumphs of Time: English antiquaries of the seventeenth century* (Oxford, 1995), 22–48, 43–45; Richard Helgerson, 'The land speaks', in Richard Helgerson, *Forms of Nationhood: The Elizabethan writing of England* (Chicago, IL, 1992), 107–47.

51. Stan Mendyk, 'Early British chorography', *SCJ* 17 (1986), 459–81.

52. Holinshed, *Chronicles*, 1587, I, 45.

53. Holinshed, *Chronicles*, 1577, I, dedication.

54. Philip Schwyzer, 'John Leland and his heirs: The topography of England', in Mike Pincombe and Cathy Shrank (eds), *The Oxford Handbook of Tudor Literature, 1485–1603* (Oxford, 2009), 238–53; James P. Carley, 'Monastic collections and their dispersal', in John Barnard and D.F. McKenzie (eds), *The Cambridge History of the Book in Britain*, vol. 4: *1557–1695* (Cambridge, 2002), 339–47; C.E. Wright, 'The dispersal of the monastic libraries and the beginnings of Anglo-Saxon studies. Matthew Parker and his circle: A preliminary study', *Transactions of the Cambridge Bibliographical Society* 1 (1951), 208–37.

55. John Leland, *The laboryouse Journey*, ed. John Bale (1549), *STC* 15445, Sig. Diiii^v.

56. William Camden, *Britain, or A chorographical description* (1637), STC 4510.8, Sig. ¶4ʳ⁻ᵛ; this is a later edition of the English translation by Philemon Holland, first published in 1610. See also Angus Vine, 'Copiousness, conjecture and collaboration in William Camden's *Britannia*', *RS* 28 (2014), 225–41.

57. Thomas Gascoigne, *Here after folowith the boke callyd the myrroure of Oure Lady very necessary for all relygyous persones* (1530), STC 17542, Sig. Avᵛ–Aviʳ.

58. Richard Carew, *The Survey of Cornwall* (1602), STC 4615, Sig. ¶4ʳ.

59. *A Relation . . . of the Island of England*, ed. Charlotte A. Sneyd (London, 1847), 7, 8.

60. D.E. Eichholz, 'A Greek traveller in Tudor England', *Greece and Rome* 16 (1947), 78.

61. Christopher Maginn and Steven G. Ellis, *The Tudor Discovery of Ireland* (Dublin, 2015), 42.

62. Wyer, *The cronycle*, Sig. bvᵛ.

63. J.B. Harley, 'Maps, knowledge and power', in Cosgrove and Daniels (eds), *Iconography of Landscape*, 277–312; McRae, *God Speed the Plough*, 169–97; J.B. Harley, 'Silences and secrecy: The hidden agenda of cartography in early modern Europe', *Imago Mundi* 40 (1988), 57–58, 66–68. See also Howard Marchitello, 'Political maps: The production of cartography and chorography in early modern Europe', in Margaret J.M. Ezell and Katherine O'Brien O'Keeffe (eds), *Cultural Artifacts and the Production of Meaning: The page, the image, and the body* (Ann Arbor, MI, 1994), 13–40.

64. This was also often prompted by legal proceedings: see Whyte, *Inhabiting the Landscape*, 12.

65. Speed, *The Theatre of the empire of Great Britaine*, Sig. ¶3ʳ.

66. John Speed, *A Description of the civill warres of England* (1601), STC 23037.

67. Nigel Nicolson (ed.), *The Counties of Britain: A Tudor atlas by John Speed* (London, 1995), 13.

68. Allie W. Richeson, *English Land Measuring to 1800: Instruments and practices* (Cambridge, MA, 1966), 22, 29–30.

69. Leonard Digges, *A boke named Tectonicon* (London, 1556), STC 6849.5; Leonard and Thomas Digges, *A Geometrical practise, named Pantometria* (London, 1571), STC 6858.

70. Edward Worsop, *A Discoverie of Sundrie Errours* (1582), STC 25997, Sig. Aiiᵛ.

71. ibid., Sig. Aiiiiᵛ; B4ʳ, C4ᵛ.

72. ibid., Sig. K2ʳ⁻ᵛ.

73. *A Relation*, 20, 10–11.

74. *A Relation*, 8–9.

75. Jane Whitaker, 'An Old Arcadia: The gardens of William Herbert, 1st Earl of Pembroke, at Wilton, Wiltshire', *Garden History* 42 (2014), 147.

76. *A Relation*, 9; Harrison, *Description of England*, 422, 419; Carew, *The Survey of Cornwall*, fo. 29ᵛ.

77. *The booke of hauking, huntyng and fysshyng* (1556), STC 3310.7, Sig. Livᵛ; Miiiᵛ.

78. ibid., Sig. i ivʳ.

79. ibid., Sig. givᵛ– hjʳ.

80. Izaak Walton, *The Compleat Angler* (1661), 36–42.

81. John Lydgate, *The horse the ghoos and the sheep* (1477), STC 17018, unpaginated. See also David Lampe, 'Lydgate's laughter: "Horse, goose and sheep" as social satire', *Annuale Mediaevale* 15 (1974), 150–58.

82. Lydgate, *The horse the ghoos and the sheep*, unpaginated.

83. Thomas Blundeville, *A newe booke containing the arte of ryding*, translation of a work by Federico Grisone (1561), STC 3158.

84. Thomas Blundeville, *The fower chiefyst offices belongyng to horsemanshippe* (1566), STC 3152, Sig. Ciʳ. Grisone had noted the derivation of the word 'cavaliero' from the word 'cavallo'.

85. Blundeville, *The fower chiefyst offices belongyng to horsemanshippe*, Sig. Aiiiʳ⁻ᵛ.

86. Lydgate, *The horse the ghoos and the sheep*, unpaginated.

87. Camden, *Britain* (1637), 188–89. As Steven Gunn kindly pointed out, this bird is a chough.

88. 'The discription of a rare or rather most monstrous fishe' (1566), EBBA 32405. See also Alexandra Walsham, *Providence in Early Modern England* (Oxford, 1999), 196–97.

89. Timothy Granger, 'A moste true and marveilous straunge wonder' (1568), EBBA 32270.

90. Camden, *Britain* (1637), Sig. ¶4ʳ⁻ᵛ.

91. Joyce Youings, *Sixteenth-Century England* (London, 1984), 13.

92. *A Relation*, 31.

93. Christopher Dyer, *Making a Living in the Middle Ages: The people of Britain 850–1520* (New Haven, CT, and London, 2002), 275–76.

94. McIntosh, *A Community Transformed*, 94.

95. Jane Whittle, 'Land and people', in Wrightson (ed.), *A Social History of England*, 154–55.

96. Roger Manning, *Religion and Society in Elizabethan Sussex: A study of the enforcement of the religious settlement, 1558–1603* (Leicester, 1969), 3.

97. Joan Thirsk, 'The farming regions of England', in *The Agrarian History of England and Wales*, vol. 4: *1500–1640*, ed. Joan Thirsk (Cambridge, 1967), 1–109.

98. *A Relation*, 10.

99. Ian Blanchard, 'The miner and the agricultural community in late medieval England', *Agricultural History Review* 20 (1972), 96.

100. Ian Blanchard, 'Rejoinder: Stannator Fabulosus', *Agricultural History Review* 22 (1974), 64–65.

101. John R. Langton, 'Coal output in south-west Lancashire, 1590–1799', *Economic History Review*, second series, 25 (1972), 28-54.

102. David C. Coleman, *Industry in Tudor and Stuart England* (London, 1975), 47–48.

103. Griffiths, 'Country and town', in Herbert and Jones (eds), *Tudor Wales*, 69.

104. Joan Thirsk, 'Industries in the countryside', in Fisher, *Essays in the Social and Economic History of Tudor and Stuart England*, 74–75.

105. ibid., 75–88.

106. ibid., 70.

107. Ian W. Archer, 'Commerce and consumption', in Susan Doran and Norman L. Jones (eds), *The Elizabethan World* (Abingdon and New York, 2011), 411.

108. Youings, *Sixteenth-Century England*, 47.

109. John Pound, *Poverty and Vagrancy in Tudor England* (London, 1971), 62.

110. Steve Hindle, 'Exclusion crises: Poverty, migration and parochial responsibility in English rural communities, c.1560–1660', *Rural History* 7 (1996), 128.

111. Steve Hindle, 'Hierarchy and community in the Elizabethan parish: The Swallowfield Articles of 1596', *HJ* 42 (1999), 850.

112. McIntosh, *A Community Transformed*, 129.

113. Steve Hindle, *On the Parish? The micro-politics of poor relief in rural England, c.1550–1750* (Oxford, 2004), 306.

114. Hindle, 'Exclusion crises', 130–31.

115. Hindle, 'Hierarchy and community', 850; see also Laura Gowing, 'Ordering the body: Illegitimacy and female authority in seventeenth-century England', in Michael J. Braddick and John Walter (eds), *Negotiating Power in Early Modern Society: Order, hierarchy and subordination in Britain and Ireland* (Cambridge, 2001), 43–44; Hindle, *On the Parish?*, 319, 412; A.L. Beier, *Masterless Men: The vagrancy problem in England 1560–1640* (London, 1985), 53.

116. Nicola Whyte, 'Landscape, memory and custom: Parish identities c.1550–1700', *Social History* 32 (2007), 166–86.

117. Ronald Hutton, *The Rise and Fall of Merry England: The ritual year, 1400–1700* (Oxford, 1996), 34–36, 105; Eamon Duffy, *The Stripping of the Altars: Traditional religion in*

England, 1400–1580 (New Haven, CT, and London, 1992), 136–39, 589; Keith Thomas, *Religion and the Decline of Magic: Studies in popular beliefs in sixteenth- and seventeenth-century England* (London and New York, 1971), 62–65; Hindle, 'Beating the bounds of the parish', 205–27.

118. Whyte, 'Landscape, memory and custom', 176, 178–80.
119. Cited in Whyte, *Inhabiting the Landscape*, 67.
120. George Cavendish, *Metrical Visions*, ed. A.S.G. Edwards (Colombia, SC, 1980). Cavendish was taking inspiration from John Lydgate's *The Fall of Princes* in ventriloquizing the laments of various famous figures at their fates.
121. Justus Lipsius, *Two Bookes of Constancie*, trans. John Stradling (1595), STC 15694.7, Sig. Kiʳ; see also Mark Morford, 'The stoic garden', *Journal of Garden History* 7 (1987), 151–75; Hester Lees-Jeffries, 'Literary gardens from More to Marvell', in Michael Hattaway (ed.), *A New Companion to English Renaissance Literature and Culture* (Oxford, 2010), 379–95; Rebecca Bushnell, *Green Desires: Imagining early modern English gardens* (Ithaca, NY, 2003).
122. Katherine Myers, '"Men as plants increase": Botanical meaning in Shakespeare's *The Winter's Tale*', *Studies in the History of Gardens and Designed Landscapes* 40 (2020), 171.
123. William Shakespeare, *As You Like It*, Act II, Scene 1, l. 23; Act II, Scene 7, l. 112; Act III, Scene 2, l. 116; Anne Barton, *The Shakespearean Forest* (Cambridge, 2017), 1, 10.
124. Steven Knight and Thomas Ohlgren (eds), *Robin Hood and Other Outlaw Tales* (Kalamazoo, 2000); Malcolm A. Nelson, *The Robin Hood Tradition in the English Renaissance* (Salzburg, 1973); Barton, *Shakespearean Forest*, 70–92.
125. Clay, *Economic Expansion*, 1: 109; Paul Warde, 'Fear of wood shortage and the reality of the woodland in Europe, c.1450–1850', *HWJ* 62 (2006), 37; Andrew McRae, 'Tree-felling in early modern England: Michael Drayton's environmentalism', *Review of English Studies* 63 (2012), 411–14.
126. Oliver Rackham, *Trees and Woodland in the British Landscape* (London, 1990), 77.
127. C.E. Hart, *Royal Forest: A history of Dean's Woods as producers of timber* (Oxford, 1966), 112; Rackham, *Trees and Woodland*, 75.
128. Roy Strong, *The Renaissance Garden in England* (London, 1979).
129. John Gerard, *The Herball, or Generall historie of plantes* (1597), STC 11750, dedication (unpaginated) to William Cecil.
130. Smith, *A Discourse of the Commonweal*, 37. See also Ross Moncrieff, '"Fair Quiet, have I found thee here?" The relationship between garden settings and *otium-negotium* in sixteenth-century philosophical dialogues', *RS* 36 (2022), 395–411.
131. More, *Utopia*, 48.
132. Thomas Betson, *Here begynneth a ryght profytable treatyse* (1500), STC 1978, Sig. cvʳ.
133. Charles Quest-Ritson, *The English Garden: A social history* (London, 2001), 38.
134. Mavis Batey, 'Basing House Tudor garden', *Garden History* 15 (1987), 99.
135. Strong, *The Renaissance Garden*, 15; Paula Henderson, 'The architecture of the Tudor garden', *Garden History* 27 (1999), 54–57; Michael Leslie, 'Spenser, Sidney and the renaissance Garden', *English Literary Renaissance* 22 (1992), 10.
136. Henderson, 'The architecture of the Tudor Garden', 57–58.
137. Elisabeth Whittle, 'The Tudor gardens of St Donat's Castle, Glamorgan, South Wales', *Garden History* 27 (1999), 109–26; Ralph A. Griffiths, 'The rise of the Stradlings of St Donat's', in Ralph A. Griffiths, *Conquerors and Conquered in Medieval Wales* (Stroud, 1994).
138. John Phillips and Nicholas Burnett, 'The chronology and layout of Francis Carew's garden at Beddington, Surrey', *Garden History* 33 (2005), 157–59, 182.
139. Quest-Ritson, *The English Garden*, 40–42.
140. ibid., 18.
141. Luke Morgan, 'Garden design and experience in Shakespeare's England', in Malcolm Smuts (ed.), *The Oxford Handbook of the Age of Shakespeare* (Oxford, 2016), 679.
142. Cited in Phillips and Burnett, 'Carew's garden at Beddington', 162.

143. Christopher Dyer, 'Gardens and garden produce', in C.M. Woolgar, Dale Serjeantson and Tony Waldron (eds), *Food in Medieval England: Diet and nutrition* (Oxford and New York, 2006), 28.

144. C.M. Woolgar, 'Gifts of food in late medieval England', *Journal of Medieval History* 37 (2011), 6–18.

145. Richard Mulcaster, *The Passage of our most drad Soveraigne Lady Quene Elyzabeth* (1559), STC 7590, Sig. Eiii^v.

146. Philip Stubbes, *The Anatomie of Abuses* (London, 1583), STC 23376, Sig. M2^v.

147. ibid., Sig. M3^v.

148. Thomas Hill, *A most briefe and pleasaunt treatyse* (1563), STC 13490, Sig. Aiiii^r.

149. 'The precinct of St Mary Spital: The priory site', in F.H.W. Sheppard (ed.), *Survey of London*, vol. 27: *Spitalfields and Mile End New Town* (London, 1957), 39.

150. John Schofield, 'City of London gardens, 1500–c. 1620', *Garden History* 27 (1999), 76.

151. Quest-Ritson, *The English Garden*, 27.

152. Schofield, 'City of London gardens', 79.

153. Quest-Ritson, *The English Garden*, 27, 40.

154. Gerard, *Herball*, dedication (unpaginated).

155. G.H. Kenyon, *The Glass Industry of the Weald* (Leicester, 1967); D.W. Crossley, 'Glassmaking in Bagot's Park in the sixteenth century', *Post-Medieval Archaeology* 1 (1967), 44–83; C. Welch, 'Glass-making in Wolseley, Staffordshire', *Post-Medieval Archaeology* 31 (1997), 1–60.

156. Jeffrey S. Theis, *Writing the Forest in Early Modern England* (Pittsburgh, PA, 2009), 11; R.G. Albion, *Forests and Sea Power: The timber problems of the Royal Navy* (1926; reissued Annapolis, MD, 2000), 9, 20.

157. Rackham, *Trees and Woodland*, 67–68, 77.

158. John Manwood, *A Treatise and Discourse of the Lawes of the Forrest* (1598), STC 17291, Sig. *2^r; Keith Thomas, *Man and the Natural World* (London, 1983), 198, 201.

159. John Manwood, *A brefe collection of the lawes of the forest* (1592), STC 17290, preface.

160. ibid.

161. Clay, *Economic expansion*, 1: 2.

162. Manwood, *Treatise and Discourse*, fo. 2^{r-v}.

163. William Shakespeare, *Timon of Athens*, Act IV, Scene 1, l. 35; Barton, *Shakespearean Forest*, 8, 46.

164. Michael Holahan, 'Wyatt, the Heart's Forest, and the Ancient Savings', *English Literary Renaissance* 23 (1993), 46–80; Catherine Bates, *Masculinity and the Hunt: Wyatt to Spenser* (Oxford, 2013), 59–62.

165. Oliver Rackham, *The Illustrated History of the Countryside* (London, 2003), 21.

166. Thomas Churchyard, *The worthiness of Wales* (1587), STC 5261, Sig. F3^r.

167. Thomas, *Man and the Natural World*, 193, 196, 199.

168. Corrinne J. Saunders, *The Forest of Medieval Romance: Avernus, Broceliande, Arden* (Cambridge, 1993), 169–71, 186–95.

169. Paul Griffiths, *Lost Londons: Change, crime and control in the capital city, 1550–1660* (Cambridge, 2008), 1. See also Vanessa Harding, 'Recent perspectives on early modern London', *HJ* 47 (2004), 435–50.

170. John Patten, *English Towns, 1500–1700* (Folkestone, 1978), 227–28, 230.

171. Phil Withington, 'Urbanisation', in Wrightson (ed.), *A Social History of England*, 174–75.

172. Francis Trigge, *To the Kings most excellent Maiestie* (1604), STC 24280, Sig. A4^v–5^r.

173. Withington, 'Urbanisation', 176.

174. Muriel C. McClendon and Joseph P. Ward, 'Urban economies', in Doran and Jones (eds), *The Elizabethan World*, 428–29.

175. St Augustine, *Twelve Sermons* (1553), STC 923, Sig. Cvi^v–Cvii^r.

176. David Levine and Keith Wrightson, *The Making of an Industrial Society: Whickham 1560–1765* (Oxford, 1991), 30.

177. D.H. Heslop, G. McCombie and C. Thomson, ' "Bessie Surtees house": Two merchant houses in Sandhill, Newcastle upon Tyne', *Archaeologia Aeliana*, fifth series, 22 (1994), 1–27.

178. Patten, *English Towns*, 225–27.

179. ibid., 226.

180. Charles Phythian-Adams, *Societies, Cultures and Kinship, 1580–1850: Cultural provinces and English local history* (Leicester, 1996), 9–23.

181. McClendon and Ward, 'Urban economies', 432–33.

182. David Palliser, *Tudor York* (Oxford, 1979), 1–6.

183. Mark Brayshay, 'Royal post-horse routes in England and Wales: The evolution of the network in the later-sixteenth and early-seventeenth centuries', *Journal of Historical Geography* 17 (1991), 373–89.

184. Withington, 'Urbanisation', 183.

185. Hen. VIII, c. 17; A. Luders et al. (eds), *Statutes of the Realm*, 11 vols (1810), III, 134–35.

186. Susan Brigden, *London and the Reformation* (Oxford, 1989), 24–25.

187. John Schofield, 'The topography and buildings of London, ca. 1600', in Orlin (ed.), *Material London*, 303.

188. ibid., 300.

189. Eichholz, 'A Greek traveller', 79.

190. *A Relation*, 42.

191. E.A. Wrigley, 'Urban growth and agricultural change: England and the continent in the early modern period', *Journal of Interdisciplinary History* 15 (1985), 683–728.

192. Ian Mortimer, 'Tudor chronicler or sixteenth-century diarist? Henry Machyn and the nature of his manuscript', *SCJ* 33 (2002), 981–98.

193. John Stow, *A Survey of London*, ed. Charles L. Kingsford, 2 vols (Oxford, 1908), I, 1.

194. *Here begynneth the prologue or prohemye of the book callid Caton* (1484), STC 4853, Sig. ii[v]. This work was originally written by an unknown author called Dionysius Cato, but medieval tradition had long ascribed it to Marcus Porcius Cato. Caxton had earlier printed at least three editions of a verse translation of the work made by Benedict Burgh, canon of St Stephen's Westminster; this was his translation of a French prose version.

195. Thomas Wyatt, 'Tagus Farewell', in *Sir Thomas Wyatt: The complete poems*, 98.

196. Henry Howard, earl of Surrey, *Poems*, ed. Emrys Jones (Oxford, 1964), 30.

197. Thomas Nash, *Christs Teares Over Jerusalem* (1593), STC 18366, dedication to Lady Elizabeth Carey, Sig. *2[v].

198. ibid., Sig. Z2[r]. See also Per Sivefors, 'Prayer and authorship in Thomas Nashe's *Christs Teares Over Jerusalem*', *English: Journal of the English Association* 65 (2016), 267–79.

199. Schofield, 'Topography and buildings', 305.

200. Quoted in John Guy, *Gresham's Law: The life and world of Queen Elizabeth I's banker* (London, 2019), 142.

201. Smith, *A Discourse of the Commonweal*, 64.

202. Harrison, *Description of England*, 145–46.

203. Laura Gowing, ' "The freedom of the streets": Women and social space, 1560–1640', in Paul Griffiths and Mark Jenner (eds), *Londinopolis: Essays in the cultural and social history of early modern London, c.1500–c.1750* (Manchester, 2000), 133.

204. Keith Wrightson, *English Society, 1580–1680* (London, 1982), 28–29.

205. Gowing, ' "The freedom of the streets" ', 136.

206. Lucy Wooding, *Henry VIII* (second edition, Abingdon, 2015), 206.

207. William Birch, 'A Warnyng to Englan[d], let London begin: To repent their iniquite, and flie from their sin' (1565?), EBBA 32088.

208. Stow, *Survey of London*, II, 199.

209. Stow, *Survey of London*, I, 85.

210. Ian Archer, 'The nostalgia of John Stow', in David L. Smith, Richard Strier and David Bevington (eds), *The Theatrical City: Culture, theatre and politics in London, 1576–*

1649 (Cambridge, 1995), 17–34; Patrick Collinson, 'John Stow and nostalgic antiquarianism', in Julia F. Merritt (ed.), *Imagining Early Modern London: Perceptions and portrayals of the city from Stow to Strype, 1598–1720* (Cambridge, 2001), 27–51.

211. Stow, *Survey of London*, II, 72, 74–75.
212. Archer. 'The nostalgia of John Stow', 32–33.
213. Griffiths, *Lost Londons*, 3–4.
214. William Shakespeare, *The Tempest*, Act I, Scene 2, ll.405 and 170; Act II, Scene 1, l.113. See also Alexander Falconer, *Shakespeare and the Sea* (London, 1964); Sebastian I. Sobecki, *The Sea and Medieval English Literature* (Cambridge, 2008), 161–65.
215. Dan Brayton, 'Shakespeare and the Global Ocean', in Lynne Bruckner and Dan Brayton (eds), *Ecocritical Shakespeare* (Farnham, 2011), 174, 177–78.
216. *The miserable estate of the citie of Paris* (1590), STC 19197, Sig. A4ʳ.
217. Robert N. Swanson, *Catholic England: Faith, religion and observance before the Reformation* (Manchester, 1993), 158–59.
218. Walsham, *Reformation of the Landscape*, 56.
219. ibid., 59; Orme, 'Church and chapel', 87.
220. Eichholz, 'A Greek traveller', 76, 79.
221. David Daniell, *William Tyndale: A biography* (New Haven, CT, and London, 1994), 198; John N. King, ' "The light of printing": William Tyndale, John Foxe, John Day, and early modern print culture', *RQ* 54 (2001), 60.
222. Falconer, *Shakespeare and the Sea*.
223. John H. Parry, *The Discovery of the Sea* (New York, 1974); Peter Whitfield, *New Found Lands: Maps in the history of exploration* (London, 1998); Alfred Crosby, *Ecological Imperialism: The biological expansion of Europe, 900–1900* (second edition, Cambridge, 2015), 107–31.
224. Stephen Alford, *London's Triumph: Merchant adventurers and the Tudor city* (London, 2017), 218–19.
225. *The Travels of John Sanderson in the Levant, 1584–1602*, ed. W. Foster (London, 1931), xv–xvi, 3, 4, 8.
226. Carew, *The Survey of Cornwall*, fo. 3ʳ.
227. W.H. Clennell, 'Thomas Bodley', *ODNB*.
228. Eichholz, 'A Greek traveller', 80.
229. *L&P*, IV, Jan. 1530.
230. *By the Kynge and the Queene* (1558), STC 7883, single sheet.
231. *TRP*, II, 81–82.
232. Gordon Connell-Smith, *Forerunners of Drake* (Plymouth, 1954), 136, 139–40.
233. *TRP*, II, 228.
234. ibid., II, 232.
235. ibid., II, 235.
236. ibid., II, 244.
237. Pierre Garcie-Ferrande (trans.), *The rutter of the see* (1536), Sig. aiiᵛ–aiiiʳ.
238. E.G.R. Taylor, 'A sixteenth-century MS navigating manual in the Society's library', *The Geographical Journal* 78 (1931), 346–52.
239. Martin Cortes, trans. Richard Eden, *The arte of navigation* (1561), STC 5798.
240. Susanna De Schepper, ' "For the common good and for the national interest": Paratexts in English translations of navigational works', in Sara K. Barker and Brenda M. Hosington (eds), *Renaissance Cultural Crossroads: Translation, print and culture in Britain, 1473–1640* (Leiden, 2017), 187–88.
241. William Bourne, *A Regiment for the Sea* (1577), Sig. Aiiiʳ⁻ᵛ.
242. Richard Hakluyt, *Principall Navigations* (1589), STC 12625, frontispiece.
243. Sobecki, *The Sea and Medieval English Literature*, 145–60; Hakluyt, *Principall Navigations*, I, 187–208.
244. Pierre Nora, 'Between memory and history: Les Lieux de Mémoire', *Representations* 26 (1989), 7–24. See also Walsham, *Reformation of the Landscape*; Whyte, *Inhabiting the*

Landscape; Simon Schama, *Landscape and Memory* (New York, 1995); Raphael Samuel, *Theatres of Memory*, vol. 1: *Past and Present in Contemporary Culture* (London, 1994).

245. *Landscapes: Selected Writings of J.B. Jackson*, ed. E.H. Zube (Amherst, MA, 1970); D.W. Meinig (ed.), *The Interpretation of Ordinary Landscapes: Geographical essays* (Oxford, 1979); Michel de Certeau, *The Practice of Everyday Life*, trans. Steven Rendall (Berkeley, CA, 1980).

246. Trigge, *To the Kings most excellent Maiestie*, Sig. A4^r.

247. Richard Hoyle, '*Cromwell v. Taverner*: Landlords, copyholders and the struggle to control memory in mid-sixteenth-century Norfolk', in Hoyle (ed.), *Custom, Improvement and the Landscape in Early Modern Britain* (Farnham, 2011), 39–63.

248. Wood, *The Memory of the People*, 156–87.

249. Jayne E. Archer, Elizabeth Goldring and Sarah Knight (eds), *The Progresses, Pageants and Entertainments of Queen Elizabeth I* (Oxford, 2007).

2 'His Wit Always Quick and Ready': The reign of Henry VII

1. Geoffrey Elton, 'Henry VII: Rapacity and remorse', *HJ* 1 (1958), 21–39, and 'Henry VII: A restatement', *HJ* 4 (1961), 1–29: reprinted in Elton, *Studies in Tudor and Stuart Politics and Government*, 4 vols (Cambridge, 1974–92), I, 45–65, 66–99; see also Steven Gunn, 'Henry VII in context: Problems and possibilities', *History* 92 (2007), 301–17.

2. G.V. Scammell and H L. Rogers, 'An elegy on Henry VII', *Review of English Studies* 8 (1957), 170.

3. Thomas Elyot, *The Book of the Governor*, ed. H.H.S. Croft (London, 1883), 256–59.

4. Vergil, *Anglica Historia*, 145–47.

5. *CSP Ven.*, I, 942; *CSP Sp.*, I, 238.

6. Steven Gunn, 'The accession of Henry VIII', *HR* 64 (1991), 287.

7. J.E.B. Mayor (ed.), *The English Works of John Fisher*, EETS extra series, 27 (1876), 269.

8. Francis Bacon, *The History of the Reign of King Henry VII*, ed. Brian Thompson (London, 2007), 161–64; Jonathan L. Marwil, *The Trials of Counsel: Francis Bacon in 1621* (Detroit, MI, 1976).

9. Christine Carpenter, 'Henry VII and the English polity', in Benjamin Thompson (ed.), *The Reign of Henry VII* (Stamford, 1995), 26.

10. Bertram P. Wolffe, *The Royal Demesne in English History: The Crown Estate in the governance of the realm from the Conquest to 1509* (London, 1971), 178.

11. C.J. Harrison (ed.), 'The petition of Edmund Dudley', *EHR* 87 (1972), 86.

12. Hall, *Chronicle*, 507.

13. David Starkey, *The Reign of Henry VIII: Personalities and politics* (London, 1985), 24; David Rundle, 'A new Golden Age? More, Skelton and the accession verses of 1509', *RS* 9 (1995), 58–76.

14. Steven Gunn, *Henry VII's New Men and the Making of Tudor England* (Oxford, 2016), 34. More was criticized by Germanus Brixius for besmirching Henry VII's reputation in order to advance Henry VIII's. See 'The *Antimorus* of Germanus Brixius of Auxerre', in *The Yale Edition of the Complete Works of St Thomas More*, vol. 3, part 2: *Latin Poems* (New Haven, CT, and London, 1984), 492–95.

15. Quoted and translated in Léon-Ernest Halkin, *Erasmus: A critical biography* (Oxford, 1993), 37.

16. Richard Rex and David Butterfield, 'A newly discovered poem by Erasmus', *Humanistica Lovaniensia* 65 (2016), 170–78.

17. Sean Cunningham, *Henry VII* (London, 2007), 275.

18. *TRP*, I, 81.

19. John Fisher, *This sermon folowynge was compyled [and] sayd in the cathedrall chyrche of saynt Poule . . . the body beyinge present of the moost famouse prynce kynge Henry the vij* (1509), STC 10900, Sig. Aij^v.

20. ibid., Aiij^v.
21. Gunn, 'Henry VII in context', 301–17; Paul Cavill, *The English Parliaments of Henry VII 1485–1504* (Oxford, 2009), 5–7.
22. Stanley B. Chrimes, *Henry VII* (London, 1972), 73.
23. Cunningham, *Henry VII*, 256.
24. ibid., 257–62, 263–73; David Loades, *The Tudor Navy: An administrative, political and military history* (Aldershot, 1992).
25. Steven Gunn, *The English People at War in the Age of Henry VIII* (Oxford, 2018), 118.
26. Cunningham, *Henry VII*, 255; Steven Gunn, 'Chivalry and politics', in Sydney Anglo (ed.), *Chivalry and the Renaissance* (Woodbridge, 1990), 116–18.
27. Vergil, *Anglica Historia*, xxvi, section 4.
28. Walter Raleigh, *History of the World*, ed. Constantinos A. Patrides (London, 1971), 55–56.
29. Gary Waller, *The Virgin Mary in Late Medieval and Early Modern English Literature and Popular Culture* (Cambridge, 2011); Eva De Visscher, 'Marian devotion in the Latin west in the later middle ages', in Sarah Jane Boss (ed.), *Mary: The complete resource* (Oxford, 2007), 177–201; Lilla Grindlay, *Queen of Heaven: The assumption and coronation of the Virgin in early modern English writing* (Notre Dame, IN, 2018).
30. Fabyan, *Chronicles*, 673.
31. *Here begynneth a litill boke necessarye . . . agenst the pestilence* (1485), STC 4590, unpaginated.
32. *Nova Statuta* (1485), STC 9264; see Joseph H. Beale, 'The early English statutes', *Harvard Law Review* 35 (1922), 529–30.
33. *Thystorye and lyf of the noble and crysten prynce Charles the grete* (1485), STC 5013, Sig. avii^v.
34. *The lyf of the holy blessid vyrgyn saynt Wenefryde* (1485), STC 25853, Sig. aiij^r.
35. Hall, *Chronicle*, 421.
36. Cecil H. Clough, 'William Selling', *ODNB*.
37. TNA, will of William Pauncefoot, PROB – 11-7-208.
38. *Additional Material for the History of the Grey Friars, London*, ed. C.L. Kingsford (Manchester, 1922), 110.
39. Michael Hicks, 'The second anonymous continuation of the Crowland Abbey Chronicle 1459–86 revisited', *EHR* 122 (2007), 349–70.
40. *Ingulph's Chronicle of the Abbey of Croyland*, ed. Henry T. Riley (London, 1865), 509, 494–95.
41. BL Add. MS 7099 fo. 75^r.
42. BL Add. MS 21480 fo. 14^r.
43. ibid., fos. 2^r, 3^r, 4^r.
44. Albert F. Pollard, *The Reign of Henry VII from Contemporary Sources*, 3 vols (New York and London, 1913), I, 5.
45. C.S.L. Davies, 'Information, disinformation and political knowledge under Henry VII and early Henry VIII', *HR* 85 (2012), 228; Ralph Alan Griffiths, 'Owen Tudor [Owain *ap* Maredudd ap Tudor]', *ODNB*; Griffiths, 'Henry Tudor: The training of a king', *HLQ* 49 (1986), 199–205.
46. *Chronicle of the Abbey of Croyland*, 501.
47. Richard II, Henry VI, Edward IV and Edward V were all deposed, Henry VI twice; Richard II, Henry VI and Edward V were murdered.
48. William Shakespeare, *Richard II*, Act III, Scene 3, ll.96, 98–102.
49. 'Depuis l'age de cinq ans il avoit esté gardé et caché comme fugitif en prison'; Pollard, *Reign of Henry VII*, I, 2.
50. Michael K. Jones and Malcolm G. Underwood, *The King's Mother: Lady Margaret Beaufort, countess of Richmond and Derby* (Cambridge, 1992), 40–41.
51. Chrimes, *Henry VII*, 15.

52. Griffiths, 'Henry Tudor', 206.
53. Cunningham, *Henry VII*, 17.
54. Ralph Alan Griffiths and Roger S. Thomas, *The Making of the Tudor Dynasty* (Gloucester, 1985), 120–21, 124–26.
55. Griffiths, 'Henry Tudor', 210.
56. This prophecy had been enshrined in Geoffrey of Monmouth's *Historia Regum Britanniae*. For a more sceptical evaluation of the significance of the dragon, see Sydney Anglo, 'The *British History* in early Tudor propaganda', *Bulletin of the John Rylands Library* 44 (1961), 35–40.
57. Anglo, 'The *British History*', 20–24. Those who hoped for a more overt Welsh victory were, however, disappointed: see Philip Schwyzer, *Literature, Nationalism and Memory in Early Modern England and Wales* (Cambridge, 2004), 16–17, 30.
58. Robin Evans, 'The battle of Bosworth Field: A Welsh victory?', *HR* 44 (2002), 5–7; Beverley Smith, 'Crown and community in the principality of North Wales in the reign of Henry Tudor', *Welsh History Review* 3 (1966), 157–59.
59. Cited in Anglo, 'The *British History*', 17.
60. Vergil, *Anglica Historia*, 5; Griffiths, 'Henry Tudor', 213.
61. Raleigh, *History of the World*, 55.
62. Vergil, *Anglica Historia*, 3–5.
63. John C. Meagher, 'The first progress of Henry VII', *Renaissance Drama* 1 (1968), 46.
64. Michael Hicks, *Richard III: The man behind the myth* (London, 1991), 129.
65. Jones and Underwood, *The King's Mother*, 59–65.
66. John Fisher, *A mornynge remembraunce*, in *English Works*, 308.
67. Thomas Penn, *Winter King: The dawn of Tudor England* (London, 2011), 98.
68. Jones and Underwood, *The King's Mother*, 86.
69. ibid., 98–99.
70. ibid., 104.
71. ibid., 97, 105, 139, 143, 145; Margaret M. Condon, 'Reginald Bray', *ODNB*.
72. Cunningham, *Henry VII*, 262.
73. Nicholas Orme, 'Hugh Oldham', *ODNB*.
74. Rosemary Horrox, 'Elizabeth of York', *ODNB*.
75. Pollard, *Reign of Henry VII*, I, 47 (Henry to the earl of Ormonde).
76. ibid., I, 58.
77. Cunningham, *Henry VII*, 255–56.
78. Vergil, *Anglica Historia*, 27.
79. The betrothal of Mary to Charles of Ghent would be broken, and she later married Louis XII of France.
80. Gunn, *Henry VII's New Men*, 3, 10–13 and *passim*.
81. ibid., 26–27, 30–31; Margaret M. Condon, 'From caitiff and villain to *Pater Patriae*: Reginald Bray and the profits of office', in Michael A. Hicks (ed.), *Profit, Piety and the Professions in Late Medieval England* (Gloucester, 1990), 139, 141.
82. Gunn, *Henry VII's New Men*, 48.
83. ibid., 39–46, 50–51, 55–56, 58–59, 73–74, 131–33.
84. Cited in ibid., 103.
85. Bacon, *History*, 3.
86. Illustrated in Ian Arthurson, *The Perkin Warbeck Conspiracy, 1491–1499* (Stroud, 1994), 150.
87. *Chronicle of the Abbey of Croyland*, 512.
88. Cavill, *English Parliaments*, xiv, 245.
89. Cunningham, *Henry VII*, 51.
90. Peter Kaufman, 'Henry VII and sanctuary', *Church History* 53 (1984), 469.
91. C.H. Williams, 'The rebellion of Humphrey Stafford in 1486', *EHR* 43 (1928), 184.

92. Cunningham, *Henry VII*, 57.
93. Bernard André, *The Life of Henry VII*, ed. Daniel Hobbins (New York, 2011), 46.
94. Cavill, *English Parliaments*, 15.
95. Chrimes, *Henry VII*, 80; Michael A. Hicks, 'The Yorkshire rebellion of 1489 reconsidered', *Northern History* 22 (1986), 39–62.
96. André, *Life of Henry VII*, 45, 60.
97. Pollard, *Reign of Henry VII*, III, 43.
98. Michael J. Bennett, 'Henry VII and the northern rising of 1489', *EHR* 105 (1990), 34–59.
99. David Grummitt, 'Household, politics and political morality in the reign of Henry VII', *HR* 82 (2009), 399–400.
100. Michael J. Bennett, 'Sir William Stanley', *ODNB*; see also Barry Coward, *The Stanleys, Lords Stanley and Earls of Derby, 1385–1672: The origins, wealth and power of a landowning family* (Manchester, 1983), 12–15.
101. David Starkey, 'Intimacy and innovation: The rise of the Privy Chamber, 1485–1547', in David Starkey (ed.), *The English Court from the Wars of the Roses to the Civil War* (London, 1987), 72–76.
102. André, *Life of Henry VII*, 67–69.
103. Pollard, *Reign of Henry VII*, III, 43.
104. Nicholas H. Nicolas (ed.), *Privy Purse Expenses of Elizabeth of York: Wardrobe accounts of Edward IV* (London, 1830), xcvii.
105. Kevin Sharpe, *Selling the Tudor Monarchy: Authority and image in sixteenth-century England* (New Haven, CT, 2009), 61–62.
106. Vergil, *Anglica Historia*, 145–47.
107. Emma Cavell, 'Henry VII, the north of England, the first provincial progress of 1486', *Northern History* 39 (2002), 190.
108. D. Thomson, 'Henry VII and the uses of Italy: The Savoy hospital and Henry VII's posterity', in Thompson (ed.), *The Reign of Henry VII*, 104–16.
109. Richard Marks, 'An age of consumption: Art for England c.1400–1547', in Richard Marks and Paul Williamson (eds), *Gothic: Art for England 1400–1547* (London, 2003), 18.
110. Quoted in Christopher Wilson, 'The designer of Henry VII's chapel, Westminster Abbey', in Thompson (ed.), *The Reign of Henry VII*, 133.
111. N. Beckett, 'Henry VII and Sheen Charterhouse', in Thompson (ed.), *The Reign of Henry VII*, 117–32.
112. Sir John Fortescue, *On the Laws and Governance of England*, ed. Shelley Lockwood (Cambridge, 1997), xv–xliii. On Fortescue, see P.E. Gill, 'Politics and propaganda in 15th century England: The polemical writings of Sir John Fortescue', *Speculum* 46 (1971), 333–47; J.H. Burns, 'Fortescue and the political theory of *dominium*', *HJ* 28 (1985), 777–97.
113. Fortescue, *On the Laws and Governance of England*, 98.
114. Philip Grierson, 'The origins of the English sovereign and the symbolism of the closed crown', *British Numismatic Journal* 33 (1965), 118–34.
115. W.C. Richardson, *Tudor Chamber Administration, 1485–1547* (Baton Rouge, LA, 1952); Geoffrey Elton, *The Tudor Revolution in Government* (Cambridge, 1953), 20–30; Bertram P. Wolffe, 'Henry VII's land revenues and chamber finance', *EHR* 79 (1964), 225–54; Penry Williams, *The Tudor Regime* (Oxford, 1979), 43–52; David Starkey, 'Court and government', in Christopher Coleman and David Starkey (eds), *Revolution Reassessed: Revisions in the history of Tudor government and administration* (Oxford, 1986); J.D. Alsop, 'The structure of early Tudor finance, c.1509–1558', in Coleman and Starkey (eds), *Revolution Reassessed*; Anthony Goodman, *The New Monarchy: England 1471–1536* (Oxford, 1988), 20–23; Steven Gunn, *Early Tudor Government, 1485–1558* (Basingstoke, 1995), 144–52.
116. John Currin, '"Pro Expensis Ambassatorum": Diplomacy and financial administration in the reign of Henry VII', *EHR* 108 (1993), 602–03.

117. Gunn, *Early Tudor Government*, 122–24.
118. Cunningham, *Henry VII*, 139–40.
119. Cunningham, *Henry VII*, 141. Note that later subsidies did not ask for a fixed amount, but were assessed on the basis of wealth. See Roger S. Schofield, 'Taxation and the political limits of the Tudor state', in C. Cross, D.M. Loades and J.J. Scarisbrick (eds), *Law and Government under the Tudors: Essays presented to Sir Geoffrey Elton* (Cambridge, 1988), 227–55.
120. Cunningham, *Henry VII*, 138.
121. Steven Gunn, 'The courtiers of Henry VII', *EHR* 108 (1993), 46–47.
122. Carpenter, 'Henry VII and the English polity', 11–30.
123. David Rundle, 'Was there a Renaissance style of politics in fifteenth-century England?', in George Bernard and Steven Gunn (eds), *Authority and Consent in Tudor England* (Aldershot, 2002), 15–32.
124. *CSP Sp.*, I, 177–78.
125. See the contrasting views of Carpenter and John Watts, '"A Newe Ffundacion of is Crowne": Monarchy in the age of Henry VII', in Thompson (ed.), *The Reign of Henry VII*, 31–53.
126. John R. Lander, 'Bonds, coercion and fear: Henry VII and the peerage', in Lander (ed.), *Crown and Nobility, 1450–1509* (London, 1976), 267–300.
127. Gunn, *Early Tudor Government*, 56.
128. ibid., 123.
129. Michael Hicks, 'Attainder, resumption and coercion 1461–1529', *Parliamentary History* 3 (1984), 15–31.
130. Cunningham, *Henry VII*, 136.
131. Grummitt, 'Household, politics and political morality', 401.
132. Margaret Condon, 'Ruling elites in the reign of Henry VII', in Charles Ross (ed.), *Patronage, Pedigree and Power in Later Medieval England* (Gloucester, 1979), 109.
133. Steven Gunn, 'Henry Bourchier, second earl of Essex', *ODNB*; Gunn, 'Henry Bourchier, earl of Essex (1472–1540)', in George Bernard (ed.), *The Tudor Nobility* (Manchester, 1992), 134–79.
134. Steven Gunn, 'John de Vere, thirteenth earl of Oxford', *ODNB*.
135. Fortescue, *On the Laws and Governance of England*, 114–17.
136. Watts, 'A Newe Ffundacion', 31–53.
137. Cunningham, *Henry VII*, 146.
138. Cavill, *English Parliaments*, 246.
139. ibid., 16.
140. Fortescue, *On the Laws and Governance of England*, 6–7.
141. C.A.J. Armstrong, 'An Italian astrologer at the court of Henry VII', in Ernest F. Jacob (ed.), *Italian Renaissance Studies* (London, 1960), 433–54; Hilary M. Carey, 'Henry VII's book of astrology and the Tudor renaissance', *RQ* 65 (2012), 666–67.
142. Cavell, 'Henry VII, the north of England and the first provincial progress', 189.
143. Sydney Anglo, *Images of Tudor Kingship* (London, 1992), 20.
144. Pollard, *Reign of Henry VII*, I, 7.
145. ibid., I, 8.
146. ibid., I, 4.
147. Aysha Pollnitz, *Princely Education in Early Modern Britain* (Cambridge, 2015), 29–65.
148. Watts, 'A Newe Ffundacion', 31–53.
149. *The Receyt of the Ladie Kateryne*, ed. Gordon Kipling, EETS 296 (1990).
150. Richard B. Wernham, *Before the Armada: The emergence of the English nation, 1485–1588* (New York, 1966); Chrimes, *Henry VII*, chapter 15; Paul S. Crowson, *Tudor Foreign Policy* (London, 1973), 47–66; Susan Doran, *England and Europe, 1485–1603* (London, 1986), chapter 5; John M. Currin, 'England's international relations 1485–1509: Continuities amidst change', in Susan Doran and Glenn Richardson (eds), *Tudor England and Its Neighbours* (Basingstoke, 2005), 14–43.

151. Currin, 'England's international relations', 19–22.
152. Glenn Richardson and Susan Doran, 'Introduction', in Doran and Richardson (eds), *Tudor England and Its Neighbours*, 3.
153. Garrett Mattingley, *Renaissance Diplomacy* (Oxford and New York, 1955), 55–63, 121–32, 162–66.
154. Cited in John M. Currin, 'Henry VII and the Treaty of Redon (1489): Plantagenet ambitions and early Tudor foreign policy', *History* 81 (1996), 346.
155. John Currin, 'To play at peace: Henry VII, war against France, and the Chieregato-Flores mediation of 1490', *Albion* 31 (1999), 209–12.
156. Currin, 'Henry VII and the Treaty of Redon', 347–49.
157. Ian Arthurson, 'The king's voyage into Scotland: The war that never was', in Daniel Williams (ed.), *England in the Fifteenth Century: Proceedings of the 1986 Harlaxton Symposium* (London, 1987), 1–22.
158. Steven Gunn, David Grummitt and Hans Cools, *War, State and Society in England and the Netherlands, 1477–1559* (Oxford, 2007), 12–13.
159. Cavill, *English Parliaments*, 24.
160. Cunningham, *Henry VII*, 71–72.
161. ibid., 259–60.
162. Gunn, Grummitt and Cool, *War, State and Society*, 86.
163. Cunningham, *Henry VII*, 261.
164. Currin, 'England's international relations', 27–29.
165. Cunningham, *Henry VII*, 69.
166. Pollard, *Reign of Henry VII*, III, 2–4.
167. Currin, 'To play at peace', 211.
168. Cunningham, *Henry VII*, 253.
169. 'Les Douze Triomphes de Henry VII', in *Memorials of King Henry the Seventh*, ed. James Gairdner (London, 1858), 133, 152.
170. Leland, *De rebus Brittanicis*, V, 373–74.
171. Vergil, *Anglica Historia*, 133.
172. Cunningham, *Henry VII*, 110, 114–15.
173. Gunn, *Henry VII's New Men*, 86.

3 'With My Own Eyes to See': Early Tudor religion

1. Sean Cunningham, *Henry VII* (London, 2007), 117.
2. *The Will of King Henry VII*, ed. Thomas Astle (London, 1775), 2.
3. John Bossy, *Christianity in the West, 1400–1700* (Oxford, 1985); John Bossy, *Peace in the Post-Reformation* (Cambridge, 1998), 85–112; Lucy Wooding, 'Charity, community and Reformation propaganda', *Reformation* 11 (2006), 131–69.
4. John Mozley, *John Foxe and his Book* (London, 1940); David Loades (ed.), *John Foxe: An historical perspective* (Aldershot, 1999); D. Loades (ed.), *John Foxe and the English Reformation* (Aldershot, 1997); Christopher Highley and John N. King (eds), *John Foxe and his World* (Aldershot, 2002); David Loades (ed.), *John Foxe at Home and Abroad* (Aldershot, 2004); Elizabeth Evenden and Thomas S. Freeman, *Religion and the Book in Early Modern England: The making of John Foxe's 'Book of Martyrs'* (Cambridge, 2011).
5. Christopher Harper-Bill, 'Dean Colet's convocation sermon and the pre-Reformation Church in England', *History* 73 (1988), 191–210.
6. G.W. Bernard, *The Late Medieval English Church: Vitality and vulnerability before the break with Rome* (New Haven, CT, and London, 2012).
7. A.G. Dickens, *The English Reformation* (second edition, London, 1989); J.J. Scarisbrick, *The Reformation and the English People* (Oxford, 1984); Eamon Duffy, *The Stripping of the Altars: Traditional religion in England, 1400–1580* (New Haven, CT, and London, 1992), part 1; Christopher Haigh, *English Reformations: Religion, politics and society*

under the Tudors (Oxford, 1993); Peter Marshall, *Heretics and Believers: A history of the English Reformation* (New Haven, CT, and London, 2017).

8. Robert N. Swanson, *Church and Society in Late Medieval England* (Oxford, 1989), vii.

9. Duffy, *The Stripping of the Altars*; Scarisbrick, *The Reformation and the English People*; Katherine French, *The Good Women of the Parish: Gender and religion after the Black Death* (Philadelphia, PA, 2008); Andrew Brown, *Popular Piety in Late Medieval England: The Diocese of Salisbury, 1250–1550* (Oxford, 1995); Clive Burgess and Eamon Duffy (eds), *The Parish in Late Medieval England: Proceedings of the 2002 Harlaxton Symposium* (Donington, 2006); Haigh, *English Reformations*; Ronald Hutton, *The Rise and Fall of Merry England: The ritual year, 1400–1700* (Oxford, 1996).

10. David Aers, 'Altars of power: Reflections on Eamon Duffy's *The Stripping of the Altars*', *Literature and History* 3 (1994), 100.

11. Brown, *Popular Piety*, 223–49.

12. Shoichi Oguro, Richard Beadle and Michael Sargent (eds), *Nicholas Love at Waseda* (Cambridge, 1997), xiii.

13. Nicholas Love, *Incipit speculum vite Cristi* (1494), STC 3261, Sig. av^v. See also Michelle Karnes, 'Nicholas Love and medieval meditations on Christ', *Speculum* 82 (2007), 380–402; Jessica Hines, 'Passionate language: Models of compassion in Nicholas Love and Margery Kempe', *Journal of Medieval and Early Modern Studies* 49 (2019), 265–94; David Aers, 'The humanity of Christ: Reflections on orthodox late medieval representations', in David Aers and Lynn Staley, *Powers of the Holy: Religion, politics and gender in late medieval English culture* (Pennsylvania, PA, 1996), 15–42.

14. Ellen Ross, *The Grief of God: Images of the suffering Jesus in late medieval England* (Oxford, 1997).

15. Caroline Walker Bynum, 'The blood of Christ in the later middle ages', *Church History* 71 (2002), 685–714.

16. *Dives and Pauper* (1496), STC 19213, Sig. avii^v. See also Elizabeth Harper, ' "A token and a book": Reading images and building consensus in *Dives and Pauper*', *The Yearbook of Langland Studies* 28 (2013), 173–90.

17. *This tretyse is of love* (1493), STC 24234, Sig. Ai^r.

18. Caroline Walker Bynum, *Jesus as Mother: Studies in the spirituality of the high middle ages* (Berkeley, CA, and London, 1982), 132–33; Miri Rubin, *Corpus Christi: The eucharist in late medieval culture* (Cambridge, 1991), 303; Sarah Beckwith, *Christ's Body: Identity, culture and society in late medieval writings* (London, 1993), 58.

19. Lucy Wooding, ' "So sholde lewde men lerne by ymages": Religious imagery and Bible learning', in Robert Armstrong and Tadhg Ó hAnnracháin (eds), *The English Bible in the Early Modern World* (Leiden, 2018), 29–52; Ross, *The Grief of God*, 21.

20. Wooding, ' "So sholde lewde men lerne by ymages" ', 33–41; see also Athene Reiss, *The Sunday Christ: Sabbatarianism in English medieval wall painting* (Oxford, 2000).

21. Julian of Norwich, *Revelations of Divine Love* (Harmondsworth, 1966), 63. These words were written in the early fifteenth century, but manuscript copies achieved some limited circulation in monastic circles during the Tudor age.

22. Love, *Incipit speculum vite Cristi*, Sig. av^r.

23. David Crane, 'English translations of the *Imitatio Christi* in the sixteenth and seventeenth centuries', *RH* 13 (1975), 79–100; Maximilian von Habsburg, *Catholic and Protestant Translations of the* Imitatio Christi, *1425–1650: From late medieval classic to early modern bestseller* (Farnham, 2012).

24. Henry Littlehales (ed.), *Medieval Records of a London City Church* (London, 1905), 131.

25. Mervyn James, 'Ritual, drama and social body in the late medieval English town', *P&P* 98 (1983), 3–29.

26. Matthew Milner, *Senses and the English Reformation* (Farnham, 2011), 142.

27. French, *The Good Women of the Parish*, 88.

28. Milner, *Senses and the English Reformation*, 154–56.
29. Miriam Gill, 'Preaching and image: Sermons and wall paintings in later medieval England', in Carolyn Muessig (ed.), *Preacher, Sermon and Audience in the Middle Ages* (Brill, 2002), 155; Miriam Gill, 'Reading images: Church murals and collaboration between media in medieval England', in Silvia Bigliazzi and Sharon Wood (eds), *Collaboration in the Arts from the Middle Ages to the Present* (Aldershot, 2006), 17.
30. Bynum, 'Blood of Christ', 688–89.
31. Vincent Gillespie, 'Medieval hypertext: Image and text from York Minster', in P.R. Robinson and Rivkah Zim (eds), *Of the Making of Books: Medieval manuscripts, their scribes and readers* (Aldershot, 1997), 206–29; Kate Giles, 'Seeing and believing: Visuality and space in pre-modern England', *World Archaeology* 39 (2007), 107.
32. W.S. Melion, 'Introduction: Meditative images and the psychology of soul', in R.I. Falkenburg, W.S. Melion and T.M. Richardson (eds), *Image and Imagination of the Religious Self in Late Medieval and Early Modern Europe* (Turnhout, 2007), 2; S.C. Karant-Nunn, *The Reformation of Feeling: Shaping the religious emotions in early modern Germany* (Oxford, 2010), 19–20; David Morgan, *The Sacred Gaze: Religious visual culture in theory and practice* (Berkeley, CA, 2005), 96–110.
33. Lucy Wooding, 'Reading the crucifixion in Tudor England', in Sabrina Corbellini, Margriet Hoogvliet and Bart Ramakers (eds), *Discovering the Riches of the Word: Religious reading in late medieval and early modern Europe* (Leiden, 2015), 287–89.
34. *Here begynneth a shorte treatyse of contemplacyon taught by our lorde Jhesu cryste, or taken out of the boke of Margerie kempe of lyn* (1501), STC 14924, Sig. Aii^r.
35. Roger Bowers, *English Church Polyphony: Singers and sources from the 14th to the 17th century* (Aldershot, 1999), sections 4–6; Andrew Wathey, *Music in the Royal and Noble Households in Late Medieval England: Studies of sources and patronage* (New York, 1989).
36. Clive Burgess and Andrew Wathey, 'Mapping the soundscape: Church music in English towns, 1450–1550', *Early Music History* 19 (2000), 1–46.
37. Magnus Williamson, 'Liturgical polyphony in the pre-Reformation English parish church: A provisional list and commentary', *Royal Musical Research Chronicle* 38 (2005), 4.
38. Clive Burgess, 'For the increase of divine service: Chantries in the parish of late medieval Bristol', *JEcclesH* 36 (1985), 54–58.
39. Milner, *Senses and the English Reformation*, 107.
40. Williamson, 'Liturgical polyphony', 10–11.
41. Milner, *Senses and the English Reformation*, 108.
42. Richard Whitford, *The Pomander of prayer* (1528), STC 25421.2, Sig. Ai^v.
43. *Vitas Patrum* (1495), STC 14507, fo. Ci^v.
44. Duffy, *Stripping of the Altars*, 29–30.
45. Michelle Karnes, *Imagination, Meditation and Cognition in the Middle Ages* (Oxford, 2011), Introduction.
46. John Mirk, *Festial* (1508), STC 17971, Sig. Av^v. See also Susan Powell, 'John Mirk's *Festial* and the pastoral programme', *Leeds Studies in English* 22 (1991), 85–102.
47. Mirk, *Festial*, Sig. Av^v.
48. Elina Gertsman, *The Dance of Death in the Middle Ages: Image, text, performance* (Turnhout, 2010); Amy Appleford, *Learning to Die in London, 1380–1540* (Pennsylvania, PA, 2015). On pre-Reformation welfare generally see Christopher Dyer, 'Poverty and its relief in late medieval England', *P&P* 216 (2012), 41–78.
49. William K. Jordan, *Philanthropy in England, 1480–1660* (London, 1959); William K. Jordan, *The Charities of London, 1480–1660: The aspirations and the achievements of the urban society* (London, 1960); William K. Jordan, *The Charities of Rural England, 1480–1660: The aspirations and the achievements of the rural society* (London, 1961).
50. Cited in Barbara Harvey, *Living and Dying in Westminster, 1100–1540* (Oxford, 1993), 7.
51. ibid., 12–13.

52. ibid., 28–29.

53. Eamon Duffy, *The Voices of Morebath: Reformation and rebellion in an English village* (New Haven, CT, and London, 2001), 11.

54. Mary Erler, *Reading and Writing during the Dissolution: Monks, friars and nuns, 1530–1558* (Cambridge, 2013), Appendix 2, 148.

55. Peregrine Horden, 'Small beer? The parish and the poor and sick in later medieval England', in Burgess and Duffy (eds), *The Parish in Late Medieval England*, 342.

56. Lucy Wooding, 'From foundation to reformation, 1521–1558', in Jeremy Gregory (ed.), *Manchester Cathedral: A history of the collegiate church and cathedral, 1421 to the present* (Manchester, 2021), 53–58.

57. 'Colleges: Whittington's College', in William Page (ed.), *A History of the County of London* (London, 1909), I, 578–80; Christopher Harper-Bill (ed.), *The Register of John Morton, Archbishop of Canterbury* (Woodbridge, 1987), 18; Joseph Bergin, 'Richard Smith', *ODNB*; James Willoughby, 'The provision of books in the English secular college', in Clive Burgess and Martin Heale (eds), *The Late Medieval English College and Its Context* (Woodbridge, 2008), 155, 160–61; Joan Greatrex, 'On ministering to "certayne devoute and religiouse women": Bishop Fox and the Benedictine nuns of Winchester Diocese on the eve of the Dissolution', *SCH* 27 (1990), 223–35; Caroline Barron, 'The expansion of education in fifteenth-century London', in John Blair and Brian Golding (eds), *The Cloister and the World: Essays in medieval history in honour of Barbara Harvey* (Oxford, 1996), 236–37, 238–39; Nicholas Orme, 'The Guild of Kalendars, Bristol', *Transactions of the Bristol and Gloucestershire Archaeological Society* 96 (1978), 40–43; Lotte Hellinga, 'Prologue: The first years of the Tudor monarchy and the printing press', in John N. King (ed.), *Tudor Books and Readers* (Cambridge, 2010), 20–21; Michael K. Jones and Malcolm G. Underwood, *The King's Mother: Lady Margaret Beaufort, countess of Richmond and Derby* (Cambridge, 1992), 180–87.

58. Cited in Robert N. Swanson (ed.), *Catholic England: Faith, religion and observance before the Reformation* (Manchester, 1993), 262.

59. Peter Marshall, *The Catholic Priesthood and the English Reformation* (Oxford, 1994), 213–16.

60. Lucy Wooding, 'From Tudor humanism to Reformation preaching', in Hugh Adlington, Peter MacCullough and Emma Rhatigan (eds), *The Oxford Handbook of the Early Modern Sermon* (Oxford, 2011), 397–98.

61. Marshall, *The Catholic Priesthood*, 215.

62. Morgan Ring, 'Translating the *Legenda aurea* in early modern England', *SCH* 53 (2017), 118–31.

63. Bynum, *Jesus as Mother*, 7–8.

64. Julian of Norwich, *Revelations of Divine Love*, chapter 58; Sandra Bhattacharji, 'Julian of Norwich', in Peter Brown (ed.), *A Companion to Medieval English Literature and Culture c.1350–c.1500* (Oxford, 2009), 530–31.

65. Thomas Gascoigne, *Here after folowith the boke callyd the myrroure of Oure Lady very necessary for all relygyous persones* (1530), STC 17542, Sig. Aiv^v.

66. English versions do not survive, but we know that they existed. See Gail M. Gibson, *The Theater of Devotion: East Anglian drama and society in the late middle ages* (Chicago, IL, and London, 1989), 215n.

67. Duffy, *Stripping of the Altars*, 258. Richard Hill's commonplace book is kept at Balliol College Oxford, MS 354. See also Sarah Salih, *Versions of Virginity in Late Medieval England* (Woodbridge, 2001).

68. *A shorte treatyse . . . taken out of the boke of Margerie kempe*, Sig. Aiii^v–Aiv^r.

69. Love, *Vita Christi*, Sig. Yiiii^r.

70. Wolfgang Riehle, *The Middle English Mystics* (London, 1981), 11.

71. David Knowles, *The Religious Orders in England* (Cambridge, 1959), II, 222–23; see discussion in Gibson, *The Theater of Devotion*, 3–4.

72. French, *The Good Women of the Parish*, 103, 112–14.

73. Duffy, *The Voices of Morebath*, 25–26.
74. French, *The Good Women of the Parish*, 88.
75. ibid., 22–23, 24–26, 38–39, 43–44.
76. Katherine French, 'Women churchwardens in late medieval England', in Burgess and Duffy (eds), *The Parish in Late Medieval England*, 303.
77. Eamon Duffy, *Marking the Hours: English people and their prayers, 1240–1570* (New Haven, CT, 2006); Helen C. White, *The Tudor Books of Private Devotion* (Madison, WI, 1951); Charles C. Butterworth, *The English Primers (1529–1545): Their publication and connection with the English Bible and the Reformation in England* (Philadelphia, PA, 1953).
78. Jennifer N. Brown, *Three Women of Liège: A critical edition of and commentary on the middle English lives of Elizabeth of Spalbeek, Christina Mirabilis, and Marie d'Oignies* (Turnhout, 2008).
79. Sarah Macmillan, 'Phenomenal pain: Embodying the Passion in the *Life of Elizabeth of Spalbeek*', *Postmedieval* 8 (2017), 102–19.
80. Carol M. Meale, 'The miracles of Our Lady: Context and interpretation', in Derek Pearsall (ed.), *Studies in the Vernon Manuscript* (Cambridge, 1990), 115–36.
81. C.M. Barron, 'The "Golden Age" of women in London', *Reading Medieval Studies* 15 (1989), 35–58; Anne Crawford (ed.), *Letters of Medieval Women* (Stroud, 2002); Carol M. Meale, '". . . alle the bokes that I have of latyn, englisch and frensch": Laywomen and their books in late medieval England', in Carol M. Meale (ed.), *Women and Literature in Britain 1150–1500* (second edition, Cambridge, 1996), 128–58; Susan Powell, 'Lady Margaret Beaufort and her books', *The Library*, sixth series, 20 (1998), 197–240.
82. Eileen Power, *Medieval English Nunneries, c.1275–1535* (Cambridge, 1922), 237; see, by contrast, Jan Rhodes, 'Syon Abbey and its religious publications in the sixteenth century', *JEcclesH* 44 (1993), 11–25; Christopher de Hamel, *Syon Abbey: The library of the Bridgettine nuns and their peregrinations after the Reformation* (London, 1991); E.A. Jones and Alexandra Walsham, *Syon Abbey and Its Books: Reading, writing and religion, c.1400–1700* (Woodbridge, 2010); Felicity Riddy, '"Women talking about the things of God": a late medieval sub-culture', in Meale (ed.), *Women and Literature in Britain*, 107–11.
83. C.M. Barron, 'The education and training of girls in fifteenth-century London', in Diana E.S. Dunn (ed.), *Courts, Counties and the Capital in the Later Middle Ages* (Stroud, 1996), 139–53; Sylvia L. Thrupp, *The Merchant Class of Medieval London 1300–1500* (Ann Arbor, MI, 1962), 169–74..
84. Kathleen Ashley and Pamela Sheingorn (eds), *Interpreting Cultural Symbol: Saint Anne in late medieval society* (Athens, GA, 1900).
85. J.E.B. Mayor (ed.), *The English Works of John Fisher*, EETS extra series, 27 (1876), 294–95; Colin Richmond, *John Hopton* (Cambridge, 1981), 125, 131.
86. Carol M. Meale, 'Women's voices and roles', in Brown (ed.), *A Companion to Medieval English Literature*, 78.
87. Brenda Hosington, 'Women translators and the early printed book', in Vincent Gillespie and Susan Powell (eds), *A Companion to the Early Printed Book in Britain* (Cambridge, 2014), 249–52; see also Brenda Hosington, 'Lady Margaret Beaufort's translations as mirrors of practical piety', in Micheline White (ed.), *English Women, Religion, and Textual Production, 1500–1625* (Aldershot, 2011), 185–203. Editions of the *Mirrour* were published in 1506, 1522 and 1526.
88. *Thus endeth the doctrinal of sapyence* (1489), STC 21431, Sig. Aj^r.
89. Foxe, *A&M* (1570), 1006.
90. Lucy Wooding, 'Catholicism, the printed book and the Marian restoration', in Gillespie and Powell (eds), *A Companion to the Early Printed Book in Britain*, 307–12; John N. King, '"The light of printing": William Tyndale, John Foxe, John Day, and early modern print culture', *RQ* 54 (2001), 52–85.
91. James G. Clark, 'Humanism and reform in pre-Reformation English monasteries', *TRHS* sixth series, 19 (2009), 77–79, 80–82.

92. Roberto Weiss, *Humanism in England during the Fifteenth Century* (Oxford, 1941); see also the critique by David Rundle, 'On the difference between virtue and Weiss: Humanist texts in England during the fifteenth century', in Dunn (ed.), *Courts, Counties and the Capital*, 197–203.

93. Jonathan Woolfson, *Padua and the Tudors: English students in Italy 1485–1603* (Toronto, 1998); Anne Overell, *Italian Reform and English Reformations, c.1535–c.1585* (Aldershot, 2008); Lucy Wooding, 'Erasmus and the politics of translation in Tudor England', *SCH* 53 (2017), 132–45.

94. Aysha Pollnitz, *Princely Education in Early Modern Britain* (Cambridge, 2015), 9–12; Curry Kennedy, 'Living the *Vita Copiosa*: Erasmus's *De duplici copia* and the presence of the Protean Jesus at St Paul's School', *Journal for the History of Rhetoric* 24 (2021), 117–39.

95. John B. Gleason, *John Colet* (Berkeley, CA, and London, 1989), 8–14, 171–78.

96. Lucy Wooding, 'Encountering the Word of God in early Tudor England', *EHR* 136 (2021), 836–66; Eyal Poleg, *A Material History of the Bible, England 1200–1553* (Oxford, 2020), 57–81; Mary Dove, *The First English Bible: The text and context of the Wycliffite versions* (Cambridge, 2007).

97. *The Yale Edition of the Complete Works of St Thomas More*, vol. 6, part 1: *A Dialogue Concerning Heresies* (New Haven, CT, and London, 1981), 344.

98. ibid., 338.

99. *These ben the chapitres of thys tretyse of the seven poyntes of trewe love* (1491), STC 3305, Sig. Av^v–Avi^r.

100. Marshall, *The Catholic Priesthood*, 88; Lucy Wooding, 'Richard Whitford's *Werke for Housholders*: Humanism, monasticism and Tudor household piety', *SCH* 50 (2014), 161–73.

101. Gill, 'Preaching and image', in Muessig (ed.), *Preacher, Sermon and Audience*, 174–75.

102. Martha W. Driver, *The Image in Print: Book illustration in late medieval England and its sources* (London, 2004), 5, 6; Hellinga, 'Prologue', 21.

103. James G. Clark, *The Religious Orders in Pre-Reformation England* (Woodbridge, 2002), 23–24; James G. Clark, 'Print and pre-Reformation religion: The Benedictines and the press, c.1470–c.1550', in Julia Crick and Alexandra Walsham (eds), *The Uses of Script and Print 1300–1700* (Cambridge, 2004), 71–90.

104. Clark, 'Humanism and reform', 77.

105. Wooding, 'Richard Whitford's *Werke for Housholders*', 161–62.

106. James Clark, *The Dissolution of the Monasteries* (New Haven, CT, and London, 2021), 18–19.

107. A.G. Dickens and D. Carr (eds), *The Reformation in England to the Accession of Elizabeth I* (London, 1967), 94.

108. Marshall, *Heretics and Believers*, 38; Clark, *Dissolution of the Monasteries*, 4–6.

109. Clark, 'Humanism and reform', 57–83.

110. Richard Rex, 'The friars in the English Reformation', in Peter Marshall and Alec Ryrie (eds), *The Beginnings of English Protestantism* (Cambridge, 2002), 38–43.

111. Wooding, 'From foundation to reformation', 47–53; Clive Burgess, 'An institution for all seasons: The late medieval English college', in Burgess and Heale (eds), *The Late Medieval English College*, 10–11.

112. David Knowles and R. Neville Hadcock, *Medieval Religious Houses: England and Wales* (London, 1953), 37–38.

113. Martin Heale, 'Colleges and monasteries in late medieval England', in Burgess and Heale (eds), *The Late Medieval English College*, 67–88.

114. Jan Rhodes, 'Richard Whitford', *ODNB*; Heale, 'Colleges and monasteries', 76–80.

115. Clark, 'Humanism and reform', 60n.

116. Gibson, *Theater of Devotion*, 20.

117. D.H. Green, *Women Readers in the Middle Ages* (Cambridge, 2007), 83, 144.

118. R.J. Whitwell, 'An ordinance for Syon Library, 1482', *EHR* 25 (1910), 121.

119. Gascoigne, *Here after folowith the boke callyd the myrroure of Oure Lady*, Sig. Aii^v.

120. Alexandra da Costa, *Reforming Printing: Syon Abbey's defence of orthodoxy, 1525–1534* (Oxford, 2012).

121. Richard Day, *A booke of Christian prayers* (1578), *STC* 6429.

122. Knowles, *The Religious Orders in England*, III, 460.

123. Richard Whitford, *The rule of saynt Augustyne* (1525), *STC* 922.4, Sig. Aii^v.

124. Wooding, 'Richard Whitford's *Werke for Housholders*', 163–64.

125. Whitford, *The rule of saynt Augustyne*, Sig. A4^r; quoted in Costa, *Reforming Printing*, 13.

126. ibid.

127. Anne Dillon, *Michelangelo and the English Martyrs* (Farnham and Burlington, VA, 2012).

128. Charles S. Knighton, 'John Feckenham', *ODNB*; Philippa Tudor, 'John Feckenham and Tudor religious controversies', in Blair and Golding (eds), *The Cloister and the World*, 302–22.

129. Mary C. Erler, 'The effects of exile on English monastic spirituality: William Peryn's *Spirituall Exercyses*', *Journal of Medieval and Early Modern Studies* 42 (2012), 519–37.

130. Andy Wood, *The 1549 Rebellions and the Making of Early Modern England* (Cambridge, 2007), 13, 31.

131. Dickens and Carr (eds), *The Reformation in England*, 103.

132. From John Colet's Convocation Sermon of 1511; see J.H. Lupton, *A Life of John Colet* (London, 1887), 293–304.

133. Margaret Aston, 'Lollardy and sedition, 1381–1431', *P&P* 17 (1960), 1–44; reprinted in Margaret Aston, *Lollards and Reformers: Images and literacy in late medieval religion* (London, 1984), 1–47.

134. See, for example, Fiona Somerset, Jill C. Havens and Derrick G. Pitard (eds), *Lollards and Their Influence in Late Medieval England* (Woodbridge, 2003), part 1; Mishtooni Bose and J. Patrick Hornbeck (eds), *Wycliffite Controversies* (Turnhout, 2011), introduction.

135. Margaret Aston, 'Lollardy and the Reformation: Survival or revival', *History* 49 (1964), 149–70; reprinted in Aston, *Lollards and Reformers*, 219–42.

136. Geoffrey Martin, 'Wyclif, Lollards, and historians, 1384–1984', in Somerset, Havens and Pitard (eds), *Lollards and Their Influence*, 237–50.

137. K.B. McFarlane, *John Wycliffe and the Beginnings of English Nonconformity* (London, 1953); Anne Hudson, *The Premature Reformation: Wycliffite texts and Lollard history* (Oxford, 1988), 278–389; Aston, *Lollards and Reformers*.

138. J.A.F. Thomson, *The Later Lollards, 1414–1520* (Oxford, 1965), 244; Shannon McSheffrey, *Gender and Heresy: Women and men in Lollard communities 1420–1530* (Philadelphia, PA, 1995).

139. Swanson, *Church and Society*, 335, 343; Duffy, *Stripping of the Altars*; Paul Strohm, *England's Empty Throne: Usurpation and the language of legitimation, 1399–1422* (New Haven, CT, 1998); Richard Rex, *The Lollards* (Basingstoke, 2002); Bernard, *The Late Medieval English Church*, 216–31.

140. Ian Forrest, *The Detection of Heresy in Late Medieval England* (Oxford, 2005); R.I. Moore, *The Formation of a Persecuting Society* (second edition, Oxford, 2007); R.I. Moore, *The War on Heresy: The battle for faith and power in medieval Europe* (London, 2012).

141. Andrew E. Larson, 'Are all Lollards Lollards', in Somerset, Havens and Pitard (eds), *Lollards and Their Influence*, 59–72.

142. J. Patrick Hornbeck, *What is a Lollard? Dissent and belief in late medieval England* (Oxford, 2010).

143. Norman Tanner (ed.), *Heresy Trials in the Diocese of Norwich, 1428–31*, CS fourth series, 20 (1977), 155–56.

144. Norman Tanner (ed.), *Kent Heresy Proceedings 1511–12*, Kent Archaeological Society, Kent Records 26 (Maidstone, 1997), 11.

145. ibid., 13.
146. Norman Tanner and Shannon McSheffrey (eds), *Lollards of Coventry, 1486–1522* (Cambridge, 2003), 64–65.
147. Shannon Noelle Gayk, *Image, Text and Religious Reform in Fifteenth-century England* (Cambridge, 2010); J. Dimmick, J. Simpson and N. Zeeman (eds), *Images, Idolatry and Iconoclasm in Late Medieval England: Textuality and the visual image* (Oxford, 2002).
148. Marshall, *Heretics and Believers*, 102–04.
149. J.H. Arnold, 'Voicing dissent: Heresy trials in later medieval England', *P&P* 245 (2019), 3–37; M. Jurkowski, 'Lollardy and social status in East Anglia', *Speculum* 82 (2007), 120–52.
150. Susan Royal, *Lollards in the English Reformation: History, radicalism and John Foxe* (Manchester, 2020).
151. Lawrence M. Clopper, 'Franciscans, Lollards and reform', in Somerset, Havens and Pitard (eds), *Lollards and their Influence*, 177–96.
152. Elizabeth Schirmer, 'Canon wars and outlier manuscripts: Gospel harmony in the Lollard controversy', *HLQ* 73 (2010), 4; Wendy Scase, 'Reginald Pecock, John Carpenter, and John Colop's "common-profit" books: Aspects of book ownership and circulation in fifteenth-century London', *Medium Aevum* 61 (1992), 261–74.
153. Mary Dove (ed.), *The Earliest Advocates of the English Bible: The texts of the medieval debate* (Exeter, 2010).
154. Marshall, *Heretics and Believers*, 100.
155. John F. Davis, *Heresy and Reformation in the South East of England 1520–1559* (London, 1983), 57–65; Bernard, *The Late Medieval English Church*, 211–15.
156. Tanner (ed.), *Kent Heresy Proceedings*, x–xi.
157. ibid., 65.
158. ibid., xiii, 59, 117.
159. Robert Lutton, *Lollardy and Orthodox Religion in Pre-Reformation England: Reconstructing piety* (Woodbridge, 2011).
160. ibid., xvii–xviii, 12, xxi.
161. Tanner and McSheffrey, *Lollards of Coventry*, 64–65.
162. ibid., 65-6.
163. Scarisbrick, *The Reformation and the English People*, 17.
164. Keith Thomas, *Religion and the Decline of Magic: Studies in popular beliefs in sixteenth- and seventeenth-century England* (London and New York, 1971), 88.
165. *The Will of King Henry VII*, 2.
166. Felicity Heal, *The Gentry in England and Wales, 1500–1700* (Basingstoke, 1994), 349–55.
167. TNA E/23/4 fo. 3^{r-v}.

4 Suffering in Life and Consolation in Death

1. John Banister, *The Historie of Man* (London, 1578), STC 1359, Sig. Aij^r.
2. Patrick Collinson, 'John Stow and nostalgic antiquarianism', in Patrick Collinson, *This England: Essays on the English nation and commonwealth in the sixteenth century* (Manchester, 2011), 287–308; Ian Archer, 'The nostalgia of John Stow', in David L. Smith, Richard Strier and David Bevington (eds), *The Theatrical City: Culture, theatre and politics in London, 1576–1649* (Cambridge, 1995), 17–34; Harriet Lyon, 'A pitiful thing? The dissolution of the English monasteries in early modern chronicles', *SCJ* 49 (2018), 1037–56.
3. Margaret Aston, *Broken Idols of the English Reformation* (Cambridge, 2016); Alison Shell, 'The writing on the wall? John Ingram's verse and the dissemination of Catholic prison writing', *BCH* 33 (2016), 58–70; Ruth Ahnert, 'Writing in the Tower of London during the Reformation, c.1530–1558', *HLQ* 72 (2009), 172–78; Juliet Fleming, *Graffiti and the Writing Arts of Early Modern England* (Philadelphia, PA, 2001); Brian Hoggard,

'The archaeology of counter-witchcraft and popular magic', in Owen Davies and Willem de Blécourt (eds), *Beyond the Witch Trials: Witchcraft and magic in Enlightenment Europe* (Manchester, 2004), 167, 175–76.

4. *The Book of Common Prayer: The texts of 1549, 1559 and 1662*, ed. Brian Cummings (Oxford, 2011), 16.

5. Keith Wrightson, *Earthly Necessities: Economic lives in early modern Britain 1470–1570* (New Haven, CT, and London, 2000), 23–24, 27.

6. *Certayne sermons, or homilies* (1547), STC 13640, Sig. Fiᵛ.

7. Alfred Hassell Smith, *County and Court: Government and Politics in Norfolk, 1558–1603* (Oxford, 1974), 193.

8. Craig Muldrew, *The Economy of Obligation: The culture of credit and social relations in early modern England* (Basingstoke, 1998), 43–46; Ian W. Archer, 'Material Londoners?' in Lena Cowin Orlin (ed.), *Material London, ca. 1600* (Philadelphia, PA, 2000), 179.

9. Phil Withington, *Society in Early Modern England: The vernacular origins of some powerful ideas* (Cambridge, 2010), 104–05.

10. John Barston, *The safegarde of societie* (1576), STC 1532, Sig. Aviiiᵛ.

11. ibid., fo. 67ʳ.

12. *The Book of Common Prayer*, 24.

13. Steve Hindle, 'Hierarchy and community in the Elizabethan parish: The Swallowfield Articles of 1596', *HJ* 42 (1999), 848–49. See also Patrick Collinson, 'De republica anglorum: or history with the politics put back', in Patrick Collinson, *Elizabethan Essays* (London, 1994), 23–25.

14. Edmund Dudley, *The Tree of Commonwealth*, ed. D.M. Brodie (Cambridge, 1948). Harrison and Wilson are discussed in Keith Wrightson, *English Society, 1580–1680* (London, 1982), 19–22.

15. Thomas Smith, *De Republica Anglorum*, ed. M. Dewar (Cambridge, 1982), 74.

16. Stephen Greenblatt, *Will in the World: How Shakespeare became Shakespeare* (London, 2004), 78–80.

17. Wrightson, *English Society*, 28.

18. Wilfrid Hooper, 'The Tudor sumptuary laws', *EHR* 30 (1915), 433–49; Frances E. Baldwin, *Sumptuary Legislation and Personal Regulation in England* (Baltimore, MD, 1926); Maria Hayward, ' "Outlandish superfluities": Luxury and clothing in Scottish and English sumptuary law, fourteenth to the seventeenth century', in Giorgio Riello and Ulinka Rublack (eds), *The Right to Dress: Sumptuary laws in a global perspective, c.1200–1800* (Cambridge, 2019), 96–120.

19. Paul Griffiths, 'Masterless young people in Norwich, 1560–1645', in Paul Griffiths, Adam Fox and Steve Hindle (eds), *The Experience of Authority in Early Modern England* (Basingstoke, 1996), 148–49; Griffiths, *Youth and Authority: Formative experiences in England, 1560–1640* (Oxford, 1996), 34–61, 81–96; Alexandra Shepard, *Meanings of Manhood in Early Modern England* (Oxford, 2003), 23–38, 54–57; Roger B. Manning, *Village Revolts: Social protest and popular disturbances in England 1509–1640* (Oxford, 1988), 187–219.

20. E.A. Wrigley and R.S. Schofield, *The Population History of England, 1541–1871: A reconstruction* (Cambridge, MA, 1981), 528–29 (table A3.1).

21. Griffiths, *Youth and Authority*, 391–92.

22. Ilana Krausman Ben-Amos, *Adolescence and Youth in Early Modern England* (New Haven, CT, 1994); Natalie Zemon Davis, 'The reasons of misrule: Youth groups and charivaris in sixteenth-century France', *P&P* 50 (1971), repr. in Natalie Zemon Davis, *Society and Culture in Early Modern France* (Stanford, CA, 1975), 97–123.

23. Margaret Pelling, 'Apprenticeship, health and social cohesion in early modern London', *HWJ* 37 (1994), 41–42.

24. Wrightson, *English Society*, 32.

25. Ben-Amos, *Adolescence and Youth*, 183–84; Ian Archer, *The Pursuit of Stability: Social relations in Elizabethan London* (Cambridge, 1991), 1–9; Manning, *Village Revolts*, 187–219.

26. A.L. Beier, *Masterless Men: The vagrancy problem in England 1560–1640* (London, 1985), 10, 54–56.

27. Philip Ziegler, *The Black Death* (1969; second edition, Stroud, 2010); W.M. Ormrod and P. Lindley (eds), *The Black Death in England, 1348–1500* (Stamford, 1996); J. Hatcher, 'England in the aftermath of the Black Death', *P&P* 144 (1994), 3–35.

28. Charles M. Evans and Angela E. Evans, 'Plague – a disease of children and servants? A study of the parish records of St Peter upon Cornhill, from 1580–1605', *Continuity and Change* 34 (2019), 183–208.

29. Will Coster, *Family and Kinship in England, 1450–1800* (second edition, Abingdon, 2017), 6, 111.

30. Richard W. Hoyle, 'Rural economies under stress: "A world so altered"', in Susan Doran and Norman Jones (eds), *The Elizabethan World* (Abingdon and New York, 2011), 439. See John Hatcher, 'Understanding the population history of England', *P&P* 180 (2003), 83–130.

31. Hugh Plat, *Sundrie new and artificall remedies against famine* (1596), STC 19996, Sig. A3ʳ.

32. Hoyle, 'Rural economies', 443–47.

33. Beier, *Masterless Men*, 17.

34. Quoted in Helen C. White, *Social Criticism in Popular Religious Literature of the Sixteenth Century* (New York, 1973), 259.

35. Paul Slack, *Poverty and Policy in Tudor and Stuart England* (London, 1988), 4, 6.

36. *Narratives of the Reformation*, 231–33.

37. Slack, *Poverty and Policy*, 11–12.

38. Hoyle, 'Rural economies', 453.

39. Robert Crowley, *One and thyrtye epigrammes* (1550), STC 6088, Sig. Dvʳ⁻ᵛ.

40. Richard Day, *A booke of Christian prayers* (1578), STC 6429, fo. 53ʳ.

41. John Dove, *A sermon preached at Pauls Crosse ... interating of the second coming of Christ, and the disclosing of Antichrist* (1594), STC 7086.5, Sig. C5ʳ.

42. Beier, *Masterless Men*, 5–7; William C. Carroll, *Fat King, Lean Beggar: Representations of poverty in the age of Shakespeare* (Ithaca, NY, 1996).

43. Quoted in Beier, *Masterless Men*, 6.

44. Gamini Salgado, *The Elizabethan Underworld* (London, 1977); Arthur F. Kinny, *Rogues, Vagabonds and Sturdy Beggars* (Barre, MA, 1973); Craig Dion and Steve Mentz (eds), *Rogues and Early Modern English Culture* (Ann Arbor, MI, 2004).

45. Thomas Harman, *A Caveat or warening for Common Cursetors* (1567), STC 12787.5, dedication; see also A.L. Beier, 'On the boundaries of new and old historicisms: Thomas Harman and the literature of roguery', *English Literary Renaissance* 33 (2003), 181–200.

46. Beier, *Masterless Men*, xxi–xxii, 9.

47. Malcolm Gaskill, 'Little commonwealths II: Communities', in Keith Wrightson (ed.), *A Social History of England 1500–1750* (Cambridge, 2017), 85.

48. Keith Wrightson, 'Two concepts of order: Justices, constables and jurymen in seventeenth-century England', in John Brewer and John Styles (eds), *An Ungovernable People: The English and their law in the seventeenth and eighteenth centuries* (London, 1980), 21–46. See also Chris Briggs, 'Introduction: Law courts, contracts and rural society in Europe, 1200–1600', *Continuity and Change* 29 (2014), 3–18.

49. E.P. Thompson, *Customs in Common* (London, 1991), chapter 3; Tim Stretton, 'Women, custom and equity in the court of requests', in Jennifer Kermode and Garthine Walker (eds), *Women, Crime and the Courts in Early Modern England* (London, 1994), 170–89; Andy Wood, 'Custom, identity and resistance: English free miners and their law c.1550–1800', in Griffiths, Fox and Hindle (eds), *The Experience of Authority*, 249–85.

50. Andy Wood, 'Social conflict and change in the mining communities of north-west Derbyshire, c.1600–1700', *International Review of Social History* 38 (1993), 31–58;

see also J.R. Dias, 'Lead, society and politics in Derbyshire before the civil war', *Midland History* 6 (1981), 39–57.

51. Adam Fox, 'Custom, memory and the authority of writing', in Griffiths, Fox and Hindle (eds), *The Experience of Authority*, 102–03, 90–92.

52. Cited in ibid., 98.

53. Mervyn James, 'Ritual, drama and social body in the late medieval English town', *P&P* 98 (1983), 3–29.

54. Beat Kumin, 'Parishioners in court: Litigation and the local community, 1350–1650', in Susan Wabuda and Caroline Liztenberger (eds), *Belief and Practice in Early Modern England: A tribute to Patrick Collinson from his students* (Aldershot, 1998), 20–21.

55. Miri Rubin, *Corpus Christi: The eucharist in late medieval culture* (Cambridge, 1991), chapter 4 and 266–70.

56. Susan Brigden, 'Religion and social obligation in early sixteenth-century London', *P&P* 103 (1984), 77–78.

57. For further discussion of this, see below, chapter 6.

58. Kumin, 'Parishioners in court', 26–27.

59. Wrightson, *English Society*, 62.

60. Anthony Fletcher, *Gender, Sex and Subordination in England 1500–1800* (New Haven, CT, and London, 1995), xvi–xix, 1–99; Keith Thomas, 'The place of laughter in Tudor and Stuart England', *TLS* 7, 21 January 1977, 77; Tim Reinke-Williams, 'Misogyny, jest-books and male youth culture in seventeenth-century England', *Gender and History* 21 (2009), 324–39.

61. EBBA 32413.

62. Judith M. Bennett, 'Feminism and history', *Gender and History* 1 (1989), 259–63; Anthony Fletcher, 'Men's dilemma: The future of patriarchy in England 1560–1660', *TRHS* sixth series, 4 (1994), 61–81.

63. Shepard, *Meanings of Manhood*; Elizabeth Foyster, *Manhood in Early Modern England: Honour, sex and marriage* (Harlow, 1999); Tim Reinke-Williams, 'Manhood and masculinity in early modern England', *History Compass* 12 (2014), 685–93.

64. Bennett, 'Feminism and history', 259–63.

65. *Thomas Platter's Travels in England 1599*, ed. Clare Williams (London, 1937), 181–82; see Fletcher, *Gender, Sex and Subordination*, 3–4.

66. Cited in Chilton Latham Powell, *English Domestic Relations 1487–1683: A study of matrimony and family life in theory and practice as revealed by the literature, law and history of the period* (New York, 1917), 175.

67. Quoted in Debora K. Shuger, *Habits of Thought in the English Renaissance* (Toronto, 1997), 2.

68. Peter L. Larson, 'Widow-right in Durham, England (1349–1660', *Continuity and Change* 33 (2018), 173–201; Barbara Hanawalt, *The Wealth of Wives: Women, law, and economy in late medieval London* (Oxford, 2007); Mavis Mate, *Daughters, Wives and Widows after the Black Death: Women in Sussex, 1350–1525* (Woodbridge, 1998); Amy Erickson, *Women and Property in Early Modern England* (London, 1995); Jane Whittle, 'Inheritance, marriage, widowhood and remarriage: A comparative perspective on women and landholding in north-east Norfolk, 1440–1580', *Continuity and Change* 13 (1998), 33–72.

69. Tim Stretton, 'The people and the law', in Wrightson (ed.), *A Social History of England*, 212.

70. Garthine Walker, *Crime, Gender and the Social Order in Early Modern England* (Cambridge, 2003); Krista Kesselring, 'Bodies of evidence: Sex and murder (or gender and homicide) in early modern England, c.1500–1680', *Gender and History* 27 (2015), 255–56.

71. Wrightson, *English Society*, 92.

72. Nicholas Ling, *Politeuphuia: Wits common wealth* (1598), STC 15686, fos. 204^v–207^r.

73. Margaret Sommerville, *Sex and Subjection: Attitudes to women in early modern society* (London, 1995).
74. Cited in Coster, *Family and Kinship in England*, 65. See also Suzanne W. Hull, *Chaste Silent and Obedient: English books for women, 1475–1640* (San Marino, CA, 1982); Susan D. Amussen, *An Ordered Society: Gender and class in early modern England* (Oxford, 1988).
75. Amussen, *An Ordered Society*, 36–37.
76. *Two Elizabethan Puritan diaries*, ed. M.M. Knappen (Chicago, 1933), 73–74.
77. Ralph Houlbrooke, *The English Family, 1450–1700* (London and New York, 1984), 119; J.A. Sharpe, *Early Modern England: A Social History 1550–1760* (London, 1987), 62–69; Wrightson, *English Society*, 100.
78. C.B. Atkinson and J.B. Atkinson, 'Thomas Bentley's *The Monument of matrones* (1582): The first Anglican Prayer Book for women', *Anglican Theological Review* 74 (1992), 277–88.
79. Thomas Bentley, *Monument of matrones* (1582), STC 1892, 73–74.
80. Tim Stretton, 'Marriage, separation and the common law in England, 1540–1660', in Helen Berry and Elizabeth Foyster (eds), *The Family in Early Modern England* (Cambridge, 2007), 34.
81. 'A sermon agaynst whoredome and uncleanesse', in *Certaine sermons and homilies* (1563), STC 13651, Sig. Xi^v. The homily was not attributed to Becon in either the 1547 or 1563 edition, but it was included in the second volume of the Elizabethan edition of Becon's collected works: Becon, *Works*, vol. II (1564), fo. clvii^r.
82. Stretton, 'Marriage, separation and the common law', 19–20.
83. ibid., 25.
84. ibid., 27, 25.
85. Wrightson, *English Society*, 68; Amy Froide, *Never Married: Singlewomen in Early Modern England* (Oxford, 2005), 2–4; Christine Peters, 'Single women in early modern England: Attitudes and expectations', *Continuity and Change* 12 (1997), 325–45.
86. *Certayne sermons, or homelies*, Sig. Xii^v.
87. Peters, 'Single women', 325–26, 339–42.
88. Charmian Mansell, 'The variety of women's experiences as servants in England (1548–1649): Evidence from church court depositions', *Continuity and Change* 33 (2018), 315–38.
89. Cited in Froide, *Never Married*, 20.
90. Peters, 'Single women', 329.
91. Anne McLaren, 'Gender, religion, and early modern nationalism: Elizabeth I, Mary Queen of Scots, and the genesis of English anti-Catholicism', *AHR* 107 (2002), 739–67.
92. Ling, *Politeuphuia*, fos. 24^v–28^r.
93. Thomas Elyot, *The Boke Named the Governour* (London, 1537), STC 7636, fos. 15^v–16^r.
94. Judith Butler, *Bodies That Matter: On the discursive limits of 'sex'* (London, 1993); Laura Gowing, 'Women's bodies and the making of sex in seventeenth-century England', *Signs* 37 (2012), 813–15; Sara Read, *Menstruation and the Female Body in Early Modern England* (Basingstoke, 2013); Patricia Crawford, 'Attitudes to menstruation in seventeenth-century England', *P&P* 91 (1981), 47–73.
95. Mary E. Fissell, *Vernacular Bodies: The politics of reproduction in early modern England* (Oxford, 2004), 32.
96. Thomas Raynalde, *The Birth of mankind, otherwise named, The woman's book*, ed. Elaine Hobby (Farnham, 2009); see also Fissell, *Vernacular Bodies*, 14, 29–32, 33–35.
97. Thomas Raynalde, *The Birth of mankynde* (1565?), STC 21158, Sig. Aii^v.
98. R.S. Schofield, 'Did the mothers really die? Three centuries of maternal mortality in the world we have lost', in L. Bonfield, R.M. Smith and K. Wrightson (eds), *The World We Have Gained: Histories of population and social structure* (Oxford, 1986).

99. Sara Mendelson and Patricia Crawford, *Women in Early Modern England 1550–1720* (Oxford, 1998), 151.

100. Linda Pollock, 'Embarking on a rough passage: The experience of pregnancy in early-modern society', in Valerie Fildes (ed.), *Women as Mothers in Pre-Industrial England* (London, 1990), 46–49.

101. ibid., 39–67.

102. Thomas Bentley, *The fift lampe of virginitie* (1582), STC 1893, 134; Fissell, *Vernacular Bodies*, 48–49.

103. Juan Luis Vives, *A very fruitefull and pleasant booke called the instruction of a Christen woman*, translated Richard Hyrde (1531), STC 24857, Sig. C^{r-v}.

104. Bentley, *The fift lampe*, 129–30.

105. Laura Gowing, *Gender Relations in Early Modern England* (Harlow, 2012), 22–23.

106. Cited in ibid., 110–11.

107. Fissell, *Vernacular Bodies*, 14–15, 24–29.

108. ibid., 14–17.

109. Quoted in ibid., 28.

110. Bentley, *The fift lampe*, 98.

111. ibid., 134.

112. Gowing, *Gender Relations*, 22.

113. Lawrence Stone, *Family, Sex and Marriage in England 1500–1800* (London, 1977); Lloyd de Mause (ed.), *The History of Childhood* (London, 1976), 21.

114. Linda Pollock, *Forgotten Children: Parent–child relations from 1500 to 1900* (Cambridge, 1983).

115. Hannah Newton, *The Sick Child in Early Modern England, 1580–1720* (Oxford, 2012), 1.

116. Ralph Houlbrooke, *English Family Life, 1576–1716: An anthology from diaries* (New York and Oxford, 1988), 105–08, 137–39.

117. Richard Rainolde, *A booke called the Foundacion of rhetorike* (1563), STC 20925a.5, fos. liiii^v–lix^r. Quotations at fos. liiii^v; lviii^v–lix^r.

118. Thomas Wilson, *The Arte of Rhetorique* (1553), STC 25799, fo. 35^v.

119. J. Jones, *The Arte and Science of preserving Bodie and Soule in Healthe, Wisedome and Catholicke Religion* (1579), STC 14724, 43; Valerie Fildes, 'The age of weaning in Britain 1500–1800', *Journal of Biosocial Science* 14 (1982), 223–40.

120. Paul Griffiths, 'Surveying the people', in Wrightson (ed.), *A Social History of England*, 52–53.

121. Shulamith Shahar, *Childhood in the Middle Ages* (London, 1990), 1–2; Barbara Hanawalt, *The Ties That Bound: Peasant families in medieval England* (Oxford, 1986), 335; Barbara Hanawalt, *Growing Up in Medieval London* (New York, 1993), 6–8.

122. Nicholas Orme, 'The culture of children in medieval England', *P&P* 148 (1995), 51–53.

123. Kathryn Sather, 'Sixteenth- and seventeenth-century child-rearing: A matter of discipline', *Journal of Social History* 22 (1989), 735–43.

124. John Northbrooke, *A Treatise wherein Dicing, Dauncing, Vaine plaies or Enterludes . . . are reprooved* (1579), STC 18671, Sig. a^v.

125. Desiderius Erasmus, 'On education for children', in Erika Rummel (ed.), *The Erasmus Reader* (Toronto and London, 1990, 71, 89; Coster, *Family and Kinship in England*, 98.

126. Elyot, *The Boke Named the Governour*, fo. 26^v.

127. Contrast P. Ariès, *Centuries of Childhood* (London, 1962) with Linda Pollock, *A Lasting Relationship: Parents and children over three centuries* (London, 1987).

128. Reinke-Williams, 'Manhood and masculinity', 685–93; Shepard, *Meanings of Manhood*; Foyster, *Manhood in Early Modern England*; Fletcher, *Gender, Sex and Subordination*; Susan D. Amussen, ' "The part of a Christian man: The cultural politics of manhood in early modern England', in Susan D. Amussen and Mark Kishlansky (eds), *Political Culture and Cultural Politics in Seventeenth-Century England* (Manchester, 1995), 213–33.

129. Griffiths, *Youth and Authority*, 200–13; Alexandra Shepard, '"Swil-bols and tos-pots": Drink culture and male bonding in England, c.1560–1640', in Laura Gowing, Michael Hunter and Miri Rubin (eds), *Love, Friendship and Faith in Europe, 1300–1800* (Basingstoke, 2005), 110–30.

130. Foyster, *Manhood in Early Modern England*, 207–08; Fletcher, 'Men's dilemma', 61–81.

131. Gowing, *Gender Relations*, 22.

132. Fletcher, *Gender, Sex and Subordination*, 4–5.

133. ibid., 8.

134. Emma Smith, *This is Shakespeare* (London, 2019), 7–21; Fletcher, 'Men's dilemma', 64–66.

135. Anthony Fitzherbert, *The Boke of Husbandrie* (1548), STC 10999, fos. 65ʳ–66ʳ.

136. Tim Stretton, 'Women', in Doran and Jones (eds), *The Elizabethan World*, 340.

137. Mendelson and Crawford, *Women in Early Modern England*, 124.

138. Gowing, *Gender Relations*, 37.

139. Mendelson and Crawford, *Women in Early Modern England*, 128, 140–41.

140. Alexandra Shepard, 'From anxious patriarchs to refined gentlemen? Manhood in Britain, circa 1500–1700', *JBS* 44 (2005), 281–95.

141. Bernard Capp, '"Jesus wept" but did the Englishman? Masculinity and emotion in early modern England', *P&P* 224 (2014), 78, 76.

142. Laura Gowing, *Domestic Dangers: Women, words and sex in early modern London* (Oxford, 1998), 109–10, chapters 3 and 4; Martin Ingram, *Carnal Knowledge: Regulating sex in England, 1470–1600* (Cambridge, 2017), 72–73.

143. William Shakespeare, *The Taming of the Shrew*, Act V, Scene 2, ll. 151–58.

144. David Underdown, 'The taming of the scold: The enforcement of patriarchal authority in early modern England', in Anthony Fletcher and John Stevenson (eds), *Order and Disorder in Early Modern England* (Cambridge, 1985); M.S. Kimmel, 'The contemporary "crisis" of masculinity in historical perspective', in H. Harry Brod (ed.), *The Making of Masculinities: The new men's studies* (Boston, MA, 1987), 121–37.

145. Martin Ingram, '"Scolding women cucked or washed?": A crisis in gender relations in early modern England?', in Kermode and Walker (eds), *Women, Crime and the Courts*, 48–80; Gowing, *Domestic Dangers*, 28–29.

146. Foyster, *Manhood in Early Modern England*, 209–10.

147. Bentley, *The fift lampe*, 79–80.

148. Beier, *Masterless Men*, 93–95.

149. Steven Gunn, *The English People at War in the Age of Henry VIII* (Oxford, 2018), 19–20.

150. ibid., 100.

151. Mervyn James, 'English politics and the concept of honour, 1485–1642', *P&P* Supplement 3 (1978) argued for the duel as a medieval legacy; for the argument that it was a Renaissance import, see Markku Peltonen, *The Duel in Early Modern England: Civility, politeness and honour* (Cambridge, 2003).

152. Thomas Churchyard, *Churchyards challenge* (1593), STC 5220, 59–60.

153. Gunn, *The English People at War*, 96.

154. *The Colloquies of Erasmus*, trans. Craig R. Thompson (Chicago and London, 1965), 271.

155. Gunn, *The English People at War*, 114.

156. Craig Muldrew, *Food, Energy and the Creation of Industriousness* (Cambridge, 2011).

157. *Nova Statuta* (1485), STC 9264.

158. Margaret Pelling, *The Common Lot: Sickness, medical occupations and the urban poor in early modern England* (London, 1998), 41; Lucy Wooding, *Henry VIII* (second edition, Abingdon, 2015), 72.

159. Gervase Rosser, 'Going to the fraternity feast: Commensality and social relations in late medieval England', *JBS* 33 (1994), 431.

160. Felicity Heal, 'Food gifts, the household and the politics of exchange in early modern England', *P&P* 199 (2008), 41–70.

161. Paul S. Lloyd, *Food and Identity in England, 1540–1640: Eating to impress* (London, 2015), 41.

162. Joan Thirsk, *Food in Early Modern England: Phases, fads, fashions 1500–1760* (London, 2007), 3.

163. Lloyd, *Food and Identity*, 37, 41.

164. Thirsk, *Food in Early Modern England*, 9, 25.

165. William Harrison, *The Description of England*, ed. G. Edelen (Washington, DC, and London, 1994), 216.

166. St Augustine, *Twelve Sermons* (1553), *STC* 923, Sig. Cvi^v–Cvii^r.

167. Quoted in Andy Wood, *Faith, Hope and Charity: English neighbourhoods, 1500–1640* (Cambridge, 2020), 55.

168. David M. Palliser, *Tudor York* (Oxford, 1979), 63.

169. Plat, *Sundrie new and artificall remedies*, Sig. A3^r.

170. Thirsk, *Food in Early Modern England*, 20–22.

171. Peter Clark, *The English Alehouse* (London, 1983); Martha Carlin, ' "What say you to a piece of beef and mustard": The evolution of public dining in medieval and Tudor London', *HLQ* 71 (2008), 199–217.

172. Felicity Heal, *Hospitality in Early Modern England* (Oxford, 1990).

173. Andrew Borde, *Hereafter foloweth a compendyous regyment or a dyetary of helthe* (1542), *STC* 3378.5, Sig. Ciii^v.

174. Heal, *Hospitality*, 5.

175. ibid., 68–69.

176. Christopher Dyer, *A Country Merchant 1495–1520: Trading and farming at the end of the middle ages* (Oxford, 2012), 27.

177. Lloyd, *Food and Identity*, 24.

178. Thomas Betson, *The Syon Abbey Herbal: The last monastic herbal in England, c. AD 1517*, ed. John Adams and Forbes Stuart (London, 2015).

179. Pelling, *The Common Lot*, 47.

180. Thirsk, *Food in Early Modern England*, 32–33.

181. *Desiderata Curiosa: or, A Collection of Divers Scarce and Curious Pieces, Relating Chiefly to Matters of English History*, ed. Francis Peck, 2 vols (London, 1779), I, 49; cited in Heal, 'Food gifts', 67.

182. *Lisle Letters*, III, 500; IV, 144–45.

183. ibid., III, 395.

184. Heal, 'Food gifts', 66.

185. Lloyd, *Food and Identity*, 41–43.

186. Thirsk, *Food in Early Modern England*, 13; Thomas Elyot, *The Castell of Helth* (1539), *STC* 7643, fos. 33^v–34^r.

187. Pollock, 'Embarking on a rough passage', 50, 54.

188. Lloyd, *Food and Identity*, 78–79.

189. Elyot, *The Castell of Helth*, fos. 34^v–35^r.

190. Lloyd, *Food and Identity*, 41.

191. Alec Ryrie, *Being Protestant in Reformation Britain* (Oxford, 2013), 195–99.

192. *APC*, XXVI, 384.

193. Ryrie, *Being Protestant*, 341–44.

194. Thirsk, *Food in Early Modern England*, 34.

195. Richard Gardiner, *Profitable Instructions for the Manuring, Sowing and Planting of Kitchen Gardens*, *STC* 11570.5 (1599), Sig. D2^v.

196. ibid. Sig. A2^r–v.

197. Elyot, *The Castell of Helth*, fo. 47^r.

198. Borde, *Dyetary of helthe*, Sig. Dii^r–v.

199. Erickson, *Women and Property*, 64.

200. Laura Gowing, 'The twinkling of a bedstaff: Recovering the social life of English beds, 1500–1700', *Home Cultures: The Journal of Architecture, Design and Domestic Space* 11 (2014), 275–304.

201. Erasmus, *De civilitate*, trans. Robert Wytyngton (London, 1532), Sig. D2ᵛ.

202. Borde, *Dyetary of helthe*, Sig. Divʳ⁻ᵛ.

203. Roger Ekirch, *At Day's Close: Night in times past* (London, 2005).

204. Gowing, 'The twinkling of a bedstaff', 289.

205. Frank E. Brown, 'Continuity and change in the urban house: Developments in domestic space organisation in seventeenth-century London', *Comparative Studies in Society and History* 28 (1986), 580.

206. Katherine Crawford, *European Sexualities, 1400–1800* (Cambridge, 2007), 1.

207. Wooding, *Henry VIII*, 253.

208. Banister, *The Historie of Man*, fo.88ᵛ.

209. Borde, *Dyetary of helthe*, Sig. Diiiᵛ–Divʳ.

210. Fletcher, *Gender, Sex and Subordination*, 6–7.

211. Mendelson and Crawford, *Women in Early Modern England*, 24–25.

212. ibid., 106–07; Laura Gowing, 'Secret births and infanticide in seventeenth-century England', *P&P* 156 (1997), 87–115; Bernard Capp, *When Gossips Meet: Women, family and neighbourhood in early modern England* (Oxford, 2003), chapter 4.

213. Crawford, *European Sexualities*, 233.

214. Helen Berry and Elizabeth Foyster, 'Childless men in early modern England', in Berry and Foyster (eds), *The Family in Early Modern England*, 165; *The Book of Common Prayer* (1559), *STC* 16293.3, Sig. Tiiʳ.

215. Quoted in Berry and Foyster, 'Childless men', 172.

216. Gowing, *Gender Relations*, 17, 18–19.

217. Audrey Eccles, *Obstetrics and Gynaecology in Tudor and Stuart England* (London, 1982), chapter 5; Angus McLaren, *Reproductive Rituals: The perception of fertility in England from the sixteenth century to the nineteenth century* (London, 1984), 19–21.

218. 'A sermon agaynst whoredome and uncleanesse', in *Certaine sermons and homilies*, Sig. Tivʳ.

219. Ingram, *Carnal Knowledge*, 2, 88.

220. Ronald B. Bond, ' "Dark deeds darkly answered": Thomas Becon's homily against whoredom and adultery, its contexts, and its affiliations with three Shakespearean plays', *SCJ* 16 (1985), 195–97.

221. William Shakespeare, *Measure for Measure*, Act I, Scene 3, ll. 19–20.

222. Bond, ' "Dark deeds darkly answered" ', 196.

223. Gowing, *Gender Relations*, 15.

224. Crawford, *European Sexualities*, 232–33.

225. Ingram, *Carnal Knowledge*, 35–36, 125–26, 129–30, 138–39, 150–55.

226. ibid., 153–54.

227. Thomas Beard, *The theatre of Gods iudgements* (London, 1597), *STC* 1659, 359–60.

228. Marie H. Loughlin, *Same-Sex Desire in Early Modern England, 1550–1735: An anthology of literary texts and contexts* (Manchester and New York, 2014); Alan Bray, *Homosexuality in Renaissance England* (London, 1982); Alan Bray, 'Homosexuality and the signs of male friendship in Elizabethan England', *HWJ* 29 (1990), 1–19; Valerie Traub, *The Renaissance of Lesbianism in Early Modern England* (Cambridge, 2002).

229. Gowing, *Gender Relations*, 20; Ingram, *Carnal Knowledge*, 34.

230. Gowing, 'The twinkling of a bedstaff', 288; Alan Sinfield, '*Poetaster*, the author, and the perils of cultural production', in Orlin (ed.), *Material London*, 87.

231. Ingram, *Carnal Knowledge*, 33–38.

232. Mendelson and Crawford, *Women in Early Modern England*, 20–21, 242–52; Gowing, *Gender Relations*, 20–21, 103–04; Leo Africanus, *A geographical historie of Africa*, trans. John Pory (1600), 148–49.

233. Steven Peele, 'A proper new balade expressyng the fames, Concerning a warning to al London dames' (1571?), EBBA 32413.

234. Pelling, *The Common Lot*, 5–6.

235. Andrew Cunningham and Ole Peter Grell, *The Four Horsemen of the Apocalypse* (Cambridge, 2001), 275.

236. Thomas Nashe, *Christs Teares Over Jerusalem* (1593), Sig. Z2^{r-v}. See also Alexandra Walsham, *Providence in Early Modern England* (Oxford, 1999), 160.

237. Paul Slack, *The Impact of Plague in Tudor and Stuart England* (London, 1985), 40 n84.

238. ibid., 38.

239. ibid., 39 n80.

240. John Balmford, *A short dialogue concerning the plagues infection* (London, 1603), STC 1338, Sig. A2^v.

241. William Shakespeare, *Romeo and Juliet*, Act V, Scene 2, l. 10.

242. Thomas Cogan, *The haven of healthe* (1589), STC 5480, 268–69.

243. Rick Bowers, 'Antidote to the plague: Thomas Dekker's storytelling in *The Wonderfull Yeare* (1603)', *English Studies* 73 (1992), 229–39.

244. Andrew Wear, 'Fear, anxiety and the plague in early modern England: Religious and medical responses', in John R. Hinnells and Roy Porter (eds), *Religion, Health and Suffering* (London, 1999), 339–63.

245. Bruce Boehrer, 'Early modern syphilis', *Journal of the History of Sexuality* 1 (1990), 197–214; M.A. Waugh, 'Venereal diseases in sixteenth-century England', *Medical History* 17 (1973), 192–99.

246. William Shakespeare, *The Tempest*, Act I, Scene 1, ll. 41–42.

247. Margaret Pelling, *The Common Lot*, 1.

248. Deborah E. Harkness, *The Jewel House: Elizabethan London and the scientific revolution* (New Haven, CT, and London, 2007), 57.

249. Paul Slack, 'Mortality crises and epidemic disease in England 1485–1610', in Charles Webster (ed.), *Health, Medicine and Mortality in the Sixteenth Century* (Cambridge, 1979), 19–21.

250. Elyot, *The Castell of Helth*, fo. 21^r.

251. Pelling, *The Common Lot*, 29–30; Wear, 'Fear, anxiety and the plague', 339–63; Michael MacDonald, *Mystical Bedlam: Madness, anxiety and healing in seventeenth-century England* (Cambridge, 1981), 2–3.

252. Borde, *Dyetary of helthe*, Sig. Aiii^r.

253. MacDonald, *Mystical Bedlam*, 4–6.

254. Jan Frans van Dijkhuizen, 'Partakers of pain: Religious meanings of pain in early modern England', in Jan Frans van Dijkhuizen and Karl A.E. Enenkel (eds), *The Sense of Suffering: Constructions of physical pain in early modern culture* (Leiden and Boston, 2008), 189–220.

255. Andrew Wear, 'Puritan perceptions of illness in seventeenth-century England', in Roy Porter (ed.), *Patients and Practitioners: Lay perceptions of medicine in pre-industrial society* (Cambridge, 1985), 55–99; Alexandra Walsham, 'In sickness and in health: Medicine and inter-confessional relations in post-Reformation England', in C. Scott Dixon, Freist Dagmar and Mark Greengrass (eds), *Living with Religious Diversity in Early Modern Europe* (Aldershot, 2009), 161–82; Newton, *The Sick Child*, 17–20.

256. Pelling, *The Common Lot*, 31–32.

257. Femke Molekamp, *Women and the Bible in Early Modern England: Religious reading and writing* (Oxford, 2013), 41–42.

258. Banister, *The Historie of Man*, Sig. Biiij^v.

259. *The Syon Abbey Herbal*, ed. Adams and Forbes, 37–38.

260. Borde, *Dyetary of helthe*, Sig. Aiii^v–Aiiii^r.

261. *A treatyse of fysshynge wyth an angle, By Dame Juliana Berners*, ed. Piscator (Edinburgh, 1885), 2.

262. Quoted in R.W. Maslen, 'The healing dialogues of Doctor Bullein', *The Yearbook of English Studies* 38 (2008), 121–22.

263. Christopher Sutton, *Disce Mori: Learne to Die* (London, 1601), *STC* 23474, Sig. A12ʳ.

264. David Cressy, *Birth, Marriage and Death: Ritual, religion, and the life-cycle in Tudor and Stuart England* (Oxford, 1997), 381.

265. Archer, 'Material Londoners?', 178.

266. Richard Whitford, *A dayly exercyse and experyence of dethe* (1537), *STC* 25414, Sig. Aiiᵛ.

267. Thomas Playfere, *The Meane in Mourning* (1596), *STC* 20015, 59, 60.

268. M.C. O'Connor, *The Art of Dying Well: The development of the* Ars Moriendi (New York, 1942); N.I. Beaty, *The Craft of Dying: A study in the literary tradition of the* Ars Moriendi *in England* (New York, 1970); D.W. Atkinson, *The English* Ars Moriendi (New York, 1992); Cressy, *Birth, Marriage and Death*, 389–93; Amy Appleford, *Learning to Die in London, 1380–1540* (Philadelphia, PA, 2014). See also Thomas Becon, *The Sicke mannes Salve*, in J. Ayre (ed.), *Prayers and Other Pieces of Thomas Becon* (Cambridge, 1844), 188.

269. Stretton, 'Marriage, separation and the common law', 21–25.

270. Plat, *Sundrie new and artificiall remedies*, Sig. A3ʳ.

271. Banister, *The Historie of Man*, Sig. Aijʳ.

272. ibid., Sig. Aijʳ⁻ᵛ.

5 'Glorious Knight and Christian King': The reign of Henry VIII

1. Alfred F. Pollard, *Henry VIII* (revised edition, London, 1905); J.J. Scarisbrick, *Henry VIII* (London, 1968); Diarmaid MacCulloch (ed.), *The Reign of Henry VIII: Politics, policy and piety* (Basingstoke, 1995); David Starkey, *The Reign of Henry VIII: Personalities and politics* (London, 1985); George W. Bernard, *The King's Reformation: Henry VIII and the remaking of the English Church* (New Haven, CT, and London, 2005); Lucy Wooding, *Henry VIII* (second edition, Abingdon, 2015).

2. Greg Walker, *Writing under Tyranny: English literature and the Henrician Reformation* (Oxford, 2005); George W. Bernard, 'The tyranny of Henry VIII', in George Bernard and Steven Gunn (eds), *Authority and Consent in Tudor England* (Aldershot, 2002), 113–29.

3. Pollard, *Henry VIII*; Geoffrey Elton, 'King of hearts', in Elton, *Studies in Tudor and Stuart Politics and Government*, 4 vols (Cambridge, 1974–92), I, 104; Thomas Freeman and Susan Doran, *The Tudors and Stuarts on Film: Historical perspectives* (Basingstoke, 2008), 46–59.

4. Starkey, *The Reign of Henry VIII*; Wooding, *Henry VIII*; Bernard, *The King's Reformation*; Diarmaid MacCulloch, *Thomas Cromwell: A life* (London, 2018).

5. Kevin Sharpe, *Selling the Tudor Monarchy: Authority and image in sixteenth-century England* (New Haven, CT, 2009); Thomas Betteridge and Suzannah Lipscomb (eds), *Henry VIII and the Court: Art, politics and performance* (Farnham, 2013); Steven Gunn and Phillip Lindley (eds), *Cardinal Wolsey: Church, state and art* (Cambridge, 1991). See also David Starkey (ed.), *The Inventory of King Henry VIII* (London, 1998).

6. Steven Gunn, *Charles Brandon, Duke of Suffolk, c. 1484–1545* (Oxford, 1988).

7. Diarmaid MacCulloch, *Thomas Cranmer: A life* (New Haven, CT, and London, 1996), 360–61.

8. Garrett Mattingly, *Catherine of Aragon* (London, 1963), 308.

9. Eric Ives, *The Life and Death of Anne Boleyn* (Oxford, 2004), 358.

10. Isobel Thornley, 'Treason by words in the fifteenth century', *I* 32 (1917), 556–61; Isobel Thornley, 'The treason legislation of Henry VIII', *TRHS* third series, 9 (1917), 97–123.

11. Elton, *Tudor Constitution*, 62.

12. Cited in Susan Brigden, 'Henry VIII and the crusade against England', in Betteridge and Lipscomb (eds), *Henry VIII and the Court*, 234, 215.

13. George Bernard, 'Reflecting on the King's Reformation', in Betteridge and Lipscomb, *Henry VIII and the Court*, 9–10, 26.

14. Edmund Dudley, *The Tree of Commonwealth*, ed. D.M. Brodie (Cambridge, 1948), 103–04.

15. Steven Gunn, 'The accession of Henry VIII', *HR* 64 (1991), 279.

16. ibid., 279, 287.

17. *TRP*, I, 81.

18. Gunn, 'The accession of Henry VIII', 280.

19. *The Correspondence of Erasmus, 2: Letters 142–297*, trans. R.A.B. Mynors and D.F.S. Thomson, in Wallace K. Ferguson (ed.), *Complete Works of Erasmus* (Toronto, ON, 1975), Epistle 215: 16–18.

20. David Starkey, 'Intimacy and innovation: The rise of the Privy Chamber, 1485–1547' in David Starkey (ed.), *The English Court from the Wars of the Roses to the Civil War* (London, 1987), 71–118.

21. Steven Gunn, 'The early Tudor tournament', in David Starkey (ed.), *Henry VIII: A European court in England* (London, 1991), 47.

22. Wooding, *Henry VIII*, 61.

23. ibid., 63.

24. Colin Fewer, 'John Lydgate's *Troy Book* and the ideology of prudence', *The Chaucer Review* 38 (2004), 229–45.

25. John B. Gleason, *John Colet* (Berkeley, CA, and London, 1989), 257–59.

26. Scarisbrick, *Henry VIII*, 105–06.

27. J.G. Russell, *Peacemaking in the Renaissance* (London, 1986), Appendix A, 'Richard Pace's oration', 238.

28. Glenn Richardson, *The Field of Cloth of Gold* (New Haven, CT, and London, 2013).

29. ibid., 1–6.

30. Geoffrey Moorhouse, *Great Harry's Navy* (London, 2005); David Loades, *The Tudor Navy: An administrative, political and military history* (Aldershot, 1992).

31. Hall, *Chronicle*, 535.

32. M. Merriman, 'Italian military engineers in Britain in the 1540s', in Sarah Tyacke (ed.), *English Map-making, 1500–1650: Historical essays* (London, 1983), 57–67; L.R. Shelby, *John Rogers: Tudor military engineer* (Oxford, 1967); H.M. Colvin, *The History of the King's Works*, vol. IV (London, 1982).

33. John Guy, 'The rhetoric of counsel in early modern England', in Dale Hoak (ed.), *Tudor Political Culture* (Cambridge, 1995), 292–310.

34. Robert Applebaum, '*Utopia* and Utopianism', in Andrew Hadfield (ed.), *The Oxford Handbook of English Prose 1500–1640* (Oxford, 2013), 253–58; Quentin Skinner, 'Sir Thomas More's *Utopia* and the language of renaissance humanism', in Anthony Pagden (ed.), *The Languages of Political Theory in Early Modern Europe* (Cambridge, 2001), 123–57.

35. Sharpe, *Selling the Tudor Monarchy*, 92; see also Muriel St Clare Byrne, *The Letters of Henry VIII: A selection, with a few other documents* (London, 1936), 149, 164.

36. Elton, 'King of hearts', 104; Eric Ives, *Faction in Tudor England* (revised edition, London, 1987); Ives, *The Life and Death of Anne Boleyn*; Starkey, *The Reign of Henry VIII*.

37. *The Correspondence of Erasmus, Letters 142–297, 1501–1514*, ed. R.A.B. Mynors, D.F.S. Thomson and Wallace K. Ferguson (Toronto, 1975), 249–50.

38. Thomas Elyot, *The Boke Named the Governour* (London, 1537), STC 7636, fo. 154ᵛ.

39. Greg Walker, *Persuasive Fictions: Faction, faith and political culture in the reign of Henry VIII* (Aldershot, 1996), 13–14.

40. Peter Gwyn, *The King's Cardinal: The rise and fall of Thomas Wolsey* (London, 1990); Bernard, *The King's Reformation*; Wooding, *Henry VIII*, esp. 87–95.

41. Gwyn, *The King's Cardinal*, 361–62.

42. Roger S. Schofield, 'Taxation and the political limits of the Tudor state', in C. Cross, D.M. Loades and J.J. Scarisbrick (eds), *Law and Government under the Tudors: Essays presented to Sir Geoffrey Elton* (Cambridge, 1988), 255.

43. G.W. Bernard, *War, Taxation and Rebellion in early Tudor England: Henry VIII, Wolsey, and the Amicable Grant of 1525* (Brighton, 1986); Wooding, *Henry VIII*, 122–23.

44. James McConica (ed.), *The History of the University of Oxford*, vol. III: *The Collegiate University* (Oxford, 1986), 67.

45. Mattingly, *Catherine of Aragon*; Ives, *The Life and Death of Anne Boleyn*, 205–45; J. Mueller, 'Katherine Parr and her circle', in Mike Pincombe and Cathy Shrank (eds), *The Oxford Handbook of Tudor Literature, 1485–1603* (Oxford, 2009), 222–30.

46. Richardson, *The Field of Cloth of Gold*, 60, 65.

47. Wooding, *Henry VIII*, 84–85.

48. Hall, *Chronicle*, 526.

49. Thomas P. Campbell, *Henry VIII and the Art of Majesty: Tapestries at the Tudor court* (New Haven, CT, and London, 2007).

50. Felicity Heal, *The Power of Gifts: Gift-exchange in early modern England* (Oxford, 2014), 87–120.

51. N.H. Nicolas (ed.), *The Privy Purse Expenses of King Henry the Eighth* (1827), 282, 28, 5.

52. James Carley, *The Books of Henry VIII and his Wives* (London, 2004), 111–13.

53. Walker, *Writing under Tyranny*, 9.

54. Juan Luis Vives, *The Education of a Christian Woman: A sixteenth-century manual*, ed. C. Fantazzi (Chicago, IL, 2000), 45.

55. Glenn Richardson, 'The French connection: Francis I and England's break with Rome', in Glenn Richardson (ed.), *The Contending Kingdoms: France and England 1430–1700* (Aldershot, 2008), 95.

56. Starkey (ed), *Henry VIII: A European court in England*.

57. Wooding, *Henry VIII*, 52.

58. A.A. Chibi, *Henry VIII's Conservative Scholar: Bishop John Stokesley and the divorce, Royal Supremacy and doctrinal reform* (Bern, 1997); A.A. Chibi, *Henry VIII's Bishops: Diplomats, administrators, scholars and shepherds* (Cambridge, 2003); Glyn Redworth, *In Defence of the Church Catholic: The life of Stephen Gardiner* (Oxford, 1990).

59. Virginia Murphy, 'The literature and propaganda of Henry VIII's first divorce', in MacCulloch (ed.), *The Reign of Henry VIII*, 138.

60. John Guy, 'Thomas Wolsey, Thomas Cromwell and the reform of Henrician government', in MacCulloch (ed.), *The Reign of Henry VIII*, 37.

61. The relevant passages were Leviticus 18:16 and 20:21. The contradictory passage in Deuteronomy was 25:5.

62. Murphy, 'The literature and propaganda of Henry VIII's first divorce', 138–39.

63. Richard Rex, 'The earliest use of Hebrew in books printed in England: Dating some works of Richard Pace and Robert Wakefield', *Transactions of the Cambridge Bibliographical Society*, 9 (1990), 517–18, 521–22.

64. Bernard, *The King's Reformation*, 6–9; see also Sharpe, *Selling the Tudor Monarchy*, 91.

65. Sharon L. Jansen, *Political Protest and Prophecy under Henry VIII* (Woodbridge, 1991).

66. Diane Watt, 'Elizabeth Barton', *ODNB*.

67. Sharon L. Jansen, 'Elizabeth Barton: "The Holy Maid of Kent"' and 'Elizabeth Barton and political prophecy', in Sharon L. Jansen (ed.), *Dangerous Talk and Strange Behavior: Women and popular resistance to the reforms of Henry VIII* (Basingstoke, 1996), 41–56, 57–75; Alan Neame, *The Holy Maid of Kent* (London, 1971).

68. Ives, *The Life and Death of Anne Boleyn*, 161–62.

69. Dale Hoak, 'The iconography of the crown imperial', in Hoak (ed.), *Tudor Political Culture*, 54–103.

70. Wooding, *Henry VIII*, 186.

71. A.G. Dickens and D. Carr (eds), *The Reformation in England to the Accession of Elizabeth I* (London, 1967), 50–51.

72. Thornley, 'The treason legislation', 104–11.

73. For the debate over the coherence and consistency of Henry's religious objectives, contrast Diarmaid MacCulloch, 'Henry VIII and the reform of the Church', in

MacCulloch (ed.), *The Reign of Henry VIII*, 159–80, with George W. Bernard, 'The making of religious policy, 1533–1546: Henry VIII and the search for the Middle Way', *HJ* 41 (1998), 321–49.

74. *A Necessary Doctrine and Erudition for any Christian Man* (1543), in Gerald Bray (ed.), *The Institution of a Christian Man* (Cambridge, 2018), 30.

75. Lucy Wooding, 'From Tudor humanism to Reformation preaching', in Hugh Adlington, Peter MacCullough and Emma Rhatigan (eds), *The Oxford Handbook of the Early Modern Sermon* (Oxford, 2011), 341–44.

76. Xanthe Brooke, 'Henry VIII revealed: Holbein's portrait and its legacy', in Xanthe Brooke and David Crombie (eds), *Henry VIII Revealed: Holbein's portrait and its legacy* (London, 2003), 10–17.

77. Philip Pouncey, 'Girolamo da Treviso in the service of Henry VIII', *Burlington Magazine* 95 (1953), 208–11.

78. Thomas Elyot, *The dictionary* (1538), STC 7659, Sig. Aiiᵛ. See also Susan Brigden, *London and the Reformation* (Oxford, 1989), 266; Hall, *Chronicle*, 539; Walker, *Persuasive Fictions*, 16.

79. Dickens and Carr (eds), *The Reformation in England*, 29.

80. George W. Bernard, 'The piety of Henry VIII', in N. Scott Amos, Henk van Nierop and Andrew Pettegree (eds), *The Education of a Christian Society: Humanism and the Reformation in Britain and the Netherlands* (Aldershot, 1999), 62–88.

81. Richard Rex, *Henry VIII and the English Reformation* (Basingstoke, 1993); see also Rex, 'The crisis of obedience: God's word and Henry's Reformation', *HJ* 39 (1996), 863–94.

82. Geoffrey Elton, *Policy and Police: The enforcement of the Reformation in the age of Thomas Cromwell* (Cambridge, 1972), 90–93.

83. ibid., 375.

84. Richard Rex and Colin Armstrong, 'Henry VIII's ecclesiastical and collegiate foundations', *HR* 75 (2002), 395–98.

85. Richard W. Hoyle, *The Pilgrimage of Grace and the politics of the 1530s* (Oxford, 2001).

86. J. Gwynfor Jones, *Early Modern Wales, c.1525–1640* (Basingstoke, 1994), chapter 2; W.R.B. Robinson, 'The Tudor revolution in Welsh government', *EHR* 103 (1988), 1–20.

87. Suzannah Lipscomb, *1536: The year that changed Henry VIII* (Oxford, 2009).

88. Anthony Fletcher and Diarmaid MacCulloch, *Tudor Rebellions* (seventh edition, Abingdon, 2020), 28.

89. Bernard, *The King's Reformation*, 295–96, 298.

90. *L&P*, XI, 860.

91. *Lisle Letters*, III, 306.

92. Simon Thurley, *House of Power: The places that shaped the Tudor world* (London, 2017), 268–72.

93. Wooding, *Henry VIII*, 253.

94. Geoffrey Elton, *The Tudor Revolution in Government* (Cambridge, 1953); Geoffrey Elton, *Reform and Renewal: Thomas Cromwell and the Common Weal* (Cambridge, 1973); Geoffrey Elton, *Reform and Reformation: England 1509–1558* (Cambridge, 1977); Geoffrey Elton, 'The Tudor revolution: A reply', *P&P* 29 (1964), 26–49; Geoffrey Elton, 'A new age of reform', *HJ* 30 (1987), 709–16; Christopher Coleman and David Starkey (eds), *Revolution Reassessed: Revisions in the history of Tudor government and administration* (Oxford, 1986).

95. Starkey, *The Reign of Henry VIII*, 123; Susan Brigden, 'Popular disturbance and the fall of Thomas Cromwell and the reformers, 1539–1540', *HJ* 24 (1981), 257–78. For a view which ascribes more agency to the king than to faction, see Bernard, *King's Reformation*, 569–79; MacCulloch, *Thomas Cranmer*, 268–71.

96. *TRP*, I, 244.

97. Thomas F. Mayer, *Reginald Pole: Prince and prophet* (Cambridge, 2000); John Edwards, *Archbishop Pole* (Farnham, 2014).

98. MacCulloch, *Thomas Cranmer*, 232–34, 352–54. See also Elaine V. Beilin, 'A challenge to authority: Anne Askew', in E.V. Beilin, *Redeeming Eve: Women writers of the English renaissance* (Princeton, NJ, 1987), 29–47.

99. Elton, *Tudor Constitution*, 390.

100. MacCulloch, *Thomas Cranmer*, 249–50.

101. ibid., 354.

102. Thomas Freeman, 'One survived: The account of Katherine Parr in Foxe's "Book of Martyrs"', in Betteridge and Lipscomb (eds), *Henry VIII and the Court*, 235–54.

103. *A famous speech of King Henry the eighth* (London, 1642), Sig. A3ʳ⁻ᵛ.

104. Christopher Haigh, *The English Reformation Revised* (Cambridge, 1987), 12.

105. Ronald Hutton, 'The local impact of the English Reformations', in Peter Marshall (ed.), *The Impact of the English Reformation, 1500–1640* (London, 1997), 144.

106. Robert Whiting, 'Local responses to the Henrician Reformation', in MacCulloch (ed.), *The Reign of Henry VIII*, 203–26.

107. Cited in ibid., 207.

108. Christopher Haigh, 'Anticlericalism and the English Reformation', *History* 68 (1983), 391–407; Peter Marshall, *The Catholic Priesthood and the English Reformation* (Oxford, 1994), 222–32.

109. Marshall, *The Catholic Priesthood and the English Reformation*, 224.

110. Ethan Shagan, '"Open disputation was in alehouses": Religious debate in the diocese of Canterbury, c.1543' in Ethan Shagan (ed.), *Popular Politics and the English Reformation* (Cambridge, 2003), 197–232, quotation at 198.

111. Sharpe, *Selling the Tudor Monarchy*, 84–85, 86.

112. *National Prayers: Special worship since the Reformation*, vol. I: *Special Prayers, Fasts and Thanksgivings in the British Isles, 1533–1688*, ed. Natalie Mears, Alasdair Raffe, Stephen Taylor and Philip Williamson (Woodbridge, 2013), 25.

113. Steven Gunn, *The English People at War in the Age of Henry VIII* (Oxford, 2018), 17–18.

114. ibid., 31–34, 35.

115. *National Prayers*, 25.

116. Charles S. Knighton and David M. Loades, *Letters from the Mary Rose* (Stroud and Portsmouth, 2002); Knighton and Loades (eds), *The Anthony Roll of Henry VIII's navy: Pepys MS 2991 and British Library Add MS 22047 with related material*, Navy Records Society, occasional publications, 2 (Aldershot, 2000).

117. Moorhouse, *Great Harry's Navy*, 238.

118. R.A. Houlbrooke, 'Henry VIII's wills: A comment', *HJ* 37 (1994), 891–99; Eric Ives, 'The protectorate provisions of 1546–7', *HJ* 37 (1994), 901–14; Eric Ives, 'Henry VIII's will: A forensic conundrum', *HJ* 35 (1992), 779–804; H. Miller, 'Henry VIII's unwritten will: Grants of lands and honours in 1547', in Eric Ives, R.J. Knecht and J.J. Scarisbrick (eds), *Wealth and Power in Tudor England* (London, 1978), 87–106.

119. TNA E/23/4 fos.3r, 5v–6r.

120. M. Mitchell, 'Works of art from Rome for Henry VIII: A study of Anglo-Papal relations as reflected in papal gifts to the English king', *Journal of the Warburg and Courtauld Institutes* 34 (1971), Appendix II, 201–03.

121. Dale Hoak, 'Introduction', in Hoak (ed.), *Tudor Political Culture*, 9–10.

122. William Thomas, *The Pilgrim: A Dialogue of the Life and Action of King Henry VIII*, cited in Sharpe, *Selling the Tudor Monarchy*, 182–83.

123. Nicholas Sander, *De Origine ac Progressu Schismatis Anglicani* (1585); translated by David Lewis and published as *The Rise and Growth of the Anglican Schism* (Tunbridge Wells, 1988), 160–62, 165.

124. Wooding, *Henry VIII*, 92.

125. William Shakespeare, *King Henry VIII*, Act V, Scene 4.

126. Sharpe, *Selling the Tudor Monarchy*, 177.

6 Authority and Dissent: The balance of power

1. *Elizabeth I: Collected Works*, 343–44.
2. *TED*, iii, 12.
3. Cynthia Herrup, *The Common Peace: Participation and the criminal law in seventeenth-century England* (Cambridge, 1987), 195; Paul Griffiths, Adam Fox and Steve Hindle, Introduction, in Griffiths, Fox and Hindle (eds), *The Experience of Authority in Early Modern England* (Basingstoke, 1996), 2–7.
4. Andy Wood, *Riot, Rebellion and Popular Politics in Early Modern England* (Basingstoke, 2002), xi.
5. Cited in Christopher Hill, 'The many-headed monster in late Tudor and early Stuart political thinking', in Charles H. Carter (ed.), *From the Renaissance to the Counter-Reformation: Essays in honour of Garrett Mattingly* (London, 1966), 297.
6. Thomas More, *Utopia*, ed. George M. Logan (third edition, Cambridge, 2016), 16.
7. Lily B. Campbell (ed.), *The Mirror for Magistrates* (1938; repr. New York, 1960); Scott Lucas, 'Hall's chronicle and the *Mirror for Magistrates*: History and the tragic pattern', in Mike Pincombe and Cathy Shrank (eds), *The Oxford Handbook of Tudor Literature, 1485–1603* (Oxford, 2009), 356–71.
8. Anthony Fletcher and Diarmaid MacCulloch, *Tudor Rebellions* (seventh edition, Abingdon, 2020), 158.
9. Thomas Elyot, *The Boke Named the Governour* (London, 1537), STC 7636, fo. 1^r. (The first edition of this work was printed in 1531.)
10. Stanford Lehmberg, *Sir Thomas Elyot: Tudor humanist* (Austin, TX, 1960); Pearl Hogrefe, 'Sir Thomas Elyot's intention in the opening chapters of the "Governour"', *Studies in Philology* 60 (1963), 133–40; Greg Walker, *Writing under Tyranny: English literature and the Henrician Reformation* (Oxford, 2005), part II.
11. Elyot, *Boke Named the Governour*, fo. 4^{r-v}.
12. Steven Gunn, *Henry VII's New Men and the Making of Tudor England* (Oxford, 2016), 16–20.
13. William Harrison, *The Description of England*, ed. G. Edelen (Washington, DC, and London, 1994), 97.
14. Judith Richards, *Elizabeth I* (Abingdon, 2012), 60.
15. John Proctor, *The historie of Wyates rebellion with the order and maner of resisting the same* (London, 1554), STC 20407, fo. 54^{r-v}.
16. *Elizabeth I: Collected Works*, 59.
17. John Rastell, *Of Gentylnes and Nobylyte* (1525), STC 20723, Sig. Civ^r.
18. George Bernard, *War, Taxation and Rebellion in early Tudor England: Henry VIII, Wolsey, and the Amicable Grant of 1525* (Brighton, 1986), 63.
19. ibid., 56–57.
20. Andy Wood, *Faith, Hope and Charity: English neighbourhoods, 1500–1640* (Cambridge, 2020), 106.
21. Michael J. Braddick and John Walter, 'Introduction. Grids of power: Order, hierarchy and subordination in early modern society', in Michael J. Braddick and John Walter (eds), *Negotiating Power in Early Modern Society: Order, hierarchy and subordination in Britain and Ireland* (Cambridge, 2001), 1–5. See also Bob Scribner, 'Is a history of popular culture possible?', *History of European Ideas* 10 (1989), 175–91.
22. Malcolm Gaskill, *Crime and Mentalities in Early Modern England* (Cambridge, 2000), 27.
23. Braddick and Walter, 'Introduction', 11.
24. Keith Wrightson, 'The politics of the parish in early modern England', in Griffiths, Fox and Hindle (eds), *The Experience of Authority*, 10–46.
25. Patrick Collinson, '*De republica anglorum*, or history with the politics put back', in Patrick Collinson, *Elizabethan Essays* (London, 1994), 1–30.
26. Anthony Fletcher, 'Honour, reputation and local office-holding in Elizabethan and Stuart England', in Anthony Fletcher and John Stevenson (eds), *Order and Disorder in Early Modern England* (Cambridge, 1985), 92–115.

27. Braddick and Walter, 'Introduction', 12–13.
28. Thomas Middleton, *Blurt, Master-Constable*, in A.H. Bullen (ed.), *The Works of Thomas Middleton* (London, 1885), I, 78. I am grateful to John Amabilino for this reference.
29. Thomas Smith, *De Republica Anglorum*, ed. M. Dewar (Cambridge, 1982), 88.
30. More, *Utopia*, 14.
31. *Richard II*, Act III, Scene 2, ll. 56–57.
32. Edmund Dudley, *The Tree of Commonwealth*, ed. D.M. Brodie (Cambridge, 1948), 103–04.
33. Jennifer Loach, 'The function of ceremonial in the reign of Henry VIII', *P&P* 142 (1994), 42–68; Fiona Kisby, ' "When the king goeth a procession": Chapel ceremonies and services, the ritual year, and religious reforms at the early Tudor court, 1485–1547', *JBS* 40 (2001), 44–75.
34. Marc Bloch, *The Royal Touch: Sacred monarchy and scrofula in England and France*, trans. J.E. Anderson (London, 1973); Sydney Anglo, *Images of Tudor Kingship* (London, 1992), 19–20; Kisby, ' "When the king goeth a procession" ', 62–63.
35. Ronald Hutton, 'The English Reformation and the evidence of folklore', *P&P*, 148 (1995), 108.
36. James Turrell, 'The ritual of royal healing in early modern England: Scrofula, liturgy and politics', *Anglican and Episcopal History* 68 (1999), 3–36.
37. William Tooker, *Charisma Sive Donum Sanationis* (London, 1597), STC 24118, quote on 105 ('Deus est optimus et maximus medicus omnium'); see also C.D. O'Malley, 'Tudor medicine and biology', *HLQ* 32 (1968), 14–15.
38. Elyot, *The Boke Named the Governour*, fo. 95^{r-v}.
39. Campbell (ed.), *Mirror for Magistrates*; C.S. Lewis, *English Literature in the Sixteenth Century* (Oxford, 1954), 240; Scott C. Lucas, *'A Mirror for Magistrates' and the Politics of English Reformation* (Amherst, MA, 2009); Harriet Archer and Andrew Hadfield (eds), A Mirror for Magistrates *in Context: Literature, history and politics in early modern England* (Cambridge, 2016).
40. Desiderius Erasmus, *The Education of a Christian Prince*, trans. and ed. Lisa Jardine (Cambridge, 1997), 4–5.
41. ibid., 23–24.
42. Walker, *Writing under Tyranny*, 181–95; Lehmberg, *Sir Thomas Elyot*, 117; Alistair Fox, 'Sir Thomas Elyot and the humanist dilemma', in Alistair Fox and John Guy (eds), *Reassessing the Henrician Age: Humanism, politics, and reform, 1500–1550* (Oxford, 1986), 66–67. See also Joanne Paul, 'The use of Kairos in renaissance political philosophy', *RQ* 67 (2014), 51–55.
43. William Westerman, *Two assize sermons* (1600), STC 25282, Sig. A6^v–A7^r.
44. *William Lambarde and Local Government*, ed. Conyers Read (New York, 1962), 69.
45. *EHD* V(A), 243–44.
46. 'Henry VII: Parliament of 1485, text and translation', ed. Rosemary Horrox, in C. Given-Wilson et al. (eds), *The Parliament Rolls of Medieval England*, vi-267.
47. Quoted in Ian Archer, 'Popular politics in the sixteenth and early seventeenth centuries', in Paul Griffiths and Mark Jenner (eds), *Londinopolis: Essays in the cultural and social history of early modern London, c.1500–c.1750* (Manchester, 2000), 35.
48. Kevin Sharpe, *Selling the Tudor Monarchy: Authority and image in sixteenth-century England* (New Haven, CT, 2009), 95–96.
49. Archer, 'Popular politics', 34–35.
50. John Pylbarough, *A Commemoration of the Inestimable Graces and Benefits of God* (1540), STC 20521, Sig. Aii^v; Aiv^v.
51. 'Act for the exoneration of exactions paid to the see of Rome', in Elton, *Tudor Constitution*, 351.
52. Fletcher and MacCulloch, *Tudor Rebellions*, 57, 93.
53. Quentin Skinner, *The Foundations of Modern Political Thought*, vol. 2: *The Age of Reformation* (Cambridge, 1978), chapter 7.

54. George Abbot, *An exposition upon the prophet Ionah* (1600), STC 34, 66.

55. See the papal bull 'Regnans in Excelsis', reprinted in Elton, *Tudor Constitution*, 414.

56. Matilda may have laid claim to the throne in 1135, but she was never crowned queen and did not exercise authority in practice.

57. Alice Hunt and Anna Whitelock (eds), *Tudor Queenship: The reigns of Mary and Elizabeth* (Basingstoke, 2010); Susan Doran and Thomas Freeman (eds), *Mary Tudor: Old and new perspectives* (Basingstoke, 2011); Susan Doran and Thomas S. Freeman (eds), *The Myth of Elizabeth* (Basingstoke, 2003).

58. Judith M. Richards, '"To promote a woman to beare rule": Talking of queens in mid-Tudor England', *SCJ* 29 (1997), 101–21; Anne McLaren, 'Gender, religion, and early modern nationalism: Elizabeth I, Mary Queen of Scots, and the genesis of English anti-Catholicism', *AHR* 107 (2002), 739–67.

59. 'Sir Thomas Smith's oration for and against the Queen's Marriage', in John Strype, *The Life of the Learned Sir Thomas Smith* (Oxford, 1820), Appendix III, 10–11.

60. 'Queene Maries Oration', in Holinshed, *Chronicles* (1577), IV, 1729.

61. Robert Miola, 'Julius Caesar and the tyrannicide debate', *RQ* 38 (1985), 271–89.

62. Ben Jonson, *Sejanus His Fall*, ed. Philip J. Ayres (Manchester, 1990), Act I, ll. 407–09.

63. See Michael Hicks, *English Political Culture in the Fifteenth Century* (London and New York, 2002), 3–6; George Bernard, 'The continuing power of the Tudor nobility', in George Bernard, *Power and Politics in Tudor England* (Aldershot, 2000), 38–44.

64. Older arguments about the 'rise of the gentry' have now been comprehensively dismissed, but see Richard H. Tawney, 'The rise of the gentry, 1558–1640', *EconHR*, x, part 2 (1940), and 'Postscript', *EconHR*, second series, vii, part 1 (1954); Hugh Trevor-Roper, 'The gentry, 1540–1640', *EconHR Supplements*, 1 (1953). See also Julian Cornwall, 'The early Tudor gentry', *EconHR*, new series, 17 (1965), 456–75.

65. Christine de Pisan, *Here begynneth the booke whiche is called the body of polycye* (1521), Sig. ai^v.

66. ibid., Sig. gii^v.

67. Laurence Humfrey, *The nobles or of nobilitye* (London, 1563), STC 13964, Sig. Aiii^r.

68. Rastell, *Of Gentylnes and Nobylyte*, Sig. Aiii^v.

69. John Hale, *England and the Italian Renaissance: The growth of interest in its history and art* (revised edition, London, 1996), 4.

70. Stephen Alford, *Burghley: William Cecil at the court of Elizabeth I* (New Haven, CT, and London, 2008), 191–92.

71. *L&P*, XI, 705 (1); Fletcher and MacCulloch, *Tudor Rebellions*, 142.

72. *L&P*, XI, 705 (4); Richard Hoyle, *The Pilgrimage of Grace and the Politics of the 1530s* (Oxford, 2001), 457–58.

73. Pisan, *Body of polycye*, Sig. hiii^r.

74. Christine Carpenter, *Locality and Polity: A study of Warwickshire landed society, 1401–1499* (Cambridge, 1992), 85–86; Felicity Heal and Clive Holmes, *The Gentry in England and Wales, 1500–1700* (Basingstoke, 1994), 166–89; M.J. Braddick, *State Formation in Early Modern England, c.1550–1700* (Cambridge, 2000), 27–46; Steve Hindle, *The State and Social Change in Early Modern England, 1550–1640* (Basingstoke, 2000), 3–15.

75. Janet Dickinson, 'Nobility and Gentry', in Susan Doran and Norman Jones (eds), *The Elizabethan World* (Abingdon and New York, 2011), 288.

76. Neil Younger, 'Securing the monarchical republic: The remaking of the lord lieutenancies in 1585', *HR* 84 (2011), 261–62.

77. Roger Manning, *Religion and Society in Elizabethan Sussex: A study of the enforcement of the religious settlement, 1558–1603* (Leicester, 1969), 221–23; Michael Questier, *Catholicism and Community in Early Modern England: Politics, aristocratic patronage and religion, c. 1550–1640* (Cambridge, 2006), 169–78; for a more pessimistic assessment, see also Curtis Breight, 'Caressing the great: Viscount Montague's entertainment of Elizabeth at Cowdray, 1591', *Sussex Archaeological Collections* 127 (1989), 147–66.

78. Barry Coward, *The Stanleys, Lords Stanley and Earls of Derby, 1385–1672* (Manchester, 1983), 97–98, 149–50.

79. ibid., 96.

80. Alfred Hassell Smith, *County and Court: Government and Politics in Norfolk, 1558–1603* (Oxford, 1974), 23–44.

81. Quoted in Dickinson, 'Nobility and gentry', 290.

82. Paul Van Brunt Jones, *The Household of a Tudor Nobleman* (Urbana, IL, 1917), Appendix B, 242. See also Susan Doran, 'The finances of an Elizabethan nobleman and royal servant: A case study of Thomas Radcliffe, 3rd earl of Sussex', *BIHR* 61 (1988), 293.

83. Suzanne Westfall, *Patrons and Performance: Early Tudor household revels* (Oxford, 1990), 2–4.

84. ibid., 10–11.

85. Jones, *Household of a Tudor Nobleman*, 240.

86. K. Mertes, 'The household as a religious community', in J.T. Rosenthal and C. Richmond (eds), *People, Politics and Community in the Later Middle Ages* (Gloucester, 1987), 124–26.

87. Westfall, *Patrons and Performance*, 15.

88. Carpenter, *Locality and Polity*, 242.

89. Paul Slack, *Poverty and Policy in Tudor and Stuart England* (London, 1988), 20–21.

90. Coward, *The Stanleys*, 95.

91. Dickinson, 'Nobility and gentry', 285.

92. Retha M. Warnicke, 'Family and kinship relations at the Henrician court', in Dale Hoak (ed.), *Tudor Political Culture* (Cambridge, 1995), 35–36.

93. J. Gwynfor Jones, *Early Modern Wales, c.1525–1640* (Basingstoke, 1994), 13–14.

94. George Bernard, *The Power of the Early Tudor Nobility: A study of the fourth and fifth earls of Shrewsbury* (Brighton, 1985), 177–78; see, too, Bernard, 'The rise of Sir William Compton, early Tudor courtier', *I* 96 (1981), 754–77.

95. Diarmaid MacCulloch, *Thomas Cromwell: A Life* (London, 2018), 422, 540.

96. Janet Dickinson, 'Nobility and gentry', 285–86; Alford, *Burghley*, 145–46, 209–10, 301–02.

97. Dickinson, 'Nobility and gentry', 286.

98. Kenneth A. Fowler, 'Sir John Hawkwood and the English *condottieri* in Trecento Italy', *RS* 12 (1998), 131–48; Stephen Cooper, *Sir John Hawkwood: Chivalry and the art of war* (Barnsley, 2008).

99. Anna Bryson, *From Courtesy to Civility: Changing codes of conduct in early modern England* (Oxford, 1998).

100. Quoted in Katherine Duncan-Jones, *Sir Philip Sidney, Courtier Poet* (New Haven, CT, 1991), 303.

101. ibid., 296–303.

102. Humfrey, *The nobles or of nobilitye*, Sig. Aiiiʳ.

103. Edmund Spenser, *The Faerie Queene* (Harmondsworth, 1978), prefatory letter to Sir Walter Raleigh, 15.

104. Susanne Wofford, 'The Faerie Queene, Books I–III', in Andrew Hadfield (ed.), *The Cambridge Companion to Spenser* (Cambridge, 2001), 114–15, 118, 196. See also William Schofield, *Chivalry in English Literature: Chaucer, Mallory, Spenser and Shakespeare* (Oxford, 1912), 149–55; Elizabeth Heale, *The Faerie Queene: A reader's guide* (Cambridge, 1987), 15.

105. Jones, *Early Modern Wales*, 49–51; Ralph A. Griffiths, *Sir Rhys ap Thomas and His Family: A study in the Wars of the Roses and early Tudor politics* (Cardiff, 1993).

106. Alexandra Gajda, *The Earl of Essex and Late Elizabethan Political Culture* (Oxford, 2012), 175–80.

107. A.H. Nelson, *Monstrous Adversary: The life of Edward de Vere, 17th earl of Oxford* (Liverpool, 2003).

108. Albert F. Pollard, *The Reign of Henry VII from Contemporary Sources*, 3 vols (New York and London, 1913), I, 48–49.
109. *The boke of noblesse*, ed. J.G. Nicols ((New York, 1972), 76–78.
110. Sir Humphrey Gilbert, *Queene Elizabethes Achademy* (EETS e.s. 8, 1869), 3–7.
111. Steven Gunn, *The English People at War in the Age of Henry VIII* (Oxford, 2018), 1–16.
112. Penry Williams, 'The crown and the counties', in Christopher Haigh, *The Reign of Elizabeth I* (Basingstoke, 1984), 129–31.
113. John Aylmer, *An Harborowe for Faithfull and Trewe Subiectes* (1559), STC 1006, Sig. Pʳ⁻ᵛ.
114. MacCulloch, *Thomas Cromwell*, 526.
115. Machiavelli, *The arte of warre . . . set forthe in Englishe by Peter Whitehorne* (1562), STC 17164, Sig. aiijʳ⁻ᵛ, aivʳ.
116. Neil Younger, 'The practice and politics of troop-raising: Robert Devereux, second earl of Essex, and the Elizabethan regime', *I* 127 (2012), 566–67.
117. Bernard, *Power of the Early Tudor Nobility*, 181.
118. See George Bernard (ed.), *The Tudor Nobility* (Manchester, 1992), in which all seven chapters focus on men.
119. Barbara Harris, *English Aristocratic Women, 1450–1550* (Oxford, 2002); James Daybell (ed.), *Women and Politics in Early Modern England, 1450–1700* (London, 2004); M.F. Harkrider, *Women, Reform and Community in Early Modern England: Katherine Willoughby, duchess of Suffolk, and Lincolnshire's godly aristocracy, 1519–1580* (Woodbridge, 2008); Amanda Herbert, *Female Alliances: Gender, identity and friendship in early modern Britain* (New Haven, CT, and London, 2014); Nicola Clark, *Gender, Family and Politics: The Howard women, 1485–1558* (Oxford, 2018).
120. Jeri McIntosh, *From Heads of Household to Heads of State: The pre-accession households of Mary and Elizabeth Tudor, 1516–1558* (New York, 2008).
121. Barbara Harris, 'Sisterhood, friendship and the power of English aristocratic women, 1450–1550', in Daybell, *Women and Politics*, 21–50.
122. Harris, *English Aristocratic Women*, 5–6.
123. Barbara Harris, 'Defining themselves: English aristocratic women, 1450–1550', *JBS* 49 (2010), 739.
124. Michael Jones and Malcolm Underwood, *The King's Mother: Lady Margaret Beaufort, countess of Richmond and Derby* (Cambridge, 1992), 40.
125. Barbara Harris, 'A new look at the Reformation: Aristocratic women and nunneries, 1450–1540', *JBS* 32 (1993), 89–113.
126. Clark, *Gender, Family and Politics*, 5.
127. Harris, 'Defining themselves', 734–36.
128. Pauline Croft, 'Libels, popular literacy and public opinion in early modern England', *HR* 68 (1995), 276.
129. Andrew Hadfield, *Edmund Spenser: A life* (Oxford, 2014), 293.
130. Gajda, *The Earl of Essex*, 178.
131. Edward P. Thompson, *Whigs and Hunters: The origins of the Black Act* (London, 1975), 265–67.
132. Conrad Russell, 'Parliamentary history in perspective, 1604–1629', *History* 61 (1976), 1.
133. Jennifer Loach, *Parliament under the Tudors* (Oxford, 1991), 54; although see also Paul Cavill, 'Debate and dissent in Henry VII's parliaments', *Parliamentary History* 25 (2006), 161, which questions Loach's view.
134. Elton, *Tudor Constitution*, 270.
135. Loach, *Parliament under the Tudors*, 24–42.
136. ibid., 29.
137. John S. Roskell, *The Commons and their Speakers, 1376–1523* (Manchester, 1965), 74.
138. Archer, 'Popular politics', 32.
139. Sharpe, *Selling the Tudor Monarchy*, 161; David Dean, 'Parliament', in Doran and Jones (eds), *The Elizabethan World*, 113–14.

140. Strype, *The Life of the learned Sir Thomas Smith*, 192. The discourse was written in manuscript, not printed.

141. Loach, *Parliament under the Tudors*, 5.

142. M.A.R. Graves, *The Tudor Parliaments* (London, 1985), 19–20.

143. See Jones, *Early Modern Wales*, 80–82.

144. Stanford Lehmberg, *The Reformation Parliament, 1529–1536* (Cambridge, 1970). See also Paul Cavill, 'Anticlericalism and the early Tudor parliament', *Parliamentary History* 34 (2015), 14–29; Richard Rex, 'Jasper Fyloll and the enormities of the clergy: Two tracts written during the Reformation parliament', *SCJ* 31 (2000), 1043–62.

145. Henry VIII, c.21 (1534); cited in Elton, *Studies in Tudor and Stuart Politics and Government*, 4 vols (Cambridge, 1974–92), II, 32.

146. *EHD* V(A), 317.

147. ibid., 323.

148. ibid., 323–25.

149. Smith, *De Republica Anglorum*, 78.

150. Richard Hooker, *Of the Laws of Ecclesiastical Polity*, ed. Arthur S. McGrade (Cambridge, 1989), 192.

151. Aylmer, *An Harborowe*, Sig. H3^v–H4^r.

152. Jones, *Early Modern Wales*, 86.

153. Herrup, *Common Peace*, 5–7.

154. Christopher W. Brooks, *Law, Politics and Society in Early Modern England* (Cambridge, 2008), 13.

155. *The Boke of Justices of Peas* (London, 1505), STC 14862, Sig. Av^v–Avi^r, Bii^v, Ci^{r-v}.

156. Ralph A. Houlbrooke, *Church Courts and the People during the English Reformation 1520–1570* (Oxford, 1979); Martin Ingram, *Church Courts, Sex and Marriage in England, 1570–1640* (Cambridge, 1987); Martin Ingram, *Carnal Knowledge: Regulating sex in England, 1470–1600* (Cambridge, 2017).

157. Daniel Kornstein, *Kill All the Lawyers? Shakespeare's legal appeal* (Lincoln, NE, 2005); O. Hood Phillips, *Shakespeare and the Lawyers* (London and New York, 1972); Paul Raffield, 'A discredited priesthood: The failings of common lawyers and their representation in seventeenth century satirical drama', *Law and Literature* 17 (2005), 365–95.

158. Erika Rackley, 'Reassessing Portia: The iconic potential of Shakespeare's woman lawyer', *Feminist Legal Studies* 11 (2003), 25–44; I. Ward, *Shakespeare and the Legal Imagination* (London, 1999).

159. Christopher W. Brooks, *Pettyfoggers and Vipers of the Commonwealth: The 'lower branch' of the legal profession in early modern England* (Cambridge, 2009), 265.

160. Wilfred R. Prest, *The Inns of Court under Elizabeth I and the Early Stuarts, 1590–1640* (London, 1972).

161. Christopher W. Brooks, *Lawyers, Litigation and English Society since 1450* (London, 1998), 68, 71. See also J.H. Baker, 'Personal actions in the high court of Battle Abbey, 1450–1602', *Cambridge Law Journal* 51 (1992); Ingram, *Church Courts, Sex and Marriage in England*, 69; Houlbrooke, *Church Courts and the People during the English Reformation*, 273–74.

162. Brooks, *Lawyers, Litigation and English Society*, 71; Laura Gowing, 'Language, power and the law: Women's Slander litigation in early modern England', in Jenny Kermode and Garthine Walker (eds), *Women, Crime and the Courts in Early Modern England* (London, 1994), 26–47; Amy Erickson, *Women and Property in Early Modern England* (London, 1995); Tim Stretton, *Women Waging Law in Elizabethan England* (Cambridge, 1998); Laura Gowing, *Domestic Dangers: Women, words and sex in early modern London* (Oxford, 1998).

163. Thomas Wilson, *The Arte of Rhetorique* (London, 1585), STC 25806, 38.

164. Christopher W. Brooks, 'Litigants and attorneys in the King's Bench and Common Pleas, 1560–1640', in J.H. Baker (ed.), *Legal Records and the Historian* (London, 1978), 41–59.

165. James Sharpe, 'The people and the law', in Barry Rea (ed.), *Popular Culture in Seventeenth-Century England* (London, 1985), 244–70; Cynthia Herrup, 'Law and morality in seventeenth-century England', *P&P* 106 (1985), 102–23.

166. Wrightson, 'The politics of the parish', 23.

167. Brooks, *Lawyers, Litigation and English Society*, 191.

168. Keith Wrightson, 'Two concepts of order: Justices, constables and jurymen in seventeenth-century England', in John Brewer and John Styles (eds), *An Ungovernable People: The English and their law in the seventeenth and eighteenth centuries* (London, 1980), 21–46.

169. David Sugarman, 'Law, law-consciousness and lawyers as constitutive of early modern England', in Michael Lobban, Joanne Begiato and Adrian Green (eds), *Law, Lawyers and Litigants in Early Modern England: Essays in memory of Christopher W. Brooks* (Cambridge, 2019), 33.

170. A.L. Beier, *Masterless Men: The Vagrancy Problem in England, 1560-1640* (London, 1985), 164–69; Joanna Innes, 'Prisons for the poor: English bridewells, 1555–1800', in Francis Snyder and Douglas Hay (eds), *Labour, Law, and Crime: A historical perspective* (London, 1987), 42–61.

171. Paul Griffiths, 'Contesting London Bridewell, 1576–1580', *JBS* 42 (2003), 283–315.

172. Herrup, *Common Peace*, 194.

173. Jonathan Barry and Christopher W. Brookes (eds), *The Middling Sort of People* (Basingstoke, 1994); see also Hindle, *The State and Social Change, passim.*

174. Wood, *Faith, Hope and Charity*, 83.

175. Quoted in Hindle, *The State and Social Change*, 94.

176. Wrightson, 'Two concepts of order', 21–22.

177. Steve Hindle, 'Exhortation and entitlement: Negotiating inequality in English rural communities, 1550–1650', in Braddick and Walter (eds), *Negotiating Power in Early Modern Society*, 116–17.

178. Bernard, *War, Taxation and Rebellion*, 118.

179. Roger B. Manning, 'Violence and social conflict in mid-Tudor rebellions', *JBS* 16 (1977), 20.

180. Fletcher and MacCulloch, *Tudor Rebellions*, 68, 83.

181. Quoted in Wood, *Faith, Hope and Charity*, 109.

182. *TED*, iii, 18–19.

183. Hall, *Chronicle*, 587.

184. Krista J. Kesselring, 'Rebellion and disorder', in Doran and Jones (eds), *The Elizabethan World*, 382.

185. Edward P. Thompson, 'The moral economy of the English crowd in the eighteenth century', *P&P* 50 (1971), 76–136.

186. Roger B. Manning, *Village Revolts: Social protest and popular disturbances in England, 1509-1640* (Oxford, 1988).

187. Cathy Shrank, 'Trollers and dreamers: Defining the citizen-subject in sixteenth-century cheap print', *The Yearbook of English Studies* 38 (2008), 102–18.

188. Peter Lake and Steven Pincus, 'Introduction: Rethinking the public sphere in early modern England', in Peter Lake and Steven Pincus (eds), *The Public Sphere in Early Modern England* (Manchester, 2007), 6; Paulina Kewes, 'The 1553 succession crisis reconsidered', *HR* 90 (2017), 465–85.

189. John Walter, 'Public transcripts, popular agency and the politics of subsistence in early modern England', in Braddick and Walter (eds), *Negotiating Power in Early Modern Society*, 125–28.

190. Latimer, *Sermons*, I, 109.

191. Leonard Wright, *A Summons for Sleepers* (London, 1589), STC 26034.7, 4.

192. J. Sears McGee, 'Leonard Wright', *ODNB*.

193. *A famous speech of King Henry the eighth* (London, 1642), Sig. A4^{r-v}.

194. Archer, 'Popular politics', in Griffiths and Jenner (eds), *Londinopolis*, 29.

195. Susan Brigden, *London and the Reformation* (Oxford, 1989), 551.
196. ibid., 605; A.G. Petti (ed.), *The Letters and Dispatches of Richard Verstegan, c.1550–1640*, CRS 52 (1959), 223.
197. Wrightson, 'The politics of the parish', 12.
198. *Elizabeth I: Collected Works*, 337.

7 From Utopia to Babel: The beginning of reformation

1. Foxe, *A&M* (1563), Preface to the Quene.
2. William Tyndale, *Obedience of a Christian Man*, ed. David Daniell (London, 2000), 3.
3. David Daniell, *The Bible in English* (New Haven, CT, and London, 2003), 134, 135, 160. See also Brian Cummings, 'The problem of Protestant culture: Biblical literalism and literary biblicism', *Reformation* 17 (2012), 183–89.
4. J. Simpson, *Burning to Read: English fundamentalism and its Reformation opponents* (Cambridge, 2007), 24; Christopher Hill, 'William Tyndale and English history', in Christopher Hill, *Intellectual Origins of the English Revolution Revisited* (Oxford, 1997), 312–17.
5. Lucy Wooding, 'Encountering the Word of God in early Tudor England', *I* 136 (2021), 836–66.
6. Arthur G. Dickens, *The English Reformation* (second edition, London, 1989).
7. Christopher Haigh, *Reformation and Resistance in Tudor Lancashire* (Cambridge, 1975); J.J. Scarisbrick, *The Reformation and the English People* (Oxford, 1984); Christopher Haigh (ed.), *The English Reformation Revised* (Cambridge, 1987); Eamon Duffy, *The Stripping of the Altars: Traditional Religion in England, 1400–1580* (New Haven, CT, and London, 1992); Christopher Haigh, *English Reformations: Religion, politics and society under the Tudors* (Oxford, 1993).
8. Caroline Barron and Christopher Harper-Bill (eds), *The Church in Pre-Reformation Society* (Woodbridge, 1985); Robert N. Swanson, *Church and Society in Late Medieval England* (Oxford, 1989); Miri Rubin, *Corpus Christi: The eucharist in late medieval culture* (Cambridge, 1991); Duffy, *Stripping of the Altars*, part 1; George W. Bernard, *The Late Medieval English Church: Vitality and vulnerability before the break with Rome* (New Haven, CT, and London, 2012).
9. Simon Fish, *Supplicacyon for the Beggers*, ed. Frederick J. Furnivall (1871), 8, 9. See also Steven W. Haas, 'Simon Fish, William Tyndale, and Sir Thomas More's Lutheran conspiracy', *JEcclesH* 23 (1972), 125–36; Tyndale, *Obedience of a Christian Man*, 29, 40.
10. Alec Ryrie, 'Counting sheep, counting shepherds: The problem of allegiance in the English Reformation', in Peter Marshall and Alec Ryrie (eds), *The Beginnings of English Protestantism* (Cambridge, 2002), 84–110. See also A.G. Dickens, 'The early expansion of Protestantism into England, 1520–1558', in Peter Marshall (ed.), *The Impact of the English Reformation, 1500–1640* (London, 1997); for a contrary view, see Haigh, *English Reformations*.
11. Thomas Harding, *A Reiondre to M. Iewels Replie* (Antwerp, 1566), STC 12760, Sig. CCCi'; H. Robinson (ed.), *Original Letters Relative to the English Reformation* (Cambridge, 1846–47), vol. I, 309–11. See also Hendrik de Vocht, 'Thomas Harding', *I* 35 (1920), 233–44.
12. Diarmaid MacCulloch, *Thomas Cranmer: A life* (New Haven, CT, and London, 1996), 585.
13. Patrick Collinson, *The Birthpangs of Protestant England: Religious and cultural change in the sixteenth and seventeenth centuries* (Basingstoke, 1988), ix.
14. Fish, *Supplicacyon for the Beggers*, 7, 2, 6.
15. Christopher Marsh, *Popular Religion in Sixteenth-Century England* (Basingstoke, 1998), 9–12.
16. MacCulloch, *Thomas Cranmer*; John Edwards, *Archbishop Pole* (Farnham, 2014).
17. Diarmaid MacCulloch, 'Two dons in politics: Thomas Cranmer and Stephen Gardiner, 1503–1533', *HJ* 37 (1994), 1–22.

18. Edwards, *Archbishop Pole*; Dermot Fenlon, *Heresy and Obedience in Tridentine Italy: Cardinal Pole and the counter-reformation* (Cambridge, 2000); Thomas F. Mayer, *Reginald Pole: Prince and prophet* (Cambridge, 2000).

19. John O'Malley, *Trent: What happened at the council* (Cambridge, MA, 2013).

20. Diarmaid MacCulloch, 'The impact of the English Reformation', *HJ* 38 (1995), 152.

21. Peter Marshall, *Heretics and Believers: A history of the English Reformation* (New Haven, CT, and London, 2017).

22. David Cressy, *Bonfires and Bells: National memory and the Protestant calendar in Elizabethan and Stuart England* (London, 1989); Tessa Watt, *Cheap Print and Popular Piety 1550–1640* (Cambridge, 1991); Alexandra Walsham, *Providence in Early Modern England* (Oxford, 1999).

23. Peter Marshall, 'Evangelical conversion in the reign of Henry VIII', in Marshall and Ryrie (eds), *Beginnings of English Protestantism*, 20–22.

24. Richard Rex, 'The friars in the English Reformation', in Marshall and Ryrie (eds), *Beginnings of English Protestantism*, 45–46, 43.

25. J.F. Davis, 'The trials of Thomas Bylney and the English Reformation', *HJ* 24 (1981), 787–88. See also Thierry Wanegffelen, *Ni Rome, ni Genève: Des fidèles entre deux chaires en France au xvie siècle* (Paris, 2006).

26. Peter Marshall, *Religious Identities in Henry VIII's England* (Aldershot, 2006), chapter 9.

27. Peter Marshall, 'The naming of Protestant England', *P&P* 214 (2012), 87–128.

28. Miles Huggarde, *The Displaying of the Protestantes* (1556), STC 13557.

29. Greg Walker, 'Saint or schemer? The 1527 heresy trial of Thomas Bilney reconsidered', *JEcclesH* 40 (1989), 219–38.

30. Timothy 1:15.

31. Foxe, *A&M* (1563), 520. It has been argued that Bilney described his conversion this way in order to appeal to Cuthbert Tunstall's humanist sensibilities, but his account expressed widespread expectations concerning the transformative power of Scripture. See Greg Walker, *Persuasive Fictions: Faction, faith and political culture in the reign of Henry VIII* (Aldershot, 1996), 160–62.

32. Davis, 'The trials of Thomas Bylney', 775–90.

33. Walker, *Persuasive Fictions*, 143.

34. M. van Duijn, 'Targeting the masses: The *Delft Bible* (1477) as printed product', in Wim Francois and A. Den Hollander (eds), *'Wading Lambs and Swimming Elephants': The Bible for the laity and theologians in the late medieval and early modern era* (Leuven, 2012), 1–19; A. Gow, 'Challenging the Protestant paradigm: Bible reading in lay and urban contexts of the later middle ages', in Thomas J. Heffernan and Thomas E. Burman (eds), *Scripture and Pluralism: Reading the Bible in the religiously plural worlds of the middle ages and renaissance* (Leiden, 2005), 161–91. See also Nicholas of Lyra, *The Senses of Scripture*, ed. P.D.W. Krey and L. Smith (Leiden, 2000), 11; B.T. Chambers, *Bibliography of French Bibles: Fifteenth and sixteenth century French language editions of the Scriptures* (Geneva, 1983), xi; Andrew Gow, 'The contested history of a book: The German Bible in the later middle ages and Reformation in legend, ideology and scholarship', *Journal of Hebrew Scriptures* 9 (2009), 2–37.

35. David Daniell, *William Tyndale: A biography* (New Haven, CT, and London, 1994), 47–48; Charles Sturge, *Cuthbert Tunstal: Churchman, scholar, statesman, administrator* (London, 1938), 51–57; Damian R. Leader, *A History of the University of Cambridge*, vol. 1 (Cambridge, 1988), 300.

36. Charles Butterworth and Allan Chester, *George Joye, 1495?–1553: A chapter in the history of the English Bible and the English Reformation* (Philadelphia, PA, 1962).

37. *The Newe Testament dylygently corrected . . . by Willyam Tindale* (1534), STC 2826, Sig. **iiii^r–**viii^r.

38. Gergely M. Juhasz, *Translating Resurrection: The debate between William Tyndale and George Joye in its historical and theological context* (Leiden, 2014).

39. George W. Bernard, *The King's Reformation: Henry VIII and the remaking of the English Church* (New Haven, CT, and London, 2005), 278-9

40. Peter Marshall and Alec Ryrie, 'Introduction', in Marshall and Ryrie (eds), *The Beginnings of English Protestantism*, 5–6.

41. MacCulloch, *Thomas Cranmer*, 173–92; Andrew Pettegree, *Marian Protestantism: Six studies* (Aldershot, 1996); Andrew Pettegree, *Foreign Protestant Communities in Sixteenth-Century London* (Oxford, 1986); Ole Peter Grell, *Calvinist Exiles in Elizabethan and Stuart England* (Aldershot, 1996).

42. Rex, 'The friars in the English Reformation', 39–43, 44–48.

43. Euan Cameron, *Enchanted Europe: Superstition, reason and religion, 1250–1700* (Oxford, 2010); Helen L. Spencer, *English Preaching in the Late Middle Ages* (Oxford, 1993), 143–44, 291–94, 305–06; Robyn Malo, *Relics and Writing in Late Medieval England* (Toronto, 2013), 127–47.

44. J.A.F. Thomson, 'Orthodox Religion and the Origins of Lollardy', *History* 74 (1989), 39–55.

45. Marshall, 'Evangelical conversion', 35–36.

46. Brian Hanson, *Reformation of the Commonwealth: Thomas Becon and the politics of evangelical change in Tudor England* (Göttingen, 2019), 30.

47. Thomas Becon, *The iewel of ioye* (London, 1550), STC 1733, Sig. D2ᵛ, D6ᵛ.

48. Marshall, 'Evangelical conversion', 21.

49. ibid., 24–25.

50. Alec Ryrie, *Being Protestant in Reformation Britain* (Oxford, 2013), 20–23.

51. *Certayne sermons, or homelies* (1547), STC 13640, Sig. Aivᵛ.

52. Marshall, 'Evangelical conversion', 26–28; Ryrie, *Being Protestant*, 89–90.

53. Cited in A.G. Dickens and D. Carr (eds), *The Reformation in England to the Accession of Elizabeth I* (London, 1967), 23.

54. Hanson, *Reformation of the Commonwealth*.

55. John Bale, *The Image of Both Churches* (1547), Sig. Aiiʳ⁻ᵛ. See also Leslie P. Fairfield, *John Bale: Mythmaker for the English Reformation* (West Lafayette, IN, 1976); Peter Happé, *John Bale* (New York, 1996).

56. Genesis 11:1–9.

57. Rory McEntegart, *Henry VIII, the League of Schmalkalden and the English Reformation* (Woodbridge, 2002).

58. 'Ten Articles', in Gerald Bray (ed.), *Documents of the English Reformation* (third edition, Cambridge, 2019), 142.

59. MacCulloch, *Thomas Cranmer*, 289.

60. *A famous speech of King Henry the eighth* (London, 1642), Sig. A4ʳ.

61. Bernard, *The King's Reformation, passim*.

62. and 35 Hen. VIII, c. 1; A. Luders et al. (eds), *Statutes of the Realm*, 11 vols (1810), III, 894–97.

63. *VAI*, II, 126.

64. *The order of the communion* (London, 1548), STC 16456.5, Sig. Aiiᵛ.

65. Diarmaid MacCulloch, *Tudor Church Militant: Edward VI and the Protestant Reformation* (London, 1999), 167–70.

66. MacCulloch, *Thomas Cranmer*, 386–92.

67. Brian Cummings, 'Introduction', in Brian Cummings (ed.), *The Book of Common Prayer: The texts of 1549, 1559 and 1662* (Oxford, 2011), xii–xiii.

68. MacCulloch, *Thomas Cranmer*, 505.

69. Pettegree, *Foreign Protestant Communities*, 26–30; Robinson (ed.), *Original Letters*, I, 17.

70. Robinson (ed.), *Original Letters*, I, 79.

71. Duffy, *Stripping of the Altars*, 472–75.

72. *The boke of common prayer* (1552), STC 16281, Sig. Piiiᵛ.

73. MacCulloch, *Thomas Cranmer*, 501–02, 518–20.

74. ibid., 512–13, 517, 525–30.
75. Aude de Mézerac-Zanetti, 'Reforming the liturgy under Henry VIII: The instructions of John Clerk, bishop of Bath and Wells', *JEcclesH* 64 (2013), 96–111; Geoffrey Elton, *Policy and Police: The enforcement of the Reformation in the age of Thomas Cromwell* (Cambridge, 1972), 236; Bernard, *The King's Reformation*, 179.
76. Duffy, *Stripping of the Altars*, 418–19.
77. Ryrie, 'Counting sheep, counting shepherds', 96.
78. Peter Marshall, 'The rood of Boxley, the blood of Hailes and the defence of the Henrician Church', *JEcclesH* 46 (1995), 689–96.
79. Peter Marshall, 'Papist as heretic: The burning of John Forest, 1538', *HJ* 41 (1998), 351–74.
80. Duffy, *Stripping of the Altars*, 384.
81. William Turner, *The rescuynge of the romishe fox* (Bonn, 1545), STC 24355, Sig. A8ᵛ.
82. Rex, 'The friars in the English Reformation', 57.
83. Quoted in Ryrie, 'Counting sheep, counting shepherds', 88.
84. Elton, *Policy and Police*, 236; Bernard, *The King's Reformation*, 179; Duffy, *Stripping of the Altars*, 416.
85. A.G. Dickens, 'Robert Parkyn's narrative of the Reformation', *I* 62 (1947), 65–66.
86. Duffy, *Stripping of the Altars*, 381.
87. John Strype, *Ecclesiastical Memorials*, 3 vols (London, 1822), I, part 2, 260–66.
88. Marshall, *Heretics and Believers*, 222.
89. *Two notable sermones lately preached at Pauls Crosse* (1544), STC 5106.5, Sig. Ciiᵛ.
90. Peter Marshall, 'Mumpsimus and sumpsimus: The intellectual origins of a Henrician bon mot', *JEcclesH* 52 (2001), 512–20; George Bernard, 'The making of religious policy, 1533–1546: Henry VIII and the search for the Middle Way', *HJ* 41 (1998), 321–49.
91. *The metynge of Doctor Barons and doctor Powell at Paradise gate* (1548), STC 1473.
92. Susan Brigden, *London and the Reformation* (Oxford, 1989), 427.
93. Dickens, 'Robert Parkyn's narrative', 66–70.
94. Duffy, *Stripping of the Altars*, 463.
95. K.L. Wood-Legh, *Perpetual Chantries in Britain* (Cambridge, 1965); Alan Kreider, *English Chantries: The road to dissolution* (Cambridge, MA, 1979).
96. Clive Burgess, ' "By quick and by dead": Wills and pious provision in late medieval Bristol', *I* 142 (1987), 837–58; Clive Burgess, ' "A fond thing vainly invented": An essay on purgatory and pious motive in later medieval England', in Susan Wright (ed.), *Parish, Church and People* (London, 1988), 56–84; Peter Marshall, *Beliefs and the Dead in Reformation England* (Oxford, 2002).
97. Scarisbrick, *The Reformation and the English People*, 87–88.
98. ibid., 81–84.
99. Duffy, *Stripping of the Altars*, 459.
100. Marsh, *Popular Religion*, 59.
101. Robert Crowley, *An information and petition against the oppressors of the poor commons of this realm* (1548), reprinted in *The Select Works of Robert Crowley*, ed. J.M. Cowper (London, 1872). See also John W. Martin, 'The publishing career of Robert Crowley: A sidelight on the Tudor book trade', *Publishing History* 14 (1983), 85–98.
102. Robert Crowley, 'The Waie to Wealth', in *Select Works*, 145.
103. *Pyers plowmans exhortation unto the lordes, knightes and burgoysses of the Parlyamenthouse* (1550), STC 19905, Sig. Aiʳ.
104. *Pyers plowmans exhortation*, Sig. Aiᵛ–Aiiʳ.
105. *A Supplication of the poore commons* (1546), STC 10884, Sig. aivᵛ.
106. Crowley, *Select Works*, 133, 143.
107. Strype, *Ecclesiastical Memorials*, I, part 2, 262; Ryrie, 'Counting sheep, counting shepherds', 102–03.

108. Cuthbert Scot, *Two notable sermones lately preached* (1544), *STC* 5106.5, Sig. Hiiii^v.
109. Paul Whitfield White, 'The *Pammachius* Affair at Christ's College, Cambridge, in 1545', in Peter Happé and Wim Hüsken (eds), *Interludes and Early Modern Society: Studies in gender, power and theatricality* (Amsterdam and New York, 2007), 261–90.
110. Brigden, *London and the Reformation*, 267.
111. Miles Coverdale, *A confutacion of that treatise* (Zurich, 1541), *STC* 5888, Sig. C5^r; Hugh Latimer, 'Sermon of the Plough', in Latimer, *Sermons*, I, 60.
112. Brigden, *London and the Reformation*, 273.
113. Luders et al. (eds), *Statutes of the Realm*, III, 894.
114. William Peryn, *Thre godlye and notable sermons, of the sacrament of the aulter* (1546), *STC* 19785.5, Sig. Aii^{r-v}.
115. Susan Brigden, 'Youth and the English Reformation', *P&P* 95 (1982), 38–40.
116. Patrick Collinson, 'Night schools, conventicles and churches: Continuities and discontinuities in early Protestant ecclesiology', in Marshall and Ryrie (eds), *Beginnings of English Protestantism*, 226.
117. Thomas Freeman, 'Dissenters from a dissenting Church: The challenge of the Freewillers, 1550–1558', in Marshall and Ryrie (eds), *Beginnings of English Protestantism*, 129–56.
118. Collinson, 'Night schools, conventicles and churches', 227.
119. J.W. Martin, 'English Protestant separatism at its beginnings: Henry Hart and the free-will men', *SCJ* 7 (1976).
120. Freeman, 'Dissenters from a dissenting Church', 155.
121. Catharine Davies, *A Religion of the Word: The defence of the Reformation in the reign of Edward VI* (Manchester, 2002), 67–68.
122. Roger Hutchinson, *The Image of God, or laie mans boke* (1550), *STC* 14020.
123. Davies, *A Religion of the Word*, 74.
124. Hanson, *Reformation of the Commonwealth*, 42.
125. Quoted in Marsh, *Popular Religion*, 201.
126. Lucy Wooding, 'Remembrance in the eucharist', in Andrew Gordon and Thomas Rist (eds), *The Arts of Remembrance in Early Modern England: Memorial cultures of the Post Reformation* (Farnham, 2013), 26–27, 31–33; Brigden, *London and the Reformation*, 266.
127. Wooding, *Rethinking Catholicism in Reformation England* (Oxford, 2000), chs 1–3.
128. Marsh, *Popular Religion*, 52.
129. Caroline Walker Bynum, *Christian Materiality: An essay on religion in late medieval Europe* (New York, 2011).
130. *Writings and Disputations of Thomas Cranmer*, ed. John E. Cox (Cambridge, 1844), 229.
131. Robinson, *Original Letters*, I, 76.
132. Cummings, 'Introduction', xxiii.
133. John Hooper, *A declaration of the ten holy comaundementes* (Zurich, 1549), *STC* 13746, fo. lxxviii.
134. *VAI*, II, 241–42.
135. Cummings, 'Introduction', xxxvii.
136. Foxe, *A&M* (1570), 1006.
137. Andrew Pettegree, 'Printing and the Reformation: The English exception', in Marshall and Ryrie (eds), *Beginnings of English Protestantism*, 160–69.
138. *The Byble in Englyshe* (second edition, London, 1540), *STC* 2070, Sig. +i^r.
139. Lucy Wooding, 'Catholicism, the printed book, and the Marian restoration', in Vincent Gillespie and Susan Powell (eds), *A Companion to the Early Printed Book in Britain, 1476–1558* (Woodbridge, 2014), 309–12.
140. Maria Dowling and Joy Shakespeare (eds), 'Religion and politics in mid-Tudor England through the eyes of an English Protestant woman: The recollections of Rose Hickman', *BIHR* 55 (1982), 97.

141. A.G. Dickens, *Lollards and Protestants in the Diocese of York 1509–1558* (Oxford, 1959), 29.

142. Alexandra Walsham, 'Preaching without speaking: Script, print and religious dissent', in Alexandra Walsham and Julia Crick (eds), *The Uses of Script and Print, 1300–1700* (Cambridge, 2004), 211–34.

143. Alexandra Walsham, '"Domme preachers"? Post-Reformation English Catholicism and the culture of print', *P&P* 168 (2000), 70–123.

144. Richard Carew of Antony, *The Survey of Cornwall*, ed. Frank E. Halliday (London, 1953), 196. See also Ryrie, 'Counting sheep, counting shepherds', 109.

145. Robert Whiting, *The Blind Devotion of the People: Popular religion and the English Reformation* (Cambridge, 1989), 39.

146. Scarisbrick, *The Reformation and the English People*, 81.

147. Brigden, *London and the Reformation*, 425.

148. Crowley, *Select Works*, 137.

8 Edward VI and the Trials of the Young Josiah

1. Wriothesley, *Chronicle*, I, 64.

2. ibid., 66–67.

3. Jennifer Loach, *Edward VI* (New Haven, CT, 1999), 5–6.

4. The common assertion that Edward VI was born by caesarean section seems to be without basis in evidence: see Samuel Lurie, 'Was Queen Jane Seymour (1509–1537) delivered by a cesarian section?', *Endeavour* 41 (2017), 23–28.

5. Charlotte Bolland and Tarnya Cooper (eds), *The Real Tudors: Kings and queens rediscovered* (London, 2014), 68. See also Aysha Pollnitz, *Princely Education in Early Modern Britain* (Cambridge, 2015), 139.

6. Diarmaid MacCulloch, *Tudor Church Militant: Edward VI and the Protestant Reformation* (London, 1999), 8.

7. Pollnitz, *Princely Education*, 141.

8. 'Certayne Brife Notes of the Controversy Betwene the Dukes of Somerset and the Duke of Nor[t]humberland', in Ian Archer, George Bernard, Simon Adams, Mark Greengrass, Paul Hammer and Fiona Kisby (eds), *Religion, Politics and Society in Sixteenth-Century England* (Cambridge, 2003), 129–30.

9. Ecclesiastes 10:16. See John N. King, *English Reformation Literature: The Tudor origins of the Protestant tradition* (Princeton, NJ, 1982), 161–62.

10. PRO, E/23/4/, fo. 12^r.

11. E.A. Wrigley and R.S. Schofield, *The Population History of England, 1541–1871: A reconstruction* (Cambridge, MA, 1981), 528.

12. Paul Slack, 'Social policy and the constraints of government, 1547–58', in Jennifer Loach and Robert Tittler, (eds), *The Mid-Tudor Polity, c. 1540–1560* (London, 1980), 95–96.

13. Robert Whiting, *The Reformation of the English Parish Church* (Cambridge, 2010), 59.

14. Chantries Act 1545, 37 Hen. VIII, c. 4; A. Luders et al. (eds), *Statutes of the Realm*, 11 vols (1810), III, 988–93.

15. Steven Gunn, *The English People at War in the Age of Henry VIII* (Oxford, 2018), 94.

16. *TED*, ii, 187.

17. John Heywood, *The proverbs and epigrams of John Heywood (A.D. 1562)* (1867), 189.

18. *TED*, ii, 187.

19. Wriothesley, *Chronicle*, II, 1.

20. Anthony Fletcher and Diarmaid MacCulloch, *Tudor Rebellions* (seventh edition, Abingdon, 2020), 151, 157–58.

21. Robert Fabyan, *The chronicle of Fabian whiche he nameth the concordaunce of histories* (London, 1559), *STC* 10664, Sig. AAAiᵛ. See also Barrett L. Beer, 'John Kyngston and Fabyan's Chronicle (1559)', *Library* 14 (2013), 199–207.
22. Loach, *Edward VI*, 29.
23. *Chronicle of Edward VI*, 4.
24. Diarmaid MacCulloch, *Thomas Cranmer: A life* (New Haven, CT, and London, 1996), 328–32; MacCulloch, *Tudor Church Militant*, 8; Diarmaid MacCulloch, 'Parliament and the Reformation of Edward VI', *Parliamentary History* 34 (2015), 387.
25. Eric Ives, 'Henry VIII's will: A forensic conundrum', *HJ* 35 (1992), 779–804; Ralph Houlbrooke, 'Henry VIII's wills: A comment', *HJ* 37 (1994), 89–109; Eric Ives, 'The protectorate provisions of 1546–7', *HJ* 37 (1994), 901–14; Loach, *Edward VI*, 18–25.
26. Roger Bowers, 'The vernacular litany of 1544 during the reign of Henry VIII', in George Bernard and Steven Gunn (eds), *Authority and Consent in Tudor England* (Aldershot, 2002), 151–78. On Edward's tutoring, see Pollnitz, *Princely Education*, 142; Loach, *Edward VI*, 14; Bernard, *The King's Reformation*, 591; J.J. Scarisbrick, *Henry VIII* (London, 1968), 475.
27. Winifred C. Tennant and Helen Suggett, 'Croes Naid', *National Library of Wales Journal* 7 (1951), 102–15.
28. *Chronicle of Edward VI*, 3.
29. Pollnitz, *Princely Education*, 143.
30. John F. McDiarmid, 'John Cheke's preface to *De Superstitione*', *JEcclesH* 48 (1997), 109–12, 117–19; Pollnitz, *Princely Education*, 143–46.
31. Pollnitz, *Princely Education*, 147.
32. Narasingha Prosad Sil, 'Sir Anthony Denny: A Tudor servant in office', *Renaissance and Reformation*, new series, 8 (1984), 190–201.
33. Foxe, *A&M* (1563), 871; see also Glyn Redworth, *In Defence of the Church Catholic: The life of Stephen Gardiner* (Oxford, 1990), 231–47.
34. Susan Brigden, 'Henry Howard, earl of Surrey, and the "Conjured League"', *HJ* 37 (1994), 519, 522.
35. PRO, E/23/4/, fos. 12ʳ–14ʳ.
36. L.P. Fairfield, *John Bale: Mythmaker for the English Reformation* (West Lafayette, IN, 1976).
37. MacCulloch, *Tudor Church Militant*, 14, 57–104.
38. Erasmus, *A very pleasaunt and fruitful Diologe called the Epicure*, trans. Philip Gerard (1545), *STC* 10460, Sig. Aiiiᵛ, Aiiiiᵛ.
39. ibid., Sig. Aviʳ.
40. *The Byble, that is to say all the holy Scripture* (1549), *STC* 2077, dedication.
41. ibid.
42. *Certain Sermones, or homilies* (1547), *STC* 13638.5, Sig. Oivʳ⁻ᵛ.
43. MacCulloch, *Tudor Church Militant*, 147 and fn.
44. MacCulloch, *Thomas Cranmer*, 364–65.
45. Thomas Cranmer, *Miscellaneous Writings and Letters* (Cambridge, 1846), 126–27.
46. Loach, *Edward VI*, 158, 180–89; MacCulloch, *Tudor Church Militant*, 23–38.
47. Margaret Aston, *The King's Bedpost: Reformation and iconography in a Tudor group portrait* (Cambridge, 1994).
48. Thomas S. Freeman, 'Providence and prescription: The account of Elizabeth in Foxe's "Book of Martyrs"', in Susan Doran and Thomas S. Freeman (eds), *The Myth of Elizabeth* (Basingstoke, 2003), 27–55.
49. Loach, *Edward VI*, 14–16, 136–39.
50. *CSP Sp.*, X, 209–12, 258–60; *Chronicle of Edward VI*, 55–56; Loach, *Edward VI*, 133–34.
51. *Chronicle of Edward VI*, 185–90.
52. ibid., 179.
53. ibid., 5–8.

54. A.F. Pollard, *England under Protector Somerset* (London, 1900; reprinted 1966); quoted in Loach, *Edward VI*, xi. See also W.K. Jordan, *Edward VI: The young king. The protectorship of Duke Somerset* (London, 1968).

55. Geoffrey Elton, 'The good duke', in Elton, *Studies in Tudor and Stuart Politics and Government*, 4 vols (Cambridge, 1974–92), I, 233–37; M.L. Bush, *The Government Policy of Protector Somerset* (London, 1975); Dale Hoak, 'Rehabilitating the duke of Northumberland: Politics and political control, 1549–53', in Loach and Tittler (eds), *The Mid-Tudor Polity*, 29–51.

56. H. Miller, 'Henry VIII's unwritten will: Grants of lands and honours in 1547', in Eric Ives, R.J. Knecht and J.J. Scarisbrick (eds), *Wealth and Power in Tudor England* (London, 1978), 87.

57. G.W. Bernard, 'The downfall of Sir Thomas Seymour', in George Bernard (ed.), *The Tudor Nobility* (Manchester, 1992), 212–40.

58. 'A "Journall" of matters of state', in Archer et al. (eds), *Religion, Politics and Society in Sixteenth-Century England*, 54.

59. *Chronicle of Edward VI*, 6.

60. Quoted in Bernard, 'The downfall of Sir Thomas Seymour', 234.

61. Loach, *Edward VI*, 45–46.

62. *The copie of a letter sent to all those Preachers, whiche the Kynges Maiestie hath licensed to preache* (1548), STC 9181.5, Sig. Aiiʳ–Aiiiʳ.

63. M.H. Merriman, *The Rough Wooings: Mary Queen of Scots 1542–1551* (East Linton, 2000); Gervase Phillips, *The Anglo-Scots Wars 1513–1550* (Woodbridge, 1999).

64. Wriothesley, *Chronicle*, II, 3.

65. Michael J. Braddick, *The Nerves of State: Taxation and the financing of the English state* (Manchester, 1996).

66. Gunn, *The English People at War*, 8–9.

67. Bush, *The Government Policy of Protector Somerset*; David L. Potter, 'The Treaty of Boulogne and European diplomacy, 1549–50', *HR* 55 (1982), 61.

68. R.B. Outhwaite, *Inflation in Tudor and Early Stuart England* (second edition, London, 1982); F.J. Fisher, 'Influenza and inflation in Tudor England', *Economic History Review*, second series, 18 (1965), 120–29.

69. Isaiah 1:22.

70. Latimer, *Sermons*, I, 137.

71. *TED*, ii, 187.

72. Jordan, *Edward VI: The young king*, 306, 415, 427–32. It has also proved possible to take a Marxist interpretation here: see Jim Holstun, 'Utopia pre-empted: Kett's rebellion, ommuning, and the hysterical sublime', *Historical Materialism* 16 (2008), 5–53.

73. Geoffrey Elton, 'Reform and the "commonwealth-men" of Edward VI's reign', in P. Clark, A. Smith and N. Tyacke (eds), *The English Commonwealth: Essays presented to Joel Hurstfield* (Leicester, 1979), 23–38; B.L. Beer and R.J. Nash, 'Hugh Latimer and the lusty knave of Kent: The commonwealth movement of 1549', *BIHR* 52 (1979), 175–78; Phil Withington, *The Politics of Commonwealth: Citizens and freemen in early modern England* (Cambridge, 2005).

74. C.S.L. Davies, 'Slavery and Protector Somerset: The Vagrancy Act of 1547', *EconHR*, second series, 19 (1966), 533–49. The act did also make some more positive provisions: see Marjorie McIntosh, *Poor Relief in England, 1350–1600* (Cambridge, 2012), chapter 5.

75. Latimer, *Sermons*, I, 101. See also Andy Wood, *The Memory of the People: Custom and popular senses of the past in early modern England* (Cambridge, 2013), 65–66.

76. Catharine Davies, *A Religion of the Word: The defence of the Reformation in the reign of Edward VI* (Manchester, 2002), 6, 140–46, 162–68.

77. Loach, *Edward VI*, 40.

78. Stephen Alford, *Kingship and Politics in the Reign of Edward VI* (Cambridge, 2002), 76.

79. Richard Grafton, *A chronicle at large and meere history of the affayres of Englande* (1569), *STC* 12147, 1311–12.
80. Gunn, *The English People at War*, 67, 145.
81. *The Letters of William, Lord Paget of Beaudesert, 1547–63*, ed. Sybil M. Jack and Barrett L. Beer, *Camden Miscellany XXV*, CS fourth series, 13 (London, 1974), 18, 33.
82. ibid., 20.
83. ibid., 22.
84. Bush, *The Government Policy of Protector Somerset*, 102.
85. Gordon R. Batho, 'Syon House: The first two hundred years', *Transactions of the London and Middlesex Archaeological Society* 19 (1958), 7–8.
86. John N. King, *English Reformation Literature*, 109. See also Bush, *The Government Policy of Protector Somerset*, 100–12; for a more sceptical view of Somerset's piety, see Loach, *Edward VI*, 42–47.
87. Bush, *The Government Policy of Protector Somerset*, 109.
88. Loach, *Edward VI*, 43.
89. MacCulloch, *Tudor Church Militant*, 103–04.
90. MacCulloch, 'Parliament and the Reformation of Edward VI', 389–91.
91. Margaret Aston, *England's Iconoclasts*, vol. 1: *Against Laws and Images* (Oxford, 1988), 258–59, 255; Susan Brigden, *London and the Reformation* (Oxford, 1989), 426–33.
92. BL Add. MS 5464 fo. 4ʳ: 'la source de tout mal et la fontaine de toute abhomination et vray filz du diable'.
93. Alford, *Kingship and Politics*, 101–15.
94. Walter Lynne, *A most necessarie treatise, declaring the beginning and ending of all poperie* (London, 1548), *STC* 17116, Sig. E3ʳ. See also Alford, *Kingship and Politics*, 102–05; MacCulloch, *Thomas Cranmer*, 402–03; John N. King, *Tudor Royal Iconography: Literature and art in an age of religious crisis* (Princeton, NJ, 1989), 166.
95. MacCulloch, 'Parliament and the Reformation of Edward VI', 387.
96. M. Thomas, 'Tunstal: Trimmer or martyr?', *JEcclesH* 24 (1973), 342–43. See also Elizabeth Biggs, 'Durham Cathedral and Cuthbert Tunstall: A cathedral and its bishop during the Reformation, 1530–1559', *JEcclesH* 71 (2018), 64–68; C. Sturge, *Cuthbert Tunstal: Churchman, scholar, statesman, administrator* (London, 1938).
97. MacCulloch, *Thomas Cranmer*, 412–14, 462–69, 505–08.
98. Loach, *Edward VI*, xvi.
99. Fletcher and MacCulloch, *Tudor Rebellions*, 54–55.
100. Sybil Jack, 'Sir William Cavendish', *ODNB*.
101. Fletcher and MacCulloch, *Tudor Rebellions*, 67–69.
102. John Edwards, *Mary I: England's Catholic queen* (New Haven, CT, and London, 2011), 67–69.
103. Fletcher and MacCulloch, *Tudor Rebellions*, 152.
104. ibid., 151–53.
105. ibid., 61–62.
106. Eamon Duffy, *The Voices of Morebath: Reformation and rebellion in an English village* (New Haven, CT, and London, 2001), 2–4, 8–9.
107. ibid., 24–25, 37, 74–76.
108. John Cooper, *Propaganda and the Tudor State: Political culture in the West Country* (Oxford, 2003).
109. Fletcher and MacCulloch, *Tudor Rebellions*, 157.
110. Ethan Shagan, 'Protector Somerset and the 1549 rebellions: New sources and new perspectives', *her* 114 (1999), 34–63; see the replies by M.L. Bush, 'Protector Somerset and the 1549 rebellions: A post-revision questioned', and George Bernard, 'New perspectives or old complexities', *EHR* 115 (2000), 103–12, 113–20.
111. J. Strype, *Ecclesiastical Memorials*, 3 vols (London, 1822), II, part 2, 432.
112. *Chronicle of Edward VI*, 18.

113. Susan Brigden, 'The letters of Richard Scudamore to Sir Philip Hoby, 1549–1555', *Camden Miscellany XXX*, CS fourth series, 39 (London, 1990), 81–83.

114. David M. Loades, *John Dudley, Duke of Northumberland, 1504–1553* (Oxford, 1996).

115. Dale Hoak, *The King's Council in the Reign of Edward VI* (Cambridge, 1976), 43–45, 231–39; A.J. Slavin, 'The fall of Lord Chancellor Wriothesley: A study in the politics of conspiracy', *Albion* 7 (1975), 265–86.

116. Hoak, *The King's Council*, 241; H. James, 'The aftermath of the 1549 coup and the earl of Warwick's intentions', *BIHR* 62 (1989), 91–97.

117. Hoak, *The King's Council*, 241–58.

118. Alford, *Kingship and Politics*, 138–40.

119. ibid., 170.

120. Quoted in ibid., 137.

121. W.K. Jordan, *Edward VI: The threshold of power* (London, 1970), 532–34.

122. *Chronicle of Edward VI*, 23.

123. Hoak, 'Rehabilitating the duke of Northumberland', 41–42; Stanford E. Lehmberg, *Sir Walter Mildmay and Tudor Government* (Austin, TX, 1964), 28–39.

124. Loach, *Edward VI*, 111–13; J. Alsop, 'The revenue commission of 1552', *HJ* 22 (1979), 511–33; W.C. Richardson (ed.), *The Report of the Royal Commission of 1552* (Morgantown, WV, 1974).

125. *Chronicle of Edward VI*, 21–22.

126. ibid., 43.

127. Eamon Duffy, *The Stripping of the Altars: Traditional religion in England, 1400–1580* (New Haven, CT, and London, 1992), 472–75.

128. MacCulloch, *Tudor Church Militant*, 106–07.

129. ibid., 109–14.

130. Heinrich Bullinger, *The Christen state of matrimonye* (Antwerp, 1541), trans. Miles Coverdale, *STC* 4045.

131. A.G. Dickens, 'The marriage and character of Archbishop Holgate', *EHR* 52 (1937), 428–42.

132. MacCulloch, *Tudor Church Militant*, 134–35.

133. *VAI*, II, 214.

134. R.V., *The old faith of Great Britain, and the new learning of England* (1549), Sig. Ci^v. See also Lucy Wooding, 'Encountering the Word of God in early Tudor England', *EHR* 136 (2021), 836–66.

135. *The copie of a letter*, Sig. Avi^v.

136. Machyn's *Diary*, 35.

137. Alford, *Kingship and Politics*, 168; Hoak, *King's Council*, 231–58. See also 'Certayne Brife Notes', 123.

138. Loach, *Edward VI*, 11.

139. ibid., 160–62.

140. Alford, *Kingship and Politics*, 171–72.

141. Peter Jensen, 'The life of faith in the teaching of Elizabethan Protestants', unpublished DPhil thesis, University of Oxford (1979).

142. Whitney Jones, *The Mid-Tudor Crisis, 1539–1563* (London, 1973); Jennifer Loach and Robert Tittler, 'Introduction', in Loach and Tittler (eds), *The Mid-Tudor Polity*, 6–7.

9 'The Vigour of Invention': Renaissance words

1. Simon Thurley, 'Nonsuch Palace', *Country Life* cxcix 31, 11 August 2005; Simon Thurley, *House of Power: The places that shaped the Tudor world* (London, 2017), 268–72.

2. Susan Doran, 'Virginity, divinity and power: The portraits of Elizabeth I', in Susan Doran and Thomas Freeman (eds), *The Myth of Elizabeth* (Basingstoke, 2003), 189–90. See also Paulina Kewes, 'Godly queens: The royal iconographies of Mary and Elizabeth',

in Alice Hunt and Anna Whitelock (eds), *Tudor Queenship: The reigns of Mary and Elizabeth* (Basingstoke, 2010), 47–62.

3. *The Romane historie written by T. Livius of Padua*, translated by Philemon Holland (1600), *STC* 16613, Preface to the Reader.

4. Antony Colynet, *The true history of the civill warres of France* (1591), *STC* 5590, Sig. A4ʳ.

5. John Manwood, *A treatise and discourse of the lawes of the Forrest* (London, 1598), fo. 1ʳ.

6. Cited in E. Armstrong, *A Ciceronian Sunburn: A Tudor dialogue on humanistic rhetoric and civic poetics* (Columbia, NY, 2006), 8.

7. Roger Ascham, *The Scholemaster* (London, 1570), *STC* 832, Sig. Liiiʳ; see also Aysha Pollnitz, *Princely Education in Early Modern Britain* (Cambridge, 2015), 241–63.

8. John-Mark Philo, 'Elizabeth I's translation of Tacitus: Lambeth Palace Library, MS 683', *Review of English Studies* 71 (2020), 44–73.

9. Juliet Fleming, *Graffiti and the Writing Arts of Early Modern England* (Philadelphia, PA, 2001), 60; Catherine Belsey, 'Invocation of the visual image: Ekphrasis in *Lucrece* and beyond', *Shakespeare Quarterly* 63 (2012), 180.

10. Arthur Bourcher, *A worthy Myrrour* (1577?), EBBA 36305; reprinted 1589, EBBA 32090.

11. Ralph Norris, 'A warning to London by the fall of Antwerp' (1555–84?), EBBA 32411; William Elderton, 'The panges of Love' (1559), EBBA 32224; see also Lindsay Reid, 'Translating Ovid's *Metamorphoses* in Tudor balladry', *RQ* 72 (2019), 537–81.

12. Emma Smith, *This is Shakespeare* (London, 2019), 90.

13. Thomas Campbell, *Henry VIII and the Art of Majesty: Tapestries at the Tudor court* (New Haven, CT, and London, 2007), 277–81.

14. William Shakespeare, *Julius Caesar*, Act III, Scene 2; see Freyja Cox Jensen, *Reading the Roman Republic in Early Modern England* (Brill, 2012), 6.

15. Domenico Lovascio, ' "Of higher state / Than monarch, king or world's great potentate": The name of Caesar in early modern English drama', *Early Modern Literary Studies* 19 (2016), 1–25.

16. Blair Worden, *The Sound of Virtue: Philip Sidney's Arcadia and Elizabethan politics* (New Haven, CT, and London, 1996), 9, 20.

17. Stephen Greenblatt, 'Introduction', in Stephen Greenblatt (ed.), *The Forms of Power and the Power of Forms in the Renaissance* (Norman, OK, 1982), 5.

18. Debora K. Shuger, *Habits of Thought in the English Renaissance* (Toronto, 1997), 1–3, 9–10.

19. David J.B. Trim, 'The art of war: Martial poetics from Henry Howard to Philip Sidney', in Mike Pincombe and Cathy Shrank (eds), *The Oxford Handbook of Tudor Literature, 1485–1603* (Oxford, 2009), 587–605.

20. Daniel R. Woolf, *The Social Circulation of the Past: English Historical Culture 1500–1730* (Oxford, 2003); Keith Thomas, *The Perception of the Past in Early Modern England* (London, 1983).

21. F.J. Levy, *Tudor Historical Thought* (San Marino, CA, 1967), 237–85; Wyman Herendeen, *William Camden: A life in context* (Woodbridge, 2007).

22. Daniel Woolf and Jane Wong Yeang Chui, 'English vernacular historical writing and Holinshed's *Chronicles*', in Malcolm Smuts (ed.), *The Oxford Handbook of the Age of Shakespeare* (Oxford, 2016), 219.

23. Annabel Patterson, *Reading Holinshed's Chronicles* (Chicago, 1994); Felicity Heal, Ian Archer and Paulina Kewes (eds), *The Oxford Handbook of Holinshed's Chronicles* (Oxford, 2013).

24. Nicholas Popper, 'European historiography in English political culture', in Smuts (ed.), *Oxford Handbook of the Age of Shakespeare*, 241.

25. Rivkah Zim, *English Metrical Psalms: Poetry as praise and prayer, 1535–1601* (Cambridge, 1987); Hannibal Hamlin, *Psalm Culture and Early Modern English Literature* (Cambridge, 2004).

26. Stephen Greenblatt, *Renaissance Self-Fashioning: From More to Shakespeare* (Chicago, 1980), chapter 3; Susan Brigden, *Thomas Wyatt: The Heart's Forest* (London, 2012), 278–79.

27. William A. Sessions, *Henry Howard, the Poet Earl of Surrey: A life* (Oxford, 1999); Susan Brigden, 'Henry Howard, earl of Surrey, and the "Conjured League"', *HJ* 37 (1994), 507–37; Hannibal Hamlin, 'Piety and poetry: English psalms from Miles Coverdale to Mary Sidney', in Pincombe and Shrank (eds), *Oxford Handbook of Tudor Literature*, 208–11.

28. Micheline White, 'Protestant women's writing and congregational psalm singing: From the song of the exiled "Handmaid" (1555) to the countess of Pembroke's *Psalmes* (1599)', *Sidney Journal* 23 (2005), 61–82; Beth Quitslund, 'Teaching us how to sing: The peculiarity of the Sidney Psalter', *Sidney Journal* 23 (2005), 83–110; Hannibal Hamlin, ' "The highest matter in the noblest form": The influence of the Sidney Psalms', *Sidney Journal* 23 (2005), 133–57.

29. Margaret Spufford, *Small Books and Pleasant Histories: Popular fiction and its readership in seventeenth-century England* (Cambridge, 1981); Barry Reay, *Popular Cultures in England 1550–1750* (London, 1998), 36–70; Adam Fox, *Oral and Literate Culture in England, 1500–1700* (Oxford, 2000).

30. E.L., *Romes Monarchie* (London, 1596), *STC* 21296; see Alexandra Gajda, 'Henry Savile and the Elizabethan Court', *Erudition and the Republic of Letters* 6 (2021), 32–60.

31. Andy Wood, *The Memory of the People: Custom and popular senses of the past in early modern England* (Cambridge, 2013); Nicola Whyte, *Inhabiting the Landscape: Place, custom and memory, 1500–1800* (Oxford, 2009).

32. Alan Bryson, 'Elizabethan verse libel', in Smuts (ed.), *Oxford Handbook of the Age of Shakespeare*, 481–82, 488–89.

33. Brian Cummings, 'Print, popularity and the *Book of Common Prayer*', in Emma Smith and Andy Kesson (eds), *Elizabethan Top Ten: Defining print popularity in early modern England* (Farnham, 2013), 135–44. On metrical psalms, see Beth Quitslund, *The Reformation in Rhyme: Sternhold, Hopkins and the English metrical psalter, 1547–1603* (Aldershot, 2008); Christopher Marsh, *Music and Society in Early Modern England* (Cambridge, 2010), 391–453; Hannibal Hamlin, *Psalm Culture in Early Modern England* (Cambridge, 2004), 19–50. On sermons, see Arnold Hunt, *The Art of Hearing: English preachers and their audiences, 1590–1640* (Cambridge, 2010); Hugh Adlington, Peter McCullough and Emma Rhatigan (eds), *The Oxford Handbook of the Early Modern Sermon* (Oxford, 2011).

34. Catherine Richardson, 'Household manuals', in Smith and Kesson (eds), *Elizabethan Top Ten*, 169–78.

35. Robert Cleaver, *A godlie forme of householde government* (London, 1598), *STC* 5383, 13.

36. Bernard Capp, *English Almanacs 1500–1800: Astrology and the popular press* (Ithaca, NY, 1979); Louis Curth, *Almanacs, Astrology and Popular Medicine, 1550–1700* (Manchester, 2007).

37. Adam Smyth, 'Almanacs and ideas of popularity', in Smith and Kesson (eds), *Elizabethan Top Ten*, 130; Smyth, *Autobiography in Early Modern England* (Cambridge, 2010), 35–38.

38. Femke Molekamp, *Women and the Bible in Early Modern England: Religious reading and writing* (Oxford, 2013), 41.

39. Keith Thomas, 'The place of laughter in Tudor and Stuart England', *TLS* 7, 21 January 1977.

40. Philip Sidney, *An Apology for Poetry (or The Defence of Poesy)*, ed. R.W. Maslen (third edition, Manchester, 2002), 112.

41. Andrew Hiscock, ' "Hear my tale or kiss my tail!": *The Old Wife's Tale, Gammer Gurton's Needle*, and the popular cultures of Tudor comedy', in Pincombe and Shrank (eds), *Oxford Handbook of Tudor Literature*, 733–48; see also Stephen J. Krahl, 'The medieval origins of the sixteenth-century English jest-books', *Studies in the Renaissance*

13 (1966), 166–83; F.P. Wilson, 'The English jest-books of the sixteenth and early seventeenth centuries', in H. Gardner (ed.), *Shakespearian and other Studies* (Oxford, 1969), 285–324; Linda Woodbridge, 'Jest books, the literature of roguery, and the vagrant poor in renaissance England', *English Literary Renaissance* 33 (2003), 201–10.

42. Bart van Es, *Shakespeare in Company* (Oxford, 2013), 163–94. See also D. Wiles, *Shakespeare's Clown: Actor and text in the Elizabethan playhouse* (Cambridge, 1987).

43. Tessa Watt, *Cheap Print and Popular Piety 1550–1640* (Cambridge, 1991), part 1; Marsh, *Music and Society*, chapters 5 and 6.

44. Marsh, *Music and Society*, 228. See also G. Pollard, 'John Dorne as an Oxford bookbinder', in D. Pearson (ed.), *Oxford Bookbinding 1500–1640* (Oxford, 2000), 201–10.

45. William Shakespeare, *The Winter's Tale*, Act IV, Scene 4, l.288.

46. Marsh, *Music and Society*, 257; Watt, *Cheap Print and Popular Piety*, 16–17.

47. Nicholas Bownde, *The doctrine of the sabbath* (1595), STC 3436, 242.

48. Harold Love and Arthur F. Marotti, 'Manuscript transmission and circulation', in David Loewenstein and Janel Mueller (eds), *The Cambridge History of Early Modern English Literature* (Cambridge, 2001), 55–80; Julia Crick and Alexandra Walsham (eds), *The Uses of Script and Print, 1300–1700* (Cambridge, 2004), 7–11.

49. Thomas F. Mayer, *Reginald Pole: Prince and prophet* (Cambridge, 2000), 13–33.

50. P.S. Donaldson (ed.), *A Machiavellian Treatise* (Cambridge, 1975); Felix Raab, *The English Face of Machiavelli: A Changing interpretation, 1500–1700* (London, 1964), 48–51, 52–53.

51. Henry R. Woudhuysen, *Sir Philip Sidney and the Circulation of Manuscripts 1558–1640* (Oxford, 1996), 207; Arthur F. Marotti, *Manuscript, Print and the English Renaissance Lyric* (Ithaca, NY, 1995). See also P. Beal, *Index of English Literary Manuscripts*, vol. I: *1450–1625* (Ithaca, NY, and London, 1980).

52. J. Gibson, 'Letters', in M. Hattaway (ed.), *A Companion to English Renaissance Literature and Culture* (Oxford, 2000), 615–19.

53. James Daybell, *The Material Letter in Early Modern England: Manuscript letters and the culture and practice of letter-writing, 1512–1635* (Basingstoke, 2012); James Daybell, *Women Letter-writers in Tudor England* (Oxford, 2006); James Daybell (ed.), *Early Modern Women's Letter Writing, 1450–1700* (Basingstoke, 2001).

54. For a detailed and spirited account of the difficulties involved, see Thomas Freeman and Elizabeth Evenden, *Religion and the Book in Early Modern England: The making of John Foxe's 'Book of Martyrs'* (Cambridge, 2010), 6–32.

55. Richard L. Hill, *Papermaking in Britain 1488–1988: A short history* (London, 1988), 50.

56. Cited in Freeman and Evenden, *Religion and the Book*, 23.

57. See B.P. Davies, 'John Day', in J.K. Bracken and J. Silver (eds), *The British Literary Book Trade, 1475–1700* (Detroit, MI, 1996), 78–93; C.L. Oastler, *John Day, the Elizabethan Printer* (Oxford, 1975); J. Roberts, 'Bibliographical aspects of John Foxe', in D. Loades (ed.), *John Foxe and the English Reformation* (Aldershot, 1997), 36–51; Freeman and Evenden, *Religion and the Book*, 15, 112–13.

58. Lisa Jardine and Anthony Grafton, ' "Studied for action": How Gabriel Harvey read his Livy', *P&P* 129 (1990), 30–78.

59. This interpretation echoed that of Justus Lipsius; see Alexandra Gajda, 'The Gordian Knot of policy: Statecraft and the prudent prince', in Smuts (ed.), *Oxford Handbook of the Age of Shakespeare*, 291.

60. Popper, 'European historiography', 241.

61. Alexandra Walsham, 'The spider and the bee: The perils of printing for refutation in Tudor England', in John N. King (ed.), *Tudor Books and Readers* (Cambridge, 2010), 163–90.

62. William Sherman, *Used Books: Marking readers in the English renaissance* (Philadelphia, PA, 2008).

63. Morgan Ring, 'Annotating the *Golden Legend* in early modern England', *RQ* 72 (2019), 816-62.

64. David Loades, 'The theory and practice of censorship in sixteenth-century England', *TRHS* fifth series, 24 (1974), 141-57.

65. Richard Rex, 'The English campaign against Luther in the 1520s', *TRHS* fifth series, 39 (1989), 85-106.

66. John Fisher, *The sermon of Iohn the bysshop of Rochester made agayn the pernicious doctryn of Martin luther* (1521), *STC* 10894, Sig. Aii^r.

67. ibid., Sig. Bv^v.

68. Richard Rex, *The Theology of John Fisher* (Cambridge, 1991), 78-92.

69. Elizabeth, c. 15; A. Luders et al. (eds), *Statutes of the Realm*, 11 vols (1810), IV, part 1.

70. Catharine Davies, *A Religion of the Word: The defence of the Reformation in the reign of Edward VI* (Manchester, 2002).

71. Lucy Wooding, *Rethinking Catholicism in Reformation England* (Oxford, 2000), 114-51; William Wizeman, *The Theology and Spirituality of Mary Tudor's Church* (Aldershot, 2006), 47-49.

72. Peter Marshall, 'The rood of Boxley, the blood of Hailes and the defence of the Henrician Church', *JEcclesH* 46 (1995), 693-95; Tracey Sowerby, '"All our books do be sent into other countreys and translated": Henrician polemic in its international context', *EHR* 121 (2006), 1271-99; Corinna Streckfuss, 'England's reconciliation with Rome: A news event in early modern England', *HR* 82 (2009), 62-73.

73. Leonard Nathan, 'The course of the particular: Surrey's Epitaph on Thomas Clere and the fifteenth-century lyric tradition', *The English Renaissance* 17 (1977), 3-12; Sheldon Zitner, 'Surrey's "Epitaph on Thomas Clere": Lyric and history', in Chaviva Hosek and Patricia Parker (eds), *Lyric Poetry: Beyond new criticism* (Ithaca, NY, 1985), 106-15.

74. Andrew Pettegree, 'Centre and periphery in the European book world', *TRHS* sixth series, 18 (2008), 101-28.

75. Julia Boffey, 'Wynkyn de Worde, Richard Pynson, and the English printing of texts translated from French', in Jennifer Britnell and Richard Britnell (eds), *Vernacular Literature and Current Affairs in the Early Sixteenth Century* (Aldershot, 2000), 171-83.

76. Mary Beth Winn, *Antoine Vérard: Parisian publisher, 1485-1512* (Geneva, 1997); John Macfarlane, *Antoine Vérard* (London, 1900).

77. Lotte Hellinga, 'Prologue: The first years of the Tudor monarchy and the printing press', in King (ed.), *Tudor Books and Readers*, 18.

78. Alexandra Gillespie, 'Caxton and the invention of printing', in Pincombe and Shrank (eds), *Oxford Handbook of Tudor Literature*, 24.

79. Thomas Freeman, 'Publish and perish: The scribal culture of the Marian martyrs', in Crick and Walsham (eds), *The Uses of Script and Print*, 235-54; E.J. Baskerville, *A Chronological Bibliography of Propaganda and Polemic Published in England between 1553 and 1558* (Philadelphia, PA, 1979), 34-87; Peter Milward, *Religious Controversies of the Elizabethan Age: A survey of printed sources* (London, 1977).

80. Fred Schurink (ed.), *Tudor Translation* (Basingstoke, 2011), 2-3; Zim, *English Metrical Psalms*; Linda P. Austern, Kari B. McBride and David L. Orvis (eds), *Psalms in the Early Modern World* (Farnham, 2016).

81. Thomas Gascoigne, *Here after folowith the boke callyd the myrroure of Oure Lady very necessary for all relygyous persones* (1530), *STC* 17542, Sig. Av^v.

82. Laurence Humphrey, *Interpretatio Linguarum* (1559).

83. Ascham, *The Scholemaster*, fo. 33^{r-v}.

84. Tania Demetriou and Rowan Tomlinson (eds), *Culture of Translation in Early Modern England and France, 1500-1660* (Basingstoke and New York, 2015), 1-3.

85. Lisa F. Parmelee, *Good Newes from Fraunce: French Anti-League propaganda in late Elizabethan England* (Woodbridge, 1996); David Randall, *English Military News Pamphlets, 1513-1637* (Tempe, AZ, 2011); Joad Raymond, 'News', in Susan Doran and Norman Jones (eds), *The Elizabethan World* (Abingdon and New York, 2011), 495-510.

86. Warren Boutcher, '"Who-taught-thee-Rhetoricke-to-deceive-a-maid?": Christopher Marlowe's *Hero and Leander*, Juan Boscan's *Leandro*, and renaissance vernacular humanism', *Comparative Literature* 52 (2000), 11–52; Anne Lake Prescott, 'Mary Sidney's *Antonius* and the ambiguities of French history', *The Yearbook of English Studies* 38 (2008), 216–33.

87. *The historie of Philip de Commines Knight* (1596), STC 5602, Sig. A2ʳ.

88. Hamlin, 'Piety and poetry', 205.

89. Samuel Daniel, *Musophilus* (1599), cited in Stephen Greenblatt, *Learning to Curse: Essays in early modern culture* (New York and London, 2007), 22.

90. Edmund Spenser, *The shepheardes calender* (1581), STC 23090, Sig. ***iiᵛ.

91. Edmund Spenser, *A View of the Present State of Ireland*, ed. W.L. Renwick (London, 1934), 87–88.

92. Joan Simon, *Education and Society in Tudor England* (Cambridge, 1966), 103.

93. Cox Jensen, *Reading the Roman Republic in Early Modern England*; J.W. Binns, *Intellectual Culture in Elizabethan and Jacobean England: The Latin writings of the age* (Leeds, 1990); Malcolm Smuts, 'Court-centred politics and the uses of Roman historians, c.1590–1630', in Kevin Sharpe and Peter Lake (eds), *Culture and Politics in Early Stuart England* (Basingstoke, 1993), 21–44; Daniel Cademan and Andrew Duxfield, 'Rome and home: The cultural uses of Rome in early modern English literature: An introduction', *Early Modern Literary Studies* 19 (2016), 1–15; David Norbrook, *Poetry and Politics in the English Renaissance* (London, 1984).

94. Demetriou and Tomlinson (eds), *Culture of Translation*, 5

95. Clifford Ronan, '*Antike Roman': Power symbology and the Roman play in early modern England* (Athens, GA, and London, 1995), 165–85.

96. Warren Chernaik, *The Myth of Rome in Shakespeare and his Contemporaries* (Cambridge, 2011), 9.

97. Margaret Tudeau-Clayton, 'What is my nation? Language, verse and politics in Tudor translations of Virgil's *Aeneid*', in Pincombe and Shrank (eds), *Oxford Handbook of Tudor Literature*, 389–90; Jessica Winston, 'English Seneca: Heywood to *Hamlet*', in Pincombe and Shrank (eds), *Oxford Handbook of Tudor Literature*, 472.

98. Quoted in Alexandra Gajda, *The Earl of Essex and Late Elizabethan Political Culture* (Oxford, 2012), 216.

99. ibid., 220–21.

100. Desiderius Erasmus, *The Education of a Christian Prince*, trans. and ed. Lisa Jardine (Cambridge, 1997), 5.

101. T.W. Baldwin, *Shakspere's Small Latine and Lesse Greeke*, 2 vols (Urbana, IL, 1944); Rebecca W. Bushnell, *A Culture of Teaching: Early modern humanism in theory and practice* (Ithaca, NY, 1996); Peter Mack, *Elizabethan Rhetoric: Theory and practice* (Cambridge, 2002); Andrew Wallace, *Virgil's Schoolboys: The poetics of pedagogy in renaissance England* (Oxford, 2010); Lynn Enterline, *Shakespeare's Schoolroom* (Philadelphia, PA, 2012); see also Colin Burrow, *Shakespeare and Classical Antiquity* (Oxford, 2013), 22–23.

102. E.A.J. Honigmann, 'Shakespeare's Plutarch', *Shakespeare Quarterly* 10 (1959), 25–33; Emrys Jones, *The Origins of Shakespeare* (Oxford, 1977); Patrick Gray, *Shakespeare and the Fall of the Roman Republic: Selfhood, stoicism and civil war* (Edinburgh, 2018).

103. Lawrence Stone, 'The educational revolution in England, 1560–1640', *P&P* 28 (1964), 41–80; Nicholas Orme, *Medieval Schools: From Roman Britain to renaissance England* (New Haven, CT, and London, 2006), 118–27; Andrew Breeze and J. Glomski, 'An early treatise upon education: Leonard Cox's *De Emendenda Iuventute (1526)*', *Humanistica Louvaniensia* 40 (1991), 112–67.

104. Quoted in Peter Mack, 'Rhetorical training in the Elizabethan grammar school', in Smuts (ed.), *Oxford Handbook of the Age of Shakespeare*, 201–02; see also Pollnitz, *Princely Education*, 88.

105. Freyja Cox Jensen, 'Intellectual developments', in Doran and Jones (eds), *The Elizabethan World*, 512.

106. Rosemary O'Day, *Education and Society, 1500–1800: The social foundations of education in early modern Britain* (London, 1982), 42, 31.
107. ibid., 33.
108. Kenneth Charlton, *Education in Renaissance England* (London, 1965), 95.
109. Desiderius Erasmus, 'On education for children', in Erika Rummel (ed.), *The Erasmus Reader* (Toronto and London, 1990), 90.
110. Anon., *An ABC for children* (1570), STC 19.5.
111. ibid., Sig. Biv^{r-v}.
112. Quoted in Mack, 'Rhetorical training', 205.
113. Pollnitz, *Princely Education*, 208.
114. O'Day, *Education and Society*, 14.
115. ibid., 11.
116. Thomas Elyot, *The Boke Named the Governour* (1531), STC 7635, fo. 30^v.
117. Nicholas Orme, 'John Holt (d.1504), Tudor grammarian', *The Library*, sixth series, 18 (1996), 283–305.
118. Lisa Jardine and Anthony Grafton, *From Humanism to the Humanities: Education and the liberal arts in fifteenth- and sixteenth-century Europe* (London, 1986), 123–28, 136–42.
119. Rhodri Lewis, 'Francis Bacon and ingenuity', *RQ* 67 (2014), 113–63; see also Zakya Hanafi, *The Monster in the Machine: Magic, medicine and the marvellous in the time of the scientific revolution* (Durham, NC, 2000); Jonathan Sawday, *Engines of the Imagination: Renaissance culture and the rise of the machine* (London, 2007).
120. *The Whole Works of Roger Ascham*, ed. J.A. Giles (3 vols) (London, 1865–67), I, part 1, 191–92.
121. Jardine and Grafton, *From Humanism to the Humanities*, 138–39.
122. Nigel Wilson, 'The name Hythlodaeus', *Moreana* XXIX, 110 (June 1992), 33.
123. Thomas More, *Utopia*, ed. George M. Logan, trans. Robert M. Adams (third edition, Cambridge, 2016), 16.
124. ibid., 113.
125. Ian Green, *The Christian's ABC: Catechisms and catechizing in England, c. 1530–1740* (Oxford, 1996).
126. Thomas Hood, *The use of both the globes, celestiall, and terrestriall most plainely delivered in forme of a dialogue* (1592), STC 13698.
127. *A ritch storehouse or treasurie for nobilitye and gentlemen* (1570), STC 23408, fo. 5^v. Colin Burrow suggests that this was one of the texts read by Shakespeare: see Burrow, 'Shakespeare', in Patrick Cheney and Philip Hardie (eds), *The Oxford History of Classical Reception in English Literature*, Vol. 2: *1558–1660* (Oxford, 2015), 26.
128. Pauline Croft, 'Libels, popular literacy and public opinion in early modern England', *HR* 68 (1995), 267.
129. Thomas Elyot, *Pasquil the playne* (1533), Sig. Ai^v.
130. Paulina Kewes, 'Romans in the mirror', in Harriet Archer and Andrew Hadfield (eds), *A Mirror for Magistrates in Context: Literature, history and politics in early modern England* (Cambridge, 2016), 126–46.
131. More, *Utopia*, 16–17.
132. *The Yale Edition of the Complete Works of St Thomas More*, vol. 1: *English Poems* (New Haven, CT, and London, 1973), 177–79.
133. *English Historical Documents, 1485–1558*, ed. C.H. Williams (London, 1967), V, 276.
134. Thomas Becon, *The Jewel of joye* (London, 1550), STC 1733, Sig. G3^{r-v}.
135. Christopher Warley, 'Reforming the reformers: Robert Crowley and Nicholas Udall', in Pincombe and Shrank (eds), *The Oxford Handbook of Tudor Literature*, 273–90.
136. Paulina Kewes, 'History and its uses', in Paulina Kewes (ed.), *The Uses of History in Early Modern England* (San Marino, CA, 2006), 5–6.
137. Blair Worden, 'Historians and poets', in Kewes, *Uses of History*, 77–78.
138. Conyers Read, *Sir Francis Walsingham*, 3 vols (Oxford, 1925), I, 18.

139. Quoted in Chernaik, *Myth of Rome*, 17.
140. Alastair J.L. Blanshard and Tracey A. Sowerby, 'Thomas Wilson's Demosthenes and the politics of Tudor translation', *International Journal of the Classical Tradition* 12 (2005), 46–80, quotation at 63.
141. Annabel Patterson, *Censorship and Interpretation: The conditions of writing and reading in early modern England* (reprint edition, Madison, WI, 1991), 18 and *passim*.
142. Worden, *Sound of Virtue*, 7–12, and *passim*.
143. Katherine Duncan-Jones, *Sir Philip Sidney, Courtier Poet* (New Haven, CT, 1991), 162–67; Patterson, *Censorship*, 48.
144. Barrett L. Beer, 'John Ponet's *Shorte Treatise of Politike Power* reassessed', *SCJ* 21 (1990), 373–84; Barbara Peardon, 'The politics of polemic: John Ponet's *Short Treatise of Politic Power* and contemporary circumstance, 1553–1556', *JBS* 22 (1982), 35–49; Ryan J. Croft, 'Sanctified tyrannicide: Tyranny and theology in John Ponet's *Shorte Treatise of Politike Power* and Edmund Spenser's *The Faerie Queene*', *Studies in Philology* 108 (2011), 538–71; see also Quentin Skinner, *The Foundations of Modern Political Thought*, vol. 2: *The Age of Reformation* (Cambridge, 1978), 221–24.
145. Wooding, *Rethinking Catholicism*, 195–96.
146. John Guy, 'The 1590s: The second reign of Elizabeth I', in John Guy (ed.), *The Reign of Elizabeth I: Court and culture in the last decade* (Cambridge, 1995), 1–19; Julia M. Walker (ed.), *Dissing Elizabeth: Negative representations of Gloriana* (Durham, NC, 1998).
147. Worden, *Sound of Virtue*, 110.
148. Cyndia Susan Clegg, *Press Censorship in Elizabethan England* (Cambridge, 1997), 203–08; David Womersley, 'Sir Henry Savile's translation of Tacitus and the political interpretation of Elizabethan texts', *Review of English Studies* 42 (1991), 313–42; Gajda, *The Earl of Essex*, 227–33; Andrew Hadfield, 'War poetry and counsel in early modern Ireland', in Brendan Kane and Valerie McGowan-Doyle (eds), *Elizabeth I and Ireland* (Cambridge, 2014), 239–60.
149. Andrew Hadfield (ed.), *Literature and Censorship in Renaissance England* (Basingstoke, 2001). See also Peter Lake, *Bad Queen Bess? Libels, secret histories, and the politics of publicity in the reign of Queen Elizabeth I* (Oxford, 2016).
150. Read, *Sir Francis Walsingham*, I, 18–19.
151. Daniel Wakelin, 'Stephen Hawes and courtly education', in Pincombe and Shrank (eds), *Oxford Handbook of Tudor Literature*, 54. See also A.S.G. Edwards, *Stephen Hawes* (Boston, MA, 1983).
152. Gajda, *The Earl of Essex*, 219; Paul E.J. Hammer, 'The earl of Essex, Fulke Greville and the employment of scholars', *Studies in Philology* 91 (1994), 167–80.
153. Joan Kelly-Gadol, 'Did women have a renaissance', in Renate Bridenthal, Claudia Koonz and Susan Stuard (eds), *Becoming Visible: Women in European history* (Boston, MA, 1977), 176.
154. Theresa Coletti, '"Did women have a renaissance?" A medievalist reads Joan Kelly and Aemilia Lanyer', *Early Modern Women* 8 (2013), 249–59.
155. Margaret King, *Women of the Renaissance* (Chicago, IL, 1991); Constance Jordan, *Renaissance Feminism: Literary texts and political models* (Chicago, IL, 1990); Elaine Beilin, *Redeeming Eve: Women writers of the English renaissance* (Princeton, NJ, 1987); Wendy Wall, *The Imprint of Gender: Authorship and publication in the English renaissance* (Ithaca, NY, 1993); Kate Chedgzoy, Suzanne Trill and Melanie Hansen (eds), *Voicing Women: Gender and sexuality in early modern writing* (Keele, 1996); Linda Woodbridge, *Women and the English Renaissance: Literature and the nature of womankind, 1540–1620* (Chicago, IL, 1984).
156. Desiderius Erasmus, *A devoute treatise upon the Pater noster* (1526), STC 10477, Sig. aii^r–biii^v.
157. Thomas More to William Gunnell, cited in Sherrin Marshall Wyntjes, 'Women in the Reformation era', in Bridenthal, Koonz and Stuard, *Becoming Visible*, 170.

158. William Harrison, *The Description of England*, ed. G. Edelen (Washington, DC, and London, 1994), 228.

159. Alistair Fox, 'The decline of literary patronage in the 1590s', in Guy (ed.), *The Reign of Elizabeth I*, 231.

160. Gemma Allen, *The Cooke Sisters: Education, piety and politics in early modern England* (Manchester, 2013); Gemma Allen (ed.), *The Letters of Lady Anne Bacon* (Cambridge, 2014); Gemma Allen, 'Women as counsellors in sixteenth-century England: The letters of Lady Anne Bacon and Lady Elizabeth Russell', in James Daybell and A. Gordon (eds), *Women and Epistolary Agency in Early Modern Culture, 1450–1690* (London, 2016).

161. Megan Hickerson. 'Gospelling sisters "goinge up and downe": John Foxe and disorderly women', *SCJ* 35 (2004), 1035–51.

162. Proverbs 41:10, 17.

163. *The first examination of Ann Askew with the elucidation of John Bale* (1546), STC 848, Sig. Aii^v.

164. Ann Lake Prescott, 'The pearl of the Valois and Elizabeth I: Marguerite de Navarre's *Miroir* and Tudor England', in Margaret P. Hannay (ed.), *Silent but for the Word: Tudor women as patrons, translators and writers of religious works* (Kent, OH, 1985), 61–76.

165. Jane Anger, *Jane Anger, Her Protection for Women* (1589), STC 644, Sig. B3^v. See also Joan Kelly, 'Early feminist theory and the "Querelle des Femmes", 1400–1789', *Signs* 8 (1982), 4–28. For the debate on authorship, see Helen Andras Kahin, 'Jane Anger and John Lyly', *Modern Language Quarterly* 8 (1947), 31–35; Woodbridge, *Women and the English Renaissance*, 63–66; Diane Purkiss, 'Material girls: The seventeenth-century woman debate', in Clare Brant and Diane Purkiss (eds), *Women, Texts and Histories, 1575–1760* (London, 1992), 69–101; A. Lynne Magnusson, 'Nicholas Breton reads Jane Anger', *RS* 7 (1993), 291–300.

166. Betty Travitsky, 'The lady doth protest: Protest in the popular writings of renaissance Englishwomen', *English Literary Renaissance* 14 (1984), 261.

167. Isabella Whitney, *The copy of a letter* (1567), STC 25439, Sig. A(6)^v.

168. Patricia Phillippy, 'The maid's lawful liberty: Service, the household, and "Mother B" in Isabella Whitney's *A Sweet Nosegay*', *Modern Philology* 95 (1998), 439–62; Ann Margaret Lange, *Writing the Way Out: Inheritance and appropriation in Aemilia Lanyer, Isabella Whitney, Mary (Sidney) Herbert and Mary Wroth* (Bern and Oxford, 2011); Wendy Wall, 'Isabella Whitney and the Female legacy', *ELH* 58 (1991), 35–62.

169. Cora Fox, 'Isabella Whitney's Nosegay and the smell of women's writing', *The Senses and Society* 5 (2010), 131–43.

170. Lindsay Ann Reid, 'The brief Ovidian career of Isabella Whitney: From Heroidean to Tristian complaint', in Sarah C.E. Ross and Rosalind Smith (eds), *Early Modern Women's Complaint: Gender, form and politics* (London, 2020), 89–113; Kirk Melnikoff, 'Isabella Whitney and the stalls of Richard Jones', in Valerie Wayne (ed.), *Women's Labour and the History of the Book in Early Modern England* (London, 2020), 145–61.

171. Ann Rosalind Jones, 'Assimilation with a difference: Renaissance women poets and literary influence', *Yale French Studies* 62 (1981), 135.

172. Peter Stallybrass, 'Patriarchal territories: The body enclosed', in Margaret Ferguson, Maureen Quilligan and Nancy Vickers (eds), *Rewriting the Renaissance* (Chicago, IL, 1986), 123–42.

173. Juan Luis Vives, *A very frutefull and pleasant boke called the Instruction of a Christen woman* (1529), STC 24856.5, Sig. Eii^v.

174. Wall, 'Isabella Whitney', 47.

175. Hannay (ed.), *Silent but for the Word*, 1–2.

176. Margaret P. Hannay, 'Re-revealing the psalms: Mary Sidney, countess of Pembroke, and her early modern readers', in Linda P. Austern, Kari B. McBride and David L. Orvis (eds), *Psalms in the Early Modern World* (Farnham, 2011), 231.

177. Vives, *Instruction of a Christen woman*, preface by Richard Hyrd, Sig. Aii^v–Aiii^r.

178. Hannay, *Silent but for the Word*, 2. This was the phrase employed by the first woman ever to be granted a doctorate, Elena Cornaro Piscopia, at the University of Padua in 1678; Piscopia was quoting Sophocles whilst giving an hour-long Latin oration, so we might conclude that the statement was intended as irony.

179. ibid., 9; Brenda M. Hosington, 'Englishwomen's translations of Protestant texts', in Schurink (ed.), *Tudor Translation*, 133–35.

180. John Jewel, *An Apology or answere in defence of the Church in England*, Sig. ii^r. See Alice Ferron, '"The ornament of a woman is silence": Censorship, mediation, and female authorship in Tudor and Stuart England', unpublished PhD thesis, University College London (2015).

181. Deborah Uman and Bélen Bistué, 'Translation as collaborative authorship: Margaret Tyler's *The Mirrour of Princely Deedes and Knighthood*', *Comparative Literature Studies* 44 (2007), 298–323; Tina Kronitiris, 'Breaking barriers of genre and gender: Margaret Tyler's translations of *The Mirrour of Knighthood*', *English Literary Renaissance* 18 (1988), 19–39.

182. Edward Wilson-Lee, 'Women's weapons: Country house diplomacy in the countess of Pembroke's French translations', in Demetriou and Tomlinson (eds), *Culture of Translation*, 128–44.

183. Neil Rhodes, 'Pure and common Greek in early Tudor England', in Neil Rhodes, *Common: The development of literary culture in sixteenth-century England* (Oxford, 2018), 58–59.

184. Jardine and Grafton, '"Studied for Action"'; Gajda, *The Earl of Essex*, chapter 6.

185. Quoted in Gajda, *The Earl of Essex*, 225.

186. Sidney, *Apology for Poetry*, 92, 89, 94, 93.

187. ibid., 116, 100, 91, 93, 95.

188. Arthur F. Kinney, *Markets of Bawdrie: The dramatic criticism of Stephen Gosson* (Salzburg, 1974); Arthur F. Kinney, 'Stephen Gosson's art of argumentation in *The Schoole of Abuse*', *Studies in English Literature, 1500–1900*, 7 (1967), 41–54; Stephen S. Hilliard, 'Stephen Gosson and the Elizabethan distrust of the effects of drama', *English Literary Renaissance*, 9 (1979), 225–39.

189. Stephen Gosson, *The Schoole of Abuse* (1579), fos. 2^r, 14^v–15^r.

190. William Shakespeare, *A Midsummer Night's Dream*, Act V, Scene 1, ll. 8–9, 13–18, 24–28.

191. William Shakespeare, *Hamlet*, Act II, Scene 2, l. 265.

10 The Problem of Queenship: The reign of Mary I

1. Robert Wingfield, 'The *Vita Mariae Reginae* of Robert Wingfield of Brantham', ed. Diarmaid MacCulloch, *Camden Miscellany XXVIII*, CS fourth series, 29 (London, 1984), 253.

2. A.G. Dickens, 'Robert Parkyn's narrative of the Reformation', *EHR* 62 (1947), 77–78.

3. Wingfield, *Vita Mariae*, 269.

4. Juan Paez de Castro, 'A diary of events', in C.V. Malfatti (ed.), *The Accession, Coronation and Marriage of Mary Tudor as Related in Four Manuscripts of the Escorial* (Barcelona, 1956), 67; Richard Grafton, *A chronicle at large and meere history of the affayres of Englande* (London, 1569), STC 12147, 1332.

5. Richard Hoyle, 'Agrarian agitation in mid-sixteenth century Norfolk: A petition of 1553', *HJ* 44 (2001), 223–38.

6. J. Mychel, *A breviat cronicle* (1555), STC 9971, Sig. Oii^r.

7. Judith Richards, 'Mary Tudor as "sole quene"? Gendering Tudor monarchy', *HJ* 40 (1997), 895–924.

8. Jane Dawson, *John Knox* (New Haven, CT, and London, 2016); Susan Felch, 'The rhetoric of biblical authority: John Knox and the question of women', *SCJ* 26 (1995), 805–22; Robert Healey, 'Waiting for Deborah: John Knox and four ruling queens', *SCJ* 25 (1994), 371–86; Rosalind Marshall, *John Knox* (Edinburgh, 2000).

9. Constance Jordan, 'Woman's rule in sixteenth-century British political thought', *RQ* 40 (1987), 421–51.

10. Alexander Samson, *Mary and Philip: The marriage of Tudor England and Habsburg Spain* (Manchester, 2020), 3–4.

11. David Hume, *A History of England*, 8 vols (Dublin, 1788), IV, 462–63. See also Thomas Freeman, 'Inventing Bloody Mary: Perceptions of Mary Tudor', in Susan Doran and Thomas Freeman (eds), *Mary Tudor: Old and new perspectives* (Basingstoke, 2011), 78–100.

12. A.F. Pollard, *The History of England from the Accession of Edward VI to the Death of Elizabeth* (London, 1913), 172.

13. Foxe, *A&M* (1576), 2030.

14. Diarmaid MacCulloch, *Suffolk and the Tudors: Politics and religion in an English county, 1500–1600* (Oxford, 1986), 80.

15. Anna Whitelock and Diarmaid MacCulloch, 'Princess Mary's household', *HJ* 50 (2007), 271–75; the evidence of Mary's ostentatious Catholic loyalties rather contradicts the claim in the same article (at 269) that Mary drew a veil over her religion during her attempt to seize the throne in July 1553.

16. Machyn's *Diary*, 34. See also Ian Mortimer, 'Tudor chronicler or sixteenth-century diarist? Henry Machyn and the nature of his manuscript', *SCJ* 33 (2002), 983–1001.

17. *Chronicle of Queen Jane and Queen Mary*, 9; Wingfield, *Vita Mariae*, 255.

18. Wingfield, *Vita Mariae*, 258–59, 263–64.

19. Machyn's *Diary*, July 1553, 35–36.

20. *The copie of a pistel* (London, 1553), STC 20188, Sig. AI^v–Aii^r.

21. Gemma Allen, *The Cooke Sisters: Education, piety, and politics in early modern England* (Manchester, 2013).

22. Richard Taverner, *An oration gratulatory* (London, 1553), Sig. Av^v–Avi^r; Aiii^v; see also the discussion in Alice Hunt, 'The monarchical republic of Mary I', *HJ* 52 (2009), 566–67.

23. Richard Beard, *A Godly psalme of Marye Queene* (London, 1553), STC 1655, Sig. Av^r; Aiv^v.

24. Amy Appleford, 'Shakespeare's Katherine of Aragon: Last medieval queen, first recusant martyr', *Journal of Medieval and Early Modern Studies*, 40 (2010), 149–72.

25. Susan Brigden, *London and the Reformation* (Oxford, 1989), 525.

26. Mary's proclamation from early July 1553; see John Edwards, *Mary I: England's Catholic queen* (New Haven, CT, and London, 2011), 97.

27. ibid., 87–88.

28. Wingfield, *Vita Mariae*, 252.

29. Robert Tittler, *The Reign of Mary I* (London, 1983), 84.

30. Edwards, *Mary I*, 90–91.

31. Whitelock and MacCulloch, 'Princess Mary's household', 283–84.

32. *CSP Sp.*, XI, 96.

33. Machyn's *Diary*, 36.

34. Antonio de Guaras, *The Accession of Queen Mary*, ed. Richard Garnett (1892), 96.

35. Mychel, *A breviat cronicle*, Sig. Oi^r.

36. John Elder, *The copie of a letter* (1555), STC 7552, Sig. D (mislabelled E) vi^v.

37. Wingfield, *Vita Mariae*, 222.

38. Guaras, *Accession*, 99.

39. *TRP*, II, 16–17, footnotes 5–32.

40. Sarah Duncan, *Mary I: Gender, power, and ceremony in the reign of England's first queen* (New York and Basingstoke, 2012), 27–28.

41. Sydney Anglo, *Spectacle, Pageantry, and Early Tudor Policy* (second edition, Oxford, 1997), 320–21.

42. *TRP*, II, 11.

43. David M. Loades, *The Life and Career of William Paulet (c.1475–1572): Lord treasurer and first marquis of Winchester* (Aldershot, 2008); James D. Alsop and David M. Loades, 'William Paulet, first marquis of Winchester: A question of age', *SCJ* 18 (1987), 333–41.

44. Diane Willen, *John Russell, First Earl of Bedford: One of the king's men*, RHS Studies in History 23 (London, 1981); George W. Bernard, *The Power of the Early Tudor Nobility: A study of the fourth and fifth earls of Shrewsbury* (Brighton, 1985).

45. Anna Whitelock, 'A woman in a man's world: Mary I and political intimacy, 1553–1558', *Women's History Review* 16 (2007), 325–29.

46. John Strype, *Ecclesiastical Memorials*, 3 vols (Oxford, 1822), III, part 2, 536–50.

47. Whitelock, 'A woman in a man's world', 324.

48. Richards, 'Mary Tudor as "sole quene"?', 899.

49. Wingfield, *Vita Mariae*, 275–76.

50. Giovanni Commendone, 'Events of the kingdom of England', in Malfatti (ed.), *The Accession, Coronation and Marriage of Mary Tudor*, 34; see also Duncan, *Mary I*, 33.

51. Alice Hunt, 'The reformation of tradition', in Alice Hunt and Anna Whitelock (eds), *Tudor Queenship: The reigns of Mary and Elizabeth* (Basingstoke, 2010), 65; Richards, 'Mary Tudor as "sole quene"?', 902.

52. Leland, *De rebus Brittanicis*, IV, 219–20.

53. Duncan, *Mary I*, 35.

54. Quoted in Edwards, *Mary I*, 139.

55. *CSP Sp.*, XI, 238.

56. Hunt, 'The monarchical republic', 559–64.

57. David Loades, *Mary Tudor: A life* (Oxford, 1989), 210 n73.

58. John N. King, *Tudor Royal Iconography: Literature and art in an age of religious crisis* (Princeton, NJ, 1989), 219.

59. *CSP Ven.*, VI, 428.

60. Holinshed, *Chronicles* (1577), IV, 1731.

61. John Christopherson, *An exhortation to all menne to take hede and beware of rebellion* (1554), Sig. Qi^v.

62. Alice Hunt and Anna Whitelock, 'Introduction: Partners both in throne and grave', in Hunt and Whitelock (eds), *Tudor Queenship*, 1–7.

63. *TRP*, II, 3, 18.

64. Foxe, *A&M* (1583), 1335.

65. David Loades, 'The personal religion of Mary I', in David Loades and Eamon Duffy (eds), *The Church of Mary Tudor* (Aldershot, 2006), 16.

66. Whitelock and MacCulloch, 'Princess Mary's household', 271.

67. *CSP Sp.*, IX, 298; D.P. Dymond and Clive Paine, *The Spoil of Long Melford Church: The Reformation in a Suffolk parish* (Ipswich, 1992), 49.

68. Dickens, 'Robert Parkyn's narrative', 79.

69. J.J. Scarisbrick, *The Reformation and the English People* (Oxford, 1984), 104.

70. Wingfield, *Vita Mariae*, 272.

71. Samson, *Mary and Philip*, 36.

72. See for example *TRP*, II, 42, 49, 71.

73. Loades, 'The personal religion of Mary I', 18.

74. *TRP*, II, 12.

75. Stephen Gardiner, *De vera obedientia: An oration made in Latine*, trans. Michael Wood (Rome [in fact London], 1553), *STC* 11585.

76. Thomas F. Mayer, *Reginald Pole: Prince and prophet* (Cambridge, 2000); John Edwards, *Archbishop Pole* (Farnham, 2014).

77. A. Pollnitz, 'Religion and translation at the court of Henry VIII: Princess Mary, Katherine Parr and the *Paraphrases* of Erasmus', in Doran and Freeman (eds), *Mary Tudor*, 123–37.

78. Quoted in Loades, 'The personal religion of Mary I', 13.
79. Roger Edgeworth, *Sermons very fruitfull, godly and learned* (London, 1557), *STC* 7482, fo. lxxxv^r; see also Janet Wilson (ed.), *'Sermons very fruitfull, godly and learned' by Roger Edgeworth: Preaching in the Reformation, c.1535–c.1553* (Cambridge, 1993).
80. Edgeworth, *Sermons very fruitfull*, fo. xxxii^r.
81. John Standish, *A discourse* (1555), *STC* 23208, Sig. Aiii^{r-v}.
82. Christopherson, *An exhortation to all menne*, Sig. Qviii^v.
83. Quoted in Matthew Tibble, *Nicolaus Mameranus: Poetry and politics at the court of Mary Tudor* (Leiden, 2020), 39; Corinna Streckfuss, 'England's reconciliation with Rome: A news event in early modern Europe', *HR* 82 (2009), 62.
84. Gary Gibbs, 'The queen's Easter pardons, 1554: Ancient customs and the gift of Thucydides', in Valerie Schutte and Sarah Duncan (eds), *The Birth of a Queen: Essays on the quincentenary of Mary I* (New York, 2016), 113–33.
85. Streckfuss, 'England's reconciliation', 62–73.
86. Eamon Duffy, *The Stripping of the Altars: Traditional Religion in England, 1400–1580* (New Haven, CT, and London, 1992), 537–43.
87. *The copie of a pistel*, Sig. Aviii^r.
88. Corinna Streckfuss, '"Spes Maxima Nostra": European propaganda and the Spanish match', in Hunt and Whitelock (eds), *Tudor Queenship*, 145–57.
89. Wingfield, *Vita Mariae*, 279, 293, 274.
90. Alexander Samson, 'Power sharing: The co-monarchy of Philip and Mary', in Hunt and Whitelock (eds), *Tudor Queenship*, 162–63.
91. *TRP*, II, 19, 22.
92. Tibble, *Nicolaus Mameranus*, 37.
93. Elder, *Copie of a letter*, Sig. Dvii^v–viii^r.
94. *TRP*, II, 24.
95. Renard to Charles V, *CSP Sp.*, XI, 363–64.
96. Anthony Fletcher and Diarmaid MacCulloch, *Tudor Rebellions* (seventh edition, Abingdon, 2020), 95.
97. M. Anne Overell, 'A Nicodemite in England and Italy: Edward Courtenay, 1548–56', in David M. Loades (ed.), *John Foxe at Home and Abroad* (Aldershot, 2004), 117–35.
98. De Castro, 'A diary of events', 68.
99. Quoted in Duncan, *Mary I*, 155.
100. R.E. Ham, 'The autobiography of Sir James Croft', *BIHR* 50 (1977), 53.
101. Fletcher and MacCulloch, *Tudor Rebellions*, 94.
102. ibid., 101.
103. W.J. Tighe, 'Courtiers and politics in Elizabethan Herefordshire: Sir James Croft, his friends and his foes', *HJ* 32 (1989), 259.
104. David M. Loades, *Two Tudor Conspiracies* (Cambridge, 1965), 107; cited in ODNB.
105. *Chronicle of Queen Jane and Queen Mary*, 49–50.
106. John Proctor, *The historie of Wyates rebellion* (1554), *STC* 20407, address to the reader.
107. Edwards, *Mary I*, 189.
108. Duncan, *Mary I*, 77.
109. Edwards, *Mary I*, 190, 192.
110. Duncan, *Mary I*, 83.
111. ibid., 109–10.
112. Richards, 'Mary Tudor as "sole quene"?', 914.
113. Christopherson, *An Exhortation to all menne*, Sig. Mv^{r-v}.
114. Quoted in Samson, *Mary and Philip*, 105.
115. Duncan, *Mary I*, 95.
116. Roy Strong, 'Hans Eworth: A Tudor artist and his circle' and 'Hans Eworth reconsidered', in Roy Strong, *The Tudor and Stuart Monarchy: Pageantry, painting, iconography*, 3 vols (Woodbridge, 1995), I, 135–45, 147–52.
117. Duncan, *Mary I*, 100–02.

118. Samson, *Mary and Philip*, 105, 132.
119. Elder, *Copie of a letter*, Sig. Cv^v.
120. Samson, *Mary and Philip*, 105–06.
121. *An Acte for the repeale of certayne Actes made in the tyme of kyng Edwarde the sixt* (1553), STC 7852.
122. *TRP*, II, 12, 6.
123. Edmund Bonner, *A profitable and necessarye doctrine* (1554), STC 3283.3, Sig. Ti^r. See also Lucy Wooding, 'The Marian restoration and the mass', in Loades and Duffy (eds), *The Church of Mary Tudor*, 227–57.
124. *A plaine and godlye treatise*, Sig. Ai^v.
125. Strype, *Ecclesiastical Memorials*, III, part 2, 482. See also Eamon Duffy, 'Cardinal Pole Preaching: St Andrew's Day 1557', in Loades and Duffy (eds), *The Church of Mary Tudor*, 187–200.
126. L.W. Whatmore and W. Sharp (eds), *Archdeacon Harpsfield's Visitation, 1557* (London, 1950), I, 5–6.
127. Duffy, *Stripping of the Altars*, 526, 555–64.
128. BL MS Cotton Titus Cvii fo. 120^v.
129. BL Lansdowne MS 96, fo. 25^r.
130. E. Russell, 'Marian Oxford and the Counter-Reformation', in Caroline Barron and Christopher Harper-Bill (eds), *The Church in Pre-Reformation Society* (Woodbridge, 1985), 218–20.
131. Quoted in Claire Cross, 'The English universities, 1553–58', in Loades and Duffy (eds), *The Church of Mary Tudor*, 70.
132. See Rex H. Pogson, 'Reginald Pole and the priorities of government in Mary Tudor's Church', *HJ* 18 (1975), 3–20; David Loades, *The Reign of Mary Tudor* (London, 1991), 272, 276, 293; Christopher Haigh, *English Reformations: Religion, politics and society under the Tudors* (Oxford, 1993), 224; Diarmaid MacCulloch, *The Later Reformation in England, 1547–1603* (Basingstoke, 1990), 20. For the contrary view, see Duffy, 'Cardinal Pole preaching', 176–200.
133. Pole to Carranza, 20 June 1558, in *Epistolarum Reginald Poli*, ed. A.M. Quirini, 5 vols (Brescia, 1744–57), V, 69–76; excerpt translated in Duffy, 'Cardinal Pole preaching', 181. See also Dermot Fenlon, 'Pole, Carranza and the pulpit', in John Edwards and Ronald W. Truman (eds), *Reforming Catholicism in the England of Mary Tudor: The achievement of Friar Bartolemé Carranza* (Aldershot, 2005), 81–97.
134. *CSP Sp.*, XIII (1954), 366, 370.
135. William Wizeman, *The Theology and Spirituality of Mary Tudor's Church* (Aldershot, 2006), 141–42.
136. Charles S. Knighton, 'Westminster Abbey restored', in Loades and Duffy (eds), *The Church of Mary Tudor*, 81.
137. Edwards, *Mary I*, 213–14.
138. David Loades, 'The Marian Episcopate', in Loades and Duffy (eds), *The Church of Mary Tudor*, 34, 36.
139. Mayer, *Reginald Pole*, 314–15.
140. Cross, 'The English universities', 66.
141. Russell, 'Marian Oxford and the Counter-Reformation', 212–27.
142. Wizeman, *Theology and Spirituality*, 21.
143. Loades, 'The Marian Episcopate', 42, 43, 47.
144. W.G. Torrance, *The History of Alleyne's Grammar School, Uttoxeter, 1558–1958* (Hanley, 1959); D.M. De Salis and R.K. Stephens, *'An Innings Well Played': The story of Alleyne's School, Stevenage, 1558–1989* (Stevenage, 1989).
145. Eamon Duffy, *Fires of Faith: Catholic England under Mary Tudor* (New Haven, CT, 2009), 6. See also Philippa Tudor, 'John Feckenham and Tudor religious controversies', in J. Blair and B. Golding (eds), *The cloister and the world: Essays in medieval history in honour of Barbara Harvey* (Oxford, 1996), 302–22.

146. Wizeman, *Theology and Spirituality*, 140–43; Darryl Mark Ogier, *Reformation and Society in Guernsey* (Woodbridge, 1996), 41–42, 56.

147. Knighton, 'Westminster Abbey restored', 81.

148. Dom René Kollar, 'The Oxford Movement and the heritage of Benedictine monasticism', *Downside Review* 101 (1983), 281–90; Christopher de Hamel, *Syon Abbey: The library of the Bridgettine nuns and their peregrinations after the Reformation* (London, 1991); E.A. Jones and Alexandra Walsham (eds), *Syon Abbey and its Books: Reading, writing and religion, c.1400–1700* (Woodbridge, 2010).

149. 'The legatine constitutions of Cardinal Pole, 1556', in G. Bray (ed.), *The Anglican Canons, 1529–1947* (Woodbridge, 1998), 95.

150. ibid., 107.

151. Standish, *The triall of the supremacy*, Sig. Tviii^v.

152. Bray (ed.), *The Anglican Canons*, 109; Bonner, *A profitable and necessarye doctrine*, Sig. I^r.

153. Patrick Collinson, 'Truth and legend: The veracity of John Foxe's "Book of Martyrs"', in Patrick Collinson, *Elizabethan Essays* (London, 1994),151–77.

154. Duffy, *Fires of Faith*, 7.

155. Thomas Freeman, 'Burning zeal: Mary Tudor and the Marian persecution', in Doran and Freeman (eds), *Mary Tudor*, 171–205.

156. Commendone, 'Events of the kingdom of England', 28.

157. *The Saying of John, late Duke of Northumberland upon the Scaffold* (London, 1553); see also W.K. Jordan and M.R. Gleason, 'The saying of John, late duke of Northumberland upon the scaffold, 1553', *Harvard Library Bulletin* 23 (1975), 324–55.

158. Narasingha Prosad Sil, 'The rise and fall of Sir John Gates', *HJ* 24 (1981), 929–43.

159. David Loades, *John Dudley, Duke of Northumberland, 1504–1553* (Oxford, 1996), 266, 270–71.

160. Strype, *Ecclesiastical Memorials*, III, part 2, 537–38.

161. Paul Slack, 'Mortality crises and epidemic disease in England, 1485–1610', in Charles Webster (ed.), *Health, Medicine and Mortality in the Sixteenth Century* (Cambridge, 1979).

162. Paul Slack, *Poverty and Policy in Tudor and Stuart England* (London, 1988), 119–20.

163. *TRP*, II, 71–72, 73–74.

164. R.H. Tawney and Eileen Power (eds), *Tudor Economic Documents* (London, 1924), I, 150.

165. *TRP*, II, 53–55.

166. ibid., II, 17.

167. C.E. Challis, *The Tudor Coinage* (Manchester, 1978), 116–17.

168. *TRP*, II, 8–9, 19–20.

169. Robert Tittler, 'The emergence of urban policy, 1536–58', in Jennifer Loach and Robert Tittler (eds), *The Mid-Tudor Polity, c.1540–1560* (London, 1980), 84.

170. Andy Wood, *The Memory of the People: Custom and popular senses of the past in early modern England* (Cambridge, 2013), 111.

171. Robert Tittler, 'The incorporation of boroughs, 1540–1558', *History* 62 (1977), 24, 29–30, 35–36.

172. Tittler, 'The emergence of urban policy', 89–90.

173. Slack, 'Social policy and the constraints of government, 1547–58', in Loach and Robert (eds), *The Mid-Tudor Polity*, 103–04.

174. Edwards, *Archbishop Pole*, 218–19.

175. Slack, 'Social policy and the constraints of government', 111–12.

176. Natalie Zemon Davis, 'Poor relief, humanism and heresy', in Natalie Zemon Davis, *Society and Culture in Early Modern France: Eight essays* (Stanford, CA, 1975), 17–20; Brian Pullan, *Rich and Poor in Renaissance Venice: The social institutions of a Catholic state, to 1620* (Oxford, 1971).

177. Wood, *The Memory of the People*, 79–80; Anon., *A plaine and godly treatise for the instruccion of the symple and unlerned people* (London, 1555), *STC* 17629, Sig. Av^v.
178. *A plaine and godly treatise*, Sig. Av^v–Avi^r.
179. *A notable Oration made by John Venaeus a Parisien*, trans. John Bullingham (London, 1554), *STC* 24633.5, Sig. Cij^{r-v}.
180. Edwards, *Mary I*, 180.
181. Samson, *Mary and Philip*, 13.
182. Peter Barber, *The Queen Mary Atlas: Commentary* (London, 2005); see also David Loades, 'The Queen Mary atlas', *The Antiquaries Journal* 86 (2006), 445–46.
183. C.S.L. Davies, 'England and the French war, 1557–9', in Loach and Tittler, *The Mid-Tudor Polity*, 159–83.
184. Edwards, *Mary I*, 313–14.
185. Davies, 'England and the French war', 162–63.
186. Benjamin Redding, 'English naval expansion under the French threat, 1555–1564', *International Journal of Maritime History* 28 (2016), 640–53.
187. Duffy, *Fires of Faith*, 7, 186.
188. Edwards, *Mary I*, 318–19.
189. Slack, 'Mortality crises', 31–32.
190. Edwards, *Mary I*, 326–27.
191. Thomas Mayer (ed.), *The Correspondence of Cardinal Pole*, Vol. 3: *A Calendar, 1555–1558: Restoring the English Church* (Aldershot, 2004), no. 2311.
192. Edwards, *Archbishop Pole*, 239–40.
193. Mayer, *Reginald Pole*, 344.
194. Quoted in Edwards, *Archbishop Pole*, 278.
195. Mayer, *Reginald Pole*, 346–47.
196. Strype, *Ecclesiastical Memorials*, III, part 2, 536–50.

11 Imagining the Other: Europe and the wider world

1. J.A. Williamson, *Maritime Enterprise, 1486–1558* (Oxford, 1913), 307–37; Thomas S. Willan, *The Muscovy Merchants of 1555* (Manchester, 1953); Thomas S. Willan, *The Early History of the Russia Company, 1553–1603* (Manchester, 1956); Kenneth R. Andrews, *Trade, Plunder and Settlement: Maritime enterprise and the genesis of the British Empire* (Cambridge, 1984), 64–71; David M. Loades, *England's Maritime Empire: Seapower, commerce and policy, 1490–1690* (Harlow, 2000), 56–57, 66–68; Kit Mayers, *North-East Passage to Muscovy: Stephen Borough and the first Tudor explorations* (Stroud, 2005).
2. Nandini Das, 'Early modern travel writing (2): English travel writing', in Nandini Das and Tim Youngs (eds), *The Cambridge History of Travel Writing* (Cambridge, 2019), 77–92; Robert Lutton, 'Pilgrimage and travel writing in early sixteenth-century England: The pilgrimage accounts of Thomas Larke and Robert Langton', *Viator* 48 (2017), 333–57; Daniel Carey and Claire Jowitt (eds), *Richard Hakluyt and Travel Writing in Early Modern Europe* (Farnham, 2012); John Gallagher, *Learning Languages in Early Modern England* (Oxford, 2019).
3. Harry Kelsey, *Sir Francis Drake: The queen's pirate* (New Haven, CT, 1998); Kenneth R. Andrews, *Drake's Voyages: A re-assessment of their place in Elizabethan maritime expansion* (London, 1967); John Sugden, *Sir Francis Drake* (London, 1996); Samuel Bawlf, *The Secret Voyage of Sir Francis Drake, 1577–1580* (London, 2003); Derek Wilson, *The World Encompassed: Drake's great voyage 1577–1580* (London, 1998).
4. Holinshed, *Chronicles* (1587), VI, 1.
5. Felicity Heal and Henry Summerson, 'The genesis of the two editions', in Felicity Heal, Ian W. Archer and Paulina Kewes (eds), *The Oxford Handbook of Holinshed's Chronicles* (Oxford, 2013), 3–5.
6. Thomas Smith, *A Discourse of the Commonweal of this Realm of England*, ed. Elizabeth Lamond (Cambridge, 1929), 27.

7. Robert W. Karrow, *Mapmakers of the Sixteenth Century and Their Maps: Bio-bibliographies of the cartographers of Abraham Ortelius, 1570* (Chicago, IL, 1993).

8. Abraham Ortelius, *An epitome of Ortelius his Theater of the world* (1601), STC 18857, Sig. A4ᵛ.

9. Clare Howard, *English Travellers of the Renaissance* (London, 1914); John Parker, *Books to Build an Empire: A bibliographical history of English overseas interests to 1620* (Amsterdam, 1965); Andrew Hadfield, *Literature, Travel and Colonial Writing in the English Renaissance, 1545-1625* (Oxford, 1998).

10. Richard Hakluyt, *The Principall Navigations* (London, 1589), STC 12625. See also Sandra Young, 'Richard Hakluyt's voyages: Early modern print culture and the global reach of Englishness', *SCJ* 49 (2018), 1057-80; Carey and Jowitt (eds), *Richard Hakluyt and Travel Writing*; A. Payne, '"Strange, remote and farre distant countreys": The travel books of Richard Hakluyt', in Robin Myers and Michael Harris (eds), *Journeys Through the Market: Travel, travellers and the book trade* (Folkestone, 1999), 1-37; Richard Helgerson, 'The voyages of a nation', in Richard Helgerson, *Forms of Nationhood: The Elizabethan writing of England* (Chicago, IL, 1992), 149-91; G.D. Ramsay, 'Clothworkers, merchants adventurers and Richard Hakluyt', *EHR* 92 (1977), 504-21.

11. E.H. Thompson, 'Elizabethan economic analysis: Fynes Moryson's account of the economics of Europe', *History of Economic Ideas* 3 (1995), 1-25; Mareile Pfannebecker, '"Lying by authority": travel dissimulations in Fynes Moryson's *Itinerary*', *RS* 31 (2017), 569-85.

12. George Abbot, *A Briefe Description of the whole world* (1599), STC 24, Sig. A2ʳ.

13. Robert Saltwood, *A comparyson bytwene iiij byrdes* (1533), STC 21647, Sig. Diiijʳ.

14. *A Relation ... of the Island of England*, ed. Charlotte A. Sneyd (London, 1847), 20-21.

15. John Aylmer, *An harborowe for faithfull and trewe subiectes* (1559), STC 1005, Sig. P4ʳ; Helen Hackett, 'Introduction', in Helen Hackett (ed.), *Early Modern Exchanges: Dialogues between nations and cultures, 1550-1750* (Farnham, 2015), 1.

16. John Banister, *The Historie of Man* (London, 1578), STC 1359, Sig. Biijʳ.

17. John Strype, *Ecclesiastical Memorials*, 3 vols (Oxford, 1822), III, part 2, 484.

18. Hackett, 'Introduction', 2; Gallagher, *Learning Languages in Early Modern England*, 23.

19. Hackett, 'Introduction', 5.

20. Nigel Goose, '"Xenophobia" in Elizabethan and early Stuart England: An epithet too far?', in Nigel Goose and Lien Luu, *Immigrants in Tudor and Early Stuart England* (Brighton and Portland, OR, 2005), 110-35.

21. John Alcock, *In die Innocencium sermo pro episcopo puerorum* (1498), STC 293, Sig. biijʳ.

22. Ranulf Higden, *Here endeth the discripcion of Britayne ...* (1480), STC 13440a, ca. iii. Further editions were published in 1498 and 1528.

23. Christopher Taylor, 'Global circulation as Christian enclosure: Legend, empire and the nomadic Prester John', *Literature Compass* 11 (2014), 445-59; Robert Silverberg, *The Realm of Prester John* (London, 2001); Lev N. Gumilev, *Searches for an Imaginary Kingdom: The legend of the kingdom of Prester John*, trans. Robert E.F. Smith (Cambridge, 1987); Nicholas Jubber, *The Prester Quest* (London, 2005).

24. Abbot, *Briefe Description*, Sig. F3ʳ.

25. William Shakespeare, *Much Ado About Nothing*, Act II, Scene 1, l. 226.

26. Thomas Blundeville, *The fower chiefyst offices belongyng to horsemanshippe* (1566), STC 3152, fo. 5ʳ.

27. William Thomas, *A Historie of Italie* (London, 1549), STC 24018, fo. 73ʳ⁻ᵛ.

28. Lewis Lewkenor, *The Commonwealth and Government of Venice* (London, 1599), STC 5642, Sig. A3ʳ.

29. Michael Wyatt, *The Italian Encounter with Tudor England: A cultural politics of translation* (Cambridge, 2009), 159-63.

30. Roger Ascham, *The Scholemaster* (London, 1570), *STC* 832, fo. 23^{r-v}.
31. ibid., fo. 26^v.
32. ibid., fo. 30^r; see also Hadfield, *Literature, Travel and Colonial Writing*, 18.
33. Lewis Lewkenor, *A Discourse of the Usage of the English Fugitives by the Spaniard* (1595), *STC* 15563; see also William S. Maltby, *The Black Legend in England: The development of anti-Spanish sentiment, 1558–1660* (Durham, NC, 1971), 93; Hadfield, *Literature, Travel and Colonial Writing*, 48–49.
34. Dominic Baker Smith, 'Antonio Buonvisi and Florens Wilson: A European friendship', *Moreana* 43 (2006), 82–108; Elizabeth McCutcheon, '"The apple of my eye": Thomas More to Antonio Bonvisi, a reading and a translation', *Moreana* 18 (1981), 37–56.
35. Frederick E. Smith, 'A "fownde patrone and second father" of the Marian Church: Antonio Buonvisi, religious exile and mid-Tudor Catholicism', *BCH* 34 (2018), 222–46.
36. Maria Dowling and Joy Shakespeare (eds), 'Religion and politics in mid-Tudor England through the eyes of an English Protestant woman: The recollections of Rose Hickman', *BIHR* 55 (1982), 94–102.
37. Maurice Chauncy, *History of the Sufferings of Eighteen Carthusians* (London, 1890), 42.
38. Tracey A. Sowerby, 'Richard Pate, the Royal Supremacy and reformation diplomacy', *HJ* 54 (2011), 265–85; Frederick E. Smith, *Transnational Catholicism in Tudor England* (Oxford, 2022), 1.
39. Heiko Oberman, 'Europa Afflicta: The reformation of the refugees', in Andrew Pettegree (ed.), *The Reformation: Critical concepts in historical studies* (London, 2004), 156–72; Geert Janssen, 'The Counter-Reformation of the refugee: Exile and the shaping of Catholic militancy in the Dutch revolt', *JEcclesH* 63 (2012), 671–92; Nicholas Terpstra, *Religious Refugees in the Early Modern World: An alternative history of the Reformation* (New York, 2015).
40. Silke Muylaert, *Shaping the Stranger Churches: Migrants in England and the troubles in the Netherlands, 1547–1585* (Leiden, 2021).
41. Caroline Bowden, 'The English convents in exile and their neighbours: Extended networks, patrons and benefactors', in Hackett (ed.), *Early Modern Exchanges*, 227.
42. Liesbeth Corens, *Confessional Mobility and English Catholics in Counter-Reformation Europe* (Oxford, 2018), 2–4.
43. H. Hamlin, 'Strangers in strange lands: Biblical models of exile in early modern England', *Reformation* 15 (2010), 63–81.
44. Carrie E. Euler, 'Bringing reformed theology to England's "rude and simple people": Jean Véron, minister and author outside the stranger church community', in Randolph Vigne and Charles Littleton (eds), *From Strangers to Citizens: The integration of immigrant communities in Britain, Ireland, and colonial America, 1550–1750* (Brighton, 2001), 17–24.
45. S.K. Barker, '"Newes lately come": European news books in English translation', in S.K. Barker and Brenda Hosington (eds), *Renaissance Cultural Cross-roads: Translation, print and culture in Britain, 1473–1640* (Leiden, 2013), 229f.
46. Christoph Strohm, 'Discipline and integration: Jan Laski's Church Order for the London Strangers' Church', in Vigne and Littleton (eds), *From Strangers to Citizens*, 25–37; Andrew Pettegree, *Foreign Protestant Communities in Sixteenth-Century London* (Oxford, 1986), 31–35, 44, 47.
47. Patrick Collinson, 'Europe in Britain: Protestant strangers and the English Reformation', in Vigne and Littleton (eds), *From Strangers to Citizens*, 57–67.
48. Steve Rappaport, *Worlds Within Worlds: Structures of life in sixteenth century London* (Cambridge, 1989), 15.
49. Joseph P. Ward, 'Fictitious shoemakers, agitated weavers and the limits of popular xenophobia in Elizabethan London', in Vigne and Littleton (eds), *From Strangers to Citizens*, 80–87.

50. Pettegree, *Foreign Protestant Communities*, 11, 16–17, 299.
51. ibid., 15.
52. Nigel Goose, 'Immigrants in Tudor and early Stuart England', in Goose and Luu (eds), *Immigrants in Tudor and Early Stuart England*, 29.
53. ibid., 15.
54. Paul Griffiths, 'Surveying the people', in Keith Wrightson (ed.) *A Social History of England, 1500–1750* (Cambridge, 2017), 51.
55. ibid., 22, 24–25.
56. Peter Fraser, 'Slaves or free people? The status of Africans in England, 1550–1750', in Vigne and Littleton (eds), *From Strangers to Citizens*, 254–60. On the history of black people in early modern England more generally, see Kenneth Little, *Negroes in Britain: A study of racial relations in English society* (London, 1972); James Walvin, *Black and White: The negro and English society 1555–1945* (London, 1973); Nigel File and Chris Power, *Black Settlers in Britain 1555–1958* (London, 1981); Jagdish S. Gundara and Ian Duffield, *Essays on the History of the Blacks in Britain: From Roman times to the mid-twentieth century* (Aldershot, 1992); Kim F. Hall, *Things of Darkness: Economics of race and gender in early modern England* (Ithaca, NY, and London, 1995).
57. Peter Fryer, *Staying Power: The history of black people in Britain* (London and New York, 1984), 4–5; Kate J.P. Lowe and Tom F. Earle (eds), *Black Africans in Renaissance Europe* (Cambridge, 2005).
58. Miranda Kaufmann, *Black Tudors: The untold story* (London, 2017), 8–9, 46–53; Gustav Ungerer, 'Recovering a black African's voice in an English lawsuit: Jacques Francis and the salvage operations of the Mary Rose and the Sancta Maria and Sanctus Edwardus, 1545–c.1550', *Medieval and Renaissance Drama in England* 17 (2005), 255–71.
59. Imtiaz Habib, *Black Lives in the English Archives, 1500–1677* (London, 2008), 9–13, 46–47.
60. ibid., 39, 40–44; Imtiaz Habib, 'Othello, Sir Peter Negro, and the blacks of early modern England', *Literature, Interpretation, Theory* 9 (1998), 15–30. Habib's identification is challenged in Ungerer, 'Recovering a black African's voice', 267 n4.
61. Quoted in Habib, *Black Lives*, 23–25.
62. Fryer, *Staying Power*, 8; Marika Sherwood, 'Blacks in Tudor England', *Black and Asian Studies Association Newsletter* 40 (2004), 41; Edward Scobie, *Black Britannia: A history of blacks in Britain* (Chicago, IL, 1972), 5–8.
63. Habib, *Black Lives*, 81, 95–97.
64. ibid., 197–98, 207–08; Kaufmann, *Black Tudors*, 247–48.
65. Samuel H. Baron, *Explorations in Muscovite History* (Aldershot, 1991); Danila Sokolov, 'Reading diplomacy across the archives: English and Russian reports on Giles Fletcher the elder's embassy to Muscovy (1588–1589)', *Journal of Medieval and Early Modern Studies* 50 (2020), 587–608.
66. Giles Fletcher, *Of the Russe common wealth* (1591), STC 11056, Sig. A3ᵛ–A4ʳ.
67. Felicity Stout, *Exploring Russia in the Elizabethan Commonwealth: The Muscovy Company and Giles Fletcher, the elder (1546–1611)* (Manchester, 2015).
68. Roger Ascham, *A report and discourse . . . of the affairs and state of Germany* (1570), STC 830, fo. 1ᵛ.
69. Poland and Lithuania had been joined together by a personal union since 1386; a constitutional union was achieved in 1569. English commentators tended to refer simply to 'Poland', however.
70. Anita G. Sherman, 'Poland in the cultural imaginary of early modern England', *Journal for Early Modern Cultural Studies* 15 (2015), 57–58; Andrew Hadfield, *Shakespeare and Republicanism* (Cambridge, 2005), 26; Markku Peltonen, *Classical Humanism and Republicanism in English Political Thought, 1570–1640* (Cambridge, 1995), 102–18.
71. Sebastian Sobecki, 'John Peyton's A Relation of the State of Polonia and the accession of King James I, 1598–1603', *EHR* 129 (2014), 1079–97.

72. Janusz Tazbir, *A State without Stakes: Polish religious toleration in the sixteenth and seventeenth centuries*, trans. A.T. Jordan (New York, 1973), 31–32; Wiktor Weintraub, 'Tolerance and intolerance in old Poland', *Canadian Slavonic Papers* 13 (1971), 32; Harry E. Dembkowski, *The Union of Lublin: Polish federalism in the golden age* (Boulder, CO, and New York, 1982), 1.

73. Thomas Starkey, *A Dialogue between Pole and Lupset*, ed. Thomas F. Mayer (London, 1989), 119.

74. Peltonen, *Classical Humanism and Republicanism*; David Norbrook, *Poetry and Politics in the English Renaissance* (London, 1984), chapters 8–10.

75. See the discussion in Hadfield, *Literature, Travel and Colonial Writing*, 49–58.

76. Lewkenor, *The Commonwealth and Government of Venice*, Sig. A3^r.

77. Thomas, *Historie of Italie*, fos. 78^v–79^r.

78. Lewkenor, *The Commonwealth and Government of Venice*, 40.

79. Fynes Moryson, *An Itinerary* (1617), STC 18205, part 1, 4.

80. Ascham, *Report and discourse*, fo. 5^v.

81. Moryson, *Itinerary*, part 1, 7–8.

82. Ascham, *Report and discourse*, fo. 2^v.

83. Peter Marshall, '"The rood of Boxley, the blood of Hailes and the defence of the Henrician Church", *JEcclesH* 46 (1995), 689–96; Tracey Sowerby, '"All our books do be sent into other countries and translated": Henrician polemic in its international context', *EHR* 121 (2006), 1271–99.

84. Janet Backhouse, 'A salute to the Tudor rose', in Anny Raman and Eugène Manning (eds), *Miscellanea Martin Wittek* (Leuven, 1993), 1–14; David R. Carlson, 'The Italian Johannes Opicius on Henry VII of England's 1492 invasion of France: Historical witness and antique convention', *RS* 20 (2006), 520–46.

85. Peter Marshall, 'The other black legend: The Henrician Reformation and the Spanish people', *EHR* 116 (2001), 31–49.

86. Reginald Pole, *Pole's Defense of the Unity of the Church*, trans. and ed. Joseph Dwyer (Westminster, MD, 1965), 282.

87. Corinna Streckfuss, 'England's reconciliation with Rome: A news event in early modern Europe', *HR* 82 (2009), 65.

88. Pietro Martire d'Anghiera, trans. Richard Eden, *The Decades of the New World* (1555), STC 647, title page.

89. Hadfield, *Literature, Travel and Colonial Writing*, 6–12.

90. Fletcher, *Of the Russe common wealth*, fos. 7^r–10^v.

91. Quoted in D.B. Quinn and A.N. Ryan, *England's Sea Empire, 1550–1642* (London, 1983), 38.

92. ibid., 21–22; Andrews, *Trade, Plunder and Settlement*, 4–5.

93. Andrews, *Trade, Plunder and Settlement*, 5–6.

94. Higden, *Here endeth the discripcion of Britayne . . .*, ca. iii.

95. William Caxton, *Here endeth this doctrine at Westmestre* (1480), STC 24865, fo. 2^r.

96. Moryson, *Itinerary*, part 1, 3.

97. Andrews, *Trade, Plunder and Settlement*, 7–8.

98. Kit Mayers, *The First English Explorer: The life of Anthony Jenkinson (1529–1611) and his adventures on the route to the Orient* (Kibworth Beauchamp, 2016); Kurosh Meshkat, 'The journey of Master Anthony Jenkinson to Persia, 1562–1563', *Journal of Early Modern History* 13 (2009), 209–28; H.R. Huttenbach, 'Anthony Jenkinson's 1566 and 1567 missions to Muscovy reconstructed from unpublished sources', *Canadian-American Slavic Studies* 9 (1975), 179–203.

99. Abraham Hartwell, *A Reporte of the Kingdome of Congo* (1597), STC 16805, 3.

100. L.P. Jackson, 'Elizabethan seamen and the African slave trade', *Journal of Negro History* 9 (1924), 1–17.

101. J.A. Williamson, *Hawkins of Plymouth: A new history of Sir John Hawkins and of the other members of his family prominent in Tudor England* (London, 1969).

102. P.E.H. Hair and Robin Law, 'The English in Western Africa to 1700', in Nicholas Canny (ed.), *The Oxford History of the British Empire*, vol. 1: *The Origins of Empire: British overseas enterprise to the close of the seventeenth century* (Oxford, 1998), 246–47.

103. Andrews, *Trade, Plunder and Settlement*, 119–21.

104. Jackson, 'Elizabethan seamen', 16.

105. Habib, *Black Lives*, 69.

106. *Shakespeare's Europe: A survey of the condition of Europe at the end of the 16th century; being unpublished chapters of Fynes Moryson's* Itinerary *(1617)*, ed. Charles Hughes (London, 1903), 14.

107. David Gwyn, 'Richard Eden: Cosmographer and alchemist', *SCJ* 15 (1984), 13–34; Howard Marchitello, 'Recent studies in Tudor and early Stuart travel writing', *English Literary Renaissance* 29 (1999), 326–47; C.J. Kitching, 'Alchemy in the reign of Edward VI: An episode in the careers of Richard Whalley and Richard Eden', *BIHR* 44 (1971), 308–15.

108. Christopher Heaney, 'Marrying Utopia: Mary and Philip, Richard Eden, and the English alchemy of Spanish Peru', in Jorge Canizares-Esguerra (ed.), *Entangled Empires: The Anglo-Iberian Atlantic, 1500–1830* (Philadelphia, PA, 2018), 85–104; David A. Boruchoff, 'The politics of providence: History and empire in the writings of Pietro Martire, Richard Eden, and Richard Hakluyt', in Anne J. Cruz (ed.), *Material and Symbolic Circulation between England and Spain, 1554–1604* (Aldershot, 2008), 103–22.

109. Richard Eden, 'The preface to the reader' in *The decades of the new worlde*, reproduced in Edward Arber (ed.), *The First Three English Books on America* (Birmingham, 1885), 50.

110. Quoted in David Potter, 'England and Europe, 1558–1585', in Susan Doran and Norman Jones (eds), *The Elizabethan World* (Abingdon and New York, 2011), 616.

111. George Best, *A true discourse of the late voyages of discoverie* (London, 1578), STC 1972, 29.

112. Andrews, *Trade, Plunder and Settlement*, 2–3.

113. Quinn and Ryan, *England's Sea Empire*, 19–22, 27–38.

114. Amanda J. Snyder, 'Pirates, exiles and empire: English seamen, Atlantic expansion and Jamaican settlements, 1558–1658', unpublished PhD thesis, Florida International University (2013); Kenneth Andrews, *Elizabethan Privateering: English privateering during the Spanish War, 1585–1603* (Cambridge, 1964).

115. James A. Williamson, *The Cabot Voyages and Bristol Discovery under Henry VII*, Hakluyt Society, second series (Cambridge, 1962); Alwyn A. Ruddock, 'John Day of Bristol and the English voyages across the Atlantic before 1497', *Geographical Journal* 132 (1966), 225–33. See also Evan T. Jones, 'Alwyn Ruddock: John Cabot and the discovery of America', *HR* 81 (2008), 224–54.

116. Andrews, *Trade, Plunder and Settlement*, 45.

117. Quinn and Ryan, *England's Sea Empire*, 19.

118. Stephen Alford, *London's Triumph: Merchant adventurers and the Tudor city* (London, 2017), 68.

119. Quinn and Ryan, *England's Sea Empire*, 28–29.

120. ibid., 35–38.

121. Quoted in Ken MacMillan, 'Exploration, trade and empire', in Doran and Jones (eds), *The Elizabethan World*, 650.

122. Helgerson, *Forms of Nationhood*; David Armitage, *The Ideological Origins of the British Empire* (Cambridge, 2000); David Armitage, 'The Elizabethan idea of empire', *TRHS* sixth series, 14 (2004), 269–77.

123. Quinn and Ryan, *England's Sea Empire*, 22–23.

124. Richard Hakluyt, *Divers Voyages Touching the Discovery of America* (1582), dedication.

125. Jane Dawson, 'William Cecil and the British dimension of early Elizabethan foreign policy', *History* 74 (1989), 196–216; Roger A. Mason 'Scotland, Elizabethan England and the idea of Britain', *TRHS* sixth series, 14 (2004), 279–93.

126. Roger Ascham, *English Works*, ed. W.A. Wright (Cambridge, 1904), 51.

127. Hartwell, *A Reporte of the Kingdome of Congo*, Sig. ♠3ʳ.

128. Peter J. French, *John Dee: The world of an Elizabethan magus* (London, 1972), 180–99; Frances A. Yates, *Astraea: The imperial theme in the sixteenth century* (London, 1975); Christopher Hodgkins, *Reforming Empire: Protestant colonialism and conscience in British literature* (Columbia, MO, and London, 2002), 10–32; Glyn Parry, 'John Dee and the Elizabethan British Empire in its European context', *HJ* 49 (2006), 643–75.

129. Michael L. Oberg, 'Tribes and towns: What historians still get wrong about the Roanoke ventures', *Ethnohistory* 67 (2020), 579–602; Brandon Fullam, *The Lost Colony of Roanoke: New perspectives* (Jefferson, NC, 2017); David B. Quinn, *Set Fair for Roanoke: Voyages and colonies 1584–1606* (Chapel Hill, NC, 1985); Andrew T. Powell, *Grenville and the Lost Colony of Roanoke: The first English colony of America* (Leicester, 2011).

130. Quinn, *Set Fair for Roanoke*, 5–12.

131. *A copie of the last advertisement that came from Malta of the miraculous deliverie of the isle from the longe sieg of the Turke* (1565), STC 17214; *A short forme of thankesgeving to God for the delyverie of the Isle of Malta* (1565), STC 16509.

132. *A short forme of thankesgeving*, collect (unpaginated).

133. *National Prayers: Special worship since the Reformation*, vol. I: *Special Prayers, Fasts and Thanksgivings in the British Isles, 1533–1688*, ed. Natalie Mears, Alasdair Raffe, Stephen Taylor and Philip Williamson (Woodbridge, 2013), 10.

134. Cited in Paul Ayris, 'Preaching the last crusade: Thomas Cranmer and the "Devotion" money of 1543', *JEcclesH* 49 (1998), 699.

135. Noel Malcolm, *Useful Enemies: Islam and the Ottoman Empire in western political thought, 1450–1750* (Oxford, 2019), 101–02; Sabine Lucia Müller, 'William Harborne's embassies: Scripting, performing and editing Anglo-Ottoman diplomacy', in Sabine Schülting, Sabine Lucia Müller and Ralf Hertel (eds), *Early Modern Encounters with the Islamic East: Performing cultures* (Farnham, 2012), 11–26; Susan Skilliter, 'William Harborne, the first English ambassador 1583–1588', in W. Hale and A.I. Bagis (eds), *Four Centuries of Turco-British Relations: Studies in diplomatic, economic and cultural affairs* (Walkington, 1984), 10–25; Susan Skilliter, *William Harborne and the Trade with Turkey, 1578–1582: A documentary study of the first Anglo-Ottoman relations* (Oxford, 1977).

136. Pauline Croft, ' "The state of the world is marvellously changed": England, Spain and Europe 1558–1604', in Susan Doran and Glenn Richardson (eds), *Tudor England and Its Neighbours* (Basingstoke, 2005), 178.

137. Potter, 'England and Europe, 1558–1585', 613.

138. Tracey Sowerby, 'Early modern diplomatic history', *History Compass* 14 (2016), 441–56; Tracey Sowerby and Jan Hennings (eds), *Practices of Diplomacy in the Early Modern World, c.1410–1800* (London, 2017); Isabella Lazzarini, *Communication and Conflict: Italian diplomacy in the early renaissance, 1350–1520* (Oxford, 2015); P.M. Dover (ed.), *Secretaries and Statecraft in the Early Modern World* (Edinburgh, 2016); Sanjay Subrahmanyam, *Courtly Encounters: Translating courtliness and violence in early modern Eurasia* (Cambridge, 2012); E. Natalie Rothman, *Brokering Empire: Trans-imperial subjects between Venice and Istanbul* (Ithaca, NY, 2012); John Watkins, 'Toward a new diplomatic history of medieval and early modern Europe', *Journal of Medieval and Early Modern Studies* 38 (2008), 1–14.

139. Garrett Mattingly, *Renaissance Diplomacy* (Oxford and New York, 1955); F. Jeffrey Platt, 'The Elizabethan "Foreign Office" ', *The Historian* 56 (1994), 725–40.

140. J.P.D. Cooper, *The Queen's Agent: Francis Walsingham at the court of Elizabeth I* (London, 2011), 95–96.

141. Felicity Heal, 'Presenting noble beasts: Gifts of animals in Tudor and Stuart diplomacy', in Sowerby and Hennings (eds), *Practices of Diplomacy in the Early Modern World*, 187–88. On Horsey, see also L.E. Berry and R.O. Crummey, *Rude and Barbarous*

Kingdom: Russia in the accounts of sixteenth-century English voyagers (Madison, WI, 1968); Robert Croskey, 'The composition of Sir Jerome Horsey's "Travels"', *Jahrbücher für Geschichte Osteuropas* 26 (1978), 362–75.

142. Heal, 'Presenting noble beasts', 193–94.

143. Lisa Jardine and Jerry Brotton, *Global Interests: Renaissance art between east and west* (London, 2000), 49–60.

144. Albert F. Pollard, *The Reign of Henry VII from Contemporary Sources*, 3 vols (New York and London, 1913), III, 44.

145. *CSP Sp.*, II, 301.

146. Steven G. Ellis, *Ireland in the Age of the Tudors, 1447–1603: English expansion and the end of Gaelic rule* (London, 1998); Steven G. Ellis, *Tudor Frontiers and Noble Power: The making of the British state* (Oxford, 1995); Ciaran Brady, *The Chief Governors: The rise and fall of reform government in Tudor Ireland, 1536–1588* (Cambridge, 1994); J.G. Crawford, *Anglicizing the Government of Ireland: The Irish Privy Council and the expansion of Tudor rule, 1556–1578* (Dublin, 1993); Nicholas Canny, *From Reformation to Restoration: Ireland, 1534–1660* (Dublin, 1987); Ciaran Brady and Raymond Gillespie (eds), *Natives and Newcomers: The making of Irish colonial society, 1534–1641* (Dublin, 1986); Nicholas Canny, *The Elizabethan Conquest of Ireland: A pattern established, 1565–76* (Hassocks, 1976).

147. Susan Brigden, *New World, Lost Worlds* (London, 2000), 258.

148. Hiram Morgan, '"Never any realm worse governed": Queen Elizabeth and Ireland', *TRHS* sixth series, 14 (2004), 305.

149. Francis Bacon, *The History of the Reign of King Henry VII*, ed. Brian Thompson (London, 2007), 20.

150. Christopher Maginn and Steven G. Ellis, *The Tudor Discovery of Ireland* (Dublin, 2015), 116.

151. Eric Haywood, 'Humanism's priorities and empire's prerogatives: Polydore Vergil's description of Ireland', *Proceedings of the Royal Irish Academy* 109 (2000), 195–237.

152. Hiram Morgan, 'Giraldus Cambrensis and the Tudor conquest of Ireland', in Hiram Morgan (ed.), *Political Ideology in Ireland, 1541–1641* (Dublin, 1999), 22–44.

153. Michael Richter, *Medieval Ireland: The enduring tradition* (Dublin, 1988), 166–67.

154. Maginn and Ellis, *Tudor Discovery*, 42–44.

155. ibid., 143.

156. Norbrook, *Poetry and Politics*, 128.

157. Andrew Hadfield, 'Rethinking early-modern colonialism: The anomalous state of Ireland', *Irish Studies Review* 7 (1999), 14–16.

158. ibid., 16–19.

159. Ciaran F. Brady, 'Spenser's Irish crisis: Humanism and experience in the 1590s', *P&P* 91 (1986), 17–49; Patricia Coughlan (ed.), *Spenser and Ireland: An interdisciplinary perspective* (Cork, 1989); Richard A. McCabe, *Spenser's Monstrous Regiment: Elizabethan Ireland and the poetics of difference* (Oxford, 2002).

160. Steven G. Ellis, *Ireland's English Pale, 1470–1550: The making of a Tudor region* (Woodbridge, 2021).

161. Brigden, *New Worlds, Lost Worlds*, 19–21.

162. ibid., 257.

163. ibid., 22.

164. Ciaran Brady, *Shane O'Neill* (Dundalk, 1996).

165. Andrew Hadfield, 'The impact of Sir Thomas Smith', in Hackett (ed.), *Early Modern Exchanges*, 171.

166. Higden, *Here endeth the discripcion of Britayne*, cc. xxij, xxiiij.

167. Alan Ford, 'Apocalyptic Ireland, 1580–1641', *Irish Theological Quarterly* 78 (2013), 131–32.

168. Quoted in Morgan, '"Never any realm worse governed"', 301.

169. Canny, *The Elizabethan Conquest of Ireland*; Brady, *The Chief Governors*.

170. Quoted in Brigden, *New Worlds, Lost Worlds*, 239.

171. Hadfield, 'The impact of Sir Thomas Smith', 165–81.

172. John Patrick Montaño, 'Cultural conflict and the landscape of conquest in early modern Ireland', *Canadian Journal of Irish Studies* 40 (2017), 127 and n30.

173. Thomas Herron, *Spenser's Irish Work: Poetry, plantation and colonial reformation* (Aldershot, 2007), 48.

174. See the commemorative poem, 'The Tumulus of Thomas Smith killed in Ireland'; see also Hiram Morgan, 'The colonial adventure of Sir Thomas Smith in Ireland', *HJ* 28 (1985), 261–78; Hadfield, 'The Impact of Sir Thomas Smith', 171–72.

175. Brigden, *New Worlds, Lost Worlds*, 155–56.

176. David Edwards, 'Ireland: Security and conquest', in Doran and Jones (eds), *The Elizabethan World*, 182; see also David Edwards, 'The escalation of violence in sixteenth-century Ireland', in David Edwards, Padraig Lenihan and Clodagh Tait (eds), *Age of Atrocity: Violence and political conflict in early modern Ireland* (Dublin, 2007), 34–78.

177. Mary Ann Lyons, *Franco-Irish Relations, 1500–1610: Politics, migration and trade* (Woodbridge, 2003), 116–19.

178. Hiram Morgan, *Tyrone's Rebellion: The outbreak of the Nine Years' War in Tudor Ireland* (Dublin, 1993); John McGurk, *The Elizabethan Conquest of Ireland: The burdens of the 1590s crisis* (Manchester, 1997).

179. Morgan, '"Never any realm worse governed"', 308; Brigden, *New Worlds, Lost Worlds*, 20.

180. Hiram Morgan, 'Faith and fatherland in sixteenth-century Ireland', *History Ireland* 3 (1995), 17.

181. Croft, 'Libels, popular literacy and public opinion', 270–71.

182. Brigden, *New Worlds, Lost Worlds*, 321, 344–45.

183. John Speed, *The Theatre of the empire of Great Britaine* (1611), STC 23041, Sig. ¶4ʳ.

184. William Camden, *Britain, or A chorographical description* (1637), STC 4510.8, Sig. ¶4ʳ⁻ᵛ; this is a later edition of the English translation by Philemon Holland first published in 1610.

185. *The Voyages and Colonising Enterprises of Sir Humphrey Gilbert*, ed. David B. Quinn (London, 2010), II, 420. Also see David Armitage, 'Literature and empire', in Canny (ed.), *The Oxford History of the British Empire*, vol. 1: *The Origins of Empire*, 107.

186. Matthew Dimmock, 'Awareness and experiences of the outside world', in Doran and Jones (eds), *The Elizabethan World*, 672.

12 The Invention of Gloriana: The reign of Elizabeth I

1. Elizabeth's speech to the delegates of parliament, 12 November 1586, in *Elizabeth I: Collected Works*, 194.

2. Elizabeth's 'golden speech' of 1601, in *Elizabeth I: Collected Works*, 342.

3. Malcolm Smuts, 'Organized violence in the Elizabethan monarchical republic', *History* 99 (2014), 418–43.

4. Peter Lake, 'Puritanism, (monarchical) republicanism, and monarchy; or John Whitgift, antipuritanism, and the "invention" of popularity', *Journal of Medieval and Early Modern Studies* 40 (2010), 463–95.

5. See Rosamund Oates, 'Puritans and the "monarchical republic"', *EHR* 127 (2012), 819–43.

6. For discussions of Elizabeth's representation, see John N. King, 'Queen Elizabeth I: Representations of the Virgin Queen', *RQ* 43 (1990), 30–73; Catherine Loomis, *The Death of Elizabeth I: Remembering and reconstructing the Virgin Queen* (New York, 2010); Mary Hill Cole, *The Portable Queen: Elizabeth I and the politics of ceremony* (Amherst, MA, 2000); Anna Riehl, *The Face of Queenship: Representations of Elizabeth I* (New York, 2010); Kevin Sharpe, *Selling the Tudor Monarchy: Authority and image in*

sixteenth-century England (New Haven, CT, 2009), chapters 9–12; Paulina Kewes, Godly Queens: the royal iconographies of Mary and Elizabeth', and Susan Doran, 'Elizabeth I: An Old Testament king', in Alice Hunt and Anna Whitelock (eds), *Tudor Queenship: The reigns of Mary and Elizabeth* (Basingstoke, 2010), 47–62, 95–110.

7. Elizabeth's gender and its impact on her authority is a subject much debated: see, for example, Susan Bassnett, *Elizabeth I: A feminist perspective* (Oxford, 1998); Susan Frye, *Elizabeth I: The competition for representation* (New York, 1993); Susan Doran, *Monarchy and Matrimony: The courtships of Elizabeth I* (London, 1996); Louis Montrose, *The Subject of Elizabeth: Authority, gender and representation* (Chicago, IL, 2006).

8. Carole Levin, *The Heart and Stomach of a King: Elizabeth I and the politics of sex and power* (second edition, Philadelphia, PA, 2013), ix–x.

9. Leah Marcus, 'Shakespeare's comic heroines, Elizabeth I, and the political uses of androgyny', in Mary Beth Rose (ed.), *Women in the Middle Ages and the Renaissance: Literary and historical perspectives* (Syracuse, NY, 1986), 135–53; Allison Heisch, 'Queen Elizabeth I: Parliamentary rhetoric and the exercise of power', *Signs* 1 (1975), 31–55; Allison Heisch, 'Queen Elizabeth I and the persistence of patriarchy', *Feminist Review* 4 (1980), 45–54.

10. Catherine Belsey, *The Subject of Tragedy: Identity and difference in renaissance drama* (New York, 1985), 180.

11. Mary Thomas Crane, ' "Video et taceo": Elizabeth I and the rhetoric of counsel', *Studies in English Literature, 1500–1900* 28 (1988), 4.

12. Patrick Collinson, 'Pulling the strings: Religion and politics in the progress of 1578', in Jayne E. Archer, Elizabeth Goldring and Sarah Knight (eds), *The Progresses, Pageants and Entertainments of Queen Elizabeth* (Oxford, 2007), 124.

13. *Elizabeth I: Collected Works*, 190.

14. Susan Doran and Thomas Freeman, 'Introduction', in Susan Doran and Thomas Freeman (eds), *The Myth of Elizabeth* (Basingstoke, 2003), 1–19. On early seventeenth-century representations of Elizabeth, see Anne Barton, 'Harking back to Elizabeth: Ben Jonson and Caroline nostalgia', *English Literary History* 48 (1981), 706–31; D.R. Woolf, 'Two Elizabeths? James I and the late queen's famous memory', *Canadian Journal of History* 20 (1985), 167–92; John Watkins, ' "Old Bess in the ruff": Remembering Elizabeth I, 1625–1660', *English Literary Renaissance* 30 (2000), 95–116.

15. Doran and Freeman, 'Introduction', 16.

16. Julia M. Walker (ed.), *Dissing Elizabeth: Negative representations of Gloriana* (Durham, NC, 1998); Tracey Sowerby, 'The coronation of Anne Boleyn', in Thomas Betteridge and Greg Walker (eds), *The Oxford Handbook of Tudor Drama* (Oxford, 2012), 386–401

17. Quoted in Thomas Freeman, 'Providence and prescription: The account of Elizabeth in Foxe's "Book of Martyrs" ', in Doran and Freeman (eds), *The Myth of Elizabeth*, 39.

18. Patrick Collinson, 'William Camden and the anti-myth of Elizabeth: Setting the mould?', in Doran and Freeman (eds), *The Myth of Elizabeth*, 79–83.

19. Elisa Oh, 'The silences of Elizabeth I and Shakespeare's Isabella', *English Literary Renaissance* 45 (2015), 352–54; Cole, *The Portable Queen*, 151.

20. For discussions of authorship, see Henry R. Woudhuysen, 'The queen's own hand: A preliminary account', and Steven W. May, 'Queen Elizabeth prays for the living and the dead', in Peter Beal and Grace Ioppolo (eds), *Elizabeth I and the Culture of Writing* (London, 2007), 1–27, 201–11. For a less cautious view, see William P. Haugaard, 'Elizabeth Tudor's book of devotions: A neglected clue to the queen's life and character', *SCJ* 12 (1986), 79–106. For works by Elizabeth, see *Elizabeth I: Collected Works*; Leah Marcus, Janel Mueller and Mary Beth Rose, *Elizabeth I: Autograph compositions and foreign language originals* (Chicago, IL, 2003); Janel Mueller and Joshua Scodel, *Elizabeth I: Translations, 1544–1589* (Chicago, IL, 2009) and Janel Mueller and Joshua Scodel, *Elizabeth I: Translations, 1592–1598* (Chicago, IL, 2009).

21. *Elizabeth I: Collected Works*, 46. Both Foxe and Holinshed attributed this couplet to 1558. See also Ilona Bell, 'Elizabeth Tudor: Poet', *Explorations in Renaissance Culture* 30 (2004), 2–5.
22. *Elizabeth I: Collected Works*, 200, 201–02. See also Crane, '"Video et taceo"', 10–11.
23. Susan Doran (ed.), *Elizabeth: The Exhibition at the National Maritime Museum* (London, 2003), 12–13.
24. Susan Doran, *Elizabeth and Her Circle* (Oxford, 2015), 20–22; Maria Dowling (ed.), 'William Latymer's Chronickille of Anne Bulleyne', *Camden Miscellany XXX*, CS fourth series, 39 (London, 1990), 48–65.
25. See John N. King, 'The royal image, 1535–1603', in Dale Hoak (ed.), *Tudor Political Culture* (Cambridge, 1995), 120–32; Roy C. Strong, *Gloriana: The portraits of Queen Elizabeth I* (London, 1987); Kewes, 'Godly queens', 47–62; Doran, 'Elizabeth I: An Old Testament king', 95–110.
26. Doran, *Elizabeth and Her Circle*, 24.
27. *Elizabeth I: Collected Works*, 5–6.
28. ibid., 9.
29. Sheila Cavanagh, 'The bad seed: Princess Elizabeth and the Seymour incident', in Walker (ed.), *Dissing Elizabeth*, 9–29; George W. Bernard, 'The downfall of Sir Thomas Seymour', in George W. Bernard (ed.), *The Tudor Nobility* (Manchester, 1992), 212–40.
30. *Elizabeth I: Collected Works*, 24.
31. ibid., 48.
32. Doran, *Monarchy and Matrimony*, 18–19.
33. Patrick Collinson, 'Elizabeth I', *ODNB*.
34. 'Count Feria to King Philip II, 14 November 1558', in *EHD* V(A), 5–6.
35. Sir John Hayward, *Annals of the First Four Years of the Reign of Queen Elizabeth*, ed. J. Bruce, CS first series, 7 (London, 1840), 1. Cited in Collinson, 'Elizabeth I'.
36. *Elizabeth I: Collected Works*, 52.
37. Elizabeth Russell, 'Mary Tudor and Mr Jorkins', *HR* 63 (1990), 263–76.
38. 'The device for the alteration of religion', in *EHD* V(A), 26–29.
39. Patrick Collinson, *The Elizabethan Puritan Movement* (London, 1967, repr. Oxford 2004), 30.
40. 'Sir Nicholas Throckmorton's advice', ed. J.E. Neale, *EHR* 65 (1950), 94–95, 93.
41. 'Count Feria to King Philip II, 14 November 1558', 6.
42. Diarmaid MacCulloch, 'Parliament and the Reformation of Edward VI', *Parliamentary History* 34 (2015), 383–84.
43. A.J. Slavin, 'Sir Ralph Sadler and Master John Hales at the hanaper: a sixteenth-century struggle for property and profit', *BIHR* 38 (1965), 31–47.
44. 'An oration by John Hales, 1558/9', in *EHD* V(A), 23.
45. John Knox, *The First Blast of the Trumpet Against the Monstruous Regiment of Women* (Geneva, 1558), STC 15070, fo. 9^{r-v}.
46. Brett Usher, 'John Aylmer', *ODNB*.
47. Levin, *The Heart and Stomach of a King*, 11.
48. Jane Dawson, *John Knox* (New Haven, CT, 2015), 173.
49. Knox, *The first blast of the trumpet*, fo. 2^r.
50. Dawson, *John Knox*, 171–75.
51. Mary Beth Rose, *Gender and Heroism in Early Modern English Literature* (Chicago, IL, 2002); Alexandra Walsham, '"A very Deborah?": The myth of Elizabeth I as a providential monarch', in Doran and Freeman (eds), *The Myth of Elizabeth*, 145–46; Levin, *The Heart and Stomach of a King*, 121.
52. Susan Doran, 'The queen', in Susan Doran and Norman Jones (eds), *The Elizabethan World* (Abingdon and New York, 2011), 47–48.
53. *Elizabeth I: Collected Works*, 55; Walsham, '"A very Deborah"?', 145.
54. Patrick Collinson, *Elizabethan Essays* (London, 1994), 114.

55. Susan Doran, 'Elizabeth I's religion: The evidence of her letters', *JEcclesH* 51 (2000), 698.
56. Doran, 'The queen', in Doran and Freeman, *Elizabethan World*, 38.
57. 'An oration by John Hales, 1558/9', 22–23.
58. Richard DeMolen, 'Richard Mulcaster and Elizabethan pageantry', *Studies in English Literature, 1500–1900* 14 (1974), 209–21.
59. Richard Mulcaster, *The Passage of our most drad Soveraigne Lady Quene Elyzabeth* (1559), STC 7590, Sig. Eiiiiʳ.
60. Collinson, *The Elizabethan Puritan Movement*, 31.
61. 'The device for the alteration of religion', 27.
62. Dale Hoak, 'The coronations of Edward VI, Mary I, and Elizabeth I, and the transformation of the Tudor monarchy', in C.S. Knighton and Richard Mortimer (eds), *Westminster Abbey Reformed, 1540–1640* (Aldershot, 2003), 114–51.
63. *The Zurich Letters: comprising the correspondence of several English bishops and others*, ed. H. Robinson, 2 vols., Parker Society (Cambridge, 1842–45), I, 4. See also Millar Maclure, *The Paul's Cross Sermons, 1534–1642* (Toronto, 1958); Torrance Kirby, 'The public sermon: Paul's Cross and the culture of persuasion in England, 1534–1570', *Renaissance and Reformation* 31 (2008), 3–30; Mary Morrissey, *Politics and the Paul's Cross Sermons, 1558–1642* (Oxford, 2011).
64. Arnold Hunt, 'Preaching the Elizabethan settlement', in Hugh Adlington, Peter McCullough and Emma Rhatigan (eds), *The Oxford Handbook of the Early Modern Sermon* (Oxford, 2011), 367–69.
65. 'The device for the alteration of religion', 28.
66. J.E. Neale, *Elizabeth and her Parliaments*, vol. I: *1559–1581* (London, 1953), chapters 1–3.
67. Norman Jones, 'Elizabeth's first year: The conception and birth of the Elizabethan political world', in C. Haigh (ed.), *The Reign of Elizabeth I* (Basingstoke, 1984), 36–39, 41–48; Diarmaid MacCulloch, 'The latitude of the Church of England', in Ken Fincham and Peter Lake (eds), *Religious Politics in Post-Reformation England* (Woodbridge, 2006), 41–59; Norman Jones, *Faith by Statute: Parliament and the settlement of religion, 1559* (London, 1982); Christopher Haigh, *Elizabeth I* (London, 1988), 30–32; W.S. Hudson, *Cambridge and the Elizabethan Settlement of 1559* (Durham, NC, 1980).
68. Peter Marshall and John Morgan, 'Clerical conformity and the Elizabethan settlement revisited', *HJ* 59 (2016), 1–22.
69. Margaret Christian, 'Elizabeth's preachers and the government of women: Defining and correcting a queen', *SCJ* 24 (1993), 561–76.
70. Collinson, *The Elizabethan Puritan Movement*, 61.
71. Quoted in ibid., 30.
72. Collinson, *Elizabethan Essays*, 42.
73. *The remains of Edmund Grindal*, ed. William Nicholson (Parker Society, Oxford, 1843), 387.
74. Collinson, *The Elizabethan Puritan Movement*, 71–83.
75. Oates, 'Puritans and the "monarchical republic"', 831.
76. ibid., 831–32.
77. *VAI*, III, 27–28.
78. ibid., 23.
79. ibid., 21.
80. John Morwen, 'An addicion with an apologie to the causes of brinnynge of Paules Church', printed in *The burnynge of Paules church in London in the yeare of oure Lord 1561* (London, 1563), STC 19931, Sig. Aiiiʳ⁻ᵛ. See the discussion of these exchanges in Alexandra Walsham, *Providence in Early Modern England* (Oxford, 1999), 232–34.
81. Karl Gunther, 'Rebuilding the temple: James Pilkington, Aggeus and early Elizabethan puritanism', *JEcclesH* 60 (2009), 689–707; James Pilkington (attrib.), *The true report of the burnyng of the steple and church of Poules in London* (London, 1561), STC 19930, Sig. Aviiiʳ.
82. Morwen, 'An addicion with an apologie', Sig. Aiiiiʳ.

83. Doran, *Monarchy and Matrimony*, 3.
84. Haigh, *Elizabeth I*, 10–11. See also Carole Levin, ' "We shall never have a merry world while the Queene lyveth": gender, monarch and the power of seditious words', in Walker (ed.), *Dissing Elizabeth*, 77–95.
85. *Elizabeth I: Collected Works*, 57.
86. Norman Jones, *Birth of the Elizabethan Age: England in the 1560s* (Oxford, 1993), 132.
87. *Zurich Letters*, II, 1–2.
88. Quoted in Wallace MacCaffrey, *The Shaping of the Elizabethan Regime* (London, 1969), 139.
89. Doran, *Monarchy and Matrimony*, 11.
90. Susan Doran, 'Why did Elizabeth not marry?', in Walker (ed.), *Dissing Elizabeth*, 43.
91. Doran, *Monarchy and Matrimony*, 40–46.
92. L.J. Taylor-Smither, 'Elizabeth I: A psychological profile', *SCJ* 15 (1984), 47–70.
93. Blair Worden, *The Sound of Virtue: Philip Sidney's* Arcadia *and Elizabethan Politics* (New Haven, CT, and London, 1996), 91. See also 'Sir Thomas Smith's oration for and against the Queen's Marriage', in John Strype, *The Life of the Learned Sir Thomas Smith* (Oxford, 1820), Appendix III, 10–11.
94. *Elizabeth I: Collected Works*, 57–58.
95. Doran, 'The queen', 42.
96. See Doran, 'Why did Elizabeth not marry?', 30–59.
97. 'Count Feria to King Philip II, 14 November 1558', 9.
98. Doran, 'Why did Elizabeth not marry?', 34–35.
99. *Elizabeth I: Collected Works*, 57.
100. ibid., 302–03.
101. 'The device for the alteration of religion', 28.
102. *Zurich Letters*, I, 8.
103. For discussions of factionalism, see Simon Adams, 'Faction, clientage and party: English politics, 1550–1603', *History Today* 32 (1982), 339; Simon Adams, 'Eliza enthroned? The court and its politics', in Haigh (ed.), *The Reign of Elizabeth I*, 55–77. For the suggestion that Elizabeth's gender impeded the business of government, see Crane, ' "Video and taceo" ', 1–15; Anne McLaren, *Political Culture in the Reign of Elizabeth I: Queen and commonwealth 1558–1585* (Cambridge, 1999).
104. Quoted in Natalie Mears, 'The council', in Doran and Jones (eds), *The Elizabethan World*, 66.
105. Patrick Collinson, 'Puritans, men of business, and parliaments', in Collinson, *Elizabethan Essays*, 75.
106. Quoted in ibid., 69.
107. *Elizabeth I: Collected Works*, 52.
108. See Geoffrey R. Elton, 'Tudor government: The points of contact. II. The Council', *TRHS* fifth series, 25 (1975), 195–211, reprinted in Geoffrey R. Elton, *Studies in Tudor and Stuart Politics and Government*, 4 vols (Cambridge, 1974–92), III, 3–57.
109. See Adams, 'Eliza enthroned?', 55–78.
110. Penry Williams, 'Court and polity under Elizabeth I', *Bulletin of the John Rylands University Library* 65 (1983), 265, 267.
111. Norman L. Jones, 'William Cecil, Lord Burghley, and managing with the men-of-business', *Parliamentary History* 34 (2015), 45–61; Stephen Alford, *Burghley: William Cecil at the court of Elizabeth I* (New Haven, CT, and London, 2008).
112. Cited in Alford, *Burghley*, 89.
113. *The Letters of Lord Burghley, William Cecil, to his son Sir Robert Cecil, 1593–1598*, ed. William Acres, CS fifth series, 53 (Cambridge, 2017), 98.
114. Stephen Alford, 'Reassessing William Cecil in the 1560s', in John Guy (ed.), *The Tudor Monarchy* (London, 1997), 233–52; Jane Dawson, 'William Cecil and the British dimension of early Elizabethan foreign policy', *History* 74 (1989), 196–216.

115. For the picture of Cecil as a grave and honourable statesman, see Conyers Read, *Mr Secretary Cecil and Queen Elizabeth* (London, 1955), and *Lord Burghley and Queen Elizabeth* (London, 1960). For a more recent evaluation acknowledging the driving force of Cecil's Protestantism, see Stephen Alford, *Burghley*.

116. Alford, *Burghley*, 37.

117. On John Cheke, see John McDiarmid, '"To content god quietlie": The troubles of Sir John Cheke under Queen Mary', in Elizabeth Evenden and Vivienne Westbrook (eds), *Catholic Renewal and Protestant Resistance in Marian England* (Farnham, 2015), 185–227. On Mildred Cooke, see Gemma Allen, *The Cooke Sisters: Education, piety and politics in early modern England* (Manchester, 2013).

118. Alford, *Burghley*, 104. See also Malcolm R. Thorp, 'William Cecil and the Antichrist: A Study in anti-Catholic ideology', in Malcolm R. Thorp and Arthur J. Slavin (eds), *Politics, Religion and Diplomacy in Early Modern Europe* (Kirksville, MO, 1994), 289–304; Alford, 'Reassessing William Cecil in the 1560s', 233–53.

119. Dawson, 'William Cecil and the British dimension of early Elizabethan foreign policy'; Stephen Alford, *The Early Elizabethan Polity: William Cecil and the British succession crisis, 1558–1569* (Cambridge, 1998); Patrick Collinson, 'The Elizabethan exclusion crisis and the Elizabethan polity', *Proceedings of the British Academy* 84 (1994), 51–92.

120. Quoted in Stephen Alford, 'The political creed of William Cecil', in John F. McDiarmid (ed.), *The Monarchical Republic in Early Modern England: Essays in response to Patrick Collinson* (Aldershot, 2007), 87.

121. ibid., 83–84.

122. Quoted in ibid., 84.

123. Quoted in J.N. Neale, *Queen Elizabeth* (London, 1934), 103.

124. Quoted in Read, *Mr Secretary Cecil and Queen Elizabeth*, 161.

125. John Guy, 'Introduction: The 1590s', in John Guy (ed.), *The Reign of Elizabeth I: Court and culture in the last decade* (Cambridge, 1995), 1.

126. Quoted in Mears, 'The council', 65–66.

127. Quoted in Neale, *Queen Elizabeth*, 215.

128. Quoted in Catherine Bates, *The Rhetoric of Courtship in Elizabethan Language and Literature* (Cambridge, 1992), 45.

129. On the importance of gifts and the pageantry of gift-giving within relationships of power, see Louis A. Montrose, 'Gifts and reasons: The contexts of Peele's *Araygnement of Paris*', *English Literary History* 47 (1980), 433–61; Louis A. Montrose, ' "Eliza, Queene of sheapheardes", and the Pastoral of Power', *English Literary Renaissance* 10 (1980), 153–82; David Bergeron, *English Civic Pageantry 1558–1642* (London, 1971; repr. Tempe, AZ, 2003); Jean Wilson, *Entertainments for Elizabeth I* (Woodbridge, 1980); Patricia Fumerton, *Cultural Aesthetics: Renaissance literature and the practice of social ornamentation* (Chicago, IL, 1991), 31–43.

130. Felicity Heal, 'Giving and receiving on royal progress', in Archer, Goldring and Knight (eds), *The Progresses, Pageants and Entertainments*, 57.

131. ibid., 60.

132. Frances Yates, 'Elizabethan chivalry: The romance of the Accession Day tilts', in Frances Yates, *Astraea: The imperial theme in the sixteenth century* (London, 1975), 88–111.

133. Heal, 'Giving and receiving on royal progress', 55.

134. Patrick Collinson, 'Bishop Richard Bancroft and the succession', in Susan Doran and Paulina Kewes (eds), *Doubtful and Dangerous: The question of succession in late Elizabethan England* (Manchester, 2014), 93–94.

135. Quoted in Arnold Hunt, 'The succession in sermons, news and rumour', in Doran and Kewes (eds), *Doubtful and Dangerous*, 162.

136. Guy, 'Introduction: The 1590s', 4.

137. Brett Usher, 'Queen Elizabeth and Mrs Bishop', in Doran and Freeman (eds), *The Myth of Elizabeth*, 200–20.

138. Doran, *Elizabeth and Her Circle*, 46–58, 63–64.
139. Quoted in Collinson, 'Pulling the strings', 125.
140. Cole, *The Portable Queen*, 4–5.
141. ibid., 52.
142. Collinson, 'Pulling the strings', 126–33. See also Zillah Dovey, *An Elizabethan Progress: The queen's journey into East Anglia, 1578* (Stroud, 1996).
143. *Calendar of State Papers Spanish (Simancas)*, vol. 1: *1558–67*, 50–51.
144. 'Count Feria to King Philip II, 14 November 1558', 6.
145. Cavanagh, 'Princess Elizabeth and the Seymour incident', 15.
146. Doran, 'Why did Elizabeth not marry?', 31.
147. Carole Levin, '"We shall never have a merry world"', 88–89.
148. Doran, *Monarchy and Matrimony*, 72.
149. Levin, '"We shall never have a merry world"', 89.
150. Hannah Betts, '"The Image of this Queene so quaynt": The pornographic blazon 1588–1603', in Walker (ed.), *Dissing Elizabeth*, 153–184.
151. MacCaffrey, *Shaping of the Elizabethan Regime*, 268–80.
152. Aislinn Muller, 'Transmitting and translating the excommunication of Elizabeth I', *SCH* 53 (2017), 210–22.
153. *A fourme of common prayer to be used . . . necessarie for the present tyme and state* (1572), *STC* 16511, Sig. Aii^r.
154. *TRP*, II, 345.
155. ibid., II, 363.
156. David Cressy, *Agnes Bowker's Cat: Travesties and transgressions in Tudor and Stuart England* (Oxford, 2000), 9–10, 21–22.
157. Alford, *The Early Elizabethan Polity*, 182–208; Christopher Hill, 'The many-headed monster in late Tudor and early Stuart political thinking', in Charles Carter (ed.), *From the Renaissance to the Counter-Reformation: Essays in honour of Garrett Mattingly* (London, 1966), 296–324.
158. Cressy, *Agnes Bowker's Cat*, 33, 43.
159. Krista J. Kesselring, *The Northern Rebellion of 1569: Faith, politics and protest in Elizabethan England* (Basingstoke, 2010), 3–8 and *passim*; see also Anthony Fletcher and Diarmaid MacCulloch, *Tudor Rebellions* (seventh edition, Abingdon, 2020), 102–16.
160. Kesselring, *The Northern Rebellion*, 46–48
161. Cuthbert Sharp, *The Rising in the North: The 1569 rebellion*, ed. Robert Wood (Durham, 1975), 20.
162. Krista J. Kesselring, 'Mercy and liberality: The aftermath of the 1569 Northern Rebellion', *History* 90 (2005), 213–35; Kesselring, *The Northern Rebellion*, vii, 119–20, 122–26, 129–31.
163. Richard Rex, *Elizabeth: Fortune's bastard?* (Stroud, 2007), 9–11.
164. *TRP*, II, 323–25.
165. Aislinn Muller, *The Excommunication of Elizabeth: Faith, politics and resistance in post-Reformation England, 1570–1603* (Brill, 2020), 41–56.
166. Thomas Drant, *Two sermons Preached . . . at Windsor* (London, 1570), *STC* 7171.5, Sig. K^r.
167. *TRP*, II, 341.
168. ibid., II, 347.
169. *Elizabeth I: Collected Works*, 127.
170. Penry Williams, *The Tudor Regime* (Oxford, 1979), 381.
171. ibid., 392–93.
172. Geoffrey Elton, *Tudor Constitution*, 72–73.
173. Collinson, *The Elizabethan Puritan Movement*, 191.
174. Thomas Bentley, *The Monument of matrones*, quoted in Collinson, 'Elizabeth I', *ODNB*. See also Colin B. Atkinson and Jo B. Atkinson, 'The identity and life of Thomas

Bentley, compiler of *The monument of matrones* (1582)', *SCJ* 31 (2000), 323–48; Colin B. Atkinson and Jo B. Atkinson, 'Thomas Bentley's *The monument of matrons* (1582): The first Anglican Prayer Book for women', *Anglican Theological Review* 74 (1992), 277–88; John N. King, 'Thomas Bentley's Monument of Matrons: the earliest anthology of English women's texts', in Pamela J. Benson and Victoria Kirkham (eds), *Strong Voices, Weak History: Early women writers and canons in England, France and Italy* (Ann Arbor, MI, 2005), 216–38.

175. Freeman, 'Providence and prescription', 27–55.

176. Norman Jones, 'Parliament and the governance of Elizabethan England: A review', *Albion* 19 (1987), 327–46.

177. Collinson, 'Puritans, men of business, and parliaments', 60.

178. ibid., 70–74.

179. Natalie Mears, 'Counsel, Public debate and queenship: John Stubb's *The discoverie of a gaping gulf*, *HJ* 44 (2001), 629–50.

180. Collinson, 'Puritans, men of business and parliaments', 68–69.

181. Collinson, *The Elizabethan Puritan Movement*, 168–76.

182. ibid., 175.

183. *The remains of Edmund Grindal*, 376–90.

184. Patrick Collinson, 'The downfall of Archbishop Grindal and its place in Elizabethan political and ecclesiastical history', in Patrick Collinson, *Godly People: Essays on English Protestantism and Puritanism* (London, 1983), 371–98.

185. Peter Lake, '"The monarchical republic of Queen Elizabeth I" (and the fall of Archbishop Grindal) revisited', in McDiarmid (ed.), *The Monarchical Republic*, 139–44.

186. Cressy, *Agnes Bowker's Cat*, 51–71.

187. Collinson, 'The Elizabethan exclusion crisis'; Mears, 'Counsel, public debate, and queenship', 629–50.

188. Doran, *Monarchy and Matrimony*, 160–61.

189. Ilona Bell, '"Sovereaigne Lord of lordly Lady of this land": Elizabeth, Stubbs and the *Gaping Gulf*, in Walker (ed.), *Dissing Elizabeth*, 99–117. See also Peter Lake, *Bad Queen Bess? Libels, secret histories, and the politics of publicity in the reign of Queen Elizabeth I* (Oxford, 2016), 98–103.

190. Wallace MacCaffrey, *Queen Elizabeth and the Making of Policy, 1572–1588* (Princeton, NJ, 1981), 255–66.

191. Doran, *Monarchy and Matrimony*, 79, 146; Worden, *The Sound of Virtue*, 103–04.

192. 'The bond of association', in *Elizabeth I: Collected Works*, 184.

193. Collinson, *Elizabethan Essays*, 48–51; David Cressy, 'Binding the nation: The bonds of association, 1584 and 1696', in DeLloyd J. Guth and John W. McKenna (eds), *Tudor Rule and Revolution: Essays for G.R. Elton from his American friends* (Cambridge, 1982), 217–36.

194. Collinson, *Elizabethan Essays*, 48–51; Cressy, 'Binding the nation', 217–36.

195. Lisa Jardine, *The Awful End of William the Silent: The first assassination of a head of state with a handgun* (London, 2005).

196. Patrick Collinson, 'The monarchical republic of Queen Elizabeth I', *Bulletin of the John Rylands Library* 69 (1987), 394–424; Jonathan McGovern, 'Was Elizabethan England really a monarchical republic?', *HR* 92 (2019), 515–28.

197. Quentin Skinner, *Liberty before Liberalism* (Cambridge, 1998), 89–90; Markku Peltonen, *Classical Humanism and Republicanism in English Political Thought 1570–1640* (Cambridge, 1995); Anne McLaren, *Political Culture in the Reign of Elizabeth I*; Alford, *The Early Elizabethan Polity*.

198. Lake, '"The monarchical republic of Queen Elizabeth I"', 135; see also Lake, 'Puritanism, (monarchical) republicanism, and monarchy', 463–64.

199. Guy, 'Introduction: The 1590s', 12–13. On Thomas Cartwright, see Stephen A. Chavura, 'Mixed constitutionalism and parliamentarism in Elizabethan England: The

case of Thomas Cartwright', *History of European Ideas* 41 (2015), 318–37; Collinson, *Godly People*, 340–41.

200. Hugh Plat, *Sundrie new and artificiall remedies against famine* (1596), STC 19996, Sig. A2ʳ.

201. On the difficulties of the 1590s, see Wallace MacCaffrey, *Elizabeth I: War and politics, 1588–1603* (Princeton, NJ, 1992); Guy (ed.), *The Reign of Elizabeth I*; Ian Archer, 'The 1590s: Apotheosis or nemesis of the Elizabethan regime?', in A. Briggs and D. Snowman (eds), *Fins de Siecle: How centuries end* (New Haven, CT, 1996), 65–98; Alexandra Gajda, 'Political culture in the 1590s: The "second reign of Elizabeth"', *History Compass* (2010), 88–100.

202. David Trim, 'The context of war and violence in sixteenth-century English society', *Journal of Early Modern History* 3 (1999), 233–55.

203. Neil Younger, 'Securing the monarchical republic: The remaking of the lord lieutenancies in 1585', *HR* 84 (2011), 1–18; see also Neil Younger, *War and Politics in the Elizabethan Counties* (Manchester, 2012).

204. Jenny Wormald, *Mary Queen of Scots: A study in failure* (London, 1988); see also the review by Michael Lynch, 'Mary Queen of Scots: A new case for the prosecution', *JEcclesH* 41 (1990), 69–73.

205. *Elizabeth I: Collected Works*, 201.

206. Jan Glete, *Warfare at Sea, 1500–1650: Maritime conflicts and the transformation of Europe* (London, 2002), 161, 164; M.J. Rodriguez-Salgado and Simon Adams (eds), *England, Spain and the Gran Armada, 1585–1604* (Edinburgh, 1991).

207. Neil Younger, 'If the Armada had landed: A reappraisal of England's defences in 1588', *History* 93 (2008), 328–54.

208. See Joseph L. Black (ed.), *The Martin Marprelate Tracts: A modernized and annotated edition* (Cambridge, 2008). For the debate on authorship, see Leland Carlson, *Martin Marprelate, Gentleman: Master Job Throckmorton laid open in his colors* (San Marino, CA, 1981); Collinson, *The Elizabethan Puritan Movement*, 391–97.

209. Joseph L. Black, 'The Martin Marprelate Tracts (1588–89) and the popular voice', *History Compass* 6 (2008), 1091–106; Eric D. Vivier, 'John Bridges, Martin Marprelate, and the rhetoric of satire', *English Literary Renaissance* 44 (2014), 3–35.

210. Quoted in Collinson, *The Elizabethan Puritan Movement*, 393. See also Joseph L. Black, '"Handling religion in the style of the stage": Performing the Marprelate controversy', in Jane Hwang Degenhardt and Elizabeth Williamson (eds), *Religion and Drama in Early Modern England: The performance of religion on the renaissance stage* (Farnham, 2011), 153–74.

211. *An epistle to the terrible priests of the Convocation House*, ed. John Petheram (London, 1842), 2.

212. Joad Raymond, *Pamphlets and Pamphleteering in Early Modern Britain* (Cambridge, 2003), 11.

213. Sandeep Kaushik, 'Resistance, loyalty and recusant politics: Sir Thomas Tresham and the Elizabethan state', *Midland History* 21 (1996), 37–72.

214. William Allen, *A true, sincere and modest defence, of English Catholiques* (1584), STC 373, 103. This work was also published in Latin as *Ad Persecutores Anglos pro Catholicis*, translated by William Reynolds. It was a reply to William Cecil's *The Execution of Iustice in England* (1583) and in turn prompted the reply from Thomas Bilson, *The True Difference betweene Christian Subiection and Unchristian Rebellion* (1585), STC 3071.

215. Allen, *A true, sincere and modest defence*, 89.

216. Bilson, *True Difference*, 313.

217. Peter Lake, 'The theatre and the "post-Reformation public sphere"', in Malcolm Smuts (ed.), *The Oxford Handbook of the Age of Shakespeare* (Oxford, 2016), 186–87; Andy Kesson and Emma Smith, 'Introduction: Towards a Definition of Print Populariy', in Emma Smith and Andy Kesson (eds), *Elizabethan Top Ten: Defining print popularity in early modern England* (Farnham, 2013), 3–4, 6–8.

218. Guy, 'Introduction: The 1590s', 8–9.
219. J. Walter, 'A "rising of the people"? The Oxfordshire Rising of 1596', *P&P* 107 (1985), 90–143.
220. R. Doleman [Robert Persons], *Newes from Spayne and Holland* (Antwerp, 1593); R. Doleman [Robert Persons], *A Conference about the Next Succession to the Crowne of Ingland* (Antwerp, 1594 [1595]). For the attribution, see A.F. Allison and D.M. Rogers, *The Contemporary Printed Literature of the English Counter-Reformation between 1558 and 1649*, 2 vols (Aldershot, 1989–1994), II, 124. See also Paulina Kewes, 'Parliament and the principle of elective succession in Elizabethan England', in Alexandra Gajda and Paul Cavill (eds), *Writing the History of Parliament in Tudor and Early Stuart England* (Manchester, 2018), 108–09.
221. *APC*, XXVI, 385.
222. *APC*, XXVI, 384.
223. Walsham, *Providence in Early Modern England*, 210–11.
224. Steve Hindle, *On the Parish? The micro-politics of poor relief in rural England, c.1550–1750* (Oxford, 2004), 227–28.
225. Quoted in Ian Archer, *The Pursuit of Stability: Social relations in Elizabethan London* (Cambridge, 1991), 198.
226. J. Gwynfor Jones, *Early Modern Wales, c.1525–1640* (Basingstoke, 1994), 191–92.
227. William Camden, *The history of the most renowned and victorious Princess Elizabeth* (fourth edition, 1688), 556; quoted in Paul Hammer, 'Robert Devereux, earl of Essex', *ODNB*.
228. Smuts, 'Organized violence', 422.
229. Paul Hammer, 'The use of scholarship: The secretariat of Robert Devereux, second earl of Essex, c.1585–1601', *EHR* 109 (1994), 26–51.
230. Leonard Digges, *An Arithmeticall Militare Treatise named Statioticos* (London, 1579), *STC* 6848, 138.
231. Hugh Gazzard, '"Those graue presentments of antiquitie": Samuel Daniel's *Philotas* and the earl of Essex', *Review of English Studies* 51 (2000), 423–50; Lesel Dawson, 'The earl of Essex and the trials of history: Gervase Markham's *The Dumbe Knight*', *Review of English Studies* 53 (2002), 344–64; Richard McCoy, '"A dangerous image": The earl of Essex and Elizabethan chivalry', *Journal of Medieval and Renaissance Studies* 13 (1983), 313–29.
232. *A lamentable ditty composed upon the death of Robert Lord Devereux, late earle of Essex* (1635), *STC* 6792.
233. Alexandra Gajda, *The Earl of Essex and Late Elizabethan Political Culture* (Oxford, 2012), 258.
234. J.B. Black, *The Reign of Elizabeth, 1558–1603* (Oxford, 1936), 1.
235. *Elizabeth I: Collected Works*, 15.
236. ibid., 347–48.

13 A World Divided

1. John Hooker [John Vowell], *The description of the citie of Excester*, ed. W.J. Harte, J.W. Schopp and H. Tapley-Soper, 3 vols., Devon and Cornwall Record Society (Exeter, 1919–47), II, 91–94.
2. Holinshed, *Chronicles* (1587), III, 183.
3. Natalie Zemon Davies, 'The rites of violence: Religious riot in sixteenth-century France', *P&P* 59 (1973), 51–91; see also Natalie Zemon Davies, 'Writing "The rites of violence" and afterward', *P&P* 214, suppl. 7 (2012), 8–29.
4. Christopher Marsh, *Popular Religion in Sixteenth-Century England* (Basingstoke, 1998), 11.
5. Alexandra Walsham, *Charitable Hatred: Tolerance and intolerance in England, 1500–1700* (Manchester, 2006), 3–4, 228–29, 232–33.

6. Brad Gregory, *Salvation at Stake: Christian martyrdom in Europe* (Cambridge, MA, 1999); Anne Dillon, *The Construction of Martyrdom in the English Catholic Community, 1535–1603* (London, 2002).

7. Patrick Collinson, 'The politics of religion and the religion of politics in Elizabethan England', in Patrick Collinson, *This England: Essays on the English nation and common-wealth in the sixteenth century* (Manchester, 2011), 42.

8. Robert Whiting, *The Blind Devotion of the People: Popular religion and the English Reformation* (Cambridge, 1989).

9. Thomas Watson, *Holsome and Catholyke doctryne* (London, 1558), *STC* 25112, fo. xlix^r.

10. Edwin Sandys to Heinrich Bullinger, December 1558, in *The Zurich Letters: comprising the correspondence of several English bishops and others*, ed. H. Robinson, 2 vols, Parker Society (Cambridge, 1842–45), II, 5.

11. Rudolph Gualter to Queen Elizabeth, January 1559, *Zurich Letters*, II, 7.

12. ibid., 9–10.

13. *Zurich Letters*, I, 1.

14. See Alec Ryrie, 'Thomas Sampson', *ODNB*; Patrick Collinson, *The Elizabethan Puritan Movement* (London, 1967), 73.

15. *Zurich Letters*, I, 2.

16. Patrick Collinson, 'Nicholas Bacon and the Elizabethan *Via media*', *HJ* 23 (1980), 258–61.

17. Louise Campbell, 'A diagnosis of religious moderation: Matthew Parker and the 1559 settlement', in Luc Racaut and Alec Ryrie (eds), *Moderate Voices in the European Reformation* (Aldershot, 2005), 32–50.

18. Richard Bancroft, *A sermon preached at Paules Crosse* (1588), *STC* 1346, 11.

19. ibid., 5.

20. Ethan Shagan, *The Rule of Moderation: Violence, religion and the politics of restraint in early modern England* (Cambridge, 2011), 7, and *passim*.

21. Amanda C. Jones, '"Commotion time": The English risings of 1549', unpublished PhD thesis, University of Warwick (2003), 261–64.

22. John Jewel to Peter Martyr, March 1559, *Zurich Letters*, I, 10.

23. Brian Cummings (ed.), *The Book of Common Prayer: The texts of 1549, 1559 and 1662* (Oxford, 2011),137. See also Eamon Duffy, *The Stripping of the Altars: Traditional Religion in England, 1400-1580* (New Haven, CT, and London, 1992), 567.

24. Stuart Clark, *Vanities of the Eye: Vision in early modern European culture* (Oxford, 2007).

25. Lucy Wooding, 'Reading the crucifixion in Tudor England', in Sabrina Corbellini, Margriet Hoogvliet and Bart Ramakers (eds), *Discovering the Riches of the Word: Religious reading in late medieval and early modern Europe* (Leiden, 2015), 294–97.

26. Patrick Collinson, 'The Elizabethan exclusion crisis and the Elizabethan polity', reprinted in Collinson, *This England*, 84. Collinson draws here on Gerald Bowler, '"An axe or an acte": The parliament of 1572 and resistance theory in early Elizabethan England', *Canadian Journal of History* 19 (1984), 349–59, who argues a more assertive case than Richard L. Greaves, 'Concepts of political obedience in late Tudor England: Conflicting perspectives', *JBS* 22 (1982), 23–34. See also Rosamund Oates, 'Puritans and the "monarchical republic"', *EHR* 127 (2012), 825.

27. Quentin Skinner, *The Foundations of Modern Political Thought*, vol. 2: *The Age of Reformation* (Cambridge, 1978), 221–22.

28. Alan P.F. Sell, 'Varieties of English separatist and dissenting writings', in Roger D. Sell and A.W. Johnson (eds), *Writing and Religion in England, 1558-1689: Studies in community-making and cultural memory* (Farnham, 2009), 25–46; Stephen Brachlow, *The Communion of Saints: Radical puritan and separatist ecclesiology, 1570-1625* (Oxford, 1988).

29. See Christopher Marsh, *The Family of Love in English Society, 1550-1630* (Cambridge, 1994); Christopher Carter, 'The Family of Love and its enemies', *SCJ* 37

(2006), 651–72; Douglas FitzHenry Jones, 'Mischievous information: Apostasy, rituals of telling, and the sixteenth-century Family of Love', *Church History* 87 (2018), 740–67; Joseph W. Martin, 'Elizabethan familists and English separatism', *JBS* 20 (1980), 53–73.

30. Douglas FitzHenry James, 'Debating the literal sense in England: The scripture-learned and the Family of Love', *SCJ* 45 (2014), 897–920.

31. Christopher Marsh, ' "Godlie matrons" and "loose-bodied dames": Heresy and gender in the Family of Love', in David Loewenstein and John Marshall (eds), *Heresy, Literature and Politics in Early Modern English Culture* (Cambridge, 2006), 59–81.

32. David Wootton, 'Deities, devils and dams: Elizabeth I, Dover harbour and the Family of Love', *Proceedings of the British Academy* 162 (2009), 45–67.

33. Alistair Hamilton, *The Family of Love* (Cambridge, 1981), 24–34.

34. Marsh, *The Family of Love*, 66–68.

35. *VAI*, III, 9, 25, 23.

36. John Jewel to Peter Martyr (undated), *Zurich Letters*, I, 23.

37. Marsh, *Popular Religion in Sixteenth-Century England*, 61.

38. ibid., 87.

39. Jonathan Willis, 'Protestant worship and the discourse of music in Reformation England', in Natalie Mears and Alec Ryrie (eds), *Worship and the Parish Church in Early Modern Britain* (Farnham, 2013), 131–50; Alec Ryrie, *Being Protestant in Reformation Britain* (Oxford, 2013), 356–57.

40. Arnold Pritchard, *Catholic Loyalism in Elizabethan England* (London, 1979).

41. Lucy Wooding, 'The Marian restoration and the mass', in D.M. Loades and Eamon Duffy (eds), *The Church of Mary Tudor* (Aldershot, 2006), 227–57.

42. Foxe, *A&M* (1570), 1992.

43. Peter Marshall and John Morgan, 'Clerical conformity and the Elizabethan settlement revisited', *HJ* 59 (2016), 1–22.

44. Duffy, *The Stripping of the Altars*, 572; Rosemary O'Day, 'Thomas Bentham: A case study in the problems of the early Elizabethan episcopate', *JEcclesH* 23 (1962), 137–59.

45. Angela Ranson, André Gazal and Sarah L. Bastow (eds), *Defending the Faith: John Jewel and the Elizabethan Church* (University Park, PA, 2018); Greg Peters, 'A "pretensed and counterfeit holiness" or sowers of "spiritual things"? John Jewel and Thomas Harding on monasticism, *Downside Review* 134 (2016), 11–24; John E. Booty, *John Jewel as Apologist of the Church of England* (London, 1963); Christian Coppens, *Reading in Exile: The libraries of John Ramridge (d.1568), Thomas Harding (c.1572) and Henry Joliffe (d.1573), Recusants in Louvain* (Cambridge, 1993).

46. On Welsh Catholics in exile, see J. Gwynfor Jones, *Early Modern Wales, c.1525–1640* (Basingstoke, 1994), 140–42; Lloyd Bowen, 'Information, language and political culture in early modern Wales', *P&P* 228 (2015), 151–52.

47. *VAI*, III, 333. See also Mark Rankin, 'Richard Topcliffe and the book culture of the Elizabethan Catholic underground', *RQ* 72 (2019), 492–536.

48. A.J. Loomie, 'Owen Lewis (1533–1594)', *ODNB*.

49. Susan Doran, *Monarchy and Matrimony: The courtships of Elizabeth I* (London, 1996), 91–92.

50. Sandeep Kaushik, 'Resistance, loyalty and recusant politics: Sir Thomas Tresham and the Elizabethan state', *Midland History* 21 (1996), 37–62.

51. Francis Young, 'Sir Thomas Tresham and the Christian cabala', *BCH* 35 (2020), 145–68.

52. Peter Marshall, 'Religious exiles and the Tudor State', *SCH* 43 (2007), 263–84, 268. On the less successful assimilation of the exiles in Paris, see Katy Gibbons, 'No home in exile? Elizabethan Catholics in Paris', *Reformation* 15 (2010), 115–31.

53. Liesbeth Corens, 'Saints beyond borders: Relics and the expatriate English Catholic community', in Jesse Spohnholz and Gary K. Waite (eds), *Exile and Religious Identity, 1500–1800* (London, 2014), 25–38; Katy Gibbons, ' "An unquiet estate abroad":

The religious exile of Catholic noble and gentlewomen under Elizabeth I', in Fiona Reid and Katherine Holden (eds), *Women on the Move: Refugees, migration and exile* (Newcastle, 2010), 43–58.

54. See Robert Persons, *A Brief Discours contayning certayne reasons why Catholiques refuse to goe to Church* (1580), STC 19394.

55. Liesbeth Corens, *Confessional Mobility and English Catholics in Counter-Reformation Europe* (Oxford, 2018).

56. Alexandra Walsham, 'Miracles and the Counter-Reformation mission to England', *HJ* 46 (2003), 779–815.

57. William Allen, *A briefe historie* (1582), STC 369.5, Sig. Dvii^v.

58. Thomas S. Freeman and Thomas F. Mayer (eds), *Martyrs and Martyrdom in England, c.1400–1700* (Woodbridge, 2007); Ceri Sullivan, '"Oppressed by the force of truth": Robert Persons edits John Foxe', in David Loades (ed.), *John Foxe: An historical perspective* (Aldershot, 1999), 154–66; Katy Gibbons, 'English Catholics and the continent', in Malcolm Smuts (ed.), *The Oxford Handbook of the Age of Shakespeare* (Oxford, 2016), 367–68; Dillon, *The Construction of Martyrdom*; Susannah Breitz Monta, *Martyrdom and Literature in Early Modern England* (Cambridge, 2005); Alison Shell, 'Martyrs and confessors in oral culture', in Alison Shell, *Oral Culture and Catholicism in Early Modern England* (Cambridge, 2007), 114–48; Thomas M. McCoog, 'Construing martyrdom in the English Catholic community, 1582–1602', in Ethan Shagan (ed.), *Catholics and the 'Protestant Nation': Religious Politics and Identity in Early Modern England* (Manchester, 2005).

59. Victor Houliston, Ginevra Crosignani and Thomas McCoog (eds), *The Correspondence and Unpublished Papers of Robert Persons, SJ,* vol. 1: *1574–1588* (Toronto, 2018), 246–47. See also Gregory, *Salvation at Stake,* 283.

60. Anne Dillon, 'Praying by number: The Confraternity of the Rosary and the English Catholic community, c.1580–1700', *History* 88 (2003), 451–71; Lisa McClain, *Lest We Be Damned: Practical innovation and lived experience among Catholics in Protestant England, 1559–1642* (New York, 2003); Alexandra Walsham, '"Domme preachers"? Post-Reformation English Catholicism and the culture of print', *P&P* 168 (2000), 72–123; Emilie Murphy, 'Music and Catholic culture in Post-Reformation Lancashire: Piety, protest and conversion', *BCH* 32 (2015), 492–525; James Kelly and Susan Royal (eds), *Early Modern English Catholicism: Identity, memory and Counter-Reformation, c.1570–1800* (Leiden and Boston, MA, 2016).

61. Francis Edwards, *Robert Persons: The biography of an Elizabethan Jesuit, 1546–1610* (St Louis, MO, 1995); J.H. Pollen (ed.), 'The memoirs of Father Robert Persons', in *Miscellanea II*, CRS 2 (1906), 12–218; J.H. Pollen (ed.), 'The memoirs of Father Persons', in *Miscellanea IV*, CRS 4 (1907), 1–161; Thomas McCoog, *The Society of Jesus in Ireland, Scotland and England, 1541–1588: 'Our way of proceeding?'* (Leiden, 1996).

62. Mitchell Leimon and Geoffrey Parker, 'Treason and plot in Elizabethan diplomacy: The "Fame of Edward Stafford" reconsidered', *EHR* 111 (1996), 1134–58.

63. M.J.M. Innes, 'Robert Persons, popular sovereignty, and the late Elizabethan succession debate', *HJ* 62 (2019), 57–76.

64. Jones, *Early Modern Wales,* 163, 166–69; Bowen, 'Information, language and political culture in early modern Wales', 150–52.

65. Peter Marshall and Geoffrey Scott (eds), *Catholic Gentry in English Society: The Throckmortons of Coughton from Reformation to emancipation* (Farnham, 2009), 5–6. See also Leland Carlson, *Martin Marprelate, Gentleman: Master Job Throckmorton laid open in his colors* (San Marino, CA, 1981); for a different interpretation see Patrick Collinson, 'Job Throckmorton', *ODNB*.

66. Keith Wrightson, 'The politics of the parish in early modern England', in Paul Griffiths, Adam Fox and Steve Hindle (eds), *The Experience of Authority in Early Modern England* (Basingstoke, 1996), 18–22; Ian Archer, *The Pursuit of Stability: Social relations in Elizabethan London* (Cambridge, 1991), 74–92; Susan Brigden, 'Religion and social obligation in early sixteenth-century London', *P&P* 103 (1984), 67–69.

67. *Certayne sermons, or homelies* (1547), STC 13640, Sig. K2j^r; Edmund Bonner, *Homilies* (1555), *STC* 3285.8, fo. 22^r. See also Lucy Wooding, 'Charity, community and Reformation propaganda', *Reformation* 11 (2006), 131–69, quotations at 131–32.

68. John Bossy, *Peace in the Post-Reformation* (Cambridge, 1998), 73–100.

69. Quoted in Archer, *Pursuit of Stability*, 84.

70. John Mirk, *Festial* (1508), *STC* 17971, fo. xiii^v.

71. Alexandra Walsham, 'Inventing the Lollard past: The afterlife of a medieval sermon in early modern England', *JEcclesH* 58 (2007), 628–55.

72. Cummings, *The Book of Common Prayer*, 133; Alexandra Walsham, 'Supping with Satan's disciples: Spiritual and secular sociability in Post-Reformation England', in Nadine Lewycky and Adam Morton (eds), *Getting Along?: Religious identities and confessional relations in early modern England: Essays in honour of Professor W.J. Sheils* (Farnham, 2012), 36.

73. Edmund Coote, *The English schoole-master* (1630), *STC* 5714, 38.

74. Marsh, *Popular Religion in Sixteenth-Century England*, 25-6.

75. Susan Brigden, *London and the Reformation* (Oxford, 1989), 28.

76. Cummings, *The Book of Common Prayer*, 19.

77. *A famous speech of King Henry the eighth, made in the Parliament House* (London, 1642), Sig. A3^v.

78. *Injunctions* (1547), *STC* 10093.7, Sig. Cij^r; Thomas Cranmer, *A Defence of the True and Catholike doctrine of the sacrament* (1550), *STC* 6002, Sig. C3^{r-v}.

79. John Churchson, *A brefe treatyse* (1556), *STC* 5219, Sig. Bi^r; Edmund Bonner, *A profitable and necessarye doctrine* (1555), *STC* 3285.5, fo. 74^r.

80. Latimer, *Sermons*, I, 421.

81. John Bullingham, 'Epistle Dedicatorie', in his translation of John Venaeus, *A notable Oration* (1555), *STC* 24633.5, Sig. Aiii^r.

82. Watson, *Holsome and Catholyke doctryne*, fo. 132^r.

83. George Gifford, *A briefe discourse of certaine points . . . which may bee termed the countrie divinitie, with a manifest confutation of the same*; hereafter, *Countrie Divinitie* (London, 1582), *STC* 11846. See also Dewey D. Wallace, 'George Gifford, puritan propaganda and popular religion in Elizabethan England', *SCJ* 9 (1978), 27–50; Scott McGinnis, *George Gifford and the Reformation of the Common Sort: Puritan priorities in Elizabethan religious life* (Kirksville, MO, 2004).

84. Gifford, *Countrie Divinitie*, fo. 2^r.

85. ibid., fo. 65^v.

86. Marsh, *Popular Religion in Sixteenth-Century England*, 5; Latimer, *Sermons*, I, 201.

87. John Craig, 'Sermon reception', in Hugh Adlington, Peter McCullough and Emma Rhatigan (eds), *The Oxford Handbook of the Early Modern Sermon* (Oxford, 2011), 187.

88. Ian Green, 'Preaching in the parishes', in Adlington, McCullough and Rhatigan (eds), *The Oxford Handbook of the Early Modern Sermon*, 138.

89. ibid., 143; Rosamund Oates, *Moderate Radical: Tobie Matthew and the English Reformation* (Oxford, 2018); William J. Sheils, 'An archbishop in the pulpit: Tobie Matthew's preaching diary, 1606–1622', *SCH* 12 (1999), 381–405.

90. Ian Green, 'Teaching the Reformation: The clergy as preachers, catechists, authors and teachers', in Scott Dixon and Luise Schorn-Schütte (eds), *The Protestant Clergy of Early Modern Europe* (Basingstoke, 2003), 160.

91. Quoted in Marsh, *Popular Religion in Sixteenth-Century England*, 52.

92. Gifford, *Countrie Divinitie*, fo. 26^r.

93. Ryrie, *Being Protestant in Reformation Britain*, 354, 351.

94. Arnold Hunt, *The Art of Hearing: English preachers and their audiences, 1590–1640* (Cambridge, 2010), 68–69.

95. ibid., 229–34.

96. McGinnis, *George Gifford and the Reformation of the Common Sort*, 5–7.

97. Bernard Gilpin, *A godly sermon preached in the court at Greenwich* (1581), STC 11897, 33.

98. ibid., 40.

99. *Certayne sermons, or homelies* (1547), Sig. Aii^r, Lii^r–Liii^r.

100. Martin Ingram, 'The reform of popular culture? Sex and marriage in early modern England', in Barry Reay (ed.), *Popular Culture in Seventeenth Century England* (London, 1988), 129–65; Martin Ingram, 'Reformation of manners in early modern England', in Griffiths, Fox and Hindle (eds), *The Experience of Authority*, 47–88; Margaret Spufford, 'Puritanism and social control?', in Anthony Fletcher and John Stevenson (eds), *Order and Disorder in Early Modern England* (Cambridge, 1985), 41–57; Ronald Hutton, *The Rise and Fall of Merry England: The ritual year 1400–1700* (Oxford, 1996).

101. Alan Macfarlane, 'Illegitimacy and illegitimates in English history', in Peter Laslett, Karla Oosterveen and Richard M. Smith (eds), *Bastardy and its Comparative History: Studies in the history of illegitimacy and marital nonconformism in Britain, France, Germany, Sweden, North America, Jamaica and Japan* (Cambridge, MA, 1980), 75; Martin Ingram, 'Reformation of manners', 66.

102. Alec Ryrie, 'Counting sheep, counting shepherds: The problem of allegiance in the English Reformation', in Peter Marshall and Alec Ryrie (eds), *The Beginnings of English Protestantism* (Cambridge, 2002), 84–110.

103. Marsh, *Popular Religion in Sixteenth-Century England*, 4–5.

104. Christopher Marsh, '"At it ding dong": Recreation and religion in the English belfry, 1580–1640', in Mears and Ryrie (eds), *Worship and the Parish Church*, 157.

105. A.G. Dickens and D. Carr (eds), *The Reformation in England to the Accession of Elizabeth I* (London, 1967), 15.

106. Eamon Duffy, *The Voices of Morebath: Reformation and rebellion in an English village* (New Haven, CT, and London, 2001), 91–96.

107. David Marcombe, 'Bernard Gilpin: Anatomy of an Elizabethan legend', *Northern History* 16 (1980), 20–39.

108. Green, 'Preaching in the parishes', 145–46.

109. Robert Whiting, *The Reformation of the English Parish Church* (Cambridge, 2010),

110. Barrett L. Beer, 'John Stow and the English Reformation, 1547–1559', *SCJ* 16 (1985), 260–61, 263–64, 266, 271.

111. Tara Hamling, 'Old Robert's girdle: Visual and material props for Protestant piety in Post-Reformation England', in Jessica Martin and Alec Ryrie (eds), *Private and Domestic Devotion in Early Modern Britain* (Farnham, 2012), 135–63.

112. Tara Hamling, *Decorating the Godly Household: Religious art in post-Reformation Britain* (New Haven, CT, and London, 2010), 212–16.

113. Jonathan Willis, *The Reformation of the Decalogue: Religious identity and the Ten Commandments in England, c.1485–1625* (Cambridge, 2017), 297–331.

114. *VAI*, III, 255.

115. ibid., 256–67.

116. Peter Marshall, *Beliefs and the Dead in Reformation England* (Oxford, 2002), 150–51.

117. Lucy Wooding, 'Remembrance in the eucharist', in Andrew Gordon and Thomas Rist (eds), *The Arts of Remembrance in Early Modern England: Memorial cultures of the Post-Reformation* (Farnham, 2013), 25–28.

118. Marshall, *Beliefs and the Dead*, 182–83; Whiting, *The Reformation of the English Parish Church*, 221–22.

119. John Craig, 'Bodies at prayer in early modern England', in Mears and Ryrie (eds), *Worship and the Parish Church*, 173.

120. Marsh, '"At it ding dong"', 153, 165.

121. Malcolm Gaskill, 'Little commonwealths II', in Keith Wrightson (ed.), *A Social History of England, 1500–1750* (Cambridge, 2017), 95.

122. Charlotte-Rose Millar, *Witchcraft, the Devil and Emotions in Early Modern England* (London, 2017); Darren Oldridge, *The Devil in Tudor and Stuart England* (Stroud, 2010); Nathan Johnstone, *The Devil and Demonism in Early Modern England* (Cambridge, 2006).

123. For an introduction to this subject, see Keith Thomas, *Religion and the Decline of Magic: Studies in popular beliefs in sixteenth- and seventeenth-century England* (London and New York, 1971); Alan Macfarlane, *Witchcraft in Tudor and Stuart England: A regional and comparative study* (London, 1970); James Sharpe, *Instruments of Darkness: Witchcraft in England, 1550–1750* (London, 1997); Malcolm Gaskill, *Crime and Mentalities in Early Modern England* (Cambridge, 2000), 33–79; Malcolm Gaskill, 'Witchcraft trials in England', in Brian P. Levack (ed.), *The Oxford Handbook of Witchcraft in Early Modern Europe and Colonial America* (Oxford, 2013), 283–99.

124. Clive Holmes, 'Popular culture? Witches, magistrates and divines in early modern England', in Steven L. Kaplan (ed.), *Understanding Popular Culture: Europe from the middle ages to the nineteenth century* (Berlin, 1984), 85–111.

125. Annabel Gregory, 'Witchcraft, politics and "good neighbourhood" in early seventeenth-century Rye', *P&P* 133 (1991), 31–66; Peter Elmer, 'Towards a politics of witchcraft in early modern England', in Stuart Clark (ed.), *Languages of Witchcraft: Narrative, ideology and meaning in early modern culture* (Basingstoke, 2001), 101–18.

126. Stuart Clark, 'Protestant demonology: Sin, superstition and society (c.1520–c.1640)', in Bengt Ankarloo and Gustav Henningsen (eds), *Early Modern European Witchcraft: Centres and peripheries* (Oxford, 1990), 45–81; Holmes, 'Popular culture?', 85–111.

127. Clive Holmes, 'Women: Witnesses and witches', *P&P* 140 (1993), 45–78; Jennifer Kermode and Garthine Walker (eds), *Women, Crime and the Courts in Early Modern England* (London, 1994); Alison Rowlands, 'Witchcraft and gender in early modern Europe', in Levack (ed.), *The Oxford Handbook of Witchcraft*, 449–67; Susan Amussen, 'The gendering of popular culture in early modern England', in Tim Harris (ed.), *Popular Culture in England c.1500–1850* (London, 1995).

128. Sharpe, *Instruments of Darkness*, 105–27. See also Gregory Durston, *Witchcraft and Witch Trials: A history of English witchcraft and its legal perspectives, 1542 to 1736* (Chichester, 2000); James Sharpe, 'Women, witchcraft and the legal process', in Kermode and Walker (eds), *Women, Crime and the Courts*, 106–24.

129. Marion Gibson, *Reading Witchcraft: Stories of early English witches* (London, 1999); Tessa Watt, *Cheap Print and Popular Piety, 1550–1640* (Cambridge, 1991); Peter Lake and Michael Questier, *The Antichrist's Lewd Hat: Protestants, papists and players in Post-Reformation England* (New Haven, CT, and London, 2002); Sandra Clarke, *The Elizabethan Pamphleteers: Popular moralistic pamphlets 1580–1640* (London, 1983).

130. Stuart Clark, *Thinking with Demons: The idea of witchcraft in early modern Europe* (Oxford, 1997).

131. See Jonathan Barry, 'Introduction: Keith Thomas and the problem of witchcraft', in Jonathan Barry, Marianne Hester and Gareth Roberts (eds), *Witchcraft in Early Modern Europe: Studies in culture and belief* (Cambridge, 1996), 1–45; Gaskill, 'Witchcraft trials in England', 283–89. See also Keith Thomas, 'The relevance of social anthropology to the historical study of English witchcraft', in Mary Douglas (ed.), *Witchcraft Confessions and Accusations* (London, 1970), 47–81; William Monter, 'Re-contextualizing British witchcraft', *Journal of Interdisciplinary History* 35 (2004), 105–11; Malcolm Gaskill, 'Witchcraft and evidence in early modern England', *P&P* 198 (2008), 33–70.

132. Quoted in Andy Wood, *Faith, Hope and Charity: English neighbourhoods, 1500–1640* (Cambridge, 2020), 188–89.

133. James Hitchcock, 'George Gifford and puritan witch beliefs', *Archiv für Reformationsgeschichte* 58 (1967), 90–99; Alan Macfarlane, 'A Tudor anthropologist: George Gifford's *Discourse* and *Dialogue*', in Sydney Anglo (ed.), *The Damned Art: Essays in the literature of witchcraft* (London, 1977), 140–55; Scott McGinnis,

'"Subtiltie" exposed: Pastoral perspectives on witch belief in the thought of George Gifford', *SCJ* 33 (2002), 665–86.

134. George Gifford, *A dialogue concerning witches and witchcraft* (1593), STC 11850, dedication.

135. Hen. VIII, c. 8; see C. L'Estrange Ewen, *Witch Hunting and Witch Trials: The indictments for witchcraft from the records of 1373 assizes held for the home circuit AD 1559–1736* (London, 1929), 13–15.

136. Sharpe, *Instruments of Darkness*, 29–30.

137. ibid., 89–90; Norman Jones, 'Defining superstitions: Treasonous Catholics and the Act against Witchcraft of 1563', in Charles Carlton, Robert Woods, Mary Robertson and Joseph Block (eds), *State, Sovereigns and Society in Early Modern England* (Stroud, 1998), 187–203.

138. Eliz., c.16; in Ewen, *Witch Hunting and Witch Trials*, 15–18.

139. *A Rehearsall both straung and true* (1579), STC 23267, Sig. Aii^r.

140. On familiars, see Sharpe, *Instruments of Darkness*, 70–79; Alexandra Walsham, *Providence in Early Modern England* (Oxford, 1999), 190; Holmes, 'Popular culture?', 85–111; Greg Warburton, 'Gender, supernatural power, agency and the metamorphoses of the familiar in early modern pamphlet accounts of English witchcraft', *Parergon* 20 (2003), 95–118.

141. *A Rehearsall both straung and true*, Sig. Aii^v.

142. Glyn Parry, 'John Dee, alchemy and authority in Elizabethan England', in Marcus K. Harmes and Victoria Bladen (eds), *Supernatural and Secular Power in Early Modern England* (Farnham, 2015), 17–40; Stephen Clucas, 'Dreams, prophecies and politics: John Dee and the Elizabethan court, 1575–85', in Susan J. Wiseman, Katharine Hodgkin and Michelle O'Callaghan (eds), *Reading the Early Modern Dream: The terrors of the night* (London, 2007), 67–80; Frances Yates, 'Renaissance philosophers in Elizabethan England: John Dee and Giordano Bruno', in Hugh Lloyd-Jones, Valerie Pearl and Blair Worden (eds), *History and Imagination: Essays in honour of H.R. Trevor-Roper* (London, 1981), 104–14.

143. See Thomas, *Religion and the Decline of Magic*, chapter 8.

144. Gifford, *A dialogue concerning witches and witchcraft*, Sig. D4$^{r–v}$. See also Sharpe, *Instruments of Darkness*, 66.

145. Malcolm Gaskill, 'Witchcraft and power in early modern England: The case of Margaret Moore', in Kermode and Walker (eds), *Women, Crime and the Courts*, 125–45; reprinted in Brian P. Levack (ed.), *New Perspectives on Witchcraft, Magic and Demonology*, vol. 3: *Witchcraft in the British Isles and New England* (New York, 2001), 301–22.

146. Sally Parkin, 'Witchcraft, women's honour and customary law in early modern Wales', *Social History* 31 (2006), 301–02

147. ibid., 311, 316.

148. W.W., *A true and iust recorde* (1592), STC 24922, Sig. A3$^{r–v}$.

149. David Wootton, 'Reginald Scot', *ODNB*.

150. Brinsley Nicholson (ed.), *The Discoverie of Witchcraft by Reginald Scot, Esquire* (1886); see the dedication to Prince Leopold.

151. Reginald Scot, *Discoverie of witchcraft* (1584), STC 21864, Sig. Aiij^r.

152. ibid., Sig. Aiiij^r.

153. Philip Almond, *England's First Demonologist: Reginald Scot and 'The Discoverie of Witchcraft'* (London, 2011), 4.

154. ibid., 9.

155. Scot, *Discoverie of witchcraft*, Sig. Aij^v.

156. ibid., Sig. Aij^r.

157. ibid., Sig. Aij^v.

158. John Jewel, *The Works of John Jewel, bishop of Salisbury*, ed. J. Ayre, 4 vols (Cambridge, 1845-50), IV, 1167.

159. See Clark, *Thinking with Demons*, chapter 3.

160. Jewel, *Works*, IV, 1168.

161. On Stapleton, see M.R. O'Connell, *Thomas Stapleton and the Counter-Reformation* (New Haven, CT, and London, 1964).

162. Stanislaus Hosius, *Of the Expresse Worde of God*, trans. Thomas Stapleton (Louvain, 1567), *STC* 13889, fo. 9ᵛ.

163. Roger Lovatt, 'The "Imitation of Christ" in late medieval England', *TRHS* fifth series, 18 (1968), 97–121; J. Sears McGee, 'Conversion and the Imitation of Christ in Anglican and Puritan writing', *JBS* 15 (1976), 21–39; David Crane, 'English translations of the *Imitatio Christi* in the sixteenth and seventeenth centuries', *RH* 13 (1975), 79–100; Maximilian von Habsburg, *Catholic and Protestant Translations of the* Imitatio Christi, *1425–1650: From late medieval classic to early modern bestseller* (Farnham, 2012).

164. Brad Gregory, 'The "True and Zealouse Service of God": Robert Parsons, Edmund Bunny, and *The First Booke of the christian Exercise*', *JEcclesH* 45 (1994), 267. See also Ronald Corthell, 'Politics and devotion: The case of Robert Persons vs. Edmund Bunny, author of *A Book of Christian Exercise*', *Journal of Jesuit Studies* 1 (2014), 558–71; Victor Houliston, 'Why Robert Persons would not be pacified: Edmund Bunny's theft of *The Book of Resolution*', in Thomas McCoog (ed.), *The Reckoned Expense: Edmund Campion and the early English Jesuits: Essays in celebration of the first centenary of Campion Hall, 1896–1996* (Woodbridge, 1996), 159–77.

165. Walsham, '"Domme preachers?"', 120–23.

166. *Of the imitation of Christ three, both for wisedome and godlines, most excellent bookes* (London, 1592), *STC* 23979, Sig. B1ʳ.

167. Debora Shuger, 'Protesting Catholic Puritan in Elizabeth England', *JBS* 48 (2009), 600–01, 605.

168. ibid., 618; Patrick Collinson, *Godly People: Essays on English Protestantism and Puritanism* (London, 1983), 147; Pauline Croft, 'The new English Church in one family: William, Mildred and Robert Cecil', in Stephen Platten (ed.), *Anglicanism and the Western Christian Tradition: Continuity, change and the search for communion* (Norwich, 2003), 74–78.

169. Leif Dixon, *Practical Predestinarians in England, c.1590–1640* (Farnham, 2014).

170. Ryrie, *Being Protestant in Reformation Britain*, 27–32, 38–41.

171. Stapleton, preface to the translation of Hosius, *Of the Expresse Worde of God*, Sig. *4ʳ⁻ᵛ.

172. Thomas Harding, *An Answere to Maister Iuelles chalenge* (1564), *STC* 12758, 161.

173. William Lawson, *A New Orchard and Garden* (1618), *STC* 15329, 1.

14 The Drama of Life and the Politics of Performance

1. Edward Muir, *Ritual in Early Modern Europe* (second edition, Cambridge, 2005), 252–87.

2. James Sharpe, *Crime in Early Modern England 1550–1750* (London, 1984), 23; Cynthia Herrup, *The Common Peace: Participation and the criminal law in seventeenth-century England* (Cambridge, 1987), 194.

3. Andy Wood, *Riot, Rebellion and Popular Politics in Early Modern England* (Basingstoke, 2002), 119.

4. Paul Slack, 'The response to plague in early modern England: Public policies and their consequences', in John Walter and Roger Schofield (eds), *Famine, Disease and the Social Order in Early Modern Society* (Cambridge, 1991), 169.

5. Martin Ingram, 'Ridings, rough music and the "reform of popular culture" in early modern England', *P&P* 105 (1984), 81–90.

6. Martin Ingram, *Carnal Knowledge: Regulating sex in England, 1470–1600* (Cambridge, 2017), 296–97.

7. Thomas Betteridge and Greg Walker, 'Introduction', in Thomas Betteridge and Greg Walker (eds), *The Oxford Handbook of Tudor Drama* (Oxford, 2012), 4–8, 11.

8. William Ingram, *The Business of Playing: The beginnings of the adult professional theater in Elizabethan England* (Ithaca, NY, 1992).

9. Michael Walzer, 'On the role of symbolism in political thought', *Political Science Quarterly* 82 (1987), 194–95.

10. For the conception of the 'theatre state', see Clifford Geertz, *Negara: The theatre state in nineteenth-century Bali* (Princeton, NJ, 1980), also Clifford Geertz, 'Centers, kings and charisma: Reflections on the symbolics of power', in Joseph Ben-David and Terry Nicholas Clark (eds), *Culture and Its Creators: Essays in Honor of Edward Shils* (Chicago, IL, 1977), and Clifford Geertz, 'Politics past, politics present', in Clifford Geertz, *The Interpretation of Cultures: Selected essays* (second edition, New York, 2000), 327–41.

11. Stephen Orgel, *Spectacular Performances: Essays on theatre, imagery, books and selves in early modern England* (Manchester, 2011), 7–35.

12. *Elizabeth I: Collected Works*, 189.

13. David Bevington, *Tudor Drama and Politics* (Cambridge, MA, 1968), 6; see also John C. Meagher, 'The first progress of Henry VII', *Renaissance Drama* 1 (1968), 45–73.

14. Susan Brigden, *Thomas Wyatt: The Heart's Forest* (London, 2012), 471, 488.

15. Henry Howard, earl of Surrey, *Poems*, ed. Emrys Jones (Oxford, 1964), 31, ll. 10–11.

16. Steve Hindle, *The State and Social Change in Early Modern England, 1550–1640* (Basingstoke, 2000), 116–17.

17. John Northbrooke, *The poore mans Garden* (1582), *STC* 18667, Sig. ¶3ʳ.

18. *A Mirror for Magistrates* (1559), *STC* 1247, Sig. Ciiiᵛ.

19. William Shakespeare, *Hamlet*, Act II, Scene 2, ll. 584–88.

20. George Cavendish, 'Life and death of Cardinal Wolsey', in Richard Sylvester and Davis P. Harding (eds), *Two Early Tudor Lives* (New Haven, CT, and London, 1962), 18, 17.

21. C.S.L. Davies, 'Popular religion and the Pilgrimage of Grace', in Anthony Fletcher and John Stevenson (eds), *Order and Disorder in Early Modern England* (Cambridge, 1985), 75, 77–78.

22. Roger Manning described early modern popular uprisings as 'primitive': see his *Village Revolts: Social protest and popular disturbances in England, 1509–1640* (Oxford, 1988), 1–6. For an alternative view, see Wood, *Riot, Rebellion and Popular Politics*.

23. Keith Wrightson, 'The politics of the parish in early modern England', in Paul Griffiths, Adam Fox and Steve Hindle (eds), Paul Griffiths, Adam Fox and Steve Hindle (eds), *The Experience of Authority in Early Modern England* (Basingstoke, 1996), 10–46.

24. Peter Marshall, *Heretics and Believers: A history of the English Reformation* (New Haven, CT, and London, 2017), 13, 445.

25. John Walter, 'Authority and protest', in Keith Wrightson (ed.), *A Social History of England, 1500–1750* (Cambridge, 2017), 230.

26. William Shakespeare, *Richard III*, Act III, Scene 5, l. 5.

27. Sydney Anglo, *Spectacle, Pageantry and Early Tudor Policy* (Oxford, 1969); Thomas Betteridge and Suzannah Lipscomb (eds), *Henry VIII and the Court: Art, politics and performance* (Farnham, 2013); Kevin Sharpe, *Selling the Tudor Monarchy: Authority and image in sixteenth-century England* (New Haven, CT, 2009); John N. King, *Tudor Royal Iconography: Literature and art in an age of religious crisis* (Princeton, NJ, 1989).

28. Roy Strong, *Art and Power: Renaissance festivals 1450–1650* (Woodbridge, 1984); see the more sceptical view put forward by Sydney Anglo, *Images of Tudor Kingship* (London, 1992), 130.

29. Hall, *Chronicle*, 506.

30. Malcolm Smuts, 'Public ceremony and royal charisma', in A.L. Bier, David Cannadine and James M. Rosenheim (eds), *The First Modern Society: Essays in English history in honour of Lawrence Stone* (Cambridge, 1989), 73.

31. Marc Bloch, *The Royal Touch: Sacred monarchy and scrofula in England and France*, trans. J.E. Anderson (London, 1973); David J. Sturdy, 'The royal touch in

England', in Heinz Duchhardt, Richard A. Jackson and Sturdy (eds), *European Monarchy: Its evolution and practice from Roman antiquity to modern times* (Stuttgart, 1992), 171–84.

32. Alice Hunt, *The Drama of Coronation: Medieval ceremony in early modern England* (Cambridge, 2008), 33, 38

33. Jennifer Loach, 'The function of ceremonial in the reign of Henry VIII', *P&P* 142 (1994), 46–47.

34. For an account of both the fundamental continuities and the nuanced changes and adaptations to the rite and its significance, see Hunt, *The Drama of Coronation*, 5–6, 173–77.

35. ibid., 6.

36. Richard Mulcaster, *The Passage of our most drad Soveraigne Lady Quene Elyzabeth* (1559), *STC* 7590, Sig. Aii^v.

37. ibid., Sig. Aii^r; Biiii^v.

38. David Trim, 'War, soldiers and high politics under Elizabeth I', in Malcolm Smuts (ed.), *The Oxford Handbook of the Age of Shakespeare* (Oxford, 2016), 82–102.

39. Janette Dillon, *Performance and Spectacle in Hall's Chronicle* (London, 2002), 45–47.

40. Hall, *Chronicle*, 830.

41. Susan Frye, 'The myth of Elizabeth at Tilbury', *SCJ* 23 (1992), 95–114.

42. David J.B. Trim, '"Knights of Christ"? Chivalric culture in England c.1400–c.1550', in D.J.B. Trim and Peter J. Balderstone (eds), *Cross, Crown and Community: Religion, government and culture in early modern England 1400–1800* (Bern, 2004), 86; see also Steven Gunn, 'Henry VIII's foreign policy and the Tudor cult of chivalry', in Charles Giry-Deloison (ed.), *Francois 1er et Henri VIII: deux princes de la renaissance* (Lille, 1996), 25–35.

43. John Edwards, *Mary I: England's Catholic queen* (New Haven, CT, and London, 2011), 84.

44. Frances Yates, *Astraea: The imperial theme in the sixteenth century* (London, 1975), 88–111.

45. Greg Walker, *Plays of Persuasion: Drama and politics in the age of Henry VIII* (Cambridge, 1991), 18.

46. Penry Williams, *The Tudor Regime* (Oxford, 1979), 365.

47. Paul Griffiths, 'Secrecy and authority in late sixteenth- and seventeenth-century London', *HJ* 40 (1997), 940.

48. Michael J. Braddick, 'Administrative performance: The representation of political authority in early modern England', in Michael J. Braddick and John Walter (eds), *Negotiating Power in Early Modern Society: Order, hierarchy and subordination in Britain and Ireland* (Cambridge, 2001), 171; Anthony Fletcher, 'Honour, reputation and local office-holding in Elizabethan and Stuart England', in Fletcher and Stevenson (eds), *Order and Disorder in Early Modern England*, 92.

49. Malcolm Gaskill, 'Little commonwealths II: Communities', in Wrightson (ed.), *A Social History of England*, 89.

50. Andy Wood, *Faith, Hope and Charity: English neighbourhoods, 1500–1640* (Cambridge, 2020), 88–89.

51. Griffiths, 'Secrecy and authority', 927.

52. Quoted in Laura Gowing, 'Gender and the language of insult in early modern London', *HWJ* 35 (1993), 1.

53. Steve Hindle, 'Exhortation and entitlement: Negotiating inequality in English rural communities, 1550–1650', in Braddick and Walter (eds), *Negotiating Power in Early Modern Society*, 116.

54. E.P. Thompson, 'The moral economy of the English crowd in the eighteenth century', *P&P* 50 (1971), 76–78.

55. ibid.; E.P. Thompson, *Customs in Common* (London, 1991), 305–36; Ralph Houlbrooke, 'Women's social life and common action in England from the fifteenth

century to the eve of the civil war', *Continuity and Change* 1 (1986), 171–89; Sara Mendelson and Patricia Crawford, *Women in Early Modern England, 1550–1720* (Oxford, 1998), chapter 7.

56. Martin Ingram, *Church Courts, Sex and Marriage in England, 1570–1640* (Cambridge, 1987), chapter 10; James Sharpe, 'Defamation and sexual slander in early modern England: The church courts at York', *Borthwick Papers* 58 (York, 1980).

57. Gowing, 'Gender and the language of insult', 3–4.

58. Walter, 'Authority and protest', 230-1; John Walter, 'Faces in the crowd: Gender and age in the early modern English crowd', in Helen Berry and Elizabeth Foyster (eds), *The Family in Early Modern England* (Cambridge, 2007), 99, 111–13.

59. Walter, 'Authority and protest', 231.

60. Glenn Richardson, *The Field of Cloth of Gold* (New Haven, CT, and London, 2013).

61. Maria Hayward, 'Fashion, finance, foreign politics and the wardrobe of Henry VIII', in Catherine Richardson (ed.), *Clothing Culture, 1350–1650* (Aldershot, 2004), 166.

62. Steven Gunn, *Charles Brandon* (second edition, Stroud, 2016), 22–23.

63. Maria Hayward, *Dress at the Court of King Henry VIII* (Leeds, 2007), 10.

64. Quoted in Smuts, 'Public ceremony and royal charisma', 71.

65. Ann Rosalind Jones and Peter Stallybrass, *Renaissance Clothing and the Materials of Memory* (Cambridge, 2000), 2–6; Susan Vincent, *Dressing the Elite: Clothes in early modern England* (Oxford, 2003).

66. Quoted in Braddick and Walter (eds), *Negotiating Power in Early Modern Society*, 12.

67. Sarah Johanesen, 'That *silken Priest*: Catholic disguise and anti-popery on the English mission (1569–1640)', *HR* 93 (2020), 38–43, quotation at 42.

68. *TRP*, II, 190.

69. Joanna Crawford, 'Clothing distributions and social relations, c.1350–1500', in Richardson (ed.), *Clothing Culture*, 156–57.

70. Ulinka Rublack, *Dressing Up: Cultural identity in renaissance Europe* (Oxford, 2010).

71. David Cressy, 'Gender trouble and cross-dressing in early modern England', *JBS* 35 (1996), 438–65; R. Valerie Lucas, '*Hic Mulier*: The female transvestite in early modern England', *Renaissance and Reformation* 12 (1988), 65–84.

72. Quoted in Lucas, '*Hic Mulier*', 69.

73. Christina Bosco Langert, 'Hedgerows and petticoats: Sartorial subversion and anti-enclosure protest in seventeenth-century England', *Early Theatre* 12 (2009), 119–25.

74. Eamon Duffy, *Fires of Faith: Catholic England under Mary Tudor* (New Haven, CT, 2009), 123.

75. Smuts, 'Public ceremony and royal charisma', 73.

76. Mulcaster, *The Passage of our most drad Soveraigne Lady Quene Elyzabeth* (1559), Sig. Aii'.

77. Mervyn James, 'English politics and the concept of honour, 1485–1642', *P&P* Supplement 3 (1978), 44.

78. See Douglas Hay, Peter Linebaugh, John G. Rule, E.P. Thompson and Cal Winslow, *Albion's Fatal Tree: Crime and society in eighteenth-century England* (New York, 1975); see also Walter, 'Authority and protest', 224.

79. James Sharpe, '"Last dying speeches": Religion, ideology and public execution in seventeenth-century England', *P&P* 107 (1985), 157–59, 165; James, 'English politics and the concept of honour', 5.

80. William Harrison, *The Description of England*, ed. G. Edelen (Washington, DC, and London, 1994), 187.

81. Malcolm Gaskill, *Crime and Mentalities in Early Modern England* (Cambridge, 2000), 40.

82. Lacey B. Smith, 'English treason trials and confessions in the sixteenth century', *Journal of the History of Ideas* 25 (1954), 471–98.

83. ibid., 472.
84. ibid., 474.
85. Eric Ives, *The Life and Death of Anne Boleyn* (Oxford, 2004), 343.
86. Smith, 'English treason trials', 477.
87. For the debate on this, see Ives, *The Life and Death of Anne Boleyn*; also see George Bernard, *Anne Boleyn: Fatal attractions* (New Haven, CT, 2011), 161–82.
88. Ives, *The Life and Death of Anne Boleyn*, 343.
89. Hindle, *State and Social Change*, 123–24.
90. *The Yale Edition of the Complete Works of St Thomas More*, vol. 12: *A Dialogue of Comfort against Tribulation* (New Haven, CT, and London, 1976), 137.
91. Smith, 'English treason trials', 485.
92. Sharpe, 'Last dying speeches', 157.
93. ibid.
94. Alexandra Gajda, *The Earl of Essex and Late Elizabethan Political Culture* (Oxford, 2012), 45–46; Fritz Levy, 'The theatre and the court in the 1590s', in John Guy (ed.), *The Reign of Elizabeth I: Court and culture in the last decade* (Cambridge, 1995), 287–95.
95. Hindle, *The State and Social Change*, 119.
96. Gaskill, *Crime and Mentalities*, 205–06.
97. Machyn's *Diary*, 36. See also Ian Mortimer, 'Tudor chronicler or sixteenth-century diarist? Henry Machyn and the nature of his manuscript', *SCJ* 33 (2002), 983–1001.
98. Hall, *Chronicle*, 590.
99. Maria Hayward, ' "We should dress us fairly for our end": The significance of the clothing worn at elite executions in England in the sixteenth century', *History* 101 (2016), 223.
100. C. L'Estrange Ewen, *Witch Hunting and Witch Trials: The indictments for witchcraft from the records of 1373 assizes held for the home circuit AD 1559–1736* (London, 1929), 16–17.
101. Fletcher, 'Honour, reputation and local office-holding', 101.
102. Foxe, quoted in Duffy, *Fires of Faith*, 110.
103. Christopher Brooks, *Law, Politics and Society in Early Modern England* (Cambridge, 2008), 400.
104. Ingram, *Carnal Knowledge*, 289.
105. ibid., 286.
106. Duffy, *Fires of Faith*, 115.
107. ibid., 114–15.
108. Diarmaid MacCulloch, *Thomas Cranmer: A life* (New Haven, CT, and London, 1996), 455; John Calvin, *An Epistle . . . to the Right Noble Prince Edwarde Duke of Somerset* (1550), STC 4407; see also M.L. Bush, *The Government Policy of Protector Somerset* (London, 1975), 110 n71.
109. Calvin, *An Epistle*, Sig. Bvi^v–Bvii^r.
110. Ingram, *Carnal Knowledge*, 293, 296.
111. ibid., 297.
112. Hindle, *The State and Social Change*, 23–24.
113. Ingram, 'Ridings, rough music and the "reform of popular culture" ', 81–90.
114. Keith Thomas, 'The Place of Laughter in Tudor and Stuart England', *TLS*, 21 January 1977, 77–79. See also Stuart Clark, 'Inversion, misrule and the meaning of witchcraft', *P&P* 87 (1980), 98–127.
115. Peter Burke, *Popular Culture in Early Modern Europe* (third edition, Farnham, 2009), 271–80.
116. Miri Rubin, *Corpus Christi: The eucharist in late medieval culture* (Cambridge, 1991), 274.
117. Richard Beadle, ' "Devoute Ymaginacioun" and the dramatic sense', in Shoichi Oguro, Richard Beadle and Michael G. Sargent (eds), *Nicholas Love at Waseda* (Cambridge, 1997), 13.

118. Rubin, *Corpus Christi*, 271.
119. Peter Happé, *John Bale* (New York, 1996).
120. Patrick Collinson, 'From iconoclasm to iconophobia', in Peter Marshall (ed.), *The Impact of the English Reformation, 1500–1640* (London, 1997), 284–85.
121. ibid.; see also Lewis Wager, *A new enterlude* (1566), edition ed. F.I. Carpenter (1904); see also John N. King, *English Reformation Literature: The Tudor origins of the Protestant tradition* (Princeton, NJ, 1982), 278–83.
122. Gervase Babington, *A Very Fruitfull Exposition of the Commaundements* (1583), STC 1095, 316–17. See also Alison Shell, *Shakespeare and Religion* (London, 2010), chapter 1.
123. Quoted in Collinson, 'From iconoclasm to iconophobia', 288.
124. Philip Stubbes, *The Anatomie of Abuses* (London, 1583), STC 23376, Sig. Lvᵛ.
125. John Northbrooke, *A Treatise wherein Dicing, Dauncing, Vaine Playes or Enterluds with other idle pastimes . . . are reproved*, STC 18670 (1577), 65.
126. Emma Rhatigan, 'Preaching venues', in Hugh Adlington, Peter McCullough and Emma Rhatigan (eds), *The Oxford Handbook of the Early Modern Sermon* (Oxford, 2011), 104–05.
127. ibid., 107.
128. ibid., 110.
129. ibid., 88–89; Susan Wabuda, *Preaching During the English Reformation* (Cambridge, 2002), 40–41.
130. Thomas Wilson, *The Arte of Rhetorique* (1553), STC 25799, fo. 2ᵛ.
131. ibid., fos. 35ᵛ; 97ʳ.
132. Patrick Collinson, *The Religion of Protestants: The Church in English society: 1559–1625* (Oxford, 1982), 244–45.
133. Hall, *Chronicle*, 586.
134. Lucy Wooding, *Henry VIII* (second edition, Abingdon, 2015), 219.
135. MacCulloch, *Thomas Cranmer*, 532.
136. Arnold Hunt, *The Art of Hearing: English preachers and their audiences, 1590–1640* (Cambridge, 2010), 58–59.
137. George Gifford, *Sermon on the Parable of the Sower* (1582), STC 11863, Sig. Aviiᵛ.
138. William Weston, *The Autobiography of an Elizabethan*, ed. Philip Caraman (London, 1955), 164–65.
139. Patrick Collinson, *Godly People: Essays on English Protestantism and Puritanism* (London, 1983), 467–98; see also P.S. Seaver, *The Puritan Lectureships: The politics of religious dissent, 1560–1662* (Stanford, CA, 1970).
140. Gifford, *Sermon on the Parable of the Sower*, Sig. Aviᵛ–Aviiʳ.
141. Henry Smith, 'The art of hearing', in *Thirteene Sermons upon several textes of Scripture* (1592), STC 22717; Wilhelm Zepper, *The Art or Skil, Well and Fruitfullie to Heare the Holy Sermons of the Church* (1599), STC 26124.5, trans. Thomas Wilcox.
142. Zepper, *The Art or Skil*, 50.
143. Hunt, *The Art of Hearing*, 19.
144. M.A. Overell, 'Peter Martyr in England, 1547–1553: An alternative view', *SCJ* 15 (1984), 87–104.
145. Norman Jones, 'Elizabeth's first year: The conception and birth of the Elizabethan political world', in C. Haigh (ed.), *The Reign of Elizabeth I* (Basingstoke, 1984), 42–43.
146. John Udall, *The State of the Church of Englande laide open* (1588), STC 24506, Sig. 3ʳ⁻ᵛ; 2ʳ.
147. K.S. van Eerde, 'Robert Waldegrave: The printer as agent and link between sixteenth-century England and Scotland', *RQ* 34 (1981), 40–78.
148. Martin Marprelate (pseud.), *Oh read over D. John Bridges . . . an Epistle* (1588), STC 17454, 22.

149. Joseph Black, 'The rhetoric of reaction: The Martin Marprelate Tracts (1588–89), anti-Martinism, and the uses of print in early modern England', *SCJ* 28 (1997), 710, 712, 713–25; see also E.K. Chambers, *The Elizabethan Stage* (Oxford, 1923), IV, 229–33.

150. Kristen Poole, 'Saints alive! Falstaff, Martin Marprelate, and the staging of puritanism', *Shakespeare Quarterly* 46 (1995), 47–75.

151. Daniel Hahn, 'Elizabeth Crofts', *ODNB*; see also Susan Brigden, *London and the Reformation* (Oxford, 1989), 548.

152. Natalie Zemon Davies, 'The rites of violence: Religious riot in sixteenth-century France', *P&P* 59 (1973), reprinted in Natalie Zemon Davies, *Society and Culture in Early Modern France* (Stanford, CA, 1976), 152–87.

153. Christopher Marlowe, *Massacre*, Scene 5, ll. 42–47.

154. ibid., Scene 21, l. 6.

155. Julia Briggs, 'Marlowe's *Massacre at Paris*: A reconsideration', *Review of English Studies* 34 (1983). See also Karen Cunningham, 'Renaissance execution and Marlovian elocution: The drama of death', *PMLA* 105 (1990), 209–22; Frank Adolino, ' "In Paris? Mass, and well remembered!": Kyd's *The Spanish Tragedy* and the English reaction to the St Bartholomew's Day Massacre', *SCJ* 21 (1990), 401–09; Molly Smith, 'The theater and the scaffold: Death as spectacle in *The Spanish Tragedy*', *Studies in English Literature, 1500–1900* 32 (1992), 217–32.

156. W.S. Streitberger, 'Adult playing companies to 1583', in Richard Dutton (ed.), *The Oxford Handbook of Early Modern Theatre* (Oxford, 2009), 20.

157. Suzanne Westfall, *Patrons and Performance: Early Tudor household revels* (Oxford, 1990).

158. Eleanor Rycroft, 'Morality, theatricality and masculinity in *The Interlude of Youth* and *Hick Scorner*', in Betteridge and Walker (eds), *The Oxford Handbook of Tudor Drama*, 475–77.

159. Walker, *Plays of Persuasion*, 7.

160. Helen Hackett, *A Short History of English Renaissance Drama* (London, 2012), 43.

161. *TRP*, II, 115–16.

162. Hackett, *A Short History of English Renaissance Drama*, 2–3.

163. Janette Dillon, 'Tamburlaine', in Betteridge and Walker (eds), *The Oxford Handbook of Tudor Drama*, 584.

164. Tiffany Stern, 'The theatre of Shakespeare's London', in Margreta De Grazia and Stanley Wells (eds), *The New Cambridge Companion to Shakespeare* (Cambridge, 2010), 45–46.

165. William Ingram, 'The economics of playing', in David S. Kastan (ed.), *A Companion to Shakespeare* (Oxford, 1999), 320, 324.

166. Ian Archer, 'The city of London and the theatre', in Dutton (ed.), *The Oxford Handbook of Early Modern Theatre*, 397.

167. Richard Dutton, *Shakespeare, Court Dramatist* (Oxford, 2016), 13–14.

168. ibid., 16.

169. ibid., *passim*.

170. Hackett, *A Short History of English Renaissance Drama*, 58.

171. Archer, 'City of London', 409.

172. ibid., 410–11.

173. Alan Somerset, 'How chances it they travel? Provincial touring, playing places, and the King's Men', *Shakespeare Survey* 47 (1994), 46.

174. Dutton, *Shakespeare, Court Dramatist*, 33.

175. Hackett, *A Short History of English Renaissance Drama*, 64.

176. Stern, 'The theatre of Shakespeare's London', 49.

177. Henry Woudhuysen, 'Shakespeare's writing: From manuscript to print', in De Grazia and Wells (eds), *The New Cambridge Companion to Shakespeare*, 34–35.

178. Charles Nicholl, *The Reckoning: The murder of Christopher Marlowe* (London, 1992); Paul E.J. Hammer, 'A reckoning reframed: The "murder" of Christopher Marlowe

revisited', *English Literary Renaissance* 26 (1996); M.J. Trow and Talieson Trow, *Who Killed Kit Marlowe? A contract to murder in Elizabethan England* (Stroud, 2001); Park Honan, *Christopher Marlowe: Poet and spy* (Oxford, 2006), chapter 10; Ian Donaldson, *Ben Jonson: A life* (Oxford, 2011), 132–38.

179. Stubbes, *Anatomie of Abuses*, Sig. Lviii^{r–v}.

180. Greg Walker and Henry James, 'The politics of Gorboduc', *English Historical Review* 110 (1995), 105–21.

181. *Lives and Letters of the Devereux Earls of Essex*, ed. Walter Bourchier Devereux, 2 vols (1853), II, 99.

182. *A fourme of common prayer to be used ... necessarie for the present tyme and state* (1572), Sig. Aii^r.

183. Christopher Marlowe, *Tamburlaine*, Act V, Scene 1, l. 131; *Tamburlaine II*, Act III, Scene 5, l. 121.

184. Oscar Brownstein, 'The popularity of baiting in England before 1600: A study in social and theatrical history', *Educational Theatre Journal* 21 (1969), 237–50.

185. *TRP*, II, 115.

186. Dutton, *Shakespeare, Court Dramatist*, 25–26.

187. Bevington, *Tudor Drama*, 12.

188. 'Act of Uniformity, 1559', in Elton, *Tudor Constitution*, 402.

189. Levy, 'The theatre and the court', 286–87.

190. Gajda, *The Earl of Essex*, 204.

191. ibid., 237–38; Fritz Levy, 'Hayward, Daniel and the beginning of politic history in England', *HLQ* 50 (1987), 1–34; Hugh Gazzard, '"Those graue presentments of antiquitie": Samuel Daniel's *Philotas* and the earl of Essex', *Review of English Studies* 51 (2000), 423–50.

192. David S. Kastan, *Shakespeare after Theory* (London, 1999), chapter 6; Louise Montrose, 'Shakespeare, the stage, and the state', *SubStance* 25 (1996), 46–67.

193. Stephen Greenblatt, *Shakespearean Negotiations: The circulation of social energy in renaissance England* (Berkeley, CA, 1988), 64–65.

194. Dutton, *Shakespeare, Court Dramatist*.

195. Richard Dutton, *Mastering the Revels: The regulation and censorship of English renaissance drama* (London, 1991).

196. Janet Clare, 'Censorship', in A.F. Kinney (ed.), *The Oxford Handbook of Shakespeare* (Oxford, 2012), 278–83.

197. Dutton, *Shakespeare, Court Dramatist*, 31–32; Clare, 'Censorship', 276–77; William Ingram, *A London Life in the Brazen Age: Francis Langley, 1548–1602* (Cambridge, MA, 1978), 167–96.

198. Misha Teramura, 'Richard Topcliffe's informant: New light on *The Isle of Dogs*', *Review of English Studies* 68 (2017), 44–59.

199. Thomas Nashe, *A Countercuffe Given to Martin Junior* (1598), *STC* 19456.5, Sig. Aiiij^r.

200. David Lawton, 'Christopher Marlowe, *Doctor Faustus*', in Betteridge and Walker (eds), *The Oxford Handbook of Tudor Drama*, 168, 171.

201. Thomas Lodge and Robert Greene, *A Looking Glasse for London, and for England* (London, 1594), *STC* 16679, Sig. I4^v. See also Anat Feinberg, 'The representation of the poor in Elizabethan and Stuart drama', *Literature and History* 12 (1986), 153.

202. Anna Riehl Bertolet, 'The "blindness of the flesh", in Nathaniel Woodes' *The Conflict of Conscience*', in Betteridge and Walker (eds), *The Oxford Handbook of Tudor Drama*, 144.

203. Quoted in Rycroft, 'Morality, theatricality, and masculinity', 470–71.

204. Stephen Gosson, *The Schoole of Abuse* (London, 1579), *STC* 12098.

205. ibid., Sig. B3^r. See also Efterpi Mitsi, 'Myth and metamorphoses in Stephen Gosson's *Schoole of Abuse*', *English: Journal of the English Association* 60 (2011), 108–23.

206. Gosson, *Schoole of Abuse*, Sig. C2^v.

207. ibid., Sig. C4^v.

208. Somerset, 'How chances it they travel?', 45.

209. Dutton, *Shakespeare, Court Dramatist*, 16.
210. Somerset, 'How chances it they travel?', 50–52, 56–57.
211. Ingram, 'The economics of playing', 326; Stern, 'The theatre of Shakespeare's London', 51.
212. Pamela Allen Brown, *Better a Shrew than a Sheep: Women, drama and the culture of jest in early modern England* (Ithaca, NY, 2003), 2.
213. ibid., 15, 43–52.
214. Sally-Beth MacLean, 'Hocktide: A reassessment of a popular pre-Reformation festival', in Meg Twycross (ed.), *Festive Drama* (Cambridge, 1996), 233–41; Ronald Hutton, *The Rise and Fall of Merry England: The ritual year, 1400–1700* (Oxford, 1996), 120, 229.
215. Andrew Brown, *Popular Piety in Late Medieval England: The Diocese of Salisbury, 1250–1550* (Oxford, 1995), 84.
216. Barbara Hanawalt, *The Ties That Bound: Peasant families in medieval England* (Oxford, 1986), 188–267.
217. Katherine L. French, '"To free them from binding": Women in the late medieval English parish', *Journal of Interdisciplinary History* 27 (1997), 387–412.
218. Houlbrooke, 'Women's social life and common action', 171–89.
219. Quoted in French, '"To free them from binding"', 411.
220. Hyder E. Rollins, 'The black-letter broadside ballad', *PMLA* 34 (1919), 319.
221. Joy Wiltenburg, *Disorderly Women and Female Power in the Street Literature of Early Modern England and Germany* (Charlottesville, VA, 1992), 27–31, 38–39; Christopher Marsh, *Music and Society in Early Modern England* (Cambridge, 2010), 228, 281–82.
222. Dianne Dugaw, 'Heroines gritty and tender, printed and oral, late-breaking and traditional: Revisiting the Anglo-American female warrior', in Patricia Fumerton, Anita Guerrini and Kris McAbee (eds), *Ballads and Broadsides in Britain, 1500–1800* (Farnham, 2010), 278–81.
223. Patricia Demers, 'On first looking into Lumley's Euripides', *Renaissance and Reformation* 23 (1999), 25–42; David Greene, 'Lady Lumley and Greek tragedy', *The Classical Journal* 36 (1941), 537–47; Stephanie Hodgson Wright, 'Jane Lumley's *Iphigenia at Aulis: multum in parvo*, or, less is more', in S.P. Cerasano and Marionne Wynne-Davies (eds), *Readings in Renaissance Women's Drama: Criticism, history, and performance, 1594–1998* (London, 1998), 129–41; Elaine V. Beilin, 'Lady Jane Lumley', in Cerasano and Wynne-Davies (eds), *Readings in Renaissance Women's Drama*, 125–28; Frank Crane, 'Euripides, Erasmus and Lady Lumley', *The Classical Journal* 39 (1944), 223–28.
224. Marie-Alice Belle and Line Cottegnies (eds), *Robert Garnier in Elizabethan England: Mary Sidney Herbert's* Antonius *and Thomas Kyd's* Cornelia (Cambridge, 2017), Introduction, 1–11, 19–49; Paulina Kewes, '"A fit memorial for the times to come": Admonition and topical application in Mary Sidney's *Antonius* and Samuel Daniel's *Cleopatra*', *Review of English Studies* 63 (2012), 243–64.
225. Hackett, *A Short History of English Renaissance Drama*, 184–85.
226. John Rainolds, *Th'overthrow of stage-plays* (1599), *STC* 20616, 16. See also J.W. Binns, 'Women or transvestites on the Elizabethan stage? An Oxford controversy', *SCJ* 5 (1974), 95–119.
227. Michael Shapiro, *Gender in Play on the Shakespearean Stage: Boy heroines and female pages* (Ann Arbor, MI, 1994).
228. Hackett, *A Short History of English Renaissance Drama*, 172.
229. Valerie Wayne, 'Refashioning the shrew', *Shakespeare Studies* 17 (1985), 170–74.
230. Emma Smith, *This is Shakespeare* (London, 2019), 7–21; Anthony Fletcher, 'Men's Dilemma: The future of patriarchy in England 1560–1660', *TRHS* sixth series, 4 (1994), 64–66. See also Coppelia Kahn, '*The Taming of the Shrew*: Shakespeare's mirror of marriage', *Modern Language Studies* 5 (1975), 88–102; Irene G. Dash, *Wooing, Wedding and Power: Women in Shakespeare's plays* (New York, 1981).

231. Margaret Loftus Ranald, 'The performance of feminism in *The Taming of the Shrew*', *Theatre Research International* 19 (1994), 214.

232. Richard Levin, 'Women in the renaissance theatre audience', *Shakespeare Quarterly* 40 (1989), 165–74; Linda Woodbridge, *Women and the English Renaissance: Literature and the nature of womankind, 1540–1620* (Chicago, IL, 1984), 250–52; Andrew Gurr, *Playgoing in Shakespeare's London* (Cambridge, 1987), 50–80.

233. Brown, *Better a Shrew than a Sheep*, 8–9.

234. Quoted in Hackett, *A Short History of English Renaissance Drama*, 175.

235. Carolyn R.S. Lenz, Gale Greene and Carol T. Neely (eds), *The Woman's Part: Feminist criticism of Shakespeare* (Urbana, IL, 1980); Marilyn French, *Shakespeare's Division of Experience* (New York, 1981); Linda Bamber, *Comic Women, Tragic Men: A study of gender and genre in Shakespeare* (Stanford, CA, 1982); Lisa Jardine, *Still Harping on Daughters: Women and drama in the age of Shakespeare* (Brighton, 1983).

236. Dash, *Wooing, Wedding and Power*; Juliet Dusinberre, *Shakespeare and the Nature of Women* (London, 1975).

237. Kate Chedgzoy, 'Marlowe's men and women: Gender and sexuality', in Patrick Cheney (ed.), *The Cambridge Companion to Christopher Marlowe* (Cambridge, 2004), 245–61.

238. Richard Sherry, *A treatise of the figures of grammer and rhetorike* (1555), STC 22429, fo. 2ᵛ.

239. T. French Baumlin, 'Thomas Wilson', in Edward A. Malone (ed.), *British Rhetoricians and Logicians, 1500–1660. First series* (Detroit, MI, 2001), 282–305.

240. Wilson, *The Arte of Rhetorique* (1553), Sig. Aiiᵛ.

241. Wolfgang G. Müller, 'Directions for English', in Michael Pincombe and Cathy Shrank (eds), *The Oxford Handbook of Tudor Literature, 1485–1603* (Oxford, 2011), 313–14.

242. Cicero, 'Orator' in *Brutus; Orator*, trans. H.M. Hubbell (London, 1939), 356–57.

243. Philip Sidney, *An Apology for Poetry (or The Defence of Poesy)*, ed. R.W. Maslen (third edition, Manchester, 2002), 94; George Puttenham, *The Arte of English Poesie* (1589), STC 20519.5.

244. Quoted in Williams, *The Tudor Regime*, 359.

245. Puttenham, *The Arte of English Poesie*, 6.

246. Anthony Munday, *A second and third blast of retrait from plaies and theaters* (1580), STC 21677, 95–96.

247. Donna B. Hamilton, *Anthony Munday and the Catholics, 1560–1633* (Aldershot, 2005).

248. Munday, *A second and third blast*, 96.

249. Michael O'Connell, *Idolatrous Eye: Iconoclasm and theater in early modern England* (Oxford, 2000), 34.

250. Hunt, *The Art of Hearing*, 11.

251. O'Connell, *Idolatrous Eye, passim*.

252. The case made by Thomas M. Greene, 'Ceremonial play and parody in the renaissance', in Susan Zimmerman and Ronald F.E. Weissman (eds), *Urban Life in the Renaissance* (Newark, DE, 1989), 281–93, is overstated. See, too, Stephen Greenblatt, 'Shakespeare and the exorcists', in Stephen Greenblatt, *Shakespearean Negotiations*, 94–128.

253. Kent Cartwright, 'Dramatic theory and Lucres' "Discretion": The plays of Henry Medwall', in Pincombe and Shrank (eds), *The Oxford Handbook of Tudor Literature*, 37–38. See also S.-B. MacLean and A.H. Nelson, 'New light on Henry Medwall', *Leeds Studies in English* 28 (1997), 77–98.

254. Henry Medwall, *Here is conteyned a godely interlude of Fulgens Cenatoure of Rome. Lucres his doughter.* (1513?), Sig. biᵛ–biiᶦ.

255. 'Introduction', in Betteridge and Walker (eds), *The Oxford Handbook of Tudor Drama*, 13.

256. Quoted in Levy, 'The theatre and the court', 274.

257. Peter Lake, 'The theatre and the "post-Reformation public sphere"', in Smuts (ed.), *The Oxford Handbook of the Age of Shakespeare*, 179–99; Blair Worden, 'Ben Jonson among the historians', in Peter Lake and Kevin Sharpe (eds), *Culture and Politics in*

Early Stuart England (Basingstoke, 1993), 67–89.

258. Lake, 'The theatre and the "post-Reformation public sphere"', 188.

259. Peter Lake, *How Shakespeare Put Politics on the Stage: Power and succession in the history plays* (New Haven, CT, 2016), x–xi, 38–58, and *passim*; Peter Lake and Steven Pincus, 'Introduction: Rethinking the public sphere in early modern England', in Peter Lake and Steven Pincus (eds), *The Public Sphere in Early Modern England* (Manchester, 2007), 1–30. It could be argued that the mid-Tudor period had also fostered the development of 'an adjudicating public': see Paulina Kewes, 'The 1553 succession crisis reconsidered', *HR* 90 (2017), 465–85.

260. Walter Raleigh, 'On the life of man', in John Hollander and Frank Kermode (eds), *The Literature of Renaissance England* (Oxford, 1973), 339.

Afterword

1. *Orders, thought meete by his Maiestie, and his Privie Counsell, to be executed throughout the counties of this realme, in such townes, villages, and other places, as are, or may be hereafter infected with the plague* (1603), STC 9209, Sig. A3^r–A4^r.

2. Viviana Comensoli, '"This straunge newes": Plague writing, print culture, and the invention of news in Thomas Dekker's *The Wonderfull Yeare* (1603)', in Simon F. Davies and Puck Fletcher (eds), *News in Early Modern Europe: Currents and connections* (Leiden and Boston, MA, 2014).

3. Thomas Dekker, *The Wonderfull Yeare* (1603), STC 6535, 20–21.

4. ibid., 10–11.

5. William Perkins, *The foundation of Christian religion gathered into six principles* (1592), STC 19710.5, Sig. A2^v.

SUGGESTIONS FOR FURTHER READING

For those with access to a university or research library the *Bibliography of British and Irish History* is an invaluable search tool, as is the *Oxford Dictionary of National Biography*.

Tudor politics

On individual monarchs, the following would be a good place to start: S.B. Chrimes, *Henry VII* (London, 1972); Sean Cunningham, *Henry VII* (London, 2007); J.J. Scarisbrick, *Henry VIII* (London, 1968); Lucy Wooding, *Henry VIII* (second edition, Abingdon, 2015); Jennifer Loach, *Edward VI* (New Haven, CT, 1999); Diarmaid MacCulloch, *Tudor Church Militant: Edward VI and the Protestant Reformation* (London, 1999); John Edwards, *Mary I: England's Catholic queen* (New Haven, CT, and London, 2011); Alexander Samson, *Mary and Philip: The marriage of Tudor England and Habsburg Spain* (Manchester, 2020); Patrick Collinson, *Elizabeth I* (Oxford, 2007); Judith Richards, *Elizabeth I* (Abingdon, 2012).

For broader discussions of these regimes, see Benjamin Thompson (ed.), *The Reign of Henry VII* (Stamford, 1995); Steven Gunn, *Henry VII's New Men and the Making of Tudor England* (Oxford, 2016); Diarmaid MacCulloch (ed.), *The Reign of Henry VIII: Politics, policy and piety* (Basingstoke, 1995); David Starkey, *The Reign of Henry VIII: Personalities and politics* (London, 1985); George W. Bernard, *The King's Reformation: Henry VIII and the remaking of the English Church* (New Haven, CT, and London, 2005); Steven Gunn, *Early Tudor Government, 1485–1558* (Basingstoke, 1995); Steven Gunn, *The English People at War in the Age of Henry VIII* (Oxford, 2018); Richard Rex, *Henry VIII and the English Reformation* (Basingstoke, 1993); Stephen Alford, *Kingship and Politics in the Reign of Edward VI* (Cambridge, 2002); W.K. Jordan, *Edward VI: The young king* (London, 1968); W.K. Jordan, *Edward VI: The threshold of power* (London, 1970); Alice Hunt and Anna Whitelock (eds), *Tudor Queenship: The reigns of Mary and Elizabeth* (Basingstoke, 2010); Susan Doran and Thomas Freeman (eds), *Mary Tudor: Old and new perspectives* (Basingstoke, 2011); Elizabeth Russell, 'Mary Tudor and Mr Jorkins', *HR* 63 (1990), 263–76; Sarah Duncan, *Mary I: Gender, power, and ceremony in the reign of England's first queen* (New York and Basingstoke, 2012); Susan Doran and Thomas Freeman (eds), *The Myth of Elizabeth* (Basingstoke, 2003); Christopher Haigh (ed.), *The Reign of Elizabeth I* (Basingstoke, 1984); Carole Levin, *The Heart and Stomach of a King: Elizabeth I and the politics of sex and power* (second edition, Philadelphia, PA, 2013); Julia M. Walker (ed.), *Dissing Elizabeth: Negative representations of Gloriana* (Durham, NC, 1998); Susan Doran and Paulina Kewes (eds), *Doubtful and Dangerous: The question of succession in late Elizabethan England* (Manchester, 2014).

On political iconography and display, see Kevin Sharpe, *Selling the Tudor Monarchy: Authority and image in sixteenth-century England* (New Haven, CT, and London, 2009); Thomas Betteridge and Suzannah Lipscomb (eds), *Henry VIII and the Court: Art, politics and performance* (Farnham, 2013); Glenn Richardson, *The Field of Cloth of Gold* (New Haven, CT, and London, 2013); Thomas P. Campbell, *Henry VIII and the Art of Majesty: Tapestries at the Tudor court* (New Haven, CT, and London, 2007); Felicity Heal, *The Power of Gifts: Gift-exchange in early modern England* (Oxford, 2014); Jennifer Loach, 'The function of ceremonial in the reign of Henry VIII', *P&P* 142 (1994), 42–68; Sydney Anglo, *Images of Tudor Kingship* (London, 1992); John King, *Tudor Royal Iconography: Literature and art in an age of religious crisis* (Princeton, NJ, 1989); Jayne E. Archer, Elizabeth Goldring and Sarah Knight (eds), *The Progresses, Pageants and Entertainments of Queen Elizabeth I* (Oxford, 2007); Mary Hill Cole, *The Portable Queen: Elizabeth I and the politics of ceremony* (Amherst, MA, 2000); Alice Hunt, *The Drama of Coronation: Medieval ceremony in early modern England* (Cambridge, 2008).

On the political role of women, see Barbara Harris, *English Aristocratic Women, 1450– 1550* (Oxford, 2002); James Daybell (ed.), *Women and Politics in Early Modern England, 1450–1700* (London, 2004); M.F. Harkrider, *Women, Reform and Community in Early Modern England: Katherine Willoughby, duchess of Suffolk, and Lincolnshire's godly aristocracy, 1519–1580* (Woodbridge, 2008); Amanda Herbert, *Female Alliances: Gender, identity and friendship in early modern Britain* (New Haven, CT, and London 2014); Nicola Clark, *Gender, Family and Politics: The Howard Women, 1485–1558* (Oxford, 2018); Michael Jones and Malcolm Underwood, *The King's Mother: Lady Margaret Beaufort, countess of Richmond and Derby* (Cambridge, 1992).

On political culture, see Michael Hicks, *English Political Culture in the Fifteenth Century* (London and New York, 2002); Dale Hoak (ed.), *Tudor Political Culture* (Cambridge, 1995); Krista J. Kesselring, *Mercy and Authority in the Tudor State* (Cambridge, 2003). David Starkey (ed.), *The English Court from the Wars of the Roses to the Civil War* (London, 1987) looks at the role of the Privy Chamber. On parliaments, see Jennifer Loach, *Parliament under the Tudors* (Oxford, 1991); although see also Paul Cavill, 'Debate and dissent in Henry VII's parliaments', *Parliamentary History* 25 (2006), also Stanford Lehmberg, *The Reformation Parliament, 1529–1536* (Cambridge, 1970). On the exercise of authority more broadly, see Michael J. Braddick and John Walter (eds), *Negotiating Power in Early Modern Society: Order, hierarchy and subordination in Britain and Ireland* (Cambridge, 2001); Patrick Collinson, *De republica anglorum: Or, history with the politics put back* (Cambridge, 1990); also in Collinson, *Elizabethan Essays* (London, 1994), 1–30; Paul Griffiths, Adam Fox and Steve Hindle (eds), *The Experience of Authority in Early Modern England* (Basingstoke, 1996); Felicity Heal and Clive Holmes, *The Gentry in England and Wales, 1500–1700* (Basingstoke, 1994), 166–89; M.J. Braddick, *State Formation in Early Modern England, c.1550–1700* (Cambridge, 2000), 27–46; Steve Hindle, *The State and Social Change in Early Modern England, 1550–1640* (Basingstoke, 2000). On Wales, see J. Gwynfor Jones, *Early Modern Wales, c.1525–1640* (Basingstoke, 1994); Glanmor Williams, *Renewal and Reformation: Wales c.1415–1642* (Oxford, 1993); and Simone Clarke and Michael Roberts (eds), *Women and Gender in Early Modern Wales* (Cardiff, 2000). Steven G. Ellis, *The Frontiers of Noble Power: The making of the British state* (Oxford, 1995) compares the far north of England and the Irish pale.

The role of the legal system is discussed in Christopher W. Brooks, *Law, Politics and Society in Early Modern England* (Cambridge, 2008). For church courts, see Ralph A. Houlbrooke, *Church Courts and the People during the English Reformation 1520–1570* (Oxford, 1979); Martin Ingram, *Church Courts, Sex and Marriage in England, 1570–1640* (Cambridge, 1987); Martin Ingram, *Carnal Knowledge: Regulating sex in England, 1470–1600* (Cambridge, 2017). On women and the law, see Jenny Kermode and Garthine Walker (eds), *Women, Crime and the Courts in Early Modern England* (London, 1994); Tim Stretton, *Women Waging Law in Elizabethan England* (Cambridge, 1998). Resistance and rebellion are explored in Anthony Fletcher and Diarmaid MacCulloch, *Tudor Rebellions* (seventh edition, Abingdon, 2020); Roger B. Manning, *Village Revolts: Social protest and popular disturbances in England 1509–1640* (Oxford, 1988); Andy Wood, *Riot, Rebellion and Popular Politics in Early Modern England* (Basingstoke, 2002).

Life and death

On the English landscape, see W.G. Hoskins, *The Making of the English Landscape* (London, 1955) and Oliver Rackham, *The History of the Countryside* (second edition, London, 1995). For agrarian history, see *The Agrarian History of England and Wales*, vol. 4: *1500–1640*, ed. Joan Thirsk (Cambridge, 1967). For the impact of the Tudors on the landscape, see Alexandra Walsham, *The Reformation of the Landscape: Religion, identity, and memory in early modern England and Ireland* (Oxford, 2011); David Gaimster and Roberta Gilchrist (eds), *The Archaeology of the Reformation, 1480–1580* (Leeds, 2003). On perceptions of the landscape, see Andy Wood, *The Memory of the People: Custom and popular senses of the past in early modern England* (Cambridge, 2013); Nicola Whyte, *Inhabiting the Landscape: Place, custom and memory, 1500–1800* (Oxford, 2009); Harriet Lyon, *Memory and the Dissolution of the Monasteries in Early Modern England* (Cambridge, 2021); Andrew McRae, *God Speed the Plough: The representation of agrarian England, 1500–1660* (Cambridge, 1996).

On society, start with Keith Wrightson, *English Society, 1580–1680* (London, 1982); Keith Wrightson (ed.), *A Social History of England 1500–1750* (Cambridge, 2017); J.A. Sharpe, *Early Modern England: A social history 1550–1760* (London, 1987). Indispensable is Keith Wrightson, 'Two concepts of order: Justices, constables and jurymen in seventeenth-century England', in John Brewer and John Styles (eds), *An Ungovernable People: The English and their law in the seventeenth and eighteenth centuries* (London, 1980), 21–46. For the history of domestic life and material culture, see Christopher Dyer, *Making a Living in the Middle Ages: The people of Britain 850–1520* (New Haven, CT, and London, 2002); Tara Hamling and C. Richardson (eds), *Everyday Objects: Medieval and early modern material culture and its meanings* (Abingdon, 2010); Tara Hamling and Catherine Richardson, *A Day at Home in Early Modern England: Material culture and domestic life, 1500–1700* (New Haven, CT, 2017).

On community, see Andy Wood, *Faith, Hope and Charity: English neighbourhoods, 1500–1640* (Cambridge, 2020); Cynthia Herrup, *The Common Peace: Participation and the criminal law in seventeenth-century England* (Cambridge, 1987); Ronald Hutton, *The Rise and Fall of Merry England: The ritual year, 1400–1700* (Oxford, 1996); Craig Muldrew, *The Economy of Obligation: The culture of credit and social relations in early modern England* (Basingstoke, 1998); Phil Withington, *Society in Early Modern England: The vernacular origins of some powerful ideas* (Cambridge, 2010); Susan Brigden, 'Religion and social obligation in early sixteenth-century London', *P&P* 103 (1984).

On London, see Steve Rappaport, *Worlds Within Worlds: Structures of life in sixteenth century London* (Cambridge, 1989); Lena Cowen Orlin (ed.), *Material London, ca. 1600* (Philadelphia, PA, 2000); Paul Griffiths, *Lost Londons: Change, crime and control in the capital city, 1550–1660* (Cambridge, 2008); Paul Griffiths and Mark S.R. Jenner (eds), *Londinopolis: Essays in the cultural and social history of early modern London, c.1500–c.1750* (Manchester, 2000); David L. Smith, Richard Strier and David Bevington (eds), *The Theatrical City: Culture, theatre and politics in London, 1576–1649* (Cambridge, 1995); Julia F. Merritt (ed.), *Imagining Early Modern London: Perceptions and portrayals of the city from Stow to Strype, 1598–1720* (Cambridge, 2001); Ian Archer, *The Pursuit of Stability: Social relations in Elizabethan London* (Cambridge, 1991).

Regarding the economy, see F.J. Fisher (ed.), *Essays in the Social and Economic History of Tudor and Stuart England* (Cambridge, 1961); David C. Coleman, *Industry in Tudor and Stuart England* (London, 1975); Keith Wrightson, *Earthly Necessities: Economic lives in early modern Britain 1470–1570* (New Haven, CT, and London, 2000). For the role of women in the economy, see Barbara Hanawalt, *The Wealth of Wives: Women, law, and economy in late medieval London* (Oxford, 2007); Mavis Mate, *Daughters, Wives and Widows after the Black Death: Women in Sussex, 1350–1525* (Woodbridge, 1998); Amy Erickson, *Women and Property in Early Modern England* (London, 1995). On poverty, see John Pound, *Poverty and Vagrancy in Tudor England* (London, 1971); Steve Hindle, *On the*

Parish? The micro-politics of poor relief in rural England, c.1550–1750 (Oxford, 2004); A.L. Beier, *Masterless Men: The vagrancy problem in England 1560–1640* (London, 1985); Paul Slack, *Poverty and Policy in Tudor and Stuart England* (London, 1988); Marjorie McIntosh, *Poor Relief in England, 1350–1600* (Cambridge, 2012).

On gender, see Laura Gowing, *Gender Relations in Early Modern England* (Harlow, 2012); Anthony Fletcher, *Gender, Sex and Subordination in England 1500–1800* (New Haven, CT, and London, 1995; Alexandra Shepard, *Meanings of Manhood in Early Modern England* (Oxford, 2003); Elizabeth Foyster, *Manhood in Early Modern England: Honour, sex and marriage* (Harlow, 1999); Tim Reinke-Williams, 'Manhood and masculinity in early modern England', *History Compass* 12 (2014), 685–93; Susan D. Amussen, *An Ordered Society: Gender and class in early modern England* (Oxford, 1988); Amy Froide, *Never Married: Singlewomen in early modern England* (Oxford, 2005); Sara Mendelson and Patricia Crawford, *Women in Early Modern England 1550–1720* (Oxford, 1998). Regarding the family, see Helen Berry and Elizabeth Foyster (eds), *The Family in Early Modern England* (Cambridge, 2007); Will Coster, *Family and Kinship in England, 1450–1800* (second edition, Abingdon, 2017); Mary E. Fissell, *Vernacular Bodies: The politics of reproduction in early modern England* (Oxford, 2004); Bernard Capp, *When Gossips Meet: Women, family and neighbourhood in early modern England* (Oxford, 2003). For same-sex relationships, see Marie H. Loughlin, *Same-Sex Desire in Early Modern England, 1550–1735: An anthology of literary texts and contexts* (Manchester and New York, 2014); Alan Bray, *Homosexuality in Renaissance England* (London, 1982); Alan Bray, 'Homosexuality and the signs of male friendship in Elizabethan England', *HWJ* 29 (1990), 1–19; Valerie Traub, *The Renaissance of Lesbianism in Early Modern England* (Cambridge, 2002).

On crime, see James Sharpe, *Crime in Early Modern England 1550–1750* (London, 1984); Malcolm Gaskill, *Crime and Mentalities in Early Modern England* (Cambridge, 2000); Garthine Walker, *Crime, Gender and the Social Order in Early Modern England* (Cambridge, 2003); Laura Gowing, *Domestic Dangers: Women, words and sex in early modern London* (Oxford, 1998); Anthony Fletcher and John Stevenson (eds), *Order and Disorder in Early Modern England* (Cambridge, 1985); Jenny Kermode and Garthine Walker (eds), *Women, Crime and the Courts in Early Modern England* (London, 1994).

Holiness and heresy

Essential introductory reading is Peter Marshall, *Reformation England, 1480–1642* (third edition, 2022). For a broad framework, see John Bossy, *Christianity in the West, 1400–1700* (Oxford, 1985). For a detailed account, see Peter Marshall, *Heretics and Believers: A history of the English Reformation* (New Haven, CT, and London, 2017).

To understand the pre-Reformation Church, Eamon Duffy's *The Stripping of the Altars: Traditional religion in England, 1400–1580* (New Haven, CT, and London, 1992) should be combined with George W. Bernard's, *The Late Medieval English Church: Vitality and vulnerability before the break with Rome* (New Haven, CT, and London, 2012). Also see Katherine French, *The Good Women of the Parish: Gender and religion after the Black Death* (Philadelphia, PA, 2008); Andrew Brown, *Popular Piety in Late Medieval England: The diocese of Salisbury, 1250–1550* (Oxford, 1995); Clive Burgess and Eamon Duffy (eds), *The Parish in Late Medieval England: Proceedings of the 2002 Harlaxton Symposium* (Donington, 2006); Ellen Ross, *The Grief of God: Images of the suffering Jesus in late medieval England* (Oxford, 1997); Miri Rubin, *Corpus Christi: The eucharist in late medieval culture* (Cambridge, 1991); Sarah Beckwith, *Christ's Body: Identity, culture and society in late medieval writings* (London, 1993); Shannon Noelle Gayk, *Image, Text and Religious Reform in Fifteenth-century England* (Cambridge, 2010); J. Dimmick, J. Simpson and N. Zeeman (eds), *Images, Idolatry and Iconoclasm in Late Medieval England: Textuality and the visual image* (Oxford, 2002).

On monasticism, see David Knowles, *The Religious Orders in England*, vol. 3 (Cambridge, 1959); Mary Erler, *Reading and Writing during the Dissolution: Monks, friars and nuns, 1530–*

1558 (Cambridge, 2013); David Knowles and R. Neville Hadcock, *Medieval Religious Houses: England and Wales* (London, 1953); James Clark, *The Dissolution of the Monasteries* (New Haven, CT, and London, 2021). On Lollardy, see Margaret Aston, *Lollards and Reformers: Images and literacy in late medieval religion* (London, 1984); Jill C. Havens and Derrick G. Pitard (eds), *Lollards and Their Influence in Late Medieval England* (Woodbridge, 2003); Mishtooni Bose and J. Patrick Hornbeck (eds), *Wycliffite Controversies* (Turnhout, 2011); Anne Hudson, *The Premature Reformation: Wycliffite texts and Lollard history* (Oxford, 1988); Robert Lutton, *Lollardy and Orthodox Religion In Pre-Reformation England: Reconstructing piety* (Woodbridge, 2011); J.A.F. Thompson, *The Later Lollards, 1414–1520* (Oxford, 1965); Shannon McSheffrey, *Gender and Heresy: Women and men in Lollard communities 1420–1530* (Philadelphia, PA, 1995); Ian Forrest, *The Detection of Heresy in Late Medieval England* (Oxford, 2005); J. Patrick Hornbeck, *What is a Lollard? Dissent and belief in late medieval England* (Oxford, 2010). For the later significance of Lollardy, see Susan Royal, *Lollards in the English Reformation: History, radicalism and John Foxe* (Manchester, 2020).

To understand the place of John Foxe in Tudor religious thought, see David Loades (ed.), *John Foxe: An historical perspective* (Aldershot, 1999); David Loades (ed.), *John Foxe and the English Reformation* (Aldershot, 1997); Christopher Highley and John N. King (eds), *John Foxe and his World* (Aldershot, 2002); David Loades (ed.), *John Foxe at Home and Abroad* (Aldershot, 2004); Elizabeth Evenden and Thomas S. Freeman, *Religion and the Book in Early Modern England: The making of John Foxe's 'Book of Martyrs'* (Cambridge, 2011).

On Protestantism, see Peter Marshall and Alec Ryrie (eds), *The Beginnings of English Protestantism* (Cambridge, 2002); Alec Ryrie, *Being Protestant in Reformation Britain* (Oxford, 2013); Patrick Collinson, *The Birthpangs of Protestant England: Religious and cultural change in the sixteenth and seventeenth centuries* (Basingstoke, 1988); Peter Marshall, 'The naming of Protestant England', *P&P* 214 (2012), 87–128; Andrew Pettegree, *Marian Protestantism: Six studies* (Aldershot, 1996); Catherine Davies, *A Religion of the Word: The defence of the Reformation in the reign of Edward VI* (Manchester, 2002); John N. King, *English Reformation Literature: The Tudor origins of the Protestant tradition* (Princeton, NJ, 1982); Femke Molekamp, *Women and the Bible in Early Modern England: Religious reading and writing* (Oxford, 2013); Natalie Mears and Alec Ryrie (eds), *Worship and the Parish Church in Early Modern Britain* (Farnham, 2013).

On post-Reformation Catholic history, see Alexandra Walsham, *Church Papists: Catholicism, conformity and confessional polemic in early modern England* (Woodbridge, 1993); Michael Questier, *Catholicism and Community in Early Modern England: Politics, aristocratic patronage and religion, c.1550–1640* (Cambridge, 2006); Peter Lake and Michael Questier, *The trials of Margaret Clitherow: Persecution, martyrdom and the politics of sanctity in Elizabethan England* (London, 2011); Sandeep Kaushik, 'Resistance, loyalty and recusant politics: Sir Thomas Tresham and the Elizabethan state', *Midland History* 21 (1996), 37–72; Ethan H. Shagan (ed.), *Catholics and the 'Protestant Nation': Religious politics and identity in early modern England* (Manchester, 2005); Victor Houliston, *Catholic Resistance in Elizabethan England: Robert Person's Jesuit polemic, 1580–1610* (Aldershot, 2007); Alexandra Walsham, *Catholic Reformation in Protestant Britain* (Farnham, 2014); Liesbeth Corens, *Confessional Mobility and English Catholics in Counter-Reformation Europe* (Oxford, 2018).

On the popular experience of religious change, begin with Keith Thomas, *Religion and the Decline of Magic: Studies in popular beliefs in sixteenth- and seventeenth-century England* (London and New York, 1971). An excellent survey is Christopher Marsh, *Popular Religion in Sixteenth-Century England* (Basingstoke, 1998). J.J. Scarisbrick, *The Reformation and the English People* (Oxford, 1984) was one of the first to challenge the received wisdom on the Reformation. See also Alexandra Walsham, *Providence in Early Modern England* (Oxford, 1999); David Cressy, *Bonfires and Bells: National memory and the Protestant calendar in Elizabethan and Stuart England* (London, 1989); Tessa Watt, *Cheap Print and Popular Piety 1550–1640* (Cambridge, 1991); Jessica Martin and Alec Ryrie (eds), *Private and Domestic*

Devotion in Early Modern Britain (Farnham, 2012). Susan Brigden, *London and the Reformation* (Oxford, 1989), gives a detailed and sympathetic account of the complexities of religious change in the capital. On sermons, see Hugh Adlington, Peter MacCullough and Emma Rhatigan (eds), *The Oxford Handbook of the Early Modern Sermon* (Oxford, 2011), Arnold Hunt, *The Art of Hearing: English preachers and their audiences, 1590–1640* (Cambridge, 2010).

On the visual and material culture of religion, see Tara Hamling, *Decorating the Godly Household: Religious art in post-Reformation Britain* (New Haven, CT, and London, 2010); David J. Davis, *Seeing Faith, Printing Pictures: Religious identity during the English Reformation* (Turnhout, 2013). On the emergence of toleration, see Alexandra Walsham, *Charitable Hatred: Tolerance and intolerance in England, 1500–1700* (Manchester, 2006).

On witchcraft, see Alan Macfarlane, *Witchcraft in Tudor and Stuart England: A regional and comparative study* (London, 1970); James Sharpe, *Instruments of Darkness: Witchcraft in England, 1550–1750* (London, 1997); Malcolm Gaskill, *Crime and Mentalities in Early Modern England* (Cambridge, 2000), 33–79; Brian P. Levack (ed.), *The Oxford Handbook of Witchcraft in Early Modern Europe and colonial America* (Oxford, 2013), 283–99; William Monter, 'Re-contextualizing British witchcraft', *Journal of Interdisciplinary History* 35 (2004), 105–11; Malcolm Gaskill, 'Witchcraft and evidence in early modern England', *P&P* 198 (2008), 33–70

Renaissance culture

The cultural history of Tudor England is particularly well served by the Oxford Handbook series: see Thomas Betteridge and Greg Walker (eds), *The Oxford Handbook of Tudor Drama* (Oxford, 2012); Mike Pinchcombe and Cathy Shrank (eds), *The Oxford Handbook of Tudor Literature, 1485–1603* (Oxford, 2009); Andrew Hadfield (ed.), *The Oxford Handbook of English Prose 1500–1640* (Oxford, 2013); Malcolm Smuts (ed.), *The Oxford Handbook of the Age of Shakespeare* (Oxford, 2016); Richard Dutton (ed.), *The Oxford Handbook of Early Modern Theatre* (Oxford, 2009); Ian Archer, Felicity Heal and Paulina Kewes (eds), *The Oxford Handbook of Holinshed's Chronicles* (Oxford, 2013). Also see Stephen Greenblatt, *Renaissance Self-Fashioning: From More to Shakespeare* (Chicago, 1980); Debora K. Shuger, *Habits of Thought in the English Renaissance* (Toronto, 1997); David Loewenstein and Janel Mueller (eds), *The Cambridge History of Early Modern English Literature* (Cambridge, 2001). For classical influences, see Andrew Hadfield, *Shakespeare and Republicanism* (Cambridge, 2005); Markku Peltonen, *Classical Humanism and Republicanism in English Political Thought, 1570–1640* (Cambridge, 1995); Colin Burrow, *Shakespeare and Classical Antiquity* (Oxford, 2013); Patrick Gray, *Shakespeare and the Fall of the Roman Republic: Selfhood, stoicism and civil war* (Edinburgh, 2018); Peter Mack, *Elizabethan Rhetoric: Theory and practice* (Cambridge, 2002); Andrew Wallace, *Virgil's Schoolboys: The poetics of pedagogy in renaissance England* (Oxford, 2010).

On the significance of print, see Vincent Gillespie and Susan Powell (eds), *A Companion to the Early Printed Book in Britain* (Cambridge, 2014); Micheline White (ed.), *English Women, Religion, and Textual Production, 1500–1625* (Aldershot, 2011); Alexandra Walsham and Julia Crick (eds), *The Uses of Script and Print, 1300–1700* (Cambridge, 2004); Aysha Pollnitz, *Princely Education in Early Modern Britain* (Cambridge, 2015); Emma Smith and Andy Kesson (eds), *Elizabethan Top Ten: Defining print popularity in early modern England* (Farnham, 2013); John N. King (ed.), *Tudor Books and Readers* (Cambridge, 2010); Fred Schurink (ed.), *Tudor Translation* (Basingstoke, 2011); Tania Demetriou and Rowan Tomlinson (eds), *Culture of Translation in Early Modern England and France, 1500–1660* (Basingstoke and New York, 2015); Annabel Patterson, *Censorship and Interpretation: The conditions of writing and reading in early modern England* (reprint edition, Madison, WI, 1991); Andrew Hadfield (ed.), *Literature and Censorship in Renaissance England* (Basingstoke, 2001). On popular print, see Margaret Spufford, *Small Books and Pleasant Histories: Popular fiction and its readership in seventeenth-*

century England (Cambridge, 1981); Barry Reay, *Popular Cultures in England 1550–1750* (London, 1998), 36–70; Adam Fox, *Oral and Literate Culture in England, 1500–1700* (Oxford, 2000).

On attitudes to history, see Daniel R. Woolf, *The Social Circulation of the Past: English historical culture, 1500–1730* (Oxford, 2003); Paulina Kewes (ed.), *The Uses of History in Early Modern England* (San Marino, CA, 2006); Keith Thomas, *The Perception of the Past in Early Modern England* (London, 1983). For the connections between literature and politics, see Peter Lake, *How Shakespeare Put Politics on the Stage* (New Haven, CT, 2016); Lisa Jardine and Anthony Grafton, ' "Studied for action": How Gabriel Harvey read his Livy', *P&P* 129 (1990), 30–78; Alexandra Gajda, *The Earl of Essex and Late Elizabethan Political Culture* (Oxford, 2012); Paul Hammer, 'The earl of Essex, Fulke Greville, and the employment of scholars', *Studies in Philology* 91 (1994), 167–80. See also Kevin Sharpe, *Reading Revolutions: The politics of reading in early modern England* (New Haven CT, and London, 2000).

On drama, see Suzanne Westfall, *Patrons and Performance: Early Tudor household revels* (Oxford, 1990); Richard Dutton, *Shakespeare, Court Dramatist* (Oxford, 2016); Helen Hackett, *A Short History of English Renaissance Drama* (London, 2012); Pamela Allen Brown, *Better a Shrew than a Sheep: Women, drama and the culture of jest in early modern England* (Ithaca, NY, 2003); Andrew Gurr, *Playgoing in Shakespeare's London* (Cambridge, 1987).

On women authors, see Margaret P. Hannay (ed.), *Silent But for the Word: Tudor women as patrons, translators and writers of religious works* (Kent, OH, 1985); Margaret King, *Women of the Renaissance* (Chicago, IL, 1991); Constance Jordan, *Renaissance Feminism: Literary texts and political models* (Chicago, IL, 1990); Elaine Beilin, *Redeeming Eve: Women writers of the English renaissance* (Princeton, NJ, 1987); Wendy Wall, *The Imprint of Gender: Authorship and publication in the English renaissance* (Ithaca, NY, 1993); Kate Chedgzoy, Suzanne Trill and Melanie Hansen (eds), *Voicing Women: Gender and sexuality in early modern writing* (Keele, 1996); Lynn Woodbridge, *Women and the English Renaissance: Literature and the nature of womankind, 1540–1620* (Chicago, 1984); Gemma Allen, *The Cooke Sisters: Education, piety and politics in early modern England* (Manchester, 2013); James Daybell and A. Gordon (eds), *Women and Epistolary Agency in Early Modern Culture, 1450–1690* (London, 2016); Valerie Wayne (ed.), *Women's Labour and the History of the Book in Early Modern England* (London, 2020); Sarah C.E. Ross and Rosalind Smith (eds), *Early Modern Women's Complaint: Gender, form and politics* (London, 2020).

The wider world

A good introduction is Susan Doran and Glenn Richardson (eds), *Tudor England and Its Neighbours* (Basingstoke, 2005). On the early stages of empire, see Kenneth R. Andrews, *Trade, Plunder and Settlement: Maritime enterprise and the genesis of the British Empire* (Cambridge, 1984); Nicholas Canny (ed.), *The Oxford History of the British Empire*, vol. 1: *The Origins of Empire: British overseas enterprise to the close of the seventeenth century* (Oxford, 1998); Andrew T. Powell, *Grenville and the Lost Colony of Roanoke: The first English colony of America* (Leicester, 2011). On the growth of trading networks, see David M. Loades, *England's Maritime Empire: Seapower, commerce and policy, 1490–1690* (Harlow, 2000); Felicity Stout, *Exploring Russia in the Elizabethan Commonwealth: The Muscovy Company and Giles Fletcher, the Elder (1546–1611)* (Manchester, 2015); Stephen Alford, *London's Triumph: Merchant adventurers and the Tudor city* (London, 2017); Derek Wilson, *The World Encompassed: Drake's great voyage 1577–1580* (London, 1998).

On travel writing and cultural encounters, see Daniel Carey and Claire Jowitt (eds), *Richard Hakluyt and Travel Writing in Early Modern Europe* (Farnham, 2012); John Gallagher, *Learning Languages in Early Modern England* (Oxford, 2019); Helen Hackett (ed.), *Early Modern Exchanges: Dialogues between nations and cultures, 1550–1750* (Farnham, 2015); Andrew Hadfield, *Literature, Travel and Colonial Writing in the English Renaissance, 1545–1625* (Oxford, 1998). For diplomacy, see Tracey Sowerby, 'Early modern diplomatic history', *History Compass* 14 (2016), 441–56; Tracey Sowerby and Jan Hennings (eds), *Practices of Diplomacy in the Early Modern World, c.1410–1800* (London, 2017).

With regard to immigrant communities, see Nigel Goose and Lien Luu, *Immigrants in Tudor and Early Stuart England* (Brighton and Portland, OR, 2005); Andrew Pettegree, *Foreign Protestant Communities in Sixteenth-Century London* (Oxford, 1986). On the history of black people in early modern England, see Kenneth Little, *Negroes in Britain: A study of racial relations in English society* (London, 1972); James Walvin, *Black and White: The negro and English society 1555–1945* (London, 1973); Nigel File and Chris Power, *Black Settlers in Britain 1555–1958* (London, 1981); Jagdish S. Gundara and Ian Duffield, *Essays on the History of the Blacks in Britain: From Roman times to the mid-twentieth century* (Aldershot, 1992); Kim F. Hall, *Things of Darkness: Economics of race and gender in early modern England* (Ithaca, NY, and London, 1995); Peter Fryer, *Staying Power: The history of black people in Britain* (London and New York, 1984); Kate J.P. Lowe and Tom F. Earle (eds), *Black Africans in Renaissance Europe* (Cambridge, 2005); Miranda Kaufmann, *Black Tudors: The untold story* (London, 2017); Imtiaz Habib, *Black Lives in the English Archives, 1500–1677* (London, 2008).

For Ireland, see Susan Brigden, *New World, Lost Worlds* (London, 2000); Steven G. Ellis, *Ireland in the Age of the Tudors, 1447–1603: English expansion and the end of Gaelic rule* (London, 1998); Ciaran Brady, *The Chief Governors: The rise and fall of reform government in Tudor Ireland, 1536–1588* (Cambridge, 1994); J.G. Crawford, *Anglicizing the Government of Ireland: The Irish Privy Council and the expansion of Tudor rule, 1556–1578* (Dublin, 1993); Nicholas Canny, *From Reformation to Restoration: Ireland, 1534–1660* (Dublin, 1987); Ciaran Brady and Raymond Gillespie (eds), *Natives and Newcomers: The making of Irish colonial society, 1534–1641* (Dublin, 1986); Nicholas Canny, *The Elizabethan Conquest of Ireland: A pattern established, 1565–76* (Hassocks, 1976).

INDEX